S0-AJQ-674

The Complete Letters of Henry James

1855–1872

VOLUME 2

The Complete Letters of Henry James

GENERAL EDITORS

Pierre A. Walker, Salem State College, Greg W. Zacharias, Creighton University (Project Director)

ASSOCIATE EDITORS

Kendell C. Kennedy, Tara D. Knapp, Roberta A. Sheehan

EDITORIAL ASSISTANTS

Katherine Crooks, Jennifer Eimers, Josi Freire, John Funchion, Tatiana M. Holway, Kurt Shoemaker, Laura Smith, Jay Spina

EDITORIAL BOARD

Michael Anesko, The Pennsylvania State University, Millicent Bell, Boston University, Susan Gunter, Westminster College (Salt Lake City), Steven Jobe, Hanover College (Indiana), George Monteiro, Brown University, Rayburn Moore, University of Georgia

ADVISORY GROUP

Daniel Mark Fogel, University of Vermont, Robert Gale, University of Pittsburgh, Richard Hocks, University of Missouri–Columbia, Philip Horne, University College London, Bay James, Newbury, Massachusetts, Henry James, Dublin, New Hampshire, Fred Kaplan, City University of New York, David McWhirter, Texas A&M University, Lyall H. Powers, University of Michigan, Roberta A. Sheehan, Quincy, Massachusetts, Adeline Tintner, New York City, Cheryl Torsney, West Virginia University, Ruth Bernard Yeazell, Yale University

The Complete Letters
of
Henry James, 1855–1872

VOLUME 2

Henry James

Edited by Pierre A. Walker and
Greg W. Zacharias

University of Nebraska Press
Lincoln and London

COMMITTEE ON
SCHOLARLY EDITIONS

AN APPROVED EDITION

MODERN LANGUAGE
ASSOCIATION OF AMERICA

© 2006 by the University of Nebraska Press
All rights reserved. Manufactured in the United
States of America. Set in Linotype Janson Text
by Tseng Information Systems, Inc. Book designer
R. Eckersley.

♾

Library of Congress Cataloging-in-Publication Data
James, Henry, 1843–1916.
[Correspondence. Selections]
The complete letters of Henry James, 1855–1872 /
Henry James ; edited by Pierre A. Walker and
Greg W. Zacharias ; with an introduction by
Alfred Habegger.
p. cm. — (The complete letters of Henry James)
Includes bibliographical references and index.
ISBN-13: 978-0-8032-2584-8 (v. 1 : cl. : alk. paper)
ISBN-10: 0-8032-2584-9 (v. 1 : cl. : alk. paper)
ISBN-13: 978-0-8032-2607-4 (v. 2 : cl. : alk. paper)
ISBN-10: 0-8032-2607-1 (v. 2 : cl. : alk. paper)
1. James, Henry, 1843–1916—Correspondence.
2. Authors, American—19th century—
Correspondence. 3. Authors, American—
20th century—Correspondence. I. Walker,
Pierre A. II. Zacharias, Greg W., 1958– III. Title.
PS2123.A4 2006
813'.4—dc22   2005036366

In memory of Adeline R. Tintner

Contents

Illustrations

Acknowledgments

A commitment to the editing, annotation, and publication of an edition of more than ten thousand Henry James letters is, of course, no small matter in terms of effort, scope, or cost. The Center for Henry James Studies at Creighton University, Salem State College, grants from the Gilbert C. Swanson Foundation, a Summer Fellowship and a Fellowship for College Teachers and Independent Scholars from the National Endowment for the Humanities, a sabbatical fellowship from the American Philosophical Society, a Mellon Fellowship to the Harry Ransom Humanities Center at the University of Texas at Austin, a fellowship from the Bibliographical Society of America, and individual contributions of time and money have contributed to making work on this volume possible.

In addition to the general editors, associate editors, editorial assistants, editorial board, and advisory group of *The Complete Letters of Henry James*, many individuals have contributed to this volume and to this edition. Hélène Hossenlopp Morandi, Maria Teresa Vanderboegh, David Vanderboegh, Lorie Vanchena, and Geoffrey Bakewell assisted with translations. Chris Mounsey of King Alfred's College took time off from his own research to check directory listings for us at the British Library. Ann-Marie Priest of Central Queensland University contributed her expertise during a visit to the James Center in 2001. Chiara Calzetta Jaeger, of the Comité Arpad Szenes-Vieira da Silva, and Rosella Mamoli Zorzi, of the University of Venice, Ca'Foscari, patiently answered questions about Venetian Italian. Ignas K. Skrupskelis and Elizabeth M. Berkeley, the editors of *The Correspondence of William James*, were very generous in sharing information. Alfred Habegger agreed to take time away from Emily Dickinson, to return to the field in which he previously worked so brilliantly and to write the introduction to *The Complete Letters of Henry James, 1855–1872*. On top of that, he gave our transcriptions of the letters and our annotations a rigorous inspection and provided numerous, valuable suggestions and caught many errors. For all this, we are most grateful.

Many kind and dedicated librarians have been extremely helpful to us as we checked and rechecked manuscripts in their archives. The Houghton Library at Harvard University holds the largest collection of manuscripts of Henry James's letters (almost four thousand), and the staff of its reading room makes the Houghton Library the most pleasant rare-book and manuscript library we know to work in. Very special thanks to Susan Halpert, Elizabeth Falsey, Denison Beach, Jennie Rathbun, Tom Ford, Emily Walhout, Rachel Howarth, Joseph Zajac, Brent Landau, and Regina Laba for their continued help and encouragement. After the Houghton, the Special Collections department at Colby College's Miller Library holds the largest collection of manuscripts of early Henry James letters. The current special collections librarian, Patricia Burdick, went the extra mile for us, checking the manuscript of James's letter to Lilla Cabot for a watermark, and her predecessor, Nancy Reinhardt, was generous in her assistance when we transcribed, checked, and photographed manuscripts in the reading room. Inge Dupont, McKenna Lebens, and Sylvie Merian, in the reading room at the Pierpont Morgan Library, New York City, were also very helpful. Christine Nelson, curator of literary and historical manuscripts at the Morgan, went out of her way to check the manuscript of James's 21 March [1872] letter to John S. Clark for a watermark, which allowed us to establish the year of the letter's composition. David Ferris, David Warrington, and Michael Austin, of Special Collections at Harvard's Law School Library, were helpful when we had to work with the manuscripts of James's letters to Oliver Wendell Holmes Jr. Michala Biondi, Jim Moske, John Stinson, Valerie Wingfield, and Melanie Yolles of the Manuscripts and Archives Division of the New York Public Library were also most helpful when we worked with the manuscripts of letters by James in the William Conant Church Papers. At the New-York Historical Society, Melissa Haley assisted the examination of the letters there to John La Farge, and the late Mary A. (Mrs. Henry A.) La Farge very kindly granted permission to examine, photocopy, and publish these manuscripts.

Some of James's earliest letters survive only on a microfilm made at Duke University, we believe, around the time Virginia Harlow wrote her dissertation (later her biography) on Thomas Sergeant Perry. Robert Byrd and Linda McCurdy, of Duke University, helped us obtain a copy of this precious microfilm. All letters from Duke University are from the Henry James Letters in the Thomas Sergeant Perry Papers (on microfilm 215-01-1), Rare Book, Manuscript, and Special Collections Library, Duke University, Durham, North Carolina. Ann Hyde and Karen S. Cook assisted our work at the Kenneth Spencer Library at the University of Kansas. We are grateful to Ms. Lilla Lyon for granting permission to publish Lilla Cabot Perry's note written on Henry James's late May 1870 or 1871 letter.

By creating his monumental *Calendar of the Letters of Henry James*, Steven H. Jobe made it possible to begin to imagine editing and publishing all of James's letters. Moreover, he transcribed and photographed the manuscripts of James's letters held by the University of Kansas and provided us with copies of material from the Edel Archive at the McLennan Library at McGill University.

Creighton University has been generous in its support of the letters project and the Center for Henry James Studies. Special thanks go to Rev. Michael Morrison, S.J., former president; to Rev. John Schlegel, S.J., the current president; to the former vice president for academic affairs, Charles Dougherty; to the current vice president for academic affairs, Christine Wiseman; to former deans of the Arts College, Michael Proterra, S.J., and Albert Agresti, S.J., and current dean, Timothy R. Austin. In addition, Barbara Braden, dean of the Graduate School, and colleagues Bryan Le Beau, Robert Dornsife, Bridget Keegan, Brent Spencer, Shari Stenberg, Jackie Masker, Robert Whipple, and Zbigniew Bialas, each in their own way, have been generous in their support of *The Complete Letters of Henry James*. Andrew Helgeson, Gina Mahaffey, Sarah Stanley, Kelly Steenholdt, and Nathan Weinert provided important support for the project in the Center for Henry James Studies.

Patricia Buchanan and Anita Shea, English department chair and dean of Arts and Sciences, respectively, at Salem State College, have been very generous in their support of work on this project. The office of Salem State College's vice president of academic affairs has provided much appreciated support from the Faculty/Librarian Research Support Fund.

The Gilbert C. Swanson Foundation, Inc., of Omaha has supported the project from the very beginning. The executive director of the Swanson Foundation, Richard E. O'Toole, believed in the project before almost anyone and deserves special thanks. Special thanks too to Lee Fenicle, Alan James, and Paul Bloede for their support.

The University of Nebraska Press has made an unprecedented commitment to *The Complete Letters of Henry James*. Our thanks go to those at the press with whom we have worked and continue to work, especially, Willis Regier, Daniel Ross, Douglas Clayton, M.J. Devaney, Ladette Randolph, and Richard Eckersley.

Our deepest thanks go to Bay James, on behalf of the James family, and to Leslie A. Morris, curator of manuscripts in the Harvard College Library, on behalf of the president and fellows of Harvard College, for permission to publish those letters still under copyright.

Abbreviated General Editors' Introduction

We intend *The Complete Letters of Henry James* to be as useful to as broad a range of readers as possible, given the limitations of print reproduction. One cannot anticipate what biographical or historical details or stylistic idiosyncrasies contained in any given letter may be of value to users of the edition. The general editors of this edition, therefore, believe that our duty is "to be as complete as possible," as James wrote in another context ("Art" 521). By being as complete as possible, we enable the opportunity for study of any aspect of James's letters. An inclusive edition of the letters enriches by its range and detail our understanding of James's life and the lives of his correspondents, his use of language, and his importance to our cultural legacy.

The goal of this edition is to provide an inclusive, reliable, available, and easily read scholarly and critical text for all extant letters, telegrams, and notes written by Henry James. We aim to represent the letter text, thus evidence of the compositional process represented by it, with the greatest precision possible in a format that is easy to read and understand. Where reliability (in terms of the meaningful details of the historical document itself) is in tension with readability, we give priority to reliability. Informing this view is a conviction that historical documents are fundamentally different from such "literary texts" as poems and novels and therefore must be edited and published differently. We do not correct slips or other errors in the letters, preferring instead to render what James wrote whenever possible.

The manuscripts of James's letters show that James was a spontaneous letter-writer who evidently wrote rapidly, for they contain a substantial number of changes and corrections. The position and apparent sequence of James's cancellations, corrections, and insertions indicate that he adjusted, shaped, and sharpened his meaning as he wrote, working just ahead of his pen, when he caught an error or clarified meaning at all. Those changes, made as he drove himself to answer letter after letter received and to open new paths of communication, reveal James's mind in action. They also record the way in which James responded to individual correspondents and rhetorical situations. As we considered the changes, it seemed important to us that those changes—in addition to James's final intention, as it were—were themselves interesting because he obviously changed meaning for a reason. And such changes could hold an interest all their own, just as they would for those who read the original letters. In the same way shifts and turns of meaning are signaled by changes, so too do mistakes and errors of carelessness and other idiosyncrasies carry meaning. To omit those details would be to misrepresent the letter James wrote and his correspondent read. Thus we sought an approach to editing the letters that would enable us to represent what James wrote; that is, what appears on the letter page and what the letter recipient read so that readers of this edition might use the edited letters more nearly as they would James's own letters. The most suitable approach we found is plain-text editing, developed by Robert H. Hirst for *Mark Twain's Letters*.

We rationalize our decision to present the letters in a plain-text style, in part, in terms of G. Thomas Tanselle's point that "the posting of a letter is equivalent to the publication of a literary work, for each activity serves as the means by which a particular kind of communication is directed to its audience" ("The Editorial Problem" 204). Henry James indicated his preference for a "definitive" letter as soon as he sealed an envelope and sent it through the mail. We see no reason, then, to alter the meaningful elements of what James wrote and a letter's recipient read. In "Recent Editorial Discussion and the Central Questions of Editing," Tanselle elaborated the concept by arguing that "readers are not normally prevented from understanding a text by oddities and inconsistencies of punctuation and spelling, and when these irregularities are characteristic of the author what is the point of altering them? It is hard to see why editors think they are accomplishing anything by straightening out the details of spelling and punctuation in a letter or journal simply for the sake of tidying it up" (58).

As much as we hope that this edition can function to communicate to readers a substantial amount of the meaning of James's originals, no edition of letters can represent all details of the original documents. Plain-text does not attempt to render a facsimile of the letter text. It enables us to represent meaningful details of the text of the historical document. At the same time, by using commonly understood editorial symbols in combination with a record of emendations and other textual notes, we provide the reader with a highly reliable and readable edition. By including in the edited text cancellations, insertions, and other changes seen in the manuscripts and typescripts and by representing these manuscript details with similar ones in the typography, plain-text editing enables users to read the edited letters nearly as they would the originals, without having to reconstruct them by way of an apparatus or specially memorized editing marks or by having to decipher James's handwriting. By representing textual details of the letter, rather than the letter writer's final intentions only, plain-text editing enables readers to see when and where in a letter James changed his mind or altered an emphasis.

Our aim is to help our readers experience something of the moment of composition, which only a careful examination of the manuscript can offer fully. Our position on this aspect of the editorial rationale is based on Tanselle's critique of modernization and his argument that editors of historical documents should preserve a writer's deletions and, by extension, other meaningful features of the holograph, in a scholarly edition, for then "the editor allows the reader to have the same experience" as the original reader of the historical document ("Editing of Historical Documents" 50–51). A letter differs from such literary texts as poems or novels in the way that it should be read and understood because in a letter there is no "final" or published text other than the one which the writer sealed in an envelope and put into the mail (Tanselle, "Problem" 204). "Drafts" and "revisions" in the form of authorial changes may be contained in a single letter text rather than in a series of separate drafts.

The texts of the letters that appear in this edition are reproduced essentially as they were written and sent, without correction or normalization, including cancellations, as long as that text can be intelligibly transcribed with typographical features available to the editors via the page design. If what might be a significant feature of the manuscript can be transcribed and included in the edition, it will be.

Reading particular idiosyncratic elements of Henry James's handwriting is a challenge because many of the letter forms — "a," "u," "o," and "v," or "T" and "I," for example — often look alike. To distinguish them, one must first remember the range of ambiguous letter forms and then consider the possible combinations in the context of an entire word or individual words in the context of its own sentence — only then can one can begin to read James's hand accurately.

An example of understanding the context of a particular letter form appears in James's [7], 8, 9 March 1870 missive to William, in which he writes: "<u>i.e.</u> that poor Jno. La Farge were with me sharing my enjoyment of this English scenery — enjoying it that is, on his own . . ." The next word is either "hook" or "book" because of the similarity of James's "h" to his "b." An investigation of both "on his own hook" and "on his own book" uncovered the contemporary colloquialism, "by one's own hook," the definition of which suited James's sense perfectly. Thus we rendered the word.

An unfamiliar proper name may pose a problem because one might lack an immediate context in which to understand critical letter forms. For example, because James's majuscule "I" and "T" were formed alike at the time, we couldn't know if James was referring in his 28 November 1871 letter to George Abbot James to "<u>Mr. I. Cook, Tailor, London</u>" or "<u>Mr. T. Cook.</u>" In the 1870 *Post Office London Directory*, we found the following listing: "Thomas William Cook, Tailor, 8 Clifford st., Old Bond st. W" (772). No mention of any other tailor named Cook could be found, so we adopted the reading "T. Cook."

There are instances of James's handwriting where we have not been able to find neat solutions. Special problems include words that may or may not end in a final "s," words in the middle of a sentence that may or may not be capitalized, and such compound words as *anything, somewhere,* and *everyone,* which may be one or two words. Understanding James's habits regarding capitalization in a particular letter, knowing James's good knowledge of English grammar, and mapping his letter-spacing habits provide ways to understand other difficulties of James's hand.

Knowledge of usage frequencies, surveyed through electronic searches for particular word combinations across more than one thousand transcribed letters also helps rationalize decisions when faced with two possibilities. For example, James closed his 18 February 1870 letter to Grace Norton by writing vertically across the complete next-to-last page: "believe me dear Grace—unutterably" or "unalterably," "yours." The fourth and fifth letters of this word are both crossed, but because James is regularly very imprecise about crossing his *t*'s, we could not be sure by the usual ways of analysis whether he wrote double "t" or "lt"; there are countless other examples of "lt" combinations that can only be read as such and in which both letters are crossed. Furthermore, "u" and "a" often look alike, so we cannot be certain that the third letter is one or the other. Either reading, "unutterably" or "unalterably," fits the context of the closing. We decided to render "unutterably" after we made a search for both words, unutterably and unalterably, in our electronic files of all the letters up through 1875. Unalterably does not appear at all in any of these letters, whereas unutterably appears five times. Therefore we felt that it was not atypical of James to use the word unutterably and, as a result, that this would be the more likely reading. Unfortunately, Grace Norton's letters to James do not survive, and none of his other letters to her offers a further clue.

One significant feature is cancellation. James frequently cancels material with one or more lines. When these are legible, we represent them as struckthrough text (~~cancel~~, ~~cancel~~, etc.). We represent illegible, canceled letters with the mark we use to indicate illegible single letter characters, ◇, struckthrough: ~~◇~~. (When a series of canceled characters with space on either side is illegible to the point that we cannot determine the number of characters, we represent it with a ▬▬▬.)

James also canceled words and letters within words by overwriting them. This we represent by giving the overwritten word or part of a word as struckthrough text followed by the word that results after the overwriting. James would also blot out letters or words before the ink dried and then sometimes overwrite the blot. In the letters' texts, we indicate blotting as struckthrough text. Since the precise nature of James's change is never entirely obvious from how we have represented overwriting and blotting out, all cases of overwriting and blotting receive an explanation in the textual commentary.

When a literal representation of a cancellation of a single character in the original letter is easily readable, we prefer that representation. For example, in his 16 April [1869] letter to his sister, Alice,

James wrote "sensations" and then canceled the final "s" by crossing it out twice. We represent this as "sensation~~s~~." While it is true that James in essence canceled the entire word, "sensations," and replaced it with "sensation" when he crossed out the final "s," representing the change as "~~sensations~~ sensation" would not, in our judgment, aid readability and would also be a less accurate representation of the manuscript.

In all cases do we preserve James's spelling and punctuation. Such preservation not only shows James's use of American and English word forms, his attention or lack of attention to certain words, but also may suggest that in certain instances James might have misspelled a word deliberately to create a pun or other humorous effect. His use of "Mewport" for "Newport" and "sich" for "such" in his 13 May 1860 and 27 March [1868] letters to Thomas Sergeant Perry and "probaly" for "probably" and "har" for "hear" in his 21 May [1867] letter to his brother, William, are typical examples. James also used variant spellings that are less common in the early twenty-first century: for instance, "shew," "despatch," "fulness," or "dulness," and we preserve these variant spellings, as we do those in other languages. James would, on occasion, inadvertently misspell words. Inadvertent misspellings are indicated as such in the corresponding textual commentary so that it is clear to our readers that the slip was James's. Deliberate misspellings and variant spellings in English and other languages receive no commentary. We provide no textual commentary on James's misspellings of proper names, unless comprehension is otherwise severely compromised. We do, however, provide the correct spelling of the name in any explanatory notes.

We indicate inadvertent repetition of a word caused by a line or page break by a note in the textual commentary. We do not gloss inadvertent omissions of words or midline repetitions, and readers should assume these to be James's.

We report all cases of end-line hyphenation in the textual notes when the hyphenation does not occur by coincidence at the end of a line in the edited text. Thus whenever an end-line hyphenation occurs in the edited text and does not receive an emendation note, readers should assume that that hyphenation occurs at the end of a line in the copytext as well.

James's use of the apostrophe in these early letters is irregular and does not always conform to today's conventions. We cannot know in any instance if James's errors were the result of carelessness, convention, or a poor understanding of the appropriate uses of apostrophes. Whatever the reasons, we believe that it is important not to correct or standardize his use of the apostrophe. When there is doubt about the placement of an apostrophe, we give James the benefit of the doubt and represent that placement according to his best usage. Where there is no doubt of his placement, we show it as it appears in his hand.

James often, but not always, linked the personal pronoun, "I," to the following word, especially in the combinations "I had" and "I have." Having concluded that this link is not meaningful and that representing James's habit of linking the words would make reading the printed letter awkward, we have silently inserted a space in these instances. For the same reasons, we have also systematically and silently inserted a space in James's signature, between "James" and "jr." when James, as he often did, linked them.

James very rarely wrote out "and." He instead wrote an abbreviated ampersand like the one used by such contemporaries as Samuel Clemens, Charles Eliot Norton, and William James. Consistent with our presenting James's abbreviated words and names as he wrote them in his letters, we represent James's abbreviated ampersand with the *&* symbol.

Recurrent stylistic idiosyncrasies are meaningful. One such idiosyncrasy is James's way of emphasis by underlining once, twice, three times, sometimes with a flourish, occasionally with a circle around or a wavy line beneath a word or phrase, for a particular degree of emphasis. We render those forms of emphasis as James did. Just as we work to represent the meaning inherent or, perhaps, explicit in the range of cancellations, so do we represent as literally as possible the meanings inherent in the range of James's means of showing emphasis.

Since we do not follow James's line endings, we don't preserve in the edited letter text his hyphenated words. Those hyphenations are preserved, however, in the textual commentary and are reported as emendations. Line breaks are recorded also in the textual commentary when a break could help to explain an awkwardness in a letter. For example in his [7], 8, 9 March 1870 letter to William James,

Henry James wrote "income—" at the end of one line and began the next with "—let it lie warm." Yet the meaning of the dashes—should they be rendered as a double-em dash, like a hyphenated word, or as two separate single ems, like two words separated by the line break?—was not clear. Thus we wanted to preserve the possible importance of the line break in a textual note to give interested readers the opportunity to decide for themselves.

James's drawings are reproduced in as close to the original relationship with the text as possible, given the nature of typography and publishing restrictions.

James tends in these early letters to avoid indentation to mark a subject change in his letters. Instead, like many of his generation, James relied on a dash for a range of meanings. He could use it following a period to mark a new subject. He could use it within a sentence to mark a parenthetical thought. He could use it between sentences to mark a shift but not a subject change. In addition, James did not seem to relate the length of the dash to its meaning. Thus a dash marking emphasis cannot be distinguished in terms of its length from one marking a transition between subjects. Because James seems not to have related meaning to length, because we couldn't be sure in every case—or even in most cases—of the dash's particular function, and because we thought it likely that not all of James's own correspondents could have understood his idiosyncratic meaning, we represent all such dashes as one-em dashes and thus represent them without distinguishing their function. Our readers will have to determine for themselves, just as James's did, whether a dash between sentences indicates a new paragraph, as it were, or not. Here, as elsewhere, we remain consistent with James's own practice in his letters.

We follow James's indentations in terms of their relation to each other (see Hirst, "Editing Mark Twain"). Thus, we give James's shortest indentation one standard indentation space. We give his next longest one two, next longest after that three, and so on. Where James places a line or series of lines against the right margin of his paper, so do we.

We represent material inserted interlineally by James, and usually signaled in his letters with a caret, with a caret preceding the insertion and a bracketed caret to mark the end of the insertion. When James inserted material interlineally but omitted a caret, we supply in square brackets the initial caret to mark the start of the inserted material. A second bracketed caret marks the end of the interlineal insertion. In our transcriptions, interlineal insertions always appear after the cancellations above which James placed them, even in cases when James placed the caret to the left of the deletion. In so doing, we favor in our transcriptions a sequential rather than a spatial representation of James's text. Intralineal insertions are noted in the textual commentary.

When nearing the end of his letter and also the end of available blank space on his page, James would, in the convention of his time, finish his letter in the margin of a page or across a page. This we note.

The header to each letter provides the full name of the correspondent on the first line, the full date on the second line, the form of the source text (ALS, TLC, etc.) and the name of its repository on the third line, and, if applicable, the catalog number of the source text on the fourth line. Square brackets in the first line indicate a recipient's married name, if she wasn't married at the time of the letter's writing and is better known to history or in James's biography by her married name. (Thus, Lilla Cabot [Perry] but not Elizabeth Boott [Duveneck].) Square brackets in the second line indicate the editors' insertion of dates not written on the letter itself. Square brackets in the header's fourth line are a part of the archival information.

When we arrive at a conjectural date through an examination of internal letter evidence or when that evidence does not contradict a date arrived at by earlier scholars, we let that date stand without comment. When we redate a previously published letter, especially if James left it partially or wholly undated, we explain in our notes the reason for our dating.

Our aim in dating letters is to arrive at the best date or range of dates possible given the evidence provided in the letter (and occasionally the stationery) itself. Of course, all such dating is to one degree or another conjectural. The articulation of multiple dates over which a letter was written deserves a few words of explanation. We give the dates of a letter written over the course of more than one day, when each day is indicated in the letter itself either by an actual date written or when the letter gives evidence that there were starts and stops in composition, with a comma separating the dates on which the letter was written (e.g., 26, 29 July [1869]). When the letter gives a temporal cue of time separating the writing of sections of the letter ("yesterday," "last night," "two days ago") but the date of the writing is not written in the letter, the implied dates are given in square brackets ([7], 8, 9 March 1870). When it is clear from evidence in the letter that James began writing the letter late one day and finished it, without a marked break, on the next, the dating is given with an en dash.

We use the ✉ sign in the letter's header to indicate the presence of an envelope with a given letter. That ✉ sign recurs before the previous publication information to signal a description of the address and postal cancellation stamp(s).

We translate foreign phrases that we judge might not be familiar for many of our readers. We offer these translations in the informational notes. Our approach to annotation in general is to provide information that will help our readers understand not only some of what we judge James's reader might have known but also, when it will help provide a useful context, what we know about people, places, and subjects to which James referred. While no set of notes will satisfy every reader, if we err, we prefer to err on the side of providing too much information, as it were, rather than too little. Overall, we hope that our notes will provide a way for readers to develop for themselves insights into James's letters, life, and time.

The two volumes of *The Complete Letters of Henry James, 1855–1872,* contain 161 letters, of which 52 are published for the first time. Each letter is followed by previous publication information or a note that there is no previous publication.

The full version of this introduction is given in volume 1.

Chronology

appear in the *Nation*, and "Travelling Companions" is published in the *Atlantic Monthly*.

1871: CAMBRIDGE

"A Passionate Pilgrim" appears in the *Atlantic Monthly*.
First novel, *Watch and Ward*, serialized in the *Atlantic Monthly*, August–December.
Late summer, HJ visits Canada, traveling from Niagara to Quebec. Howells asks him to serve as occasional art reviewer for the *Atlantic Monthly;* articles begin to appear the following year.

1872: CAMBRIDGE

HJ expresses a wish to return to Europe. He makes plans to accompany Alice and Aunt Kate there and proposes travel articles for the *Nation*. May 11, they depart on the *Algeria*.

Symbols and Abbreviations

SYMBOLS USED IN THE EDITED LETTERS

✉ indicates the presence of an envelope with the original letter.

▬ represents the cancellation of an illegible sequence of letters, probably a word.

◊ represents an illegible character.

[∧] at the end of a phrase indicates the end of material inserted interlineally; at the beginning of a phrase it indicates the beginning of material inserted interlineally when HJ did not write a caret.

FAMILY NAME ABBREVIATIONS

AJ	Alice James
AK	Catharine Walsh (Aunt Kate)
GWJ	Garth Wilkinson James (Wilky, Wilkie)
HJ	Henry James
MWJ	Mary Walsh James
RJ	Robertson James (Rob, Robbie, Bob)
Sr.	Henry James Sr.
WJ	William James

COPY-TEXT FORM ABBREVIATIONS USED

AL	Autograph letter, not signed
ALS	Autograph letter, signed
Mf	Microfilm of lost manuscript
MS Photocopy	Photocopy of lost manuscript
TLC	Typed letter copy of lost manuscript

The Complete Letters of Henry James

1855–1872

VOLUME 2

1869

CHARLES ELIOT NORTON
[18 May 1869]
ALS Houghton
bMS Am 1088 (3848)

5

Tuesday
Genève, Pension Bovet
    aux Pâquis.
Dear Charles—

M'y voici! & tempted to lose as little time as possible in letting   10
you know it—lest you should feel like asking me to do any thing
for you. I had as pleasant a journey to Paris as was compatible
with a very disorganized condition on the ~~journey~~| channel. But
with my feet on my native heath so to speak, I soon recuperated
& enjoyed the run from Boulogne. In Paris I spent a day—a   15
portion of it in the Salon wh. contrasts characteristically enough
with the R. A. Paris struck me as a perfect ~~g~~ flare & glare of
mechanical splendor. I came here by night—from 8 p.m to 10.
am.—a trying & fatiguing journey. I am already installed in the
~~ino~~ inevitable pension with half a dozen dear Americans.   20
Geneva looks charming & I can't but think you'll find it so. I am
told that there are many houses—some delightful—but that they
are going rapidly. Are you in communication with any one here?
If not I might, on your authorization, say a word to the agent. I
do hope you~~r~~ are not going to back out (excuse my vulgarity.)   25
for without you~~r~~, the Dismal looms portentous. Farewell! I have
only just time to catch the mail. Address me as above—ie.
Pension Bovet, aux Pâquis, Genève. Give my love to all your
household & dont hesitate to appeal to the feeble energies of
    Your most well disposed & faithful   30
        H. James jr.

No previous publication

    ∾

3

3.11 any thing • any | thing

3.12 pleasant • pleas= | ant

3.13 ~~journey~~ channel • [channel *overwrites* journey]

3.17 ~~g~~ flare • [f *overwrites* g]

3.20 ~~ino~~ inevitable • [e *overwrites illegible letter*]

3.25 you~~r~~ • [r *blotted out*]

∽

3.2 [18 May 1869] • Date based on information about HJ's travels to Geneva, narrated in HJ's [19] May [1869] letter to his mother, and about the Nortons' travels to Switzerland described in Charles Eliot Norton's letters of 27 May 1869 and 3 June 1869 to HJ (Houghton bMS Am 1094 [370, 371]). "Tuesday" fell on 18 May in 1869. HJ's letter to his mother describes his arrival in Geneva on "Sunday" May 16 and his moving into the Pension Bovet "on Tuesday morng." May 18. The Nortons arrived at Antwerp on May 26, and Charles Eliot Norton wrote HJ on May 27 from there, telling of their planned departure the next day for Cologne and arrival in Basel on May 31 or June 1, where he hoped "we may find a note from you." (HJ's May 31 letter to Norton in fact begins: "It's a great pleasure at last to get your letter, wh. arrived half an hour ago, ∂ to feel that we are neighbors again," thus acknowledging the 27 May letter from Antwerp.) Norton also apologizes in the 27 May 1869 letter for not having had time before leaving London to answer "your very pleasant ∂ kind note" (which would be the "Tuesday" letter). Clearly the "Tuesday" letter predates HJ's May 31 letter, and since the Nortons had arrived in Switzerland by Tuesday, June 1 (Norton's 3 June 1869 letter to HJ from Lausanne states: "We reached here safely last night"), HJ could only conceivably have written the "Tuesday" letter on May 18 or May 25, but May 25 is not possible, since the Nortons would have already left London and would not have received it.

3.7 Pension Bovet • Madame Bovet operated a "pension d'étrangers" (pension for foreigners) at Pâquis, 27 (Catalan 35); Baedeker's *Switzerland* for 1869 indicates that Geneva pensions typically charged between eighty-five and three hundred francs a month (178).

3.10 M'y voici! • Here I am!

3.17 R. A. • Royal Academy, London.

MARY WALSH JAMES
[19] May [1869]
ALS Houghton
bMS Am 1094 (1758)

✉   5

Genève. Pension Bovet
    aux Pâquis.
    Wednesday May 17(?)

                                                10

Dearest mamman de mon coeur.

   I wrote a week ago from London, just before crossing to
Paris. Since then I have again travelled by flood & field & again
relapsed into a "regular boarder". The most distinct impression
present in my mind is of how much can be done in a week. I left   15
London at 10 a.m of Friday & reached Paris at 8.30 p.m.—
tolerably <u>maladif</u> on the channel—better at Boulogne & best at
Paris. Boulogne looked as if I had left it yesterday—<u>rien n'y
manquait</u>, except that it was much smaller. Of course I saw only
the little bit from the boat to the Station. At Paris I went to the   20
Grand Hotel—a horrible place—a little Paris within the big—&
a big New-York inside of that—a complication of terrors. I was
obliged to stop over the whole day as there is but one train—the
night express, to Geneva. I spent my time in walking the streets,
whereby I was vastly struck with their magnificence. The place   25
has turned into a perfect monotony of glaring would-be
monumental splendor. Flare & glare are the only words it
suggests—the reflection of torrid asphalte & limestone by day &
the feverish torrents of gaslight by night. Napoleon has <u>tué
la nuit</u> Victor Hugo would say. Tell Willy that I spent some time 30
at the <u>Salon</u>, the average tone of which is much less clever than I
supposed. A very fine Courbet, tho', a hunting piece—& an
immense lot of ◊ promiscuous ability. But it did me good
afterwards to stroll through the eternal Louvre. I enjoy the

masters quite as much as I hoped. They are so respectable, in this profligate modern world—oh the tumult, the splendor, the crazy headlong race for pleasure—& the stagnant gulfs of misery to be seen in two great capitals like London & Paris. Mankind

5 seems like the bedevilled herd of swine in the Bible, rushing headlong into the sea.—<u>Enfin</u>, I left Paris Saturday evening at 8.30 & after a very tough night of it reached this place at 10.30 ∧a.m.[∧] of Sunday. I went to the Ecu—still the excellent Ecu of the past. On the Monday I bestirred myself for a <u>pension</u> & on

10 Tuesday morng. (yesterday) came here. You remember this place probably—the abode of Mr. Giles & Mrs. Clayson—who by the way is now here—somewhat elderly, but elegant in her ruins. I came near going to ⋄ a house further along the <u>Pâquis</u>, kept by M<u>me</u> Oefterdinger, the daughter of M<u>me</u> Buscarlet, now

15 apparently a second time a widow & the perfect image of her mother. The situation was charming but the room poor. Here, I have a large room on the <u>rez de chaussée</u> for 6 frs daily, including wine. The company is small, American & puerile. But we shall see. Mme Bovet & her daughters seem very obliging &

20 good—intelligent even—since they are great readers of V. Cherbuliez. <u>À propos</u> he lives in Geneva & there is a young German in the house who knows & dines with him. <u>J'ai bien envie de me faire presenter</u>. My French astounds me—its goodness is ~~equally~~ equalled only by its badness. I can be terribly

25 <u>spirituel</u>, but I can't ask for a candlestick.—Geneva looks very pleasant & has kept all its old specialty of blue—that of the lake, river & mountains. But I apprehend the dull—not to say the dismal, until the season opens & I run against some acquaintance. <u>Par bonheur</u> I have my dear Nortons who are

30 probabling coming in ten days, if they can get a house.—I have as yet not got your mail of this week. I write this to go <u>via</u> Bremen, for which I must post it now, & at the same time shall stop at Lombard ∧&[∧] Odier's to ask for my letters from London. Direct in future to them <u>via</u> Bremen: I am told it is the

best way. I feel my weekly palpitations at letter-time. I assure
you dearest mother, they are violent. I am chronically,
desperately, mournfully, shamelessly homesick. I'm very glad to
◇ get on the Continent; but on leaving England I find I like it
even better—more cordially—than I fancied. It's so healthy, so   5
honnête ɟ above all, so comfortable. I realize now the blessings
of its admirable cookery—enough in itself to preserve the virtue
ɟ maintain the empire of a great people. With that ɟ t̶h̶e̶i̶r̶
ᴧher[ᴧ] bath-tubs England may take her stand. À propos of these
matters you will admit that in the week my strength has been   10
well-tested. The old story: I am so well for it that it can be called
nothing but ◇ better. If from you all I can only get as good news
as I send! I adore you all—if that will do any good. Tell Willy to
scribble a line in pencil whenever he can. From Alice I expect
great things, at least ten pages for instance, to day ɟ from father, 15
after his last promises, in proportion—I fully count upon a line
from A. K. from Queenstown. Farewell. Your devoted son H.

✉

Bremen   20
    Mrs. Henry Ja[mes]
      Cambridge
        Mass.
    Etats Unis d'Amérique
Front postmark: GENEVE| 19 V 69 I *Back postmarks:* BASEL| 25
20 V [69] *and* LAU[SANNE]| 19 V [69]. *Someone (possibly WJ)
has written in ink on the back of the envelope:* Geneva. May 17ᵗʰ|
1869 *and in pencil, someone (possibly WJ) has drawn three profiles, of
a man with a mustache, a clean-shaven man, and a man with a beard.*

No previous publication

  ∾

  5.11 mamman • [*misspelled*]

  5.12 London • Lon= | don

5.33 ⬦ promiscuous • [p *overwrites illegible letter*]

6.13 ⬦ a • [a *overwrites illegible letter*]

6.18 American • Ameri= | can

6.19 daughters • daugh= | ters

6.21 Cherbuliez • Cher= | buliez

6.24 ~~equally~~ equalled • [ed *overwrites* y]

6.25 candlestick • candle= | stick

6.29 acquaintance • acquain- | tance

7.4 ⬦ get • [g *overwrites illegible letter*]

7.12 ⬦ better • [b *overwrites illegible letter*]

7.16 promises, in proportion—I fully count • [*written across the letter's fifth page*]

7.16–17 upon a line from A. K. from Queenstown. Farewell. Your devoted son H. • [*written up the left margin of the letter's first page*]

        ∾

5.9 Wednesday May 17(?) • May 17 was a Monday in 1869; since the envelope to this letter is postmarked May 19, and since HJ refers to "Tuesday (yesterday)," he clearly wrote the letter on Wednesday, May 19.

5.11 mamman de mon coeur • mammy of my heart.

5.17 <u>maladif</u> • <u>seedy</u>.

5.18 Boulogne looked [. . .] yesterday • The Jameses resided in Boulogne-sur-Mer during the summer of 1857 and from December 1857 to May 1858.

5.18–19 <u>rien n'y manquait</u> • <u>nothing was missing</u>.

5.29–30 <u>tué la nuit</u> • <u>killed the night</u>.

5.32 A very fine Courbet, tho', a hunting piece • According to the 1869 Salon catalog, Gustave Courbet exhibited two paintings: *L'hallali du cerf, épisode de chasse à courre par un temps de neige* and *La sieste, pendant la saison des foins; montagne du Doubs* (*Explication* 571–72); HJ refers to the first of these two paintings.

6.6 <u>Enfin</u> • <u>Finally</u>.

6.8 the Ecu • The Ecu de Genève.

6.14 M<u>me</u> Buscarlet • Baedeker's *Switzerland* for 1869 includes in the lists of Geneva pensions: "Mme. Buscarlet (200–250 fr.), Quai du Mont Blanc 9" (178).

6.17 <u>rez de chaussée</u> · <u>ground floor</u>.

6.22–23 <u>J'ai bien envie de me faire presenter.</u> · <u>I really would like to be introduced</u>.

6.25 <u>spirituel</u> · <u>witty</u>.

6.29 <u>Par bonheur</u> · <u>Luckily</u>.

6.33 Lombard ∧&[∧] Odier's · HJ's mailing address and banker during the beginning of his stay was Lombard, Odier, and Company, Geneva.

7.6 <u>honnête</u> · <u>honest</u>.

7.17 A. K. · Aunt Kate.

ALICE JAMES   15
29 May 1869
ALS Houghton
bMS Am 1094 (1555)

Geneva May 29<u>th</u> '69.   .   20

My dearest Sister—

  I wrote to mother about ten days ago, just after my arrival in this place—since when I have been counting strongly on news from home. I received last week a note from Bob—or rather a   25
letter & a most amiable one. But this week, nothing! I trudge over to the Bankers almost daily, but return with blighted hopes. A few days ago I heard from A. K. from Dublin, in apparently good spirits. When I shall encounter the party I know not, but wait resignedly. You will of course have heard from A. K. & will   30
be getting more frequent news of her movements than I. The most charming news in Bob's letter, sweet sister, was the mention he made in of ⋄ your prowess & energy! Long may it last! Why doesn't mother give a party for your coming out?—I

9

have but little to tell you, for Geneva has not as yet been fertile
in sensations. In fact, it is not to be concealed that it is decidedly
dull. When once you get used to its delightful beauty, you have
come to the end of the chapter. I nevertheless manage to get
5   along very comfortably. Each successive day in one way or
another takes care of itself & behold, tomorrow I shall have been
here a fortnight. The chief drawback has been a deal of showery
weather, which is now at a dismal climax. I have been afraid that
coming here as early as I did will give me rather too long a
10   summer (3 mos & ½) in Switzerland & felt some regret that I
didn't remain in Paris, as I at first intended, till the 1ˢᵗ July,
where in the Louvre, if nowhere else, I could have spent a vast
amount of time. But the weeks will look after themselves even as
the days, I suppose & when the season fairly opens, I shall be
15   likely to find considerable diversion. I foresee however, that my
enjoyment of this precipitous land will depend largely on two
circumstances—my meeting a certain amount of available
society & my developing some serious ability to use my legs. In
both respects the promise is good. If I don't wander too far
20   from the highway of travel I shall be certain to encounter a lot
of fellow-strangers. As for walking I have good reason to hope
that I may yet turn out a walker. I have been trying my paces
since my arrival here & with distinguished success: there is
indeed, except reading, little to do but walk. I walked out to
25   Ferney the other day, visited the château of the illustrious V. &
returned on the top of a 'bus. But it was the next day that I
shewed what is in me. I started forth for an innocent walk to the
Junction, which you remember & which I duly reached. Thence
I pursued the bank of the Arve to Carouge & thence meandered
30   thro' a long dense Avenue of acacias to Lancy. There, striking
boldly forth, I approached the base of the great Salève, & ~~trug~~
trudged along a very good stretch of lovely road to the village of
Veirier, which lies at the foot of the smaller Salève. Ask Willy if
he remembers the Pas-de-l'-Echelle. I advanced boldly thro' the

Village, measured the ascent with an unflinching eye ᵺ then
deliberately scaled it. It's a stiff half-hour's work. At the summit
I entered the Village of Monnetier, reposed a while in the shade
ᵺ quaffed a beaker of wine. I then descended the pas-de l'echelle
ᵺ trudged back to Geneva by the straight course— —about a   5
third of the distance of the round-a-bout way I had come. If I
had come by the same road, I would have easily been in a state
to push up to the summit of the great Salève. But this will be for
another time. I got home at about 7 p.m. after a nice little stroll
of about seven hours. Of course I was mortally tired. The next   10
day, too, I was decidedly languid. But the third day, ma toute-
belle, I was unmistakeably better—i.e. better than before I
undertook the walk: ᵺ on the 4ᵗʰ, if I had had a companion, I
would gladly have gone ᵺ done it over again. Since then I have
taken divers minor promenades. All hereabouts it's ⋄ lovely   15
walking country. The roads are as smooth ᵺ ~~level~~ ∧hard[∧] as
parquets—the trees ᵺ hedges ▬▬▬ full of the prime of summer
ᵺ the mountainous horizon everywhere. It's almost as beautiful
as England, with all the strange difference between French
verdure ᵺ English—the same as the difference between the   20
faces. Day before yesterday, I made a charming day of it. I
started forth at 10. am. in the steamer ᵺ made the entire circuit
of the lake, returning here at 7.30 p.m. I had an hour ᵺ ½ ashore
at Villeneuve where I dined, celestially, at the delicious hotel
Byron, off a fillet of beef ᵺ petits pois, with an omellette aux   25
confitures. There, by the way, is a sign of my regeneracy—that I
eat pease. Later in the season I hope to spend a fortnight at the
H. B., as I'm told they take you en pension. —My house here is
comfortable, but stupid. The company is two ∧old[∧] English
ladies, with their daughter, a rather nice, ~~decidely~~ decidedly   30
clever ᵺ somewhat untidy young person of a marrigeable age;
two "Southern ladies" with a strong negro accent, who keep
their rooms, Mrs. Clayson ᵺ a young German of studious habits
ᵺ infantile conversation. Mrs Clayson is harmless, but hugely

uninteresting ~~&~~ of ~~Mrs~~ Miss Cranford I have already sounded the depths. So I live in the hope of better things. I have a very nice room on the <u>rez-de chaussée</u>, opening into the good old garden. I can be here but a week longer as Mme Bovet is to move

5   over to a new campagne on the other side of the lake & of course I wish to shirk the déménagement. I expect the Nortons soon to turn up, which will be an improvement. With their assistance I hope to remain here till ~~June~~ July 1st—of course in new quarters.—So much, dearest child, for myself & my own

10   everlasting fussifications, of wh., by this time, you must be quite sick. In the absence of any recent news from home, I can only indulge in the usual good wishes for your bien-être. I want very much to learn about your arrangements for the summer—good luck to them. I do hope Willy & you may find them profitable &

15   that father will not be quite so expatriated as last year. As for mother, with the first sniff of country air I suppose she will begin to frisk & prance. Is Wilky at home? If so I wish he could drop me a line & trust me for an answer. Give him my love & a punch in the stomach. Tell Willy I mean soon to write to him—

20   especially ᴧin reply to₍ᴧ₎ his remarks in his last, about studying German. Give my remembrances to friends & such—love to Mrs. Lombard. Commend me most filially to my parents, write to me still & believe me your brother, as happy in your amendment as in his own—H.

No previous publication

∾

9.24 strongly • strong= | ly

9.25 received • re= | ceived

9.27 return • re= | turn

9.29 encounter • en= | counter

9.33 ~~in~~ of • [of *overwrites* in]

9.33 ◊ your • [yo *overwrites illegible letter*]

10.1 fertile • fer= | tile

10.2 decidedly • de= | cidedly

10.4 chapter • chap= | ter

10.5 successive • suc= | cessive

10.6 tomorrow • to= | morrow

10.10 Switzerland • Switzer= | land

10.15 considerable • consid= | erable

10.16 enjoyment • enjoy= | ment

10.17 certain • cer= | tain

10.31–32 ~~trug~~ trudged • [d *overwrites* g]

10.34 boldly • bold= | ly

11.5 — — • — | —

11.12 unmistakeably • [*misspelled*]

11.13 undertook • un= | dertook

11.17 ■■■■■ full • [full *overwrites illegible word*]

11.18 mountainous • moun= | tainous; [ous *inserted*]

11.21 charming • charm= | ing

11.24 Villeneuve • Ville= | neuve

11.30 ~~decidely~~ decidedly • [dly *overwrites* ly]

11.31 untidy • un= | tidy

11.31 marrigeable • [*misspelled*]

12.1 ~~Mrs~~ Miss • [is *overwrites* rs]

12.6 Nortons • Nor= | =tons

12.8 ~~June~~ July • [ly *overwrites* ne]

12.10 everlasting • ever= | lasting

12.11 recent • re= | cent

12.24 amendment • amend= | ment

∽

9.23 I wrote to mother about ten days ago • See HJ to MWJ, [19] May [1869].

9.25 Bob • RJ.

9.28 A. K. • Aunt Kate.

10.25 Ferney • A village five miles north of Geneva, where Voltaire resided from 1759 to 1777.

10.25 illustrious V. • Voltaire.

10.29–30 Carouge [. . .] Lancy • Suburbs of Geneva.

10.31 the great Salève • Mt. Salève, ridge (1176 m) just south of the Swiss-French border.

10.33 Veirier • Veyrier, on the Swiss border with France, at the foot of Mt. Salève.

10.34 Pas-de-l'Echelle • Murray's 1867 *Alps of Savoy and Piedmont* describes this as "a very steep path, practicable only on foot, partly formed by steps cut in the rock" (173).

11.3 Monnetier • French village connected by Pas-de-l'Echelle to Veyrier and a midpoint on the ascent of the Mt. Salève.

11.11–12 ma toute-belle • my pretty one.

11.24 Villeneuve • City at the easternmost tip of the Lake of Geneva.

11.24–25 the delicious hotel Byron • The 1867 Murray for the *Alps* describes this hotel: "Between Chillon and Villeneuve, 10 minutes' walk from either, and a little above the lake, stands the *Hôtel Byron*, a large and well-managed hotel and pension, table-d'hôte liberal, and great cleanliness and civility; rooms lofty and airy. Hotel prices for passing travellers: charge for pension, $7\frac{1}{2}$ fr. a day in summer, $5\frac{1}{2}$ fr. in winter. This is the best stopping-place at the E. end of the lake" (185); the 1869 Baedeker for *Switzerland* gives the price of a table d'hôte meal at the Hotel Byron as four francs and calls it "handsome" (197).

11.25 petits pois • green peas.

11.25–26 omellette aux confitures • omelet with jam.

11.28 en pension • board and lodging.

12.3 rez-de chaussée • ground floor.

12.5 campagne • place in the country.

12.6 déménagement • move.

12.12 bien-être • well-being.

12.20–21 his remarks in his last, about studying German • In his 23 April 1869 letter to HJ, WJ wrote:

I have found myself realizing of late very intensely how much I had gained by the knowledge of German, more than I ever appreciated at the time. It is a really classical & cosmopolitan literature, compared to which French & Engl. both seem in very important respects provincial.

I take back all I ever said to you about it being no matter if you never
shd. learn it. I wd. give a good deal if I cd. have learned it 10 years ago—
it wd. have saved me a great many lost steps and waste hours. The common currency of german thought is of a so much higher denomination
than that of Engl. and Fr. that a mind of equal power playing the game
of life with that coin for counters accomplishes far more with an equal
exertion. (*CWJ* 1: 66–67)

12.22 Mrs. Lombard · The Lombards were family friends (Strouse
142).

WILLIAM JAMES
30, 31 May 1869
ALS Houghton
bMS Am 1094 (1931)

Geneva May 30ᵗʰ 69. (Sunday.)

Dear Brother Bill—

I wrote to Alice yesterday ☞ remarked en passant that I meant
soon to write to you. As I have just discovered that I ~~have~~ forgot
to enclose this photograph—as it's a dismal rainy day ☞ I am
confined within doors, the moment seems propitious for my
design. Not that I have any wondrous things to tell; I was
thinking more especially of the recommendation in your last
note, with regard to studying German. Your words go to my
heart. The thing on earth I should most like to do would be to
make a bee-line for some agreeable German town ☞ plunge into
the ⬦⬦⬦ speech ☞ the literature of the land. I would give my head
to be able to use it. But it's painfully evident that I can do
nothing of the kind for many a month to come. I know that you
didn't suggest it as an immediate project but ~~you~~ that you chiefly
wished to remind me of its intrinsic importance. I have no doubt
whatever of the truth of what you say ☞ and I hope one of these
days to act upon your advice. But the day looks distant. I am no

nearer being able to read with impunity than I was when I left
home. The fact of my feeling the old familiar seediness owing to
having tried it ~~dur~~ a little more than usual during these last days
while confined to the house by the rain, shews me plainly

5   enough that I must ₍ₐ₎still₍ₐ₎ interpose a little ease—or in other
words a long interval of idleness. I have come to the conclusion
that I must modify in a considerable degree the programme with
which I came abroad—I remember that I wrote to father from
London that I thought a year of travelling would go far towards

10   making me a well man. If I felt any doubt then of the truth of
the statement it has been removed by the experience of the last
fortnight. Movement, & more movement & still movement—"de
l'audace et encore de l'audace et ⋄ toujours de l'audace"—seems
to be the best—the only prescription for my ills. It's the idea I

15   came abroad with, only more so. Instead of a few long quiet
sojourns I must make short sojourns & more of them; that is
what I mean by "travelling." I can very well stay in a place until I
have exhausted its material sights & resources & in some places
of course this would ~~resolve~~ ₍ₐ₎imply₍ₐ₎ a comparatively long stay

20   (Paris & various Italian towns.) But when I have "done" the place
so thoroughly that there is nothing left but to fall back upon my
own society, it will be my best interest to leave it & take up with
another. I feel that it is in my power to "do" any place, quietly, as
thoroughly as it can be done. If this is not the case my ~~de~~

25   condition & my destiny are a decidedly tough problem; for I
have established it as an ~~ee~~ absolute certainty that I can't sit &
read, & between sitting & standing I know of no middle state.
These reflections have been forcibly suggested by my life in this
place, in which there is so little external diversion that (in spite

30   of considerable walking & two expeditions in particular wh. I
described to Alice) I am reduced to the old <u>tête à tête</u> with my
back—greatly to the detriment of both of us. I think it therefore
necessary to face the situation & read it aright. Do communicate
these views to father & mother & invoke their blessing on my

theory. What I wish is firmly to establish it as a theory, even should my practice not diverge very widely from that which I originally contemplated. It will certainly not be extravagant & I shall be at best a very tame traveller. I was slightly disappointed at mother's reply in her last to my remarks about going to Scotland & at her apparent failure to suspect that it was not as a spree but as ~~an~~ part of an <u>absolute</u> <u>remedy</u> that I thought of the journey. I doubtless neglected to give a hint of this, however, & my lovely mammy was further justified by my erroneous estimate of my expenses. That she should have thought it necessary to place a veto on my proposition, nevertheless proves the necessity of my thus defining my situation. I want to feel free to use my means to circulate as largely as necessity pure & simple seems to dictate. I have no desire to be restless or fanciful or wasteful. I wish simply to feel at liberty ∧to[∧] spend my letter of credit rather more rapidly than I at first anticipated; & I shall by no means feel so blissfully commissioned until I have brought the sacred influences of home into harmony with my idea & ensured them against being shocked by my apparent extravagance & inconstancy. I want father & mother to write & say that they understand & approve my representations. They cannot overestimate my perfect determination to spend my money only as wisely as it was generously given & any future use I make of it will give me tenfold greater satisfaction for receiving ∧beforehand[∧] some slight propulsion from them. — In all this I have no fixed plan whatever; it is not a matter of plans, but simply of that one general tendency. I may turn out after all, to have done not very differently from what I should have done without all this contortion of spirit. I shall hang on to a place till it has yielded me its last drop of life-blood. I promise you, there shall be a method in my madness. In this way I hope to get a good deal for my money & ◇ to make it last a long time. How long I know not. When it is gone I shall come home ⧸ ∧a new man;[∧] I shall of course not ask for more. But I incline to think

5

10

15

20

25

30

17

that on this basis I shall get no regular study out of my present residence in Europe, even if I stay, as I hope to do, two years. If I am ever to spend any time in Germany it will be later, on my own responsibility. On the other hand, tho' I get no study, I

5 think I shall absorb a good deal of "general culture." I feel as if, in this way, I have already made a good beginning. ~~The~~ I have enjoyed the little I have seen in the way of pictures ¦ in a manner to suggest that, if I take all I find, I may lay the basis of a serious interest in art & of knowledge which may be of future use to me.

10 I embrace this idea with a desperate grasp—tho' after all ~~these~~ there may be nothing in it. If I knock two more years out of my life, as regards study, it will bring me to 28—rather a late period to begin a course of reading—assuming even that I am then able to study. If therefore I have made anything of a start in the

15 knowledge of the history of art (& if I haven't "reacted") it will be so much time gained. But to do anything here at present, implies infinite labor & research & this is but a passing vision. Indeed I have no right to concern myself with what lies <u>au delà</u> this season of idleness; my present business—strange destiny!—

20 is simply to be idle. I shall have no plans but from month to month. My present notion is to remain here until I am irresistibly prompted to depart; then to go ∧to[∧] the hotel Byron at Villeneuve & stay as long as I can; then to go to some other place & then to finish the summer if possible at St. Moritz,

25 where I hope to be fortified by the air. In case Switzerland proves too much for me ∧<u>or</u> too little, rather,[∧] before the summer is over I shall finish it elsewhere. While in England I conceived the design of giving up Paris next winter & going to Italy in stead, where I should have a better chance to circulate &

30 carry out my programme. In Paris, a year later, I may be in a condition to do something in the way of study—for which (~~m~~ that is for reading) making every allowance for all the practicable diversions of the place, I should have a deal of time left on my hands. With this view I made up my mind to secure

6 weeks of Paris at present by staying there to the 1st July. But
I subsequently decided to come directly here & have perhaps
thereby added to my summer at one end what I shall have to
take off at the other. If I have had enough of Switzerland by the
middle of August, I shall perhaps go to P. & stay till the middle   5
of October & thence proceed via Marseilles & Leghorn to Italy.
But all this is black darkness & my prattle is superfluous. One
would think that I ~~didn't~~ ∧wasn't to[∧] write to you every blessed
week. — Pray tell father & mother for their satisfaction that I
have in hand (i.e. my letter of credit represents) £867 & that   10
upon this sum I build my adventures. It seems to me a good
broad foundation. It will not be likely to diminish as rapidly as it
has done in the last three months, owing both to lower prices &
greater experience. 31st. I have kept this over till to day but have
little to add. I have told the long story because I felt a need of ◇◇   15
opening myself & taking hold of my situation. I don't forget that
you too have a "situation" of your own. I wish I could prescribe
for it as well. I wish I heard from you oftener, but don't write a
line but when you feel like it. Give my love to father & mother &
bid them be charitable to the egotism of my letter. I am fighting   20
a very egotistical enemy. Farewell. Tout à toi H. J. jr
I don't know what you generally do with my letters — but read
this to no one out of the family.

Previous publication: *CWJ* 1: 74–77

∾

15.19   yesterday • yester= | day
15.20   ~~have~~ forgot • [forg *overwrites* have]
15.21   photograph • photo= | graph
15.25   studying • study= | ing
15.28   ◇◇◇ speech • [spe *overwrites illegible letters*]
15.29   painfully • pain= | fully
15.31   suggest • sug= | gest
15.31   ~~you~~ that • [that *overwrites* you]

15.32 importance • im= | portance

15.33 whatever • what= | ever

16.3 ~~dur~~ a little • [a l *overwrites* dur]

16.4 confined • con= | fined

16.12 Movement • Move= | =ment

16.13 ◊ toujours • [t *overwrites illegible letter*]

16.14 prescription • pres= | cription

16.16 sojourns • so= | =journs

16.24–25 ~~de~~ condition • [co *overwrites* de]

16.26 an • [n *inserted*]

16.26 ~~ce~~ absolute • [ab *overwrites* ce]

16.33 communicate • communi= | cate

17.7 ~~an~~ part • [pa *overwrites* an]

17.15 wasteful • waste- | ful

17.22 cannot • can= | not

17.30 promise • pro= | mise

17.32 ◊ to • [to *overwrites illegible letter*]

17.33 ¦ ∧ • [∧ *overwrites* ,]

18.6 ~~The~~ I have • [I h *overwrites* The]

18.10–11 ~~these~~ there • [re *overwrites* se]

18.18 <u>au delà</u> • [*misspelled*]

18.22 irresistibly • irre= | sistibly

18.25 Switzerland • Switzer= | land

18.31–32 ~~m~~ that • [tha *overwrites* m]

19.6 proceed • pro= | ceed

19.7 superfluous • super= | fluous

19.10 represents • repre= | sents

19.15–16 ◊◊ opening • [op *overwrites illegible letters*]

19.16–23 I don't [. . .] out of the family • [*written across the letter's first page*]

~

15.19 I wrote to Alice yesterday • HJ's 29 May 1869 letter from Geneva to AJ.

15.19 en passant • casually.

15.24–25 your last note • See WJ to HJ, 23 April 1869 (*CWJ* 1: 66–67).

16.12–13 "de l'audace et encore de l'audace et ◊ toujours de l'audace" •
HJ is loosely quoting the famous 2 September 1792 speech to the Legislative Assembly by then minister of justice, Georges-Jacques Danton (1759–94), following France's defeat in the battle of Longwy, in which Danton said that, to defeat her enemies, "Pour les vaincre il nous faut de l'audace, encore de l'audace, toujours de l'audace, et la France est sauvée" (To conquer them [our enemies] we need daring, more daring, daring now and always, and France is saved).

16.30–31 two expeditions in particular wh. I described to Alice • In his 29 May 1869 letter to AJ, HJ describes a walk up part of the Mt. Salève, near Geneva, and a boat trip around Lake Geneva.

18.18 au delà • beyond.

18.22–23 hotel Byron at Villeneuve • See HJ's 29 May 1869 letter to AJ for his description of this hotel.

19.6 Leghorn • Livorno, Italy.

19.21 Tout à toi • All yours.

CHARLES ELIOT NORTON   20
31 May [1869]
ALS Houghton
bMS Am 1088 (3849)

Genève, Pension Bovet   25
    May 31ˢᵗ
Dear Charles

It's a great pleasure at last to get your letter, wh. arrived half an hour ago, ₰ to feel that we are neighbors again. I had begun to fear ◊ either that my note never reached you or that your   30
answer had miscarried. I do mightily wish I had been of your party in Antwerp: I think I should even have risked the Rubenses. I wish there were a few dozen of them in ~~Geneve~~ Geneva! I condole most heartily with Mrs. Norton ₰ Grace on

their misery at sea—but this lovely land will make it up to them. I wish I could see them reposing in peace at their journey's end.—I await you impatiently on Thursday or Friday & have little doubt but that you will discover some fashion of dwelling

5 to your taste. I'm glad you think of going into a pension: it will save you a deal of trouble. There ~~are~~ is no end of such places in this region & as many more at the other end of the lake.—a whole chain of them, in particular, from Vevey to Villeneuve. The drawback there, however, is that the air is not bracing—that

10 they are winter sojourns & decidedly hot in summer. But I am told of a certain Glion—perched aloft behind Montreux, where the air is capital & there is an excellent pension. From the lake (whence I saw it the other day), the spot looks enchanting. At Lausanne & here both, you would have, I should think, a large

15 choice. Nous verrons bien, when you come. This household Bovet is an excellent one—but rather limited & predestined to a move across the lake into smaller quarters. Of myself I have no wonders to relate—except that I am very well—which has ceased to be a wonder. Geneva is extremely pretty, but rather vacuous.

20 One feels rather sold, living in a European town which has so few ~~Eu~~ distinctively European resources:—no Antwerp spire— no Rubenses—no museum, churches, opera nor theatre.— nothing but the sense of the Alps in the distance & Calvinism in the past. Victor Cherbuliez is in Berlin!—From your saying

25 nothing to the contrary I take it that your mother & yourself are enduring your journey & Jane & Sara even rising superior. My love to all. À bientôt! Yours most faithfully & impatiently H. James jr.

No previous publication

૦૦

21.30 ◇ either • [e *overwrites illegible letter*]

21.31 miscarried • miscar= | ried

21.33–34 ~~Geneve~~ Geneva • [a *overwrites* e]

21.34 heartily • hear= | tily

22.6 ~~are~~ is • [is *overwrites* are]

22.8 particular • par= | ticular

22.21 ~~Eu~~ distinctively • distinctive= | ly; [di *overwrites* Eu]

22.27 faithfully • faith= | fully

∾

21.28 your letter • Charles Eliot Norton to HJ, 27 May 1869 (Houghton bMS Am 1094 [370]).

21.32–33 Antwerp [. . .] Rubenses • Antwerp, in northern Belgium,
where artist Peter Paul Rubens (1577–1640) lived most of his life. In his
27 May 1869 letter from Antwerp to HJ, Charles Eliot Norton writes:
"Rubens is in great force here. His pictures positively [. . .] intrude upon
you, however quietly disposed you may be. They are like blasts of a trum-
pet. I am glad there are no more of them. I admit their power,—but power
is very little in comparison with some other qualities."

22.15 Nous verrons bien • Well, we shall see.

22.27 À bientôt • See you soon.

HENRY JAMES SR. AND MARY WALSH JAMES   20
13 June [1869]
ALS Houghton
bMS Am 1094 (1759)

Geneva June 13ᵗʰ   25
        Pension Bovet—
Dearest father & mother—
    Since I last wrote I have been blessed by the receipt of two
letters, father's of May 18 & mothers of the 25ᵗʰ—a strong &
savory blast from home. I have myself delayed writing a bit   30
longer than usual because I latterly despatched two letters at
once (to Alice & Willy)—to say nothing of another to Bob. It is
a great satisfaction, beloved parents to hear from you so amply &
cheerfully. There is another Atlantic Cable, quite as stout as the

telegraph, one end of which is moored in Quincy St, ♂ the other
tied thro' one of the sad perforations of my heart. It is simply
my dear mammy's apron-string, from which I calculate never to
be detatched. The two good items in your letters were the fine
things about Alice (who, I must say I think is going a little too
far) ♂ the news of Pomfret ♂ its charms. I have no doubt it has
nothing to envy Switzerland ♂ that you will spend a delicious
summer. Don't take fire at my descriptions of affairs over here.
You, too, have your advantages. A vast deal of life here is
charming, but it is obtained at the cost of much that is not—
loneliness, the constant money question, the perpetual sense of
something alien ♂ abject in the people about you, ♂ above all a
feeling of unrest, of being an outsider, of incomplete, baffled
enjoyment as if the ~~coutrᵒ~~ country, in ~~return for your~~
~~attempt to~~ ∧resentment of your selfish irresponsible₍∧₎ attitude
towards it, were determined to give up but a fraction of its
secrets. Under these drawbacks I continue to live ♂ move.
Voyons, what I have to relate. I have taken a number of walks,
made a few excursions ♂ misdigested, alas! a few repasts. Some
days ago I went to Coppet (Mme de Stael's place) with the young
Anglaise of whom I have spoken. I am sorry to say that she is
only an apology for a really agreeable girl (an American nice
girl), but nevertheless, we made a very good afternoon of it. The
château is a very gentle ♂ ladylike piece of antiquity ♂ the park
is as pleasant as a chapter in a good french novel—a little thin
but most agreeable for a hot summer's day. A week since
(Sunday) I took such a walk as ∧quite₍∧₎ recalled the time of my
petite jeunesse. A certain young German collegian living in the
house (a most amiable fellow) proposed to me to join him ♂ an
elderly frenchman (an exile who gives him lessons) in an early
course into the country. Having ◊ pondered, I accepted ♂
behold us trudging forth at 5 ½ a.m. while the dawn was yet
young ♂ the air still smelling of night. We walked till about nine
♂ then halted at a village on the lake, where we breakfasted most

lustily under the trees of a rustic <u>café</u>. We then strolled & ~~loafd~~
loafed & lounged ~~a◆◆~~ among woods & lanes till 2 ½ p.m. when we
took the train for home. I was thus about nine hours <u>en</u>
<u>course</u>—& with the usual salutary result. I enjoyed much the
vivacity, the liquid sort of gaiety of the french exile: but was
forcibly impressed with the essential philistinism of the french
mind. It has neither shade nor silence. On the Tuesday I took
the steamer up to Vevey & spent the day with the Nortons, who
had arrived there after an enchanting journey from London <u>via</u>
Antwerp, Cologne, the Rhine, Bâle & Lausanne. I passed several
agreeable hours with them at the delicious hôtel Monnet &
returned in the evening. They have taken a house for the
summer just out of Vevey, back from the lake, where, being in
pursuit of quiet, I fancy they will find it to their hearts' content.
They kindly suggest to me to come into a farm-house near
them, but ~~the~~ I should find the tranquillity excessive & shall stick
to pensions. Besides these expeditions I have taken a number of
enchanting walks   I find that with strength, my old passion for
walking returns to me; & the ideal of happiness, to my
percption, at present is to trudge on for ever & ever, coursing
thro' green solitudes & chasing the blue horizon. The country
hereabouts is deeply, admirably charming. The trees have an
almost English immensity & luxuriance & many a road is ~~lined~~
ₐcovered₍ₐ₎ for a mile by a transparent vault of verdure. If I had
time space & language I should like to sketch some of my walks:
but I must wait till I can talk of them. They would be pleasanter
if I had a companion; it is rather dreary forever poking about
alone. I went this morning up to the Cathedral St. Pierre, to
hear the discourse of a certain pastor Cougnard who has raised
an incredible storm about his ears by the utterance of a little
mild Unitarianism. His sermon was amiable & feeble—Boston
left it behind thirty years ago.—Of course you hear from
A. Kate & you know of Mr. Perkins's death. Speaking rationally,
I should say it was a most fortunate occurrence. As Cousin H.,

maintains her projects of travel, I shall problably meet the party somewhere this summer. A. K. seems to be keenly enjoying things—exclusive of course of Mr. P.'s demise. I have been spending a great deal of time in digesting my impressions of
5 England. They are ineffaceable. Nevertheless, I <u>must</u> some day go there for a year.—Not the least delectable among the contents of father's letter were the 2 photos. Mother's is excellent; I committed follies over it. A. Kate's is decidedly inferior. Alice, now in some leisure moment¡ (w if such exist)
10 will of course be done. <u>I implore it!</u>—I had meant to drop a line to Willy, but foresee that I will not. I shall be glad when his thesis &c. are over, as I shall perhaps get a letter, & he probably some benefcial repose. I enjoin upon him a long, idle, sensual, degrading summer. I hardly take a ~~breath~~ step or draw a breath
15 wh. I don't dedicate to his memory. Thank Wilk for his postscript, but bid him write a letter. I shall probably leave this in a couple of days for the other end of the lake. I shall have been here 4 weeks & more. You shall hear forthwith of my new quarters. Many thanks to father for his adjurations to
20 enjoyment. Kisses to Alice & Mother & love to all. H. J. jr. Rec'd. the 2 Atlantics & 1 Nation. Thanks about the proof. The french phrase cut out <u>was quite right</u>!

No previous publication

&

23.34 Atlantic · Atlan= | tic
24.4 detatched · [*misspelled*]
24.14 ~~coutr◊~~ country · [ntr *overwrites* tr◊]
24.19 misdigested · misdi= | gested
24.24 ladylike · lady= | like
25.1–2 ~~loafd~~ loafed · [e *overwrites* d]
25.2 a◊◊ among · [m *overwrites illegible letters*]
25.6 philistinism · phil= | istinism
25.9 enchanting · en= | chanting
25.11 agreeable · agree= | able

25.11 delicious • de= | licious

25.16 t̶h̶e̶ I • [I *overwrites* the]

25.20 percption • [*misspelled*]

25.28 Cathedral • Cathe= | dral

26.1 problably • [*misspelled*]

26.9 ¦ (• [(*overwrites* ,]

26.9 w̶ if • [if *overwrites* w]

26.13 benefcial • [*misspelled*]

26.14 b̶r̶e̶a̶t̶h̶ step • [step *overwrites* breath]

26.15–16 post- | script • post-script

26.21–22 Rec'd. the 2 Atlantics ᵭ 1 Nation. Thanks about the proof. The french phrase cut out <u>was quite right</u>! • [*written across the letter's first page*]

∾

23.31–32 I latterly despatched two letters at once (to Alice ᵭ Willy) • HJ's 29 May 1869 letter to AJ and his 30, 31 May 1869 letter to WJ.

24.6 Pomfret • Located in the northeastern part of Connecticut, the Jameses spent their summer holiday here, in "a farmhouse pleasantly surrounded by trees" (Lewis 200).

24.18 <u>Voyons</u> • <u>Let's see</u>.

24.20 Coppet (M<u>me</u> de Stael's place) • The village of Coppet, ten miles northeast of Geneva, on the lakeshore, site of the Château of Coppet, home of French novelist and critic Anne-Louise-Germaine Necker, Madame de Staël (1766–1817), most famous for her novels *Corinne* (1807) and *Delphine* (1802), her relationship with fellow author Benjamin Constant (fictionalized in his novel *Adolphe*), and her celebrated literary salon.

24.21 Anglaise • Englishwoman.

24.28 <u>petite jeunesse</u> • <u>early youth</u>.

24.31 <u>course</u> • <u>excursion</u>.

25.3–4 <u>en course</u> • <u>on my excursion</u>.

25.8–10 the Nortons [. . .] enchanting journey [. . .] Bâle [Basel] ᵭ Lausanne • See Charles Eliot Norton's 27 May 1869 letter from Antwerp (Houghton bMS Am 1094 [370]) and his 3 June 1869 letter from Lausanne (Houghton bMS Am 1094 [371]) to HJ for a description of this journey.

25.11 the delicious hôtel Monnet • The 1869 *Switzerland* Baedeker describes this hotel: "Trois Couronnes, or *Hôtel Monnet*, on the lake [. . .], well fitted up and comfortable; [. . .] reading, smoking and billiard-rooms, warm baths" (194). The cost of a room was two to four francs per night, with meals ranging from three to four francs (194). The opening scene of *Daisy Miller* takes place in the garden of a Vevey hotel called the Trois Couronnes.

25.12–13 They have taken a house for the summer just out of Vevey • Norton describes this house, called La Pacotte, in his 6 June 1869 letter from Vevey to HJ. According to this letter, the Nortons moved into La Pacotte on 10 June 1869.

25.29 pastor Cougnard • Jean-Marc Cougnard (1821–96), pastor in Geneva (1851–65) and professor of Christian morality and practical theology from 1865 to 1896 (Heyer 445). In 1870 Cougnard lived in Geneva, at the rue des Philosophes, 12 (*Catalan* 52).

25.33 A. Kate • Aunt Kate.

25.33 Mr. Perkins's death • Leonard Perkins, husband of Helen Rodgers Wyckoff Perkins, who was MWJ's first cousin. According to his *New York Times* obituary, he died "suddenly, at Chester, England, on Sunday, May 30" ("Deaths" 5).

25.34 Cousin H. • Helen Perkins.

26.2 A. K. • Aunt Kate.

ALICE JAMES
19 June 1869
ALS Houghton
bMS Am 1094 (1556)

Hotel du Righi-Vaudois—
    Glion
        Lake of Geneva.
        June 19th '69.

My dearest Sister—

It is to thee, this week, that an irresistible impulse compels me to direct these lines, tremulous with the infernal cold. The

great mountain-prospect without is sheeted in a freezing rain—
my room feels as if in the words of M. Arnold, the glaciers had
spared to it "the soul of their white snows;" in fine all nature is
barren & horrible & if I were inclined, I could be as homesick as
you please. I have brought my portfolio to the public room   5
where there is a fire, & in the midst of an exasperating confusion
of tongues I attempt to indite a few words of decent English.—I
wrote a week ago from Geneva, announcing vaguely my
departure for this neighborhood. I have pulled up at this place,
where (to day being Saturday) I have been since Tuesday. I say   10
"pulled up"; in fact I came direct from Geneva hither. Glion is a
spot you may remember to have seen from the steamer on the
lake, perched on the mountainside above Montreux, & looking
from below like a single small châlet. In truth it is a large hotel
and a small group of houses. You reach it by a long winding   15
carriage road which ascends from Montreux—the ascent taking,
comfortably about an hour. They call it as you see the "Righi-
Vaudois." The establishment here is a large hotel=pension of
two buildings, kept in a very handsome style, where one may
stay (by the week—that is provided you stay a week to begin   20
with) to the tune of seven francs a day—which is reasonable
seeing what you get for it. The tâble d'hote is at two; ~~dinn~~
[∧]breakfast[∧] & tea when you please. The house is large & clean,
service excellent, air capital & scenery magnificent. That is it
would be, if one ~~can~~ ∧could[∧] see it. Since my arrival clouds &   25
rain have been the order of the day & I hear horrible
prognostications of their long continance & of our being booked
for a wet summer. But we shall see. The house is tolerably full—
about fifty persons—English, Germans &c—I being sole of my
race. In spite of the weather I have managed to get a few walks. 30
On Thursday, I descended to Montreux, & from there
proceeded across the country to Vevey, where I paid a visit to
the Nortons & dined with them. From Vevey at 6 p.m. I took the
steamer back to Montreux & thence walked up here. It took me

about 2½ hours to reach Vevey. Yesterday afternoon I climed a
little mountain behind the house *&* emerging from the woods,
found myself in the midst of of a grand mountain scene; ◇◇ on
one side the great purple-grey prong of the Dent de Jaman—at
5   my feet a vast green gorge plunging down to the lake *&*
commanding the wide issue of the valley of the Rhône—beyond
the Velan *&* the Dent du Midi. The mountains here are mild for
Switzerland; but they would make the fortune of tamer lands. In
fact, I can't pretend to describe the beauty of position *&*
10 approach which marks this spot. The whole ascent from the lake
is a realized vision: vast steep green slopes, smothered with wild
flowers *&* covered with fruit trees; beneath, the blue sheet of the
lake, gleaming through the leaves *&* undermining the cliff;
above, the great bosky walls of the immediate mountains
15 opposite ∧the[∧] th̶ more distant masses; of mightier Alps. I am
told there are plenty of walks *&* climbs: if the weather improves I
am not without hope of accomplishing some of the ◇ easier ones.
With the inmates of the place I have as yet formed but little
acquaintance. I enjoyed seeing the Nortons the other day *&*
20 think a little (very little) of taking a room near them for a week.
They have a nice little house, quite in the country, back of
Vevey, among the Vineyards *&* as still as the desert. But they are
great company unto themselves. The chief event since my
arrival here, is the receipt of a most blessed letter from Willy *&* a
25 note from father. I shall answer W.'s n̶o̶t̶e̶ ∧letter[∧] specifically. I
congratulate father on ◇ h̶i̶s̶ b̶o̶o̶ the termination of his book. Of
course he will send me a copy. See to it, sweet sister, that he
keeps his promise of writing. A little note like that, if nothing
more, is a great favor. Thank Willy for his excellent letter; I feel
30 at last, almost for the 1ˢᵗ time since my departure, ◇ as if some
real speech had passed between us.—Every letter brings me such
reiterated assurance of your amendment that I feel an awful
desire to get home *&* see it with my eyes. Were I there, there
were much we could do together. We could mingle the streams

of our common improvement, & walk about together hand in
hand, smiling so "peacefully." When you receive this, you will
be about starting off to Pomfret Conn. Depend upon it, it is
much better than this. Strange, as it may appear, I don't enjoy all
this half as much as I did last summer the vastly inferior charms   5
of New Hampshire. I am forever running my nose here into
the ₓ uncompromising, incomprehensible foreign-ness of things.
I ~~am~~ feel helplessly hopelessly American. The mountains
overwhelm me with their masses of European soil. The
old=world faces, manners & accents ∧about me₍∧₎ make me feel   10
like the denizen of another planet. I have conceived a horror of
the french language & delight in speaking ∧it₍∧₎ badly. And yet I
confess most of the Americans I have met revolt me by their
thinness & commonness. Fortunately we are the richest nation in
the world; otherwise we should be the poorest.—Near the fire   15
sit two gentlemen talking of the weather & telling dreadful tales
of the possible wetness of the summer. If it really sets in wet, I
think it will scarcely pay to remain. But there is time for
improvement.—For the present farewell! Love to all! Continue
to grow & prosper! I have heard nothing from Aunt Kate since   20
her mention of Mr. P.'s death.—Didn't I say to address me to
Lombard Odier & Co? <u>Mind this.</u> Ton frère dévoué
      H.

No previous publication
  ∾

28.33 compels • com= | pels

29.1 prospect • pros= | pect

29.6 exasperating • exas= | perating

29.10 Saturday • Sat= | urday

29.13 mountainside • mountain= | side

29.14 châlet • [*misspelled*]

29.17–18 Righi- | Vaudois • Righi-Vaudois

29.18 establishment • establish= | ment

29.22 tâble d'hote • [*misspelled*]

29.23 [ʌ]breakfast[ʌ] • [ʌ]break=[ʌ] | fast

29.27 continance • contin= | =ance; [*misspelled*]

30.1 climed • [*misspelled*]

30.3 ◊◊ on • [on *overwrites illegible letters*]

30.10 ascent • as= | cent

30.15 th̶ more • [m *overwrites* th]

30.17 ◊ easier • [e *overwrites illegible letter*]

30.23 themselves • them= | selves

30.26 ◊ h̶i̶s̶ b̶o̶o̶ the termination • [i *of* his *overwrites illegible letter;* the ter *overwrites* his boo]

30.30 ◊ as • [a *overwrites illegible letter*]

30.32 reiterated • re= | iterated

31.1 improvement • improve= | ment

31.7 incomprehensible • incom= | prehensible

31.8 a̶m̶ feel • [feel *overwrites* am]

31.19 farewell! • fare= | well!

31.20–23 nothing from [. . .] H. • [*written across the letter's first page*]

31.21 mention • men= | tion

෴

28.28 Glion • Town on the northeast shore of the Lake of Geneva, just above Montreux.

29.3 "the soul of their white snows" • From Matthew Arnold's "Stanzas in Memory of the Author of 'Obermann,'" in *Poems* (1853).

29.7–8 I wrote a week ago from Geneva • HJ's 13 June [1869] letter to his parents.

29.14 a large hotel • The 1869 *Switzerland* Baedeker says that, located "in a healthy and beautiful situation," the Hôtel Righi Vaudois was recommended for its whey-cure and pensions available from five to ten francs (197). The 1867 Murray for the *Alps of Savoy and Piedmont* describes the Righi Vaudois as the "largest and best situated" of the "two hotels and pensions" at Glion; it was a "new house (1867), 100 beds; comfortable, with salon, smoking-room, newspapers, [and] resident chaplain" (184).

30.4 Dent de Jaman • The Col de Jaman (1512 m), above Glion.

30.7 the Velan · Mt. Vélan (3731 m), on the Swiss-Italian border, next to the Grand Saint Bernard pass.

30.24 a most blessed letter from Willy · WJ to HJ, 1 June 1869 (see *CWJ* 1: 77–81).

30.26 his book · *The Secret of Swedenborg.*

31.21 Mr. P. · Leonard Perkins.

31.22 Ton frère dévoué · Your devoted brother.

JOHN LA FARGE   10
20 June [1869]
The New-York Historical Society
La Farge Papers
✉

                                                                      15

Hotel du Righi-Vaudois
    Glion
        Lake of Geneva
            June 20th
My very dear John —   20
    Your letter of June 3^d was handed me last night, just at a
moment when I was recording a silent oath that to day & not a
day later, I should execute my long-designed & oft-deferred
letter to you. Truly, I have most earnestly been meaning to write
to you. I felt the need of so doing. Our parting in N. Y. was so   25
hurried & unsatisfactory that I wished to affix some sort of
supplement or corrective. Happily now, what I write may be a
greeting rather than a farewell. I am deeply delighted to hear
that there is a prospect of your getting abroad this Summer.
Don't let it slip out of your hands. That your health is has   30
continued bad, I greatly regret; but I can't consider it an
unmitigated curse, if it brings you to these parts. You must have
pretty well satisfied yourself that home-life is not a remedy for
your troubles, & the presumption is strong that a certain amount

of Europe may be.—As you see I am already in Switzerland: in
fact I have been here for the past five weeks. I came directly to
Geneva (giving but a day to Paris ɟ that to the ⬦ Salon) ɟ spent
a month there; ɟ then came up to this place which is at the other
extreme of the lake, beyond Vevey, perched aloft on the
mountain side, just above the Castle of Chillon. It is what they
call a <u>hotel-pension</u>: a number of people capital air, admirable
scenery. Unhappily the weather is bad ɟ seems determined to
continue so. Heaven defend us from a rainy Summer—no
uncommon occurrence here. My actual plans are vague; they are
simply to continue in Switzerland as long as I can; but as I am
not a regular tourist I shall distribute my time between 2 or 3
places.—I enjoyed most acutely my stay in England. If you can
only touch there, I think you will find it pay. Of people I saw
very few, of course; ɟ of places no vast number, but such of the
latter as I did get a glimpse of, were awfully charming. I <u>did</u> see
Rossetti, Chas. Norton having conducted me to his studio—in
the most delicious melancholy old house at Chelsea on the river.
When I think what Englishmen <u>ought</u> to be, with such homes ɟ
haunts! Rossetti however, does not shame his advantages.
Personally, he struck me as unattractive—poor man, s̶t̶ I suppose
he was horribly bored!—but his pictures, as I saw them in his
room, I think decidedly strong. They were all large fanciful
portraits of women, of the type <u>que</u> <u>vous savez</u>, narrow, special,
monotonous, but with lots of beauty ɟ power. His chief
inspiration ɟ constant model is Mrs. W͟m Morris, (wife of the
poet) whom I had seen, a w̶o̶m̶e̶n̶ woman of extraordinary
beauty of a certain sort—a face, in fact quite made to his hand.
He has painted a dozen portraits of her—one, a̶ in particular, in
a blue gown, with her hair down, pressing a lot of lilies g̶ against
her breast—an almost great work. I told him I was your intimate
friend ɟ he spoke very admiringly of those of your drawings he
had seen.—I saw also some things of another man (tho' not
himself) one Burne Jones, a water-colorist ɟ friend of Chas.

Norton. They are very literary &c; but they have great merit. He
does Circe preparing for the arrival of Ulysses—squeezing
poison into a caldron, with strange black beasts <u>dans</u> <u>les jambes</u>:
thro' the openings of a sort of cloister you see the green salt
ocean, with the Greek galleys blowing up to land. This last part
is admirably painted. I enjoyed vastly in London the national
gallery, wh. is a much finer collection than I supposed. They
have just acquired a new Michael Angelo—Entombment of
Christ—unfinished—but most interesting, as you may imagine.
Then they have their great Titian—the ~~Bach~~ Bacchus &
Ariadne—a thing to go barefoot to see; as likewise his portrait
of Ariosto. Ah, John! what a painter. For him, methinks, I'd give
all the rest. I saw in the country (i.e. at Blenheim near Oxford &
at Wilton House near Salisbury) some magnificent Vandykes.
The great Wilton Vandyke (the Earl of Pembroke & family—an
immense canvas) is I think worth a journey to contemplate.
<u>À propos</u> of such things I oughtn't to omit to say that I dined at
Ruskin's, with the Nortons. R. ~~is~~ was very amiable & shewed his
Turners. The latter is assuredly great; but if you wish to hold
your own against exaggeration go ⋄ & see him at the National
Gallery where some thirty of his things stand adjoining the old
masters. I think I prefer Claude. He had better taste, at any
rate.—In England I saw a lot of Cathedrals—wh. are good
things to see; tho' to enjoy them properly, you mustn't take
them quite as wholesale as I was obliged to do.—You ask of my
intentions for next winter. They are as yet indefinite, & are not
firmly fixed upon Paris. That is, I am thinking a little of Italy. If
I give up Italy, however, ~~perhaps it will~~ [∧]of course I[∧] shall take
up Paris. But I do most earnestly hope we shall be able to talk it
over face-to face. Of course, if you decide to come, you will lose
no time. I wish greatly that your wife were to come with you;
short of that, I much hope that ~~th~~ your visit if it takes place, will
really pave the way for hers. Give her my love & tell her,
persuasively, that if Europe does not wholly solve the problem

35

of existence, it at least helps the flight of time — or beguiles its
duration. You give me no local or personal news, beyond that of
your illness. I hope other matters are of a more cheerful
complexion. I can hear nothing better than that you have sailed.
5   If you determine to do so write to me (Lombard, Odier & Cie,
Genève) & give your own address. Meanwhile, till further news,
farewell. Portez vous mieux, at least. Regards to J. Bancroft, if
you see him. Most affectionate messages to your wife &
youngsters & a <u>bon</u> <u>voyage</u>, if any to yourself.
10   Yours always
        H. James jr.

        ⊠

Etats Unis d'Amérique
15   John La Farge esq
        Newport
           R. I.
        Etats Unis d'Amérique

20   Postmarks: MONTREUX | 22 VI 69; NEW YORK [*faded
and mostly illegible*]; BASEL | [2]3 VI 69 — 10 | BRIEF◊ED;
GENEVE — SION | 22 VI 69

Previous publication: La Farge 176–78; *HJL* 1: 119–22; *SL* 1: 26–29; *SL* 2:
37–40

        ∾

   33.23 long-designed • long- | designed
   33.26 unsatisfactory • unsatisfac= | tory
   33.30 is has • [has *overwrites* is]
   33.31 consider • consid= | er
   33.34 presumption • pre= | sumption
   34.1 Switzerland • Switzer= | land
   34.3 ◊ Salon • [S *overwrites illegible letter*]

34.9 continue · con= | tinue

34.9 defend · de= | fend

34.21 ~~st~~ I · [I *overwrites* st]

34.27 ~~women~~ woman · [a *overwrites* e]

34.29 ~~a~~ in · [i *overwrites* a]

34.30 ~~g~~ against · [a *overwrites* g]

34.32 admiringly · admiring- | ly

35.6 national · nation= | al

35.8 acquired · ac= | quired

35.10 ~~Bach~~ Bacchus · [c *overwrites* h]

35.11 likewise · like= | wise

35.13 Blenheim · Blen= | heim

35.18 ~~is~~ was · [wa *overwrites* is]

35.20 ~~o~~ d · [d *overwrites illegible letter*]

35.24 mustn't · must= | n't

35.32 ~~th~~ your · [y *overwrites* th]

36.10-11 Yours always H. James jr. · [*written across the letter's last page*]

∾

34.6 Castle of Chillon · The medieval castle on the Lake of Geneva, between Vevey and Villeneuve, made famous in English literature by Byron's poem "The Prisoner of Chillon." In *Daisy Miller*, HJ had his narrator, Winterbourne, take Daisy to visit the castle.

34.17-18 studio [. . .] Chelsea · This London suburb is on the northern embankment of the Thames River. Dante Gabriel Rossetti lived at Tudor House, 16 Cheyne Walk.

34.24 que vous savez · that you know.

34.34 Burne Jones · English painter Sir Edward Coley Burne-Jones, First Baronet (1833-98). HJ and Burne-Jones developed a lifelong friendship. HJ later wrote reviews of his artwork in such periodicals as the *Galaxy*, the *Nation*, and the *Atlantic Monthly*.

35.1-5 He does Circe [. . .] blowing up to land · Burne-Jones's *Wine of Circe* (1863-69).

35.3 dans les jambes · at her feet.

35.8–9 Michael Angelo—Entombment of Christ • Acquired by London's National Gallery in 1868, the *Entombment* was left unfinished by Michelangelo in 1501.

35.10–11 Titian—the ~~Bach~~ Bacchus & Ariadne • Part of a larger series of commissioned works, the painting dates from 1523. The National Gallery acquired it in 1826.

35.12 Ariosto • Titian's unidentified *Portrait of a Man* has long been thought to be of Italian poet Ariosto. It was painted in 1512.

35.22 Claude • Claude Lorrain (1600–1682), French artist best known for ideal-landscape painting.

36.7 Portez vous mieux • Enjoy better health.

36.7 J. Bancroft • John Chandler Bancroft (1835–1901), American painter and businessman.

MARY WALSH JAMES
[27], 28, 30 June [1869]
ALS Houghton
bMS Am 1094 (1760)

Glion-sur-Montreux
        Hotel du Righi-Vaudois
              June 28th

My dearest Mother—

Glion last week & Glion, as you see, still. Glion has produced however, in the interval, your most amiable letter of June 7th or 8th (I conjecture: it has no date.) Besides this, it has brought forth nothing so wonderful as to be particularly described or related. Nevertheless, I can't help writing, at the risk (I persist in suspecting) of boring you by my importunity. It is a warm Sunday afternoon: I have come up to my room from dinner, & after lying down snoozingly on ~~a~~ the sofa for half an hour find a

thousand thoughts & memories of home invade my languid mind
with such pertinacity that there is nothing for it but to seize the
pen & work off my emotions. Since I last wrote, the situation has
changed very much for the better. The weather has cleared up &
we have had nearly a week of fine warm days. I have found it
possible to profit by them to my very great satisfaction. Every
afternoon I have taken a long lonely lovely ramble of some three
or four hours. The walks hereabouts are extremely numerous &
singularly beautiful. It is true that they are all more or less on
the perpendicular; nevertheless I have learned them almost all.
Judge of my improvement since M̶ leaving Malvern, where I
found the little hills a burden & a nuisance. Now I think nothing
so to speak, of a mountain, & climb one, at least, on an average
every afternoon. I should extremely like to be able to depict the
nature of this enchanting country; but to do so requires the pen
of a Ruskin or a G. Sand. Back from the lake, at Montreux,
stretches the wide deep gorge or ravine, on one side of which, on
a little plateau, this hotel is planted. Into this gorge, above, b̶l̶
below, horizontally, you can plunge to your heart's content.
Along its bottom rolls the furious course of a little mountain
river, hurrying down to the lake. Leaving the hotel & striking
into the f̶e̶i̶ fields, a winding foot-path, wandering up & down
thro' meadows & copses & orchards, leads down to a heavenly
spot where a little wooden bridge spans this tremendous little
torrent. It is smothered in the wilderness; above your head the
tangled verdure shuts out the hillsides; beneath, the racketing
stream roars and plunges far down in its channel of rocks. From
here you can cross up & ascend the opposite side of the gorge,
pursue it along its edge, to its innermost extremity, t̶o̶ where the
great mountain walls close sheer about it & make it lonely, awful
& Alpine. There you can again cross the river & return thro' the
woods to Glion. This is one walk in a dozen. I enjoy them all: I
relish keenly the freedom¡ t̶h̶e̶ of movement, the propulsion of
curiosity, the largeness & abundance of the scenery—& for that

matter its richness & gentleness too. Crossing ◇ the bridge
aforesaid & turning out toward the lake & along the hillsides
above you can walk to Vevey thro' a region of shady meadows &
slanting orchards as tranquil & pastoral as an English park.—

5 Nevertheless this is not yet real Switzerland & I am preparing to
take myself thither. I want to get into genuine ◇ Alpine air &
scenery. I went over to Vevey by train a few days since & paid a
second visit to the Nortons. I have made up my mind on leaving
this place to go & spend a week in the farm house adjoining their

10 premises. They are so utterly buried & lonely that I think they
would be somewhat grateful for my society & I can thereby do
something to pay off their hospitalities to me in London &
cancel a possibly onerous obligation. They enjoy extremely their
seclusion & rusticity & find it a very pleasant relief after

15 England. It is well they do, for it is absolute & without appeal. In
this house I shall probably remain ~~here~~ a ~~m~~ week longer. It is a
little more expensive than what I expect to find elsewhere, but it
affords a number of comforts which I am glad to have at this
stage of my ~~ini◇◇◇~~ initiation into mountain habits. A fortnight

20 hence I shall be better able to rough it. With this view I shall
proceed to the Lake of Lucerne, seek out an abode & remain
there probably to the 1ˢᵗ of September. I have about given up the
idea of going to St. Moritz. I am deterred by the stories I hear
about the extreme cold & the severity of the climate. I want the

25 air of some great altitude, but enough is as good as a feast; I
want the summer too. But of all this, you will hear when it takes
place. I duly noted your injunction to spend the summer quietly
& economically. I hope to do both—or that is, ~~in the~~ to circulate
in, so far as I do, ◇ by the inexpensive vehicle of my own legs.

30 You will by this time have received a letter written nearly a
month ago in Geneva on this matter of travelling & expenditure
containing propositions somewhat at variance with the spirit—
or rather with the letter—of the above advice. I don't know in
what manner you have replied ∧to[∧] it; exactly as you felt you

40

ought, of course. When you speak of your own increased expenses &c., I feel very guilty & selfish in entertaining any projects which look in the least like extravagance. My beloved mother. if you but knew the purity of my motives! Reflection assures me, as it will assure you, that the only economy for me is to get thoroughly well & in to such a state as that I can work. For this consummation, I will accept every thing—even the appearance of mere pleasure-seeking. A winter in Italy (if I feel 2 mos. hence as I do k now) enabling me to spend my time in a certain way, will help me on further than anything else I know of—more than a winter in Paris & of course, so long as the very semblance of application is denied me—than one in Germany. But it will by so much hasten (so I reason) the moment when I can spend a winter (◊ or some months at any rate) in Germany without damage & with positive profit. If before I left home I had been as certain as I have now become, that to pay, my visit here must at present be a real change—a real active taking hold of the matter—we could have talked oe over the subject far better than we can do in this way. In effect when I consider how completely, during the three or four months before I sailed I was obliged to give up f all reading & writing (Willy can tell you) I see that it was a very absurd extension of my hopes to fancy that mere change of place would enable me to take them up again—or that I could lead the old life with impunity in Paris more than in German Cambridge. Having lost all the time I have, you see I naturally wish to economise it. ∧what is left.[∧] When I think that a year [∧]winter[∧] in Italy is not as you call it (a winter of "recreation" but an occasion not only of physical regeneration, but of serious culture too (culture of the kind which alone I have now at 26 any time left for) I find the courage to maintain my proposition even in the face of your allusions to the need of economy at home. It takes a very honest conviction thus to plead the cause of apparently gross idleness against such grave and touching facts. I have trifled so long with my trouble that I feel as if I could afford now to be a little brutal. My lovely mother, if ever I am restored to you sound & serviceable you will find that you have not cast the pearls of your charity before a senseless beast, but before a creature with a soul to be grateful &

5   a will to act.—There are two things which I hardly need add. 1st, that of course, you will be guided in your rejoinder simply by the necessities of the case, & will quite put aside any wish to please or any fear to displease me; & 2^{d} that whether I go to I̶a̶l̶ Italy or to Paris I shall be as economical as possible. After all,

10   there are two months yet; so much discussion & protestation will strike you as premature. I may find that by the 1st of September, I am quite strong enough to face the <u>dulness</u> of Paris. <u>Wednesday</u> 30th. I left my letter standing & shall add but a few �◇◇◇ words before closing it. I have had an adventure worth

15   mentioning. On Monday evening (night before last) I agreed with three gentlemen here (2 Englishmen & a German) to make with them the ascent of a certain mountain hard-bye, by name the Rochers de Naye. (For the various localities hereabouts, by the way tell Willy to shew you M. Arnold's two poems on

20   <u>Obermann</u>). We started accordingly at midnight, in order to be on the summit to see the sunrise. We reached the top, after 4 hours steady walking—the last part by moonlight. The sunrise was ∧rather[∧] a failure owing to an excess of clouds: still, the red ball shot up with the usual splendid suddenness. The summit was

25   extremely cold—tho' we had brought a guide with overcoats &c. We descended in about half the time & reached the hotel by 7 p a.m., in time for a bath & breakfast. I was of course tired but not to excess & to day finds me all right again. The expedition was a stupid one, however, & I shall undertake no more night

30   feats. They don't pay. But the rocks of Naye are about as high as Mt. Washington. What would you have thought last summer of my starting of at midnight to scale the latter? As far as impunity is concerned I feel perpectly disposed to start off tommorrow, with a pleasant companion, o̶n̶ ̶d̶a̶o̶g̶ by daylight, on the same

errand.—I have just ~~rec⬦~~ received with gratitude, the ~~June~~ July
Atlantic. My story strikes me as the product of a former state of
being. The 2ᵈ part, I fancy, is better. I heard recently from Jno.
La Farge to the effect that he would probably come out to
Switzerland this summer. I hope much he may, but I doubt it. 5
Minny T. writes me that she <u>may</u> appear in Rome next winter.
This too I hope somewhat faintly. I hear often from A. K. who
evidently is enjoying things hugely. You must be on the point of
starting for Pomfret. Write me all about it. Address me until I
give you a more permanent address to the Nortons, <u>La Pacotte</u> 10
<u>Vevey</u>. Farewell, my dearest mother. Tell Willy I shall speedily
answer his last. My blessings upon father ⅋ Alice. Make Wilky
write. Your devoted son <u>H. James</u> jr.

Previous publication: *HJL* 1: 122–26; *SL* 2: 40–44

∾

38.34 snoozingly • snoozing= | ly

38.34 ~~a~~ the • [the *overwrites* a]

39.10 nevertheless • never= | theless

39.11 ~~M~~ leaving • [le *overwrites* M]

39.18–19 ~~bl~~ below • [e *overwrites* l]

39.19 horizontally • hori= | zontally

39.22 ~~fei~~ fields • [ie *overwrites* ei]

39.26 hillsides • hill= | sides

39.33 ~~the~~ of • [of *overwrites* the]

40.1 ⬦ the • [t *overwrites illegible letter*]

40.5 preparing • pre= | paring

40.6 ⬦ Alpine • [A *overwrites illegible letter*]

40.11 thereby • there= | by

40.12 hospitalities • hospi= | talities

40.16 ~~m~~ week • [w *overwrites* m]

40.19 ~~ini⬦⬦⬦~~ initiation • [tia *overwrites illegible letters*]

40.28 ~~in the~~ to circulate • [to cir *overwrites* in the]

40.29 ⬦ by • [b *overwrites illegible letter*]

43

40.29 vehicle • vehi= | cle

40.32 somewhat • some= | what

41.9 k̶ now • [n *overwrites* k]

41.12 application • applica= | tion

41.14 ◇ or • [o *overwrites illegible letter*]

41.18 o̶e over • [v *overwrites* e]

41.21 r̶ all • [a *overwrites* r]

41.25 G̶e̶r̶m̶a̶n̶ Cambridge • [Cambr *overwrites* German]

41.26 naturally • natu= | rally

41.28 physical • physi= | cal

42.1 lovely • love= | ly

42.8–9 I̶a̶l̶ Italy • [ta *overwrites* al]

42.14 ◇◇◇◇ words • [words *overwrites illegible letters*]

42.27 p̶ a.m. • [a *overwrites* p]

42.33 perpectly • [*misspelled*]

42.33 tommorrow • [*misspelled*]

42.34 o̶n̶ d̶a̶◇g̶ by daylight • [by *overwrites* on; y *overwrites illegible letter;* l *overwrites blotted* g]

43.1 r̶e̶◇ received • re= | ceived; [ce *overwrites illegible letter*]

43.1 J̶u̶n̶e̶ July • [ly *overwrites* ne]

43.9–13 until I give you a more permanent address [. . .] H. James jr. • [*written across the letter's first page*]

∾

38.32–33 It is a warm Sunday afternoon • Since 28 June 1869 was a Monday, Sunday afternoon would have been the 27th.

40.30–31 You will by this time have received a letter [. . .] & expenditure • See HJ to WJ, 30, 31 May 1869.

42.18 the Rochers de Naye • A mountain due east of Montreux. The 1869 *Switzerland* Baedeker describes an excursion from Montreux: "*Rochers de Naye* (6926′), the S. neighbour of the Jaman, ascent in 4 to 5 hrs., descent 3 hrs., view embracing the entire chain of the mountains of Bern, Valais and Savoy; Mont Blanc only partially visible" (198).

42.19–20 M. Arnold's two poems on Obermann • Matthew Arnold's

44

poems "Stanzas in Memory of the Author of 'Obermann'" (1852) and
"Obermann Once More" (1867).

42.31 Mt. Washington · The highest mountain in New Hampshire.

43.1-2 July Atlantic. My story · The first installment of "Gabrielle de
Bergerac" appeared in the *Atlantic Monthly* 24 (July 1869): 55-71.

43.7 A. K. · Aunt Kate.

CHARLES ELIOT NORTON
10 July [1869]   10
ALS Houghton
bMS Am 1088 (3850)

   Hotel du Righi-Scheideck
      July 10th   15
My dear Charles—
   You have doubtless been surprised at not hearing from me
before & your ladies have pronounced ~~your~~ ∧my[∧] conduct of a
piece with my performances—or my non-performance—on
previous occasions. But in truth I am not so culpable as I look. I   20
have been in perpetual motion every blessed moment since I left
you until this morning & have literally lacked time to write a
line. I seize this very earliest opportunity to let you know of my
whereabouts & my adventures. These latter have been manifold
& the way since leaving Vevey, I have drifted along from place to   25
place is either very sublime or very imbecile—I hardly know
which. After I had bidden you farewell I betook myself to Aigle
on my way, as you will remember, to Château d'Oeux. At Aigle I
spent the night & there in the silent watches of the same, I
communed with my soul & asked myself why after all I should   30
doom myself to hover forever about a part of Switzerland which
I knew tolerably well, while a vast unexplored Paradise lay
smiling in the distance. The consequence was that from one
thing to another I found myself propelled to Lucerne, where I

arrived on Thursday evening—having slept on Tuesday at the
Diablerets & on Wednesday at Zweisimmen, in the Simmenthal.
I enjoyed the journey vastly—especially those little portions
which I performed on foot. From the Diablerets, I crossed in
5   that manner over the charming little pass of the Col de Pillon &
felt sensations which recalled most keenly my distant boyish,
days when with my brother I made a little foot-journey in the
same region. From Zweisimmen I made a five hours coach-
journey to Thun—Thun the charming but the awfully hot &
10   thence proceeded in 6 hours by train to Lucerne. Lucerne is
truly delightful & seriously picturesque. It really has quite a
suggestion of that historic charm whose absence elsewhere we
have so deeply deplored. I spent yesterday morning strolling
about, staring (& I may add, perspiring) & at noon took the
15   steamer for Gersau at the further end of the lake—the station
whence you ascend to this famous ~~altitudes~~ altitude. I have quite
forgotten at what stage of my journey the intention of coming
up here clearly defined itself—or whether it ever did so at all;
but nevertheless at 5 o'clock p.m., having dined at Gersau, I
20   started on foot & after a sweltering climb of 2 ½ hours reached
the cool & crepuscular summit. Here I am then, fixed for the
present. Whether I have done well to select this residence time
alone will shew. It has its merits—& it certainly has its
drawbacks. The Rigi, as perhaps you know, has three inhabited
25   points—the Kulm, where folks go to see the sunrise—the Kalt-
bad a Water-Cure—& this Scheideck (whatever it means) a little
lower than the ~~C~~ Kulm, which is largely frequented by persons
wishing to remain some time on the summit.—I insert a graphic

& vivid diagram of the scene. I find here a vast rough-&-tumble
sort of hotel, swarming with Germans & conducted on strictly
German principles—suggesting, too, many reflections on

German idiosyncrasies—notably one to the effect that the
excellent creatures are the very ugliest members of the
European family. Such men—such women—such children! But
we will drop the painful theme.—Even the comparatively good-
looking ones suffer from the ugliness of the others ɗ are injured
ᵐ by the hideous contagion. I look ₍ᴧ₎up₍ᴧ₎ from my writing a ɗ
see a young girl sitting alone; she is decently pretty ɗ graceful:
suddenly her party comes in—half a dozen terrible specimens—
ɗ fling over her the baleful mantle of their plainness. But in
spite of their ugliness I fancy they have their points ɗ that a
certain amount of satisfaction is to be obtained in their society.
They are homely but not vulgar ɗ simple but not shabby.—How
long I shall remain here I know not. I came up to get the real
mountain air ɗ escape from the heat of the lower regions but I
am afraid that owing to its position, this place has a fair share of
heat of its own. It stands on the bare-mountain-top, rearing its
head to the sun without a tree or a bush within sight. But we
shall see. If it fails to satisfy, I can but depart. I shall of course
let you hear of any future peregrinations.—Meanwhile I am lost
in conjecture as to the state of affairs at La Pacotte. I truly hope,
to begin with, that you are feeling better than when we parted ɗ
that your amendment is final. Altho' I ⊕ inflict this
communication upon you I shall be sorry to tax your infirmity
with a reply ɗ shall find no fault with a line of female
authorship. The female heart is nothing, if not charitable—ɗ the
female pen nothing if not delightful. I trust I shall hear that
Susan is stronger ɗ—what will she permit me to call it?—more
hopeful—more "peaceful." Your mother, Jane Grace ɗ Sara
seemed i on such good terms with the complexion of things that
they can dispense with my poor good wishes. Nevertheless, in
kindness, they must accept them. I shall be deeply grateful if one
of you in a leisure moment will superscribe ɗ post afresh any
thing I may have in your hands in the way of letters. The address
is Righi–Scheideck, Lucerne. Farewell. Let me have some scrap

of news—& good news—of you & believe me, dear Charles, yours always H. James jr.

No previous publication

᷁

   46.2 Diablerets • Diable= | rets

   46.8–9 coach- | journey • coach-journey

   46.16 ~~altitudes~~ altitude • [e *overwrites* es]

   46.24 inhabited • in= | habited

   46.25–26 Kalt- | bad • Kalt-bad

   46.27 C̶ Kulm • [K *overwrites* C]

   46.34 principles • princi= | ples

   47.4–5 good- | looking • good-looking

   47.6 m̶ by • [b *overwrites* m]

   47.6 a̶ & • [& *overwrites* a]

   47.8 suddenly • sudden= | ly

   47.22 ◌̶ inflict • [i *overwrites illegible letter*]

   47.29 i̶ on • [o *overwrites* i]

   47.30 Nevertheless • Never = | theless

᷁

45.14 Hotel du Righi-Scheideck • The 1869 Baedeker for *Switzerland* describes this hotel: "magnificent view, second only to that from the Kulm" (60). Rooms cost $1\frac{1}{2}$ francs, pension 5 to 6 francs, meals $1\frac{1}{2}$ to $2\frac{1}{2}$ francs, and "whey, milk, or the chalybeate water of the Scheideck 2 fr. per week" (59).

45.27 Aigle • A town on the Rhône River, between Villeneuve and Martigny.

45.28 Château d'Oeux • Village to the northeast of Montreux and Glion; variously spelled Château d'Oeux or Château d'Oex in the 1869 *Switzerland* Baedeker (map between 146–47, 155).

46.1 Thursday evening • July 8; July 10, the date of this letter, was a Saturday.

46.1–2 the Diablerets • Les Diablerets (3210 m), east of Aigle and south of Gstaad; HJ describes his stay at the village of les Diablerets, at the foot of the north face of the mountain, in his 12, 13 July 1869 letter to WJ.

46.2 Zweisimmen • Village northeast of Gstaad, at the junction of the Ober Simmenthal and Nieder Simmenthal.

46.2 the Simmenthal • Valley of the Simme, stretching from above the village of Lenk and heading north to Spiez, where the Simme flows into the Thuner.

46.5 the charming little pass of the Col de Pillon • A pass (1546 m) east of the village of les Diablerets.

46.6–8 my distant boyish, days [. . .] region • See HJ to Thomas Sergeant Perry, 18 July 1860.

46.9 Thun • In central Switzerland on the Aare River, which there issues from the Thuner See (Lake Thun).

46.15 Gersau • Village on the northeast shore of the Lake of Lucerne.

46.24 The Rigi • The mountain ridge dominating the northeast shore of the Lake of Lucerne; its principal peaks are the Kulm (1797 m) and the Scheidegg (1699 m).

46.25–26 Kalt-bad • Kaltbad, spa and hotel on the ascent from Weggis to the Kulm. According to the 1869 *Switzerland* Baedeker, it was "in the height of summer generally full" and expensive, with a room and service around ten francs a day (58).

46.26 this Scheideck • French spelling of the German Scheidegg, a Rigi peak above Gersau.

WILLIAM JAMES
12, 13 July 1869
ALS Houghton   25
bMS Am 1094 (1932)

Righi-Scheideck (Lucerne)
        Monday July 12th '69.
My dear old Bill—   30
    The unprecedented interval of nearly two weeks ~~have~~ has elapsed since I last wrote from Glion. Meanwhile your excellent letter of June 12th has added itself to that of June 1st & made it impossible that I should now address my remarks to any one but

49

you. Meanwhile, too, adventures have piled themselves up ɮ I
am loth to let ~~any~~ another day pass lest experience should
outrun memory or memory strength of hand. My date informs
you that I have at last torn myself away from the lake of Geneva
⁵ ɮ confided my frail existence to these unknown <u>parages</u>. Some
twelve days ago ‿I‿ left the charming Glion, prepared to seek a
spot which should combine economy with something more
grand ɮ novel in the way of scenery. First, however, I betook
myself to Vevey to pay my duties to the Nortons in the shape of
¹⁰ a four days' visit, lasting from Thursday to Monday. Four days I
found as much as I could manage. I lodged in an extremely
picturesque old farm-house about ten minutes' walk from their
place—a genuine old Vaudois concern, nestling among
vineyards ɮ orchards. The Nortons are living in great simplicity
¹⁵ ɮ great contentment. I hope the latter will not forsake them, for
the former is a little excessive. Charles ɮ his wife, are both
poorly; the Swiss air seems not to agree with them. On my
leaving the Nortons, began the famous "adventures," above
mentioned, which have culminated in this mountain top. My
²⁰ plan as I quitted Vevey on the afternoon of July 5$^{\underline{th}}$, was to resort
to—Château d'Oeux a favored spot in the Canton de Vaud, back
from the lake, behind the mountains, where living is cheap,
nature beautiful ɮ Americans abundant. With this laudable
intention I betook myself to Aigle, in the Valley of the Rhone
²⁵ 1 ɮ $\frac{1}{2}$ ‿hour‿ from Vevey whence I proposed to proceed by
coach next morning to Chateau d'Oeux. At Aigle I chanced to
meet a respectable English lady, bound to the same spot ◇ who
furnished me with information which led me to modify my
views. The place was full, the pensions overflowing ɮ the air not
³⁰ particularly mountainous. I slept on it ɮ next morning decided
to proceed only as far as Comballaz (4000 feet above the sea)
half way to C. d'Oeux, where the air ~~w~~ is better ɮ
accommodation more plenteous. Meanwhile, in the watches of
the night, I ‿had‿ interrogated my ◇◇ soul ɮ inquired of it
³⁵ whether it was worth while to linger ɮ hover so long in this f

comparatively familiar & secondary part of Switzerland while
the splendid & famous regions lay blooming afar. Nevertheless I
stuck to Comballaz, & having learned that it was but a three
hours' walk & a very beautiful one, I despatched my luggage by
the mail-coach, grasped my trusty staff & at 9. a.m. ⊬ started   5
away on foot. The morning was intensely hot—I absolutely
rained perspiration; but I deeply enjoyed the walk. The road on
leaving Aigle, branches off from the Rhone valley & slowly winds
& mounts, in splendid fashion, along the beautiful Gorge des
Ormonts. Far below rushes & murmurs the usual torrent; above   10
gleams the dusty macadamized band, wandering among the
green recesses. A two hours' trudge brought me to the Village of
Sepey, where at the inn I sat me down to rest. Here, conversing
with the post-mistress, I learned that there were as yet, at the
hotel at Comballaz but three individuals—a circumstances   15
which again led me to commune with my soul. Further
researches led me to commune more devoutly; half an hour's
meditation led me to give it up. It is needless to trace the
process of thought which at this stage of my proceedings
induced me to fix upon the Diablerets—a rg region about two   20
hour's distant noted for the infernal grandeur of its scenery. It
contains a large pension, which was already well filled. I
communed awhile with the inestimable Bäddeker & found that
when I wearied of the Diablerets I could make a direct journey
to Thun & Interlaken, where I might abide permanently. Behold   25
me then awaiting the arrival of the coach of ∧at[∧] Sepey,
transferring my luggage to the post=chaise for the Diablerets,
dining & at two o'clock ⊬ starting away. I enjoyed in the chaise,
by the way, the company of an elderly & ugly Miss Bradford of
Chesnut St. Boston—a great botanist—a devotee of the   30
"Flōwra" of America. We reached the D. at about 5 o'clock—
which left me a bit before dark to examine the scene. Here
occurred a new revolution of spirit. Decidedly this was not a
place to stop at: a vast ampitheatre, surrounded by bleak

towering desolate walls of snow=crowned rock—grim, horrible
& uninteresting. The next morning, accordingly, I started on
foot for Thun. The first step was to cross the charming little
Col de Pillon—a trudge of three hours. You may imagine that
the pass is of the mildest, inasmuch as I took with me a stout
little car, for my luggage. I don't mean I dragged it myself: I
have not yet come to that. From the Col we descended into the
lovely Simmenthal (Berne) by the little village of Gesteig, where
I stopped to rest & dine. This walk to Gesteig was deeply
delightful ₍ₐ₎Here,₍ₐ₎ At the inn at Gesteig I met four lovely
young Englishmen—the flower of the earth.—I am getting, by
the way, absolutely to adore the English. At this place, my
brother, there came over me a rich & vivid recollection of the
little foot=journey we made together years ago, when we had no
aches & pains. As I sat in the little German-Swiss dining room, I
could almost fancy you at my side & myself ten years younger.
From Gesteig in the afternoon I took a waggon to
Zweisimmen—a three hours' ride & a very pretty one. Here,
before dark, I still had time for an hour's walk in the
"Environs₁" & spent the night at a very good inn. Next morning
at 5.45 I started in the ₍ₐ₎coupé of the₍ₐ₎ mail-coach for Thun,
which we reached, thro' a most adorable country, at about 10.30.
This gave me a chance for further meditating & communing—so
that when we reached Thun & I had walked about for an hour &
found it, thro' extremely pretty, deplorably low & hot & reflected
that Interlaken was in this respect identical & furthermore that it
was a shame to come to Switzerland to bury one's self in Valleys
when breezy steeps & summits were at one's disposal—when I
had compressed these arduous cogitations & perambulations
into the space of an hour, I was quite ready to proceed to the
station & take my ticket for Lucerne <u>Via</u> Berne & depart at a
quarter past twelve. The journey to Lucerne was of six hours—
six of the hottest & grimiest I ever spent. I never enjoyed a wash
so much as that in which I indulged at the gorgeous

Schweizerhof. Here I dined, strolled a bit in the dark & retired to
rest. Now during that busy hour at Thun I had fixed upon this
Rigi-Scheideck as the goal of my future efforts. I had made a
note of it ˄in[˄] England at the urgent recommendation of a
gentleman at Malvern & I found it qualified in Bädeker as the   5
most frequented spot of the kind in Switzerland—bracing,
comfortable, & "plein de calme & de repos." ~~On rising~~ ˄Having
breakfasted[˄] therefore on Friday morning, I devoted & hour & a
half to perambulating the mysteries of Lucerne—a charming
little old town, but given over body & soul to tourists. I then   10
departed at 11.40. in the steamer for Gersau, at the further end
of the lake. The ~~scenery of~~ ˄mountains about[˄] the lake were all
shrouded in a hot haze, but they loomed out in dim grandeur,
out-crowding & overtopping each other. At Gersau I landed,
dined & reposed a while previous to ascending the mountain. The   15
Rigi as you probably know, rises directly above the lake, thus:

From the Kulm where people go to see the sunrise, it stretches a
long undulating back to this Scheideck, a second summit, to
which you mount from Gersau. From Gersau, accordingly,
having previously charged my luggage on the back of a sweating
peasant, I began at 5. p.m. to trudge upwards. I reached the   25
Scheideck in about 2 hrs.' & ½ steady walk. Here I find a large
rough-&-tumble sort of hotel, planted on the naked summit &
crowded with Germans. Having telegraphed from Gersau I am
fortunate enough to get a room—a little box of a place, but
sufficient. I have as yet been here but ~~four~~ [˄]2[˄] days & am   30
unable to say how I shall like things. At any rate I shall give
them a fair trial. The obvious drawback is the total absence of
shade & the violent glare produced by the "view" & by the clouds
being as much below as above you. Nevertheless owing to the

great elevation (I believe about 6.000 feet.) the air even at noonday is light ♃ cool ♃ stirring—it has a sort of flavor. The house is
conducted on strictly German principles—breakfast at 8; dinner
at 12 ½; coffee at 5 ½ supper at 7 ½. But the fare is very good ♃
5   plentiful. As ∧for[∧] the walks, I have as yet ~~but~~ reconnoitred but
little. They must be all rather stiff climbing. But I assure you I
am not afraid of them; ♃ by the time I write again, I hope to
have some high deeds to relate. ◈◈ My sketch of my journey will
shew you that a considerable amount of fatigue ♃ exertion has
10   been my portion. It is the same story. On each succeeding day I
felt myself better ♃ capable ∧of[∧] more. There were moments
when I would have greeted with enthusiasm the proposition of
an amiable ♃ intelligent youth to undertake with him an
extended walking-tour. Indeed the chief abatement of my
15   pleasure was having to do it all alone. So as I say, I make have
some startling performances to relate. Your diagnosis of my
back in your last seems to me as good as another ♃ I don't
profess to understand the matter any better than you. I think
however I ~~am to~~ have a glimpse of the course it is to run before
20   it returns to sanity. Namely 3 stages. 1° A stage in which exercise
must go on increasing until it entirely predominates ♃ attains its
maximum—even to not sleeping, if necessary. 2° A stage in
which sitting, reading, writing ♃c. may be gradually ~~increased~~
introduced ♃ allowed to share its empire. 3° A stage in which
25   they will hold their own against it ♃ subsist on ∧an[∧] equal ♃
finally a superior footing. But I shall certainly never get beyond
having to be minutely cautious [Excuse the accidental
irregularity of my pages]
in the distribution of my time ♃ use of my strength. When this
30   last stage will come I know not.—But to return a moment to
actual plans. I am already satisfied that I must not expect myself
to spend the summer on this spot. It is s too peculiar in its
nature ♃ the exclusively German character of its habitués will
afford me so little society ♃ conversation, that I must finish the

season somewhere else. In this emergency I have returned to St.
Moritz, which I wrote you that I had abandoned, ~~I~~ chiefly on
acct. of the cold. ⋄ The perpetual confirmation of my belief that
my powers of locomotion are steadily on the increase,
emboldens me to think that I may by constant movement depise
the temperature. So I wrote last evening to Leslie Stephen, who
is staying there to ask him to try & hire me a room ~~before~~ ₍ₐ₎for₍ₐ₎
three weeks hence. He may be unsuccessful; but we shall see. —
& now enough of my own plans & my own doings. I have
unwound this string of homely details in the belief that it may
amuse mother & Alice & gratify their feminine love of the
minute & the petty. I wish one of them would treat me to an
equally keen analysis of your situation at Pomfret, which you
must have already reached. Since leaving Vevey I have been
without my letters & ⋄⋄ am starving for news from home. I
actually <u>gloat</u> over the prospect of to-morrow's mail. Meanwhile
I have stayed my stomach by reading over your two inestimable
letters, above mentioned. There is much in them to respond to,
but I am fagged by this long scribble. I deeply relish & enjoy all
your remarks about German. A little of your knowledge would
stand me in very good stead up here. I hope to heaven your
mind & body are both well rid of your examination. I feel that
in all I tell of my own amendment I constantly anticipate as it
were, & reply to any news of your continued suffering. I feel as
if every ~~walking~~ I take is a burning & shining light, for your
encouragement, & I confess I don't understand how in the face
of the phenomenon of my conduct you can feel any serious
doubt or dejection. All expression of such doubt I savagely
resent. But I shall suspend further judgement until the summer
is over. May you enjoy it calmly, lazily & selfishly! I got a letter
from H. Bowditch, assuming that I was coming to Bonn & that
we might go to Switzerland together. He comes Aug. 1ˢᵗ. I hope I
may meet him. I have not heard in 2 weeks from Aunt K. She is
probably enjoying herself vastly. She will lay up treasure for the

rest of her life. Is father's book yet out? I of course count in
some way or other on a copy. I hope to morrow to get letters
from both Alice & him. My blessings on them both! I suppose
Mother is frisking & frolicking as usual, on being turned into the
fields. Imprint a kiss upon her lovely brow. I am perpetually
shedding tears over ₍ₐ₎her₍ₐ₎ patches in my night-shirts stockings
&c.—Farewell!—Thy brother

H. J. jr

P. S. My one intellectual feat is having read J. S. Mill on the
subjection of women at Vevey.—Tuesday. 13ᵗʰ I can hardly put
too strongly the good effect of my rovings of last week.
Yesterday afternoon I ascended with a young Englishman a very
pretty little mountain near by, with a lovely view of the whole
lake from the top: a matter of about 5 hours in all, including rest
on the top. To day I think of walking down to Gersau, taking
boat to Lucerne, to ~~making~~ make a purchase, & returning &
walking back in the afternoon. Good-bye!—
Where is Wilky? how is he to spend the summer? make him
write.—

Previous publication: *CWJ* 1: 84–90

ॐ

49.31 ~~have~~ has • [s *overwrites* ve]
49.32 Meanwhile • Mean= | while
50.2 ~~any~~ another • [o *overwrites blotted* y]
50.6 prepared • pre= | pared
50.27 ◊ who • [w *overwrites blotted letter*]
50.32 ~~w~~ is • [is *overwrites* w]
50.34 ◊◊ soul • [soul *overwrites blotted letters*]
50.35–51.1 f comparatively • [c *overwrites* f]
51.1 familiar • fam- | iliar
51.15 circumstances • [s *blotted out*]
51.19 proceedings • proceed= | ings
51.20 Diablerets • Diable= | rets

51.20 ~~rg~~ region · [e *overwrites* g]

51.27 post=chaise · post= | chaise

51.34 ampitheatre · [*misspelled*]

52.1 snow=crowned · snow= | =crowned

52.2 uninteresting · unin= | teresting

52.7 descended · descen= | ded

52.14 foot=journey · foot= | journey

52.20 ╎ · [*blotted out*]

52.27 Switzerland · Switzer= | land

53.15 previous · pre= | vious

54.1–2 noon- | day · noon-day

54.8 ◇◇ My · [My *overwrites illegible letters*]

54.9 considerable · consider= | able

54.21 predominates · pre= | dominates

54.23–24 ~~increased~~ introduced · [troduc *overwrites* creas]

54.27–28 [Excuse the accidental irregularity of my pages] · [*HJ's*
brackets; written across the letter's twelfth page*]

54.32 s too · [too *overwrites* s]

54.34 conversation · con= | versation

55.1 emergency · emer= | gency

55.2 ~~I~~ chiefly · [h *overwrites* I]

55.3 ◇ The · [T *overwrites illegible letter*]

55.3 perpetual · per= | petual

55.5 depise · [*misspelled*]

55.14 already · al= | ready

55.15 ◇◇ am · [am *overwrites illegible letters*]

55.20 knowledge · knowl= | edge

55.22 examination · examina= | tion

55.25 walk~~ing~~ I · [I *overwrites blotted* ing]

55.26 confess · con= | fess

56.16 ~~making~~ make · [e *overwrites* i; ng *struck through*]

∽

49.32 since I last wrote from Glion · HJ's [27], 28, 30 June 1869 letter
from Glion to MWJ is his most recent extant letter to his family.

49.32–33 your excellent letter of June 12ᵗʰ [. . .] that of June 1ˢᵗ • See *CWJ* 1: 77–84.

50.5 parages • surroundings.

50.13 Vaudois concern • Characteristic of the canton of Vaud.

50.31 Comballaz • La Comballaz, a small village in the canton of Vaud. The 1869 *Switzerland* Baedeker states that it is "much frequented for its mineral spring and invigorating mountain air" (155).

51.9–10 Gorge des Ormonts • The 1869 *Switzerland* Baedeker notes that the gorge was "a valley surrounded by picturesque, wooded mountains, and studded with innumerable houses and chalets, known collectively as Ormont-dessus" (156).

51.12–13 Village of Sepey • The principal village in the lower part of the Ormont Valley.

51.20–21 region about two hour's distant noted for the infernal grandeur of its scenery • According to the 1867 Murray for the *Alps*, the Diablerets were noted for massive landslides, and, as a result, the inhabitants had so named the region "because they regard it as the vestibule of hell" (196).

51.26–27 Sepey [. . .] the Diablerets • The 1869 *Switzerland* Baedeker describes this part of HJ's journey (though in the opposite direction): "From the Hôtel des Diablerets the traveller ascends the valley of the Grande Eau for ½ hr, [passing through the village of Sepey,] and then enters a lateral valley by a bridle-path" (156).

52.7–8 the lovely Simmenthal • The 1869 *Switzerland* Baedeker describes much of the itinerary HJ followed:

From the Bernese Oberland to the lake of Geneva the following beautiful route is strongly recommended to *pedestrians* (27 hrs. from Interlaken to Aigle; the whole journey may be performed on horseback; guides superfluous, except between Adelboden and Lauenen). [. . .]. On foot in 8 hrs. over the Col de Pillon ([. . .] or by carriage from the Hôtel des Diablerets or from Sepey) to Aigle [. . .] whence the traveller may proceed by railway to the Lake of Geneva, or to Martigny, or Sion in the Valley of the Rhone. (153)

52.8 village of Gesteig • Spelled Gsteig in the contemporary guidebooks.

52.13–14 the little foot=journey we made together years ago • See HJ
to Thomas Sergeant Perry, 18 July 1860.

52.18–20 Zweisimmen [. . .] a very good inn • The 1869 *Switzerland*
Baedeker lists two inns at Zweisimmen, the Bär and the Krone (154).
The 1867 Murray for the *Alps* lists the Lion and the Krone, but considers
neither "good" (140).

52.31 Lucerne • According to the 1869 *Switzerland* Baedeker, Lucerne
is "the capitol of the canton, popul. 11,673 (683 Prot.), [and] is situated on
the Reuss where it emerges from the lake" (50).

52.34–53.1 the gorgeous Schweizerhof • Hotel fronting the Lake of
Lucerne, in the center of Lucerne. It is described in the 1869 *Switzerland*
Baedeker as having rooms from two francs, with meals ranging from one
to $4\frac{1}{2}$ francs (49).

53.5–7 qualified in Bädeker [. . .] calme & de repos." • The 1869 *Switzerland* Baedeker notes that the "Scheideck is a charming retreat, quiet and
peaceful, forming a great contrast to the incessant bustle of the Kulm"
(65). The 1869 *La Suisse* Baedeker renders this last phrase "une retraite
charmante, pleine d'un calme et d'un repos" (67).

53.7 plein de calme & de repos • quiet and restful.

54.16–17 Your diagnosis of my back in your last • See WJ's 12 June 1869
letter to HJ (*CWJ* 1: 82), in which WJ writes: "The condition of your
back is totally incomprehensible to me."

55.31 H. Bowditch • Henry Pickering Bowditch was a medical school
classmate of WJ's and a cousin of Fanny Dixwell's. After earning his medical degree in 1868, Bowditch went to Europe and became a physiologist
and a well-respected researcher. In 1871 he accepted Charles W. Eliot's
offer to teach physiology at Harvard. Throughout both of their careers,
WJ and Bowditch remained friends. WJ had written HJ on 12 June 1869:
"Henry Bowditch writes me fm. Bonn where he is to spend the summer,
and hopes you may come there. He is an honest man" (*CWJ* 1: 83).

56.1 father's book • *The Secret of Swedenborg*, about which WJ wrote HJ
on 1 June: "Father has finished his book, wh. will be printed July 1ˢᵗ" (*CWJ*
1: 80).

56.9–10 J. S. Mill on the subjection of women • John Stuart Mill's *The*

Subjection of Women (1869) was reviewed by WJ in the *North American Review* 109 (Oct. 1869): 556–65.

5   HENRY JAMES SR. AND MARY WALSH JAMES
17, [18], 20 July [1869]
ALS Houghton
bMS Am 1094 (1761)

10   Righi Scheideck July 17<u>th</u> Sunday.

My cherished parents—
    I received several days since your two letters of June 21 & 22. I
particularly enjoyed of course father's flattering citations from
15   the <u>Tribune</u> & am deeply grateful for his own expressions of
pleasure in my tales. I feel as if I should do much better now & as
if some months hence I should ₐdo₍ₐ₎ better still. A couple of
days later ~~co~~ came an excellent letter from Willy (June 28<u>th</u>)
containing ~~rem~~ critical remarks &c. I wont answer it just now but
20   merely thank him for it. So much has happened since that the
notions with which I wrote the things have quite faded out of ·
memory & I should be quite at loss to explain their obscurities or
justify their ~~sch~~ shortcomings. They are the poor unripe fruits
of the house of bondage—& as such let them ~~ob~~ sink into
25   oblivion. Willy's criticisms were, nevertheless most valuable &
will certainly profit me much in the future.—More pleasant
however than any of this ~~news~~ talk about my literature was your
truly benignant response to my inquiries of some 6 weeks ago as
to my movements & expenses. Be assured that if you thus
30   appreciate my needs, I appreciate your kindness. I feel that it
puts me on the right footing with regard to ~~amende~~ amendment
& I feel a deeper sense than I can say of my blessed good
fortune. I mean to take myself in hand with a fresh gripe & put
myself thro'. It's a long tough struggle, this contest with so

dogged & firmly seated ◊ an enemy, but I shall not leave him as I
found him. My letter of a week ago is now well on the way to
you & before you get this you will have learned the
circumstances of my coming to this place & my 1ˢᵗ impressions
of it. I am now in my second week here & will probably finish it.   5
A longer stay is rather impracticable. The air is magnificent &
the view immense & sublime; but there the merits end. There is
no shade, little comfort & ◊ only one walk. The house is quite as
rude & crude as anything at home & I occupy perforce a room no
larger than a closet. The table, however is abundant & solid—too   10
solid for any but German stomachs. We have two dinners a
day—one at 12 ½ & the other, under the specious disguise of a
supper, at 7 ½! This Rigi is a mountain immense in extent & we,
being at one end of of it, the walk in question is to the <u>Culm</u>, or
great summit at the other extremity, with a diversion, on the   15
way, to a third hotel, the <u>Kaltbad</u>—a charming spot. The walk to
the Culm & back, however is a good five hours. I took it
yesterday, by way of the <u>Kaltbad</u>, (where I found Mrs. Otto
Dresel's name on the books & asked for her, but she was out)
which made (stopping to dine) a good seven hours of it. Then   20
there is the descent to Gersau, on the lake. That too I have
made, between dinner & supper: an hour & ½ down & 2 ½ up.
The return however is such a very tough grind that it is not a
journey to be lightly undertaken. I spoke ~~of~~ ₍ₐ₎in₍ₐ₎ my last of
meaning to go down, proceed to Lucerne & return before   25
evening, but I find that to get the proper boat I must leave
without my breakfast & altogether make rather a heavy day of it.
So I shall spend two or three days at Gersau on leaving here &
give myself a chance to explore the lake. As for the view, it is
decidedly more than I can talk about. It is vast, changing,   30
cloudy, chaotic. I am writing these lines at 4 p.m. under the
piazza of the hotel, the one little shady spot where all the
lodgers huddle together & fiercely dispute the little beer-stained
tables. The great mountain prospect opposite—above, below, is

veiled in a faintly purple haze out of which fitfully gleam the
snowy horrors of the Bernese Oberland. Beneath us lie three
blue-bosomed lakes—Lucerne, Zug & Lauwertz & a little to one
side the raw dismembered shoulder of a mountain from which
5   fifty years ago ◊ an avalanche rolled & crushed the little Village
of Goldau. So you see we are lodged far aloft in the world of ~~co~~
clouds & peaks & the desolate spaces of air—amid the silence, the
chilliness & ~~be~~ bareness. You will probably understand me well
enough if I express a certain aversion to all this awful grandeur.
10   Switzerland ends by flattening down my spirits ~~awfully.~~
[∧]dreadfully.[∧] It's no country, I'm convinced, for a man with a
"◊ back or with nerves: no country at all events, for a man to
visit alone unless he's a Thoreau or an Obermann. I have as yet
been very unlucky in the way of finding (, or rather of missing)
15   companions ~~⅜~~ & having walked now a good deal almost wholly
alone I have acquired a sort of susceptibility to these inhuman
steeps & brooding solitudes which at moments amounts to a
positive craven fear. I went the other afternoon (I mentioned
∧it[∧] in my last) with a very rational young Englishman up ~~th~~ a
20   mountain near at hand which has an extremely sad & inaccessible
summit—quite a dizzy climb to reach it. Being with him it was
well enough, but I can readily imagine that with my own
~~company~~ timorous ∧spirit[∧] for all support, I might have ended
with an attack of hysterics. If you are sensitive to the mountains
25   tho', the only way evidently to get over it is to take the rudest
liberties with them & rob them of their mysteries. You can never
feel especially imaginative about a bit of steepness you have
trudged up & baptized in your perspiration.—I believe I
mentioned in my last that I had made up my mind to try St.
30   Moritz & had written to Leslie Stephen to kindly attempt to get
me a room. But altho' a week has passed I have got no answer; so
I shall take other steps & hope at any rate to be there by the end
of the month.—Tuesday, 20th I was interrupted on Sunday &
have now time to add but a few words—being rather fagged &

stiff from a long excursion yesterday—which was nevertheless very jolly while it lasted. I went with a very jolly botanizing English parson who is staying here, down to Gersau; thence took boat to Brunnen (20 minutes) ¦ ∧d∧ thence walked about 3 miles to the good old town of ~~Schytz.~~ Se Schwytz—a vast, dignified, antique, empty place—a bit of old Switzerland; here we dined lightly & started to turn about the shoulder of the Rigi & came up the opposite side. This gave us a level walk of about an hour, to start with, & then a long, hard upward grind of about four more over a very pathless & rugged ascent—so that there is the wherewithal to feel a little used up to day. To morrow I shall be all right again. But the day was, I think, the pleasantest I have spent in Switzerland—perfect summer weather, a beautiful country, & a certain flavor of enterprise & adventure.—This is turning out by the way, a very hot summer here. I hope that at home your'e not having a second edition of last.—I hope, when I next hear to get some news of Pomfret—would I were there! My enjoyment of yesterday, however, makes me unsay my complaints, just above. Switzerland is a great place, after all.— By this time, you must have heard again from Aunt Kate. I haven't heard in 3 weeks, but shall write immediately. Your letters have made me determine definitely to go to Italy about September 1st, if not sooner. On August 15th, I shall have been 3 months in ~~Italy~~ ∧Switzerland∧—quite as long a time as I feel like giving to it. I hope to be able to go direct from St. Moritz, over the Bernina or the Splügen.—Thank W. much for Pratt's good letter. I'm afraid his journey's too much of a job for me. At all events, I couldn't undertake it alone. But I do hope to get to Sicily. I'm sorry J. L. F. is not to come abroad. If we could have been together a bit here I think I should have enjoyed his society. Greet my dear sister: my next letter shall be to her. Farewell. Once more let me breathe out my satisfaction in your letters. I embrace you.—Your son—H. J. jr.

No previous publication

∾

60.18 e~~o~~ came • [a *overwrites* o]

60.19 ~~rem~~ critical • [crit *overwrites* rem]

60.23 s~~ch~~ shortcomings • [h *overwrites* ch]

60.24 ~~ob~~ sink • [s *overwrites* ob]

60.27 ~~news~~ talk • [talk *overwrites* news]

60.29 movements &̷ expenses • [&̷ *inserted*]; ex= | penses

60.31 ~~amende~~ amendment • [m *overwrites* e]

60.33 myself • my= | self

61.1 ◊ an • [a *overwrites illegible letter*]

61.6 impracticable • im= | practicable

61.8 comfort • [m *inserted*]

61.8 ◊ only • [o *overwrites illegible letter*]

61.18 yesterday • yes= | terday

61.33 together • to= | gether

62.5 ◊ an • [a *overwrites illegible letter*]

62.6–7 e~~o~~ clouds • [l *overwrites* o]

62.8 ~~be~~ bareness • [a *overwrites* e]

62.12 "◊ <u>back</u> • [" *blotted out*; b *overwrites illegible letter*]

62.15 companions • com= | panions

62.19 ~~th~~ a • [a *overwrites* th]

62.23 ~~company~~ timorous • [timorous *overwrites* company]

62.33 interrupted • inter= | rupted

63.4 ⌐∧ • [∧ *overwrites* ;]

63.5 S~~c~~ Schwytz • [Sch *overwrites* Sc]

63.22 definitely • de= | finitely

63.26–28 Thank W. much for Pratt's [. . .]. At all • [*written across the letter's first page*]

63.28–29 events, I couldn't [. . .] J. L. F. is not to • [*written across the letter's second page*]

63.29–31 come abroad. [. . .] enjoyed his society. • [*written across the letter's third page*]

63.31–32 Greet my dear sister [. . .] let me breathe • [*written across the letter's fourth page*]

63.32-33 out my satisfaction [. . .]. Your son—H. J. jr. • [*written across the letter's seventh page*]

༄

60.10 July 17ᵗʰ Sunday • 17 July 1869 was a Saturday, but HJ speaks of being "interrupted on Sunday" (62.33) and refers to "Tuesday, 20th" (62.33), and 20 July 1869 was a Tuesday.

60.14-15 father's flattering citations from the Tribune • Two reviews of HJ's short stories appeared in the 18 June 1869 *New-York Tribune*. The first notes: "Mr. Henry James, jr's, 'A Light Man' is a powerful, painful study, in strong contrast with the sweetness and purity of his Mlle. de Bergerac, in the *Atlantic*. How many men have we—how many are there—who could write two stories, each so clever and yet so different?" ("New Publications" 6). The second review says:

> Mr. Henry James, jr's, "Gabrielle de Bergerac" of which we have only the first part, is full of promise for the future, and of fine performance in the present. We have no story writer in America who writes at once so delicately and so strongly as Mr. James. His style, with perhaps a suspicion of French epigram too much, is almost faultless as an expression of his idea, his power of description is a gift of serenity and artistic skill, and his character-drawing is a treat in this generation of daubers and slashers. Gabrielle de Bergerac bids fair to make a red letter in this young author's calendar—and in ours, too, for that matter. (6)

60.28-29 my inquiries of some 6 weeks ago as to my movements & expenses • See HJ to WJ, 30, 31 May 1869.

61.2-5 My letter of a week ago [. . .] my coming to this place & my 1ˢᵗ impressions of it • See HJ to WJ, 12, 13 July 1869.

61.14 the Culm • The 1867 Murray for the *Alps* gives both Culm and Kulm as spellings for the Rigi peak above Weggis (45).

61.18-19 Mrs. Otto Dresel • Wife of Otto Dresel (ca. 1826–90), German concert pianist and composer who, after 1852, resided primarily in Boston with her.

62.5-6 avalanche [. . .] Village of Goldau • The 1869 *Switzerland* Baedeker notes the following: "On approaching Goldau [. . .], traces of the disastrous landslip of the Rossberg, which completely buried this large and wealthy village, may be observed. [. . .] The summer of 1808 [*sic, actually*

1806] had been very rainy. On Sept. 2nd about 5 p.m. one of these strata [. . .] was precipitated from a height of 3000′ into the valley below, swallowing up four villages with about 500 of their inhabitants, and converting the smiling landscape into a scene of desolation" (55).

62.13 Obermann • The title character of *Obermann* (1804), the influential romantic novel by Étienne Pivert de Senancour (1770–1846), inhabited a remote Alpine village. It is not clear whether HJ knew Senancour's Obermann or only knew him through later works he inspired, like George Sand's *Lélia* (1833), Balzac's *Le Lys dans la vallée* (1836), Sainte-Beuve's *Volupté* (1834), or Arnold's "Stanzas in Memory of the Author of 'Obermann'" (1852) and "Obermann Once More" (1867). In his [27], 28, 30 June [1869] letter to MWJ, HJ refers her to Matthew Arnold's two poems on Obermann.

62.18–20 I went the other afternoon (I mentioned ∧it[∧] in my last) with a very rational young Englishman up ~~th~~ a mountain near at hand • See HJ to WJ, 12, 13 July 1869.

62.28–31 I mentioned in my last that I had made up my mind to try St. Moritz ~~&~~ had written to Leslie Stephen to kindly attempt to get me a room • See HJ to WJ, 12, 13 July 1869.

63.4 Brunnen • City east of Gersau, on a bend of the Lake of Lucerne or Vierwaldstätter See. Described in the 1869 *Switzerland* Baedeker as "the port of the canton of Schwyz, perhaps the most beautifully situated place on the Lake of Lucerne, of late years much frequented, and suitable for a stay of some duration" (70).

63.5 Schwytz • The 1869 *Switzerland* Baedeker describes Schwyz as "a straggling town (5780 inhab., 53 Prot.), the capitol of the canton, and [. . .] is picturesquely situated at the foot and on the *Mythen*" (56).

63.26 Bernina or the Splügen • Bernina Pass (2328 m), generally closed by snow from November to May, lies 16 km southeast of Saint Moritz. Of the Splügen Pass, the 1869 *Switzerland* Baedeker notes: "10,748′, ascent 3–4 hrs., not unattended with danger; the view extends N. to Suabia, S. to Milan, whence this mountain is visible" (356).

63.26 W. • WJ.

63.29 J. L. F. • John La Farge.

ALICE JAMES
26, 29 July [1869]
ALS Houghton
bMS Am 1094 (1557)

5

Gersau ∧Hotel Müller,₍∧₎ Lake of Lucerne July 26.
My dearest Sister.

   Altho' little enough has happened since a week ago when I last
wrote home, yet as the usual period has elapsed & the influences
of the scene are of a kind to drive a poor creature for comfort   10
where he can best find it, I cant help beginning, at least, another
scrawl & addressing it to the sister of my childhood—a little
love-letter, at any rate, is if nothing more interesting. The rain is
descending in steady sounding sheets & the dismal heavens are
grey with the promise of a deluge. I have read till I'm tired,   15
paced the corridors amid the graceless chatter of ugly Germans
till I'm depressed in spirit & sought in vain for relief in
conversation. The people in the house are all German save an
amiable but rather stiff & conservative English parson & his
sister, a couple of English ladies & an American family of so   20
repulsive a type that I blush to associate with them. So I sit me
down to confer awhile with the lovely child, the thought of
whom alone can afford consolation as her presence alone will
restore me to happiness. Switzerland in bad weather is a very sad
affair, for here if you can't be under the sky, the purpose of life is   25
defeated. Bent as I am upon a savage economy of my various
resources I regard every day as lost in which I don't get some
sort of walk. However, I should be sorry to grumble. For a
month now, (since the cessation of the June rains) we have been
having splendid skies & this is only the second day of the storm.   30
I shall teach my spirit to drink deep of the sunshine by enduring
the gloom with fortitude.—To day is Monday: I came down
from the Rigi on S Friday evening after a very satisfactory
fortnight. But I had come to an end of my privileges &

determined to seek fresh fields. I am making a halt at this place,
where there is a capital & very moderate hotel=pension, a sort of
mate to that on the mountain above, to give myself a chance to
make one or two expeditions on the lake, which it is a pity I

5 should miss, before going to St. Moritz. As yet, however the rain
has balked me. I have partly agreed with a very amiable young
Englishman whom I met on the Rigi (& who has been some time
in America) to have him join me tomorrow & ~~journey with me
to the Eng~~ proceed [∧]in[∧] his company. We shall make a day's

10 railway journey to a certain place called <u>Coire</u> & thence it is my
magnificent ambition to walk some forty miles by a two day's
relay to St. Moritz. My appetite for walking is becoming quite
huge & I shall soon be fit for nothing else. When I was last at
Lucerne (Saturday) I came to ~~a~~ the point & invested in a pair of

15 mountain-boots—& if you please, in a knapsack—a very light
one. What will come of them, time will shew. In my last letter I
spoke of a long walk I had taken with the Chaplain of the Rigi
hotel & of my feeling somewhat done by it. Lest you should fear
I had hurt myself let me hasten to add that on the second day

20 after I achieved very nearly the mate to it, in company with
Middlemore the young Englishman aforesaid. What started me
was the need to go to Lucerne ~~to~~ on account of another break in
my famous watch (thro' no carelessness either) & wh. I sadly
begrudged paying 15 frs. to have repaired. So I came down to

25 Gersau at 7 a.m. took the boat (~~at~~ 2 hours [∧]&[∧] ½) for L., spent a
couple of hours walking about there, & thence took the boat
back to Weggis, further up the lake, whence you ascend to the
Rigi-Cùlm. The day was infernally hot but we tugged up a three
hour's ascent to the <u>Kaltbad</u> & thence proceeded in an hour [∧]&[∧]

30 ¼ along the mountain to the Scheideck, wh. we reached at
9 p.m. All this is to ~~assure~~ [∧]shew[∧] you what I am up to & to
suggest that the boots & the knapsack may yet be of use.—Much
of my time ◇◇◇◇ during the last ten days (tell father & mother) I
have spent in pondering the contents of their two letters which I

answered last week & scanning the future in the light of their generosity. I feel at times as if it made life almost too grave a thing ∧to bear,[∧] to have ∧it[∧] enriched & embroidered by such liberal providential hands. I dont think I couldn't entertain you better, if I were able to do it than in describing my secret wrestlings & wranglings over my plans. If I only had some friend or trustworthy acquaintance who knew Switzerland it would save me a vast deal of worry. I feel as if I couldn't afford in time money or strength to make mistakes & by dint of ardently contemplating every conceivable side of a question I am apt to get my intellects tied into an inextricable knot. Yesterday, for instance I had one of my grand spasms. I sat at the tâble d'hôte next to a very clever English lady of the better sort (who complained that her sad fate was to be ~~the~~ only the wife of a peer's¦ second son) & who gave me a dreadful turn ~~m~~ by depicting the scarcity of rooms & the high prices at St. Moritz. Behold me unstrung, unhinged, for the day. After dinner I "conversed" awhile with the head of the American family of which I spoke, who is fresh from the Black Forest. He railed bitterly at Switzerland & vaunted the latter region ⋄ so roundly that il ~~ne~~ ~~m~~ n'en fallut pas davantage to set me agog about Wildbad, which Willy used to preach to me. As it is only some eight hours journey hence I was for a moment tempted f to forswear these puzzling Alps & hie me to its lovely shades. Add to this that ever since fairly deciding to go to Italy my spirit yearns & tends to it in the most hungry fashion & I detect ~~it th~~ in my secret heart a timid hope that ~~if~~ I shall not like the Engadine & so be driven after a fortnight over one of the great passes into the land of art & romance. Much as I enjoy Switzerland in many ways I am loth (having now been here some 9 weeks) to spend a longer time in the contemplation of pure nature, while so much of peculiar & distinctive Europe lies outspread in the distance. There was another moment when I thought gravely of crossing over the St. Gothard (I am just on the route) & going down to

spend the month of August at the Baths of Lucca, which are said
to be so charming & adjourning thence, September 1<u>st</u> to Venice.
Now as I write I feel as if I am detained, as much as anything by
a mere vague pusillanimity. The thing sounds too wild & rich &

5   enchanting. But in point of fact there is reason for it. The
argument against it is of course that Italy is too hot to be healthy
in the month of August. It is not however—it can't be—hotter
than the Swiss valleys & as ◈◈ for the Swiss mountain-tops in one
important respect—tho' only one—I find them pernicious. ~~They~~

10   The ∧air[∧] deprives me of sleep. I have got an Italian Bäddeker &
read in it the most seductive page about the Baths of Lucca &
looked the place out on the map & conned all the names of the
near-lying romantic old towns. Upon my word I have talked
myself into another spasm. But an hour hence I shall be all

15   right—& meanwhile this is a harmless pastime. What I shall do
probably is to start in a day or two for the Engadine & stop not
at St. Moritz but at Pontresina some 4 miles distant a cheaper &
~~left~~ less crowded place. I shall do what walking I can <u>en route</u> &
after I get there, remain as long as I find it wise & thence start

20   for Italy. You had better therefore address your letters to Venice,
care of <u>M. M. Schielin</u>, <u>Frères</u>, bankers, where some 5 weeks
hence I shall find them awaiting me. Owing to the present
uncertainty of my movements there is a little suspension of their
coming in. I nevertheless received some 5 days ago father's little

25   note from Cambridge on his return from Pomfret, telling of the
burglar & of poor Wilky's scorched back. Bully ∧for[∧] both of
them! I trust the former has ere this been slain & that Wilky is
all right again. Thank father heartily for his note—a little from
him goes a great way. I have been watching for the letter from P.

30   which he said he had forgotten to post, but it hasn't turned up﹔
But I do hope I am to get some account of your situation &
fixings. <u>Thursday.</u> 29<u>th</u> I have left my letter standing till to-day &
tho' it seems so vague & stupid, I shall send it. I am still lingering
at this place—tho' as the heat continues, I begin to pant again

for the altitudes. I have passed two very pleasant days. On
Tuesday I roamed forth & took a very great walk—that is I
truged from here all along the lakeside (a splendid carriage road
scraped into the base of the mountain) to Flüelen & thence to
the quaint & charming town of Altorf—where Tell shot—or   5
didn't shoot—his arrow; thence back to Flüelen on foot &
thence by boat to Gersau: in all a walk, I should say, of <u>fifteen</u>
good miles. I ~~was~~ got very tired, but I enjoyed it. Altorf, for a
Swiss town, is delightful & <u>what</u> a dinner I did make at the
excellent inn! On the morrow (to gently woo away the stiffness   10
that ensu[ ] on such an exploit) I took the boat to Lucerne to
call on a Miss Ward & sister, late of the hotel Pelham Boston,
whom I met at ~~the~~ Glion & whom I may not have mentioned.
They are very amiable women, rather sad & lonely (the elder a
great musician) & accompanied by a charming little Roxbury   15
cousin. They are staying at an extremely nice "Kùrort," some
3 miles from Lucerne, & with them I found Mrs. Huntington &
tw[o] [da]ughters late of Cambridge, who spoke affectionately of
you & mother. The elder Miss H. ravished my soul by her sweet
American solidity. There is nothing on earth, after all, to   20
compare with the young American female of gentle nurture. My
spirits soar quite as much when I encounter good Americans as
they sink when I meet base ones—who alas! are numerous.—
Don't jeer at me when I tell you that my plans are again
dissolved. The Engadine is knocked on the head by a letter I   25
received yesterday from Leslie Stephen in answer to one I wrote
3 weeks ago & which had but recently come to him. He dissuades
me so strongly from trying it, that I give it up. In fact there isn't
a room to be had. I shall stay here till Monday (making ten day's
in all.) L. S. very kindly gives me an itinerary for a foot-journey   30
of about four weeks. I may perhaps try a small fraction of it—
but be sure I shall do nothing imprudent. I do nothing but with
sanitary motives. I doubt not but that thro' much tribulation I
shall enter into the [k]ingdom of health—where I shall find you
on the threshold to receive me!—Tout à toi H. J. jr.   35

P. S. I had meant to enclose a little note for Willy—but I must wait till next week.—

No previous publication

☙

67.8 happened • hap= | pened

67.13 i̶s̶ if • [f *overwrites illegible letter*]

67.33 S̶ Friday • [F *overwrites* S]

67.33 satisfactory • satis= | factory

68.4 expeditions • expedi= | tions

68.8–9 j̶o̶u̶r̶n̶e̶y̶ ̶w̶i̶t̶h̶ ̶m̶e̶ ̶t̶o̶ ̶t̶h̶e̶ ̶E̶n̶g̶ proceed ₍ₐ₎in₍ₐ₎ his company • [proceed *overwrites* journey; his company *overwrites* me to the Eng]

68.14 a̶ the • [th *overwrites* a]

68.22 t̶o̶ on • [on *overwrites* to]

68.25 a̶t̶ 2 • [2 *overwrites* at]

68.33 ◇◇◇◇ during • [during *overwrites illegible letters*]

69.8 couldn't • [n't *inserted*]

69.15 m̶ by • [b *overwrites* m]

69.20 ◇ so • [s *overwrites illegible letter*]

69.21 m̶ n'en • [n *overwrites* m]

69.23 f̶ to • [t *overwrites* f]

69.26–27 i̶t̶ ̶t̶h̶ in my • [in my *overwrites* it th]

69.27 i̶f̶ I • [I *overwrites* if]

70.8 ◇◇ for • [fo *overwrites illegible letters*]

70.9–10 T̶h̶e̶y̶ The ₍ₐ₎ • [₍ₐ₎ *overwrites* y]

70.18 l̶e̶f̶t̶ less • [ss *overwrites* ft]

71.3 truged • [*misspelled*]

71.8 w̶a̶s̶ got • [got *overwrites* was]

71.11 ensu[ ] • [*ms. damaged*]

71.13 t̶h̶e̶ Glion • [Glion *overwrites* the]

71.18 tw[o] • [*ms. damaged*]

71.18 [da]ughters • [*ms. damaged*]

71.33 doubt • [t *inserted*]

71.34 [k]ingdom · [*ms. damaged*]

∾

67.6 Hotel Müller · The 1869 *Switzerland* Baedeker notes that this hotel has "gardens and lake-baths," charging six francs a day for pension (70).

67.8–9 when I last wrote home · The last extant letter is HJ to Sr. and MWJ, 17, [18], 20 July [1869].

68.2–3 a sort of mate · The same Mr. Müller owned the Hôtel Müller in Gersau and the Hotel Rigi-Scheideck (Baedeker, *Switzerland* [1869] 70).

68.10 Coire · The French name for the eastern Swiss town of Chur.

68.27 Weggis · Town on the northeast shore of the Lake of Lucerne and to the northwest of Gersau.

68.34–69.1 I answered last week · HJ to MWJ and Sr., 17, [18], 20 July [1869].

69.21 il ne m n'en fallut pas davantage · no more was needed.

69.22 Wildbad · Mineral spring and watering place in Germany.

69.27 Engadine · The Inn River valley, northeast of St. Moritz.

69.34 St. Gothard · The St. Gotthard Pass connects the cantons of Uri and Ticino; it is an important part of one of the principal routes through the Alps, from Switzerland to Italy.

70.10–11 I have got an Italian Bäddeker & read in it the most seductive page about the Baths of Lucca · The 1868 Baedeker of *Northern Italy as Far as Leghorn* gives the following description:

The Baths of Lucca, known in the middle ages, about 12 M. distant from the town (diligence and omnibus several times daily in $2\frac{1}{2}$ hrs., fare 3 fr.; carr. 15 fr.), are situated to the N. in a mountainous district, on the small river *Lima*. An excursion there and back may easily be accomplished in one day if Lucca be quitted at an early hour. The town is quitted by the Porta Sta. Maria. The road leads N. by the bank of the Serchio, the impetuous water of which is confined between lofty embankments. The road to the beautiful *Villa Marlia* (p. 334) diverges to the r. The Serchio is then crossed by the bridge of *Muriano*, decorated with figures of saints, and a charming hilly district traversed. [. . .] The valley of the Lima is cool and well shaded, affording healthy and

delightful quarters for the summer. Many beautiful excursions may
be made among the neighbouring mountains, thus to the bridge *Della
Maddalena*, to the village of *Lugliano*, to the old watch-tower *Bargilio*,
affording a magnificent prospect in clear weather. [. . .] The casino,
or *Ridotti*, stands on an eminence in the vicinity. Near it is the *Nuovo
Ospedale*, erected by the Russian Prince Nicholas Demidoff. (334–35)

70.17 Pontresina · Town eight kilometers east of St. Moritz, in the
Bernina Valley.

71.4 Flüelen · Located on the southeast shore of the Lake of Lucerne.

71.5 Altorf · An alternative spelling for Altdorf, a town just south of
the Lake of Lucerne.

71.5-6 Tell shot [. . .] his arrow · The legendary William Tell was
supposed to have been born in Altdorf.

71.12 Miss Ward *&* sister, late of the hotel Pelham Boston · Ellen M.
and Judy E. Ward, who in 1867 resided at the Hotel Pelham, at the corner
of Boylston and Tremont Streets, Boston.

71.16 Kùrort · Health resort.

71.17 Mrs. Huntington · Possibly Ellen Greenough Huntington
(1814–93). She was the second wife of Charles Phelps Huntington and
sister-in-law to Francis Boott. The Huntingtons resided in Florence.

71.35 Tout à toi · All yours.

WILLIAM JAMES
12 August [1869]
ALS Houghton
bMS Am 1094 (1933)

Gersau, Lucerne, Hotel Müller.

J August 12<u>th</u>

Dearest Bill—When I wrote to father a couple of days since
from Interlaken I had no idea that I should so soon be writing

again from this place. On the morning after my letter was
written however, a slight change befell in my plans—caused by a
variety of circumstances—the setting in of bad weather—the
need of a little rest—the development of a slight affection in my
right ankle (wh. immediate use might aggravate)—& finally a   5
vague sort of collapse of physical enthusiasm. So instead of then
& there pushing on over the Gemmi (wh. I had already done) I
came immediately in one day over the <u>Brünig</u> to this place, to
pick up my luggage & reorganize my programme. It seemed to
me somewhat unwise to be pushing southward, without my   10
effects only to give myself the labor of the upward journey again
prior to starting afresh. Owing to my foot I thought it best not
to ◊ try to walk the Brünig, but was fortunate enough to meet at
Brienz with a frenchman & his wife with whom I went shares in
the hire of a vehicle. We drove over yesterday, ~~comp~~   15
comfortably in 8 hours—<u>plus</u> two more for me from Lucerne
he◊◊◊ hither. I shall give my foot a day or two's rest & then,
having forwarded my luggage to <u>Milan</u> start off again with my
knapsack. It's quite as I expected: a few days interval brings out
strongly the good effects of this doughty climbing. When I get   20
home I shall tear your diploma in twain & prescribe to you a
course of ~~of~~ the same treatment. It ought to take rank among
the regular stock remedies.—It takes something of an effort to
get up steam to do the thing alone: but I shall find even this
better than leaving it undone. I may not as I ~~wish~~ ∧announced,[∧]   25
cross the St. Gotthard, as that from here is a matter of only a
couple of days. I <u>may</u> go down to the Simplon—& I may
~~scramble~~ ∧push[∧] on to Zermatt & scramble thence over the
Monte Moro. I shall see when I get under way. But I shall make
with great directness for the Italian Lakes, as I grudge spending   30
any more money on Switzerland. I have been having quite a
correspondence with H. P. Bowditch upon the possibility of our
joining forces, wh. I much wished: but am disappointed as he
doesn't even enter Switzerland till the twentieth. I received to

day most gratefully a <u>Nation</u> of July 22$^{\underline{d}}$, but am still, thro' my cursed awkwardness, without my recent letters. I hope however to receive them in a day or two. —The tenor of this & my last letters has been very dull—owing to the fact that in walking you

5 quite sweat the rhapsodical faculty out of you & have no eloquence left for talk. Mountain-climbing is an awfully silent process. I nevertheless should be very glad to be able to give you some hint of one or two of my sensations—the great snow- ~~worl~~ &-ice-world I gazed upon from the summit of the Titlis—& the

10 spectacle before me when, on the summit of the Wengern-Alp I sat on the bench outside the inn & surveyed, directly ~~before me~~ ‸opposite‸₍∧₎, the towering gleaming pinnacles of the Silberhorn, the Eiger, the Mönch &c—both views admirably favored by a cloudless air. But you'll readily excuse me. Wait till I get into

15 Italy—& then I'll dip my pen in purple & gold. I have been reading T. Gautier's <u>Italia</u>. <u>Le</u> <u>brave</u> <u>homme</u>! —The only thing worth now putting into words is just what I can't—~~my~~ the deep satisfaction in being able to do all this healthy trudging & climbing. It <u>is</u>—it <u>is</u> a pledge, a token of some future potency.

20 Amen! What ‸I‸₍∧₎ especially wait for in my letters is some news of you—your Pomfret₎ life—habits, improvement. I'm absolutely faint & sick for home news. From Aunt Kate I have heard nothing for a long time. I'm afraid I have missed some letter she has sent. It may yet turn up. She is not yet in

25 Switzerland, inasmuch as her party were to be in Paris on the Emperor's fête, 15$^{\underline{th}}$ August. Farewell my brother. I'd give my right hand for an hour's talk with you—lying ~~under~~ ‸in‸₍∧₎ some afternoon shade, beneath a Connecticut sky! I hope you & Alice get some drives. Ask her if the she remembers that one she & I

30 had last summer, that evening, at Littleton? —at Littleton it used to be Switzerland, —& now it's Littleton! Where & how is Wilky—fat & faithless one! Mother, I hope, is well & idle & free to roam where she likes. I wish I could take her a sail down here into the Bay of Uri. By this time I suppose father's book is out. ◈

Send any notices as well as the vol. Direct as I wrote a fortnight
since: ₍ₐ₎M. M.₍ₐ₎ <u>Schielin</u> <u>frères</u>, <u>Banquiers</u>

    Venice

      Italy.

      Tout à toi   5

  <u>H. James</u> jr.

Previous publication: *CWJ* 1: 90–92

∞

74.31 J̶ August · [A *overwrites* J]

75.11 upward · up= | ward

75.13 ◊ try · [t *overwrites illegible letter*]

75.15-16 c̶o̶m̶p̶ comfortably · [f *overwrites* p]

75.17 h̶e̶◊◊ hither · [ither *overwrites* e◊◊◊]

75.19 knapsack · knap= | sack

75.22 o̶f̶ the · [th *overwrites* of]

76.8-9 w̶o̶r̶l̶ ꝺ- · [ꝺ- *overwrites* worl]

76.17 m̶y̶ the · [the *overwrites* my]

76.25 Switzerland · Switzer= | -land

76.34–77.1 ◊ Send · [S *overwrites illegible letter*]

∞

75.8 the <u>Brünig</u> · The Brünigpass (1002 m), on the principal route from
Interlaken to Lucerne.

75.14 Brienz · A town on the northeast shore of the Brienzer Sea and
between Interlaken and the Brünigpass.

75.27 the Simplon · The Simplon Pass (2005 m), one of the principal
Alpine passes; it connects Brig, in the canton of Valais, and Domodossola,
Italy.

75.28 Zermatt · Only "a village with 424 inhab." in the late nineteenth
century (Baedeker, *Switzerland* [1869] 287).

75.28–29 over the Monte Moro · Monte Moro Pass (2868 m), east of
Zermatt and south of Saas-Fee, north of the Valle Anzasca in Italy.

76.9 the summit of the Titlis · Titlis (3239 m), south of Gersau and
east of Interlaken.

76.10 the summit of the Wengern-Alp • Part of the Kleine Scheidegg, between Wengen and the Eiger and Jungfrau.

76.12 the Silberhorn • Part of the Jungfrau (4158 m).

76.13 the Eiger • Mt. Eiger (3970 m).

76.13 the Mönch • Mt. Mönch (4099 m).

76.16 T. Gautier's Italia • Théophile Gautier published *Italia* in 1852.

76.16 Le brave homme! • The good man!

76.25–26 the Emperor's fête • August 15, 1869, was the one hundredth anniversary of Napoleon I's birth.

76.30 Littleton • Littleton, New Hampshire, in the White Mountains, was a popular summer destination.

76.34 the Bay of Uri • The southeasternmost section of the Lake of Lucerne.

77.5 Tout à toi • All yours.

CHARLES ELIOT NORTON
17 August [1869]
ALS Houghton
bMS Am 1088 (3851)

Gersau Lucerne August 17th

My dear Charles—

I am very much obliged to you for your note of information & suggestion about Italy, which found me weather-bound in this stupid little spot. We have been having a week of such persistently rainy days as to make departure impossible & as even yet there is no look of mercy in the skies I don't know how much longer I may be imprisoned. Between my lame foot (now I think once more serviceable) & these adverse heavens I have lost so much time in mere waiting that when I start I think it will be directly over the St. Gotthard to Italy, without attempting to

78

embrace any more of Switzerland. I have been here now more
than three months & feel a decided sensation of satiety. I quite
intend to linger a week or ten days by Lugano, Como &
Maggiore & to ramble among their shores as much as my
strength & the temperature will permit.—More, however, than
for your hints & recommendations, I thank you for the
delightful news that you are to spend the winter in Florence.
À la bonne heure. I had resigned myself to prospective solitude
& gloom but these good tidings exonerate me from that virtuous
patience. I most sincerely trust that Italy will be quite as good
for you as Mr. Simon pronounced Dresden to be bad. With your
letter came one from Jane which had been lying at Zermatt, in
which the announcement is first made—making me fiercely
regret the absence of this happy knowledge, which would have
gone far to console me for the dismal weather. I shall make more
or less directly for Venice (as much as possible on foot)—
stopping at as many as I may of the smaller towns you mention.
Turin I'm afraid I shall have to leave till my upward journey,
when I shall enter France. I shall probably be going to Florence
abou just before the time of your arrival & count upon you to
commission me for overtures & arrangements.—Your note stirs
up my languid pulses to ◊◊ so strongly & makes me so impatient
to put these terrible Alps behind me that I may be quietly of the
bad taste of starting off in the rain—i.e. this evening or
tomorrow. At any rate you shall hear from me when I once fairly
arrive on Italian soil.—My letters finally arrived from Zermatt &
forcibly impressed me with my obligations to Jane & you. They
contained little news. Among them was a charming long one
from Howells requesting his especial regards to all of you.
(In the August Atlantic is an extremely good sketch from his
pen of the "Jubilee". Your hostile attitude toward your native
land may disable you from enjoying it; but your innocent &
unsophisticated ladies will read it with pleasure.)—Congratulate
Sara most warmly upon her resolution to stay with you; instead

of the note of farewell which I meditated I feel strongly prompted to write her a letter of thanks. — I'm very much afraid that your'e not as well as you ought to be. If so, why linger among those hateful hills? Why not come Southward without
5 loss of time? But j'en parle à mon aise. Excuse the presumption of one who is neither a parent nor a householder. I enclose a scrap for Grace & my love to all invidually. You say nothing of Susan: I suppose she is resigned to missing Germany. It's very pleasant to be able again to write farewell without feeling that it
10 means something so dreadful. — Faithfully yours H. James jr.

No previous publication

∽

78.27 suggestion • sug= | gestion
78.31 imprisoned • im= | prisoned
79.8 prospective • pros= | pective
79.20 ~~abou~~ just • [just *overwrites* abou]
79.22 ~~to~~ ⟡⟡ so strongly • [so stro *overwrites* t *and illegible letters*]
80.7 invidually • [*misspelled*]

∽

78.26–27 your note of information & suggestion about Italy • See Norton's 14 August 1869 letter from Vevey to HJ (Houghton bMS Am 1094 [373]).

79.8 À la bonne heure • Marvelous.

79.28–29 a charming long one from Howells • Howells's 26 June, 18, 24 July 1869 letter from Cambridge to HJ (see Anesko 64–68).

79.30–31 sketch from his pen of the "Jubilee" • The National Peace Jubilee, held in Boston in June 1869, was the subject of Howells's "Jubilee Days," *Atlantic Monthly* 24 (August 1869): 245–54.

80.5 j'en parle à mon aise • but it is easy for me to say so.

ALICE JAMES
31 August [1869]
ALS Houghton
bMS Am 1094 (1558)

5

Hotel Belle-Vue
    Cadenabbia
(August 31ˢᵗ) Lago di Como.
My dearest old Sister—

Your wonderment & anxiety as to my fate has perhaps by   10
this time reached the stage of perfect indifference. I confess I
have well-nigh given it time to do so. My excuse is the very
best—& one that that will quite reconcile ~~me~~ you to my guilt:—I
have ˰been˰ roaming & rambling—walking & scrambling so
hard & so constantly that I have not had time to sit down & write   15
such a letter as I deemed consonant to the situation. Voyons: où
en étais-je when I last wrote? Great heavens, since that dim &
distant day what an age has elapsed? I was at Gersau, if I mistake
not, on my return ~~for~~ from the Oberland, waiting for the Rain
to ~~go~~ ~~&~~ stop & for my letters to come. Well finally the rain did   20
go—& one blissful evening my letters did come & flattened me
out beneath the weight of my joy—one from father, one from
mother, & one from you. One delightful long one too from
Howells—as well as an <u>Atlantic</u> with No. 2 of my story. I read &
re-read them—groaned & moaned & howled over them all the   25
evening & ~~th~~ took them to bed with me and renewed the scene at
intervals during the night. Mother's was especially delicious: but
I can't stand such another. I shall shuffle off this stale old tourist-
coil & go leaping home in the simple spirit of childhood. Since
then another dreary blank has elapsed but I count most devoutly   30
upon finding treasure laid up for me in Venice, thro' Jane
Norton's charitable hands. At the same moment I got your
letters came one also, long-delayed from Aunt Kate. Her
announcement of her party's projected movements led me to go

up to Lucerne in the hope of meeting them—where I spent two
days in the vain expectation of their arrival, & then, the weather
having settled fair, despatched my luggage to Milan, shouldered
my knapsack, took the steamer down the lake to Flüelen & com
5   began to trudge over the St. Gotthard. At Lucerne, by the way, I
met Dana Horton (who used to be at Cambridge you know & to
frequent the Sedgwicks' tea-fights)—he is now in Europe,
having his head-quarters with G. P. Marsh American Minister at
Florence.) (I mustn't forget to mention that I also met that very
10 sweet Mrs. Otto Dresel with her stupid husband & that she sent
especial messages to father & mother.) I partially agreed with
Horton to meet him & some cousins of his at Bel-Alp (or rather
on it—'tis in the clouds) in the higher Valais & proceed with
them to Zermatt. I walked in two days from Flüelen to
15 Hospenthal—the greater part of the Swiss ascent of the St.
Gotthard—a most lovely journey with glorious weather. At the
latter place I diverged to the right & crossed the Furka pass to
the Rhone Glacier—a wondrous silent cataract of snow ∧framed
clean in the rocks &[∧] rolling down straight out of the blue of
20 heaven & expiring at your feet, at the inn door. Here having
dined I started to cross the Grimsel & proceed thence to the
Aeggishorn & Bel-Alp: excuse all these stupid names: I give as
few as possible. But about an hour up the Grimsel, I suddenly
collapsed & was obliged to return. I didn't just then quite
25 understand the rationale of it, but I did later. 'Twas partly
(excusez ce detail) a disordered stomach & partly that I had
exhausted myself by carrying my knapsack from Lucerne. At all
events I renounced the idea of meeting Horton & that afternoon
took the diligence (5 hours.) for Brieg—the foot of the Simplon
30 pass. Here of course I slept & the next morning rose in my might
at 4.30, & having procured an individual to carry my sack (wh.
by the way a little forethought, tho' at some inconvenience,
would have enabled me to send by the dile diligence) began to
streak away over this famous road. This day on the whole was ◊

somehow the pleasantest I have known in Switzerland. The
superb weather—the ~~serene~~ ∧clean[∧] unclouded views—the
rapture of finding my strength returned to me with interest—
the rest & dinner at the Hospice on the summit, with a dozen
mild picturesque priests—& above ∧all,[∧] the sense of going   5
down into Italy—the delight of seeing the north slowly melt into
the south—of seeing Italy gradually crop up in bits & vaguely
latently betray itself—until finally, at the little frontier Village
of Isella where I spent the night, it lay before me warm & living
& palpable (<u>warm</u>, especially)—all these fine things bestowed   10
upon the journey a delightful flavor of romance. It was
moreover, a great day's work—about 33 miles from Brieg to
Isella. I'll not pretend to conceal that that I was slightly
fatigued. Nevertheless I was up betimes the next morning to
catch the diligence on its way on to Domo d'Ossola (the   15
terminus of the pass) & thence to the Lago Maggiore. I had a
ride of 6 hours to Baveno on the shore of the Lake. Down,
down—on, on into Italy we went—a rapturous progress thro' a
wild luxuriance of corn & vines & olives & figs & mulberries &
chesnuts & frescoed villages & clamorous beggars & all the good   20
∧old[∧] Italianisms of tradition. At Baveno is a vast, cool, dim
delicious hotel, with a great orange-haunted terrace on the lake.
I had a ∧cold[∧] bath in a great marble tank, I dined & touched up
my toilet, & then as the afternoon began to wane, took a little
boat at the terrace-stairs, lay ~~at~~ out at my length beneath the   25
stripèd awning & had myself pulled out to those delicious absurd
old Borromean islands—the Isola Madre & the Isola Bella. I'll
not treat you to a graphic description or a keen analysis. Theyr'e
a quaint mixture of tawdry flummery & genuine beauty—a sort
of tropical half-splendid, half-slovenly Little Trianon &   30
Hampton Court. The most striking feature of Italian scenery ~~is~~
∧seems to be[∧] this same odd mingling of tawdriness &
splendor—the generous profuse luxuriance of nature & the
ludicrous gingerbread accessories of human contrivance. But I

shall develop this pregnant theme hereafter. I think of beginning
a series of desultory letters to the <u>Nation</u> & I shall touch off this
region. At Baveno ◊ I felt in the 1ˢᵗ place so relaxed by the heat &
in the second, so fortified & excited by my few days walking in

5 Switzerland that I resolved again to cross the Alps—& simply do
what I could from day to day—nourishing a vague hope
however, of being able to proceed thro' the Engadine & Tyrol &
er recross ~~them~~ ₍ₐ₎into Italy₍ₐ₎ at by the great Stelvio pass. So
having slept at Baveno I took the early boat to Magadino at the

10 head of the lake & thence walked (a sweltering ten miles) to
Bellinzona, a charming dirty suffocating old town, where the St.
Gotthard & San Bernadino roads converge. The next morning, I
chose the latter—with a companion of course for my knapsack.
The Bernadine is a lovely pass—but it turned out an awful

15 grind. Partly thro' e misinformation & miscalculation I had
~~unnder~~ underestimated the length of the ascent & mistimed my
feeding-hour—& the result was a day of truly heroic fatigue.
There is something strange & wild & curious in the sensation of
great weariness in the midst of the lonely, silent irridescent

20 beauty of these Italian Alps & now that it's all over I'm not sorry
to have known it. I lay that night—(I unfortunately can't say I
slept) at San Bernadino, a village on the Italian slope just below
the summit & the next morning pursued my way (less than four
hours) to the Village of Splügen, where I was glad to halt & rest

25 & where I diverted myself the rest of the day, as I lay supine,
with Mrs. Stowe's <u>Old Town</u>, which I found kicking about, &
which struck me under the circumstances as a work of singular &
delicious perfection. From Splügen next morning I went bravely
thro' the famous <u>Via Mala</u>—a fine bit, in its way, to Tusis, ~~where~~

30 (a good five hour's trudge) where I stopped at the ◊ inn &
communed with my soul—to say nothing of my body. We all
three had a little breakfast together & unanimously agreed that
our poor old legs were very tired & had become conscious of an
obstinate chronic aching. We noted with immense satisfaction

however that it was simply our legs & that our much-tried back
was holding out bravely In fact this was the case. These poor
long-suffering limbs have been worked so hard all summer in the
service of their weaker brother that they have finally begun to
cry mercy & to suggest that they too are mortal. So I gave up the
Engadine, the Tyrol & all the rest of it & sadly took a vehicle
back to Splügen. The next morning I entrusted my knapsack to
the diligence & started off over the Splügen pass to Chiavenna—
which I reached at about the end of eight hours. ⌇ Toward the
end of the walk my legs betrayed such a tendency to s actually _se_
dérober _sous_ _moi_ that I was glad to think I hadn't counted on
them for further service. At Chiavenna where I spent the night I
was again in Italy—amid Italian beauty heat & dirt. I took the
following morning the diligence to Colico—a wofully hot &
dusty drive. Thence the steamer for two hours to this delicious
~~stop~~ spot, where I have been since 4 p.m. yesterday. _Non_—it's
too rapturous. Nothing is wanting but to feel fluttering at my
side in the soft Italian breeze, some light muslin drapery of the
sister of my soul. It's the place of places to enjoy _à_ _deux_ & it's a
shame to be here in gross melancholy solitude. In its general
presentment & contour the Lake of Como strikes me as hardly
superior to the finest Swiss lakes—but it's when you come to the
details—the swarming shimmering prodigality of the
landscape—that you stand convinced & enchanted before Italy &
summer. I may find it too hot here to stay, but I shall be glad to
have had at least this glimpse of a potent southern August. I
took yesterday after my arrival as the sun began to sink, a five
miles' stroll along the shore of the lake—following a broad foot-
road that leads thro the most enchanting variety ₍ₐ₎of₍ₐ₎ scenes—
past the fantastic iron gates of idle, pretentious villas, dozing in
a perpetual _siesta_ amid the grey-green boskage of their parks—
between vineyard ~~walks walls~~ ₍ₐ₎walls₍ₐ₎ all hedged & overtopped
with the flaunting wealth of their vinery—thro' the arcades of
dirty little villages with houses of pink and blue & orange, where

at a fruit stall you may buy for six cents as many luscious
peaches, pears, grapes and ambrosial figs as you can possibly, as
Artemus Ward says, conceal about your person. — The only blot
upon the scene is the excessive heat which quite forbids moving
about & leads me to apprehend that — a considerable amount of
locomotion being needful to my welfare — I may have come
hither too early in the season. In fact I'm already feel a good
deal of my stout Swiss starch taken out of me. I shall tomorrow
go on to Milan to get my luggage & shall then see how I feel &
how things look. I have laid in such a capital stock of strength of
& satisfaction in Switzerland that I shall be sorry to be
compelled to see it diminished & if I find it is melting away
beneath a southern sun I shall not scruple to quietly execute a
little scheme which all your combined affection & sagacity will
not pronounce unwise & which I father's & mother's last letters
make me feel I may do, if needful, with an easy conscience: <u>i.e.</u>
cross over from Verona into Southern Germany & make a tour
thro ‸Trent₍ᴧ₎ Innsbruck, Vienna, Salzburg, Augsburg,
Nuremburg, & Munich — all well-worth seeing. I can then come
back to Italy a month hence & begin my winter. Address your
letters still, as before enjoined, to <u>MM.</u> <u>Schielin</u> <u>frères</u>,
<u>Venice</u>. — Even if I take another route I shall find means to get
them. I shall then look upon this dip into Italy as simply the
~~usual accompaniment~~ little run southward which the walker in
Switzerland usually winds up with. My pedestrian developments
have more or less modified my prospects & projects. I hope to
‸be₍ᴧ₎ able, in walking, to get so much diversion & to save so
much money that I may strike out freely in at certain times &
places. I already have distant visions of doing England in bits,
next summer on foot. But I'll not bother you with these greedy
shadows & ghosts of my egotism: you have listened to a long
enough tale. — And now for your dear old domestic selves. I lack
<u>affreusement</u> a letter from Willy; <u>pourvu</u> that there only be one
in Venice! I enjoyed immensely your & mothers' account of that

blessed Pomfret. Every little bit of tittle-tattle seems written like the word's on Belshazzar's wall. To-day I suppose you are moving back to Cambridge—rested, I devoutly hope, a ɗ healed ɗ comforted. What the summer has done for Willy, I can only conjecture ~~all~~ and this I'm afraid to do too freely. At least, I trust, as much as he hoped. Let him never, night ɗ day, forget to reflect how wretched a being I ~~was~~ once was. ~~Th~~ To do this ɗ as little else as possible—this is best counsel I can give him at present.—It is very jolly to hear of Wilky's ɗ Bob's getting up their muscle for rowing. Heaven reward them. Just now I believe only in muscle. I read yesterday in the <u>Times</u> the news of the defeat of the Harvard crew on the Thames. I had expected nothing else. When I was in ~~Eng~~ ₍ₐ₎London₍ₐ₎ I saw the stupendous crowd of spectators come surging along Picadilly on its return from the Oxford ɗ Cambridge match—ɗ I have since felt in my bones that the land which produced that awful host would certainly produce a proportionate crew—a crew of immeasurable British "go", such as would outdo our ~~Y~~ gallant meagre Yankees.—I don't see why Bob shouldn't make a ~~gallant~~ ₍ₐ₎capital₍ₐ₎ oarsman: he's so "splendidly formed" about the chest ɗc.—I shall find in your next letters I suppose some news of the cotton crops=good news, I beseech you.—I'm much obliged to you for your compliments ɗ to mother for hers, about my story. I'm more obliged still to father, for the decent figure, which thanks to his revision, ~~they~~ ₍ₐ₎it₍ₐ₎ makes in print. It all strikes me as amusingly thin ₍ₐ₎ɗ₍ₐ₎ watery—I mean as regards its treatment of the Past. Since coming abroad ɗ seeing relics, monuments ɗc, I've got a strong sense of what a grim old deathly reality it was, ɗ how little worth one's while it is to approach it with a pen unless your mind is <u>bourré</u> with facts on the subjects—how little indeed it is worth-while at all to treat it imaginatively. You can <u>imagine</u> nothing so impressive as Queen's Elizabeth's battered old tomb in Westminster. The present ɗ the immediate future seem to me the best province of fiction—the latter especially—

the future to which all our actual modern tendencies & leanings seem to build a sort of ~~et~~ ætherial pathway. But excuse all these bad images & crude notions. This is a long letter for one sitting—another San Bernadino.—Farewell. Its hideous to have
5 so much family ~~a~~ & yet to ~~m~~ be here alone in ~~b~~ all this beauty. But I'm too tired to write another word, except my love to all— & especially to my sweet little sister.

H. James jr.

Previous publication: *HJL* 1: 126–33

∾

81.13 ~~me~~ you • [you *overwrites* me]

81.19 ~~for~~ from • [rom *overwrites* or]

81.20 ~~go &~~ stop • [stop *overwrites* go &]

81.26 ~~th~~ took • [o *overwrites* h]

82.4–5 ~~com~~ began • [bega *overwrites* com]

82.7 now • [w *inserted*]

82.22 Aeggishorn • Aeggis- | horn

82.32 inconvenience • in= | convenience

82.33 ~~dile~~ diligence • [i *overwrites* e]

82.34–83.1 ◇ somehow • [s *overwrites illegible letter*]

83.1 pleasantest • pleasant= | est

83.25 ~~at~~ out • [ou *overwrites* at]

83.31–32 ~~is~~ ∧ • [∧ *overwrites* is]

84.3 ◇ I • [I *overwrites illegible letter*]

84.4 fortified • forti= | fied

84.8 ~~cr~~ recross • [re *overwrites* cr]

84.8 ~~at~~ by • [by *overwrites* at]

84.15 ~~c~~ misinformation • [m *overwrites* c]

84.16 ~~unnder~~ underestimated • [deres *overwrites* nder]

84.30 ◇ inn • [i *overwrites illegible letter*]

85.9 ~~C~~ Toward • [T *overwrites* C]

85.10 ~~s~~ actually • [a *overwrites* s]

85.16 ~~stop~~ spot • [pot *overwrites* top]

88

85.21 presentment • pre= | sentment

85.28-29 foot- | road • foot-road

85.32 ~~walks walls~~ • [l *overwrites* k]

86.7 I'~~m~~ already • [al= | ready; al= *overwrites* 'm]

86.10-11 ~~of~~ ɗ • [ɗ *overwrites* of]

86.14 affection • affec= | tion

86.15 ~~I~~ father's • [f *overwrites* I]

86.18 Augsburg • Augs= | burg

86.19 well-worth • well- | worth

86.26 prospects • pros= | pects

86.28 ~~in~~ at • [at *overwrites* in]

87.3 ~~a~~ ɗ • [ɗ *overwrites* a]

87.5 ~~all~~ and • [nd *overwrites* ll]

87.7 ~~Th~~ To • [o *overwrites* h]

87.18 ~~Y~~ gallant • [g *overwrites* Y]

88.2 ~~et~~ ætherial • [æth *overwrites* et]

88.5 ~~a~~ ɗ • [ɗ *overwrites* a]

88.5 ~~m~~ be • [b *overwrites* m]

88.5 ~~b~~ all • [a *overwrites* b]

∾

81.6 Hotel Belle-Vue • According to the 1869 *Switzerland* Baedeker, the Bellevue charged two francs for a room, four francs for dinner, and seven francs for pension (382).

81.8 Lago di Como • Lake Como.

81.16-17 Voyons: où en étais-je • Let's see: where was I?

81.22-23 one from mother • MWJ to HJ, 24, 25 July [1869], Houghton bMS Am 1093.1 (34).

81.23-24 One delightful long one [. . .] Atlantic with No. 2 of my story • The second installment of "Gabrielle de Bergerac" appeared in the August 1869 *Atlantic Monthly* (231-41); with his 26 June, 18, 24 July 1869 letter to HJ (Anesko 64-68), William Dean Howells enclosed "an August [*Atlantic*] by this post" (68).

82.6 Dana Horton • Samuel Dana Horton (1844-95) enjoyed a relatively short career as a diplomat working with the American minister in Florence before the unification of Italy.

82.8 G. P. Marsh • George Perkins Marsh (1801–82), American attorney and politician; Marsh was appointed by Lincoln in 1861 to be the first U.S. minister to Italy.

82.12 Bel-Alp • Village (2094 m) above Brig, on a southern spur of the Aletschorn, and to the southwest of (and separated by the Aletsch Glacier from) the Eggishorn.

82.15 Hospenthal • Also spelled Hospental, a village near Andermatt, at the crossroads for the routes to the Furka pass and Grimselpass (and into the Canton of Valais), the St. Gotthard pass (toward the Ticino and Italy), the Oberalpass (to Switzerland's easternmost Canton of Gaubünder), and the road from Altdorf and Lucerne (Baedeker, *Switzerland* [1869] 79).

82.17 Furka pass • The 1869 *Switzerland* Baedeker notes that the "pass, seldom entirely free from snow, descends abruptly on both sides, and lies between two peaks, bearing a fanciful resemblance to the prongs of a fork (furca)" (138).

82.18–21 Rhone Glacier [. . .] having dined • According to the 1869 *Switzerland* Baedeker, "The *Glacier of the Rhone, imbedded between the *Gelmerhorn* and *Gersthorn* (10,450′) on the W., and the *Galenstock* (11,801′) on the E., is 18 M. long, and rises in a terrace-like form, resembling a gigantic waterfall suddenly arrested in its career by the icy hand of some Alpine enchanter. Above it towers the Galenstock. At its base is the *Hôtel du Glacier du Rhône*, a substantially built house, where travellers from the Grimsel, Furca and the Rhone Valley frequently halt for dinner" (137).

82.22 Aeggishorn • Today spelled Eggishorn, this mountain (2927 m) is on the north side of the Rhone and to the northeast of Brig.

82.26 excusez ce detail • sorry to mention it.

82.29 Brieg • Today spelled Brig, it is a large town in the Rhone Valley at the foot of the Simplon pass.

83.8–9 Village of Isella • HJ would later appropriate details of his journey from Switzerland to Italy in "At Isella" (*Galaxy*, August 1871), which is set in this Italian border village: "Here, as everywhere, I was struck with the mere surface-relation of the Western tourist to the soil he treads. He filters and trickles through the dense social body in every possible direction, and issues forth at last the same virginal water drop. Go your way, these antique houses seemed to say, from their quiet courts and gardens; the road is yours and welcome, but the land is ours. You may pass and stare and wonder, but you may never know us" (242).

83.15 Domo d'Ossola • Today spelled Domodossola.

83.17 Baveno • On the western bank of Lake Maggiore facing the Borromean Islands. According to the 1869 *Switzerland* Baedeker, while in Baveno, "as it is not a post station, travellers are accommodated in the passing diligence only when seats are vacant. Diligence daily between Pallanza and Domo d'Ossola" (260).

83.27 Isola Madre *&* the Isola Bella • These two islands, with Isola di San Giovanni and Isola dei Pescatori, form the Isole Borromeo, or Borromean Islands, in Lake Maggiore, northwestern Italy.

83.30–31 Little Trianon *&* Hampton Court • The Petit Trianon, situated on the grounds of Versailles near Paris, was built for Marie Antoinette in the early eighteenth century. Hampton Court, dating from the twelfth century, is best known as the palace of King Henry VIII and is located on the northern bank of the Thames in Surrey.

84.8 Stelvio pass • Directly north of Lago di Garda, on the border of Switzerland.

84.9 Magadino • "Consisting of two villages, the Upper and Lower, [it] is situated on the N. bank of *Lago Maggiore*, at the mouth of the *Ticino*, in a marshy district" (Baedeker, *Switzerland* [1869] 367).

84.11 Bellinzona • Located east of the northernmost tip of Lago Maggiore, the city is "one of the three capitals of the canton of Tessin" (Baedeker, *Switzerland* [1869] 83).

84.12, 14, 22 San Bernadino, Bernadine, San Bernadino • HJ probably means San Bernardino, the village and pass in the western Graubünden.

84.16 underestimated the length of the ascent • A thirty-eight-mile ascent, with an additional twenty-five miles (40 km) to Splügen.

84.26 Mrs. Stowe's Old Town • Harriet Beecher Stowe's *Oldtown Folks* published in 1869.

84.29 the famous Via Mala • The 1869 *Switzerland* Baedeker notes:

The limestone-rocks rise almost perpendicularly on both sides to a height of 1600′. A short distance from the entrance, near the *Känzeli*, the retrospective view is very fine. About 1 $\frac{1}{2}$ m. from Thusis is a *Gallery*, 200′ in length, penetrating the solid and perpendicular rock. Immediately beyond it is a partially open gallery, over which the rocks project. The roaring river is visible at the bottom of the gorge, from the point where the side-wall ceases and the wooden railings recommence. The retrospective, through the narrow and gloomy defile, of the solitary tower of Hohen-Roetien, and the sunny slopes of the Heinzenberg beyond, is singularly beautiful. (353–54)

84.29 Tusis · An alternative spelling of Thusis, a village halfway between San Bernardino and Chur.

85.8 Chiavenna · "An ancient town with 3000 inhab., charmingly situated on the *Maira*, at the mouth of the Val Bregaglia" (Baedeker, *Switzerland* [1869] 358).

85.10–11 se dérober sous moi · give way beneath me.

85.14 Colico · A town situated on the northern shore of Lago di Como. According to the 1869 *Switzerland* Baedeker, "Travellers should avoid passing the night here, the situation being unhealthy" (358).

85.19 à deux · with someone else.

86.18 Trent · An alternative spelling of Trento, a city along the Adige River.

86.33 affreusement · desperately.

86.33 pourvu · let's hope.

87.2 Belshazzar's wall · See the story of Daniel, Belshazzar, and the apocalyptic writing on the wall (Daniel 5.7–8).

87.9–20 Wilky's & Bob's getting up their muscle for rowing [. . .] I don't see why Bob shouldn't make a ~~gallant~~ ₍ₐ₎capital₍ₐ₎ oarsman · MWJ had written, in her 24, 25 July [1869] letter, that GWJ and Arthur Sedgwick "had gone off on a rowing trip up the coast," during which "Arthur's wherry was upset," and that RJ

has abandoned the pen and taken up the oar. He has been enrolled as a member of the "Western Boating Club", and is going into training at once, to enable him to take part in the great match for next year— He is to give up every leisure moment; all society; all the luxuries of the table for the coming year to this end—so great is his enthusiasm that there is no telling but that we may have the honor of numbering among us the Champion oarsman of the West! (Houghton bMS Am 1093.1 [34])

87.23 to mother for hers • MWJ had written, in her 24, 25 July [1869] letter, that AJ has "told you what an enthusiasm there is about your last story— I have taken more pleasure in it than in any thing you have ever written— The last part darling Harry was exquisite— Mʳ Boott is one of your most ardent admirers— He predicts for you a great future!"

87.23–27 my story [. . .] treatment of the Past • "Gabrielle de Bergerac" is set primarily in pre-Revolutionary France.

87.30 bourré • crammed.

87.32–33 Queen's Elizabeth's [. . .] Westminster • Queen Elizabeth I (b. 1533, r. 1558–1603) is buried in the north aisle of the chapel of Henry VII at Westminster Abbey in London.

MARY WALSH JAMES
10, 12 September 1869
ALS Houghton
bMS Am 1094 (1762)   20

Brescia Italia
          Sept. 8 10ᵗʰ (?) '69
               (Friday,)
Madre carissima—   25
     I despatched last week a long letter to Alice, which you will not have received until after a silence so portentous that I shrink from the thought of trifling with your affections by again allowing this life of perpetual motion to interfere with my correspondence. So altho', o̶n̶ this blessed evening finds me a   30
good deal outwearied with the lovely sights of this ancient town of Brescia I still summon my flickering energies &̶ grasp at the pen, to scrawl at least a few words before I lapse into insensibility. Moreover, at the present rate, my adventures multiply so fast that if I wish to project some faint image of   35

them on the pure maternal apprehension I must do so before
they all squeeze each other out of shape. Ah, beloved mother, if
I could convey to you some truly living & vivid notion of the
heavenly beauty of this magical Italy I should be doing a good
5   deed—◊◊ in fact a great one. It's very well talking, but words tell
nothing—I've been absorbing things so lustily during the past
fortnight that I ought to have a great deal to say; but somehow it
seems useless to try.—I wrote to Alice immediately after my
arrival on the lake of Como. I remember I spoke very strongly of
10 the heat & expressed the apprehension that it might ∧drive[∧]
▄▄▄▄▄ me away. Fine talk: I should like to see the heat (th or the
cold) that can ◊ now expel me from this enchanting land. I felt
the temperature the more for having come out of the
mountains; but I immediately got used to it. M Besides,
15 intrinsically it is no greater than ∧that of[∧] our own summer
weather—& now in short I am perfectly comfortable. I think I
failed duly to dwell upon the ~~the~~ enchantments & ravishments of
the Lake of Como. Or rather I had just got there & didn't yet
comprehend them. But I spent four complete days there which I
20 shall always think of ~~has~~ as having been cunningly ~~in◊~~
interpolated into the gross fabric of common existence out of
some waste hours of Paradise. It's a good old world after all; it
reconciles you to it & to a ~~believe~~ belief in the general ~~in+~~
integrity of things to find a place not only keeping all the
25 promises ∧& pretensions[∧] of its fame but actually inventing &
extemporizing new & peculiar delights for your especial
benefit—as I'm sure the Lake of Como did for me—just as I'm
sure that no one ever learned more of its secrets than I—poor
shabby I, skulking about among its villas in weather-stained
30 walking gear, ~~his~~ my toilet recruited from the most exiguous
knapsack. The infernal part of it was tho' that I had no one at
my side whom I loved & esteemed. A mother—a mere mother—
or even a sister—in the absence of a more impassioned object—
would have served my turn. But I here lay it down as an especial

axiom in travelling: don't go to the Italian lakes alone. It's a
brutal waste of opportunity. I took up with Mrs. & Miss Peet of
New-York—Miss P. a gentle dark eyed thing with rather less of
the "peculiar accent" of our native land than <u>most</u>—in fact a
very nice girl. I had a couple of delicious walks along the ⁵
lakeside—one, in particular, long, luminous, memorable,
crowded with visual episodes of the most admirable sort. I did
three Villas—one, especially, the day I left:—<u>enfin</u> remind to
tell you about ᴧit₍ᴧ₎ when I get home. The proper humdrum way
to have left ~~Cann~~ Cadenabbia would have been to take the ¹⁰
steamer quietly to the town of Como, at the southern end of the
lake—a sail of two hours. But I'm not one of your soulless
senseless drudges, in the matter of travelling. I got my head ɴ
<u>montée</u> ~~in~~ over a description in Bäddeker of a way afoot to
Como, inland, over the hills. So tho' the distance is at least ¹⁵
thirty miles, I shouldered my knapsack, crossed the lake to
Bellagio, & started about 1. p.m. I did the 1ˢᵗ ~~th~~ half of the route
that afternoon—thro' as lovely a country as eye ever beheld—
low mountain scenery, ~~turning~~ ₍ᴧ₎half₍ᴧ₎ smothered in its
fertility—or at least its <u>redundancy</u>—luxuriance & grace going ²⁰
hand in hand. Elegance & grace seem to me the ~~featu~~ distinctive
features, as I get know it, of Italian landscape. England is ᴧfar₍ᴧ₎
deeper & richer in ◇◇◇◇ tone & Switzerland in its lower portions,
far broader & ◇ more various. But upon the face of this Italian
summer there reigns the most enchanting feminine smile. ²⁵
England is a good married matron, Switzerland a magnificent
man ⚲ & Italy a beautiful dishevelled nymph of fable.—I lay
that night at a very squalid little village inn & pushed on the next
morning to Como, thro' a much less interesting country, under
a very hot sun & in a state of severe fatigue. The fact is that ³⁰
walking in Italy is a very different matter from the same work in
the Alps; & I have for the present made my last journey on foot.
At Como I spent a day: it contains a most delightful cathedral—
small but absolutely perfect. I devoured it with my eyes; I doubt

if there's any of it left. Thence last Sunday I took train (in an
hour ꝺ ½) for Milan where I spent five busy days. I saw there
pretty much all that is worth seeing, ꝺ I think ~~of can~~ [∧]I can[∧]
lay my hand on my heart (or on my <u>Murray</u>; they are now
5   identical) ꝺ say that I know Milan. I climbed to the tip-top of
the Cathedral—which by the way is a very pretty piece of
immensity. But the sight of sights—the one thing I saw in Milan
to speak of is a certain famous picture—Raphaël's Marriage of
the Virgin, in the Brera Gallery, whereof you may remember the
10   engraving, in the Boudoir at the Tweedies'. 'Tis a great work ꝺ
Raphael was an enviable fellow to have been able to see things
about him, as in that picture—let alone <u>do</u> them. I think if I
could so see them, I should be almost content to let the doing
go. I beheld like-wise Leonardo's great <u>Cenacolo</u>—the Last
15   Supper—horribly decayed—but sublime in its ruins. The mere
<u>soul</u> of the picture survives—the form, the outline; but this is
the great thing—being as the container to the contained.
There's something unspeakably grand in the simplicity of these
blurred ꝺ broken relics of a magnificent design—a sentence by
20   the way which only half conveys my thought. I'll tell you 'tother
half when I get home. I took the train one morning ꝺ spent a
day at Pavia—a large portion of it at the renowned <u>Certosa</u>
(Chartreuse) which Murray pronounces "the most magnificent
monastery in the world"—a statement to the absolute truth—ꝺ
25   the relative inadequacy—of which I fervently testify. The great
feature is the church—a thing of dazzling splendor. ~~Th~~ At the
end of a long grassy court rises its façade, which I remember thus:

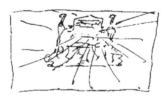

—a perfect bedazzlement of ornament, elegance ꝺ grace. The
interior is all of a piece—a great storehouse of riches. Pavia

itself is a mild old city of the past, with a long list of churches which Murray condemns you to see. Having done two or three however I shirked the rest & preferred to wander at my ease along a delicious old moated rampart which surveys the teeming plain of Lombardy. This morning I came hither from Milan, arriving at noon. I forthwith let myself loose upon the town and went about devouring (<u>des yeux</u> only alas! except a <u>glass</u> of beer) until the stroke of ~~eigh~~ six. Brescia is extremely rich. It has one pearl of great price, contained in an excellent museum of antiquities—a ~~famous~~ ∧wondrous[∧] Greek statue of Victory in B bronze, disinterred 40 years since in Brescian soil. Chas. Norton adjured me to make a point of stopping to see ◊ it & I thank him heartily. It is indeed, as he says, one of the things which most give one an idea of what art can be & do. As you sit & look at it your purified intellect leaves your puny body & soars back to Greece & to the heroic age of art & spurns with ɍ light retreating heel the vile abortions of this modern time. I wish I could give you some visible presentment of this magnificent creature.—◊ Willy may know of her already, thro' photos. or description. She is of about the size of the Venus of Milo, but younger, more slender, prettier, & magnificently winged. Her left foot rests on a helmet & on the knee slightly elevated is placed a shield, sustained by the left outstretched hand, on which she is making a record. She is not a panting human victory, inflated with success, but a calm immortal muse who was in the secrets of the gods & knew beforehand ~~whom~~ ∧how[∧] it would be. Look at her from what side you will she is equally beautiful—divinely dignified & yet with a certain lightness, to match her great wings. I have been seeing too, some great pictures: a ~~great~~ ∧famous[∧] Raphael—~~man~~ the Man of Sorrows—small in dimensions, but Raphaelesque in merit. Then in two churches an admirable Paul Veronese & two transcendent Titians. My faith in Titian (~~had~~ so ~~be~~ firmly established in London) had been a little shaken by some indifferent specimens at Milan. But now that I see him again at his best I proclaim that there is but one painter & his name is Titian. I don't quite know what I do with Raphael. I'll arrange it when I get time. ~~The~~ ◇◇ Brescia is a most charming old place, ~~not~~ feeling not a bit

5 ∧apparently[∧] the burden of its mediaevalism & <u>Italianissimo</u> in color & aspect. When you come abroad again (as I mean you shall, dear mammy) you will ~~know~~ ∧learn[∧] what that means.) Foremost among its buildings stands ~~a~~ an incredibly beautiful Town-hall of the 16<u>th</u> century—a vast piece of gold-smith's work

10 in marble.—<u>Verona</u>, <u>Sunday</u>, 12<u>th</u>. <u>Albergo</u> <u>delle</u> <u>Due</u> <u>Torre</u>. Yes, this is Verona & I supped last night where Juliet at the masque saw her loved Montagu. I came hither yesterday at noon (2 hours) from Brescia, where on the morning after the above was written I tarried a couple of hours to get another glance of that

15 lovely <u>Victory</u>. Lovely she is & I enclose a small photo. of her for W. I furthermore visited a private gallery of much merit in a vast decayed old <u>palazzo</u> & came away thinking excellently well of Brescia. I doubt whether elsewhere in so small a space there are collected so many good things.—Verona however is a

20 splendid magnified Brescia. Ruskin, I believe, deems it the most picturesque town in Europe. I had a brief ramble yesterday & got a general sense of a world of architectural wonders. Properly to see the place would take many patient days; but I shall take it easy & do what I can in a couple. The great central marvel is of

25 course the famous Roman Arena which I examined yesterday. It's stupendously impressive & interesting & wofully dwarfs & vulgarizes the later beauties of the place. Those ancient Latins certainly had a manner <u>qui</u> <u>n'était qu'à eux</u>. Then there is a most charming little signorial <u>piazza</u> of the renaissance—small,

30 compact & elegant as if it were made for a lot of ~~the~~ Picturesque Italians to play at the civic virtues. Besides this there is no end of churches—some 40 in number, & the streets are absolutely thick with extraordinary fragments & relics. And then there are the <u>Tombs</u> of the <u>Scaligers</u>—I like the phrase! Altogether I shall

have work ⬦ for a couple of days: I shall devote a third to
<u>Mantua</u>—an hour distant by rail. Of course I get very tired.
This sort of work is a thousand times more exhausting than
Swiss mountains. But every one <u>does</u> get tired ⅋ a considerable
portion of my fatigue belongs simply to the common lot. On the   5
p̶ other part I keep a rigorous watch.—

So much for Italy ⅋ me. Thro' all this I am supported by the
prospect of letters at Venice. On September 1ˢᵗ I meditated on
your all coming back to Cambridge. How well I remember my
own return there a year ago! Farewell, dearest mother. Give   10
these two photos. to W. ⅋ tell him to refresh himself in the
contemplation of eternal beauty. Just now they are all I can do
for him. Lay me at the feet of father ⅋ Alice—⅋ then pick me up
again for yourself.

   Ton fils <u>H. James jr</u>   15
  P.S. What of M. Temple's coming to Italy?

No previous publication

❧

93.23 8̶ 10ᵗʰ • [10 *overwrites* 8]

93.30 o̶n̶ this • [th *overwrites* on]

94.5 ⬦⬦ in • [in *overwrites illegible letters*]

94.7 somehow • some= | how

94.11 � me • [me *overwrites illegible word*]

94.11 t̶h̶ or • [or *overwrites* th]

94.12 ⬦ now • [n *overwrites illegible letter*]

94.14 M̶ Besides • [B *overwrites* M]

94.20 h̶a̶s̶ as • [as *overwrites* has]

94.20-21 i̶n̶⬦ interpolated • [t *overwrites illegible letter*]

94.23 b̶e̶l̶i̶e̶v̶e̶ belief • [f *overwrites* ve]

94.23 i̶n̶⧺ • [*blotted out*]

94.24 integrity • [in *inserted*]

94.30 h̶i̶s̶ my • [my *overwrites* his]

95.10 C̶a̶n̶n̶ Cadenabbia • [de *overwrites* nn]

95.13–14 n̶ <u>montée</u> • [m *overwrites* n]

95.14 i̶n̶ over • [ov *overwrites* in]

95.17 t̶h̶ half • [h *overwrites blotted* th]

95.21 f̶e̶a̶t̶u̶ distinctive • [dist *overwrites* featu]

95.23 ◇◇◇◇ tone • [tone *overwrites illegible letters*]

95.24 ◇ more • [m *overwrites blotted illegible letter*]

95.27 ⊬ ɟ • [ɟ *overwrites* —]

96.18 unspeakably • un= | speakably

96.26 T̶h̶ At • [At *overwrites* Th]

96.33 ornament • orna= | =ment

97.8 e̶i̶g̶h̶ṭ six • [six *overwrites* eigh.]

97.11 B̶ bronze • [b *overwrites* B]

97.12 ◇ it • [i *overwrites illegible letter*]

97.16 ꝛ light • [l *overwrites* r]

97.19 ◇ Willy • [W *overwrites illegible letter*]

97.23 outstretched • out= | stretched

97.26 beforehand • before= | hand

97.30 m̶a̶n̶ the • [the *overwrites* man]

97.32 transcendent • trans= | cendent

97.33 h̶a̶d̶ so • [so *overwrites* had]

97.33 b̶e̶ firmly • [fi *overwrites* be]

98.3–4 T̶h̶e̶ ◇◇ Brescia • [Bresc *overwrites* The *and illegible letters*]

98.4 n̶o̶t̶ feeling • [feel *overwrites* not]

98.5 mediaevalism • mediaeval= | ism

98.5 <u>Italianissimo</u> • [o *inserted*]

98.8 buildings • buil= | dings

98.8 a̶ an • [an *overwrites* a]

98.22 architectural • architec= | tural

98.30 t̶h̶e̶ Picturesque • [Pic *overwrites* the]

99.1 ◇ for • [f *overwrites illegible letter*]

99.4 considerable • consid= | erable

99.5 simply • sim= | ply

∾

93.22 Brescia Italia · The 1868 *Northern Italy* Baedeker says of Brescia: "The town, with 35,000 inhab. and numerous iron-works, is delightfully situated at the base of the Alps" (193).

93.25 Madre carissima · Dearest mother.

93.26 I despatched last week a long letter to Alice · HJ's 31 August [1869] letter.

94.8–9 I wrote to Alice immediately after my arrival on the lake of Como · HJ's 31 August [1869] letter was written from Cadenabbia.

95.8 enfin · in any case.

95.14 montée · worked up.

95.14–16 a way afoot to Como, inland, over the hills. So tho' the distance is at least thirty miles · In effect, Baedeker describes a pedestrian itinerary which would have taken HJ from Bellaggio to Civenna, Canzo, Erba, and Como, "by land, very agreeable for pedestrians, and especially recommended for the return-journey to those who have not quitted the steamboat on their route to Como. There is a carriage-road the whole way, but the hilly portion between Canzo [. . .] and Bellaggio may be traversed almost as quickly on foot as by carriage" (*Switzerland* [1869] 386).

96.6 Cathedral · According to the 1868 *Northern Italy* Baedeker, the Cathedral of Milan "is termed by the Milanese the eighth wonder of the world, and is, next to St. Peter's in Rome and the cathedral at Seville, the largest church in Europe. [. . .] The dome is 201 ft. in height, the tower 339 ft. above the pavement" (145–46).

96.8–9 Raphaël's Marriage of the Virgin · *The Marriage of the Virgin* (1504), also called Sposalizio, was Raphael's first major work and depicts the marriage of Joseph and Mary. According to the 1868 *Northern Italy* Baedeker, the painting was in room 251 of the Brera Gallery in the Palazzo di Brere, Milan (151).

96.14–15 Leonardo's great Cenacolo—the Last Supper · Located in the former refectory of Santa Maria delle Grazie. The decay results from the technique Leonardo used: tempera painted onto a base on the stone wall. The base soon became loosened from the wall, and attempts to halt the decay were not successful until after World War II.

96.22 the renowned Certosa · The Certosa, or Carthusian monastery, of Pavia, also known as the Certosa della Beata Vergine delle Grazie, was founded in 1396.

96.23-24 which Murray pronounces "the most magnificent monastery in the world" • HJ refers to the 1866 Murray's *Northern Italy*, which calls the Certosa of Pavia "the most splendid monastery in the world" (232).

96.34-97.2 Pavia [. . .] a long list of churches which Murray condemns you to see • Murray's *Northern Italy* lists ten: the Duomo, or Cathedral, of San Stefano and the churches of San Michele, Santa Maria del Carmine (or San Pantaleone), San Francesco, Santa Maria de Canepanova, San Pietro in Cielo d'Oro, San Teodoro, San Marino, San Lanfranco, and San Salvatore (236, 238-40).

97.7 des yeux • with my eyes.

97.10 Greek statue of Victory • A bronze winged Statue of Victory, approximately six feet in height, housed among other antiquities found near and in Brescia at the Museo Patrio.

97.11-12 Chas. Norton • HJ refers to Charles Eliot Norton's letter of 14 August 1869, from Vevey.

97.20 Venus of Milo • Created sometime in the second century B.C.E., the statue was found on the Greek island of Melos in 1820. It was bought by France and moved to the Louvre in 1821.

97.30-31 the Man of Sorrows • Raphael's Pietà, in the Galleria Tosi or Museo Civico.

97.32-33 in two churches an admirable Paul Veronese & two transcendent Titians • Brescia's Church of Santa Afra, erected in 1580, has a painting by Titian of Christ and the adulteress above its north door and Paolo Veronese's *Martyrdom of St. Afra* above the north altars; Titian's five-section altarpiece, representing the Resurrection, St. Sebastian, St. Rochus, St. Nazarus, and St. Celsus, was in the Church of Santi Nazaro e Celso, erected in 1780 (Baedeker, *Northern Italy* 196).

98.8-9 an incredibly beautiful Town-hall • The Palazzo Municipio, or Communale, also called La Loggia, built by Formentone in 1508 and completed by Jacopo Sansovino and Palladio in the later sixteenth century.

98.10 Albergo delle Due Torre • The 1868 Baedeker for *Northern Italy* indicates a room was 3 French francs, light 1 franc, breakfast 1 ½ francs, dinner 4 francs, and attendance 1 franc (203); the 1866 Murray for *North-ern Italy* describes the inn as "very comfortable, the best for families; a good table-d'hôte at 2 o'clock, 5 fr.: the manager, Luigi Bellini, is a most intelligent person" (288); it adjoined the Church of Santa Anastasia.

98.11–12 **I supped last night where Juliet at the masque saw her loved Montagu** • Casa di Giulietta 23 is the locally reputed address of Shakespeare's Juliet Capulet. The small inn-house, once known as *il Cappello*, was built in the early thirteenth century.

98.16 **W.** • WJ.

98.25 **Roman Arena** • Built in the first century, the amphitheater in Verona is the third largest surviving.

98.28 <u>qui n'était qu'à eux</u> • <u>which was theirs only</u>.

98.28–29 **a most charming little signorial** • The Piazza dei Signori.

98.33–34 the <u>Tombs of the Scaligers</u> • Tombs of the della Scala or Scaligeri family, who ruled Verona during the late thirteenth to late fourteenth century.

99.15 **Ton fils** • Your son.

99.16 **M. Temple's coming to Italy** • Minny Temple, who was desperately ill with tuberculosis, planned on and off in 1869 to go to Europe.

HENRY JAMES SR.
17 September [1869]
ALS Houghton
bMS Am 1094 (1763)   25

Venice, Hotel Barbesi

Sept. 17<u>th</u>

Dear father—

I have as yet hardly more than time to let you know by this   30
hasty scrawl that I have at last arrived among these blessed
isles—in fact that I have been here two days. My 1<u>st</u> act, the
morning after my arrival was to take a gondola to the bankers &
ask for my letters. They were not as numerous as I had hoped—

but there were enough of them to create a little heaven—within
this larger heaven—about me: one from you of Aug. 27$\underline{\text{th}}$, from
Cambridge, one from mother from Pomfret & one from Willy,
do., which seemed to have suffered great delay & mischance,
5   having been soaked to death with salt water;—not however that
I couldn't easily read it. Its date was the last of July & in case of
his having wondered at my not having got it before, tell him I
couldn't possibly have read it with greater rapture than just as I
did. I bade my gondolier turn into the Grand Canal, & there
10 stretched in voluptuous ease beneath my awning, as we lapsed &
swerved & gurgled along this glorious liquid path, I devoured the
paternal, maternal, fraternal words. Ah, je vous aime bien, allez!
Your letters were full of good things & good news. The Lord be
praised for your blissful Summer at Pomfret! Willy's statement
15 of his mild improvement caused me to howl again! May it
proceed with inexorable consistency. The only bad bit in your
letter was ~~abou~~ what you say about poor Wilky's crop & the
worm. I had just been reading in the Times an article
celebrating the fine crop of the year & was fancying him happy
20 in a comfortable harvest. Poor dear boy; if this gorgeous ~~&~~
wicked old Venice had any consolation for him he should have
it.—I wrote you last from Verona, where I spent three excellent
days. The place is full of admirable things, such as ought to be
quietly studied & enjoyed. The great arena lords it over the
25 whole with stupendous Roman inelegance. But after this come
two other great works of which I wish (a wish now likely to
become chronic) I might enclose you proper photographs: ~~T~~ the
tombs of the Scaligers & the Ch. of San Zenone. The former are
a little group of monumental ◇ sepulchres in a little mediaeval
30 church-yard in the heart of the old city & exhibit I ~~think~~
ᴧfancy₍ᴧ₎ a denser ◇◇◇◇ accumulation of artistic labor & deep
aesthetic intent than can anywhere else be found in the same
compass. The atmosphere in the little iron-bound circle which
encloses them seems absolutely thick & heavy with research &

beauty. The whole thing is tremendously serious. San Zenone is about the most worshipful & religious edefice I have yet beheld:—a beauty so vast & tranquil, so chaste & formal that it wrings tears from the eyes. On my way from Verona I spent 24 hours at Vicenza. It is easily described by saying that Vicenza is Palladio—the place having been his home & the great scene of his operations. What one looks at is the outsides of about a hundred palaces—the town swarms with 'em. I enjoyed them vastly, but since coming here & getting hold of a vol. of Ruskin's Stones of V., I find he pronounces Palladio infamous & I must blot out that shameful day. Of Venice generally I shall attempt to say nothing, as yet—unless how astonishingly well one knows the place without having been here. Atmospherically it is a good deal like Newport. I have already contrived to see a good many pictures—having been to the 3 strongholds—the ducal Palace, the Academy & the Scuola of San Rocco. It's all a perfect bedazzlement of genius. I hope soon to write Willy a good letter about the various "artists." He may be interested to know en attendant that the proud Titian already trembles, nay actually sinks, in the scale. There is a greater than he in the terrible Tintoretto—& a greater than either possibly in the sublime John Bellini. Titian's famous things here—the Assumption, the presentation of the little Virgin are disappointing. But of all this anon.—Gondolas are celestial. I have one by the day: the gondolier is my slave & creature. It's most imperial. I have been two afternoons to the Lido at sunset: I say no more.—If you see Howells tell him I have a letter on the stocks. I'm glad to hear your news of your book. You will of course mail or in some way despatch a copy to me. Address it & address all future letters (jusquà nouvel ordre) Care MM. Em. Fenzi & Cie ₍ₐ₎Banquiers₍ₐ₎ Florence. (I re-write: Em. Fenzi & Cie.) I shall stay here at least a couple of weeks. I thought of taking a lodging, but looked at some & found them dearer than the hotel & besides very lonely. I had heard neither of Kitty Emmet's baby nor of Elly's husband.

May they both turn out satisfactory. I hope Kitty is better &
prospering. But I don't a bit like Elly marrying that Methusaleh.
Is Minny coming abroad? Has J. L. sailed? I get no news of
A. K. I fancy they are now in Milan, on their way to Florence.

5   The mosquitoes are infernal, ₐhere₍ₐ₎ just now & they will
probably take Venice on their exit. Thank Mother & W. for their
letters, & Alice for that wh. she of course has written & is now
en route. Thank you, dear dad, for everything. I get no ₐmore₍ₐ₎
Nations: where is the hitch? Yours till I write again H. J. jr.

Previous publication: Horne 24–27

∞

104.4   mischance • [*first* c *inserted*]

104.17   ~~abou~~ what • [wha *overwrites* abou]

104.20   comfortable • com= | fortable

104.20–21   ~~&~~ wicked • [w *overwrites* &]

104.27   ~~T~~ the • [t *overwrites* T]

104.29   ⬦ sepulchres • [s *overwrites illegible letter*]

104.29   mediaveal • [*misspelled*]

104.31   ⬦⬦⬦ accumulation • [accu *overwrites illegible letters*]

105.2   edefice • [*misspelled*]

105.17   bedazzlement • bedazzle= | ment

105.30   jusquà • [*misspelled*]

∞

103.27   Venice, Hotel Barbesi • The 1868 Baedeker for *Northern Italy*
says: "Hotel Barbesi, in the *Palazzo Zucchelli*, on the Grand Canal, opposite
the church della Salute, new" (227).

104.3   one from mother from Pomfret • Presumably MWJ's letter of
8 August 1869.

104.12   Ah, je vous aime bien, allez! • Ah, I love you well, you know!

104.18   the Times an article • The 9 September 1869 *Times* article,
written by an unnamed American correspondent, reads: "All the important cotton-growing States of the country are said to report improvement
in the general condition and promise of the cotton crop as compared

with the statements made in the July report of the Department. [. . .] Florida reports an average condition of the crop and 25 per cent increased acreage" (5).

104.22 I wrote you last from Verona · HJ's 10 September 1869 letter from Brescia, to MWJ, was completed in Verona on 12 September.

104.28 Ch. of San Zenone · In *Italian Hours*, HJ describes the church as "a structure of high antiquity and of the most impressive loveliness. The nobly serious character of San Zenone is deepened by its single picture — a masterpiece of the most serious of painters, the severe and exquisite Mantegna" (346).

105.6 Palladio · Andrea Palladio was one of the most renowned and influential architects of the sixteenth century. Palladianism follows the principles of classical antiquity exalting clarity, order, and symmetry.

105.9–10 Ruskin's Stones of V. · John Ruskin's *Stones of Venice*, complete in three volumes (1851–53).

105.15 the ducal Palace · Located in St. Mark's Square, the palace was the Doge's residence and was connected, by the Bridge of Sighs, to a prison across the canal.

105.16 Academy · The Accadémia delle Belle Arti exhibited Titian's *Assumption* among other Italian paintings by Veronese, Bellini, and Tintoretto.

105.16 Scuola of San Rocco · The Scuola di San Rocco in Venice houses numerous Tintorettos and Titians.

105.18–19 en attendant · in the meantime.

105.21–22 John Bellini · Giovanni Bellini (1430–1516).

105.26 Lido · Island between the Venice lagoon and the Adriatic Sea on which fashionable resorts were built.

105.28 your book · *The Secret of Swedenborg*.

105.30 jusquà nouvel ordre · until I tell you otherwise.

105.34 Kitty Emmet's baby · Katherine Temple Emmet gave birth to a boy, William, in July 1869.

105.34 Elly's husband · Ellen James Temple (1850–1920) married her cousin Christopher Temple Emmet (1822–84) on 16 September 1869.

106.3 J. L. • John La Farge.

106.4 A. K. • Aunt Kate.

106.6 W. • WJ.

JOHN LA FARGE

21 September [1869]

New-York Historical Society

La Farge Papers

10   ✉

Venice, Hotel Barbesi, Sept. 21.

My dear John.—

Tho' I am tired with much writing I must answer your

15 letter of Aug. 26$^{\underline{th}}$ without loss of time—in the hope that I may
be able to say something to accelerate your coming abroad. I was
very sorry your original plan had to be abandoned & sorry again
that your wife & children are not to come. I can't but agree with
you tho', that if you are to come with full benefit, you should

20 come without care. I can't help thinking that a 6 months' or a
year's stay here would do you great good. I speak from my own
daily experience. As regards expense I consider it on my own
part as a species of investment, destined to yield later in life
sufficient returns in the way of work to repay me. Can't you do

25 the same? Of course the point is to raise ready money; &
certainly it is better not to come than to come on such slender
means that you have to be constantly preoccupied, to the
detriment of a free appreciation of things, with the money
question. You are right I think in not particularly caring to see

30 any special country—& in longing generally for something
European. Even if you only saw a portion of England, you
would be richly rewarded. The more I see of the continent, the
more I value England. It is striking how as a mere place for
sight-seeing—a home of the picturesque—she holds her own

against Italy. It may be that I think so chiefly because my 1ˢᵗ stay
was there ɟ my enjoyment enhanced by novelty. Nevertheless
the only very violent wish I entertain with regard to my travels
is that I may get 3 more months of England before my return.—
Not however that Italy is not unspeakably fair ɟ interesting—ɟ
Venice perfectly <u>Italianissima</u>. I extremely wish we were here
likely to meet ɟ see some things together. Here, especially one
needs a companion ɟ intellectual sympathy. Properly to see
things you need to talk~~ing~~ about them, ɟ we should do much
talking ɟ seeing. I hope to be in Italy 5 or 6 mos. more: you
might still get here. I have already eaten a good slice of the feast.
I came over the Alps by Maggiore ɟ Como, Milan, Pavia,
Brescia, Verona ɟ Vicenza; ɟ I have been a ~~mo~~ week among
these happy isles. I have seen a vast number of paintings, palaces
ɟ churches ɟ received far more "impressions" than I know what
◇ to do with. One needs a companion to help him to dispose of
this troublesome baggage. Venice is quite the Venice of ones
dreams, but it remains strangely the Venice of dreams, more
than of any appreciable reality. The mind is bothered with a
constant sense of the exceptional character of the city: you can't
reconcile it with common civilization. It's awfully sad too in its
inexorable decay. Newport by the way is extremely like it in
atmosphere ɟ color, ɟ the other afternoon, on the sands at the
Lido, looking out over the dazzling Adriatic, I fancied I was
standing on Easton's beach. It's treasures of course are
numerable, ɟ I have seen but a small fraction. I have been
haunting chiefly the ducal palace ɟ the ◇◇ Academy ɟ putting
~~over~~ [ʌ]off[ʌ] the churches. Tintoretto is omnipresent ɟ well-nigh
omnipotent. Titian I like less here than in London ɟ elsewhere.
He is strangely unequal. P. Veronese is great ɟ J. Bellini greater.
Perfect felicity I find nowhere but in the manner of the Ducal
Palace ɟ bits of other palaces on the Gd. Canal. One thing
strangely strikes me; viz. that if I were an "<u>artist</u>" all these
immortal daubers would have anything but a directly

discouraging effect upon me. On the contrary: they are full of
their own peculiar compromises, poverties & b̂etises, & are as far
off from the absolute as Miss Jane Stuart. —I go hence to
Florence, <u>via</u> Bologna, in about 10 days. I hope to remain some
5   time at F., to see Rome & Naples & possibly have a glimpse of
Sicily. I must stay my hand just now. I only wanted to let you
know that if you find it possible to come within a short time, I
should like well to do some travelling in your company. Offering
counsel is repugnant to the discreet mind; yet I can't but say that
10   I should predict serious good of your coming. Steady sight
seeing is ∧extremely[∧] fatiguing, but there is a way of taking it
easy—such as I—theretically—practice. —I think of spending
from March 15ᵗʰ o͟f ₍∧₎to₍∧₎ May 15ᵗʰ in France—(Paris
Normandy & Brittany;) going during the next 2 mos. thro'
15   Belgium Holland & the Rhine & then going for 3 mos. to
England. —I shall then either make up my mind to return (I
shall have been abroad about a year & 8 mos.) or if I feel up to
any serious reading shall make straight back to Dresden; &
spend the Winter. There you have my "line of march" as far as
20   'tis defined. But it's not in the least fixed. —I hope your wife &
young ones are well & that you've been having a decently
entertaining & comfortable summer. I wish I were hereditary
possessor of t͟h one of these old palazzi. I would make it over to
you for a year's occupancy. The gondola by the way is a thing
25   divine. Did you ever get my letter from Glion, in June? You
don't mention it? Thank Sargy for his good intentions in
∧regard to₍∧₎ writing to w͟r͟i͟t͟i͟n͟g ₍∧₎me—₍∧₎ infernal asphalte.
Farewell. Let me hear from you hopefully & believe me yours
always H. James jr. ·
30   The Nortons are to spend this winter in Florence. —

✉

<u>Stati Uniti di America</u>
<u>Via Ostenda</u>

John L Farge esq
   Newport
    R. I.
    Etats Unis d'Amérique

Front postmark: VENEZIA | 21 | SET | 69 | 4 S
Back postmark: MILANO STAZ. | 22 | SET | 69 | 10 M

Previous publication: La Farge 178–80; *HJL* 1: 133–35

∾

108.23 investment • in= | vestment

109.5 unspeakably • un= | speakably

109.8 sympathy • sym- | pathy

109.13 m◊ week • [we *overwrites* m◊]

109.16 ◊ to • [to *overwrites illegible letter*]

109.27 ◊◊ Academy • [Ac *overwrites illegible letters*]

110.12 theretically • [*misspelled*]

110.23 th one • [on *overwrites* th]

∾

108.14–15 your letter of Aug. 26ᵗʰ • La Farge to HJ, 26 August [1869] (Houghton bMS Am 1094 [316]).

109.6 Italianissima • eminently Italian.

109.25 Easton's beach • Beach just to the east of the center of Newport; Purgatory and Paradise are immediately to its east.

109.32 Gd. Canal • Grand Canal.

110.2 bêtises • silly things.

110.3 Miss Jane Stuart • Jane Stuart, daughter of American portrait painter Gilbert Stuart, and a lesser-known portrait artist herself.

110.25 my letter from Glion, in June • HJ to La Farge, 20 June 1869.

110.26 Sargy • Thomas Sergeant Perry.

WILLIAM JAMES
25, 26, [27] September [1869]
ALS Houghton
bMS Am 1094 (1934)

5

Venice Hotel Barbesi Sept. 25<u>th</u>
My dear Bill—I wrote to father as soon as I arrived here &
mentioned my intention of sending you some copious account
of my impressions of ~~the~~ Venice. I have since then written to
10   J. LaFarge (briefly) & to Howells & worked off in some degree
the Éblouissement of the 1<u>st</u> few days. I have a vague idea that I
may write some notes for the Atlantic or the Nation; but at the
risk of knocking the bottom out of them, I feel that I must
despatch you a few choice remarks—although I'm too tired to
15   plunge deeply into things.—Among the letters which I found
here on my arrival was a most valuable one from you, of the last
of July, which made me ache to my spirit's core t for half an
hour's talk with you. I was unutterably gladdened by your
statement of your improvement. Three days since however came
20   a letter from Mother of Sept. 6<u>th</u>, speaking of a slight decline,
since your return home. As she also mentions, however, your
meaning to go to Newport & Lennox I trust you had not lost
courage. I hope next to hear that you have made your visits & are
the better for them. Give Mother unutterable thanks for her
25   letter: my only complaint is that I don't get one like it every day.
But I can't be at home & abroad both. I have now been here
nearly two weeks & have experienced that inevitable
reconciliation to things which six months of Europe cause to
operate so rapidly & smoothly, no matter what the strangeness of
30   things may be. A little stare—a little thrill—a little curiosity, &
then all is over. You subside into the plodding blasé, homesick
"doer" of cities. Venice is magnificently fair & quite, to my
perception, the Venice of Romance & fancy. Taine, I remember,
somewhere speaks of "Venice & Oxford—the two most

picturesque cities in Europe." I personally prefer Oxford; it told
me deeper & richer things & than any I have learned here. It's as
if I had been born in Boston: I cant for my life frankly surrender
myself to the Genius of Italy—or the Spirit of the South—or
whatever one may call the confounded thing; but I nevertheless   5
feel it in all my pulses. If I could only write as I might talk I
should have no end of things to tell you about my last days in
Switzerland & especially my descent of the Alps—that mighty
summer's day upon the Simplon when I communed with I~
immensity & sniffed Italy from afar. This Italian tone of things   10
which I then detected, lies richly on my soul & gathers
increasing weight, but it lies as a cold & foreign mass—never to
be absorbed & appropriated. The meaning of this superb image
is ∧that[∧] I feel I shall never look at Italy—at Venice for
instance—but from without; whereas it seemed to ƀ me at   15
Oxford & in England generally that I was breathing the air of
home. Ruskin recommends the traveller to frequent & linger in a
certain glorious room at the Ducal ~~place~~ palace, where
P. Veronese revels on the ceilings & Tintoret rages on the walls,
because he "no where else will enter so deeply into the heart of   20
Venice." I̶ But I feel as if I might sit there forever (as I sat there a
long time this morning) & only feel more & more my inexorable
Yankeehood. As a puling pining Yankee however, I ◇ enjoy
things deeply. What you will most care to hear about is the
painters; so I shall not feel bound to inflict upon you any tall   25
writing about the canals & palaces; the more especially as with
regard to them, photographs are worth ~~soming~~ something; but
with regard to the pictures comparatively nothing—rapport à la
couleur—which is quite half of Venetian painting. The first
thing that strikes you, when you come to sum up, after you been   30
to the D. P. & the Academy is that you have not half so much
been seeing ~~painters a~~ paintings as painters. The accumulated
mass of works by a few men drives each man home to your
senses with extraordinary force. This is especially the case with

the greatest of them all—Tintoretto—so much so that he ends
by becoming an immense perpetual moral presence, brooding
ₐover₍ₐ₎ the scene & worrying the mind into some species of
reponse & acknowledgment. I have had more eyes & more
5   thoughts ~~of~~ ₐfor₍ₐ₎ him than for anything else in Venice; & in
future, I fancy, when I recall the place, I shall remember chiefly
the full-streaming dazzling light of the heavens & Tintoretto's
dark range of colour. Ruskin truly says that it is well to devote
yourself here solely to three men—P. Veronese, Tintoretto &
10 J. Bellini; inasmuch as you can see sufficient specimens of the
rest (including Titian—amply) elsewhere but must come here
for even a notion of these. This is true of the three, but
especially of Tintoretto—whom I finally see there is nothing for
me to do but to admit (& have done with it) to be the biggest
15 genius (as far as I yet know) who ever wielded a brush. Once do
this & you can make your abatements; but if Shakespeare is the
greatest of poets Tintoretto is assuredly the greatest of painters.
He belongs to the same family & produces very much the same
effect. He seems to me ~~he has~~ to have seen into painting to a
20 distance unsuspected by any of his fellows: I don't mean into its
sentimental virtues or didactic properties but into its simple
pictorial capacity. Imagine Doré a 1000 times refined in quality
& then as many times multiplied in quanity & you may have a
sort of notion of him. But you must see him here at work like a
25 great wholesale decorator to form an idea of his boundless
invention & his passionate energy & ~~the~~ of the extraordinary
possibilities of color—for he begins ■■■■ by striking you as
the poorest & ends by impressing you as the greatest of colorists.
Beside him the others are the simplest fellows in the world. ₐFor
30 the present₍ₐ₎ I give up Titian altogether. He is not adequately
represented here. His <u>Assumption</u> strikes me as a magnificent
second-rate picture; his presentation of the Virgin is utterly
killed by another of Tintoretto's. I fancy you must see him in
England, Madrid &c. P. Veronese is really great, in a very simple

fashion. He seems to have had in his head a ~~splendid~~ ∧perfect[∧]
realization of a world in which all things were interfused with a
sort of silvery splendor delicious to look upon. He is thoroughly
undramatic & "impersonal." A splendid scene in the concrete
was ∧enough[∧] for him & when he paints anything of a story the   5
whole action seems to rest suspended in order to look handsome
& be painted. If I weren't a base Anglo-Saxon ∧&[∧] a coward
slave, I should ask nothing better than his <u>Rape of Europa</u> in the
D. P., where a great rosy blonde, gorgeous with brocade & pearls
& bouncing with salubrity ~~a~~ & a great mellow splendor of sea &   10
sky & nymphs & flowers do their best to demoralize the world
into a herd of Theophile Gautiers. The great beauty of ~~T. G.~~
P. Veronese is the perfect unity & placidity of his talent. There is
not a whit of struggle, nor fever, nor longing for the
unattainable; simply a glorious sense of the look of things out of   15
doors—of heads & columns against the sky, of the lustre of satin
& of the beauty of looking up & seeing things lifted into the light
above you. He is here chiefly found in the ceilings, where he is
perfectly at home, & delights to force you to break your back to
look at him—& wonder what sort of a back <u>he</u> must have had.   20
John Bellini, a ~~great~~ painter of whom I had no conception—one
of the early Venetians—is equally great & simple in his ∧own[∧]
far different way. He has everything on a great scale—
knowledge color & expression. He is the 1<u>st</u> "religious" painter I
have yet seen who has made me understand that there can be—   25
or that there once was at least, such a thing as pure religious art.
I always fancied it more or less an illusion of the critics. But
Bellini puts me to the blush. How to ~~the~~ define his "religious"
quality I know not; but he really makes you believe that his
genius was essentially consecrated to heaven & that each of his   30
pictures was a genuine act of worship. This is the more
interesting because his piety prevails not the least against his
science & his pictorial energy. There is not a ray in his works of
debility or vagueness of conception. In vigor breadth & richness

he is a thorough Venetian. His best pictures here possess an extraordinary perfection. Everything is equal—the full deep beauty of the expression—the masterly—the more than masterly firmness ∂ purity of the drawing—∂ the ◇ undimmed,

5 unfathomed lucidity ∂ richness of the coloring. And then over it all ~~the~~ a sort of pious deference has passed ∂ hushed ∂ smoothed ∂ polished ∧it[∧] ~~it~~ till the effect is one of unspeakable purity. He has hardly more than ∧one[∧] subject—the Virgin ∂ Child, alone, or enthroned ∂ attended with Saints ∂ cherubs; but you will be

10 slow to tire of him, for long after you've had enough of his piety there is food for delight in the secret marvels of his handling. It gives one a strong sense of the vastness ∂ strangeness of art, to compare these 2 men, Bellini ∂ Tintoretto—to reflect upon their almost equal greatness ∂ yet their immense dissimilarity, so

15 that the great merit of each seems to have been that he possesses just those qualities the absence of which, apparently, ensures his high place to the other.—T̶ But to return to Tintoretto. I'd give a great deal to be able to fling down a dozen of his pictures into prose of corresponding force ∂ color. I strongly urge you to look

20 up in vol 3ᵈ of Ruskin's <u>Stones</u> (last appendix) a number of magnificent descriptive pages ~~about~~ ∧touching[∧] his principal pictures. (The whole appendix by the way, with all its exasperating points is invaluable to the visitor here ∂ I have profited much by it.) I should be sadly at a loss to make you

25 understand in what his great power consists—the more especially as he ~~has~~ ∧offers[∧] a hundred superficial points of repulsion to the well-regulated mind. In a certain occasional imbecility ∂ crudity ∂ imperfection of drawing Delacroix is nothing to him. And then you see him at a vast disadvantage

30 inasmuch as with hardly an exception his pictures are atrociously hung ∂ lighted. When you reflect that he was willing to go on covering canvas to be hidden out of sight or falsely shown, you get some idea of the prodigality of his genius. Most of his pictures are ~~large~~ ∧immense[∧] ∂ swarming with figures;

All have suffered grievously from abuse & neglect. But there are all sorts; you can never feel that you have seen the last; & each new one throws a new light on his resources. Besides this, they are extremely unequal & ◊ it would be an easy task I fancy to collect a dozen pieces which would conclusively establish him an unmitigated bore. His especial greatness, I should be tempted to say lies in the fact that more than any painter yet, he habitually conceived his subject as an <u>actual</u> <u>scene</u>, which could not possibly have happened otherwise; not as a mere subject & fiction—but as a great fragment wrenched out of life & history, with all its natural details clinging to it & tesifying to its reality. You seem not only to look <u>at</u> his pictures, but <u>into</u> them—& this in spite of his not hesitating to open the clouds & shower down the deities & mi◊ mix up heaven & Earth as freely as his purpose demands. His <u>Miracle of St. Mark</u> is a tremendous work, with life enough in it to animate a planet. But they can't all paint a crowd, & this is as much Venetian as individual. A better specimen of his peculiar power is a simple <u>Adam & Eve</u>, in the same room, or a <u>Cain & Abel</u>, its mate, both atrociously hung— away aloft in the air. Adam sits on a bank with his back to you; Even ∧facing you,[∧] with one arm wound round a tree leans forward & holds out the apple. The composition is so simple that it hardly exists & yet the painting is so rich & expressive th◊ that it seems as if the <u>natural</u> the real, could go no further—unless indeed in the other, where Cain assaults Abel with an intent to kill more murderous & tragical than words can describe it. One of his works that has most struck me is a large <u>Annunciation</u>, immensely characteristic of ▬▬ this unlikeness to other painters. To the right sits the Virgin, starting back from her angelic visitant with magnificent surprise & terror. The Angel swoops down into the picture, leading a swarm of cherubs, not as in most cases where the subject is treated, as if he had come to pay her a pretty compliment but with a fury characteristic of his tremendous message. The greatest of all though—the greatest

picture it seemed to me as I looked at it I ever saw—is a
crucifixion in a small church. (He has treated the same subject
elsewhere on a stupendous scale; but on the whole I prefer this.)
Here ∧as usual[∧] all is original & unconventional. Ruskin
describes it far better than I can do. Monday 26ᵗʰ Having
written so much last evening, ⋄ I succumbed to slumber, & this
evening I hardly feel like resuming the feeble thread of my
discourse. I have been abroad all day bidding farewell to Venice,
for I think of leaving tomorrow or next day. I began the day with
several churches & saw two new & magnificent Tintorets & a
beautiful Titian. Then I paid a farewell visit to the Academy,
which I have got pretty well by heart—& where I saw Mr. & Mrs.
Bronson of Newport who knew me not—the latter very haggard
& pale. After wh. I took a gondola over to the Lido to look my
last at the Adriatic. It was a glorious afternoon & I wandered for
nearly two hours by the side of the murmuring sea. I was more
than ever struck with the resemblance ~~to~~ of Venice—especially
that part of it—to Newport. The same atmosphere, the same
luminosity. Standing looking out at the Adriatic with the low-
lying linked islands on the horizon was just like looking out to
sea from one of the Newport beaches, with Narragansett afar. I
have seen the Atlantic as blue & smooth & musical—almost! If
words were not so stupid & colorless, fratello mio, & sentences so
interminable & chirography so difficult, I should like to treat you
to a dozen pages more about this watery paradise. ~~Get~~ ∧Read[∧]
Theophile Gautier's Italia; its chiefly about Venice. I'm curious
to know how this enchanted fortnight will strike me, in memory
10 years hence—for altho' I've got absurdly used to it all, yet
there is a palpable sub-current of deep delight. Gondolas spoil
you for a return to common life. To begin with, in themselves
~~theyre'~~ they afford the perfection of indolent pleasure. The seat
is so soft and deep & slumberous & the motion so mild elastic &
unbroken that even if they bore you through miles of stupid
darkness. ∧you'd think its the most delectable fun.[∧] But when

they lift you thro' this rosy air, along these liquid paths, beneath
the p̶ balconies of palaces as lovely in design & fancy as they are
pathetic in their loneliness & decay—you may imagine that it's
better than walking down Broadway. I should never have
forgiven myself had I come to Venice any later in the season.
The mosquitoes are perfectly infernal—& you can't say more for
Venice than that you are willing, at this moment, for the sake of
the days she bestows to endure the nights she inflicts. But,
bating this, all else is in perfection—the weather, the
temperature & the aspect of the canals. The Venetian
population, i̶ on u̶n̶d̶e̶r̶ [∧]the[∧] water, is immensely picturesque.
In the ∧narrow[∧] streets, the ∧people[∧] are far too squalid &
offensive to the nostrils, but with a good breadth of canal to set
them off & a heavy stream of sunshine to light them up, as they
go pushing & paddling a̶ & screaming—bare chested, bare-
legged, magnificently tanned & muscular—the men at least are a
e̶f̶ very effective lot. Besides lolling in my gondola I have spent a
good deal of time in poking thro' the alleys which serve as
streets & staring about in the <u>Campos</u>—the little squares formed
about every church—some of them the most sunnily desolate,
the most grass-grown, the most cheerfully m̶e̶l̶a̶n̶c̶h̶o̶l̶y̶ ∧sad[∧]
little reliquaries of a splendid past that you can imagine. Every
one knows that the Grand Canal is a wonder; but really to feel
in your heart the ancient s̶p̶l̶e̶n̶d̶o̶r̶ ∧wealth[∧] of Venice, you
must have frequented these canalettos & campos & e̶ seen the
number & splendor of the p̶a̶l̶a̶z̶ palaces that stand rotting &
crumbling & abandoned to paupers.—If I might talk of these
things I would talk of more & tell you in glowing accents how
beautiful a thing this month in Italy has been & how my brain
swarms with pictures & my bosom aches with memories. I
should like in some neat formula to give you the <u>Italian</u>
<u>feeling</u>—& tell you just how it is that one f̶e̶e̶l̶s̶ ∧is conscious[∧]
here of the aesthetic pressure of the past. But you'll learn one
day for yourself. You'll go t̶h̶ to that admirable Verona & get

your fill ∧of[∧] it.—I wanted not only to say a 100 things about Tintoretto which I've let unsaid (indeed I've said nothing) but to gossip a bit about the other painters. Whether it is that the three great ones I've mentioned practically include all the rest or
5 not, I can't say; but (with the exception of two or three primitive members of the school, especially Carpaccio, who seem to have learned laboriously for themselves,) there flows from the great mass of the secondary fellows no very powerful emanation of genius. Immense aptitude & capital teaching—vigorous talent, in
10 fine—seem to be the amount of the matter. In them the school trenches on Vulgarity. Bonifazio, Caligiari, the two Palmas, Paris Bordone &c have all an immense amount of ability (,often of a very exquisite kind) to a comparatively small amount of originality.—Nevertheless I'm very willing to believe—in fact
15 I'm quite sure—that seen in other places, in detached examples each of them would impress & charm you very much as their betters ▬▬ do here. All of them know endless things about color: in this they are indeed exquisite. Bonifazio is a somewhat coarser Titian—a perfect ◇ Monarch of the mellow & glowing &
20 richly darksome. Paris Bordone equals him, on a slightly different range. C. Caligiari (son of P. Veronese) is a very handsome imitation of his father—& if the latter's works were destroyed, we'd vote him a great master. But what has fascinated me most here after Tintoretto & Co, are the two great
25 buildings—T̶ the Ducal Palace & St. Mark's Church. You have a general notion of what they amount to; its all you can have, until you see them. St. Mark's, within, is a great hoary shadowy tabernacle of mosaic & marble, entrancing you with its remoteness, its picturesqueness & its chiaroscuro—an immense
30 piece of Romanticism. But the Ducal Palace is as pure & perpetual as the façade of the p̶ Parthenon—& I t̶h̶i̶n̶g̶ think of all things in Venice, its the one I should have been gladdest to achieve ̶s̶h̶o̶u̶l̶d̶ [∧]—the[∧] one most worthy of civic affection & gratitude. When your'e heated & wearied to death with

Tintoretto & his feverish Bible Stories, you can come out on the
great Piazetta, between the marble columns, & grow
comparatively cool & comfortable with gazing on this work of
art which has so little to do with <u>persons</u>!
But I too am weary & hot—tho' I expect to find on my couch but
little of coolness or comfort. I have the delightful choice of
sleeping with my window open & being <u>devoured</u>—maddened,
poisoned—or closing it, in spite of the heat, & being stifled!—I
have made no allusion to the contents of mothers' letter, which I
none the less prize. I have written to Minny Temple about her
sisters. Elly's marriage strikes me as absolutely <u>sad</u>. I care not
how good a fellow T. Emmet may be: Elly deserved a younger
man. Mother says nothing about Wilky's crops. I hope ~~new~~ no
news is good news. I am not surprised to hear of Dr. Wilkinson's
being at hand. When I was in England he was evidently all ready
for a chance to sail. I'm very curious to know the impression he
made. I'm not to meet A. K. They come at present no further S.
than the Lakes.—But I <u>must</u> say good night. I mean to write you
again in a few days—<u>not</u> about painters. À toi
     H. James jr.

Previous publication: *HJL* 1: 136–44; *CWJ* 1: 92–99; Zorzi, *Palazzo
Barbaro* 57–73

∾

112.9 ~~the~~ Venice • [Veni *overwrites* the]

112.12 <u>notes</u> • [*underline blotted out*]

112.17 ~~t~~ for • [f *overwrites* t]

112.22 Lennox • [*misspelled*]

112.24 unutterable • un= | utterable

112.31 homesick • home= | sick

112.32 magnificently • magnifi= | cently

112.33 remember • re= | member

113.9-10 ~~I◊~~ immensity • [i *overwrites* I◊]

113.15 ~~b~~ me • [m *overwrites* b]

113.18 ~~place~~ palace • [alace *overwrites* lace]

113.21 ~~I~~ But • [B *overwrites* I]

113.23 ◊ enjoy • [e *overwrites blotted illegible letter*]

113.27 ~~soming~~ something • [ethin *overwrites* in]

113.32 ~~painters a~~ paintings • [ing *overwrites* ers; s *overwrites blotted* a]

114.4 reponse • [*misspelled*]

114.4 acknowledgment • acknowledg= | ment

114.5 ~~of~~ ∧ • [∧ *overwrites* of]

114.16 Shakespeare • Shakes= | peare

114.19 ~~he has~~ to have • [to *overwrites* he; v *overwrites* s]

114.20 distance • dis= | tance

114.23 quanity • [*misspelled*]

114.26 passionate • pas= | sionate

114.26 ~~the~~ of • [of *overwrites* the]

114.27 ■■■■ by • [by *overwrites illegible word*]

115.10 ~~a~~ ↲ • [↲ *overwrites* a]

116.2 extraordinary • extra- | ordinary

116.4 ◊ undimmed • [u *overwrites illegible letter*]

116.6 ~~the~~ a • [a *overwrites* the]

116.7 ~~it~~ till • [till *overwrites* it]

116.17 ~~T~~ But • [B *overwrites* T]

116.23 exasperating • exas= | perating

116.24 profited • pro- | fited

116.28 imbecility • imbecil= | ity

117.4 ◊ it • [it *overwrites blotted illegible letter*]

117.6 greatness • great= | ness

117.11 tesifying • [*misspelled*]

117.13 hesitating • hes- | itating

117.14 ~~mi◊~~ mix • [x *overwrites illegible letter*]

117.15 tremendous • tremen= | dous

117.16 can't • ['t *blotted out*]

117.18 specimen • speci= | men

117.21 Even • [n *blotted out*]

117.23 ~~th◊~~ that • [a *overwrites illegible letter*]

117.28 characteristic • charac= | teristic

117.28 ▬▬▬ this • [this *overwrites illegible word*]

118.4 unconventional • unconven- | tional

118.6 ⬦ I • [I *overwrites illegible letter*]

118.6 succumbed • suc- | cumbed

118.17 ~~to~~ of • [of *overwrites* to]

118.19–20 low- | lying • low-lying

118.30 themselves • them- | selves

118.31 ~~theyre*~~ they • [y *overwrites* yre']

119.2 ᵽ balconies • [b *overwrites* p]

119.4 Broadway • Broad= | way

119.5 myself • my- | self

119.6 perfectly • per= | fectly

119.11 ᵼ on • [o *overwrites* i]

119.15 ₐ ᑯ • [ᑯ *overwrites* a]

119.15–16 bare- | legged • bare-legged

119.17 ~~ef~~ very • [ve *overwrites* ef]

119.22 splendid • splen= | did

119.25 campos • cam- | pos

119.25 ᴇ seen • [s *overwrites* c]

119.26 ~~palaz~~ palaces • [ce *overwrites* z]

119.34 You'll • You | 'll

119.34 ~~th~~ to • [o *overwrites* h]

120.4 include • in= | clude

120.5 primitive • pri- | mitive

120.11 Bonifazio • Boni- | fazio

120.15 detatched • [*misspelled*]

120.19 ⬦ Monarch • [M *overwrites illegible letter*]

120.25 Ŧ the • [t *overwrites* T]

120.28 tabernacle • taberna- | cle

120.31 ᵽ Parthenon • [P *overwrites* p]

120.31 ~~thing~~ think • [k *overwrites* g]

120.33 affection • affec- | tion

120.34 your'e • [e *inserted*]

121.2 Piazetta • [*misspelled*]

121.13 ~~new~~ no • [o *overwrites* ew]

121.16 impression • im= | pression

∾

112.7 I wrote to father as soon as I arrived here • HJ to Sr., 17 September [1869].

112.9–10 I have since then written to J. LaFarge (briefly) • HJ to John La Farge, 21 September [1869].

112.11 Éblouissement • Wonderment.

112.20 a letter from Mother of Sept. 6th • MWJ to HJ, 6 September [1869], from Cambridge.

113.28–29 rapport à la couleur • in regard to color.

113.31 D. P. • Doge's Palace.

114.31 His Assumption • Painted in 1518 for the altar of the Church of Santa Maria Gloriosa dei Frari.

114.32 his presentation of the Virgin • *The Presentation of Mary in the Temple* (1538), painted for the Scuola della Carità.

114.33 another of Tintoretto's • Tintoretto's *Presentation of Mary* (1552–53) adorns the outer organ shutters of Madonna del Orto.

115.8 his Rape of Europa • Painted circa 1580 and now in the Anticollegio, the Doge's Palace.

116.28 Delacroix • Eugène Delacroix (1798–1863).

117.15 His Miracle of St. Mark • Sometimes known as *St. Mark Rescuing the Slave* (1548), commissioned by the Scuola Grande di San Marco.

117.18 Adam & Eve • Alternatively known as *Original Sin* (1550–53), painted for the Scuola della Trinità.

117.19 Cain & Abel • Also called *The Murder of Abel* or *Cain Killing Abel* (1550–53) and, like Tintoretto's *Adam and Eve*, painted for the Scuola della Trinità.

117.27 a large Annunciation • Painted 1578–81 and in the Scuola di San Rocco.

118.1–2 a crucifixion in a small church • Tintoretto's 1568 painting at Venice's San Cassiano.

118.2–3 the same subject elsewhere on a stupendous scale • Tintoretto's 1565 painting at Venice's Scuola di San Rocco.

118.5 <u>Monday 26<u>th</u></u> • 26 September 1869 was a Sunday; Monday was September 27.

118.12–13 Mr. & Mrs. Bronson • Arthur Bronson (1824–55) married Katharine de Kay in New York on 11 October 1855. After he began to have mental health problems in 1880, he lived separately from his wife. Katharine de Kay Bronson (1834–1901) probably first met the Jameses when she and her husband lived in Newport in the late 1850s. She would later become a close friend of Robert Browning's and of HJ's; both authors visited her at her Venice palazzino, Casa Alvisi, its guest accommodations in the neighboring Palazzo Giustiniani-Recanati, and her house, Casa La Mura, in nearby Asolo. HJ commemorated his friendship with Mrs. Bronson in his memorial article "The Late Mrs. Arthur Bronson," in the *The Critic*, reprinted as "Casa Alvisi" in *Italian Hours*.

118.23 <u>fratello</u> mio • <u>my brother</u>.

120.6 Carpaccio • Vittore Carpaccio (1460–1525/26), early Renaissance painter who earned the critical praise of John Ruskin in the nineteenth century.

120.11 Bonifazio • Bonifazio de 'Pitati (1487–1553), also known as Bonifazio Veronese.

120.11 Caligiari • Carlo (Carletto) Caliari (1570–96), son of Paolo Veronese.

120.11 two Palmas • Jacopo Negretti, known as Palma il Vecchio (1480–1528) to distinguish him from his son, Jacopo Palma il Giovane (1544–1628), who completed Titian's final work, the *Pietà*.

120.12 Paris Bordone • Bordone (1500–1571), a Venetian painter, briefly studied under Titian.

120.25 St. Mark's Church • On the eastern end of the Piazza San Marco, the church was built primarily in the eleventh century after the tutelary saint of Venice.

121.12 T. Emmet • Christopher Temple Emmet.

121.14 Dr. Wilkinson's • Dr. James John Garth Wilkinson.

121.17 A. K. • Aunt Kate.

121.19 À toi • Yours.

ALICE JAMES
6, [8] October [1869]
ALS Houghton
bMS Am 1094 (1559)

5

Hotel de l'Europe, Florence
October 6<u>th</u>(?)

Carissima Sorella—I have before me the fragment of a letter
begun yesterday at Parma, while I waited for the train, but it
10 looks so flat & stale that I shall chose a clean sheet & begin
afresh. The last news you will have got of me is contained in a
letter to Willy—despatched if I mistake not the day before I left
Venice. Yes, Venice too has become a figment of the past—she
lies like a great dazzling spot of yellow paint upon the backward
15 path of my destiny. Now that I behold her no more I feel sadly
as if I had done her wrong—as if I had been cold & insensible—
that my eyes ◊◊◊ scowled & blinked at her brightness & that with
more of self-oblivion I might have known her better & loved her
more. Wherever we go we carry with us this heavy burden of
20 our personal consciousness & wherever we stop we open it out
over our heads like a great baleful cotton ombrella, to obstruct
the prospect & obscure the light of heaven. Apparently it's in the
nature of things. To come away vaguely dissatisfied with my
Venetian sojourn is only one chapter in the lesson which this
25 hardened old ~~Italy~~ ∧Europe[∧] is forever teaching ~~yoo~~—that you
must rest content with the ~~flimsi◊◊~~ flimsiest knowledge of her
treasures & the most superficial insight into her character. I feel
sadly the lack of that intellectual outfit which is needful for
seeing Italy properly & speaking ~~a~~ a of ◊ her in words which shall
30 be more than empty sounds—the lack of facts of all sorts—
chiefly historical & architectural. A mind unprepared by the
infusion of a certain amount of knowledge of this kind,
languishes so beneath the weight of its impressions, light as they
must necessarily be—that it is ready at times to give up the game

126

as lost. ◇ Your only consolation is in the hope that you may be
able by hook or by crook to retain a few of the impressions ⅋
confront them with the facts in the leisure of subsequent
years.—Well, Venice has gone, but Florence treads fast on her
heels. I have a good deal to recount however before the   5
inexorable logic of my story brings me hither. Since leaving
Venice I'◇ I've transformed Padua, Ferrara, Bologna ⅋ Parma
from names into places—⅋ most interesting places too. At Padua
I spent twenty-four hours of immense felicity—for at Padua are
many charming things. I will speak neither of the Caffé   10
Pedrocchi, nor of the delightful old court of the University, nor
of the ch. of San Antonio, nor even of that of the Eremitani.
The great central treasure of Padua is a certain edefice known
unto men ⅋ angels as <u>Giotto's</u> <u>Chapel</u>. Padua like many other
Italian towns has perforce its Roman Arena—a vast oval   15
enclosure, quite disfurnished of its ancient fixings. The interior
has been turned in a great cornfield ⅋ orchard, save that at one
extremity sa stands a little mediaeval chapel—a mere empty
shell—lined with a series of ₍ₐ₎decorative₍ₐ₎ frescoes by the great
hand of Giotto. I say the "great" hand advisedly; no sooner have   20
you crossed the threshold than you perceive with whom you
have to deal. I ◇◇g have h̶t̶ ̶o̶f̶ ₍ₐ₎seen₍ₐ₎ nothing yet in Italy which
has caused me so to long for the penetrating judgement ⅋ genial
sympathy of my accomplished William. I have always fancied
that to say anything about Giotto was to make more or less a   25
fool of one's self ⅋ that he i̶s̶ was the especial property of the
mere sentimentalists of criticism. But he is a real complete
painter of the very strongest sort. In one respect he has never
been surpassed—in the faculty of telling a story—the mastery of
dramatic presentation. The amount of dramatic expression   30
compressed into these quaint little squares would equip a
hundred later masters. And then the simplicity—the purity—the
grace! The whole exhibition suggests more reflections than I
have time for. Happy, happy art, you say to yourself—as you

seem to see it, beneath Giotto's hand, tremble & thrill with a ◈◈
presentiment of its immense career—for the next two hundred
years what a prodigiously "good time" you are going to have! At
Ferrara I spent some five memorable hours walking about the

5   streets & tasting the exquisite quality of Ferrarese desolation &
decay. The ▬▬▬ city is immense in extent (like all these lesser
Italian towns—there's no end to their length & breadth) &
peopled I should say, to the tune of one individual to a dozen
houses. The streets are lined with mighty palaces & all coated &

10   muffled in silent grass. I got in particular a walk at sunset upon
the old ruined ramparts that enclose the town & melt away in
most pacific verdure into the ◈◈ great murmuring plain of the
Po. It was ~~unlike~~ unique: I can't ~~remember~~ render it. Some old
steel engraving, seen in childhood & re-discovered in future

15   years, comes as near to it as any thing else. ~~At~~ To Bologna I
devoted three good days—Bologna being, if you please, "quite a
place." Bologna is rich in all great gifts. A mighty public square,
with the Middle Ages & the Renaissance all frowning & smiling
together about its margin—no end of fine churches & palaces—a

20   remarkable gallery of pictures (to say nothing of a capital
hotel—unhoped for blessing!)—such is Bologna. ◈ The
physiognomy of the city is most grand gloomy & peculiar owing
to its being wholly built upon arches, like the Rue de Rivoli!
The gallery of course is the organ of the so-called Bolognese

25   school—to which, however, I should send no boy of mine whom
I wished to train up in the way he should paint. There you ~~p~~
behold the exact reversion of the spectacle you witness at
Padua—art having played itself out & living on memories,
precepts & ambitions—Guido, Domenichino, the Caracci &c. As

30   a most delightful old Frenchman whom I met ◈ at Padua said to
me, they have neither the ~~color~~ couleur Venitienne ni la
<u>belle ligne Romaine</u>" The Gallery contains a Rafael (his <u>St.</u>
<u>Cecilia</u>—we have a small photo. of Marc Antonio's engraving ~~it~~
of it) in which the belle ligne Romaine makes all things else look

tipsy. Après cela, Guido & all the rest are very clever painters. From Bologna I made a pilgrimage to Parma (where I spent the night) in order to see what there is to be seen of Coreggio. Parma was his lifelong residence & possesses some of his best works—tho' they are very few in number. He had a most divine touch—& seems to have been a sort of <u>sentimental</u> Leonardo— setting Leonardo down as "intellectual." A couple of his masterpieces at Parma perfectly <u>reek</u> with loveliness. A little infant Christ in one of them diffuses a holiness fit to convince unbelievers & confound blasphemers. I reached Florence last evening—after a long journey thro' a glorious country—the bosom of the Appenines. I have been spending the day strolling about, thro' the streets & the two Great Galleries—the Uffizi & the Pitti Palace. They are <u>incroyables</u>—& will give me work for many days. Florence strikes me very pleasantly & I should like to settle down here for a series of weeks. I am just now wrestling with the problem of exactly how I shall live. I shall not go into a <u>Pension</u> tho' I believe there are several good ones because its of the last necessity that I should escape public tables. An "apartment" looks lonesome & would not be especially cheap. I therefore think I shall remain at this hotel or go to another. Dining at a restaurant, & paying here for my room, solid breakfast & service I can live for 10 frs. a day, which is about as much I should pay at the best pension here (the only one I should be willing to go to)—tho' of course considerably more than if I were to hunt up a small room & concentrate my energies on enconomy I am very sorry to say (if you'll allow me to mention the topic) that in spite of the most religious prudence (& I have learned many things) my disgestive organs are the bane of my existence & so long as this state of things continues I must ensure myself the best conditions in the way of food & lodging. But I shall look about me & consult simply my genuine needs: I went this morning to my bankers, dreaming wildly of letters. But all was cold & dark—or would have been

but for a very pretty letter from Miss Peabody & one from Sara
Sedgwick. The Nortons are to reach here about the 22$^{\underline{d}}$ Mrs.
Huntington & her daughters (formerly of Cambridge) & Mrs.
Horatio Greenough & daughter (ditto) are here for the winter. I
◊◊ fancy there is quite a little group of Americans. J. Lorimer
Graham jr of N. Y. is Consul. I hope for letters tomorrow &
shall keep this over.

<u>Friday</u>. I found this morning at my banker's with feelings that
may be easily imagined than described mother's blessed letter of
Sept. 21$^{\underline{st}}$, telling of Dr. Wilkinson's visit &c. Also a most
characteristic & amusing one from Bob Temple. I was very sorry
to hear of father's ~~hav◊◊~~ having been so long in trouble with his
boil. I hope by this time it's all well over, for ever. Mother
speaks of his book being out, but says nothing of any plan of
sending it to me. This will not be neglected, at least. She
likewise says nothing more of Bob's (<u>our</u> Bob's) Texan plans tho'
B. T. mentions his being in N. Y. "negotiating" on the subject.
Let me hear all about it. Not a word either about Wilky's crops,
tho' she speaks of his having gone back to Florida. I don't know
whether to infer from her silence that they are good bad or
indifferent. Most sweet it is to get all your Cambridge news. Bob
Temple expresses great disgust with Elly's marriage. I must say I
can't help in some degree feeling with him. There ~~was~~ ₍ₐ₎is₍ₐ₎ that
~~p~~ remarkable charm & loveliness about Elly which seem to have
marked her for a fresher destiny. At the same time she is a very
old little person & I hope she'll not feel the weight of her
husband's years. Do write me yourself, beloved girl, & tell me yr.
impressions of all things—Dr. W., B. T., Kitty Prince &c.
Mother says you are doing nicely: I shall believe it far better if I
hear from you.—Florence pleases me passing well. I have never
seen a city, which took my fancy so fully & speedily. <u>C'est
une ville</u> <u>sympathique</u>. I took a long long walk this morning, as I
didn't feel in the mood for the Galleries. I went out to Fiesole—
"<u>my</u> Fiesole"—Mr's Brownings, of course that is,—& thence

away into the hills beyond it. ~~Lo~~ A lovely country—all pale olives *&* dark cypress—with beautiful views of Florence lying in her circle of hills like—like what?—like a chiselled jewel in a case of violet velvet! Farewell ton frère qui t'adore <u>H. J. jr.</u>

Previous publication: *HJL* 1: 144–49

ᕤ

126.17 ◊◊◊ scowled • [scow *overwrites illegible letters*]

126.25 y◊◊— • [— *overwrites* y◊◊]

126.26 ~~flimsi◊◊~~ flimsiest • [est *overwrites illegible letters*]

126.28 outfit • out= | fit

126.29 ~~a~~ of • [o *overwrites* a]

126.29 ◊ her • [h *overwrites illegible letter*]

126.31 architectural • archi= | tectural

126.34 necessarily • ne= | cessarily

127.1 ◊ Your • [Y *overwrites illegible letter*]

127.1 consolation • con= | solation

127.7 I'◊ I've • [v *overwrites illegible letter*]

127.13 edefice • [*misspelled*]

127.16 disfurnished • dis= | furnished

127.18 ~~sa~~ stands • [t *overwrites* a]

127.22 ◊◊g have • [ve *overwrites* ◊◊g]

127.26 ~~is~~ was • [wa *overwrites* is]

128.1–2 ◊◊ presentiment • [pr *overwrites illegible letters*]

128.6 ■■■■■ city • [city *overwrites illegible word*]

128.12 ◊◊ great • [gr *overwrites illegible letters*]

128.13 ~~remember~~ render it. • [nder it. *overwrites blotted* member]

128.15 ~~At~~ To • [To *overwrites* At]

128.21 ◊ The • [T *overwrites illegible letter*]

128.26–27 ~~p~~ behold • [b *overwrites* p]

128.30 ◊ at • [a *overwrites illegible letter*]

128.31 ~~color~~ couleur • [ouleu *overwrites blotted* olor]

128.31 Venitienne • [*misspelled*]

128.33–34 ~~it~~ of it • [f i *overwrites* it]

129.27 enconomy • [*misspelled*]

129.29 disgestive • [*misspelled*]

129.32 consult • con= | sult

130.5 ◊◊ fancy • [fa *overwrites illegible letters*]

130.12 ~~hav◊◊~~ having • [ing *overwrites illegible letters*]

130.24 ~~p~~ remarkable • [r *overwrites* p]

130.29 nicely • nice= | ly

131.1 ~~Lo~~ A • [A *overwrites* Lo]

131.4 ton frère [. . .] <u>H. J. jr.</u> • [*written across the letter's penultimate page*]

     ∾

126.8 Carissima Sorella • Dearest Sister.

126.11-13 The last news [. . .] before I left Venice • See HJ's 25, 26, [27] September [1869] letter to WJ.

127.10-11 Caffé Pedrocci • According to the 1868 *Northern Italy* Baedeker, the café is "opposite the University, an imposing and celebrated edifice with halls and columns of marble" (216).

127.12 ch. of San Antonio • Also called "Il Santo," the church is the burial place of Saint Anthony of Padua and was completed in 1424.

127.12 Eremitani • "An Augustine church of the middle of the 13th cent., judiciously restored a few years ago, with painted vaulting of wood, is a very long structure, and destitute of aisles, columns and pillars" (Baedeker, *Northern Italy* [1868] 218).

127.14 <u>Giotto's Chapel</u> • Giotto di Bondone (1266–1337), leading Italian painter of the late Middle Ages–early Renaissance period; in 1305-10 he decorated the Scrovegni Chapel, in Padua, which the 1868 *Northern Italy* Baedeker describes: "In a large garden adjoining the Piazza in front of the church [. . .], within the precincts of an ancient amphitheatre, is situated the *Madonna dell' Arena [. . .], a long, round-arched burial-chapel, erected in 1303. The lateral walls are completely covered with a series of **Frescoes, most of them in good preservation, by *Giotto*" (218).

128.23 Rue de Rivoli • A major street in downtown Paris, along which the Louvre, the Tuileries, and the Place du Palais-Royal are situated, running just east of the Champs-Elysées.

128.29 Guido • Guido Reni (1575–1642), Bolognese artist and student of the Carracci.

128.29 Domenichino • Dominico Zampieri, il Domenichino (1581–1641), Italian painter of Bolognese origin and a student of Ludovico Carracci.

128.29 the Caracci • Ludovico (1555–1619), Agostino (1557–1602), and Annibale Carracci (1560–1609), Bolognese artists and founders in 1585 of Bologna's Academia del Naturale (or degli Incamminiati); they influenced Guido Reni and Domenichino.

128.31–32 neither the ~~color~~ couleur Venitienne ni la <u>belle ligne Romaine</u> • neither the Venetian color nor the <u>beautiful Roman line</u>.

129.1 Après cela • Nevertheless.

129.3 Corregio • Antonio Allegri (1494–1534), or Correggio, was the most influential Renaissance painter from the school of Parma.

129.13–14 Uffizi & the Pitti Palace • At the time of HJ's travels, the Uffizi Gallery, founded by Lorenzo the Magnificent, was a comprehensive survey of Florentine schools of painting and considered especially interesting because they were exhibited in their native land. Connected to the Uffizi by the Vasari corridor, the Pitti Gallery housed the priceless treasures amassed by the Medici family.

129.14 <u>incroyables</u> • <u>incredible</u>.

130.3–4 Mrs. Horatio Greenough & daughter • Louisa Gore Greenough and her daughter, Charlotte.

130.5–6 J. Lorimer Graham jr • James Lorimer Graham (1835–76), U.S. consul to Italy after 1866 and founder of *Graham's Magazine* in New York City.

130.8 <u>Friday</u> • 8 October 1869.

130.9–10 mother's blessed letter of Sept. 21st, telling of Dr. Wilkinson's visit &c. • MWJ's 21 September [1869] letter to HJ (Houghton bMS Am 1093.1 [37]), tells of the day Dr. Garth Wilkinson spent visiting the Jameses in Cambridge.

130.10–11 a most characteristic & amusing one from Bob Temple • Robert Temple's 17 September 1869 letter to HJ.

130.12-13 father's [. . .] trouble with his boil • MWJ's 21 September [1869] letter to HJ tells of the boil Sr. had on the stump of his leg, which was preventing him from using his artificial limb.

130.14 his book • *The Secret of Swedenborg*.

130.16-17 Bob's (<u>our</u> Bob's) Texan plans tho' B. T. mentions his being in N. Y. "negotiating" on the subject • RJ had "been recommended as Treasurer & Secretary of a rail-road in Galveston Texas, with a salary of $1500," according to MWJ's 6 September [1869] letter to HJ; Robert (Bob) Temple mentioned in his letter of 17 September 1869 to HJ that RJ was "in New York negotiating for" this position.

130.17 B. T. • Robert (Bob) Temple.

130.22 Elly's • Ellen Temple.

130.28 Dr. W. • Dr. Garth Wilkinson.

130.28 Kitty Prince • Catharine (Kitty) James Prince (1834-90) was the youngest daughter of Rev. William James (1797-1868), the half brother of Sr. MWJ wrote HJ on 6 September [1869] that she had received "a note from Kitty Prince saying she is at Newton and will come and spend a few days with us"; MWJ tells of Kitty Prince's visit in her 21 September [1869] letter.

130.31-32 <u>C'est</u> une ville <u>sympathique</u> • It's a pleasant town.

130.33 Fiesole • Suburb of Florence.

131.4 ton frère qui t'adore • your adoring brother.

25 WILLIAM JAMES
7, [8] October [1869]
ALS Houghton
bMS Am 1094 (1935)

✉

30

Florence—Hotel de l'Europe
 Thursday October 7<u>th</u>
Dear W<u>m</u>.—

In writing to you some ten days since from Venice I
35 mentioned intending to write shortly again on another topic; *&*

as in a letter to Alice yesterday I threw out a hint on this topic, I
had better come to the point without delay. I ◊◊ hoped to find
here yesterday a letter from you, speaking of the receipt of a
little note I sent you just before leaving Switzerland; it had not
come however; but tho' it is probably not far distant I shall not   5
wait for it. ◊ I feel too strongly the need of emitting some cry
from the depths of my discomfort. I am sorry to have to put
things so darkly; but truth compels me to state that I have none
but the very worst news with regard to my old enemy no. 2—by
which of course I mean y̶ my unhappy bowels. Things have   10
reached that pass when I feel that something must be done—
what I know not, but I have a vague hope that you may be able
to throw some light on the subject. To begin with, it is of my
constipation, almost solely that I speak: those old attacks of pain
have almost completely disappeared—tho' t̶h̶e̶ a very small error   15
in diet is sufficient to s̶◊◊◊ start them up again. In spite of this I
suffer so perpetually ꝸ so keenly from this hideous repletion of
my belly that I feel as if my gain had been but small. That
immense improvement which I felt in England ceased as soon as
I touched the continent ꝸ tho' I have had ₄fleeting₍ₐ₎ moments   20
of relief d̶u̶r̶i̶n̶g̶ since the summer, my whole tendency,
considering my uninterrupted ꝸ vehement efforts to combats it
seems to have been to aggravation. When I reflect that after
seven months of the active, wholesome open-air life I have been
leading, I have no better tale to tell, I feel extremely miserable.   25
During this last month in Italy my sufferings seem to have come
to a climax. At Venice they came as near as possible to ◊ quite
defeating the pleasure of my stay, ꝸ the week of busy sightseeing
that I spent ө in the journey to this place has brought no
amelioration. I had great hopes of Italy in this matter—I fancied   30
I should get plenty of fruit ꝸ vegetables ꝸ that their effect would
be highly laxative. Fruit is abundant but I can eat ₄it₍ₐ₎ ◊ only in
small quantities; otherwise it produces pain. As for vegetables,
haricots verts ꝸ spinach are obtainable, but invariably fried in

grease—which quite robs them of their virtue. I have managed
on the whole to feed reasonably enough, however,—which is
only the more discouraging. I am compelled to eat a good
amount of meat. Leading the life I do, this is essential—& meat

5   is more nourishing & less crowding than other things. So I
always ◊◊◊ breakfast on a beefsteak. At dinner I have more meat
& a vegetable, which with a little fruit in the middle of the day is
my regular diet. Potatoes I long since ~~fore~~ forswore, & I am ~~not~~
now on the way to suppressing bread as nearly altogether as I

10 can. Wine I never touch—the common sorts are too bad & the
better too dear. ~~I~~ At dinner I drink Vienna beer & at breakfast
chocolate made with water. You must have been in Italy to
appreciate the repugnance that one acquires for the <u>water</u> of the
country as a beverage. Heaven knows what it passes thro' before

15 it reaches you. My bowels yearn for the <u>cuisine</u> of my own
happy land—& I think I should faint with joy at the sight a leg of
plain boiled mutton—a great mess of ◊◊ fresh vegetables—or a
basin of cracked wheat, flanked by a loaf of ~~plain~~ [ʌ]stale[ʌ]
brown bread. As regards diet however I might be worse off. The

20 régime I follow would be kindly enough for a case less cruelly
stubborn than mine. I may actually say that I <u>can't get</u> <u>a passage</u>.
My "little squirt" has ceased to have more than a nominal use.
The water either remains altogether or comes out as innocent as
it entered. For the past ten days I have become quite

25 demoralized & have been frantically dosing myself with pills. But
they too are almost useless & I may take a dozen & hardly hear of
them. In fact, I don't pretend to understand how I get on. When
I reflect upon the ʌutterly[ʌ] insignificant relation of what I get
rid of to what I imbibe, I wonder that flesh & blood can stand it.

30 ~~Upon my own~~ I find it in every way a grievous trial & my
wretched state alone prompts these outpourings. My condition
affects alike my mind & my body: it tells upon my ■■■ spirits
& takes all the lightness & freedom out of them; & more & more
as time goes by I feel what a drag it is upon my back. If I could

get a daily passage, I am sure my back would improve as rapidly
again, to say the least, as at present. To go about with this heavy
burden weighing down my loins is the worst thing in the world
for it. But this is quite a long enough recital of my miseries; I
have made it only as a preliminary to the question of practical   5
remedies. Somehow or other I must take the thing in hand. I
have regretted very much of late (how wisely I know not) that I
didn't get the opinion of some eminent London physician—or
some big Paris Authority. The memory of my happy condition
during my last month in England makes me feel as there I might   10
again find some relief. It was Malvern that started me up &
English cookery & English air that ~~again~~ helped me along
afterwards. It may surprise you to hear it—but here in this
distant Italy I find myself hankering after Malvern. If I should
return there I should submit to no treatment for my back, but   15
simply take the running sitzbaths. As I think of it (as I have done
many times) the idea assumes an enormous attraction—& the
vision of the beef & mutton ˄& the watery cauliflower[˄] of the
Malvern table & of great walks across the Malvern hills causes
my heart to beat & throb. I have good reason to believe that I   20
should suffer very much less now than I did last spring from the
monotony & dullness of the life. I can walk more & read more.—
On the other hand it would break my heart to leave Italy a
moment before I have had my fill. I fancy nevertheless that I
shall be obliged to make a very much shorter stay here than I   25
originally intended. If my condition remains as it is I shall go
thro' the country rapidly & be ready to leave it about three
months hence, instead of six. Long before then I hope to have
heard from you & if you suggest nothing more practicable I shall
think seriously of making straight for Malvern. Mention if you   30
are able to the names of a couple of the great Paris & London
doctors. In the latter place I know of Sir Wᵐ Ferguson &
Mr. Paget; but you may tell me something more to the
purpose.—Beloved brother, I hope you'll not let this dreary

effusion weigh upon your spirits. I thought it best to be frank *&*
copious. My petty miseries seem but small when I think I have
such a guide *&* friend as you, to slop over to—*&* am so divinely
blessed with means that I can freely consider of remedies *&*

5 methods. I have written not in passion but in patience. Speak to
father *&* mother of all this in such terms as you think best. I
expect a letter from you tomorrow *&* shall keep this over, so that
I may add a word. I say nothing of Florence nor of yourself. You
can both wait. —(████ B◊◊ ~~suppressed the~~ [A]every[A] ~~allusion~~

10 [A]a[A] ~~in other letters~~ ████ ████ Friday. A letter from mother
& one from B. Temple (a most amusing one) but none, oh, my
brother, from you. Mother, however, gives me your message—
that you want awfully to write, but that you've so much to say
you don't dare to begin. Allons, du courage! She says nothing

15 more about your visits to Newport *&* Lenox—from wh. I infer
that they were given up. I was extremely interested, as you may
suppose, in her mention of Dr. Wilkinson's ~~dig~~ diagnosis *&*
prescription for you. I palpitate to hear more *&* invoke the next
mail with tears in my eyes. Cut out *&* send me your notices in

20 the A N. A. R. À propos, I again receive the Nation. It comes
apparently ~~thro~~[×] ∧from[A] the office *&* always thro' Lombard *&*
Odier *&* Ө thence thro' my subsequent bankers. As it is not well
to have it ~~m~~ pass thro' so many hands *&* yet difficult to keep
making them change my address at the office, you had better

25 make them send my copy thence to you, so that you may mail it
weekly, just as you do your letters. Pray act upon this *&* if. —I
have been reading over what I wrote yesterday *&* am half-
dismayed at its dismal aspect. But I shall not change it, as it
reflects fairly the facts of the case. —To day the Malvern plan

30 seems wild *&* unnatural: tomorrow it will again seem judicious.
So oscillates the morbid human spirit. —Florence looks so
promising *&* pleasant that I feel as if it would be a delightful
thing to settle down here for a winter *&* pass the time with
pictures *&* books. I mustn't think of the books, in any serious

way, but I hope during whatever stay I make, to plunge deeply
into the pictures. I had a most interesting journey here from
Venice, tho' I have written Alice an extremely stupid letter on
the subject. To tell the truth, for some ~~time~~ ∧days[∧] past my
peculiar affliction has developed the faculty of giving me an out   5
& out <u>headache</u> & it was under this influence that I wrote. But
this is probably but temporary, "Considering," my head has
always been remarkably easy. True, I have used it so little. I hope
to write you something satisfactory about the things here.
B. Cellini's <u>Perseus</u>, in the great square, quite deserves the fuss   10
he makes about it in his book. It kills M. Angelo's <u>David</u>. But I
must knock off. Answer my question about the physicians &
above all don't let this nasty effusion prey upon your spirits.
Tout à toi <u>H. J</u> jr

15

✉

<u>Stati Uniti di America</u>
   W<u>m</u> James esq
      Quincy St.
         Cambridge   20
            <u>Mass.</u>
<u>Etats Unis</u> d'Amerique

Two postmarks: FIRENZE 9 | OTT 69 | 12 M
MILANO STAZ. | 10 OTT 69 | 10 M   25

HJ wrote, in pencil, under WJ's name and to the left of the address: "<u>Private</u>."
Other drawings and notes on the envelope are not in HJ's hand.

Previous publication: *CWJ* 1: 103–7; *WHSL* 49–51

∞

  135.2 ◇◇ hoped • [ho *overwrites illegible letters*]
  135.6 ◇ I • [I *overwrites illegible letter*]
  135.10 ~~y~~ my • [m *overwrites* y]
  135.15 ~~the~~ a • [a *overwrites* the]

135.16 ~~s◊◊◊~~ start • [tar *overwrites illegible letters*]

135.20 continent • con= | tinent

135.21 ~~during~~ since • [since *overwrites* duri]

135.21 tendency • ten= | dency

135.22 vehement • ve= | hement

135.27 ◊ quite • [q *overwrites illegible letter*]

135.29 ~~o~~ in • [i *overwrites* o]

135.32 ◊ only • [o *overwrites illegible letter*]

136.6 ◊◊◊ breakfast • [bre *overwrites illegible letters*]

136.8 ~~fore~~ forswore • [s *overwrites* e]

136.8–9 ~~not~~ now • [w *overwrites* t]

136.9 altogether • alto= | gether

136.11 ~~I~~ At • [A *overwrites* I]

136.17 ◊◊ fresh • [fr *overwrites illegible letters*]

136.32 ■■■■■■ spirits • [spirits *overwrites blotted illegible word*]

137.24 nevertheless • neverthe= | less

138.17 ~~dig~~ diagnosis • [a *overwrites blotted* g]

138.20 ~~A~~ N • [N *overwrites* A]

138.20 receive • re= | ceive

138.22 ~~O~~ thence • [th *overwrites* O]

138.23 ~~m~~ pass • [p *overwrites* m]

138.26 <u>upon this</u> ~~if.~~— • [. — *overwrites blotted* —if]

139.11 he makes [. . .]. But I • [*written across the letter's penultimate page*]

139.12–14 must knock [. . .] <u>H. J jr</u> • [*written across the letter's first page*]

139.22 <u>d'Amerique</u> • [*misspelled*]

∽

134.34 In writing to you some ten days since • HJ to WJ, 25, 26, [27] September [1869].

135.1 in a letter to Alice [. . .] a hint • See HJ to AJ 6, [8] October [1869].

135.34 <u>haricots verts</u> • <u>string beans</u>.

137.32 Sir W<u>m</u> Ferguson • Sir William Fergusson (1808–77), Scottish surgeon, professor of surgery at King's College, London (1840–70), afterward clinical professor of surgery and senior surgery at the same college; named sergeant-surgeon to the queen in 1867, elected to the council of the College of Surgeons in 1861 and president in 1870 (*Dictionary of National Biography*).

137.33 Mr. Paget • George Edward Paget (K. C. B. in 1885), physician to Addenbrooke's Hospital, bursar of Caius College, Cambridge, elected to the Royal College of Physicians, London (1839), president of the General Council of Medical Education and Registration (elected 1869) (*Dictionary of National Biography*).

138.10 Friday • 8 October 1869.

138.10–11 A letter from mother & one from B. Temple • MWJ's letter to HJ of 21 September [1869] and Bob Temple's 17 September 1869 letter.

138.14 Allons, du courage! • Come on, be brave!

138.19–20 Cut out & send me your notices in the A N. A. R. • WJ's review of Horace Bushnell's *Women's Suffrage; The Reform against Nature* (1869) and John Stuart Mill's *The Subjection of Women* (1869) appeared in the *North American Review* 109 (October 1869): 556–65.

139.3 I have written Alice • HJ's 6, [8] October [1869] letter to AJ.

139.10 B. Cellini's Perseus • Benvenuto Cellini (1500–1571) sculpted the bronze *Perseus* (1545–54) holding the head of Medusa. It is displayed in the Loggia dei Lanzi, Florence.

139.14 Tout à toi • All yours.

MARY WALSH JAMES
13, 16 [17] October [1869]
ALS Houghton
bMS Am 1094 (1764)

30

Florence Hotel de l'Europe, Oct. 13th

My darling Mammy—

I wrote to Alice only a week ago & tho' in the interval nothing has occurred to interrupt the monotony of my career, such is the   35

141

weakness of the human heart, that I must again fall a-scribbling & prattling to my dearest mamma. At the moment I wrote to Alice I received a lovely letter from you, of Sept. 21ˢᵗ—telling of Dr. Wilkinsons' visit &c. You had begun to worry (as I feared

5   you might) over that long suspension of my letters in Switzerland: but by this time your doubts will have been replaced by better feelings. I have told of my journey hither & of my 1ˢᵗ impressions of Florence. My later ones are quite as pleasant, & if I should ever feel like living awhile in Italy I fancy

10 I should choose this place. Not that it strikes me as a particularly cheerful city: its aspect—thanks to the narrowness of many of the streets & the vast cyclopean structure of many of the buildings is, rather gloomy than otherwise. But it has the gaiety of plenty of business (apparently) plenty of comfort & of

15 strangers & of an unsurpassed collection of art treasures; & then it has on all sides the loveliest <u>échappées</u> into the beautiful hills among which it lies deposited, like an egg in a nest. I have been spending my days in a p̶ regular philosophical appreciation of things. I have gone each morning to the great Uffizzi Gallery to

20 commune with the immortals & in the afternoon I have taken a good walk out into the country. I have not yet opened the chapter of churches, having been recently rather over- churched—save to stare with the proper & inevitable feelings at the magnificent many-colored, marble-plated walls & dome of

25 the Cathedral. I have not even been to see M. Angelo's Medicean statues at St. Lorenzo. I take a rare satisfaction in keeping this adventure in reserve, till my appetite is of just that temper to r̶l̶ relish the <u>haut goût</u> of the affair. A journey t̶o̶ in Italy moreover, is a great killer of impatience. You learn not only

30 to wait—but in a degree, to like to wait. So as yet I have only done the Uffizzi—& that incompletely. There is so much more to say about ₍ₐ₎it₍ₐ₎ that I can begin to even hint at, that it were easier to let i̶t̶ talking alone altogether. The great things on the whole, I suppose, are the R̶a̶f̶a̶e̶e̶ Rafaels—which give one a

feeling distinct from the works of any other painter. More, far more than others, he seems to have been a genius pure & simple, unalloyed & unmodified by the struggles of development & the teachings of experience. The succession of his famous "three manners" is apparently nothing more than the order of youth manhood & maturity. How interesting this is, at once, & how uninteresting, you must see his pictures to understand. But until you have seen them, I fancy, you lack an adequate conception of the beauty of Genius—of simple intellectual spontaneity—per se. I say its beauty—I mean its exquisite unutterable beauty. As regards meaning & character, religious feeling &c I don't believe there is much more in his works than the spectator ∧himself∧ p infuses under the inspiration of the moment—the influence that descends from them & lifts him from the level of his common point of view. What they contain, is a sort of general formal indifferent beauty. But we poor vulgarians, catalogue in hand, find it hard to conceive a man working in such magnificent freedom & in order to get a purchase on the works we furnish them provisionally with this spiritual element, ∧by∧ which in their high superiority, they neither gain nor lose. Their beauty seems a direct result of the fact that to Rafael apparently, the world was clear, tranquil & serene—he looked at things & they pleased him. You don't in the least feel about his figures as about many others—M. Angelo's especially—that they might have been ~~ugliness~~ ugly—that they have escaped it by so much more or less.—I suppose it's in the nature ∧of∧ the mind to rebel against the violent ~~dominn~~ dominance of even delightful sensations. At any rate, half out of spite to the Italian painters, two of the things that I most enjoy at the Uffizi are a magnificent Albert Dürer & a most celestial Memling or Hemling—or whatever it may be. I enjoy immensely standing before them & murmuring invidiously "Ah que c'est bien Allemand—que c'est bien Flamand!"—But you'll not care, beloved Mammy, for more of this dreary stuff. And yet to what

else shall I treat you? Except pictures & churches I see but little.
For the past 6 weeks that I have been in Italy I've ~~not~~ ∧hardly[∧]
until within a day or two exchanged five minutes' talk with any
one but the servants in the hotels & the custodians in the
churches. As far as meeting people is concerned, I've not as yet
had in Europe a very brilliant record. Yesterday I met at the
Uffizi Miss Anna Vernon of Newport & her friend Mrs. Carter
with whom I had some discourse; & on the same morning I fell
in with a somewhat seedy & sickly American, who seemed to be
▇▇▇ doing the Gallery with an awful minuteness, & who after
some conversation proposed to come & see me. He called this
evening & has just left; but he seems a vague & feeble brother & I
anticipate no wondrous joy from his acquaintance. The "hardly"
in the clause above is meant to admit two or three Englishmen
with whom I have been thrown for a few hours. One especially,
whom I met at Verona won my affections so rapidly that I was
really sad at losing him. But he has vanished leaving only a
delightful impression & not even a name—a man of about 38
with a sort of quiet perfection of English virtue about him, such
as I have rarely found in another. Willy asked me in one of his
recent letters for an "opinion" of the English, which I haven't
yet ~~h◇◇~~ had time to give—tho' at times I have felt as if it were a
theme on which I could write from a full mind. In fact, however,
I ∧have[∧] very little right to have any opinion on the matter. I've
seen far too few specimens & those ~~tw~~ too superficially. The
only thing I'm certain about is that I like them—like them
heartily. W. asked if as individuals they "kill" the individual
American. To this I would say that the Englishmen I have met
not only kill, but bury in unfathomable depths, the Americans I
have met. A set of people ◇◇ less framed to provoke national
self-complacency than the latter it would be hard to ◇◇ imagine.
~~I think~~ There is but one word to use ~~to~~ in regard to them—
vulgar, vulgar, vulgar. Their ignorance—their stingy grudging
defiant attitude towards everything European—their perpetual

reference of all things to ∧some[∧] American standard or precedent which exists only in their own unscrupulous wind-bags—& then our unhappy poverty of voice, of speech & of physiognomy—these things glare at you hideously. On the other hand, we seem a people of <u>character</u>, we seem to have energy,   5
capacity & intellectual stuff in ample measure. I What I have ⬦ hinted at as our vices are the elements of the modern man with <u>culture</u> quite left out. It's the absolute & incredible lack of <u>culture</u> that strikes you in common travelling Americans. The E̶n̶ pleasantness of the English, on the other side, comes in a   10
great measure from the fact of their each having been dipped into [*the*] crucible which gives them a sort of coating of comely f varnish & color. They have been smoothed & polished by mutual social attrition. They have manners & a language. We lack both, but particularly the latter. I have seen very "nasty" Britons,   15
certainly, but as a rule they are such as to cause your heart to warm to them. The women are at once better & worse than the men. Occasionally they are h̶a̶d̶ hard & flat & greasy & dowdy to downright repulsiveness; but frequently they have a modest matronly charm which is the perfection of womanishness & wh.   20
makes Italian & French women—& to a certain extent even our own—seem like a species of feverish highly-developed invalids. You see Englishmen, here in Italy, to a particularly good advantage. In the midst of these false & beautiful Italians they glow with the light of the great fact, that after all, they love a   25
bath-tub & they hate ⬦ a ⬦⬦ lie.—<u>16th, Sunday</u>. I <u>have</u> seen some nice Americans & I still love my country. I e̶ have called upon Mrs. Huntington [*and her*] 2 daughters—late of Cambridge—whom I met in Switzerland & who have an apartment here. The daughters more than reconcile me to the shrill voiced syrens of   30
New England's rock-bound coast. The youngest is delightfully beautiful & sweet—& the elder delightfully sweet & plain—with a plainness <u>qui vaut</u> <u>bien des</u> <u>beautés</u>. I'm to go there this evening to meet certain Perkinses who live here—or near by. With the

H.'s is a Miss Gray. I know not who she is—save that she's concentrated Brookline. The Nortons are to arrive here about a week hence. I have just got a letter from Jane. I have not heard from A. K. in a month. I owe her however a letter. I don't know

5 when we shall meet—perhaps not till the spring when we may be together in Paris. Mamman de mon âme, farewell. I have kept my letter 3 days, hoping for news from home. I hope your'e not paying me back for that silence of 6 weeks ago. Blessings on your universal heads. The lone ~~exile~~ and loving exile—H. J. jr

10 I have just read Ste. Beuve's death. I have lost my best friend.—

Previous publication: Lubbock 1: 21–23; *HJL* 1: 149–53

∾

142.6 Switzerland • Switzer= | land

142.15 unsurpassed • unsur= | passed

142.18 ~~p~~ regular • [r *overwrites* p]

142.22–23 over- | churched • over-churched

142.28 ~~rl~~ relish • [el *overwrites* l]

142.28 ~~to~~ in • [in *overwrites* to]

142.33 ~~it~~ talking • [ta *overwrites* it]

142.34 ~~Rafaee~~ Rafaels • [ae *overwrites* aee]

143.12–13 ~~p~~ infuses • [in *overwrites blotted* p]

143.15 ~~¦~~ • [*blotted out*]

143.25 ~~ugliness~~ ugly— • [y *overwrites* i *and* — *overwrites blotted* ness]

143.27 ~~dominn~~ dominance • [a *overwrites* n]

144.10 ██████ doing • [doing *overwrites illegible word*]

144.21 recent • re= | cent

144.22 ~~hoo~~ had • [ad *overwrites illegible letters*]

144.25 ~~tw~~ too • [o *overwrites* w]

144.30 ~~◊◊~~ less • [le *overwrites illegible letters*]

144.31 ~~◊◊~~ imagine • [im *overwrites illegible letters*]

144.32 ~~I think~~ There • [There *overwrites* I think]

144.32 ~~to~~ in • [in *overwrites* to]

145.2–3 wind- | bags • wind-bags

145.6 ~~I~~ What • [W *overwrites* I]

145.6–7 ⋄ hinted • [h *overwrites blotted illegible letter*]

145.10 E̶n̶ pleasantness • [pl *overwrites* En]

145.12 [*the*] crucible • [*ms. damaged; We follow Edel, who may have seen the ms. before it was torn*]

145.12–13 f varnish • [v *overwrites* f]

145.15 particularly • partic= | ularly

145.18 h̶a̶d̶ hard • [r *overwrites* d]

145.26 ⋄ a • [a *overwrites illegible letter*]

145.26 ⋄⋄ lie • [l *overwrites illegible letter and* i *overwrites blotted illegible letter*]

145.27 e̶ have • [h *overwrites* c]

145.28 [*and her*] • [*ms. damaged; We follow Edel, who may have seen the ms. before it was torn*]

146.6 Mamman • [*misspelled*]

146.9 e̶x̶i̶l̶e̶ and • [and *overwrites* exile]

146.10 I have just read Ste. Beuve's death. I have lost my best friend.— • [*written across the letter's first page*]

∾

141.34 I wrote to Alice only a week ago • HJ to AJ 6, [8] October [1869].

142.3–4 letter from you, of Sept. 21ˢᵗ—telling of Dr. Wilkinson's visit • MWJ's 21 September [1869] letter from Cambridge tells about Garth Wilkinson's two-week visit in 1869 to the northeast United States and the St. Lawrence Valley, including a day spent with the Jameses in Cambridge.

142.16 échappées • vistas.

142.25–26 M. Angelo's Medicean statues at St. Lorenzo • Monumental tombs, with sculptures of Giuliano de' Medici and Lorenzo de' Medici, the son and grandson of Lorenzo the Magnificent in the New Sacristy, Church of San Lorenzo.

142.28 haut goût • refined taste.

143.30–31 Memling or Hemling • Hans Memling (c. 1435–94), Flemish painter of the Bruges school; two of his major works at the Uffizi Gallery are *St. Benedict* (1487) and *Portrait of Benedetto Portinari* (1487).

143.32–33 Ah que c'est bien Allemand—que c'est bien Flamand! • Oh, how typically German, how typically Flemish!

145.26 16th, Sunday · 16 October 1869 was a Saturday.

145.33 qui vaut bien des beautés · that is worth many beauties.

145.34 Perkinses · Charles Callahan Perkins (1823–86), Boston art critic, and his wife, Frances D. Bruen (married 1855), had lived in Rome and Paris and kept a summer home in Newport. Perkins was one of the founders of the Boston Museum of Fine Arts.

146.4 A. K. · Aunt Kate.

146.6 Mamman de mon âme, farewell. · Mammy of my soul, farewell.

146.10 Ste. Beuve's death · Charles Augustin Sainte-Beuve died in Paris on 13 October 1869.

The last page of the ms. includes two pencil drawings on it, probably by WJ.

WILLIAM JAMES

16 [17], 19 October [1869]

ALS Houghton

bMS Am 1094 (1936)

Florence, Hotel de l'Europe
        October 16th Sunday.

My dear Wm. I wrote you a week ago a letter such as ought to be followed up, I feel, by some further communication. I don't want to incur the charge of harrowing you up—without at least raking you over. I hoped by this time to have got a letter from you; but I receive nothing but cold head-shakes from the portier. Since, then, I've undertaken this "startling exposé" of my condition, I will proceed to draw the curtain altogether. I felt very blue at having to write to you as I did; but I was glad I had done so; inasmuch as after I ⋄ had to sent my letter, matters came to a crisis which ₐmade₍ₐ₎ me feel that they were truly serious ⋄ that if you were to give me any hints the sooner I got them the better. I have just written to mother, without speaking of being unwell. But you had better let father know that I am not quite all that I should be, since if I should be obliged (as I still hope not to be, however) to do anything or go anywhere for this special reason, so much of the tiresome story may be known.—I was feeling very badly when I wrote you: <u>je ne tardai pas</u> to feel worse. For a week, owing to the state of my bowels, my head ɗ stomach had been all out of order. What I have called the "crisis" was brought on by taking 2 so-called "antibilious" pills, recommended me at the English druggists'. They failed to relieve me ɗ completely disagreed with me—bringing ₍∧₎on₍∧₎ a species of abortive diarrhoea. That is I felt the most reiterated ɗ most violent inclination to stool, without being able to effect anything save the passage of a little blood. Meanwhile my head got much worse ɗ this was accompanied by a gradual violent chill. Whereupon I took to my bed, ɗ here the chill began to merge into a fever, with cramps in my feet ɗ legs—my bowels horribly stuffed ɗ my head <u>infernal</u>. Of course I sent for the English—(or rather, as he turned out the Irish) physician. (I believe there are several here.) He ~~de~~ concentrated his energies upon getting me a stool as speedily as possible. That is he made me take an injection, of some unknown elements, which completely failed to move me. I repeated it largely—wholly in vain. He left me late in the evening, apparently quite in despair; ɗ between my abdomen ɗ my head, I passed a very hard night ɗ one such as I should be sorry to endure the repetition of. Towards morning some pills wh. he had given ₍∧₎me₍∧₎ began to procure me comparative relief, tho' my head was slow to clear up. Eventually however with reiterated pills I began to mend ɗ that afternoon went out into the air. Several days have now passed. I have seen the doctor repeatedly, as he seems inclined (to what extent as a friend ɗ to what as a doctor ɗ I ignore) to keep me ₍∧₎in₍∧₎ hand. He has prescibed me ~~so~~ a peculiar species of <u>aloetic</u> pill, to be taken an hour before dinner, wh. he hopes ~~will~~ if kept up long enough will woo me into an habitual action. <u>Je ne demande pas mieux</u>, so long as that in the interval, I can keep tolerably comfortable—which is the difficult point. He says, what is doubtless true—that my bowels have been more injured by large injections in the past, than by the abuse of medicine. He examined them (as far as he could) by the

5   insertion of his finger (horrid tale!) & says there is no palpable obstruction. He seemed surprised however that I haven't piles; you see we have always something to be grateful for. On the whole nevertheless I find it hard to make him (as I should anyone who had'n't observed it) at all understand the

10   stubbornness & extent—the length & breadth & depth, of my trouble. He indulges in plenty of vague remarks about diet, exercise & not reading—which you will admit that I have earned the right to dispense with.—Of course all this business has left me uncomfortable in the present & apprehensive ~~in~~ of the

15   future. At this present moment of my writing, I know neither how I'm to do without a stool, nor how (in spite of the doctor's pills, as yet) ~~ho~~ I am to get one. The whole matter occupies perforce (how gracefully!) the foreground of my thoughts & oppresses equally my mind & my body. It seems hardly worth

20   while to be in this great Italy on such a footing; but <u>enfin</u> circumstances are what they are; & mine might be very much worse. My trouble is a bad one, but ~~my~~ the circumstances ~~w~~ are very well; especially this of my sitting scribbling to you. Of course I feel even more than when I last wrote that some change

25   is imperative & that this state ∧of things[∧] must ▪▪▪▪ discontinue ~~you~~ <u>au plus tôt</u>. But as you see however I am not much nearer to finding an issue, & meanwhile my daily life becomes rather less than₁ more comfortable. Let me not however use too dark colors. I find the best restaurant here—the

30   Café de Paris—very sufficient to my dietetic needs. I can get ▪▪▪▪ things done quite à l'anglaise. I have entered ~~with~~ ∧into[∧] renewed engagements with myself with regard to eating & drinking, & by means of these, the doctor's pills & ~~a contrived~~ [∧]the[∧] ◇◇ same active life that I been leading so long (tho' with

only <u>this</u> <u>very</u> result against ∧which[∧] I now appeal to it!) I hope
to hold out till the dawning of some change.—But this matter of
an active life ▨▨▨▨ suggests precisely the most serious point in
these late developments. They have brought with them a rapidly
growing sense of the relation between the state of my bowels &
my <u>back</u>. My actual situation is complicated by the fact that this
recent terrible constipation has made itself <u>directly</u> felt in my
back (the lower part, across the base, loins & hips) to such a
degree that it becomes an added effort to take that amount of
exercise needful to combat this same constipation. I feel this
heaviness of the bowels across my loins more palpably &
~~unmistakea~~ unmistakably than I can express to you. I have
always felt in a general way that if my bowels were regular, my
back would be better; but it is only within the past few weeks
that I have realized keenly the connection between the two &
been able to measure the load of which my back would be
lightened if I could keep my abdomen free. Formerly I had two
∧distinct[∧] troubles—my contsipation & my pain in my back. I
now see that what I still retain of the latter is in a large degree
but another phase of the former. ~~While the former lasts~~ I draw
from this fact a stupendous hope—it shines to me as a light out
of the darkness: & I depend upon it for drawing to your mind, by
its cheering influence, the barbarity of this appeal to your
sympathies. To put it in a wor[d], I feel justified in believing that
if, by at the end of a month, (no matter how—by some miracle!)
I had established a healthy action of my bowels, my back would
by a corresponding movement have made a leap not of a <u>month</u>,
but of a year—of two, three—what you please. I should feel in
other words <u>immediately</u> an improvement which I have been
used to consider a thing of very distant days. I dont mean to say
that the relation between these two localities has always been
the same: but there came a moment on the march of
improvement ∧when[∧] the one overtook & outstripped the
other, & has ever since been clogged & held back by it.

Disengaged from this fatal grasp it would at once advance to the end of its own chain—a longer one than than I have yet ventured to fancy.—These reflections fill me with a perfectly <u>passionate</u> desire for a reformation in my bowels. I see in it not

5 only the ~~reformation~~ ◊◊◊ question of a special localized affection, but a large general change in my ~~life~~ condition ɟ a blissful renovation of my life—the reappearance above the horizon of pleasures which had well-nigh sunk forever behind that great murky pile of undiminishing contingencies to which

10 my gaze has so long been accustomed. It would ◊◊ result in the course of ₍ₐ₎a₍ₐ₎ comparatively short time, a return to repose— reading—hopes ɟ ideas—an escape from this weary word of idleness. But I needn't descant further: a word to the wise is enough.—You may imagine that there's nothing I am not ready

15 to do to compass my desire. At present the prescription seems to be that hardest of all things—to wait. Well—I'll even wait. I shall remain in Florence until one way or the other I get some news of a change. I shall do so almost <u>mechanically</u>, for I confess that in my present physica~~lly~~ condition—with this perpetual

20 oppression of the inner ɟ outer man—to enjoy things keenly is difficult. If I get no better, I shall not push on to Rome. ~~I~~ Such at least is my present disposition. It would <u>spoil</u> Rome to see it ~~in such a way~~ under this perpetual drawback. To go there simply as travelling ɟ as therefore beneficial would moreover not

25 be worthwhile, as here for some time to come I can get a sufficiency of movement. If I leave Florence <u>not</u> for Rome, I don't see what is left for me but to go to <u>Malvern</u>—a matter on wh. I touched in my last. I am not wrong I think, in attributing to Malvern ◊ my condition during the last part of my stay in

30 England; ɟ I feel now that once possessed of a similar <u>start</u>, I should not let it slip from me as before. I should, however, deeply regret being forced to take this step ɟ to turn my back upon Italy. The thought is horrible. Not only should I lose what may possibly be the most delightful ɟ valuable part of this

Italian experience; but I should find my subsequent plans grievously disarranged. It is my dearest desire to get three months of England, in the fine season, before my return—to sail if possible thence. To take them now in midwinter would of course be a poor substitute.—On the other side, if I should ~~gain~~ make a solid gain by a couple of mos. at Malvern, it would reconcile me to everything. Such a start, I say, I would undertake to keep; & with my bowels thus regenerated I would laugh Italy to scorn. I should then feel comparatively small need of leading a life of sight-seeing & should not hesitate to claim from the days a fair allowance of reading. With this consolation—I should ask f but for a moderate daily sitting—I should either remain in England (i.e. London) or resort to Paris & abide there till such a moment as I should feel prepared to venture on Germany. ~~There~~ Thence, after a sojourn the duration of which I don't now pretend to fix—I should return to Cambridge & I devoutly trust to work.—

"The thought grows frightful, 'tis so wildly dear!" All this hangs as you see—on a feeble thread—but it <u>does</u> hang.—Meanwhile I eat beans & pease & grapes ∧& figs[∧] & walk—walk—walk—in the hope of an <u>occasional</u> stool.—This is the end of my long story. I feel the better for having written it: I hope you will feel none the worse for reading it. Its because I know you not to be a maudlin & hysterical youth that I have let myself out. But dont think me a great fool if you should suddenly get a letter from me from England. I can imagine ~~my being~~ ◊ my being <u>forced</u> to fly, in desperation. For instance I don't think I could withstand the effects of another attack like that last—for tho' the "crisis" was accelerated by improper medicine I'm sure I felt all ripe for it. But I have good hopes of evading such miseries¦ ∧& remaining here—at any rate.[∧] Having opened up the subject at such a rate, I shall of course keep you informed.—To shew you haven't taken this too ill, for heaven's sake make me a letter about your own health—poor modest flower!—Commend me most lovingly

to my parents & sister. Write to me to as good purpose as
(without worrying) you may & believe me your brother <u>H. J. jr</u>

P.S. It's no more than just that the family should in some
form repay themselves for your medical education. And what is
a doctor meant for but to listen to old women's <u>doléances</u>?—
Don't lose sight of that good news about my back.

—

Give my love, when you see him to frank Washburn & tell
him I long for news of him—& that if he should ever feel like
sending me a line the gracious act would rank among benefits
remembered. Let him remember Pisa & that Florence is but a
larger sort of Pisa.

—

I get no news at all of ~~W~~ O W H. jr.—Tell him—I hate him
most damnably; I never knew till the past few mos. how much;
but that I yet think I shall write to him

19<u>th</u> I have kept my letter till today, hoping I might have one
from home to acknowledge.—But I close it, sick unto death of
vain waiting.—I see in it nothing to alter—& nothing to add save
the adjuration to <u>take it</u> <u>easy</u>!—The Malvern plan is very thin: I
don't see how I <u>can</u> leave Italy.—While there is life there is
hope.—Address me as I wrote you: MM. Em. Fenzi & Cie.
Banquiers Florence, Italy. If I go to Rome they will forward & if
I am likely to be there more than a mo. I will give you a new
address. Pray stop the <u>Atlantic</u>, coming from the office. It keeps
coming like the Nation whereof I wrote you, thro' Lombard
Odier & Cie, & after them thro' a string of Bankers who each
charge a commission I suppose. If you could have it sent you
from the office & mail it ~~yourself~~ yourselves as you do my letters
I should ~~peo~~ prefer it. I made this same request about the
Nation. If this is inconvenient, it would be better to suppress
them.

Previous publication: *SL* 2: 44–49; *CWJ* 1: 107–12

148.30 ◇ had • [h *overwrites illegible letter*]

148.30 ~~lo~~ sent • [se *overwrites* lo]

149.7 antibilious • anti- | -bilious

149.8 English • Eng- | lish

149.18 ~~de~~ concentrated • [co *overwrites* de]

149.19 speedily • spee- | dily

149.29 inclined • in- | clined

149.31 prescibed • [*misspelled*]

149.31 ~~so~~ a • [a *overwrites* so]

149.33 ~~will~~ if • [if *overwrites* wi; ll *blotted out*]

150.1 tolerably • toler= | ably

150.6 surprised • sur- | prised

150.8 nevertheless • neverthe- | less

150.14 ~~in~~ of • [of *overwrites* in]

150.17 ~~ho~~ I • [I *overwrites* ho]

150.22 ~~my~~ the • [the *overwrites* my]

150.22 circumstances • circum- | stances

150.22 ~~w~~ are • [are *overwrites* w]

150.31 ■■■■ things • [thin *overwrites illegible word*]

150.34 ◇◇ same • [sa *overwrites illegible letters*]

151.3 ■■■■ suggests • [su *overwrites illegible word and* ggests *inserted*]

151.11 heaviness • heavi- | ness

151.12 ~~unmistakea~~ unmistakably • [a *overwrites* ea]

151.12 express • ex- | press

151.18 contsipation • [*misspelled*]

151.24 wor[d] • [*ms damaged*]

152.2 than than • than | than

152.4 reformation • refor= | mation

152.5 ◇◇◇ question • [que *overwrites illegible letters*]

152.6 ~~life~~ condition • [cond *overwrites* life]

152.9 contingencies • con- | tingencies

152.10 ◇◇ result • [re *overwrites illegible letters*]

152.15 present • pre- | sent

152.18 confess • con= | fess

152.19 physical~~ly~~ • [ly *blotted out*]

152.20 oppression • op- | pression

152.21 ~~I~~ Such • [S *overwrites* I]

152.29 ◇ my • [m *overwrites illegible letter*]

153.6 ~~gain~~ make • [make *overwrites* gain]

153.12 f but • [but *overwrites* f]

153.15 ~~There~~ Thence • [nce *overwrites* re]

153.26 ~~my being~~ • [*blotted out*]

153.26 ◇ my • [m *overwrites illegible letter*]

153.30 | ∧ • [∧ *overwrites* .]

154.14 ~~W~~ O W H. jr. • [O *overwrites* W]

154.29 ~~yourself~~ yourselves • [f *struck through and* ves *inserted*]

154.30 ~~pe◇~~ prefer • [r *overwrites* e◇]

∾

148.21 October 16<u>th</u> Sunday • October 16 was a Saturday.

148.22 I wrote you a week ago • HJ's letter of 7, [8] October was posted on the 9th.

148.27 portier • porter.

148.33 I have just written to mother • HJ's 13, 16 [17] October [1869] letter to MWJ.

149.4–5 je ne tardai pas • it wasn't long before I began.

149.17 English—([. . .] Irish) physician • Dr. Duffy, who, according to Murray's 1867 *Central Italy*, was a "fellow of the College of Surgeons in Ireland, and who has practised in London, 10, Via dei Tornabuoni" (85).

149.34 Je ne demande pas mieux • I don't ask for anything more.

150.20 enfin • in the end.

150.26 au plus tôt • at the earliest.

153.18 "The thought grows frightful, 'tis so wildly dear!" • Robert Browning's "Pictor Ignotus" (1.40), from *Men and Women* (1855).

154.5 doléances • complaints.

HENRY JAMES SR.
24, 25, [26] October [1869]
ALS Houghton
bMS Am 1094 (1765)

5

Florence Hotel de l'Europe
October 24<u>th</u>

My dearest Daddy—

I feel as if I should write a very dismal letter; nevertheless, 10
write I must, tho' it be but three lines. There are moments when
I feel more keenly than ever the cheerlessness of solitude & the
bitterness of exile. Such a one is the present. The weather has
turned fearfully bleak & cold, & gloomy skies & piercing winds
are the order of the day. The dusk has fallen upon my small & 15
frigid apartment & I have lit my candle to warm my fingers—as I
begin this letter to warm my thoughts. Happy Florence is going
to ~~sup~~ ∧dine∧ en famille & to enjoy the delights of mutual
conversation.—Well; so be it: it's something to have a famille to
write to if not to dine & converse with.—I have recently come in 20
from a long walk in the Cascine—the great Bois de Boulogne of
Florence—a lovely verdurous park, skirting the Arno, with no
end of charming outlooks into the violet-bosomed hills. The
Florentine beau-monde & ◇◇◇ bourgeoisie were there in force—
& a remarkably good looking set of people they are: the latter— 25
the pedestrians—especially. ~~I'm~~ I've ∧been∧ vastly struck
throughout with the beauty of the Italian race, especially in the
men. After the hideous population of German Switzerland, they
◇◇◇◇ are ◇◇◇◇ ∧most∧ delightful to behold; & when ~~from~~
∧hand∧ ~~the bosom of~~ ∧in hand with∧ their charming smiles 30
come flowing the liquid waves of their glorious speech, you feel
positively ashamed of ~~your~~ having a Anglo-Saxon blood. Never
in my life as since I've been in Florence have I seen so many
young men of princely aspect. The charm of it all too is that's

it's the beauty of intelligence & animation quite as much as of
form & feature. — Their beauty, however, consoles me little in
my sorrow — my sorrow at the cold silence of my home — owing
to which I have had no letter — no sign or sound of life or love —
for nearly three weeks. I got a letter from mother on my arrival
here; but I've waited in vain for further news. — I seek not to
complain; but I feel lonely & we~~e~~ weak minded & if I mention
the fact cannot pretend to be indifferent. I devoutly trust the
stillness will soon be broken. — I set you all a good example by
writing even tho' I've very little to tell. My life in Florence is
very quiet & monotonous & unless I ██████ ~~to~~ go in for a ~~detailed~~
catalogue raisonné of the two great galleries, my letter must
perforce be brief. Such a catalogue indeed would be as good an
account of my time as anything I could give; inasmuch as I have
spent it chiefly in looking at pictures. I feel able to say, now with
a certain amount of truth that I <u>know</u> the Uffizi & the Pitti. How
much the wiser I am for my knowledge I hope one of these days
to learn — if not to teach. These two Galleries are ~~unutterly~~
unutterably rich & I hope before I leave Florence to transmit to
W<u>m</u>. ~~some~~ a few glittering generalities on their contents.
<u>Monday</u> evening. 25th. I was obliged to give up writing
yesterday because my room was too cold to abide. A fierce
<u>tramontana</u> has been blowing for several days & Florence is like
Boston in January. I adjourned for warmth & cheer to a very
good English reading-room near at hand; & ~~there~~ thence,
having spent an hour, I made my way across the river to call
upon Mrs. Huntington & daughters, whom I have already
mentioned. I found them seated with Mrs Horatio Greenough &
daughter round a jolly fire which it was a joy to behold. In the
centre of this rich group of my fair country-women, I spent a
very pleasant evening. To day too I have tasted of society.
Charles Norton arrived here this morning from Pisa, where he
had left his family, in quest of an apartment. I went about the
city with him & parted with him in the afternoon, he returning

to Pisa. We ~~sao~~ saw two good places—a large handsome
apartment in town ~~&~~ in the same house as the Huntingtons'—&
a most delightful old villa, a good bit out of the city gates. Chas.
inclines to the latter—& indeed with friends & books it would be
hard to contrive a brighter lovelier home: the house capacious,   5
elderly, Italian—& the garden & all the outside prospect
Italianissimi—Florence lying at your feet & the violet snow-
tipped Appenines ornamenting the distance. In one way or
another I suppose, they will settle themselves within a week. I
am very glad to have looked at that Villa, at all events. It gave   10
me a most penetrating sense of the peculiar charm of
Florence—of the general charm indeed of Italy—a charm
inexpressible, indefinable, which must be observed in its native
air, but which, once deeply felt, leaves forever its mark upon the
sensitive mind & fastens ∧it[∧] to Italian soil thro' all its future   15
wanderings by a delicate chain of longings & regrets. I wish I
could get you & mother & Alice implanted for a while in some
such habitation—feeding on its picturesqueness & drinking ~~in~~
the autumn sunshine—which like everything about Florence
seems to be ~~have a~~ colored with a mild violet, like diluted wine.   20
But it's a very silly wish. You would die of loneliness & you'd
curse your antique privacy.—I 've have placed myself half under
a promise to go down to Pisa within a day or two, to see the
Nortons 'ere they come to Florence. I hesitate somewhat to do it
because ~~when~~ ∧if[∧] I turn my back upon Florence now, I'm   25
afraid I shall turn it upon Italy altogether. I'm very sorry to say
that I'm anything but well. Not that I have any new & startling
affliction, but an old trouble which I had most confidently hoped
by this time to have got the mastery of, has settled down upon
∧me[∧] during the last six weeks with a most ~~oner~~ inexorable ~~mi~~   30
weight. Willy will tell you what it is: I wrote him on the subject
~~sooner~~ after I came to Florence. I fought a hard battle all
summer with it in Switzerland; but I left the country with a
painful sense that I hadn't gained an inch of ground. Ever since

I have been in Italy I have been rapidly losing ground & now I
have scarcely a square inch to stand on. During my stay in
Venice my journey hither & the three weeks of my being here I
have been in a very bad way. Shortly after getting here I was so
5 knocked up that I had to take to my bed & have the doctor & I
have since then been in his hands. He plies me with drugs, but
to no purpose: I only seem to get worse. But I'll not treat you to
a string of details: I recommend you to Willy for information. I
don't ˄know₍˄₎ whether to think that Italian air has anything to
10 do with the matter: I'm utterly unable to explain so violent an
aggravation of my state, in the very face of a mode of life
magnificently calculated (as one would say) to ensure a steady
improvement. But the fact remains & I must come to some sort
of terms with it. I feel as if I couldn't live on a week longer in my
15 present pernicious condition. I'm not impatient: I have given
the thing a fair chance, & my present condition, which is all that
has come of my patience, is quite unendurable. I would give a
vast deal to be able to believe that all I have to do is to hang on
in Italy & a change will come. Experience assures me that I have
20 no reason whatever to look for a change on these terms &
without a change I absolutely can't remain. It makes a sad
trouble of what ought to be a great pleasure. My malady has
done a great deal towards spoiling Florence for me: I should be
sorry to have it meddle with other places. The question is of
25 course what to do, inasmuch as I've pretty nearly exhausted
expedients. I have almost made up my mind to depart straight
from Italy & take refuge at Malvern again. The sole period of
relief that I have enjoyed since I've been abroad came to me
during the last part of my stay there & the subsequent month of
30 my travels in England. On leaving England I immediately
relapsed. I therefore feel justified in hoping that ˄if₍˄₎ I buckle
down to a good two months at M. (or whatever shorter time
may seem sufficient) I ma̶o̶ may gain a solid benefit. I have come
to this decision with much cogitation & infinite regret. In

leaving Italy now I shall be doing I think, the hardest thing I ever did. But I don't see that any other way is open to me. To be at the very gates of Rome & to turn away i requires certainly a strong muscular effort. A very faint ray of light ahead would make me advance with a rush. But I cannot undertake to see Rome as I have seen Florence: the pain would outweigh the pleasure. ◇ I no◇◇ [∧]Since[∧] I must take myself in hand the sooner I do it the better. This will be a great disappointment to your dear sympathetic souls at home, just as it is to my own: but place on the other side the chance of my recovery by going to M. There will be no Rome & no Italy like the Rome & Naples of my getting really relieved of this dismal burden. They will be utterly vulgar in comparison. You may measure the need of my bolting thus out of Italy, by the simple fact of things having reached that point that it's easier to go than to stay. Tuesday eveg† [∧]morning[∧] I was driven to bed last night by the cold & before going out this morning, I take up my shaky pen to finish my letter. It's such a dismal effusion that the sooner I bring it to a close the better. Don't revile me & above all don't pity me. Simply be as comfortable & jolly as you can yourselves & I shall get along very well. Don't wholly give up writing to me, however: such an extravagance of jollity I should wholly deprecate.—Dear father, if once I can get rid of this ancient sorrow I shall be many parts of a well man. Remember this & give me your good wishes. This trouble now is the only rock in my path: if I remove it I shall march straight ahead, I think, to health & work.—I spent a good portion of last night wondering whether I can manage not to go to Rome. Nous verrons: I shall go to Pisa for a couple of days & may there with a change of circumstances & a little society receive an impulse for the better, on which I shall perhaps try Rome for a couple of weeks. I shall drop you a line from there saying whether I am to move North or South, so that you may know where to write. Meanwhile farewell. Je vous embrasse—I squeeze you all.—I have invented

for my comfort a theory that this degenerescence of mine is ~~the~~ a result of Alice ⅃ Willy getting better ⅃ locating some of their diseases on me—so as to propitiate the fates by not turning the poor homeless infirmities out of the family. Isn't it so? I forgive
5 them ⅃ bless them.

Your ever affectionate young one
H. James jr.

Previous publication: *HJL* 1: 153–58; *SL* 2: 49–53

∾

157.19 conversation • conversa= | tion

157.24 ◇◇◇ bourgeoisie • [bo *overwrites illegible letters*]

157.26 especially • espe= | cially

157.26 ~~I'm~~ I've • [ve *overwrites* m]

157.28 population • popu- | lation

157.29 ◇◇◇◇ are • [are *overwrites illegible letters*]

157.32 ~~your~~ having • [having *overwrites* your]

157.32 ~~a~~ Anglo-Saxon • [A *overwrites* a]

158.7 ~~we◇~~ weak • [a *overwrites illegible letter*]

158.11–12 ~~detailed~~ catalogue • [catalogue *overwrites* detailed]

158.13 perforce • per= | force

158.18–19 ~~unutterly~~ unutterably • [ably *overwrites* ly]

158.20 ~~some~~ a few • [a few *overwrites* some]

158.22 yesterday • yester= | day

158.25 English • Eng= | lish

158.25 ~~there¡~~ thence • [nce *overwrites* re,]

159.1 ~~sa◇~~ saw • [w *overwrites illegible letter*]

159.2 ~~⅃~~ in • [i *overwrites* ⅃]

159.18–19 ~~in~~ the • [th *overwrites* in]

159.20 ~~have a~~ colored • [colore *overwrites* have a]

159.22 ~~'ve~~ have • [ha *overwrites* 've]

159.30 ~~oner⁄~~ inexorable • [inexor *overwrites* oner-]

159.30–31 ~~mi~~ weight • [we *overwrites* mi]

160.11 aggravation • aggrava= | tion

160.13 improvement • improve | -ment

160.33 m̶a̶ may • [y *overwrites illegible letter*]

161.3 i̶ requires • [re *overwrites* i]

161.7 ◊ I̶n̶◊◊ • [I *overwrites illegible letter;* n◊◊ *struck through*]

161.10 recovery • re- | covery

161.27 wondering • won= | dering

162.1–2 t̶h̶e̶ a • [a *overwrites* the]

162.4 infirmities • in= | firmities

∾

157.18 en famille • at home.

157.21 the Cascine • Florence's largest park.

157.21 the great Bois de Boulogne • Paris's largest park.

157.24 beau–monde • fashionable society.

158.12 catalogue raisonné • descriptive catalog.

158.23 tramontana • north wind.

158.24–25 a very good English reading-room near at hand • Vieusseux, in the Palazzo Buondelmonti, Piazza S. Trinità, was a popular reading room and lending library. It also had an extensive collection of journals and newspapers from many countries (Murray, *Central Italy* 85).

159.7 Italianissimi • most Italian.

159.7–8 snow- | tipped • snow-tipped

161.28 Nous verrons • We'll see.

161.34 Je vous embrasse • Love.

WILLIAM JAMES   25
26 October [1869]
ALS Houghton
bMS Am 1094 (1937)

Read 1ˢᵗ Florence Hotel de l'Europe   30
        October 26ᵗʰ
Dear Bill—
    I wrote you the enclosed long letter some ten days ago, but abstained from sending it, on account of its darksome purport &

in the hope that by waiting I might have better news. But I
haven't. My condition has become so intolerable that I have well
nigh made up my mind to leave Italy ꝸ fly to England—for the
reasons ꝸ with the purpose mentioned in my letter. For the past
ten days I have been in the very depths of discomfort. If it wasn't
as great as it I can imagine it being, I should say it was getting
worse. I haven't the shadow of a reason left I think, after my
long experience, for supposing that I shall encounter any
change, on this footing. Moreover, my back as I have related in
my letter, is so chronically affected by my constipated state that
there are times when I can hardly drag myself about. Half the
week I can eat but a single meal a day; I can't possibly find room
for more—ꝸ this in spite of getting very tired ꝸ passably hungry
with all my poking about. I mean therefore to return to England
in a very short time. Just at the present moment, I am undecided
as to whether I shall push on to Rome for a fortnight or depart
straightway <u>via</u> Leghorn ꝸ Marseilles. I shall advise you a couple
of days hence. I have just written to father. I have heard nothing
from home in 3 weeks. Excuse brutal brevity Your's in haste
<u>H. J.</u> jr.

Previous publication: *HJL* 1: 158; *CWJ* 1: 114

∽

163.30 <u>Read 1ˢᵗ</u> • [*inserted*]

164.5 discomfort • discom= | fort

164.19–20 Your's [. . .] <u>H. J.</u> jr. • [*written across the letter's last page*]

∽

163.33 the enclosed long letter • HJ's letter to WJ of 16 [17], 19 October
[1869].

164.18 I have just written to father • HJ's 24, 25, [26] October [1869]
letter to Sr.

WILLIAM JAMES
30 October [1869]
ALS Houghton
bMS Am 1094 (1938)

5

<u>Rome</u> Hotel d'Angleterre, Oct. 30<u>th</u>
    My dearest W<u>m</u>—

    Some four days since I despatched to you & father
respectively, from Florence, two very doleful epistles, which you   10
will in course of time receive. No sooner had I posted them
however than my spirits were ~~raised~~ revived by the arrival of a
most blessed brotherly letter from you of October ~~11~~ 8<u>th</u>, which
had been detained either by my banker or the porter of the hotel
& a little scrap from father of a later date, enclosing your review   15
of Mill & a paper of Howells—as well as a couple of <u>Nations</u>.
Verily, it is worthwhile pining for letters for 3 weeks to know the
exquisite joy of final relief. I took yours with me to the theatre
whither I went to see a comedy of Goldoni most delightfully
played & read & re-read it between the acts.—But of this anon.—   20
I went as I proposed down to Pisa & spent two very pleasant days
with the Nortons. It is a very fine dull old town—& the great
square with its four big treasures is quite the biggest thing I have
seen in Italy—or rather was, until my arrival at this well-known
locality.—I went about a whole morning with Chas. N. &   25
profited vastly by his excellent knowledge of Italian history &
art. I wish I had a small fraction of it. But my visit wouldn't have
been complete unless I had got a ramble ~~by myself~~ <u>solus</u>, which I
did in perfection. On my return to Florence I determined to
start immediately for Rome. The afternoon after I had posted   30
those two letters I took a walk out of Florence to an enchanting
old Chartreuse—an ancient monastery, perched up on top of a
hill & turreted with little cells like a feudal castle. I attacked it &
carried it by storm—i.e. obtained admission & went over it. On

coming out I swore to myself that while I had life in my body ∧I
wouldn't[∧] leave a country where adventures of that complexion
are the common incidents of your daily constitutional: but that I
∧would[∧] hurl myself upon Rome & fight it out on this line at
the peril of my existence. There I am then in the ~~Itali~~ Eternal
city. It was easy to leave Florence; the cold had become
intolerable. & the rain perpetual. I started last night & at 10 &
½ o'clock & after a bleak & fatiguing journey of 12 hours found
myself here with the morning light. There are ~~p~~ several places
on the <u>route</u> I should have been glad to see; but the weather &
my own condition made a direct journey imperative. I rushed to
~~m~~ this hotel (a very slow & obstructed rush it was I confess,
thanks to the longueurs & lenteurs of the Papal dispensation) &
after a wash & a breakfast let myself ~~self~~ loose on the city. From
midday to dusk I have been roaming the streets. Que vous en
dirai-je?—At last—for the 1ˢᵗ time—I live! It beats every thing:
it leaves the Rome of ~~f~~ your fancy—your education—nowhere.
It makes Venice—Florence—Oxford—London—seem like little
cities of paste-board. I went reeling & moaning thro' the streets,
in a fever of enjoyment. In the course of four or five hours I
traversed almost the whole of Rome & got a glimpse of
everything—the Forum the Coliseum (↙ stupendissimo!) the
Pantheon—∧the Capitol—[∧] St. Peter's—the Column of
Trajan—the Castle of St. Angelo—all the Piazzas & ruins &
monuments. The effect is something ~~indescri◊◊◊~~ indescribable.
For the 1ˢᵗ time I know what the picturesque is.—In St. Peter's I
staid some time. It's even beyond it's reputation. It was filled
with foreign ecclesiastics—great armies encamped in prayer on
the marble plains of its pavement—an inexhaustible
physiognomical study. To crown my day, on my way home, I met
his Holiness in person—driving in prodigious purple state—
sitting dim within the shadows of his coach with two uplifted
benedictory fingers—like some dusky Hindoo idol in the depths

of its shrine. Even if I should leave Rome to night I should feel that I have caught the key-note of its operation on the senses. I have looked along the grassy vista of the Appian way & seen the topmost stonework of the Coliseum sitting shrouded in the light of heaven, like the edge of an Alpine chain. I've trod the Forum & I have scaled the Capitol. I've seen the Tiber hurrying along, as swift & dirty as history! ~~I see a great~~ From the high tribune of a great chapel of St. Peter's I have heard in the papal ◇◇◇ choir a strange old man sing in a shrill unpleasant soprano. I've seen troops of little tonsured neophytes clad in scarlet, marching & counter marching & ducking & flopping, like poor little raw recruits for the heavenly host.—In fine I've seen Rome, & I shall go to bed a wiser man than I last rose—yesterday morning.—It was a great relief to me to have you at last ~~speak abou~~ give me some news of your health. Thank the Lord it's no worse. With all my I heart I rejoice that your'e going to try loafing & visiting. I discern the "inexorable logic" of the affair; courage, & you'll work out your redemption. I'm delighted with your good report of J. L. F.'s pictures. I've seen them all save the sleeping woman. I have given up expecting him here. If he does come, tant mieux. Your notice of Mill & Bushnell seemed to me (save the opening lines which savored faintly of Eugene Benson) very well & fluently written. Thank father for his ten lines: may they increase & multiply!—Of course I don't know how long I shall be here. I would give my head to be able to remain 3 months: it would be a liberal education. As it is, I shall stay, if possible, simply from week to week. My "condition" remains the same. I am living on some medicine (aloes & sulphuric acid) given me by my Florentine doctor. I shall write again very shortly. Kisses to Alice & Mother. Blessings on yourself. Address me <u>Spada</u>, <u>Flamini</u> & Cie, Banquiers, Rome. Heaven grant I may be here when your letters come. Love to father.

À toi <u>H. J. jr.</u>

Previous publication: Lubbock 1: 24–25; *HJL* 1: 159–61; *SL* 2: 54–56; *CWJ* 1: 115–18; *WHSL* 51–54

∾

165.11 receive • re= | ceive

165.12 ~~raised~~ revived • [revive *overwrites* raise]

165.13 ~~11~~ 8 • [8 *overwrites* 11]

165.28 ~~by myself~~ solus • [solus *overwrites blotted* by myself]

165.30 afternoon • after- | noon

166.5 ~~Itali~~ Eternal • [Etern *overwrites* Itali]

166.9 ~~p~~ several • [s *overwrites* p]

166.12 ~~m~~ this • [th *overwrites* m]

166.14 ~~self~~ loose • [loose *overwrites blotted* self]

166.17 ~~f~~ your • [y *overwrites blotted* f]

166.22 ∤ stupendissimo • [s *overwrites* —]

166.25 ~~indescri◇◇~~ indescribable • [bable *overwrites illegible letters*]

166.29 inexhaustible • inex= | haustible

167.7 ~~I see a great~~ From the • [From the *overwrites* I see a great]

167.8 ◇◇◇ choir • [choir *overwrites illegible letters*]

167.14 ~~abou~~ give • [give *overwrites* abou]

∾

165.6 Hotel d'Angleterre • Murray's *Rome* (1869) describes the hotel as situated

> in the Via Bocca di Leone, near the Via Condotti, [. . .] with accommo-
> dations well suited for families and bachelors, charges more moderate
> than at the Europa, Londres, &c., a most obliging landlord and secre-
> tary, and one of the best tables-d'hôte in Italy at 5 fr., including good
> wine of the country; bed-rooms 3 to 6 fr. a day, according to the floor
> on which they are situated, and the season; a sitting-room with bed and
> servant's room from 10 to 15 fr.; breakfast, with eggs, 2 fr., or cold meat,
> $2\frac{1}{2}$ fr.; id. à la fourchette, $3\frac{1}{2}$ fr.; dinner in apartments, 7 fr.; servant's
> board, 5 fr. per diem; *service*, 1 fr. per diem, and 5 fr. a month for the
> porter and facchini for a single person, 10 to 15 for families, according
> to their number. [. . .] There are attached to the hotel very comfortably
> and elegantly fitted-up sitting, music, reading (with the principal En-
> glish, American, French, and Italian newspapers), and smoking-rooms,
> baths, &c. (ix)

165.9–10 I despatched [. . .] two very doleful epistles • HJ's 24, 25, [26] October [1869] letter to his father; his 26 October [1869] letter to WJ enclosed his longer, 16 [17], 19 October [1869] letter.

165.16 a paper of Howells • William Dean Howells, "A Pedestrian Tour," *Atlantic Monthly* 24 (November 1869): 591–603.

165.19 Goldoni • Carlo Goldoni (1707–93), Venetian dramatist.

165.21–22 I went as I proposed down to Pisa & spent two very pleasant days with the Nortons • See HJ's 24, 25, [26] October [1869] letter to Sr.

165.22–23 the great square with its four big treasures • According to Murray's *Central Italy* (1867):

> The *Cathedral* at Pisa, with its *baptistery, campanile*, and the *Campo Santo*, are as interesting a group of buildings as any four edifices in the world. It has been well observed that they are "fortunate in their solitude, and their society." They group well together and are seen to advantage. Visitors to these buildings are much pestered by persons offering their services as guides, but they are quite useless. A small fee is paid to the doorkeepers of the Baptistery, Campanile, and Campo Santo: ½ a franc to each of these will be sufficient, except in the case of a large party. (15, 17)

The Campanile, or bell tower, is better known as the "Leaning Tower of Pisa."

165.25 Chas. N. • Charles Eliot Norton.

165.31–32 an enchanting old Chartreuse • La Certosa, or Charterhouse, in Val d'Ema, about two and a half miles from the Porta Romana, founded in 1341 and designed by Andrea Orcagna. The monastery was fortified, and Murray's 1867 *Central Italy* describes it: "its first aspect, with its fine Gothic windows and battlements, is much more that of a mediæval fortress than of a sacred edifice" (199). Although the Carthusian order of Val d'Ema had been suppressed, according to the same Murray guide, there were "a few monks remaining to carry on the religious ceremonies of the ch. An order from the Minister of Public Instruction, or of Grace and Justice, is necessary to see the interior" (200). HJ describes the Certosa of Val d'Ema in "An Italian Convent" (*The Independent* 2 July 1874: 3–4).

166.13 the longueurs & lenteurs • the delays and slowness.

166.13 the longueurs *&* lenteurs of the Papal dispensation • Foreigners traveling to the Papal State in 1869 needed to obtain a preliminary visa from a papal diplomatic or consular officer before entering the pontifical territory and then received an entrance visa at the frontier (Murray, *Rome* v, xiv).

166.15–16 Que vous en dirai-je? • What shall I tell you about it all?

166.22 the Forum • The Roman Forum or Forum Romanum, at the center of the city.

166.22 the Coliseum • An arena, begun in 72 C.E. and dedicated in 80 C.E.

166.22–23 the Pantheon • One of ancient Rome's best-preserved monuments, this temple was built in 27 B.C.E., rebuilt by Hadrian between 118 and 128 C.E., and dedicated in 609 C.E. as the Christian church of Santa Maria ad Martyres.

166.23 Capitol • Site of the square of palaces at the top of the Capitoline Hill, known in Italian as the Piazza del Campidoglio (Murray, *Rome* 250). Once the "spiritual as well as political capitol of Rome" (Gardner 502), consisting of the Medieval Palace of the Senators (Palazzo dei Senatori); the fifteenth-century Palace of the Conservators (Palazzo dei Conservatori), with a façade built by Michelangelo circa 1537; and the Capitol Museum (Museo Capitolino), also by Michelangelo and built at the same time; all grouped around the circa 165 C.E. equestrian bronze of Marcus Aurelius (Gardner 235, 501–3).

166.23–24 the Column of Trajan • Built by Apollodorus of Damascus in honor of the Emperor Trajan in 113 C.E. (Gardner 230).

166.24 the Castle of St. Angelo • Originally Hadrian's mausoleum of about 130 C.E. and converted into a fortress during the later Roman Empire; further fortified and expanded during the Middle Ages and Renaissance, until 1644, when it reached its definitive state.

166.31 his Holiness • Giovanni Maria Mastai Ferretti (1792–1878), Pope Pius IX from 1846 to the end of his life; he held the First Vatican Council (1869–70), which proclaimed the dogma of papal infallibility.

167.3 Appian way • Via Appia, an ancient Roman road, begun in 312 B.C.E., connecting Rome's Porta di San Sebastiano first to Capua and

then to Brundisium; it was ancient Rome's principal line of communication to the south.

167.8–9 a strange old man sing in a shrill unpleasant soprano • Probably
a reference to a castrato in the Vatican choir.

167.19 J. L. F. • John La Farge.

167.20 tant mieux • so much the better.

167.22 Eugene Benson • American painter (1839–1908) who also supported himself by writing reviews for the *Galaxy*, the *Atlantic Monthly*, and
Putnam's, among others.

167.27–29 I am living on some medicine (aloes & sulphuric acid) given
me by my Florentine doctor • See HJ's 8 November [1869] letter to WJ
for the composition of this medicine prescribed by Dr. Duffy.

167.30–31 Spada, Flamini & Cie, Banquiers, Rome • "Spada, Flamini,
and Co., successors of Torlonia and Co., Pal. Torlonia, 20, Via Condotti"
(Murray, *Rome* xviii).

167.33 À toi • Yours.

ALICE JAMES
7, 8 November [1869]   20
ALS Houghton
bMS Am 1094 (1560)

Rome Hotel de Rome
    Nov. 7ᵗʰ Sunday.   25

Beloved sister—A week ago, on my arrival here I despatched a
hasty note to Willy, telling of my few first impressions. Since
then, with time, & (I am most happy to say, an improved
physical state—thanks to my good Florentine doctor) I have   30
largely added to the stock—in many cases for your especial
benefit. The excitement of the 1ˢᵗ hours has passed away & I have
recovered the healthy mental equilibrium of the sober practical
tourist. Nevertheless Rome is still Rome at the end of a week—

or rather is more thoroughly Rome than ever. But before I
proceed with Rome, let me say that I feel poignantly that I have
quite failed of justice to that delightful admirable Florence—the
very <u>sweetest</u> among cities. In spite of being so poorly, I saw
5 more & enjoyed more while there than I managed to to tell you
of. I had planned in particular to write to W<u>m</u> a high-toned
letter on the two great Galleries—wherein I should have spoken
with infinite wisdom of certain sublime portraits by Rafael
Titian & Leonardo. I had likewise arranged a brilliant
10 discourse upon Michael Angelo's ~~Medicae~~ Medicean tombs—
the last word of Romantic art—& had collected some notes on
the characteristics of Florentine scenery. I hope to stop ◇ again
in the lovely city on my way out of Italy & I shall then perhaps
be inspired. En attendant, tell my brother not to cherish the
15 fond illusion that in seeing the photos. of M. Angelo's statues he
has <u>même</u> <u>entrevu</u> the originals. Their beauty far surpasses my
prior conception. As they sit ■■■■ brooding in their dim-
lighted chapel, exhaling silence & thought, they form, ~~the~~ I
imagine, the most impressive work of art in the world. The
20 warrior with the cavernous visage is absolutely terrible: he seems
to shed an amount of inarticulate sorrow sufficient to infect the
Universe.—& now as for this Rome, it seems a sadly vain
ambition to attempt to give you any idea of its effect upon the
mind. It's so vast so heavy, so multitudinous that you seem to
25 require all your energy simply to bear up against it. Your
foremost feeling is that of your own ignorance. In a certain way
the <u>premier</u> <u>venu</u> can enjoy the place as much as another: its
immense superficial picturesqueness appeals to the elementary
sentiments of our common nature. But at every step you feel
30 that in the line of a sort of sympathetic comprehension you are
losing something thro' your want of knowledge. It's a place in
which you needn't in the least feel ashamed of a ■■■■■
perpetual reference to <u>Murray</u>: a place in which you feel
emphatically the value of "culture." At every step in some guise

or other History ↰ confronts you ↰ the mind must make some
response: ⊘ the more intelligent the better. I have buckled down
to my work with a fair amount of resolution. In the morning I
have regularly gone to the Vatican, ↰ in the afternoon have
strolled about at hazard, seeking what I might devour, ↰   5
devouring (frequently with something of the languor of fatigue)
whatever I have found. I have seen tolerably well—i.e. got the
feeling of—some half dozen special localities, besides absorbing
incidentally a sufficiently ample sense of the general
physiognomy of Rome. The Vatican, the Museum of the   10
Capitol, the Coliseum ↰ the Baths of Caracalla ∧the Pantheon,[∧]
the Forum, ↰ the Churches of the Lateran ↰ Sta. Maria
Maggiore—such are my special acquisitions. In spite of an
immense deal of dove-tailing ↰ intermingling, Pagan ↰
Christian Rome keep tolerably distinct ↰ the ancient city is a   15
fact that you can appreciate more or less in its purity.
Appreciate, but not express! No words can reproduce the
eloquence of a Roman block of blunted ~~granite~~ ∧marble[∧] or a
mass of eternal brickwork—let alone the crowded majesty of an
original inscription. Last Sunday, the Vatican being closed, I   20
went down ↰ had a long lounge in the coliseum. The day was
magnificent ↰ the sun seemed to shine on purpose to illumine
~~the~~ its crevices ↰ set off its immensity. I climbed over the
accessible portions of the summit ↰ communed with the genius
of the spot—in the person of a heavy-souled German whom I   25
met ↰ whom I had formerly encountered on the Rigi. The
coliseum is a thing about wh. its useless to talk: it must be seen
↰ felt. But as ∧a[∧] piece of the picturesque—a province of it—it
is thoroughly ↰ simply delightful. The grassy arena with its
circle of tarnished shrines ↰ praying strollers—the sky between   30
the arches ↰ above the oval—the weeds ↰ flowers against the sky
↰c—are as charming as anything in Rome. The next day in the
afternoon I betook myself to the almost equal ruins of the Baths
of Caracalla. It was the hour of sunset ↰ I had them all to myself.

They are a collection of perfectly mountainous masses of brickwork, to the right of the Appian way. Even more than the Coliseum I think they give you a notion of the Roman <u>Scale</u>. Imagine a good second class mountain in reduced

5 circumstances — perforated & honeycombed by some terrestrial cataclysm — & you'll have an idea of these terrific ruins. Through a modern staircase in one of the columns I ascended to the roof (or what remains of it) & saw the ~~Cumo~~ Campagna bathed in the sunset. At this giddy elevation the effect is more

10 mountainous than ever. The aged masonry seems all compacted & condensed into natural stratifications & a great wilderness of trees & thickets sits blooming over the abyss. — But by far the most beautiful piece of ancientry in Rome is that simple & unutterable <u>Pantheon</u> to which I repeated my devotions

15 yesterday afternoon. It makes you profoundly regret that you are not a pagan suckled in the creed outworn that produced it. It's the most conclusive example I have yet seen of the simple sublime. Imagine simply a vast cupola with its drum, set directly on the earth & fronted with a porch of columns & a triangular

20 summit: the interior lighted by a hole in the apex of the cupola & the circumference furnished with a series of altars. The effect within is the very <u>delicacy</u> of grandeur — & more worshipful to my perception than the most mysterious & aspiring Gothic. St. Peter's, beside it, is absurdly vulgar. Taken absolutely however

25 St. Peters is extremely interesting — not quite so much so as it pretends to be — but quite enough so to give you a 1st class sensation. It's pretention, I take it, is to be the very synthesis & summit of all sensations & emotions. I can't dispose of it in three words. As a whole it's immensely picturesque. As you journey

30 thro' its various latitudes, moreover, you really feel that you stand at the heart & centre of modern ecclesiasticism: you are watching the heart-beats of the church. The past week has been a season of great performances; & but the combined absence of a dress-suit & an aversion to a crowd has prevented my going to

the Sistine Chapel, where the best of the fun has been going on.
Before I leave Rome, however, I mean to get a glimpse. A
glimpse indeed I had some three days since, when the Pope came
in state to say mass at a church opposite this hotel. I made no
attempt to enter the church: but I saw tolerably well the arrival   5
of the cardinals & ambassadors &c, & finally of the Grand
Llama in person. The whole spectacle was very handsome, but
it was precisely like a leaf out of the Middle-Ages—or even
more out of the last century—pre-revolutionary times. Its a
"merciful providence" that the spectator of all this Papistry has   10
at hand so vast a magazine of antiquity to appeal to for
purgation & relief. When you have seen that ~~bloated~~ ₐflaccid₍ₐ₎
◇◇ old woman waving his ridiculous fingers over the prostrate
multitude & have duly felt the picturesqueness of the scene—&
then turn away sickened by its absolute <u>obscenity</u>—you may   15
climb the steps of the Capitol & contemplate the equestrian
statue of Marcus Aurelius. This work, by the way, is one of the
things I have most enjoyed in Rome. It is totally admirable—the
very model of the <u>genre</u>:—so large & monumental & yet so full
of a sweet human dignity—stretching out a long thin arm in the   20
act of mild persuasive command—that ~~if~~ it affects you like an
audible personal voice out of that stony Roman past. As you
revert to that poor sexless old Pope enthroned upon his
cushions—& then glance at those imperial legs swinging in their
immortal bronze, you cry out that here at least was a <u>man</u>! But   25
the mention of this statue brings me to the Museum of the
Vatican. Here I have had great satisfactions. Before plunging
into the antiques however I took a look at Rafael, as the Vatican
shows him. It contains his ~~t~~ <u>Transfiguration</u> & his famous
<u>Stanze</u>—a series of rooms painted in fresco—the <u>School</u> of   30
<u>Athens</u>, <u>Heliodorus</u> &c. Whether I have completed my
"evolution" in the enjoyment of painting or—terrible fate!—
have got stuck fast in the middle of it—I know not: but in truth
my uppermost feeling before these works was one of the most

irresponsive sort. In a word, I was disappointed. Before Rafael's great portraits in Florence there was nothing I wouldn't have conceded to him: but as I looked at these heroic compositions I begrudged him even his proper dues. The more I see of painting & sculpture, the more I value a good portrait. In proportion to the subject, difficulties seem to me more boldly faced & more honestly solved than in "compositions." The inventive—the would-be creative—faculty, left to itself, seems sadly inclined to wander & stumble—sadly fallible. There is at the ~~Capitol~~ ₍ₐ₎Vatican₍ₐ₎ a ~~bust~~ statue of Demosthenes—you may see a cast of it at the Athenaeum—a fine wise old man with his head bent & his ~~eyes~~ ₍ₐ₎hands₍ₐ₎ dropped, holding a scroll—so perfect & noble & beautiful that it amply satisfies my desire for the ideal. Great are the Venetians: these things of Rafael makes me feel it: they stuck to the real, though in so doing they missed the belle ligne romaine. Without going into metaphysics, it is easy to say that these great works of Rafael are vitiated by their affected classicism—their elegance & coldness. I sat staring stupidly at the ~~C~~ Transfiguration—actually surprised at its thinness— asking myself whether this was the pretended greatest of pictures. Not so had I sat before the great Crucifixion of Tintoret. It's very foolish to lay down any rules or form any theories in advance. In painting you must deal with accomplished facts. There's hardly any painter who has fairly earned the name in whom I don't feel capable on occasion & on certain special grounds of taking a ~~moderate~~ ₍ₐ₎critical₍ₐ₎ interest: but I find ~~these~~ the number of those who afford me genuine spontaneous delight sifted down to a few. 1º The best Venetians—Bellini, Tintoret, Titian, Veronese & the rich Giorgione—who is entirely unrepresented in his native city & whom I learned to know in Florence. ~~ɪ~~ 2º Giotto & a ~~few specimens~~ small number of the early Italians—notably the great Orcagna in the Campo Santo at Pisa. ₍ₐ₎In₍ₐ₎ ~~ɪ~~ these primitive men, when thro' their stiffness & ignorance a ray of

genius breaks forth, it has a <u>quality</u>—a freshness & directness—
which makes it leap home to the mind like a winged arrow. 3º
The portraits of Leonardo & Rafael. Here, while ~~ther~~ their
education has made them free, their subjects have kept them
honest. What Leonardo's education has enabled him to put—
or to keep—in the physiognomy of a certain clever young
woman at Florence—it would take a Leonardo of the pen to
relate. 4º After this, <u>for</u> <u>pleasure</u>, give me any ~~n~~ amount of
good Dutch realism.—But with my good Dutch realism me
voilà loin du Vatican!—from the Apollo Belvedere & the
Laocoon. These clever pieces don't err on the side of realism.
My 1ˢᵗ movement at the Vatican was to run to the Belvedere &
get them off my conscience. On the whole they quite deserve
their fame: famous things always do, I find: even the ~~t~~
<u>Transfiguration</u> is no exception. But there are some ~~o~~ other
things on the premises which deserve their delicious
(comparative) obscurity. The Apollo is really a magnificent
youth—with far more of solid dignity than I fancied. The
Laocoon on the other hand, strikes me as ₍ₐ₎a₍ₐ₎ decidedly made
up affair & a much less complete & successful embodiment of
human anguish than that sublime <u>Niobe</u> at Florence—a perfect
image of maternity ₍ₐ₎on the rack.₍ₐ₎ ~~Broa~~ —I don't of course
mean, beloved child, to enumerate the contents of the Vatican.
Broadly, until youv'e trod those glorious halls you don't know
what sculpture is. They are immense in extent & crowded
~~of course~~ with indifferent specimens: even the really interesting
things, of course, being of various degrees of merit. Among
these, the innumerable busts & statues of the Roman Emperors
hold a foremost place. I find a particular fascination in a
magnificent statue of Augustus, excavated only some 5 years
since, in a marvellous state of preservation. Also in a ravishing
little bust of Augustus as a boy, as clear & fresh in quality as if it
dated from yesterday. He may have been an arrant knave but he
had a most interesting intellectual visage. I saw yesterday at the

Capitol the dying Gladiator, the Lycian Apollo, the Amazon ɟc—all of them unspeakably simple ɟ noble ɟ eloquent of the ⬦⬦ breadth of human genius. There is little to say or do about them, save to sit ɟ enjoy them ɟ let them act upon your nerves ɟ
5 confirm your esteem for completeness, purity ɟ perfection. After two crowded months of pictures ~~thier~~ their effect is delightfully cooling ɟ reassuring. All the roman ~~busts~~ ∧portraits[∧] give me a deep desire to plunge in to roman history—so that yesterday I narrowly escaped paying 22 frs. for
10 an English publication on the subject. But to approach it, you must have a Roman will.—Out of the high windows of the Vatican you get glimpses of all kinds of delicious Italian courts ɟ gardens. You even surprise the secrets of the papal household. I'm sure I saw one of the pontifical petticoats hanging out to
15 dry. ⬦ In the corridors ɟ stairways you likewise see the Swiss guard—glorious mediaeval warriors clad in splendid fantastic trappings of red ɟ yellow. Indeed the human picturesque in Rome is quite as rich as the architectural. The peasantry are in a decided minority ɟ to ~~see~~ get a proper notion of them I suppose
20 one must ~~pl~~ leave the city ɟ plunge into the Campagna—which I hope in some small way to do. I <u>had</u> hoped to have a good deal to do with the Campagna (in the way of afternoon walks ɟc) but it is ∧at[∧] a much greater distance from ~~the~~ any given point than I supposed. Besides there is far more than enough to do within
25 ~~Rome~~ the walls.—The human picturesque as I say, is visible in the innumerable host of soldiers ɟ priests—of whom there is about an equal swarm. You may meet in any half hour's walk ~~as many~~ a dozen as genuine squalid friars of the early church— or a dozen pale ascetics of as good a quality—as the imagination
30 could possibly desire.—<u>Monday</u> 8<u>th</u>. So much I wrote yesterday ɟ then in mercy stayed my hand. It must suffice for the present. I have made in the above no mention of letters because since leaving Florence I have received none. The next I fondly hope <u>may</u> be from you. In his last note father mentioned your having

gone with Miss T. S. to spend the day at Milton. It would
be a little more becoming I think if instead of <u>te</u> <u>livrer à</u>
<u>ces</u> <u>folles</u> <u>jouissances</u> you should <u>once in a while</u> spend a
morning in your room, writing to your poor old brother.—I am
very sorry to hear of Addy Watson's bad state. I always liked her.
She had a certain graceful way with her which I suppose her
gradual extinction doesn't diminish. If I could invent a message
proper to her condition I would send it. But I can't.
~~The Nortons~~ Jane Norton read me last summer ~~an~~ a remarkably
good & singularly <u>pathetic</u> letter from Silvia W., which made me
resolve at the time to write to her: but the flesh is weak.—Of
<u>intime</u> & personal news I have little to give beyond the fact that
for the present, as I have said, I am vastly better in body. If I can
only manage to keep so I shall feel ~~a~~ that a brighter day has
dawned.—Since sending my last letter I have changed my
hotel—much for the better. I suffered so from the cold in
Florence that I made a point of taking a room <u>with sun</u>, which I
have found here very fairly. If I were surer of my health & the
duration of my stay I would take a ∧private[∧] room or a couple
of them. Prices, this winter, however are so high in Rome, that I
fancy I should pay as much for good quarters ~~than~~ ∧as[∧] I do
here & from my lack of friends & of the language be more lonely
& less comfortable. I made a rapid & feverish excursion into a
<u>pension</u> of good repute—but what with high terms, a poor room
& a vicious <u>table</u> <u>d'hôte</u> concluded I had not changed for the
better & backed out. I should have paid 75 frs. a week, & here, I
live for about 80—dining to suit myself at a very good
restaurant. It's not cheap—but for Rome, apparently (& for
comfort) it's not dear. I have of course no company but my own,
but in the intervals of sight seeing find a rare satisfaction in the
long-denied perusal of a book. I have been reading Stendahl—a
capital observer & a good deal of a thinker. He really knows
Italy. I have no plans. There are moments when I feel as if I
should like to establish myself for the winter in Rome: at others

I feel as if (sight seeing apart) I should prefer another course. A whole winter of sight-seeing were too much of a good thing. If I were in good working order I have little doubt of ~~what I should do~~ [∧]my movements.[∧] I should (at the end of a
5 brief sojourn here ♂ a fortnight at Naples) betake myself to Florence ♂ settle there for the winter. There, with books ♂ photos., in a sunny room on that divine <u>Lung Arno</u>, I should study Italian art ♂ history. Concerning my actual course I have this vague prevision: — that I shall remain in Rome until about
10 the 10<u>th</u> ∧of December,[∧] (just after the opening of the Council) ♂ then go down to Naples for three weeks; return Northward on Jan'y 1st ♂ stop for ~~an~~ a fortnight at Florence. I shall have then spent 5 months in Italy. I should leave for France <u>via</u> Genoa ♂ Marseilles ♂ travel up to Paris by way of Avignon, Nîmes, ♂
15 Arles. In Paris I should abide for 3 mos: <u>i.e.</u> till May 1<u>st</u>. Here ceases this shadow of a scheme. If I had a <u>compagnon</u> de voyage I should prattle to him in some such strain: as I have none, I must exhale my unrest in your sympathetic ear. By May 1<u>st</u> j'aime à <u>croire</u> that I shall be able to pronounce as to my going
20 to Germany. I have a glimmering hope that I may then ♂ thence embark upon the Rhine — the stream of study. Putting Germany aside ♂ thinking only of travel, ~~then~~ [∧]I am[∧] conscious only of these definite desires. 1º To get a couple of months of Paris. Willy will scoff at this, but I have good reasons forsooth. 2º To
25 see the Flemish ♂ Dutch painters. 3º To get another glimpse of England. <u>Evening</u>. I have kept my letter ~~as~~ all day — happily: for I have the receipt of a celestial missive from mother to announce. Language cannot reveal the deep, still tremulous joy with which I possessed myself of its contents. I had been out all
30 day — since I laid away my letter after breakfast; dusk had fallen ♂ I came home tolerably done up with my work. Going into the porter's lodge for my key, my 1<u>st</u> glance was at the little case where the letters are exposed. There stood my joy, in legible black ♂ white! I brought it up to my lofty 4<u>th</u> <u>piano</u> ♂ — laid it

reasonable in Paris

carefully on the bed. I then proceeded to cleanse my self of all
soils & stains, & not before I was duly washed brushed &
refreshed did I address myself to its perusal. It contained the
very essence of my lovely mammy.—The news of Ellen's
departure gives me a real pang. You must get her back before I   5
return. She has been among the foremost objects wh. on that
happy day I have often dreamed of folding in my arms. I can't
believe but that she is destined to re-enter the family. She seems
the very keystone of the arch. All mother's little facts were most
delicious: especially the sale of "your father's" immortal work.   10
Has he yet made any money on it, or merely covered his
expenses?—Poor Wilky's caterpillar (,of which I have at last got
explicit mention) can hardly be called delicious: I'm sure I don't
know what to think about it. I hope Miss Mason yields him
some compensation: he rarely deserves it. I shall be glad to hear   15
that Minny has gone to San Francisco. I wrote her a long letter
from Venice & suppose I shall soon have an answer. I take an
awful interest in your English hat. Thereby hangs a tale! It
reminds me of a visit I paid to Mrs. Brown, Bond St. London—
& of a most lovely young shop-woman who shewed me a most   20
lovely young hat—which I came so near buying! & would have
utterly bought (you'll be gratified to hear) had I not bethought
myself to inquire the extra cost of shipping it to America: on
learning which I feared that your delicate pate ~~may~~ might ache
beneath the weight of so costly a monument. Describe it in your   25
next. If it's not ∧of green felt[∧] peaked at the summit & decked
with a little eagle's feather & with a long streaming veil, wound
about your throat—ça ne vaut rien. Tell me about all your new
things. How do you wear your hair? in those long drooping
braids' I hope: they are very pretty. If I could only get you to do   30
it in the manner of some of the busts of the roman Empresses!—
I have meant a 1000 times in the intervals of writing to send
some message to poor dear Mrs. Lombard, which mother
adjures me to do, but have always forgotten it in the decisive

act. — Tell her then that I adore her! or rather, give her my love &
tell her that I'm extremely glad to hear of her having really fixed
herself in Cambridge. I have always included her among those
missing friends who make the sadness of absence & exile &
5   should be very sorry not to find her ∧on my return[∧] still within
reach, to make the satisfaction of home. Ask her to give my
especial regards to Miss Fanny & my best hopes for her
uninterrupted recovery. — Let me beg you once for all to keep
giving my love, regards &c, in all proper quarters.* — Mother
10   says no more about Bob's Texan appointment: so I suppose it is
extinct. — I met Miss Bessy Ward lately in the street, attended by
her maid. She looked old & fat & didn't know me: but I mean
shortly to call upon them. — In the same enclosure with Mother's
letter, I got a note from A. K. announcing her arrival in Venice
15   for the 8ᵗʰ They will therefore not reach Rome before
December 1ˢᵗ. I hope I shall still be here — for A. K.'s sake at any
rate, — & Helen Ripley's. A̶ Indeed I shall receive A. K with the
wildest enthusiasm. She will b̶e̶ at last be some one to talk to.
We shall gossip mightily about home. I can easily understand
20   that she suffers from the insensibility of her companions. I have
seen specimens of unregenerate American stolidity which (if her
fellow travellers are gifted with it) make me feel for her. — But
my letter is of a perfectly barbarous length. — I'm glad Howells
shewed you what I wrote him from Venice. Goad him on to
25   answer me. They take the Daily Adv. at this hotel & I have just
read of Mr. Eliot's installation. — I enclose a note to
W. Farewell. — Love to father & Mother. I close my eyes & fancy
you going into Dr. Butler's (blessed man) — tossing your
beautiful hat — the pride of the horse-car! — & of your devoted
30   brother H. J. jr.
    * N. B. Especially to the Gurneys.

Previous publication: *HJL* 1: 161–71

ॐ

171.30 Florentine • Floren- | tine

171.34 Nevertheless • Neverthe- | less

172.5 to to • to | to

172.10 ~~Medicae~~ Medicean • [ea *overwrites* ae]

172.12 ◊ again • [a *overwrites illegible letter*]

172.17 ▰▰▰ brooding • [brooding *overwrites blotted illegible word*]

172.18 ~~the~~ I • [I *overwrites* the]

172.32-33 ▰▰▰ perpetual • [perpetual *overwrites blotted illegible word*]

173.2 ◊ the • [t *overwrites illegible letter*]

173.12 Sta. • [a *inserted*]

173.20 inscription • in= | scription

173.23 ~~the~~ its • [its *overwrites* the]

173.23 immensity • im- | mensity

174.2 brickwork • brick- | work

174.4 mountain • moun- | =tain

174.5 perforated • perfora- | ted

174.7 staircase • stair- | case

174.8 ~~Cum◊~~ Campagna • [a *overwrites* u; p *overwrites illegible letter*]

174.11 wilderness • wilder- | ness

174.15 profoundly • pro- | foundly

174.16 produced • pro= | duced

174.21 circumference • circum- | ference

174.31 ecclesiasticism • ecclesias- | ticism

174.33 ~~b~~ but • [b *overwrites* ♂]

175.13 ◊◊ old • [ol *overwrites illegible letters*]

175.16 contemplate • con= | template

175.19 monumental • monu- | mental

175.21 ~~if~~ it • [t *overwrites struck through* f]

175.29 ~~t~~ Transfiguration • [T *overwrites* t]

176.3 conceded • con= | ceded

176.10 ~~bust~~ statue • [statue *overwrites blotted* bust]

176.19 ~~C~~ Transfiguration • [T *overwrites* C]

176.27 ~~these~~ the • [e *overwrites* ese]

176.30 unrepresented • un- | represented

176.31 ƚ 2 • [2 *overwrites* 1]

176.33 ~~T~~ these • [t *overwrites* T]

176.34 primitive • primi- | tive

177.3 ~~ther~~ their • [i *overwrites* r]

177.8 ~~n~~ amount • [a *overwrites* n]

177.14-15 ~~t~~ <u>Transfiguration</u> • [T *overwrites* t]; <u>Trans-</u> | <u>figuration</u>

177.15 ⬦ other • [o *overwrites illegible letter*]

177.17 comparative • compara- | tive

177.19 decidedly • de- | cidedly

177.22 ~~Br⬦a~~ —I • [—I *overwrites blotted* Br⬦a]

177.29 particular • particu= | lar

177.33 yesterday • yes= | terday

178.2-3 ⬦⬦ breadth • [br *overwrites illegible letters*]

178.6 ~~thier~~ their • [e *overwrites* i *and* ir *overwrites blotted* er]

178.15 ⬦ In • [I *overwrites illegible letter*]

178.17 picturesque • pic- | turesque

178.19 ~~see~~ get • [get *overwrites* see]

178.20 ~~pl~~ leave • [le *overwrites struck through* pl]

178.23 ~~the~~ any • [any *overwrites* the]

178.24-25 within • [with *inserted*]

178.25 ~~Rome~~ the walls • [the wa *overwrites blotted* Rome]

178.29 imagination • imagi- | nation

179.9 ~~The Nortons~~ Jane Norton • [Jane *overwrites* The; n *over-* | *writes* ns]

179.9 ~~an~~ a • [a *overwrites* an]

179.14 ~~a~~ that • [th *overwrites* a]

180.5 myself • my= | self

180.12 ~~an~~ a • [a *overwrites* an]

180.16 <u>compagnon</u> • <u>com-</u> | <u>pagnon</u>

180.26 ~~as~~ all • [a *overwrites* as]

180.29 myself • my= | self

180.30 breakfast • break- | fast

181.20 shop-woman • shop- | woman

181.24 ~~may~~ might · [ight *overwrites blotted* ay]

182.17 ~~A~~ Indeed · [I *overwrites* A]

182.18 ~~be~~ at · [at *overwrites* be]

182.31 * N. B. Especially to the Gurneys. · [*This line is written across the letter's penultimate page*]

∽

171.24 Hotel de Rome · "*Hotel de Rome*, in the Palazzo Lozzano, Piazza di San Carlo in Corso, on a large scale; nearly 300 beds; very good. The larger apartments, salle à manger, and general sitting and smoking rooms, are handsomely fitted up; table-d'hôte 5 fr., without wine. Bedrooms from 4 to 7 fr.; dinner in apartments 7 to 10 fr. Of late years this hotel has been one of the most frequented in Rome" (Murray, *Rome* x).

171.28 hasty note to Willy · HJ's 30 October [1869] letter to WJ.

172.14 En attendant · Meanwhile.

172.16 <u>même</u> <u>entrevu</u> · <u>even had a glimpse of</u>.

172.27 the <u>premier</u> <u>venu</u> · <u>anyone</u>.

173.10-11 Museum of the Capitol · After the Vatican, the Capitoline Museum contained the finest collection of antique sculptures in Rome.

173.11 Baths of Caracalla · Also called the Antonine Baths, the ancient public baths in Rome were first begun by emperor Septimius Severus and completed by his emperor son, Caracalla, in 216 C.E.

173.12-13 the Churches of the Lateran & Sta. Maria Maggiore · The Basilica of San Giovanni in Laterano, Rome's principal church after the time of Constantine; damaged by earthquake in 896, rebuilt in 904-11, burned down in 1308 and restored, with decorations by Giotto, and frequently altered in subsequent centuries; the Basilica of Santa Maria Maggiore, founded in 352 C.E., with additions, alterations, and restorations in 432, 1292, 1575, and 1741.

174.8 Campagna · The countryside surrounding Rome.

174.32-33 The past week has been a season of great performances · According to Murray's *Rome* (lv), events on 1 November, All Saints Day, included high mass at the Sistine Chapel and music in the oratory at the Church of Santa Maria in Vallicella; events on 2 November, All Souls Day, included another high mass at the Sistine Chapel; and events on 4 November, the Feast of Saint Charles Borromeo, included a high mass in presence of the Pope at the Church of San Carlo in Corso.

175.4 a church opposite this hotel • The Church of San Carlo in Corso, designed by Martino Lunghi in 1614 and completed by Pietro da Cortona, the site of a high mass on 4 November, according to Murray's *Rome* (147).

175.16-17 the equestrian statue of Marcus Aurelius • A monumental, equestrian bronze statue, from circa 165 C.E., of Roman emperor Marcus Aurelius, who reigned 161-80 C.E., in the center of the Piazza del Campidoglio.

175.28-29 Rafael [. . .] his [. . .] Transfiguration • Raphael's last work, unfinished at his death in 1520, considered by many in HJ's day the greatest or "first oil painting in the world," according to Murray's *Rome* (239); commissioned by Giulio de' Medici, then Archbishop of Narbonne and later Pope Clement VII, for the cathedral of Narbonne, kept in the Church of San Pietro in Montorio, Rome, until 1797, moved to Paris until 1815, and then in the Picture Gallery of the Vatican Museum.

175.28-30 Rafael [. . .] his famous Stanze • Four papal apartments in the Vatican, decorated with frescoes designed (and in some cases painted) by Raphael; the Stanza della Segnatura includes Raphael's *The School of Athens* (1509-11); the Stanza d'Eliodoro (Heliodorus), painted in 1511-14, contains four scenes from the Old Testament on the ceiling and four New Testament scenes on the walls.

176.10 a ~~bust~~ statue of Demosthenes • Found at Frascati, near the ancient Tusculum, exhibited in the Braccio Nuovo, Vatican Museum.

176.11 the Athenaeum • Incorporated in 1807 with the intent to become "an establishment similar to that of the Athenaeum and Lyceum of Liverpool in Great Britain" (*Athenaeum Centenary* 24), the Boston Athenaeum is a membership library located at 10½ Beacon Street.

176.15-16 belle ligne romaine • beautiful Roman line.

176.30 Giorgione • Venetian artist of High Renaissance style, Giorgione (1477-1510) influenced a generation of artists with his landscapes.

176.32-33 the great Orcagna in the Campo Santo at Pisa • Andrea di Cione, called Andrea Orcagna (1308-68), a leading Florentine artist; the three frescoes by him in the southeast corner of the Campo Santo at Pisa depict *The Triumph of Death*, *The Last Judgment*, and *The Infernal Regions*.

177.9-10 me voilà loin du Vatican! • here I am, far from the Vatican!

177.10 Apollo Belvedere • Statue of Apollo found in the late fifteenth century near Anzio (Antium), purchased by Cardinal della Rovere (later Pope Julius II), part of the Vatican collection since its inception, and displayed in HJ's day in the fourth cabinet of the Cortile di Belvedere, Vatican Museum.

177.11 Laocoon • Executed by Rhodians Agesander, Polydorus, and Athernodorus during the Hellenistic period, the marble statue depicts Laocoön with his two sons strangled by serpents. It was recovered in 1506.

177.21 that sublime Niobe at Florence • Group of ancient statues, thought to be copies of originals by either Praxiteles or Skopas, found near Rome in 1583 and displayed since the late 1700s at the Uffizi, now in a room dedicated to the group.

177.29-31 a magnificent statue of Augustus, excavated only some 5 years since • The Augustus of Primaporta, a full-length marble made circa 20 B.C.E.; so called because it was discovered in 1863 among the ruins of the villa of Augustus's Empress, Livia, near Prima Porta; shown in the Braccio Nuova, Vatican Museum.

177.31-32 ravishing little bust of Augustus as a boy • In the Museo Chiaramonti, Vatican Museum; this bust, which Murray's *Rome* describes as "one of the most beautiful busts known" (206), was found at Ostia in the early nineteenth century.

178.1 the dying Gladiator • Roman marble copy of a Greek bronze original of circa 240 B.C.E., also known as the Dying Gaul or Dying Gladiator in HJ's day but now identified as the Dying Galatian; it is displayed in the Hall of the Dying Galatian (the Hall of the Dying Gladiator in the nineteenth century) at the Capitoline Museum; it was discovered in the Sallustian Gardens in Rome in 1622.

178.1 Lycian Apollo • The Lycian Apollo, or Apollo Citaredo, copy of an original by Praxiteles, displayed in the Hall of the Dying Gladiator at the Capitol in HJ's day; this statue of Apollo with a lyre was found at the Solfatara, on the road to Tivoli.

178.1 Amazon • Copy of an original by Phidias, found headless in the Villa d'Este, at Tivoli, and displayed in the Hall of the Dying Gladiator or Galatian; it is described in Murray's *Rome* as "one of the grandest figures of its class—much finer than the repetition in the Vatican" (263).

179.1 Miss T. S. • Theodora Sedgwick (1851–1916), sister of Arthur George Sedgwick, Susan Sedgwick Norton, and Sara Sedgwick Darwin.

179.1 Milton • Milton, Massachusetts, southern Boston suburb, where the family of Robert Sedgwick Watson (1809–88) lived.

179.2–3 te livrer à ces folles jouissances • delivering yourself up to these insane pleasures.

179.5 Addy Watson's bad state • Adelaide Howard Watson (1841–69) was one of Robert Sedgwick Watson's daughters; MWJ had written HJ (6 September [1869], Houghton bMS Am 1093.1 [36]) that "Addy Watson is rapidly sinking with lung disease and can last but a little while"; she would die six days after the composition of HJ's letter.

179.10 Silvia W. • Addy's older sister, Sylvia Hathaway Watson (1834–1917), a friend of AJ; in 1873 she married William Emerson, a distant relative of Ralph Waldo Emerson.

179.12 intime • intimate or private.

179.31–33 I have been reading Stendahl [. . .]. He really knows Italy. • Stendhal, pseudonym of Henri Beyle (1783–1842), author of *Le Rouge et le noir* (1830) and *La Chartreuse de Parme* (1839), the latter set in Italy. Beyle was French consul, first to Trieste (1831) and, for the last ten years of his life, to Civita Vecchia, near Rome; he wrote several works about Italy, including *Histoire de la peinture en Italie* (1817), *Rome, Naples et Florence en 1817* (1817, rev. 1826), *Promenades dans Rome* (1829), and *Chroniques italiennes* (1829–36). HJ contributed a review of Andrew A. Paton's *Henry Beyle (otherwise De Stendahl* [sic]): *A Critical and Biographical Study* (1874) to the 17 September 1874 issue of the *Nation*.

180.7 Lung Arno • The broad quay of the Lungarno that skirts the River Arno in Florence.

180.10 Council • HJ was in Rome when the First Vatican Council convened. The council drew the boundaries of Vatican City and declared the doctrine of papal infallibility.

180.16 <u>compagnon</u> de voyage · <u>traveling companion</u>.

180.19 <u>j'aime à croire</u> · <u>I like to believe</u>.

180.34 <u>piano</u> · <u>floor</u>.

181.4–5 Ellen's departure · Ellen, a family servant (Habegger, *Father* 449); MWJ mentions the departure of two other servants in her 21 September [1869] to HJ (Houghton bMS Am 1093.1 [37], and Catharine Walsh, in her 1 November [1869] (Houghton bMS Am 1095 [52]) letter to HJ, mentions having "had a letter from your mother and Alice, dated Oct 12ᵗʰ [. . .]. The only <u>event</u> was our good old Ellen's departure for another place. She had had trouble with the temporary incumbent in the cuisine and resolved, to your mother's great consternation, to 'make a change'. Before leaving however she had a complete break-down—poor thing! and sobbing told your mother that she would come ₍∧₎back₍∧₎ [. . .] to her if the woman she had engaged did not suit her."

181.10 the sale of "your father's" immortal work · Catharine Walsh, in her 1 November [1869] letter to HJ, relayed the news that "the first edition of the 'Secret of Swedenborg' was nearly exhausted."

181.12 Poor Wilky's caterpillar · Catharine Walsh's 1 November [1869] letter to HJ also relayed the news that "Wilk found the Caterpillar worse than ever—but his other produce was fine"; GWJ's cotton crops were regularly ruined by caterpillars (see Maher 78-108).

181.16 Minny <u>has</u> gone to San Francisco · Minny Temple, suffering from the tuberculosis that would kill her a few months later, had hoped to accompany her newly married sister, Ellen Temple Emmet, to California.

181.28 <u>ça ne</u> <u>vaut</u> <u>rien</u> · <u>it is not worth a thing</u>.

182.7 Miss Fanny · Fanny Lombard, a family friend (Strouse 142).

182.10 Bob's Texan appointment · RJ had been a candidate for a position in Galveston, Texas; see Robert Temple's 17 September 1869 (Houghton bMS Am 1094 [439]) and MWJ's 6 September [1869] (Houghton bMS Am 1093.1 [36]) letters to HJ.

182.11 Miss Bessy Ward · Daughter of Anna Barker Ward, a once close friend of Sr. (see *CWJ* 1: 399, 407, 412).

182.14 A. K. · Aunt Kate.

182.25 the Daily Adv. • The *Boston Daily Advertiser*.

182.26 Mr. Eliot's installation • Charles W. Eliot (1834–1926) was
inaugurated president of Harvard University on 19 October 1869.

182.26–27 a note to W. • HJ's 8 November [1869] letter from the Hotel
de Rome to WJ.

182.28 Dr. Butler's • Dr. David P. Butler, whose office, which included a
gymnasium for physical therapy (see HJ to WJ 13, 14 February 1870), was
at 53 Temple Place, Boston.

WILLIAM JAMES
8 November [1869]
ALS Houghton
bMS Am 1094 (1939)

15

Rome, Monday Nov. 8ᵗʰ Hotel de Rome.
Dear W.—I have written Alice so long a letter that I can only
send you 3 lines.—The purpose of them is to tell you that since
coming to Rome I have been immensely relieved of those woes
20 concerning wh. I sent you from Florence such copious bulletins.
Now that I feel better I reproach myself that I broke silence on
the subject. But I couldn't help it. My improvement is owing to
some pills which the doctor gave me just as I left Florence.
Their effect has been so truly remarkable that I enclose a copy
25 of the prescription. With a daily pill (taken before dinner) I get
a daily passage: not copious but sufficient. "And oh! the
difference to me!" I needn't dilate upon it. Whether they are a
mere temporary aid or ~~not~~ are destined to help me to a cure I
know not: as yet when I omit a pill, I miss the evacuation. But
30 their effect is so far cumulative & unattended with a reaction that
as yet I don't need to increase the dose. Without ~~them~~ this
ₐchange₍ₐ₎ I couldn't possibly have staid in Rome. It was quite
unforeseen: therefore I wrote you & probably distressed you as I
did. Their effect as yet has been so magical that I have a horror

of ~~their~~ ₍∧₎its₍∧₎ coming to a sudden explosion ɟ leaving me as bad
as before. But at least I shall ~~of~~ have seen Rome. — The virtue
seems to be in the sulfuric acid, for I had quite come to an end
of aloes. Here it is — as well as I can decipher it.

Rx aloes Barlead ʒiiss   5
    Acide Sulphur, fortissimi
       Guttas XII
  ɟ divide in pio XII — st. duas(?) mane noctique si opus sit.

  —

I can simply make a fac-simile of the man's hieroglyphics: the   10
thing has fewer details than I thought. — Do let me hear some
good news of yourself — whether thro' Garratt or whatsoever.
Wait till I get home ɟ I'll cheer ɟ comfort you. — I have tried to
give Alice ɟ a few of my impressions. — I spent yesterday a
delightful day. I went down to the Capitol ɟ had a delicious long   15
lazy stare at the Faun of Praxiteles ɟ the Antinous. They are
beyond everything. — They have a fault: they transcend the
legitimate bounds of beauty. To comprehend them becomes a
delicious pain. Later I gazed at the glorious sculptures on the
arch of Constantine. <u>Manly</u>! Thy brother   20
     H.

Previous publication: *CWJ* 1: 121–22

  ∾

  190.31 ~~them~~ this • [is *overwrites* em]

  191.2 ~~of~~ have • [h *overwrites blotted* of]

  191.5 Barlead • [*misspelled*]

  191.8 pio • [*misspelled*]

  191.8 noctique • [*misspelled*]

  191.14 ɟ a • [a *overwrites* ɟ]

  191.14 yesterday • yester- | day

  ∾

190.17 I have written Alice so long a letter • HJ's 7, 8 November [1869]
letter to AJ is eleven sheets (twenty-three pages) in manuscript.

190.20 I sent you from Florence such copious bulletins • HJ wrote three such letters to WJ from Florence dated 7, [8] October [1869]; 16 [17], 19 October [1869]; and 26 October [1869].

190.23 which the doctor gave me just as I left Florence • HJ mentions Dr. Duffy prescribed "some medicine (aloes & sulphuric acid)" in his 30 October [1869] letter to WJ.

190.26-27 "And oh! the difference to me!" • The final line of William Wordsworth's 1799 poem "She Dwelt among the Untrodden Ways."

191.5-8 Rx aloes Barlead ʒiiss | Acide Sulphur, fortissimi | Guttas XII | & divide in pio XII—st. duas(?) mane noctique si opus sit. • Rx aloe barbadensis two drams | strongest sulphuric acid | twelve drops | divide in twelve pills—immediately two (?) day and night as needed.

191.12 Garratt • Dr. Alfred Charles Garratt (1813–91). See WJ's 2 October 1869 and 25 October [1869] letters to HJ, in which WJ writes that he has gone to Dr. Garratt to begin galvanism (*CWJ* 1: 99–103 and 112–15).

191.15-16 I went down to the Capitol [. . .] Faun of Praxiteles & the Antinous • Two famous classic sculptures at the Museum of the Capitol. The Faun of Praxiteles is a copy of a statue of a satyr by Greek sculptor Praxiteles. The Antinous is a portrait-statue of a young man thought to be Antinous, lover of the Roman emperor Hadrian. It is described in Murray as an "exquisite statue" that "has commanded the admiration of all critics by its exceeding beauty" (*Rome* 263).

191.19-20 the arch of Constantine • Near the Colosseum, the Arch of Constantine was built in 312 c.e. Its sculptures, most of which were taken from earlier buildings, include part of a battle frieze, figures of prisoners, a series of Hadrianic roundels, and a set of Aurelian panels.

GRACE NORTON
11 November [1869]
ALS Houghton
bMS Am 1094 (875)

5

Rome, Hotel de Rome, Nov. 11th.

Dear Grace—Rome is sublime, but you are sublimer! Base tho' I
am, I am not insensible to the delicate insight with which you
divined that, <u>in spite</u> of my baseness & my apparent oblivion of
all human decencies, I was not only worthy but even anxious to   10
hear from you. Your letter came to me yesterday at the end of a
heavy Roman day & lightened most palpably the weight of the
twenty four hours past & to come. It doesn't do to stand too
much alone among all these swarming ghosts of the past & there
can be no better antidote to their funereal contagion than a   15
charming modern living feminine letter.—My dear Grace, I was
not only anxious to hear from you: I will say more: I will
actually assert that I was <u>worthy</u>! I have been holding my peace
neither because I was false nor fickle nor ~~faithf~~ faithless but
simply—if it's not too lame & impotent a conclusion—because   20
I've been too perpetually tired to take up a pen.—After roaming
thro' the city all day I have generally in the evening collapsed
into languor & stupefaction. Having come to Rome with very
vague previsions as to my stay I have gone roundly to work
sight-seeing, ~~Aot~~ so that in case of a proximate departure I   25
should have drunk as deeply as possible of the enchanted
draught. I have tacitly rejected the thought of putting you off
even provisionally with half a dozen lines & I have most ~~illollg~~
illogically waited until some supernatural intervention should
have compelled me to spend a morning in my room—or brought   30
he home in the evening fresh & elastic & the least bit good
company. I don't say that this is the case this evening: but we
must affect a compromise.—Your letter was all delightful, save
your mention of Charles's being unwell. What is the use of

having such a sunny haven of rest—of being master of the villa d'Elci—if you are going to overwork yourself like a <u>bourgeois</u>? Do let me hear when you next write that he is better—better even than before *&* being rapidly made over anew by the magic

5 of your home. Meanwhile give him my love *&* God-speed for a Florentine Winter.—It's poor work writing from Rome, if you pretend in the least to write up to the level of your impressions. Expect a most common-place scrawl.—I find Rome— <u>interesting</u>: I cant say more. In this quality it exceeds everything

10 I have yet seen *&* falls not a whit below my pre-conceptions. Other places are pleasing, picturesque, pretty, charming; but Rome is thoroughly serious. Heaven knows it's picturesque enough: but it has in this respect a depth of tone which makes it differ not only in degree but even in kind, from Florence *&*

15 Venice. I have been out of doors so constantly from the moment of my arrival *&* have had such a crowding multitude of impressions that my brain contains as yet but a confused mass of brilliant images which I devoutly trust will be reduced with time to some degree of harmony *&* logic: but as yet they are barely

20 available for epistolary purposes.—My s mind swarms with <u>effects</u> of all kinds—to be introduced into realistic novels yet unwritten.—But I must get rid without delay of my confession. I came hither, as I foresaw I should have to, by the night express *&* saw no more of the road than was visible between sunrise *&* 10

25 o'clock. Don't lament, however, I shall see it all in detail on my way back. After going to my hotel *&* a hasty "wash" *&* breakfast I let my self loose on the city. It was decidely one of the days of my life. I roamed about in every direction from noon till dusk *&* when I came home to dinner had pretty well taken the cream off

30 of Rome. My senses being a good deal quickened by excitement I think that if I had been compelled to depart that evening I should have felt myself to have got a good solid impression of the subject—*&* would have ventured to discuss it at an evening-party. I <u>do</u> find Rome <u>rubbishy</u>—magnificently, sublimely so.

Amid many of the heaps of rubbish I have lingered & gloated
with the fondest fascination. I spent a long sunny morning
(besides various secondary visits) lounging & maundering &
murmuring in the Coliseum; & an afternoon very much in the
same fashion at the Baths of Caracalla. I enjoyed a magnificent
sunset there, on the summit, quite by self; & I think I never had
quite so intimate à <u>tête à tête</u> with the genius of the past. We
were literally face to face—& eye-to eye. Another long sunny
cloudy breezy morning at the Palace of the Caesars which (since
you were here probably) ~~have~~ has been under the auspices of
Napoleon III ~~been~~ excavated & revealed in the most wondrous
manner. Much too have I loafed & lingered in the Forum. Two
good long stares have I had at those unutterably <u>manly</u>
sculptures which adorn the arch of Constantine. Few things tell
so well the Roman tale. Decidedly I veto Female Suffrage. Again
& again have I taken the measure of that noblest & simplest &
sweetest of statues—the kind old Marcus Aurelius at the ~~Capital~~
Capitol. It makes even Roman bronze mild & humane &
pathetic. At the Pantheon I have said at least a dozen good
round Pagan prayers. It seems to me <u>exquisitely</u> sublime & I dont
believe I shall ever get from architecture a purer cleaner
sensation. As for St. Peter's I decidedly go in for it:—tho'
indeed as you suggest I'm extremely glad "it aint no bigger." But
it <u>is</u> big without a doubt & furnishes the mind with a perfectly
satisfactory standard & example of vastness. It's internal
physiognomy strikes me as ~~really~~ immensely ~~magnificently~~ & I
should never dream of wishing it other. The glorious whole
swallows up the inglorious parts & you get one rich transcendent
effect. — To the Vatican I have paid ~~ma~~ of course many visits &
almost feel as if I ₍ₐ₎have₍ₐ₎ seen a fair portion of it. Its richness &
interest are even greater than I supposed; ◊ the great things are
more numerous & greater. That there <u>are</u> such things is certainly
a great comfort to the feeble conscientious mind. I had finally
got into a wretched muddle in the Florentine galleries with

regard to pictures ɗ painters ɗ my likes ɗ dislikes: but now that
fitful fever is ◊ quenched — ɗ these cool immortals quite make
me forget the tawdry colorists. Within the last couple of days
however I confess I have been reminded of them at a couple of
the private Galleries. I saw to day at the Doria Palace your old
man of Titian with a rose ɗ a jewel. He is well enough; but I
fancy your maturer judgement would think him the least bit of a
humbug. I fear it would enlighten you in a similar manner as to
the merits of the Empress Helena of Paul Veronese, of which
you speak. I am sorry my dear Grace to blight your young
illusions; but in compensation I commend to you the fine P. V.
at the Pitti, over a door — ◊◊ A Baptism of our Lord. I have seen
to day one really great picture — one of those works which draw
heavily⸗ on your respect, ɗ make you feel the richer for the loss:
the portrait of Innocent X, by Velasquez at the Doria Palace.
Also a Corregio — a mere sketch, but most divinely touched — ɗ a
glorious Claude which leaves Turner nowhere; car enfin it's in
good taste. This is not everything but it's much. If it were
everything, by the way, I think I should like the Transfiguration
a little better. It's well enough once in awhile I suppose, to have
a disappointment. I paid Rafael the high compliment of
choosing his immortal work as the occasion of mine: in that way
I shall be sure to remember it. M. Angelo's ᵐ Moses, on the
other hand leaves much less to be desired than I fancied. It
seems to me a work of really heroic merit. — You ask about your
old friend San Clemente. I paid him a visit the other afternoon
ɗ found him full of sweet antiquity ɗ solitude. It's since you
were here I suppose, that he has been found to have an elder
brother buried beneath the soil, on whose prostrate form he has
settled himself so placidly. I was too late to explore: but shall not
fail to return. — Too late; my dear Grace those words remind me
of the actual flight of time. You must let this hasty scribble serve
as a note of my deep enjoyment. I do wish I could put into my
poor pale words some faint reflection of the color ɗ beauty of

this glorious old world. But you have it all in memory; & then—
que dis-je?—you have in fact something very nearly as good. I
know some of the secrets of the Florentine hills: I know your
garden, your terrace, your prospect: you certainly have Italy
quite as well as I.—I am most happy to ~~know~~ learn of your   5
felicity & contentment. May it know no interruption. I trust that
Charles has exhausted ~~old~~ all possible pretexts for getting
tired—& that in common with you all, ₐhe₍ₐ₎ will elevate himself
to inventing pretexts for taking his perfect ease—troubled by no
more painful effort than once in a while to remember that I   10
think of you as you my dear Grace have done so divinely & that
in token of the same I have hereby sent you my love.—Farewell.
I sometimes ~~whis~~ wish that instead of having come to this
terrible serious Rome I were wintering ◇◇◇ peacefully in calm
aesthetic Florence. But in some fashion or other I shall put   15
Rome thro'; & then I hope shall take another look at the banks
of the Arno. Many thanks for your account of my vacant rooms.
I'm afraid it has a more liberal vacancy than I shall avail to fill:
but I shall do what I can, be sure. But at this rate you'll certainly
not accuse me of lacking the power of expansion. So with   20
Roman brevity—good bye.—Most faithfully your's H. James jr.
P.S. I have been feeling since coming to Rome, in spite of
inevitable fatigue, very much better than in Florence.—I address
to Fenzi as I don't know your proper superscription.

Previous publication: Horne 27–32

 ❧

    193.19 ~~faithf~~ faithless • [l *overwrites blotted* f]

    193.25 ~~A◇t~~ so • [so *overwrites* A◇t]

    193.28–29 ~~illollg~~ illogically • [gic *overwrites* llg]

    193.29 intervention • interven= | tion

    194.20 ~~s~~ mind • [m *overwrites* s]

    194.33–34 evening- | party • evening-party

    194.34 magnificently • magnifi- | cently

    195.7 à tête à tête • [*misspelled*]

195.10 ~~have~~ has • [s *overwrites* ve]

195.17–18 ~~Capital~~ Capitol • [o *overwrites* a]

195.26 ~~really~~ immensely • [imm *overwrites* really]

195.29 ~~ma~~ of • [of *overwrites* ma]

195.31 ⋄ the • [t *overwrites illegible letter*]

196.2 ⋄ quenched • [q *overwrites illegible letter*]

196.12 ⋄⋄ A • [A *overwrites illegible letters*]

196.23 ~~m~~ Moses • [M *overwrites* m]

197.5 ~~know~~ learn • [learn *overwrites* know]

197.7 ~~old~~ all • [all *overwrites* old]

197.13 ~~whis~~ wish • [is *overwrites* his]

197.14 ⋄⋄⋄ peacefully • [pea *overwrites illegible letters*]

197.21–24 good bye. [. . .] superscription. • [*written across the letter's last page.*]

∾

194.1–2 the villa d'Elci • The Nortons' Florence residence during the winter of 1869–70; see HJ's 24, 25, [26] October [1869] letter to Sr.

195.9 the Palace of the Caesars • The Roman Imperial palace on the Palatine was frequently altered and rebuilt during the Empire. According to Murray, during the winter and spring of 1869, "the whole of the *Area Palatina* has been laid bare, the vast *Crypto porticus* leading to the Flavian Palace from the residences of Claudius, Caligula, and Tiberius, have been cleared out, a large *Piscina* bordering on them discovered, which probably served as a fish-pond, and a great subterranean gallery beneath the Palace of Vespasian, or Aedes Publica, and the Temple of Jupitor Victor discovered, from which passages lead to the ancient *Latomiae* of the Palatine, excavated in the volcanic tufa" (lvii). Also recently discovered were "numerous painted chambers between the Flavian Palace and the huge mass of rubble-work building overlooking the Velabrum, supposed to mark the site of the *Auguratorium*" (*Rome* lvii).

195.29 the Vatican • The Vatican museums.

196.5 Doria Palace • The Palazzo Doria-Pamphili, a seventeenth-century palace built at via del Corso 305 in Rome, housed a significant Renaissance art collection.

196.5–6 your old man of Titian with a rose & a jewel • Titian's *Portrait*.

196.12 A Baptism of our Lord • HJ described this painting as "a lovely composition by Paul Veronese, the dealer of silver hues—a Baptism of Christ," in "Florentine Notes," originally published in *The Independent*, 21 May 1874: 1–2.

196.15 the portrait of Innocent X • Velázquez's *Pope Innocent X*.

196.16 a Corregio—a mere sketch • Probably Correggio's unfinished, allegorical painting *Virtue*, in the Palazzo Doria-Pamphili.

196.16–17 a glorious Claude • The Palazzo Doria-Pamphili held several Claude Lorrain works: *Landscapes with Figures*, *Landscape with a Temple of Apollo*, and *The Mill*.

196.17 car enfin • for indeed.

196.23 M. Angelo's m Moses • Michelangelo's massive *Moses*, part of the monument to Pope Julius II in San Pietro in Vincoli, stands in harsh judgment of the idolatry of the Jews.

196.26 San Clemente • The Church of San Clemente, on the Via di San Giovanni in Laterano, which connects the Coliseum and the Basilica of San Giovanni in Laterano; this is one of the oldest churches in Rome, erected in 1108 on the ruins of an even older church that was mentioned as early as 392 and destroyed in 1084.

196.28–29 he has been found to have an elder brother buried beneath the soil • Excavation of the ruins of the older Church of San Clemente had begun, according to Murray's 1869 *Rome*:

> This ancient ch. [. . .] had been long forgotten, until, in the latter
> months of 1857, some repairs having become necessary in the adjoining
> convent, [. . .] its zealous and very intelligent prior, Father Mullooly,
> came upon a wall covered with very ancient paintings at a level of nearly
> 20 ft. below the modern ch.; further research showed that this was
> the aisle of a very extensive edifice, and that it stood on massive con-
> structions of a Pagan period, some, probably, of the early times of the
> Empire. So interesting was the discovery considered, that researches
> on an extensive scale were undertaken under the direction of the prior,
> which up to the present time have resulted in the clearing out of both
> the aisles and a large portion of the nave, and in opening out the line of
> columns which divided them, and in tracing a considerable area of the
> Roman edifice, upon which it as well as the modern ch. rested. (149)

197.2 que dis-je? • what am I saying?

GRACE NORTON
18 November [1869]
ALS Houghton
bMS Am 1094 (876)

5

Rome Hotel de Rome Nov. 18<u>th</u>

My dear Grace—
　　Your in every ∧way[∧] <u>exquisite</u> letter of last Sunday has just
10　arrived & filled me with anguish & agony. To have failed to write
for so long is ignominy enough. To have you exaggerate my fault
is simply intolerable. I despatched to you several days since
(within 3, I think, after the receipt of your first letter) an epistle
which, since you haven't received it, I may venture to say was
15　both long & brilliant. Why it shouldn't have reached you I know
not. It was sent (as I was uncertain as ◇◇ to ~~the~~ your exactly
proper address) to MM. Fenzi. It was superscribed to you
simply, without mention of Charles. M.M. Fenzi may have
stupidly failed to associate you with him & have placed it aside to
20　be called for. Do, I beseech you, cause it to be asked for—as this
is the only clue I can devise as to its whereabouts. May it have
turned up since you wrote? I quite forget on what day it was
posted—but I should have supposed it might make the journey
before the moment of your writing.—If it is lost, however, I
25　can't altogether regret it, for ~~the~~ the ∧loss[∧] has made me
possessor of your second letter & of the happiness thereby
produced.—You see, after all, I <u>am</u> as bad as you would think
me—I am not only indifferent to your unhappiness—I am
actually happy in it. By which I mean that I would not for a
30　great deal have not got your letter. I am emphatically not ill—&
thereby not in need of Mrs. Ward's ministrations—a fortunate
circumstance—inasmuch as she, poor woman, is again an invalid
herself. I called upon her sometime since but being informed at
the door that she was feasting an archbishop I discreetly retired.

I immediately received from her an invitation to dine, but she
was absent from the table owing to one for her old attacks & I
learned to day from her daughters that she is still suffering. —
But enough about her — in spite of her wretchedness. That
Charles is better I am ◇ heartily rejoiced to hear — as well as that
you too are mending — which I keenly regret should have been
necessary. — I gave you the other day a few of my "impressions":
they have done nothing but increase & multiply. I do hope for
their sake, such as they were, that my letter may have turned
up. — ◇ Assuredly Rome is beyond all things. I have had since I
wrote, a long glorious drive along the Appian Way, besides an
other infinitude of strolls & lounges & stares in a dozen great
places. I went back a couple of days since to San Clemente & saw
the deeply interesting old sub-church which has recently been
recovered to the world. At San Lorenzo too I spent a charming
hour — in spite of the gorgeous bedizenments with which its
delicious antiquity is well nigh smothered away. I have been
seeing to day the grand restored Bas◇ Basilica of St. Paul (out of
the Walls) — a really sublime affair. It has been restored in a
grand sumptuous taste & is a marvel of opole opulence & beauty.
◇ But it is not only these special marvels & localities that enchant
my soul — it is all the chance beauties & delights of one's
wanderings here — the very air & light & colour of the Roman
landscape — the sky that seems to reflect the unseen campagna —
the great grassy wastes, skirted with convent walls & dotted with
a lounging soldier or a wandering monk — the cypresses the
olives, the little pallid stunted oaks (— the silence & idleness of
the scene) — the perpetual presence of the past. I go a great deal
to the Vatican. I think I should never — really never — weary of
those thoroughly healthy ◇ Masterpieces. I don't know ◇ that I
have any overwhelming favorite: Sometimes one rules the hour
& sometimes another. The sweetest thing in Rome I think is the
Antinous of the Capitol: but close to him stands the Faun of
Praxiteles (in merit I mean ʃ — as well as in fact) & close to him

the ~~Strigillarious~~ Strigillarius of the Vatican—& the
Demosthenes & the new Augustus & a certain athlete & a certain
Caryotid & a hundred more. In fact they are all profoundly
excellent & beautiful—all definite & masculine & full of character

5 & truth. "Where," exclaims the distracted modern mind—"shall
I find the real voice of the absolute?" I should direct him to the
gallery of the Vatican. Did I say anything in my last about the
Sistine Chapel? Possibly I hadn't seen it. But I have seen it
now—& tho' I am not sure that I have learned anything new

10 about the reach of human genius I think I like M. A. the better
for it. That is, the last Judgment strikes me as being a good deal
of an error; but the ceiling, as ceilings go, is decidedly great.—I
see no people, to speak of—or for that matter, to speak to. Rome
as yet is by no means crowded.—As if Rome were ever anything

15 else <u>but</u> crowded! "Crowded" is just the word. It's not the clear,
light atmosphere of Florence—but an air thick with the
presence of invisible ghosts. Upon this fine fancy I must say
good night. I wish to write on the other side a little note to
Jane.—or rather, lest I should breed a sisterly feud, let me

20 consecrate to her in the future a sheet complete & peculiar, &
beg of you to thank her for her note & for its vivid reminder of
Florentine beauty— —as well as of her own kindness.—My dear
Jane—(I'll risk the feud) I <u>do</u> know Fiesole. It was the 1ˢᵗ walk I
took from Florence. I know that cypress bordered convent

25 terrace—& all the divine prospect. I don't despair of knowing it
again, under your auspices.—May I write still a line to Sara? I
am haunted by a vile omission, which I failed to repair at Pisa.
She kindly transmitted me a message from Miss Lowell for
which I have found (as usual) no better response than silence.

30 Do beg her (if she has not yet written or when she again writes)
to invent on my behalf some pretty compliment. As that I thank
Miss L. most warmly for her good wishes toward my advantage
& gain over here, but that a message from her can only remind
me of my losses.—Farewell. Make believe you haven't received

this & write me another epistle of reproof.—Seriously—it is very disagreeable to think of your having been worried by ∧my[∧] silence. Be sure that silence is always a healthy sign. When melted & softened by illness I shall be sure to become eloquent & appealing. I'm not a stoic: <u>n'y comptez</u> <u>pas</u>—but always dear Grace your most affectionate & grateful friend

      <u>H. James</u> jr.

5

No previous publication

∽

200.12 intolerable • intoler= | able

200.16 ◇◇ to • [to *overwrites illegible letters*]

200.16 ~~the~~ your • [your *overwrites* the]

200.24 however • how- | ever

200.25 ~~th◇~~ the • [e *overwrites illegible letter*]

200.33 sometime • some- | time

201.1 immediately • imme- | diately

201.5 ◇ heartily • [h *overwrites illegible letter*]

201.10 ◇ Assuredly • [A *overwrites illegible letter*]

201.18 ~~Ba◇~~ Basilica • [s *overwrites illegible letter*]

201.20 sumptuous • sump- | tuous

201.20 ~~opole~~ opulence • [u *overwrites blotted* ol; l *overwrites* e]

201.21 ◇ But • [B *overwrites illegible letter*]

201.27 (— • [(*inserted*]

201.28 scene) • [) *inserted*]

201.30 ◇ Masterpieces • [M *overwrites illegible letter*]; Master- | pieces

201.30 ◇ that • [t *overwrites illegible letter*]

201.33 Capitol • Capi- | tol

201.34)— • [— *overwrites*)]

202.1 ~~Strigillarious~~ Strigillarius • [ius *overwrites* i◇us]

202.3 Caryotid • [*misspelled*]

202.12 decidedly • deci= | dedly

202.34–203.6 Farewell. [. . .] <u>H. James</u> jr. • [*written across the letter's first page*]

∽

200.12–13 I despatched [. . .] an epistle • HJ's letter of 11 November [1869].

200.31 Mrs. Ward • Anna Barker Ward.

201.15 San Lorenzo • The Basilica of San Lorenzo, or Church of San Lorenzo fuori le Mura, built in 578 on the burial site of Saint Lawrence, restored and altered several times up to 1864; according to Baedeker, "The front has been recently embellished with mosaics representing the founders and patrons of the church" (*Central Italy* 163).

201.18 Basilica of St. Paul (out of the Walls) • San Paolo fuori le Mura, about two kilometers outside the Porta San Paolo and on the road to Ostia, this church, originally founded in 388, was renewed, embellished, and restored many times in intervening years; before a fire in 1823, it was "the finest and most remarkable church in Rome"; Pope Leo XII's subsequent restoration left "the ancient basilica [. . .] superseded by a modern and in many respects unsightly fabric" (Baedeker, *Central Italy* 221, 222).

202.1 Strigillarius of the Vatican • The *Apoxyomenos*, a statue of an athlete cleaning himself with a strigil, or scraping iron, housed in the Braccio Nuovo.

202.2 a certain athlete • Possibly the *Apoxyomenos*, which HJ already noted, or another of the several statues of athletes housed in the Braccio Nuovo.

202.2–3 a certain Caryotid • According to the Baedeker for *Central Italy*, there are at least two caryatids in the Braccio Nuovo, the most noteworthy being "one of those executed by Diogenes for the Pantheon, restored by Thorwaldsen" (280).

202.11 the last Judgment • Michelangelo's *Last Judgment* (1534–41) on the altar wall.

202.28 Miss Lowell • Mabel Lowell, only surviving daughter of James Russell Lowell, was traveling abroad with Mr. and Mrs. Fields.

203.5 n'y comptez pas • don't count on that.

MARY WALSH JAMES
21, [22] November [1869]
ALS Houghton
bMS Am 1094 (1766)

5

Rome Hotel de Rome Nov. 21<u>st</u>
 Sunday evening.

My dearest Mother—In consideration of my last letter having
been a terrifically long one, I have let two whole weeks ebb away   10
without writing again. I find here so many uses for my time that
except in the evening it is hard to find a moment for letters, & in
the evening I am apt to be rather too jaded with my day's
exploits to take up my pen with much energy. I had hoped to
succeed in devoting this blessed Sunday morning to a long   15
homeward scribble; but I spent a large part of it in going with
Mrs. Ward to a famous Musical Mass at St. Cecilia's: this being
the eve. of that holy virgin & martyr. But of this anon. I
mentioned in my last the receipt of your dearest & sweetest of
letters. A week later I received an excellent communication from   20
Willy in answer to my 1<u>st</u> letter from Florence—written as it
seems to me, so long ago. I now, insatiable wretch as I am, begin
to crave & expect some heavenly missive from father or Alice; &
even to count the days until the revolving month shall bring me
another letter from you. Heaven speed the time!—Meanwhile I   25
am up to my neck in Rome & have to day begun the fourth week
of my stay. In spite of the dense fulness of the days the time has
passed most rapidly. I have seen, in some cases repeatedly, most
of the important ~~shows~~ shews & wonders. Would that I could
give you a twentieth part—a select condensed twentieth—of my   30
swarming impressions & emotions. Most happily, I have been
very decently well, & if the same blissful condition will outlast
my stay & accompany me to Naples I shall be immensely
thankful. Soon after writing last I called upon Mrs. Ward, but

learning that she was feasting an Archbishop I modestly
withdrew. The next day, however, I ~~discovered~~ [∧]received[∧] a
very kind note from her, bidding me to dinner, which I of course
accepted. She turned out as usual to be laid up with one of her

5 ancient attacks. But we were largely entertained by the
loquacious Miss Lily & the adorable Miss Bessy—"we" being,
beside myself, Mrs. Charles Strong of N. Y.—a very sweet &
agreeable woman whose "conversion," chiefly I believe thro'
Mrs. Ward's agency, made some noise here last Winter—& her

10 youthful & precocious daughter Miss "Pussy" Strong. Bessy
Ward spoke very joyfully of having rec'd a letter from Alice,
asked many questions about her & sent her her love. She has
grown up into a most charming creature—pretty, intelligent,
gracious & elegant—a most noble & delightful maiden—as nice a

15 girl as you often see. Her poor sister looked very feeble & jaded,
but conversed as fluently as ever. One day last week Mrs. Ward
called for me to drive, but I was absent. ⫽ Last evening I again
went to see her & had the benefit of her precious discourse for a
couple of hours. Her garrulity is something stupendous—& the

20 best that you can say of her is that she makes such garrulity
graceful⫽ ⁎ —which she ◊ certainly does, extremely. She was
very sweet & kind & obliging in her offers & sent her love to you
& father. She arranged with me to accompany her to day to the
Vesper Service (3 o'clock) at the little ch. of St. Cecilia away

25 over in the Trastevere. She duly called for me ∧in comp'y.[∧] with
Miss Ripley an ancient virgin of the f Faith, established in
Rome. The music & singing on this occasion draws great crowds
& is most divinely beautiful. Much of it was immensely florid &
profane in tone—as far at least as I could judge; but in spite of

30 the crowded & fetid church & the ▬▬▬ ~~rebellion~~ revolt
provoked in my mind by this spectacular Catholocism (for if
you don't love it here in Rome you must hate it: there is no
middle path) I truly enjoyed the performance. On our way
home, in the e◊◊◊ carriage, Mrs. Ward, who had become highly

names

excited & <u>exaltée</u>, recited with a great deal of color & warmth the
history of her conversion & the blessedness of her state. At all
points apparently she bravely takes the bull by the horns. For a
Catholic as thoroughly <u>lancée</u> & active as she, this must be a
truly <u>délicieux séjour</u>. I don't at all agree with the people who 5
assume that Rome is the place to disgust ◊ & disenchant you with
the Church. On the contrary, a faint impulse once received (an
essential premiss) Rome makes the rest of the journey all down-
hill work. The sense you get here of the great Collective church
must be far ◊ more potent than elsewhere to swallow up & efface 10
all the vile & flagrant minor offenses to the soul & the senses.
Once <u>in</u> the church you can be perfectly indifferent to the
debased & stultified priests & the grovelling peasantry: out of it
you certainly can't. But enough on this chapter. There is a better
Rome than all this—a Rome in the lingering emanation of 15
whose genius & energy I have spent many a memorable hour. It
makes all this modern ecclesiasticism, to my perception, seem
sadly hollow & vulgar. The ruins & relics & chance wayside
reminders of this ancient strength are far more numerous &
absorbing than I supposed. You come upon them in some form 20
at every step & when once encountered, they fix & fascinate the
mind. All the old Roman fragments that I've seen, of whatever
nature or dimensions, have a character & dignity that makes ◊ it
salutary ∧to[∧] ~~aoundle~~ haunt & frequent them. I wish I could
knock off with a stroke of the pen ~~an~~ a clear impression of one 25
of my days here & make you feel the interest of two or three of
the choicest spots. Its hard to say, however, what are the choicest
spots. ◊◊ Each one at the ~~moments~~ moment seems richer in
suggestions, more eloquent & thought-provoking than the last &
you surrender yourself to the absolute spell of its melancholy 30
charm. I betook myself one glorious morning a number of days
since to the mighty baths of Caracalla (of wh. I spoke in my last)
& spent a long time ∧alternately[∧] quaking among their damp
cold shadows & roasting in the sunshine which floods their

crumbling summits, as they gaze out across the Campagna. From there I went to certain <u>Columbaria</u> in the same quarter—a series of subterranean vaults recently discovered, in which the Romans <u>pigeonholed</u> or deposited on small concave shelves the

5 vases containing the ashes of their dead. They stand in a great ~~sun◊~~ sunny rubbishy Italian vineyard, whence you descend into ~~these~~ the ~~curious wells~~ dead moist air ɑ̃ the dim mildewed light of these strange funereal wells. Few things transport you so forcibly into the past. Their perfection is almost unimpaired.

10 Tier upon tier the little pigeon holes sit yawning upon you, ~~sub~~ each subscribed with its original Latin statement. From here, at the invitation of a solitary Englishman whom I encountered on the premises, I took a ~~long~~ drive along the Appian Way, as far as the tomb of Cecilia Metella—or ◊◊ ◊ rather some distance

15 beyond it. "Who was this lady?—was she chaste ɑ̃ fair?" I'm sure I don't know; but her tomb at any rate is one of the effective objects of the world. The great violet Campagna, at this point, stretching its idle breadth to the horizon known of Roman eyes—a wilderness of sunny decay ɑ̃ vacancy—must be

20 seen to be appreciated. Another day of ~~a~~ the ~~similar fashion~~ ₍ᴧ₎same tender color₍ᴧ₎ I had more recently, when I drove out to the glorious restored Basilica of St. Paul's without the Walls—ɑ̃ came home by the Pyramid of Caius Cestius—(whose mighty Roman mortality was deemed worthy of entombment in the

25 heart of ₍ᴧ₎that₍ᴧ₎ solid mountain of masonry—I went into the little sepulchral chamber ɑ̃ saw the faded frescoes ɑ̃ ~~the~~ measured the thickness of the walls)—ɑ̃ that divine little protestant Cemetery where Shelley ɑ̃ Keats lie buried—a place ~~more~~ most lovely ɑ̃ solemn ɑ̃ exquisitely full of the traditional

30 Roman quality—with the vast grey pyramid inserted into the sky on one side ɑ̃ the dark cold cypresses on the other, ɑ̃ the light bursting out between them ɑ̃ the whole surrounding landscape swooning away for very picturesqueness. Another morning I spent at the Palace of the Caesars, a vast enclosure

covering ◇ a large portion of the Palatine Hill, in which great
excavations are being carried on by the Emperor of the
French—& mighty mansions & temples & theatres restored to
the light of day & to some faint semblance of their primitive
shape. It's a most enchanting spot. You have a view of all Rome
& you wander at your will through a wilderness [∧]of[∧] evergreen
shrubbery & eternal Roman basements & partitions. One
afternoon recently towards dusk, after a day spent I don't quite
remember how, I found myself standing in a little hollow
between the foot of the Palatine & the Tiber & gazing at the
massive, battered & ugly old Arch of Janus Quadrifrons. A man
sallied forth from the neighboring shades with an enormous key
& whispered the soul-stirring name of the <u>Cloaca Maxima</u>. I
joyfully assented & he led me apart in ◇ under a series of half-
buried arches into a deeper hollow, where the great mouth of a
tunnel seemed to brood over the scene & thence introduced me
into a little covered enclosure, whence we might survey a small
section of the ancient sewer. It gave me the deepest & grimmest
impression of antiquity I have ever received. He lit a long torch
& plunged it down into the blackness. It threw a red glare on a
mass of dead black travertine & he I was assured that I was
gazing upon the masonry of Tarquinius Priscus. If it wasn't I'm
sure it ought to have been. A few days since I went to see the
strange old church of <u>San Clemente</u>, which has long passed for
one of the most curious & interesting of the early Roman
basilicas. You may judge whether its reputation was increased by
the recent discovery of a complete subterranean church, upon
whose walls as on a foundation, the later edifice was reared.
Thro' the now wholly excavated labyrinth of this primitive
tabernacle, taper in hand, I was <u>promené</u> by an old Irish monk,
who told me stories of all the blessed saints whose adventures
you may yet decipher in the most rudimentary frescoes on the
walls. But he ended by conducting me down into a dee still
deeper & darker & narrower compartment & in this triply buried

sanctuary laid my hand upon an enormous block of granite (or
what-not) & pronounced in a magnificent brogue the name of
Servius Tullius. To the non-antiquarian mind these are quite 1ˢᵗ
class sensations. Another emotion of equal value was the fruit
some three nights since of a moonlight visit to the Coliseum. I
started off by ◇ myself on foot, about 8 o'clock, beneath a
radiant evening sky. The Coliseum itself was all very well; but it
was not that that repaid me, but my halt on the square before
the ~~Ca◇◇~~ Capitol, beneath the great transfigured statue of
M. Aurelius. I like this grand old effigy better ~~evert~~ every time I
see it. It commands the sympathies somehow more than any
work of art I know. If to directly impress the soul, the heart, the
affections, to stir up by some ineffable magic the sense of all
one's human relations & of the warm surrounding presence of
human life — if this is the sign of a great work of art — this statue
is one of the very greatest. It massed itself up before me in the
~~m◇~~ magical moonlight with a truly appalling reality. — Of course
I go a great deal to the Vatican — & never without feeling
somewhat the wiser for it. The really good statues there would
gain by being looked at every day of your life, so manly &
definite & strong are they. They have no pretention, affectation,
subtlety &c. But one can't talk about them. I am buying no
photos.; but if I were, should like to send you about a
hundred. — In my last letter, I remember I let out rather savagely
on Rafael. Since then I have been back to his ~~stan~~ rooms in the
Vatican & feel rather more philosophical about the matter. I
don't think him more interesting; but I mind less his being as he
is. Evidently there are two moods for looking at pictures. One in
which the mind demands simple unqualified pleasure &
exaltation: the other critical considerate & questioning. The first
is really much the more fastidious of the two & I fancy it to ~~w~~ be
well that it should find only occasional satisfaction. When the
second is uppermost, almost any gallery is a very pleasant place.
I have seen almost all the Roman collections. Half their merit to
my taste is in their being in their delightful princely shabby old

Palaces—with their great names—Borghese, Farnese, Colonna, Corsini, Doria. Among them all I don't know that I have seen any thing very noteworthy. In the Borghese collection is a Corregio of heavenly merit—& a Titian of earthly. In the magnificent Dorian halls is the famous portrait by Velasquez of Innocent X, of wh. Taine speaks rather memorably—& a most memorable portrait it is—one of those works wh. by its heavy drain on your faculty of respect seem absolutely to exhaust it & yet to leave you only the richer for the loss. At the Corsini palace the other day, I got myself let into the Gardens where I spent a delicious hour. I did the same at the Vatican & went strolling about the sunny terraces like a wicked old Cardinal. But this is gossip enough. We are each rather tired. I wanted to say something about M the Sistine Chapel, the Moses &c—& about a rapturous little fresco of ◊◊ the e◊◊ cunning Leonardo, which I chanced upon, during a delicious random stroll, in a convent on the top of the Janiculum. But they'll keep—they've kept thus far.—This by the way is no longer last night but Su Monday afternoon.—I have just got—a richer fate than I expected, your & Willy's letters of November 1st. They are full of sympathy & advice with regard to the burden of my letters from Florence. You will by this time have learned that I've derived invaluable relief from the use of sulfuric acid, prescribed by my Florentine doctor. How long this is going to last I can't foresee; but the medicine has done [ʌ]me,[ʌ] at any rate, the immense service of letting me see Rome. As yet its effect continues very fairly; tho' I fancy that I see signs of its gradual diminution. If it will only carry me thro a fortnight at Naples! In my last letter, I remember I prattled away in fine style ◊◊ about my "plans." I have really no right to have any beyond the morrow: I should like to remain here another fortnight & then make the trip to Naples. If a month hence I am as well as I am now I shall rather feel that I am better—tho' I'm not sure how far it is just to regard as an improvement a condition wholly dependent on medicine. I have been awfully tempted to "settle"

5

10

15

20

25

30

35

in Rome for the winter; but I have lacked (I don't ∧know[∧] what
to call it) the rashness or the courage. I have amused myself by
looking at a dozen lodgings—all repulsive. They consist either
of a single room in the bosom of an Italian family—or of an
5   independent group. The latter for obvious reasons ∧—i.e.
expense—[∧] are unsuitable—& the former ~~for~~ on grounds none
the less valid, for one obliged to exact certain comforts.
Altogether, on reflection I have shrunk from binding myself
here in any way. If, after Naples I still feel like remaining in
10   Italy, I shall have Florence to turn to—Florence the lovely (&
the comfortable.) If not I shall make for Paris, where my ulterior
plans may freely develop themselves. I shall there be equidistant
from England & Germany & during any period of suspense shall
feel ~~in a good~~ ∧thats it's[∧] no loss to have a month of Paris. Tell
15   Willy that I mean to answer his two letters fully in day or so. I
meant to inclose herewith a reply to the 1ˢᵗ, but am rather tired
of writing.—Your own letter, d my dearest Mother, was an
excellent thing in letters, & very welcome your news of father
Alice & the boys. The two former I see, have tipped each other
20   the wink to neglect & ignore me.—With such conduct they will
never prosper. I'm extremely glad to hear of Minny's journey.
A. K. will probably arrive here a week hence. I should much
enjoy going about here a little with her; but I fear I shan't find
much sympathy in her "party."—Farewell. This is the home-sick
25   hour—twilight. Be sure I keep it religiously.—Love to all. Your
son of sons—
        H. James jr

Previous publication: *HJL* 1: 172–79

        ∾

    205.29 ~~shows~~ shews • [e *overwrites* o]
    205.31 impressions • im= | pressions
    206.10 precocious • pre= | cocious
    206.17 ~~&~~ Last • [La *overwrites* &]
    206.19 stupendous • stupen= | dous

206.21 ◇ certainly • [c *overwrites illegible letter*]

206.26 f Faith • [F *overwrites* f]

206.28 immensely • immense= | ly

206.30 ▬▬▬ ~~rebellion~~ • [*struck through* rebellion *overwrites illegible word*]

206.31 spectacular • spectac= | ular

206.31 Catholocism • [*misspelled*]

206.34 ~~c◇◇◇~~ carriage • [arr *overwrites illegible letters*]

207.6 ◇ ɗ • [ɗ *overwrites illegible letter*]

207.8–9 down- | hill • down-hill

207.10 ◇ more • [m *overwrites illegible letter*]

207.12 indifferent • in- | different

207.17 perception • per= | ception

207.23 ◇ it • [i *overwrites illegible letter*]

207.24 ~~a◇undle~~ haunt • [haunt *overwrites* a◇und]

207.25 ~~an~~ a clear • [a cl *overwrites* an]

207.28 ◇◇ Each • [Ea *overwrites illegible letters*]

207.28 ~~moments~~ moment • [t *overwrites* ts]

208.4 pigeonholed • pigeon= | =holed

208.6 ~~sun◇~~ sunny • [ny *overwrites illegible letter*]

208.7 ~~these~~ the • [e *overwrites* ese]

208.10–11 ~~sub~~ each • [eac *overwrites* sub]

208.12 Englishman • English= | man

208.14 ◇◇ ◇ rather • [rath *overwrites* ◇◇ ◇]

208.20 ~~a~~ the • [the *overwrites* a]

208.26–27 ~~the~~ measured • [m *overwrites* the]

208.29 ~~more~~ most • [st *overwrites* re]

209.1 ◇ a • [a *overwrites illegible letter*]

209.14 ~~in ◇~~ under • [und *overwrites* in ◇]

209.14–15 half- | buried • half-buried

209.21 ~~he~~ I • [I *overwrites* he]

209.27 subterranean • sub= | terranean

209.32 rudimentary • rudi= | mentary

209.33 ~~dee~~ still • [sti *overwrites* dee]

209.34 compartment • compart= | ment

210.6 ◊ myself • [m *overwrites illegible letter*]

210.9 ~~Ca◊◊~~ Capitol • [pi *overwrites illegible letters*]

210.10 ~~evert~~ every • [y *overwrites blotted* t]

210.17 ~~m◊~~ magical • [a *overwrites illegible letter*]

210.17 moonlight • moon= | light

210.19 somewhat • some= | what

210.25 ~~stan~~ rooms • [roo *overwrites* stan]

210.27 interesting • in- | teresting

210.31 ~~w~~ be • [be *overwrites* w]

211.14 ~~M~~ the • [th *overwrites* M]

211.15 ◊◊ the • [the *overwrites illegible letters*]

211.15 ~~e◊◊~~ cunning • [un *overwrites illegible letters*]

211.17 they've • they | 've

211.18–19 ~~Su~~ Monday • [M *overwrites* Su]

211.29–30 ◊◊ about • [ab *overwrites illegible letters*]

212.6 ~~for~~ on • [on *overwrites* for]

212.17 ~~d~~ my • [m *overwrites* d]

212.21–27 glad to hear of Minny's journey. [. . .] <u>H. James</u> jr • [*written across the letter's penultimate page*]

☙

205.9–10 my last letter having been a terrifically long one • HJ's 7, 8 November [1869] letter to AJ is twenty-three pages long (eleven sheets) in manuscript.

205.10–11 I have let two whole weeks ebb away without writing again • HJ's last surviving letters to family members are his 7, 8 November [1869] one to AJ and his 8 November [1869] one to WJ, which were mailed together.

205.17–18 St. Cecilia's: this being the eve. of that holy virgin & martyr • Santa Cecilia in Trastevere, a church dedicated to the second-century Roman martyr and patron of musicians. 22 November is Saint Cecilia's day.

205.18–20 I mentioned in my last the receipt of your dearest & sweetest of letters • HJ mentions in his 7, 8 November [1869] letter to AJ "the receipt of a celestial missive from mother."

206.6 Miss Lily & the adorable Miss Bessy · Anna Barker Ward's daughters, Elizabeth (Bessy) and Lydia (Lily).

206.7 Mrs. Charles Strong · Eleanor Fearing married Charles Edward Strong; however, the couple was estranged and Mrs. Strong resided abroad with their daughter.

206.25 Trastevere · Roman neighborhood on the opposite bank of the Tiber (Tevere, in Italian) from the Capitol and the Forum.

207.1 exaltée · ardent.

207.4 lancée · involved.

207.5 délicieux séjour · delightful stay.

208.2 Columbaria · The Columbarium of Pomponius Hylas, a structure of vaults lined with depressions for cinerary urns.

208.14 tomb of Cecilia Metella · The tomb, a monument on the Appian Way, honors the daughter-in-law of the triumvir Crassus.

208.23 Pyramid of Caius Cestius · Built during the last years of the Roman Republic (first century B.C.E.), the pyramid is 36 meters tall and located on the Via Ostiense, to the right of the Protestant Cemetery.

208.28 Cemetery where Shelley & Keats lie buried · Protestant Cemetery, Rome.

209.1 Palatine Hill · Rome was founded on Palatine Hill in 753 B.C.E., the first of the seven hills of Rome.

209.11 Arch of Janus Quadrifrons · An arch dating from the later imperial age, supposedly built in honor of Constantine the Great. It is located in the valley north of the Palatine.

209.13 Cloaca Maxima · Described in Murray's 1869 Rome as a "subterranean canal, extending from the Velabrum to the river, well known as the opening of the great common sewer of ancient Rome into the Tiber" (83).

209.22 Tarquinius Priscus · Lucius Tarquinius Priscus, the legendary fifth king of Rome who reigned from 616 to 578 B.C.E.

209.30 promené · shown around.

210.3 Servius Tullius · Son-in-law of Tarquinius Priscus, he was the sixth king of Rome and reigned from 578 to 534 B.C.E.

211.3-4 In the Borghese collection is a Corregio of heavenly merit · Possibly Correggio's Danaë.

211.15 little fresco of [. . .] cunning Leonardo • In Sant' Onofrio, the fresco of the Madonna with donor is now attributed to a disciple of Leonardo.

211.17 Janiculum • A hill on the western bank of the Tiber River, overlooking Rome.

211.20 your & Willy's letters of November 1st • See *CWJ* 1: 118–21.

212.22 A. K. • Aunt Kate.

10   WILLIAM JAMES
30 November [1869]
ALS Houghton
bMS Am 1094 (1940)

15   Rome, Hotel de Rome, Nov. 30th
Beloved William—I have before me two excellent letters from you of Oct. 25th & Nov. 1st respectively, wh. I have been meaning for some days to answer. Most welcome they have been to me & comforting to my spirit. I have felt much better for letting you
20   know out & out how I was & am very glad I did it, tho' at the time it seemed a brutal & senseless act. You have had better kn news from me since those doleful letters from Florence wh. drew forth these answers of yours. I wrote you a line telling you of the remedy finally given me by Doctor Duffy & of the blessed
25   relief I have been getting from it. I have now been ◊ a month in Rome & feel that I owe it quite to those little daily pills that I have had so great an experience. The best things however must come to an end—Surtout the best! The virtue of my pills has not quite departed but it is rapidly waning & unless I can keep
30   afloat by some other means I fear I may again relapse into Florentine depths. I went this morning to see Dr. Gould the chief American physician here, ~~who~~ ∧& he[∧] came to me this afternoon & "examined" ◊ my bowels & abdomen. On the whole he was not very satisfactory—less so than Dr. Duffy. He says
35   there is no apparent or palpable obstruction or organic disorder

in the parts; & that as far he can see I have only torpor &c. He recommended a certain ₐItalian₍ₐ₎ mineral water, a specific for this trouble, which I am to take before breakfast. He also spoke highly of the <u>Kissingen</u> waters, which he has taken himself, on the spot for two summers, for ~~the same~~ ₍ₐ₎a similar₍ₐ₎ complaint. I shall of course immediately try this Italian stuff & hope when I next write to let you hear that it works—tho' I have a fear that it succeeds only with lighter cases than mine. I suppose you are quite right in saying that I had better not attempt to consult any of the great medical swells; tho', if from these two men I got no permanent assistance I shall be rather at loss to know to whom to apply. I duly noted what you said about <u>electricity</u>. I shall be glad enough to try it, if there is any prospect of its helping me. I mentioned it to Dr. Gould, but he seemed sceptical on the subject. If you have started a battery yourself, you will perhaps have something to tell me from your own experience. Whether there is an electrician here or not, I haven't learned. I doubt it, so out of keeping is it with the general Roman tone of things. But at any rate, I should try it not here but either in ~~Rome or~~ Florence or Paris. My stay here is almost at an end. I have (very wisely, I now think) abstained from fixing myself here & I feel less inclined to ₐnow than ever—₍ₐ₎ (much—how much indeed!—as I should like to.) If this confounded thing should settle down upon me again in the same way as at Florence, I feel as if it would be decidedly harder to bear & to contend with here than elsewhere. This heavy Atmosphere is not a place to have troubles in. In view of a possible relapse I feel like using the last lingering traces of my ~~bessu~~ <u>Besserung</u> to take a run down to Naples if only for a week. I know now what it would have been to lose Rome, & the knowledge gives me a horror of missing Naples. I should start to-morrow if I were not pledged to wait for A. Kate. She arrives however to morrow & after fairly seeing her e, I suppose I can be off as soon as I please. In one way or another I hope to get a comfortable stay at Naples & to get back

to Florence. There I shall reflect upon my further movements & make up my mind either to stick fast to the Continent or to go to Malvern. What I wrote you from Florence about the relation of this matter to my back has been amply borne out ⤴ by
5   experience here. That is, with ~~th~~ my comparatively open condition, my back has been fifty per-cent more comfortable. You say that you hear of all this walking &c, but that you have yet to learn whether I am any the less conscious of my back. Very much less so. As much less so or as little ⤴ (as you please
10   to call it) as is natural in one who expects at his final & ultimate best (whenever that arrives) to stop a good bit short of perfect unconsciousness. As for being able to "study", that I have hardly tried. I have found tho' that little by little, in proportion as my bowels keep open, I am getting back the power of reading with
15   impunity. I have read in the evenings of the past week with immense pleasure—pleasure in the simple act of reading—a good thick French 8$^{\underline{vo}}$ on Italian history, & done ⌃it[⌃] far more easily & comfortably than I could have done it in those ◇ stupid months last winter before I left home. I strongly suspect that a
20   ~~perm~~ prolonged "openness" would bring me up in this respect in a most wonderful way. Altogether I may decidedly say that with regard to my back I have entered into a new stage or era. All that walking, walking & more walking can do for it, I think I have done; (~~as well as~~ ⌃& this is equally true[⌃] for my bowels.)
25   Curious as it sounds, I think walking tires me more—decidedly more—& resting—i.e. sitting, lying &c proportionetly less than they did 3 months ago. If I could reform my constipation I fancy I should find I could afford to be far more sedentary ~~than~~ now— & could afford equally to walk more for the simple pleasure of
30   change & not with the fierce monotony & feverish purpose that I have done hitherto. With regard to my sleep I am happy to say you are quite mistaken. All summer in Switzerland it was decidedly bad; but since my coming to Italy it has been gradually improving & during the past month has been

particularly good. My appetite is also excellent—tho'
(fortunately) in proportion as I tend to keep full, it diminishes.
It has become too a far more healthy & rational appetite than the
thing you know of old. I like everything now, without exception
(& am particularly fond of fat!)—In what you said in your last   5
about England & Germany I was of course immensely
interested. I quite incline to agree with you that if I were
compelled a month hence to go to England I needn't to look
upon it as a misfortune. In fact it would quite solve the problem
of my present destinies & heaven knows it would crown all my   10
longings & desires with bliss! I have been thinking a good deal
about the possibility of going to Germany for next summer but
the plan offers many objections—or rather it is subject to one—
all=important: viz: that even putting things at their ₐvery₍ₐ₎
best, I have no business to assume in myself the capacity for real   15
study within the present year: & certainly to go to Germany &
not to ₐbe₍ₐ₎ able to study fairly seems a false arrangement. ◇ I
confess I am surprised however at your saying that 15 mos. is the
minimum in wh. one could get started there: I allude of course
simply to reading. T. S. P. I should suppose at least very well   20
"started," & he, if I'm not mistaken was there for considerably
less than a year. But if one, with work, can do but little in 15
mos., one could hardly do much without it in 6. In truth I
should be sorry at this time of day to sit down & forego all hope
of ever ◇ mastering German, but on the other hand I feel as if   25
for some time to come there were things more important. Here
I am at 26 with such a waste of lost time behind me & such an
accumulated ignorance of so many of the elements & rudiments
of my own tongue, literature &c piled up in my track—& with
the practical needs of my "calling" facing me in the immediate   30
future—with these things pressing on me to such a degree that
to branch off into the awful chaos of that portentous tongue
seems simply like an increase of care ₐ& responsibility₍ₐ₎ without
an increase of means. If I were to go to England a short time

hence ₍ₐ₎ᵈ₍ₐ₎ I remain till I go home (I am talking all the while
on the basis of my return a year hence, when I shall have been
absent about 20 mos.) I shall simply be getting in a different way
a mass of impressions which, if I had hitherto been well & able
to develop myself more freely & vigorously I sh would
ₐ(probably)₍ₐ₎ have got from study or at least from more liberal
habits of reading. For mere pleasure alone, I can think of none
greater than to spend a summer wandering thro' England with a
certain freedom. It may be that the great impression England
has left on my mind is owing in a measure to its being the 1st
European country I saw—& saw just after that long moton
monotonous period of home life; & that after Italy it will seem
comparatively pale & colorless. But with all abatements; I am
sure it will yield me great delights & rich instruction. The
principal drawback I see to going there—to going anywhere in
fact—is the possible—not to say probable dearth, of society. I
feel as if "society" were yet destined to play a very large part in
lifting me fairly onto my legs. It is an agent I have never fairly
tried but I have great hopes of it. The only trouble is to get hold
of it. If I were to settle here in Rome I should probably be able
to see ₐas much as I pleased of₍ₐ₎ plenty of Americans. This one
consideration almost outweighs several weighty objections. On
the Continent alone is American Society to be found; & the
apparent inaccessibility of the Natives is so great that save this
there is little other. I get a strong feeling, while in England, of
the degree to wh. to a lonely & unassisted man society must
ₐremain₍ₐ₎ obstructed & closed—& to go there & be left wholly to
my own resources, tho it might be very pleasant for a couple of
months would be rather dreary for six. To have any but really
<u>Good</u> Society there, moreover, would be rather more intolerable
than to have none at all. If I go, I shall try & drum up a few
introductions.—Meanwhile I still get the same heavy news of
your immobility & continued wretchedness. In And yet in spite
of it I manage not to feel hopeless or even cheerless. I feel a

conviction not to be shaken that your present condition is destined regularly to play itself out. Improvement will come to you as it came to me—with a lingering & stumbling ~~oreo~~ tread— but still it will come. Little by little, inch by inch the divine messenger of relief will lay bare his countenance & when once you have seen it, you will be as one who has talked face to face with an angel. I hope you are carrying out that programme you hinted at some time since—visiting "evenings." Go thro' it doggedly & mechanically when you can't otherwise & you will know your reward. Your days are composed but of hours, by taking each hour "empirically" & disposing of it as best you can, you can get thro' a month, & at the end of a month (probably) you find some appreciable result.—But I can't write to you about your back. The subject is to me too heavy—too sickening. All I can do is to remind you of my own career. Go thro' a certain course of combined rest & motion & meanwhile keep up a devil of a waiting! Now that I am better, my own waiting & watching seems as nothing—as a mere brief fitful fever ∧—a bad dream,[∧] preceding a blissful awakening into serene reality.— Rome remains sublime to the end. My movements have been a good ∧deal[∧] curtailed of late by rainy weather: still, no day has been empty.—I have also been going a little <u>dans le monde</u>— that is I dined recently twice at Mrs. Ward's & met the second time Miss Story, daughter of the ~~selu~~ sculptor—a kind of Anglicized & highly superior Helena De Kay. Nay, really she only <u>looks</u> like H. D. K.—wh. she does very much: otherwise she is immensely <u>bon genre</u>. I went to Story's studio with Mrs. W. & saw S. in person. He was very civil & his statues very clever. I likewise received the card of George Ripley of the N. Y. <u>Tribune</u> & of course (feeling very greateful for his attention) immediately returned his visit. He was very kind & agreeable & asked lovingly about father. He is here as a species of reporter on the <u>Council</u>; but I fancy will get little satisfaction.—I have seen nothing new in Rome—but have been repeatedly to old places. The Campagna is something tremendous—but it can only be seen on horseback. The <u>Vatican</u> is inexhaustible—& the general picturesqueness of Rome something not to be defined. I have seen it pretty well & despite many pangs, am fairly ready to go. The filth that is so remote from godliness & the dead weight of the moral & political atmosphere ~~weigh~~ ∧count for[∧] somewhat on the other scale. I have ceased to get the Atlantic & Nation. I suppose you have stopped them, in pursuance of my remarks. I shall see them again at Florence. After that I shall perhaps return to the subject. Good night. Love to all. I shall write a week hence—probably from Naples.—If only I could be favored with an hour's conversation with you!—

Yours <u>H. James</u> jr.

Previous publication: *CWJ* 1: 122–27

∾

216.21–22 ~~kn~~ news • [n *overwrites blotted* kn]

216.25 ◊ a • [a *overwrites illegible letter*]

216.33 ◊ my • [m *overwrites illegible letter*]

217.28 ~~bessu~~ <u>Besserung</u> • [B *overwrites* b; er *overwrites* u]

217.33 e, • [, *overwrites blotted* e]

218.4 ⟋ by • [b *overwrites* —]

218.5 ~~th~~ my • [m *overwrites* th]

218.9 ⟋ (• [(*overwrites* —]

218.18 ◊ stupid • [s *overwrites illegible letter*]

218.20 ~~perm~~ prolonged • [rolo *overwrites* erm]

218.26 proportionetly • [*misspelled*]

219.17 ◊ I • [I *overwrites illegible letter*]

219.25 ◊ mastering • [m *overwrites illegible letter*]

220.5 ~~sh~~ would • [w *overwrites* sh]

220.11–12 ~~moton~~ monotonous • [not *overwrites blotted* ton]

220.33 ~~In~~ And • [A *overwrites* In]

221.3 ◊re◊ tread • [t *overwrites illegible letter*; a *overwrites illegible letter*]

221.24 ~~selu~~ sculptor • [ul *overwrites* lu]

221.27 immensely • immense- | ly

221.30 greateful • [*misspelled*]

222.2 inexhaustible • [e *inserted*]

222.10 perhaps • per= | haps

∽

216.16–17 letters from you of Oct. 25ᵗʰ & Nov. 1ˢᵗ • See *CWJ* 1: 112–15, 118–21.

216.23 I wrote you a line • HJ to WJ, 8 November [1869].

216.28 Surtout • Especially.

216.31 Dr. Gould • James Brewster Gould (1810–79). According to Murray's 1869 *Rome*, Dr. Gould was an American "Member of the College of Physicians and Surgeons of New York, formerly physician of the U. S. Navy, may be heard at Sinimberghi's pharmacy, 130, Via Frattina" (xx).

217.4 Kissingen waters • One of the most favored watering-places in Bavaria, Kissingen welcomed twenty-five thousand patients annually.

217.12 what you said about electricity • In his 25 October [1869] letter, WJ suggests alternative therapies for HJ's constipation: "Electricity *some*times has a wonderful effect, applied not in the piddling way you recollect last winter but by a strong *galvanic* current from the spine to the abdominal muscles, or if the rectum be paralysed one pole put inside the rectum" (*CWJ* 1: 113).

217.28 Besserung • improvement.

219.5–6 In what you said in your last about England & Germany • In his 1 November 1869 letter, WJ advises HJ to go to England rather than to Germany (*CWJ* 1: 119–20).

219.20 T. S. P. • Thomas Sergeant Perry.

221.22 dans le monde • in society.

221.24 Miss Story • Edith Story, daughter of sculptor William Wetmore Story. She married Florentine Simone Peruzzi, a descendant of the Medicis.

221.25 Helena De Kay • American artist and sister of Katharine de Kay Bronson, Helena de Kay married poet Richard Watson Gilder (1844–1909) in 1874.

221.27 <u>bon genre</u> · <u>distinguished</u>.

221.29 George Ripley · George Ripley (1802–80), an American literary critic and author; he and his wife, Sophia Willard Dana Ripley (1803–61), founded the Brook Farm commune.

HENRY JAMES SR.

7 December [1869]

ALS Houghton

10 bMS Am 1094 (1767)

Rome Hotel de Rome Dec. 7<u>th</u>

My dearest father—

15   I rec'd. yesterday a short note from Willy, in reply to mine from Florence of Nov. 26<u>th</u>—in which he speaks of your having sent me a letter to England. I have not yet ~~f~~ got your letter, but I suppose it will arrive in a few days. Meanwhile, on the eve. of my departure from Rome, I despatch you a line of thanks for
20 what I know in advance ~~your~~ it contains. I'm afraid that heavy bulletin of mine from Florence harrowed up your feelings more than was needful—~~&~~ that you fancy, since the receipt of better news from me, from this place, that I rather trifled with your sympathies. But it has been all along as much of a surprise as a
25 delight to me, to have this better news—~~&~~ I live on from day to day without any great assurance of the future. You will have been thoroughly glad to hear of my having been able to get these six comfortable weeks of Rome. I speak of the <u>comfort</u>:— of the <u>interest</u> they have yielded me, it were vain to try to speak.
30 I have sent a few rough notes in previous letters—but they are wofully apart from the tremendous truth of things! I ~~h~~ now mean to start for Naples—where I hope to be able to ~~get~~ [∧]keep[∧] ahead of my troubles till the 1<u>st</u> of January. If I do this I shall feel as if I had wrenched open with a vengeance the

niggardly fist of fate.—Aunt Kate told me to day she was writing
to mother; you will therefore ~~hear~~ have copious details of our
long-deferred meeting. It has been extremely pleasant & I have
much enjoyed having a long "jaw" with her about things at
home & abroad. She looks extremely well & jolly & I think has
enjoyed things largely—in spite of her somewhat onerous
society. Cousin Helen seems tired & a good deal flattened out ◊
in mind by European influences. Henry is a nuisance, in so far as
he confines the party to seclusion & solitude. Helen Ripley is
extremely nice & shews a very fair intelligence of what she ◊ sees
& a sufficient appreciation of things to make her a very good
companion. But for her, A. K. must have perished. I have been
about with them both a good deal during the past week & have
found it very pleasant to take all the old things easy—without
that strenuous effort to make a <u>point</u> in ~~my~~ ones experience,
~~woh~~ which one falls into when alone. We have had great drives
on the Campagna (where however it is almost a shame—a
crime—to go otherwise—than alone—as a pilgrim—with rapt
attention & ~~m~~ bated breath):—& a glorious visit to the Pamfili-
Doria Villa—a fabulous park—where the genius of Italy takes
you by the hand & leads you away out of the world & the
century—into the delicious distant background of some sweet
old picture & sends you roaming up & down thro' rapturous hills
& dales amid an incredible horizon—until you feel like some
◊◊◊◊◊ happy brute in an Aesop's fable—& come back again to
your hotel & your dinner as to the stupid moral. I have had
ₐalso₍ₐ₎ several little excursions with Helen Ripley alone & have
tasted the excellent joy of looking at ~~grea◊◊~~ great works in the
society of a sweet young woman. You never really know a first-
rate work until you have done this: nor do you know it either
until you have examined it long & often in churlish solitude &
concentrated silence. I took her this afternoon to the Santi
Apostoli to see the pope make his great annual visit to hear
~~Mass~~ Vespers. A tremendous crowd—a terrible squeezing & a

long weary waiting. I got her a ~~tolerable~~ tolerably good place however & boosted her aloft & she saw something. I only saw a little & that thro' my impiety. When the Pope, clad in ~~dazzling~~ [ʌ]shining[ʌ] ~~rop~~ robes crept up to the altar & in the midst of that

5 dazzling shrine of light, possessed himself of the Host & raised it aloft over the prostrate multitudes, I got a very good look at him by poking up my head & confronting that terrible toy.—But this will have been nothing to tomorrow—the feast of the Immaculate Concept. & the opening of the Council. Rome is

10 densely crowded & St. Peters will burst with its contents. I am to go at 6. ⋄ a.m. with H. R. We shall see what we shall see—very little I fear. A. K. & Cousin H. are to go with their Courier. But even if I see but little of the prelates, the crowd in St. Peters is always worth seeing.—The next day I leave for Naples whence I

15 shall soon write you.—I have seen Mrs. Ward several times. She is "rather" superficial. Geo. Ripley (as I think I mentioned) left his card on me & I called & found him very affable & civil. He said he had gone to see Carlyle in London & ⋄ C. had asked most <u>affectionately</u> about you. Ripley did the same. He is very sleek &

20 comfortable & a great connoisseur in hotels. He is ~~heⱺⱺ~~ here as a reporter on the Council but finds himself rather balked, I fancy, by the governmental incommunicativeness.—I have written to Willy fully more than once about my present condition & shall wait another week before writing again. I am living on

25 Medicines, wh. is a state wh. oughtn't to be prolonged needlessly. But I <u>must</u> see Naples. <u>Vedi</u> <u>Napoli</u> ⋄ e <u>poi mori</u>. I think I shall survive. Where & how I shall let you know. Meanwhile <u>don't</u> <u>worry</u>. I long for your letter: it's a long time since I've had such a one. Farewell. Thank Willy for all his good

30 advice—Kiss Mother & Alice & believe me, dear father, your loving son <u>H. James</u> jr.

No previous publication

∞

224.17 ᵣ got • [g *overwrites* r]

224.20 ~~your~~ it contains • [it c *overwrites* your]

224.27 thoroughly • thorough- | ly

224.31 ʰ now • [n *overwrites* h]

225.2 ~~hear~~ have • [av *overwrites* ear]

225.7–8 ◇ in • [i *overwrites illegible letter*]

225.10 ◇ sees • [se *overwrites illegible letter*]

225.12 companion • com- | panion

225.15 ~~my~~ ones • [ones *overwrites* my]

225.16 ~~w◇h~~ which • [hi *overwrites* ◇h]

225.19 ~~m~~ bated • [ba *overwrites* m]

225.19–20 Pamfili- | Doria • Pamfili-Doria

225.22 into • [to *inserted*]

225.24 incredible • incred- | ible

225.25 ◇◇◇◇◇ happy • [happy *overwrites illegible letters*]

225.28 ~~grea◇◇~~ great • [t *overwrites illegible letters*]

225.34 ~~Mass~~ Vespers • [Vespers *overwrites* Mass]

226.1 ~~tolerable~~ tolerably • [y *overwrites* e]

226.4 ~~rop~~ robes • [b *overwrites twice struck through* p]

226.6 multitudes, • [, *overwrites* s]

226.11 ◇ a • [a *overwrites blotted illegible letter*]

226.18 ◇ C • [C *overwrites illegible letter*]

226.19 affectionately • affection | ately

226.20 comfortable • com- | fortable

226.20 ~~he◇◇~~ here • [re *overwrites illegible letters*]

226.22 incommunicativeness • incommunicative= | ness

226.26 ◇ e • [e *overwrites illegible letter*]

226.29–31 Thank Willy for all [. . .] H. James jr. • [*written across the letter's first page*]

∾

224.15–16 mine from Florence of Nov. 26ᵗʰ • HJ probably means his 26 October letter from Florence to WJ (which was the short cover letter to the 16 [17], 19 October [1869] letter to WJ); there is no surviving 26 November 1869 letter, and HJ was in Rome, not Florence, all of

November. In addition, eleven or twelve days would not be sufficient to complete a two-way correspondence between Italy and the United States.

225.7 Cousin Helen • Helen Wyckoff Perkins.

225.8 Henry • Henry Wyckoff.

225.19-20 Pamfili-Doria Villa • The Villa Doria-Pamphíli was created between 1644 and 1652 for Prince Camillo Pamphili.

225.32-33 Santi Apostoli • The Church of Santi Apostoli was constructed on the site of a Roman temple; it was rebuilt and completely restored in 1871. The church adjoins the Palazzo Colonna.

226.8-9 feast of the Immaculate Concept. • December 8, the Immaculate Conception of the Blessed Virgin Mary.

226.11-12 H. R. [. . .] A. K. & Cousin H. • Helen Ripley, Aunt Kate, and Helen Wyckoff Perkins.

226.22-23 I have written to Willy fully more than once about my present condition • See HJ to WJ, 8 November [1869] and 30 November [1869].

226.26 Vedi Napoli ☙ e poi mori. • See Naples and then die.

20 MARY WALSH JAMES
21, 23 December [1869]
ALS Houghton
bMS Am 1094 (1768)

25 Naples—Hotel de Grande-Bretagne
Dec. 21st

My own dear mother—
    Ever since my arrival in Naples I have been struggling to
30 find a moment to write to you; but I have only laid my hand on
it now—just on the eve of my departure. I have found many
moments however to read your letter of the ~~3~~ 23d November &
Alice's of the 28th wh. came to me here some days since & filled
me with the extremity of joy. You will soon have recd. my last
35 letter from Rome telling you of my coming here on a rapid visit.

My visit has almost been made ⅋ my face is three-quarters
turned northward—i.e. to Paris <u>via</u> Rome, Florence, Genoa, the
cornice, Nice ⅋ Marseilles. I am very decently well ⅋ very
impatient to presume on my salubrity ⅋ on the hopes of greater
to make a temporary settlement somewhere. While I was in
Rome A. Kate rec'd a letter from you, written after the receipt
of those famous letters of mine from Florence, which made me
feel as if I had ~~ha◊~~ harrowed up your dear maternal soul to an
unpardonable extent. Long before this, I take comfort in
thinking, you will have been largely reassured. I have good
reason to believe that I passed in Florence the crisis of my
troubles ⅋ that I have turned a corner into smoother waters. We
shall see. Your letter was deeply interesting¡ —especially your
account of poor Bob's affair with Kitty V. B. What a strange
conjunction—⅋ what a happy disjunction! I hope they are both
getting over it. Now that Bob has his hand in, perhaps he e will
console himself with some more eligible party. I hope too poor
Kitty may light upon some strongly ⅋ celebrated swain.—Your
enclosed scrap of Wilky's letter brought strongly before my
mind his dreary ⅋ desolate state—in that distant southern clime
so different from this Neapolitan South. Beloved youth! Since
my residence abroad ⅋ my acquaintance with the pangs of
solitude ⅋ exile, I have learned to do justice, in many a
homeward reverie to <u>his</u> long fortitude ⅋ courage—as well of
course, as to the multitudinous virtues of my family in
general!—Well I've seen Naples ⅋ I am not dead—of that death
that the proverb ◊ consigns you to. I've been here some ten days,
more or less constantly <u>en course</u>. I regret to say that the
pleasure of my visit has been seriously diminished by obstinate
bad weather—⅋ that I shall probably be condemned to leave
with hardly more than a glimpse of that Southern Sunshine
which fills the sky ⅋ sea with color ⅋ calls out the latent beauty
of the place.—Yet as I sit here writing at my window I have a
great prospect before me. My hotel directly faces the sea ⅋ my

room is perched aloft in the 5th story on a terrace which commands all the immensity of the view. On each side of me the bay stretches out its mighty arms—holding in one hand the sullen mass of Vesuvius & in the other, veiled in a mist which
5 shadows forth the dimness of their classicism, the antique sites of Baiae & Cumae—all haunted with Horatian & Virgilian memories. Into its vast embrace the grey Mediterranean comes roaring & tumbling, distressed by many winds. Directly opposite, in the middle of the immensely-uplifted horizon,
10 Capri uplifts into the watery sky the vague steepness of its beautiful shape. Cast aloft over all this an immeasurable sky in which a faint sunset is ~~fight~~ fighting with a ◊◊◊◊◊ compacted army of clouds & then evoke in your mind's ears the tremendous clamor of the troubled waves—& you'll have a notion of what
15 my window treats me to. This is all well enough; but it's hard to find myself compelled solely to imagine the orthodox bay of Naples, clad in all the dazzling azure of tradition. The city is a vast swarming ugly place, with pink & blue houses & a population of terrific vileness. The <u>lazzaroni</u> have gone, but
20 their sons & younger brothers remain & for one who pretends to enter at ∧all[∧] <u>dans</u> <u>le</u> <u>réel</u> <u>de</u> <u>la vie</u> they are a depressing & forbidding sight. Heaven has cursed them with picturesqueness! In fine, Naples is a barbarous city. You feel perpetually ∧in all things[∧] the thinness of their shiny varnish of civilisation. But
25 for its glorious position it is quite the poorest & meanest ∧of[∧] Italian cities. My mind reverts with enthusiasm to such a place as that brave rich little Verona! Decidedly I go in for Northern Italy.—But I must be just. The Museum here is vast rich & admirable. It contains a hundred things of the very first
30 excellence: ~~most~~ Among them a magnificent statue of <u>Aristides</u> (a fit companion to the great Demosthenes of the Vatican) which gives one beyond all other things an impression of the high culture of the Greek sculptors—of the lofty aesthetic basis on which they worked. The good taste of this statue is a

revelation—the drapery a creation!—the dignity a thing there's no name—no measure for! There are moreover two busts found at Pompei a year ~~hence~~ ∧ago,[∧] which evoked within me to a dire extent the thievish principle lurking in our common nature. If only they had been smaller or I bigger! They are the later Brutus & the great Pompey. Excuse me: words fail me! Never was a character so deep—so individual—an interest so exquisite put into two battered blocks of stone. The Museum is especially rich in bronzes (whereof the Vatican has none)—furnished by the generous Pompei. Verily it is a great advantage for a good thing to be in Bronze. Regardez donc that ~~sitting~~ ∧resting[∧] Mercury—the grace of his leaning body—the idleness of his winged feet! It's the statue—the divinity ө—of Boyhood. To Pompei I have made two good visits—having the 2ᵈ time, happily my one Sunny day. You can't know Pompei, I fancy, until youv'e seen the Sunshine leading its silent march thro' that paradise of emptiness. That Pompei should be interesting I of course expected: it's a way so many things have! But I certainly wasn't prepared for that! What "that" is, mother dear, you must come some day & see. You cant paint a perfume & you can't write the feeling of Pompei. The sadness of the place flattens you out into nothing. Truly as M. Arnold says—"that hard Roman world," &c. "But oh, its heart⤚, its heart, was stone

And so it could not thrive!"

And so Vesuvius came down & buried it alive. Pompei is simply the great Roman world on a ~~reeud~~ reduced scale & you get there in a deeply concentrated form, the emotion you feel, diffused & diluted, in Rome.—Owing to the weather I have been unable to make the regular excursions from this place. I have done the great thing, however, I have been to Paestum & seen the Greek temples.—Thursday 23d. Rome (H. de Rome.) I was here interrupted, day before yesterday & now behold me in Rome. I arose betimes yesterday morning meaning if there was any sort of weather to go to Sorrento for the day: but I was greeted by

the vision of a sombre sky ✠ the sound of a great gale. It was no
time for the divine Sorrento: so in despair, I threw up the
enterprise ✠ caught the train for Rome. ~~So~~ I am ‸therefore[‸]
ignorant of those famous shores. But as I say, I <u>did</u> see Paestum
5 ✠ am wiser by the knowledge of that great temple of Neptune—
a ruin with all the sadness of a ruin ✠ none of its incompleteness.
It is most exquisitely noble ✠ perfect—with all its multitudinous
columns divinely present ✠ the very genius of Greece sitting
amid them in serene desolation. Paestum is something of an
10 expedition. I slept one night at antique mediaeval Salerno ✠
drove to the temples the next day—making with the return an
excursion of eleven hours—thro' a most sombre desolate
country—the scene, until recently, of much brigandage. The
second night I again slept at Salerno ✠ in the morning drove,
15 with a pleasant young Englishman whom I met at the inn, along
the beautiful bay of Salerno to the gloriously-placed town of
Amalfi—rich in memories of former greatness ✠ empire but now
sunk into the depths of the picturesque. In the evening again to
Naples. You know I ◊ suppose of the Kings being there, for the
20 winter. ◊ I saw them several times ✠ was warmly received. They
seem to lead a lonely dreary life. Arthur was just getting over a
bad attack of ~~infam~~ inflammation of the lungs ✠ looked weak ✠
delicate. He seems a very nice simple young fellow, with a head
full of facts. Cousin C. ✠ Annie are the same as of yore—
25 extremely <u>finite</u>—quiet ✠ soft ✠ practical ✠ full of a bland
absence of enthusiasm. Cousin Charlotte seems far from well.—
I find my relatives in Rome in <u>statu quo</u>—a good deal stupefied
by the wretched weather. A. Kate communicated to me a
delicious letter from you—telling of Alice's ◊◊ dissolute life ✠ of
30 your offer for the house. In both facts I rejoice. I got the other
day four very good photos. of statues in the Vatican wh. I gave
to A. K. to carry to Alice—in the hope that the contemplation
of ideal beauty may win her from her wild career. I should have
been glad to get more: but I am on the footing of buying none at

all.—As for the house I hope you may get it. I feel very kindly to
Cambridge in these days & quite agree with you that we could
ₐnot₍ₐ₎ strike our roots into a more congenial soil. <u>Bonne</u> <u>chance</u>
then with the T.s. I have just come from A. Kate's hotel, where I
left her <u>tête à tête</u> with Miss Sara Clark, who spoke   5
affectionately of father & you.—The letter father sent me to
England doesn't arrive. I mean to write to the B.'s about it.
Meanwhile I venture to hope for the appearance of another. Day
after tomorrow (Saturday) is X◊ Xmas. I shall wait over till
Monday & then start for Florence—stopping if the weather is   10
fine, at ~~Orvieto~~ Perugia & Sienna—or rather if it is <u>tolerable</u>—to
have it fine is apparently too much to ask. Now that I am leaving
Italy I feel with redoubled force its ~~eloquence & enchantment~~
enchanting eloquence & fumble over the rich contents of these
last four months as fondly as a coin-collector a bag of medals.   15
Address me care of MM. Hottinguer & Cie ₐBanquiers₍ₐ₎ Paris.
I think its Rue de Provence: but it doesn't matter. I meant to
have told you this before, but it will be almost in season to find a
letter waiting. Tell W. I meant to add a P.S. for him; but I will
write apart in a few days. Love to father & sister & to yourself,   20
beloved mother all possible greetings.
        Your devoted son
            <u>H. James jr</u>
P.S.
On reflection, I think you had better address your letters not to   25
Hottinguer but to <u>Bowles</u>, <u>Frères</u>, <u>Rue de la Paix</u>. I can trade
there, I fancy, with my Barings letter & it will be pleasanter.
H. is ◊ too d—d private & poky.

No previous publication

&

228.31 departure • de= | parture
228.32 3 23ᵈ • [2 *overwrites* 3]
229.8 ~~ha◊~~ harrowed • [r *overwrites blotted illegible letter*]

229.13 ¦ — • [— *overwrites* ,]

229.15 disjunction • disjunc= | =tion

229.16 e will • [w *overwrites* c]

229.22 acquaintance • ac= | quaintance

229.27 ◇ consigns • [c *overwrites illegible letter*]

230.12 ~~fighte~~ fighting • [i *overwrites blotted illegible letter*]

230.12 ◇◇◇◇◇ compacted • [compacted *overwrites illegible letters*]

230.22 picturesqueness • picturesque- | ness

230.24 their • [ir *inserted*]

230.30 ~~most~~ Among • [mo *overwrites* most]

230.30 magnificent • magnifi= | cent

231.1 revelation • reve= | lation

231.4 extent • ex= | tent

231.13 o— • [— *overwrites blotted* o]

231.23 ⤫ , • [, *overwrites* —]

231.26 ~~recud~~ reduced • [d *overwrites* c; c *overwrites* d]

232.2 despair • des= | pair

232.9 something • some= | thing

232.19 ◇ suppose • [s *overwrites illegible letter*]

232.20 ◇ I • [I *overwrites illegible letter*]

232.22 ~~infam~~ inflammation • [lam *overwrites* am]

232.29 ◇◇ dissolute • [di *overwrites blotted illegible letters*]; disso- | lute

233.6 affectionately • affec= | tionately

233.9 X◇ Xmas • [m *overwrites illegible letter*]

233.13-14 ~~enchantment~~ enchanting eloquence • [ing el *overwrites blotted* ment]

233.18-28 to find a letter waiting [. . .] poky. • [*written across the letter's penultimate page*]

233.28 ◇ too • [t *overwrites illegible letter*]

∾

229.14 Bob's affair with Kitty V. B. • RJ had become secretly engaged to his first cousin, Kitty Van Buren, daughter of Ellen King James and Smith Thompson Van Buren; see WJ's 14 November 1869 and 25 July 1870 letters to RJ (*CWJ* 4: 389-91, 408-10).

229.28 en course • moving around.

230.6 Baiae • A town on the Gulf of Pozzuoli, near Naples, with ruins of Roman baths and temples.

230.6 Cumae • Ancient city west of Naples, Cumae is believed to be the oldest Greek mainland colony in the West. Remains of fortifications, graves, and a cavern home of a sibyl have been discovered throughout the city and its surrounding areas.

230.19 lazzaroni • Neapolitan poor.

230.21 dans le réel de la vie • into the reality of life.

230.28 The Museum • At the time of HJ's travels, the National Museum of Naples housed one of the finest collections of antiquities in the world, including treasures excavated at Pompeii, Herculaneum, Stabiae, and Cumae.

231.11 Regardez donc • Do look at.

231.22–24 M. Arnold says —"that [. . .] not thrive!" • From Matthew Arnold's "Obermann Once More" in *New Poems* (225 ll. 13–16).

231.30 Paestum • The ancient city of Paestum, or "City of Neptune," was founded by the Greeks in about 600 B.C.E. and became a Roman colony in 273 C.E. Three remaining Greek temples are exquisitely preserved and closely rival those in Athens.

231.34 Sorrento • Sorrento is located southwest of Naples on a peninsula that separates the Bay of Naples from the Gulf of Salerno.

232.10 Salerno • Located southeast of Naples, Salerno was founded in 197 B.C.E.

232.17 Amalfi • A popular tourist spot, Amalfi lies in the ravine of the Mulini Valley, southeast of Naples.

232.19 the Kings • Maternal cousins of the Jameses, the Kings were considered the "Europeanized" relatives. Charlotte Elizabeth Sleight Matthews married Clarence W. King, a Canton, China, merchant. They had three children: William Vernon, who was killed in the American Civil War battle at Petersburg, Virginia; Annie; and Arthur. During the war, Charlotte King's sympathies strongly favored the southern cause, and the defeat of the Confederacy led the Kings to abandon the United States for Europe.

232.32 A. K. • Aunt Kate.

233.3 Bonne chance • Good luck.

233.4 with the T.s. • Sr. was arranging to buy 20 Quincy Street from the landlord, Louis Thies.

233.5 tête à tête • alone.

233.5 Miss Sara Clark • Sarah Freeman Clarke, an artist who befriended the Jameses and the Emersons.

233.7 B.'s • Baring's.

233.16 Hottinguer & Cie ₍ₐ₎Banquiers₍ₐ₎ Paris • The 1869 Paris directory *Annuaire-Almanach* lists "Hottinguer et Cie, banquiers" at 38, rue de Provence (334).

233.19 W. • WJ.

GRACE NORTON
25 December [1869]
ALS Houghton
bMS Am 1094 (877)

Rome Dec. 25th p.m.

My dear Grace—

I shall reach you probably as soon as this poor pretence of a letter—but I nevertheless can't help sending it—so that I needn't quite present myself before you in the utter nakedness of my guilt. I have before me an excellent epistle from you of a horrible month ago—since when so many things have happened to both of us that you are probably no longer the person who wrote it nor I the creature to whom it was addressed. If I had continued to be that happy individual, trust my delight & gratitude to have answered it a dozen times over. What has befallen you I hope soon to hear from your own lips, in the drawing room of the Villa D'Este. For myself, the main events of my career are that I have been to Naples for a couple of weeks

& that I have brought my visit to Rome to a close. I leave
tomorrow, rain or no—rain, for Florence the divine, <u>via</u> Assisi &
Perugia. I came back from Naples a couple of days since, my
stay being abbreviated by the wretched weather. I will make a
clean breast of it at once & declare that I saw neither Vesuvius   5
nor Sorrento. I made two vain attempts on the latter—one for
<u>your</u> sake & one for my own, but was worsted in each. So I saw ~~n~~
Naples without sunshine—but still I saw it. It is a good deal of a
place. As for Rome—by this time it's an old story. I leave it with
regret but without those pangs of outraged affection which I felt   10
on quitting Florence. But these latter pangs are soon ~~two~~ to be
healed. I daren't ask for news of you, nor express any interest in
you. 'Twill sound so affected. But I nevertheless <u>do</u> hope most
devoutly to find you well & prosperous. It would be a most
enchanting thing to find three words from you at the hotel de   15
l'Europe: but life is not a fairy tale. I hope to see you on
Wednesday or Thursday morng.—if I suffer no delay. Love to all
of you—especially your mother & Jane & Susan & Charles & Sara
& the children & Grace. <u>À bientôt</u>! Your's fitfully, but
perpetually <u>H. James</u> j[r]

No previous publication
    ∾

   236.23 probably • pro= | bably
   236.24 nevertheless • never= | theless
   236.25 myself • my= | self
   236.25 nakedness • naked= | ness
   236.27 happened • hap= | pened
   237.4 abbreviated • abbre= | viated
   237.7-8 ~~n~~ Naples • [N *overwrites* n]
   237.11 ~~two~~ to • [o *overwrites blotted* wo]
   237.20 j[r] • [*ms. damaged*]
    ∾

   236.33 Villa D'Este • The Nortons actually wintered in Florence at
Villa d'Elci (see 11 November [1869] to Grace Norton).

237.2 Assisi • In Umbria, twenty kilometers southeast of Perugia.

237.19 À bientôt! • See you soon!

5   WILLIAM JAMES
27, 28 [December 1869]; 1 January 1870
ALS Houghton
bMS Am 1094 (1941)

10   Rome, Hotel de Rome
            Nov. 27$\underline{th}$
Beloved Bill—I have just found at my bankers a long letter from
you (Dec. 5$\underline{th}$) wh. has gratified me so inexpressibly that altho' I
despatched home a document only a couple of days since, I feel
15   powerfully moved to write to you directly—the more especially
as my letter contained a promise that I would. Your letters fill
me with a divine desire to occupy for an hour that old cane-
bottomed chair before your bedroom fire. One of these days it
will hold me for many hours. I am extremely glad you like my
20   letters—& terrifically agitated by the thought that Emerson likes
them. I never manage to write but a very small fraction of what
has originally occurred to me. What you call the "animal heat"
of contemplation is sure to evaporate within half an hour. I went
this morng. to bid farewell to M. Angelo's Moses at St. Pietro in
25   Vincoli & was so tremendously impressed with its sublimity that
on my the spot my intellect gushed forth a torrent of wisdom &
eloquence; but where ₍ₐ₎is₍ₐ₎ that torrent now? I have managed
tolerably well however, wh. is the great thing to soak myself in
the various scenes & phenomena. Conclusions occasionally leap
30   full-armed from my Jovine brain, bringing with ₍ₐ₎them₍ₐ₎ an
immensely restful sense of their finality. This morng. I think I
definitively settled the matter with regard to A M. A. I believe
by the way I never defin ₍ₐ₎exp₍ₐ₎licitly assured you of the
greatness of the Moses—or of the vileness of that eo calumnious

238

photograph. ~~The Moses~~ ∧It[∧] is a work of magnificent beauty—
beauty very nearly equal to that of the statue of Lorenzo de'
Medici. ~~It~~ I now feel as if I could judge of M. A.'s merits in
tolerably complete connaissance de cause. I have seen the Great
Greek things ~~&~~; I have seen Raphael & I have ∧seen[∧] all his own
works. He has something—he retains something, after all
experience—which belongs only to himself. This transcendent
"something" invested the Moses this morning with a more
melting exalting power that I have ◊ ever perceived in a work of
art. It was a great sensation—the greatest a work can give. I sat
enthralled & fascinated by that serene Aristides at Naples: but I
stood agitated this morng. by all the forces of my soul. The
beauty of such a thing as the Aristides is in the effect achieved;
that of the Moses, the Lorenzo, the figures on the Sistine roof in
the absence of a ~~definite~~ ∧limited[∧] effect. The first take no
account of the imagination; the others the largest. They have a
soul. Alack! It's poor work talking of them; je tenais seulement
to work off something of the tremor in which they have left me,
& to gratify myself by writing down in black & white & if need be
taking my stand on it against the world, the assertion, that M. A.
is the Greatest of Artists. The question remained solely ∧as[∧]
between him & the Greeks; but this morng. settled it. The
Moses alone perhaps would n't have done it; but it did it in
combination with the vision of Lorenzo's tomb—which I had it
with the deepest distinctness. It's the triumph of feeling: the
Greeks deny it—poor stupid old Michael proclaims it sovereign
o'er a regenerate world: —& affords a magnificent ~~g~~ pretext for
making a stand against it ensuite. It's the victorious cause:
the other will never be so well plead. It behoves therefore the
generous mind to take ~~it up↓~~ ∧the latter.[∧] It was worth the
trouble going afterwards, as we did this morning, to ~~St↓~~ San
Agostino & Sta. Maria della Pace to look upon Raphael's two
wretchedly decayed frescoes of Isaiah & the Sybils, in wh. il
a voulu faire du Michel Ange. There was in him none but the

very smallest Michael Angelesque elements—I fancy that I have
found after much fumbling & worrying—much of the deepest
enjoyment & of equal dissatisfaction—the secret of his
incontestable thinness & weakness. He ~~lacked~~ ∧was incapable
5 of∧ energy of statement. This may seem to be but another
name for the fault & not an explication of it. But <u>enfin</u> this
energy—positiveness—courage—call it what you will—is a
simple ■■■■ fundamental primordial quality in the supremely
superior genius. Alone it makes the real man of action in art &
10 disjoins him effectually from the critic. I felt this morning
irresistibly how that M. Angelo's greatness lay above all in the
fact that he <u>was</u> this man of action—the greatest almost,
~~considerab~~ considering the temptation he had to be otherwise—
considering how his imagination embarrassed & charmed &
15 bewildered him—the greatest perhaps, I say, that the race has
produced. So far from perfection, so finite, so full of errors, so
broadly a target for criticism as it sits there, the <u>Moses</u>
nevertheless by the vigor with which it utters its idea, the ~~e◊◊~~
eloquence with which it tells the tale of the author's passionate
20 abjuration of the inaction of fancy & contemplation—his
willingness to let it stand, in the ~~n~~ interest of life & health &
movement as his <u>best</u> & his only possible,—by this high
transcendent spirit ∧it∧ redeems itself from ~~su~~ ~~these~~ a
subjection to its details & appeals most forcibly to the generosity
25 & sympathy of the mind. Raphael is undecided, slack &
unconvinced.—I have seen little else since my return from
Naples. I have been staying on from day to day—partly from the
general difficulty there is in leaving Rome, partly ~~from~~ for the
Xmas doings, & partly because it's a certain comfort to A. K. &
30 Helen Ripley. My departure however is fixed for tomorrow. You
will have heard from A. K. of the steady hideousness of the
weather. It tells sadly upon her party & reduces to a very small
amount the utmost that can be done in a day. I have seen very
little of the Xmas ceremonies. I got my fill so completely at the

Council of a crowd & a struggle that I made no attempt to go
out on Xmas eve. On Xmas. day I roamed about St. Peter's. ~~The~~
I ◊◊ saw nothing of the Mass or the Pope—but the crowd there
is immensely picturesque & well worth seeing. A. K. & Helen R.
(Cousin H. having been laid up for a week with a violent cold)   5
went with their Courier got beautiful places & saw to perfection.
I'm sick unto death of priests & churches. Their
"picturesqueness" ends by making you want to go ~~in~~ strongly
into political economy or the New England school system. I
conceived at Naples ₐaₐ tenfold deeper loathing than ever ~~for~~   10
ₐofₐ the hideous heritage of the past—& felt for a moment as if
I should like to devote my life to laying rail-roads & erecting
blocks of stores on the most classic & romantic sites. The age has
a long row to hoe.—Your letter was full of delightful things. I
can't too heartily congratulate you on your plan of visiting. Vous   15
allez bien voir. You will live to do great things yet.

Assisi. Tuesday Dec ₐ2ₐ8<u>th</u> Since writing the above I have
been taking a deep delicious bath of mediaevalism. I left Rome
this morning by the 6.40 a.m. train & under a villainous cloudy
sky & came along in a mortally slow train (all the better to see   20
from) thro the great romantic country which leads up to
Florence. Anything <u>more</u> romantic—more deeply & darkly ~~die~~
dyed with the picturesque & all the "happy chiaroscuro of song &
story, it would be impossible to conceive. Perpetual alternations
of the landscape of Claude & that of Salvator Rosa—an   25
unending repetition of old steel engravings—raised to the 100<u>th</u>
power. Oh ■■■ <u>Narni</u>—Oh <u>Spoleto</u>! who shall describe your
unutterable picturesqueness?—what words can shadow forth
your happy positions aloft on sinking mountain spurs—girt with
your time-fretted crumbling bastions—incrusted with the rich   30
deposit of history? I've seen such ~~&~~ ~~such~~ passages of color &
composition—such bits—such effects—as can only be
reproduced by a moan of joy. It's <u>dramatic</u> landscape. The towns
are all built alike—perched on a mountain summit & huddled

together within the dark-belted circuit of their walls. At 2.30.
after a long morning of delight (despite occasional grievous
showers) I arrived at this famous little spot—famous as the
birth-place of St. Francis & the seat of ~~a~~ that vast wondrous
5   double church of wh. you perhaps remember the description in
Taine. The town lies away up on the mountain & the church is
built sheer upon its side. I got the one little <u>carriole</u> at the
station to convey me thither & found to my delight that I had
time to see it tolerably well & get a hasty ramble thro' the terrific
10   little city before dark. I have made a magnificent afternoon of it
and I am now scribbling this in the stranger's room of the
<u>Leone d'Oro</u>, having just risen from an indigestibilissimo little
repast.—The church is a vast & curious edefice of a great deal of
beauty & even more picturesqueness—a dark cavernous solemn
15   sanctuary below—& above it as ʌanother,₍ʌ₎ high, aspiring &
filled with light—& with various sadly decayed frescoes of
Giotto. The position is glorious. A great aerial portico winds
about it & commands a tremendous view. The whole thing is
intensely mediaeval & the vocabulary of Michelet alone could
20   furnish a proper characterization of it. And if such is the ~~street~~
church—what are the strange tortuous hill-scaling little streets
of the city? Never have I seen the local color laid on so thick.
They reek with antiquity. The whole place is like a little
miniature museum of the <u>genre</u>—a condensation of the
25   elements of mediaevalism—or the effect it produces at least, a
condensation of one's impressions of them. I am to go on this
eveg. by the 8.30 train to Perugia. The man who brought me up
has promised me to return with his vehicle & convey me down
the mountain & across the plain to the station. Meanwhile
30   however, the wind howls wofully, the storm seems to be rousing
itself & our transit may perhaps be uncomfortable. But I am
bent on reaching Florence to morrow night & I wish to see
Perugia ~~tomorrow~~ in the morning. I am haunted with the
apprehension that the host has bribed the little driver <u>not</u> to

return, so that I may be kept over night.—I have vilely
calumniated the establishment: the <u>padrona</u>, with the loveliest &
most beaming Italian face I have ever seen, has just come in, to
herald the approach of the <u>vetturino</u>. Buona sera! I shall add a
word at Florence.— 5

<u>Florence</u>. Jan 1st 1870. A happy new-year! I have been here
nearly three days but have been unable until now to get at my
letter. I made with success the transit from Assisi to Perugia &
now feel as if I had up a store of thrilling little memories wh.
will last for many a year & witness many a recurrence of this 10
would-be festive day. I spent at Perugia (which I found
decorated with a snow-storm wh. would have done no discredit
to the ~~climb~~ clime of obstructed horse-cars) a morning of
unalloyed enjoyment. I put myself for the 1st time in Italy into
the hands of a valet-de-place & found him a capital investment. 15
So if there is one spot in Europe I know it's Perugia—Perugia
the antique, the high-erected—the Etruscan-walled the nobly-
palaced—the deeply darkly densely curious. It's the centre of
that fine old Umbrian school of art of which Perugino & he of
~~Umbria~~ [ʌ]Urbino[ʌ] were the brightest efflorescence & I saw 20
there a number of noble specimens of the former painter which
almost reconciled me to his eternal monotony & insipid
sweetness. What a summer could be spent in a long slow journey
of long lingering days between Florence & Rome—every town
stopped at—every landscape stared at—& lofty grim old Roman 25
<u>Cortona</u> not whizzed by in the pitiless train near the Lake of
Thrasymene barely glanced at thro a gust of cinders. With these
reflections & under these annoyances I arrived in Florence. But
~~with~~ the sweetness of Florence restores me to perfect
equanimity. I feel once more its delicate charm—I find it the 30
same ~~little~~ [ʌ]rounded[ʌ] pearl of cities—cheerful, compact,
complete—full of a delicious mixture of beauty & convenience.
There is for the moment at least a return of fine weather, but the
cold is simply devilish. The streets, the hotels, the churches &

galleries all strive to out-freeze each other. I begin to appreciate
now the mildness of Rome & Naples. Yesterday, however, the sun
was glorious & I got a good warming up in a sweet lone walk all
beside the rapid Arno to the uttermost end of the charming
5   Cascine, where, sheltered from the North by a magnificent wall
of perpetual verdure & basking full in the long-sealed smile of
the South, all happy graceful Florence was watching the old year
decline into its death-shroud of yellow & pink. I have spent a
long day with the Nortons who are established in a cold
10   capacious Villa not ∧too[∧] far from one of the city gates, to
their apparent perfect contentment. They made me as welcome
as ever & we talked about Rome & Naples. Charles seems
sufficiently well & is working in a way it does one good to see ~~to~~
so many-burdened a man work, on Italian history & Art. The
15   rest are excellent & pleasant, comme toujours. I took a turn
yesterday thro' the Uffizi & the Pitti. All my old friends there
stood forth & greeted me with a splendid good-grace. The
lustrissimo Tiziano in especial gave ∧me[∧] a glorious Venetian
welcome. I spent half an hour too in Michael Angelo's chapel at
20   San Lorenzo. Great Lorenzo sits there none the less, above that
weary Giantess who reclines at his feet, gazing at the future with
affrighted eyes & revolving the destinies of humanity. He has not
yet guessed his riddles or broken his awful stillness. — Such lines
were never conceived in other vision as Michael Angelo has
25   there wrung out of his marble. For the notion of real grandeur
we must knock at that door. — — But I am scribbling on without
remembering that before I close I must thank you for your
further ~~council~~ counsel upon what you term ∧so happily[∧] my
moving intestinal drama. I wrote you before I went to Naples
30   that I had consulted Dr. Gould, the "popular" American
physician at Rome. He recommended me a mineral water, wh. I
tried without the least success. Meanwhile however Dr. Duffy's
pills began to resume their action & at Naples (owing I think to
the concurrent ~~action~~ ∧influence[∧] of many oranges) became

name

decidedly efficacious. They are slacking up once more, but I
continue ~~you~~ to take them, wear a sort bandage & get along very
decently. Dr. Gould recommended fluid extract of senna, of wh.
I procured a supply but have as yet held off from going into it.
~~I a~~ I'm extremely glad to hear that you tested on yourself the
Virtues of the sulfuric acid. It has evidently an especial
application to this matter. I don't know where Dr. D. got hold of
it. I mean to see him again & will ask him.—Meanwhile I am
gravitating northward. You bid me not hope to escape wholly
the bore of Malvern. I don't in the least. I'm determined to get
rid of this thing before my return home, if not without Malvern,
then with it. I wish to put off my visit there till such a moment
as that when I leave, ~~I shall still~~ the season will be advanced
enough for me to remain in England without disadvantage. I
shall try & hold off therefore till the 1st of March. But you will
be hearing from me again before I leave Florence. I don't know
that there's anything more to say upon this solemn theme.—In
reading over what I have written it occurs to me that you will
reproach me with brevity & paucity of <u>data</u> regarding A. Kate.
But there is nothing very startling to communicate. The three
ladies apparently found my presence a useful distraction from
the unbroken scrutiny of each other's characters. I think they are
a little bit tired of each other & owing partly to the presence of
~~Henry~~ ∧an insane[∧] & partly to the absence of a sane, gentleman
among them, have not introduced a "foreign element" into thier
circumstances to the degree they would have liked. A. Kate's
energy, buoyancy & activity are magnificent. With a male
companion & without a courier (a very stupefying as well as a
very convenient appendage) she would have had a better chance
to exercise them. Helen R. is very observant & very American
(both for better & worse.) She regrets somewhat ∧I fancy,[∧] the
"good time" which she might have had under different
circumstances. Cousin H. seems mild & gentle & patient of her
adventures rather than actively interested in them. I did what I

could for them all but was very sorry I couldn't do more. —But I must bring this interminable scrawl to a close. —I am perpetually *&* deliciously pre-occupied with home—as little as I can help to the detriment of European emotions—but to a
5 degree wh. condemns me decidedly of being of being less in the intellect than the affections. But my intellect has a hand in it too. When you tell me of the noble working life that certain of our friends are leading in that clear American air, I hanker wofully to wind up these straggling threads of loafing *&*
10 lounging *&* drifting *&* to toss my ball with the rest. But having waited so long I can wait a little longer. —I rejoice in the felicity of M. Temple's visit—*&* deplore her disappointment with regard to Calfa. But I mean to write to her. The <u>Nation</u> has ceased to come to me; but I felt a most refreshing blast of <u>paternity</u>, the
15 other day in reading father's reply to a "Swedenborgian," in a number I saw at the bankers. But ~~when~~ ∧was[∧] there ever so cruel a father? He writes to the newspapers but not to his exiled child. I have not yet got his letter to England. I saw Ripley *&* Mrs R. on my return to Rome. The former sent his love to
20 father: the latter looked very pretty *&* related an "audience" she had had of the Queen of Wurtemburg, who was living at the same hotel. —But a truce to my gossip. Addio. A torrent of loves *&* longings to my parents *&* sister. Your brother

H.

25 P.S. Since T. S. P. is so hard at work on philology, ask him the Persian for a faithless *&* perjured friend! —

Previous publication: *HJL* 1: 179–86; *SL* 2: 56–63; *CWJ* 1: 133–40
∾
238.15 especially • especi= | ally
238.17-18 cane- | bottomed • cane-bottomed
238.26 ~~my~~ the • [the *overwrites* my]
238.28 tolerably • toler= | ably
238.32 ~~A~~ M. A. • [M *overwrites* A]

238.34 e̶o̶ calumnious • [a *overwrites* o]

239.3 I̶t̶ I • [I *overwrites* It]

239.5 ⌀; • [; *overwrites* ⌀]

239.9 ◇ ever • [e *overwrites* *illegible letter*]

239.23 perhaps • per- | haps

239.26 sovereign • sover= | eign

239.27 g̶ pretext • [p *overwrites* g]

239.29 therefore • there= | fore

239.30 ⊦ ∧ • [∧ *overwrites* .]

239.31 afterwards • after= | wards

239.31 S̶t̶⊦ San • [a *overwrites* t.]

239.33 wretchedly • wretched- | ly

240.8 ▬▬▬ fundamental • [fundamental *overwrites blotted word*]

240.10 effectually • effec= | tually

240.13 c̶o̶n̶s̶i̶d̶e̶r̶a̶b̶ considering • [in *overwrites* ab]

240.14 imagination • imagi= | nation

240.18–19 e̶◇◇ eloquence • [lo *overwrites illegible letters*]

240.21 willingness • willing= | ness

240.21 n̶ interest • [i *overwrites* n]

240.23 s̶u̶ t̶h̶e̶s̶e̶ a • [these *overwrites* su; a *overwrites* these]

240.28 f̶r̶o̶m̶ for • [or *overwrites* ro]

241.2–3 T̶h̶e̶ I • [I *overwrites* The]

241.3 ◇◇ saw • [sa *overwrites illegible letters*]

241.15 congratulate • congratu= | late

241.22–23 d̶i̶e̶ dyed • [ye *overwrites* ie]

241.27 ▬▬▬ Narni • [Narni *overwrites blotted illegible word*]

242.4 a̶ that • [th *overwrites* a]

242.12 indigestibilissmo • indiges= | tibilissmo

242.13 edefice • [*misspelled*]

242.20 characterization • characteriza= | tion

242.24 condensation • condensa= | tion

242.33 Perugia • Peru= | gia

243.11 would-be • would- | -be

243.13 c̶l̶i̶m̶b̶ clime • [e *overwrites* b]

243.14 into • [to *inserted*]

243.33 moment • mo= | ment

244.1 appreciate • ap= | preciate

244.8 into • [to *inserted*]

244.11 contentment • content= | ment

244.13–14 ~~to~~ so • [s *overwrites* to]

244.26 — — • — | —

244.28 ~~council~~ counsel • [se *overwrites* ci]

244.32 Meanwhile • Mean= | while

245.3 decently • de= | cently

245.5 ~~I a~~ I'm • [m *overwrites* a]

245.5 yourself • your= | self

245.25 thier • [*misspelled*]

245.26 circumstances • circum= | stances

246.2 interminable • intermi= | nable

246.3 perpetually • per= | petually

246.15 Swedenborgian • Swe= | denborgian

246.17 newspapers • news= | papers

246.21–26 was living [. . .] friend!— • [*written across the letter's penulti-mate page*]

∾

238.11 Nov. 27$\underline{^{th}}$ • HJ's error. The letter, clearly, was begun on December 27.

238.12–13 a long letter from you (Dec. 5$\underline{^{th}}$) • WJ's 5 December 1869 letter, from Cambridge (*CWJ* 1: 127–32).

238.13–14 I despatched home a document only a couple of days since • HJ's letter to MWJ, begun in Naples, 21 December [1869], and completed in Rome, 23 December [1869].

238.16 a promise that I would • See HJ to MWJ, 21, 23 December [1869]: "Tell W. I meant to add a P.S. for him; but I will write apart in a few days" (233.19–20).

238.20–21 Emerson likes them • Sr. circulated his son's letters among his friends, including Ralph Waldo Emerson.

238.32 M. A. • Michelangelo.

circulating
letter

239.4 connaissance de cause · knowledge of the facts.

239.17 je tenais seulement · I only wanted.

239.28 ensuite · afterward.

239.31–32 San Agostino · Built in 1479–83, this church contains Raphael's fresco of the prophet Isaiah.

239.32 Sta. Maria della Pace · Church of Santa Maria della Pace; contains Raphael's fresco *The Sybils*.

239.33–34 il a voulu faire du Michel Ange · he aimed at Michelange-lesque art.

240.6 enfin · finally.

240.29 A. K. · Aunt Kate.

241.5 Cousin H. · Helen Wyckoff Perkins.

241.15–16 Vous allez bien voir · You'll see.

241.25 Salvator Rosa · An Italian baroque painter and etcher of the Neapolitan school, Rosa (1615–73) is known for landscapes and religious and historical paintings.

241.27 Oh ▬▬▬ Narni—Oh Spoleto · Both towns are located in Umbria, central Italy.

242.4 St. Francis · Saint Francis of Assisi (c. 1181–1226).

242.4–5 that vast wondrous double church · The great Church of St. Francis of Assisi, which is actually two churches, one built upon the other. Both churches were commenced in 1228; the lower one was finished in 1232 and the upper one around 1253.

242.7 carriole · cart.

242.7–8 at the station to convey me thither · Murray indicates that the railway station is "distant about 1 $\frac{1}{2}$ m[ile]" from the town (*Central Italy* 398).

242.11–12 the Leone d'Oro · Murray's *Central Italy* indicates that "There is only one inn, properly speaking, at Assisi, the *Albergo del Leone*, in the Piazza del Vescovado, kept by Stoppini, clean rooms, civil people" (398).

242.19 Michelet · Jules Michelet (1798–1874), French historian whose works include *Histoire de France* (1833–67), *L'Oiseau* (1856), and *L'Amour* (1858).

243.2 <u>padrona</u> • <u>landlady</u>.

243.4 <u>vetturino</u> • <u>coachman</u>.

243.4 Buona sera! • Good evening!

243.15 valet-de-place • courier.

243.19 Umbrian school of art • During the Renaissance, the Umbrian school of painting produced such masters as Perugino and Pinturicchio.

243.19 Perugino • Pietro di Cristoforo Vannucci (1445–1523), early Renaissance painter from the Umbrian school and teacher of Raphael. He executed his finest works at the final stages of his career, including *Madonna and Saints* and the fresco of the *Crucifixion*.

243.20 Urbino • A town in the Marches region of Italy, seventy-five kilometers north of Perugia.

243.26 <u>Cortona</u> • Medieval city in the Tuscany region of central Italy.

243.26-27 Lake of Thrasymene • Lake Trasimeno, also called the Lake of Perugia.

244.15 comme toujours • as always.

244.18 lustrissimo Tiziano • most illustrious Titian.

244.28-29 what you term ∧so happily∧ my moving intestinal drama • A direct quote from WJ's 5 December 1869 letter to HJ (see *CWJ* 1: 127).

244.29-30 I wrote you before I went to Naples that I had consulted Dr. Gould • See HJ to WJ, 30 November [1869].

245.24 ~~Henry~~ • Henry Wyckoff.

245.30 Helen R. • Helen Ripley.

246.12-13 disappointment with regard to Calfa. • Minny Temple had been planning to travel to California for her health, to join her sister, Ellen, and brother-in-law, Christopher Temple Emmet; WJ wrote near the end of his 5 December 1869 letter to HJ: "Letter fm. Minny to Alice yest. saying Temple Emmet had telegraphed her not to come to Cal. as he was coming East in December" (*CWJ* 1: 131).

246.15 "Swedenborgian" • A letter signed "A Swedenborgian" appeared in the *Nation* attacking Sr. for his criticisms of the Swedenborgian church (25 November 1869: 458). Sr. promptly responded, and this led to another cycle of responses that concluded with Sr.'s second letter (16 December 1869: 534).

246.18–19 Ripley & Mrs R. · George and Sophia Ripley.

246.21 Queen of Wurtemburg · Grand Duchess of Russia Olga Niko-laevna Romanov (1822–92) was married to Karl I, King of Württemberg, who reigned from 1864 to 1891.

246.25 T. S. P. · Thomas Sergeant Perry.

1. Mary Walsh James. By permission of the Houghton Library, Harvard University. pfMS Am 1094.

2. William James, ca. 1869. By permission of the Houghton Library, Harvard University. pfMS Am 1092.

3. Alice James, June 1870. By permission of the Houghton Library,
Harvard University. pfMS Am 1094.

4. Alice James in Boston, 1870. By permission of the Houghton Library, Harvard University. pfMS Am 1094.

5. Minny Temple, ca. 1869. By permission of the Houghton Library, Harvard University. pfMS 1092.9.

6. The James house at 20 Quincy Street. *Cambridge Chronicle*,
November 16, 1889. Cambridge Public Library collection, Cambridge
Historical Commission.

7. Jane Norton, 1850s. Courtesy of the Society for the Preservation of New England Antiquities.

8. Grace Norton, probably 1860s. Courtesy of the Society for the Preservation of New England Antiquities.

1870

HENRY JAMES SR.
14, 17, 18, 19 January 1870
ALS Houghton
bMS Am 1094 (1769)

5

Genoa Hotel Feder Jan. ◇ 14ᵗʰ. 1870.
Dearest father—I drew from my bankers in Florence the day
before I left your excellent & most welcome letter of Dec. 22ᵈ.
You speak of ~~wr~~ having written me along with Mother & Willy,
on the receipt of my bad news from Florence. Your letter is   10
probably destined soon to come to hand. I imagine it to be the
document I am now in treaty for with the P.O. at Naples—it
having gone there after I had left the place thro' the carelessness
of my Roman bankers, & various complexities since having
clustered about its fate. When I next write I ~~p~~ hope to be able to   15
announce its arrival. Meanwhile, for the present, your last is
good enough ∧to content me[∧]—tho' it pleases you to call it a
sermon. For heaven's sake don't fear to write exactly as the spirit
moves you. I should be as sorry to have you lay any injunction
on your natural humor as to have you not write at all. Be very   20
sure that as I live more I care none the less for these wise human
reflections of yours. I turn with ◇◇ great satisfaction to any
profession of interest in the fate of collective humanity—turn
with immense relief from this wearisome European world of
idlers & starers & self-absorbed pleasure seekers. I am not   25
prepared perhaps to measure ~~yo~~ the value of your notions with
regard to the ~~amelar~~ amelioration of society, but I certainly have
not travelled a ~~years~~ in this quarter of the globe without coming
to a very deep sense of the absurdly ~~g~~ clumsy & transitory
organization of the actual social body. The only respectable   30
state of mind, indeed, is to constantly express one's perfect
dissatisfaction with it—& your letter was one of the most
respectable things I have seen in a long time. So don't be afraid
of treating me to a little philosophy. I treat myself to lots. With

your letter came two <u>Nations</u>, with your Swedenborgian letters, which I had already seen ♂, I think, mentioned. I read at the same time in ~~At~~ an Atlantic borrowed from the Nortons, your article on the Woman business—so you see I have had quite a
5 heavy blow of your genius. Your <u>Atlantic</u> Article I decidedly like—I mean for matter. I am very glad to see some one not Dr. Bushnell ♂ all that genus ~~j~~ insist. upon the distinction of sexes. As a mere piece of writing moreover I enjoyed it immensely:—I had been hoping before I left Florence to write a
10 good long "descriptive" letter to Willy; but between my various cares it never came to the light. But it's ♦ only adjourned. Florence is the one thing I mean to talk about when I reach home. Talk alone can deal with it—talk as light ♂ delicate ♂ many-shaded as its own inestimable genius. At present I feel as if
15 ~~oo~~ I could hardly speak of it: all my intellects are sunk in the one dull dismal sensation of having left it—of its holding me no more. I sit here ♂ wonder how my departure effected itself. The better man within me—the man of sympathies ♂ ideas—of soul ♂ spirit ♂ intellect, had certainly not the least little finger in the
20 business. The whole affair was brutally ♂ doggedly carried thro' by a certain base creature called Prudence, acting in the interest of a certain base organ wh. shall be nameless. The angel within me sate by with trembling fluttering wings watching these two brutes at their work. And ~~how~~ oh! how that angel longs to
25 spread those wings into the celestial blue of freedom ♂ waft himself back to the city of his heart. All day yesterday in the train as it dragged me along I could hardly believe that I was doing the hideous thing I was. Last night I spent—so to speak, in tears. To day I have been <u>more meo</u> trudging over Genoa,
30 trying hard to make it do service as an humble step-sister—a poor fifth Cousin, of my Florence. But it's wretched work. The divine little city has no mortal relationships. She has neither father nor mother, nor brother nor child. She sits alone ~~in~~ on the great ~~world~~ [∧]earth,[∧] with nothing but a lover—♂ that lover

moi!—I was there about a fortnight—making six weeks in all.
Day by day my fondness ripened into this ⋄⋄⋄ unhappy passion.
I have left my heart there & I shall be but half a man until I go
back to claim it.—I should be now however in some degree a
consoled & comforted man, dear father, if I could give you some
sufficient statement—f some faithful account, of this delightful
object of my choice. But in truth no mere account of Florence—
no catalogue of her treasures or eᵒᵒₗₗ eulogy of her charms—can
bring you to a knowledge of her benignant influence. It isn't this
that or the other thing; her pictures, her streets or her hills—its
the lovely genius of the place—its ineffable spirit—its
incalculable felicity. It's the most feminine of cities. It speaks to
you with ₐthat₍ₐ₎ same soft low voice which is such an excellent
thing in women. Other cities beside it, are great swearing
shuffling rowdies. Other cities are ₐmere₍ₐ₎ things of men &
women & bricks & ⋄ mortar. But Florence has an immortal soul.
You look into her deep grey eyes—the Florentines have great
cheap brown eyes, but the spiritual city has orbs of liquid grey—
& read the history of her early sympathies & her generous
youth—so studious, so sensitive, so human. Verily, of the history
of Florence I as yet know the ~~verily~~ very smallest amount. I
should be sorry to establish my passion on deeper foundations
than really belong to it. No—Florence is friendly to all men &
her beauty is equal to her wisdom. I spent a couple of days
before I came away in going about to take a farewell look at the
places I had more or less haunted. It was then that my heart was
wrung with its deepest pain. To know all this & yet to forswear
it—is there any sense in life, on such a basis? In point of fact,
after all, there are very few individual objects in Florence of
transcendent excellence. Michael Angelo's tombs stand first—
then the Raphael's & Titian's portraits in the Uffizi & Pitti &
then the Fra Angelico's at St. Marco & half a dozen
ₐspecimens₍ₐ₎ of the early Florentine masters ⋄ (Ghirlandaio,
~~Lippi~~ Lippo Lippi Botticelli &c) in various places. There is no

great church; no great p̶l̶ palace (a dozen capital <u>fine</u> ones) ⅋ save Leonardo, there was no great Florentine painter— (counting M. A. as a Roman)—(19<u>th</u>) which he wasn't! <u>Mentone.</u> <u>H. de Gde.</u> <u>Bretagne.</u> <u>Jan. 17<u>th</u> p.m.</u> I stayed my hand three

5 nights ago at Genoa—since when I haven't had time to add a word. To night finds me on French soil—too tired with four days of constant exertion to hope to finish my letter; which I must keep till I get to Nice ⅋ rest my bones ⅋ my mind. But I don't want to fail to make a note of my impressions at the close

10 of this memorable journey—the famous drive along the upper Riviera—the so-called Cornice Road. I had the good luck—the most blessed good fortune indeed I must f̶i̶n̶d̶ [∧]call[∧] it—to find at Genoa a return carriage to Nice—the proprietor whereof was glad to take me at about a fourth of the rate of the regular

15 journey—but little more than I should have had to pay for my <u>coupé</u> in the diligence. I left Genoa yesterday morning at 5. a.m. by train for <u>Savona</u> (2 hours) where I met my carriage, which turned out thoroughly comfortable. How can I tell you what followed? how can words express it or minds conceive it? The

20 naked facts are that I started from Savona at 8 o'clock, halted ⅋ lunched at the little sea-side village of <u>Loano</u> ⅋ slept at <u>Oneglia</u>: that I started this morning again at the same hour, lunched at <u>San Remo</u> ⅋ reached Mentone this evening at 5.: that to-morrow finally I am to take the short remnant of the drive (4 hours) to

25 Nice.—o̶f̶ [∧]Amid[∧] all that I have seen ⅋ done a̶t̶ ⅋ felt in Europe, this journey stands forth <u>triumphant</u>. I have been <u>too</u>, too happy—⅋ at the same time too utterly miserable—the latter to think that I̶ ̶h̶a̶v̶e̶ ̶n̶o̶ some parent or brother or sister w̶e̶r̶e̶ was not at my side to help to dispose of such overwhelming

30 impressions. The weather has been simply perfect—which, in this particular region means a good deal. <u>Nice</u>, <u>Grand</u> <u>Hotel</u>, <u>Jan 18<u>th</u> p.m.</u> I have carried out my programme. I spent this morning at Mentone ⅋ established myself in my carriage ∧at[∧] about one. We reached this place at five. The drive is said to be

the most beautiful part of the Riviera. Beautiful indeed it is. It
leaves the shore ꝺ climbs ꝺ winds aloft among the mountains—
giving you on one side a succession of the grandest masses of
hill-scenery, all clad in purple ꝺ snow ꝺ sh spotted ꝺ streaked
with broken lights—ꝺ on the other, seen thro' the open portals   5
of shady seaward gorges, the vast blue glitter of the
Mediterranean. But it lacks the lovely swarming detail—the
lingering, clinging Italianism of the earlier portions of the road.
Mentone is delicious ꝺ I am tout désolé to find myself in this
ugly pretentious sprawling Nice. I speak of ∧on_[∧] the evidence   10
of half an hour's stroll I got before dinner. Here Italy quite gives
it up ꝺ Imperial France reigns supreme—France which I used to
love—but somehow love no more. That passion is dead ꝺ
buried.—But what shall I tell you of this transcendent
journey?—Great heavens! That while he has breath in his body   15
ꝺ a brain in his head a man should leave that land of the
immortal gods! Never never never have I got such a sense of the
essential enchantment—the incomparable "distinction" of Italy.
Happy, thrice happy, the man who enters the country along that
road! Proportionately deep ꝺ serious the melancholy of one who   20
leaves it. No, one has not lived unless one has left Italy by the
Cornice, in the full mid-glow of enjoyment, in the divinest
weather that ever illumined the planet!—I have been journeying,
as I suppose you know, thro' a belt of eternal spring. It has been
a revelation of the possible kindness of nature. And that such a   25
power should be the power of storm ꝺ darkness ꝺ cold! The
country is a land of universal olive—a foliage as gentle ꝺ tender
as the feathers on the breast of a dove—of olives ꝺ lusty cacti ꝺ
fierce fantastic date-palms, perfect debauchees of light ꝺ heat.
Two moments stand out beyond the rest in my memory of the   30
last three days—the night I spent at Oneglia—ꝺ the two sweet
morning hours I passed at San Remo, yesterday. The 1ˢᵗ had a
peculiar sanctity from the fact that it was the ∧my_[∧] last night
on Italian soil. I still had a good long hour of day-light after

arriving & well I used it to roam thro' the little sea-side town.
But it was the moon-light which ~~was the~~ set its stamp on the
event—the biggest brightest highest moon I ever beheld—a few
pale stars looking on & the Mediterranean beneath, a sheet of
5 murmurous silver. At San Remo, as the Italian coast draws to a
close it gathers up on its lovely bosom the scattered elements of
its beauty & heart-broken at ceasing to be that land of lands, it
exhales towards the blind insensate heavens a ∧rapturous[∧]
smile, more poignant than any reproach. There is something
10 hideous in having ~~to leave~~ ∧at[∧] such a place to get back into
one's ~~carrig~~ carriage. The color of the Mediterranean there is
something unutterable—as blue as one's ⊖ has dreamed the skies
of heaven—as one seen the Rhone at Geneva. There, too, the
last sweet remnant of the beautiful Italian race looks at you with
15 kindly dark eyed wonder as you take your way to the stupid
unlovely North. I made a hundred notes of things I wanted to
describe to you but I give it all up. The details overwhelm me. I
can only bid you come & see it for yourself—come & see what
you feel as you drive thro' a wide low plantation of olives, with
20 their little tender sparkling leaves all interwoven overhead into a
filter of grey-green light & their little tender twisted stems &
trunks forming on the grassy hill-side an upper & lower horizon,
& a foot-path trodden in the grass making a vista to shew in the
distance two young Italians strolling arm in arm.—I made one
25 note, tho', which I shan't forbear to dwell upon—a note relating
to the deep gratitude I feel to the beloved parents to whom I
owe all the rich acquisitions of these inestimable days. My
second thought is always of them. 19$\underline{^{th}}$. I was so tired last night
that I knocked off just after the above little spurt of filial
30 affection. Tho' I had nominally driven from Mentone, yet so
much of the way was up the mountains that I walked for miles
together, to ease the horses: I was consequently a bit jaded by
ten o'clock. Meanwhile however, the days are treading on each
others heels & you will have been an age without hearing from

me. I don't forgive myself for not having managed to write in
Florence: it was a rare occasion lost. I did however write three
long letters, ∧the two 1ˢᵗ of₍∧₎ which you had better get hold of:
one to Mr. Boott (thro father) one to A. G. Sedgwick, & one to
M. Temple.—To night again I am rather tired & in view of this &   5
of your probable impatience will make short work with what I
have left to say.—I have spent today most pleasantly: I oughtn't
to abuse Nice, she has given me a charming day—charming,
that is, by getting away from her. I plucked up my energies after
breakfast & walked over to the beautiful little adjoining bay &   10
town of Villefranche—where my heart beat proudly at seeing a
noble American Man of War riding alone & glorious in the still
blue basin of the harbor. Once at Villefranche I walked about
promiscul promiscuously for hours (as I may say) among the
loveliest conceivable olive-shaded paths, beside the sweet blue   15
coves that look across the outer sea toward the bosky cliffs of
Italy. I took a little carriage home, just in time for dinner. I
∧have₍∧₎ never seen anything so unmitigatedly innocent & sweet
as all this coast region. It un∕ out-Italys England. I mean to
hang on as many days as I think I can afford & get some more   20
walks.—Woe betide me! All this time I see I have told you
nothing about Genoa. I was there but two days but I saw it
tolerably well, & be-walked it, I fancy, as few mortals have ever
done before. It's an extremely curious & interesting place—a
sort of prosaic Naples: full moreover of a magnificent second-   25
rate architectural picturesqueness. Lots of tremendous ornate
palaces whose rusty cornices take the afternoon light, as the sun
descends to the ocean, with a grand glaring melancholy. Of
especial sights the one chiefly worth mentioning is the beautiful
collection of paintings at the Brignole-Sale p Palace: 30
4 tremendous Vandykes. I can't write of them. Before their
immortal elegance I lay aside my plebeian pen. I enclose a
poorish photo. of the greatest (one of the early Marquises of
B.-S.) for Alice. It's not Rafael—it's not Titian; it's not an

Italian. But it <u>is</u> Vandyke—transcendant Dutchman!—I have already hinted of my probable course on leaving this place. I shall <u>filer</u> <u>sur Paris</u>, stopping en route at three ◊◊ or four places—chiefly Avignon Arles & Nîmes & be settled in Paris by

5   Feb. 1ˢᵗ—settled for three or four weeks. To this has fizzled down my youthful dream of spending <u>years</u> in the brilliant Capital! No: if I had had any extra ~~weeks~~ ₐyears₍ₐ₎ on hand I should have given them to Florence. By the 1ˢᵗ week in March I hope to have reached Malvern. But enough of projects.—These are ~~the~~

10   dreary days in respect of letters. You will have been directing I suppose to Bowles frères, as I asked you. I hope to find at least a dozen, teeming with news & health & happiness. Farewell. I read in the last <u>Atlantic</u> Lowell's poem & Howells's Article. I admire them both ₐlargely—₍ₐ₎—especially the latter. Tell H. I haven't

15   been waiting for him to write, to write again myself, but simply for the convenient moment. It will soon come. Addio. Unendliche Liebe.—Your H.

Previous publication: *HJL* 1: 187–93; *SL* 2: 64–70

༄

   255.6 ◊ 14 • [1 *overwrites illegible letter*]

   255.9 ~~wr~~ having • [ha *overwrites* wr]

   255.15 ~~p~~ hope • [h *overwrites struck through* p]

   255.18 exactly • ex= | actly

   255.22 ◊◊ great • [gr *overwrites illegible letters*]

   255.26 ~~yo~~ the • [th *overwrites* yo]

   255.27 ~~amelar~~ amelioration • [l *overwrites* lar]

   255.29 ~~g~~ clumsy • [c *overwrites* g]

   256.3 ~~At~~ an • [an *overwrites* At]

   256.7 ~~j~~ insist • [i *overwrites blotted* j]

   256.8 moreover • more= | over

   256.11 ◊ only • [o *overwrites illegible letter*]

   256.15 ~~o◊~~ I • [I *overwrites* o◊]

   256.19 intellect • [*first* e *inserted*]

256.24 ~~how~~ oh • [oh *overwrites* how]

256.33 ~~in~~ on • [o *overwrites* i]

257.6 ~~f~~ some • [s *overwrites struck through* f]

257.8 ~~eꝏll~~ eulogy • [ul *overwrites* ◊◊ll]

257.16 ◊ mortar • [m *overwrites illegible letter*]

257.22 ~~verily~~ very • [ery *overwrites* erily]

257.33 Florentine • Floren- | tine

257.33 ◊ (• [(*overwrites illegible letter*]

257.34 ~~Lippi~~ Lippo • [o *overwrites* i]

258.1 ~~pl~~ palace • [a *overwrites* l]

258.25 ~~at~~ ꝺ • [ꝺ *overwrites* at]

258.28 ~~have no~~ some • [some *overwrites* have no]

258.28 ~~were~~ was • [as *overwrites* ere]

259.4 ~~sh~~ spotted • [p *overwrites* h]

259.13 somehow • some= | how

259.20 melancholy • melan= | choly

259.22 mid-glow • mid- | glow

260.2 moon-light • moon- | light

260.9 something • some= | thing

260.11 ~~carrig~~ carriage • [a *overwrites blotted* g]

260.12 ~~one's◊~~ has • ['s *blotted out;* h *overwrites blotted illegible letter*]

260.30 affection • affec= | tion

261.14 ~~promiscul~~ promiscuously • [o *overwrites blotted* l]

261.15 olive-shaded • olive- | shaded

261.19 ~~un⁄~~ out • [out *overwrites* un-]

261.25 magnificent • magnifi= | cent

261.25–26 second- | rate • second-rate

261.26 picturesqueness • picturesque | ness

261.30 ~~p~~ Palace • [P *overwrites* p]

262.1 Dutchman • Dutch- | man

262.3 ◊◊ or • [r *overwrites illegible letter*]

∾

255.6 Hotel Feder • "Now one of the best in Genoa, very clean," with a view of the harbor, according to the 1866 Murray for northern Italy (107), located Via Bogino 9, rooms three francs and upward (Baedeker, *Northern Italy* 113).

256.3–4 your article on the Woman business • Sr.'s "The Woman Thou Gavest with Me," *Atlantic Monthly* 25 (January 1870): 66–72.

256.29 more meo • in my own way.

257.32 Fra Angelico's at St. Marco • Frà Giovanni da Fiesole, known as Beato Angelico (1400–1455), a Florentine painter, some of whose early work was for the monastery of San Marco.

257.33 Ghirlandaio • Domenico Ghirlandajo (1449–94), a Florentine painter of narrative frescoes.

257.34 Lippo Lippi • Fra Filippo Lippi (1406–69), a second-generation painter, whose works include *The Annunciation, Coronation of the Virgin*, and *Madonna with Child and Scenes from the Life of Mary*.

257.34 Botticelli • Sandro Botticelli (1445–1510) studied under Fra Filippo Lippi. Approximately fifty paintings survive that are either entirely or partially by his own hand, many which are housed at the Uffizi Gallery.

258.3 M. A. • Michelangelo.

258.3 Mentone • Menton in French, town on the French-Italian border and the Mediterranean coast.

258.4 H. de Gde. • According to the *Northern Italy* Baedeker, the Hôtel de Grande Bretagne was located facing the "E. Bay, towards the Italian frontier, pension 7–10" francs a day (127).

258.11 Cornice Road • Road through the hills overlooking the Mediterranean.

258.16 coupé in the diligence • Seat inside the stage-coach.

258.17 Savona • Town thirty-five kilometers west of Genoa.

258.21 Loano • A town in northwest Italy, on the western coast of the Ligurian Sea, southwest of Genoa.

258.21 Oneglia • A town eighty-six kilometers east of Nice and 180 kilometers west of Genoa, with only one hotel listed by the *Northern Italy* Baedeker, the Hôtel Victoria (126).

258.23 San Remo • A town fifty-nine kilometers east of Nice.

258.31 Grand Hotel • Grand Hotel Royal, rue Grimaldi, "beyond the harbour" (Baedeker, *Northern Italy* 130).

259.9 tout désolé • really sorry.

259.12 Imperial France reigns supreme • Nice became French in 1860, as a result of the same agreement between Napoleon III and the Kingdom of Piedmont by which Savoy was transferred from Piedmont to France (see HJ to Thomas Sergeant Perry, 27, 28 March [1860]).

261.11 Villefranche • A town about five kilometers east of Nice, on the Gulf of Villefranche.

261.30-31 Brignole-Sale ꝑ Palace: 4 tremendous Vandykes • The Palazzo Brignole Sale contained the most extensive collection of paintings in Genoa, including a number by Anthony Van Dyck (1599-1641), who resided in Genoa in the early 1620s. The four "tremendous" paintings are probably portraits of Jeronima Brignole Sale and her daughter, of a Prince of Orange, of Antonio Brignole Sale, and of Marchesa Paolina Adorno-Brignole.

262.3 filer sur Paris • head straight for Paris.

262.13 the last Atlantic Lowell's poem & Howells's Article • James Russell Lowell's poem "The Cathedral" and W. D. Howells's article "By Horse-Car to Boston" appeared in the *Atlantic Monthly* 25 (January 1870): 1-16 and 114-22, respectively.

262.14 H. • W. D. Howells.

262.16 Addio • Farewell.

262.17 Unendliche Liebe • Unending love.

GRACE NORTON
20 January 1870   25
ALS Houghton
bMS Am 1094 (878)

Nice Grand Hotel Jan. ~~1~~ 20ᵗʰ 1870.
Dear Grace—You see there is a Grand Hotel after all—& very   30
grand it is & full of frivolous french magnificoes whose cold
indifference makes me turn with rapture to the kindly graces of
the Villa d'Elci. A further inspection of my date, by the way,
reveals to me that I left Florence only a week ago to day.

Incredible & astounding fact! So much of sensation & emotion & perception has been crowded into these short eight days that many a slow & solemn month in my chequered career makes a wretched show beside them. You see I've seen the Riviera. But
5   you don't, you won't, you can't see <u>how</u> I've seen it! But let me be calm. First the prose & then the poetry. I departed from Florence in about the manner I expected. A glorious day, but an interminable journey. The country between Florence & Bologna which I had seen in all the glow of early autumn, was bare of the
10   better half of its beauty. In Genoa I spent two beautiful busy days—only two because the occasion presented itself of taking a certain return carriage to Nice at a marvellously reduced rate & thus voyaging at my leisure & pleasure <u>en prince</u> instead of in the ignoble <u>diligence</u>. Genoa however I saw pretty well & am
15   quite ready to subscribe to your estimate of it—or was it Jane's? The <u>quality</u> of its picturesqueness strikes me as below ‸that of₍ₐ₎ much that I have seen in Italy. But for generosity & abundance & coming in great swinging masses it is quite unsurpassed. But it's not <u>exquisite</u>, like Florence, & I think on the whole it's decidedly
20   the city to see 1ˢᵗ in Italy. Of course I saw the Vandykes. That is I saw those at the B. S. palace—but not those at the Balbi—the latter being closed on account of death in the family. But I was content with those at the Brignole-Sale & with the great one at the Pallavicini. The Marquis on horse back is a really great work
25   I think, & not at all diminished by its elegance. No more is the young fellow in the last room with his hand on his sword—such a perfect model of an interesting bloated young aristocrat of the <u>temps</u> <u>passé</u>. The effect of Vandyke's pictures seems to me a rather saddening one. He painted not like Titian & Tintoret the
30   complete solid well-rounded human creature, but a semi-factitious partial presentment of it—the Gentleman & the Lady. The human creature still survives, sound & healthy & whole: but the Gentleman & Lady in the sense in which Vandyke's patrons were such are incontestably defunct; & yet these vivid images

still remain, gazing with such implicit confidence upon a world
which doesn't care two straws for them. (I enclose you a photo.
of the Marquis. I would have got his wife too, but the
reproduction was too offensive.) From Genoa ∧i.e. Savona,[∧] to
this place I made my journey with real splendor. One of
Vandykes ~~gentleman~~ gentlemen couldn't more nobly have taken
his ease. The weather was simply divine—mild, still, ~~iridess~~
iridescent. My carriage was delightfully ~~ob~~ comfortable; my
coachman most obsequious—<u>rien n'y manquait</u>. You'll hardly
expect me to <u>describe</u> the Riviera. If it were fifty years since you
passed along it, I should count on your remembering it.
Remember it then! It's thoroughly simple, on the one hand the
grey of olives—on the other the blue of the Mediterranean. I
think on the whole I never enjoyed scenery so much. I have just
been working off my enthusiasm in a long letter home—
fortunately for you: I might have treated you to some pretty fine
writing. It's Italian up to the last. What a high-way for entering
Italy! San Remo is perhaps the biggest pearl on the string. If I
hadn't been bound by base financial ties to my coachman I don't
think I could have left it in less than a week. Mentone is very
nearly as good. I am on the point of going back there for a few
days: tomorrow will decide—probably in the negative. This
glaring parisianized Nice is rather unsatisfying. I have had two
very long & beautiful walks; but if I want to get more I must
return towards Italy or go on towards Cannes. Return towards
Italy! Delightful irony of rhetoric! I have said nothing about the
main feature of my journey after all—I mean my <u>sentiments</u>. Ah
the way Italy kept tugging at my heart! Well I know her the
better for leaving her thus. I know myself the better at least. I
know I really care for her. And for herself she puts in a heavy
claim on my future. Already I feel my bows ∧beneath her
weight[∧] settle comfortably into the water.—Nevertheless its
well your'e all at Florence to be written to & to write & thereby
persuade me that I didn't just dream of it. Are you well & happy?

Is Susan better? Are you better? Has the spring arrived? Ah happy Florentines! Out of Italy you don't know how vulgar a world it is. I detect a universal ugliness in things. Stick to Italy to the last hour. <u>Bien des</u> <u>choses</u> to every one. I shall probably be in Paris on the 1<u>st</u>. Address me <u>Bowles</u> <u>frères</u> <u>Rue de la Paix</u> & let me angelically find ten words there. Salute everything for me & believe me dear Grace

    Your devoted friend & servant

      <u>H. James jr.</u>

No previous publication

    ∾

    265.29 ‡ 20 • [*2 overwrites* 1]

    266.1 sensation • sensa= | tion

    266.11 presented • pre- | sented

    266.16 picturesqueness • picturesque= | ness

    266.30-31 semi- | factitious • semi-factitious

    266.31 presentment • pre= | sentment

    267.6 ~~gentleman~~ gentlemen • [e *overwrites* a]; gentle= | men

    267.7-8 ~~iridess~~ iridescent • [c *overwrites* s]

    267.8 ~~ob~~ comfortable • [com *overwrites blotted* ob]; com= | fortable

    267.9 obsequious • obse= | quious

    267.29 myself • my- | self

    268.4-9 be in Paris [. . .]. <u>H. James jr.</u> • [*written across the letter's first page*]

    ∾

    266.13 <u>en prince</u> • <u>like a prince</u>.

    266.14 <u>diligence</u> • <u>stagecoach</u>.

    266.21 B. S. palace • Palazzo Brignole Sale.

    266.21 Balbi • Palazzo Balbi; the collection includes half a dozen paintings by Van Dyck.

    266.23-24 the great one at the Pallavicini • Van Dyck's *Coriolanus and Veturia*, representing King James I and his family.

    266.24 the Marquis on horse back • Van Dyck's portrait of Antonio Brignole Sale on horseback, at the Palazzo Brignole Sale.

266.28 temps passé · old days.

267.9 rien n'y manquait · nothing was missing.

267.15 a long letter home · HJ's 14, 17, 18, 19 January 1870 letter to Sr.

267.25 Cannes · Twenty-five kilometers southwest of Nice.

268.4 Bien des choses · All the best.

ALICE JAMES
25, 27 January 1870
ALS Houghton
bMS Am 1094 (1561)

Avignon — Hotel d'Europe
    Jan. 25th 1870.
Beloved sister — After a terribly long silence I managed to get off
to you at Nice a letter wh. will have prepared you for ~~the new~~
my present localization. A couple of days after writing I brought
my stay at Nice to a close — simultaneously with the close
apparently of the fine weather. I managed to make a tolerably
good thing of the four or five days of my sojourn. A most
delightfully good thing might be made I am sure, by a person
addicted to long walks of a couple of months' ~~sojourn~~ ∧stay[∧] on
that enchanting coast. I would have given much to have felt free
to remain there two or three weeks. It is certainly one of the
spots of earth where nature smiles. If I had staid however I
shouldn't have stopped at Nice. I should have gone back to
Mentone: or better still I should have made a further retreat
back on to soft Italian soil & to the magic precincts of San
Remo. Delightful name! As I write the word the whole lovely
stretch of my journey from Genoa comes back to me — destined
evidently to become one of the most sacred shrines of memory.
But I mean to go back there one of these days in the vulgar flesh
as well — with my sister vulgarly by my side. But we'll not talk of
it now, but merely glance & pass. I got one fine long walk out of

Nice, away from the shore, up a lovely winding road which
vanquished a gentle mountain & wandered vaguely thro' an
unutterable forest of olives. The sweetness of olive scenery is
~~son~~ something quite indescribable. You get a suggestion of it in
5 the light among the tree-trunks in the old apple-orchards at
Newport—a suggestion but little more. All the detail here is of a
superlative delicacy. Of course I went to that wicked little
Monaco—the famous principality of six-miles square, supported
by its great gambling house. I tried to do my duty by Monaco as
10 a conscientious observer but I'm afraid I rather failed. I took the
midday train from Nice & was deposited with a cargo of
dissolute persons of both sexes, at the Casino station after half
an hour's journey. I made my way into ∧the[∧] gambling-rooms &
watched the play at the various tables with vague projects of
15 learning the <u>modus</u> <u>operandi</u> & staking a napoleon for that 1<u>st</u>
time which is always so highly profitable. After a while—
however I turned from the greedy human throng & the vulgar
chink of gold to the nobler face of the great blue ocean without
& the deeper music of its waves. Monaco out of doors is as
20 divinely beautiful as Monaco in-doors is godlessly ugly. Great
mountains, of deep & tender shades, form a glorious background
to the gleaming little promontory & come sweeping down in
great soft lines to the sea. A beautiful winding road travels close
above the shore along the coast to Mentone. I came out before
25 the Casino & looked at the melting mountains & the dazzling sky
& the laughing sea & throwing my projected <u>étude</u> <u>de moeurs</u>
quite overboard, I started off so briskly that I never stopped till I
had annihilated the seven or eight miles which intervene before
Mentone. At Mentone I dined—with appetite—at a plain little
30 restaurant, but off a series of dishes—I had a series I assure
you—prepared with real French genius. French cookery by the
way already strikes me forcibly. It makes that of other lands
seem barbarous & laughable. Of course I took the train from
Mentone back to Nice & thereby never saw Monaco again. I

promised myself to return on the morrow ɤ complete my <u>étude</u> <u>de moeurs</u> but on the morrow <u>le</u> <u>temps</u> <u>se gâta</u> ɤ I took the train for Marseille—a seven hour's journey—but which derived a certain human interest from my being thrown with an unhappy young Englishman very far gone with a grievous pulmonary trouble, travelling back home alone (tho' quite unfit to do so) ɤ whose "eternal gratitude, as he assured me, I won by paying him a few little attentions on the way, at the hotel at Marseille ɤ on our departure next morning. If the poor fellow isn't dead on the road he will have reached England by this time. At Marseille I spent simply the night, not deeming it under the circumstances (i.e bad weather ɤ my being pressed for time) worthy of a detailed inspection. I came on yesterday morning as far as Arles, which I reached by noon. ~~The~~ We left the rain behind us but we entered a land of tremendous cold—the land of the terrible <u>mistral</u>. As it was to the sweet accompaniment of the <u>mistral</u>— the howling roaring paralysing <u>mistral</u>—that I visited the ancient city of Arles, I might be accused for not finding it the most interesting spot on earth. I was continually thinking how pleasant it might ⨯ be if it were warm. But without ranking Arles as one of my 1<u>st</u> class successes I may say that it has its points. These points are as you know, its roman ruins—to which some authorities add the beauty of ◇◇ the <u>Arlésiennes</u>. But the Arlésiennes were to my perception so swollen ɤ empurpled with the mistral that I was unable to detect their traditional loveliness. And even of a warm day I fancy, they are pretty only with the relative prettiness of French women—not with the perfect ɤ peerless ɤ absolute beauty of that young American lady who sat opposite to me at the table d'hôte at Nice ɤ whose face must testify to a certain divine delicacy, after all, in the Nation that produced her. The great lion at Arles is the Roman Arena—very perfect: less massive ɤ imposing than those of Verona ∧ɤ Rome[∧] but far richer in all its horrible details of dungeons ɤ dens. Scattered over the city are various other relics

271

of more or less importance. But better than any of these is the
cloister of St. ~~Thr~~ Trophime—the Cathedral church—the
sweetest richest quaintest little Gothic cloister you can possibly
imagine—the genuine florid fantastic gothic of the North. It's
5   very pleasant on leaving Italy to be thus kindly taken by the
hand by a really exquisite monument. You feel ∧at 1st[∧] that in
doing so youv'e left everything: but such a work as this little
cloister opens a glimpse into the mighty world of great
churches. I left Arles at 7.30 in the evening ♂ came on here by 9.
10 In doing so I purposely omitted Nîmes, which is off the
railway—that is on a branch line. After mature reflection I
decided that the course of wisdom was not to attempt to do
Nîmes <u>par</u> <u>un temps</u> <u>pareil</u>—especially as I couldn't have done it
properly. The proper course for the enterprising traveller is to
15 take a carriage from Nîmes to the famous Pont du Gard ♂
thence drive across country to Avignon. But as I couldn't face
the idea of spending six hours in a carriage in the teeth of the
mistral I gave it all up. Meanwhile I dream of coming back one
of these days in the leafy month of June. Then I shall ~~go~~
20 ∧make[∧] as well the great excursion to Vaucluse, the haunt of
Petrarch which I shall forego now by the same token. These last
days have thoroughly convinced me of the folly of attempting to
do sight seeing in Winter. It's equally unkind to yourself ♂ to
the places you see. You <u>cant</u> see them fairly—you cant but carry
25 away harsh false impressions of them. It's absolutely cruel to any
place to come ♂ stare at it in the season of its hideous nakedness
♂ this is especially true of this pale <u>blafard</u> scrubby landscape of
Provence which especially needs the utmost glow ♂ exuberance
of summer. So although I've seen Avignon I dont in the least feel
30 as if I had seen the Avignon of my fancy—for Avignon if I'm not
mistaken is a place that vaguely haunts the fancy. Its
picturesqueness needs a good soft thaw. Its well enough—but
ah, I'm fresh from Italy—cruel fatal fact! There can be no
better illustration of the surpassing force of Italian scenery than

the fact that this fine old Avignon should back down before it. If
I had come here six months my delights would certainly have
been deep. I should have revelled in the paleness & tameness &
t̶h̶i̶n̶n̶e̶s̶s̶ [∧]flatness[∧] which now displeases me. But as I say one
of these days when Southern memories are dim I shall come
down from the North & greet in pleasant Avignon the formost
h̶a̶r̶b̶i̶n̶g̶e̶r̶ ∧member[∧] of the glorious sisterhood of southern
cities. Meanwhile my reason, sternly provoked tells me that the
great shapeless mass of the palace of the Popes lords it over the
city with a grim magnificence whereof it were ignoble not to
take account. I went over the palace this morning in tow of a
dingy french person who failed to impart any ∧very[∧] vivid
color to its dreary white-w̶h̶washed mutilated apartments. I did
the Musée too—with its cold brick-tiled halls & its colder
paintings of the early french school & its coldest shivering,
shuddering groaning little old concierge:—but pleasant enough
nevertheless—a real little Musée de Province. And I bewalked
the streets comme toujours until my legs n'en pouvaieent plus.
And then I came home & dined at the excellent succulent
bourgeois table d'hote, in company with several Englishmen &
an American lady with two very ugly daughters—all of a strange
denationalized aspect—of unknown antecedents, who they tell
me has been living here for the past three years. I take her to be
a Southron impoverished & exiled. This however is the wildest
conjecture. But a̶n̶ a trio of American women living at Avignon
is a phenomenon demanding explanation. It remains wrapped in
mystery. And then having dined I came up here to my high-
walled brick-paved room & caused a fire of many logs to be
created on the hearth: in the enjoyment of about a 20th part of
whose heat (the rest being consecrated to the vast receding
chimney) I have been stupidly scrawling these pages. And now
the chimney having utterly consumed the fire & my letter having
consumed the stubborn fuel of my wits I'll bid you a loving

5

10

15

20

25

30

Amer

hotel room

good night. I'm to be called to morrow in the cold darkness (horrible thought) to start for Lyons.

Paris. <u>Hotel</u> du Louvre₊ ₍ₐ₎Jan. 27th. ₍ₐ₎ I was called I did start, & here I am—since last night. My journey was without excitement.

5 The process of congelation can hardly be called an excitement. I ₍ₐ₎have₍ₐ₎ never suffered from the cold as in that dreary day's journey to Lyons. I lay a night at Lyons & came on here, in eleven hours, yesterday. It was still cold, but more endurable. I saw nothing <u>en route</u> but the dull ugly platitude of the French

10 landscape. In summer, doubtless, it's charming; but it lacks fine elements. I came on my arrival to this hotel as being on the whole the surest & most suitable. I find it much better than that horrible Gd. Hotel at which I stopped a last spring. My 1st steps this morning were of course toward Bowles Bros. <u>rapport à</u>

15 <u>mes lettres</u>. I found but one—viz. from Mother & Willy, of Dec. 28th—brief on the part of each, but such as it was I made the most of it & shall shortly reply to each of them specifically. Meanwhile thank them kindly. When I say I found but one I omit ~~one~~ a note from A. Kate, written on the eve of her

20 departure from Rome, which she says she shall not be sorry to leave, as she has not been at all well. Between her illness, the horrible weather & her lack of society, I fancy her Roman stay hasn't seemed very brilliant.—But the question is not of Rome, but of Paris. It is half-past midnight & I have just come in from

25 the <u>Gymnase</u> theatre where I have had a very exquisite pleasure. A new play by name <u>Froufrou</u> (if you can read it) & a new actress, Mlle. Desclée who has suddenly scrambled to the ◊ top of the histrionic heap. The play very clever—the actress— superlative! the whole thing admirable for finish & delicacy.

30 What a happy society where folks may turn out & take an eveg.'s amusement of that fashion. It's an education. Besides this to day I have walked about a deal & spent a long time at the Louvre. I was immensely struck with its noble splendors. Much of it was a great warm blast of Italy—a glorious gust of the south wind. For

274

Paris generally—admirable: but quite without charm—as it strikes me. I had rather live in Florence or London. But a truce to keen analysis. It's too late, too cold & I'm too tired to do anything but shut up shop. I shall probably be here about a fortnight—or until Feb. 15<u>th</u>. I shall write to mother in a very few days. Tell Willy I give his letter all the thought it deserves. Heaven bless you all. Good night petite soeur.

    Tout à toi <u>H. James</u> jr.

5

No previous publication

∾

269.16-17 ~~the new~~ my present • [my pres *overwrites* the new]

269.17 localization • localiza= | tion

269.19 apparently • ap= | parently

270.3 unutterable • unutter= | able

270.4 ~~son~~ something • [m *overwrites* n]

270.15 napoleon • na= | poleon

270.27 overboard • over- | board

270.28 annihilated • annihil= | ated

271.14 ~~The~~ We • [We *overwrites* The]

271.20 ~~+~~ be • [be *overwrites* —]

271.23 ◇◇ the • [the *overwrites* illegible letters]

272.2 ~~Thr~~ Trophime • [r *overwrites* hr]

272.32 picturesqueness • picturesque | ness

273.2 delight◇ • [*illegible letter blotted out*]

273.6 formost • [*misspelled*]

273.13 white-~~wh~~washed • [a *overwrites blotted* h]

273.18 pouvaieent • [*misspelled*]

273.20 d'hote • [*misspelled*]

273.20 with • [*inserted*]

273.25 ~~an~~ a trio • [a tr *overwrites* an]

273.26 explanation • explana= | tion

273.27-28 high- | walled • high-walled

274.3 † ʌ • [ʌ *overwrites* .]

274.13 ~~a~~ last • [l *overwrites* a]

274.19 ~~one~~ a · [a *overwrites* one]

274.22 society · soci= | -ety

274.27 ◇ top · [t *overwrites illegible letter*]

∾

269.15–16 I managed to get off to you at Nice a letter · HJ to Sr., 14, 17, 18, 19 January 1870, begun in Genoa, continued in Mentone, and completed in Nice.

270.15 a napoleon · A gold coin worth twenty francs.

270.26 étude de moeurs · a study of manners.

271.2 le temps se gâta · The weather turned bad.

271.16 mistral · A cold, powerful wind that often blows out of the Alps into Provence.

271.23 Arlésiennes · Women of Arles.

271.31–32 the Roman Arena · From the early second century of the common era.

272.1–2 the cloister of St. ~~Thr~~ Trophime · The church of St. Trophime in Arles was built between 1170 and 1180 and is an excellent example of twelfth-century romanesque architecture. In 1840 it was designated as a "monument historique," which led to a series of renovations and cleanings in 1860.

272.13 par un temps pareil · in such weather.

272.15 the famous Pont du Gard · Well-preserved Roman aqueduct between Avignon and Nîmes.

272.20–21 Vaucluse, the haunt of Petrarch · The Fontaine de Vaucluse, next to Isle-sur-Sorgues, where Petrarch once resided.

272.27 blafard · colorless.

273.18 comme toujours · as always.

273.18 n'en pouvaient plus · could take it no longer.

274.3 Hotel du Louvre · The Grand Hôtel du Louvre, located on the Rue de Rivoli, opposite the north side of the Louvre.

274.14–15 rapport à mes lettres · concerning my letters.

274.15 one [. . .] Willy · WJ to HJ, 27 December 1869 (see *CWJ* 1: 132–33).

274.25 Gymnase theatre · Gymnase Dramatique, Boulevard Bonne-Nouvelle 38, primarily used for vaudevilles and comedies.

274.26 <u>Froufrou</u> · *Froufrou* (1869), a drawing-room comedy by Henri Meilhac (1830–97) and Ludovic Halévy (1834–1908). Froufrou, a superficial wife who is jealous of her older sister, has an affair out of spite but dies forgiven by her husband.

274.27 Mlle. Desclée · HJ mentions Aimée Desclée, an actress at the Théâtre du Gymnase, in his 1876 essay "The Théâtre Français," first published in the *Galaxy* in April 1877 and subsequently reprinted a number of times: "The Gymnase, since the death of Mlle. Desclée, has been under a heavy cloud" (441).

275.7 petite soeur · little sister.

275.8 Tout à toi · All yours.

MARY WALSH JAMES
5 February [1870]   15
ALS Houghton
bMS Am 1094 (1770)

London. Charing Cross Hotel. Feb. 5.
My own dear Mother.   20
 I despatched home a letter about a week ago which will in some degree have prepared you for this superscription of the ~~above~~ ₗ ∧present.₍∧₎ I left Paris yesterday morning & after a fairly good passage of the Channel (<u>via</u> Boulogne) (during wh. however I only just managed to escape the last tribulation)   25
arrived at 7. p.m. in this brilliant metropolis. I have been poking about the streets all day, doing several needful errands; I have dined in the coffee room off the inevitable <u>régale</u> of a cut of roast beef, brussels sprouts & a pint of beer, & now I find myself in the reading room, having appropriated the ∧public₍∧₎   30
blotting-book, up to my neck in British local color & hankering by the same token wofully after my dear old Yankee kith & kin. I found at my bankers just before leaving Paris a second letter apiece from Willy & you, of I forget what date—the letters are

up in my room. Most joyful was I to ~~foo~~ get them. I have had
since leaving Florence such a plentiful lack of society that for
nearly a month I have hardly exchanged ten words with a human
creature—& to get a couple of letters reminds me agreeably that
I am not quite the isolated human particle that I am tempted to
fancy. Your letter, dearest mother, was most delightful—full of
succulent gossip about all the <u>bonnes gens</u> in Cambridge. Willy
alludes ∧scornfully[∧] in his letter to my habitual "jaunty
promise" to write to him in "a day or two"—so at present I'll
indulge in no~~w~~ promises: ~~for the p~~ but I'm much obliged to him
for his letter & as soon as I reach Malvern I <u>won't</u> answer it. It
had the inestimable merit of containing tolerably good news
about his health, which has put me in so good a humor that I
don't mind his incriminations. I made as you see a shorter stay
in Paris than I expected; a much shorter one than I should have
liked. Lo₁! when I came to prepare to go, I found that I
immensely liked the old city—~~oo~~ the new city rather. And what t
do I say to it now, after a day in this <u>beastly</u> London. Its
darkness & grime & filth & misery are ~~doubling~~ doubly
overwhelming & Paris shines from afar with the lustre of the
new Jerusalem. When I first arrived there, still haunted with the
memory of Florence I was oppressed & irritated by its
pretentious splendor & its pedantic neatness & symmetry: but
gradually its immense merits began to impress me ~~I~~ & now I
have quite succumbed to it as the perfect model of a mighty
capital. And the excellent little Hotel de l'Amirauté in the Rue
Neuve St. Augustin (recommended me on I know not whose
authority by Willy) to which I removed (~~economicly~~
economically) from the Louvre & which just as I had got to
know it well & to love it, I was obliged to leave. To live at the
H. de l'Amirauté, to spend the morng. at the Louvre, to dine
modestly (but none the less well) at some Restaurant on the
Boulevards & to go in the eveg. to the Theatre Français—or
equally good, to come back in the eveg. to your well appointed

little room ◊ put your feet into your slippers ◊ touch a match to
the little edefice of logs on your hearth, ◊ in the frequent pauses
of your book lend an ear to the whisper of a maternal ∧voice[∧]
in the fizzing of the burning wood—such—such are the
elements of a decently happy life—a life which I glanced at ◊   5
passed. I found it becoming everyday more needful that I should
get to Malvern without further delay; so I broke short off ◊
started. I left a good deal in Paris unseen ◊ undone: but I had a
very pleasant ten days—◊ three prime emotions. I saw Notre-
Dame—a far finer edefice than I supposed—a most glorious one,   10
indeed: I saw, after a fashion, the Louvre ◊ I went—(4 times) to
the Theatre Français. I feel almost like ranking these three
exhibitions on a line. The Louvre is ∧even[∧] more rich ◊
wonderful than I supposed. I should have liked to give a month
to it. I should have learned bien des choses. At the Theatre   15
Français I of course had immense pleasure—a real feast of the
intellect. Two nights I saw Molière done—more delectably ◊
deliciously than words can say. You know nothing about Molière
till you have seen him acted i̶t̶ by Régnier Got ◊ Coquelin; nor
about Emile Augier till you have seen Mlle. Favart—the no   20
longer young ◊ the never beautiful, but the supremely elegant ◊
exquisitely dramatic Mlle. Favart.—But here I am scribbling
along without coming to what I want chiefly to say. In the 1ˢᵗ of
your two last letters you touch upon a theme on which I was
myself just on the point of opening up—viz: my "plans" ◊ my   25
expenses. I have been careering along, drawing money which has
seemed furnished by some mysterious magic on which I have
been almost afraid to reflect—lest in following the golden
stream to its source I should find it flow from the great parental
lap w̶i̶t̶h̶ ̶s̶o̶m̶e̶ [∧]in[∧] obedience to something of a cruel   30
pressure. But it has been gushing forth in noble abundance ◊
still it gushes. I have been feeling for some time that I owed you
a report of the situation ◊ here it is:—I have drawn from Barings
up to the present moment £379.00 ◊ have £̶4̶9̶6̶ ∧621[∧] left in his

hands. I have been abroad eleven months & have spent (or rather have drawn, for I have £30 in my pocket) 1.895$ in gold. You say that father has sent to Barings the sum of $3.000. I don't know whether you mean in gold or in paper. In the former case, it will

5   furnish 1100$ to carry me on into next year: in the latter it little more than covers I suppose (I don't know the actual price of gold) my expenditure for the present one. This expenditure is exclusive of what father paid for my passage & of 10 sovereigns he gave me before I started. I may be considered therefore to

10   have cost you in a year about 400£. This is certainly a good round sum & as I consider it I feel a most palpable weight of responsibility & gratitude. I know thoroughly well at the same time that any difficulty on your own part must have melted away in your sense of the great good the money was doing. Have I on

15   the whole spent the money not wisely but too well? I feel unable to pronounce. At moments I have seemed to myself to be spending very moderately (considering always what I was doing)—& at others very largely. One thing I have become sensible of—that I am not a good economist, in the proper sense

20   of the word. I can dispense with things with comparative ease & alacrity—but I can't get them & do them cheap. I have for instance a strong sense of having gone about constantly giving excessive fees & paying ~~double~~ ₍∧₎extra₍∧₎ carriage-fares. On the other hand I have frittered away no money & spent none vainly

25   or at random. ~~I~~ Except a few clothes & ½ a dozen books I have ~~littered~~ ₍∧₎literally₍∧₎ bought nothing. My grand abstention & the one that has told most (in favor of my purse & against my "culture"—or at least my pleasure) has been in the matter of photographs. On your arrival in Italy it very soon becomes

30   apparent that you must take some ₍∧₎firm₍∧₎ ground in this respect. I immediately took that of leaving them wholly alone. If I had got any it would have been largely for the sake of the rapacious Willy & the voracious Alice—but I hereby notify them that I shall come home quite empty-handed. Two facts have

conspired to increase my expenses: viz: my being unwell, & my travelling alone. A companion reduces one's expenditure by at least a 3$\underline{\text{d}}$ (This tells especially in carriage-hire.) My being unwell has kept me constantly from attempting ‸in any degree‸ to rough it. I have lived at the best hotels & done things in the most comfortable way. Ah me, the stubborn fact nevertheless remains that I shall have spent £400! I might have spent less. One always might have spent less. I think on the whole I may claim this:—that I have spent little more than was needful for the full & proper fruition of my enterprise. To have kept myself on a materially narrower financial basis would have been to lay up a store of bitter memories & regrets for the future— memories of a stingy ~~timp~~ timid spirit, lagging behind rare great opportunities. As it is, (believe it as you can) I have a certain number of such ignoble memories. There are certain glorious extra-mural drives at Rome in regard to which when in future I hear folks descant upon them I must silently hang my head. The more fool you, you'll say, to have spent so much & have got so little. But really I have got a great deal. Wait till I get home & you ~~see~~ behold the glittering treasures of my conversation—my fund of anecdote—my brilliant descriptive power. I assure you, I'll keep the table in a roar. Your guests will forget to eat—& thus you'll get back your money.—To say nothing of my making your universal fortunes by the great impetus with which I shall have been launched into literature. Consider therefore what you know me to have done & what you believe me to have gained & try to think that my return will not be altogether that of the prodigal—altho' perhaps not quite either that of the <u>prodigy</u>.— As for my plans I shall wait to hear what you think of the situation before I indulge in any: wait also until I see what Malvern does for me. Unless I get thoroughly started towards a cure I frankly confess that I shall be in no state to form any project—save that of immediate return to America—where at least I ~~was~~ shall not be on the footing of striving towards a gain

∧—a gain of enjoyment I mean—[∧] which is perpetually defeated. If Malvern fails to do for me what I hope I shall therefore turn my face homeward. But ~~I have~~ my _[∧]hopes_[∧] are strong. They are perhaps in some degree a simple "sentiment"—
but sentiments propel one forward & give one a grip of a chance. If Malvern does for me I shall stay there 8 or 10 weeks. This will cost money. I shall be living there at a~~ny~~ expense of about 4£ per week. If at the end of my stay I am veritably better I shall be able to discuss my subsequent movements. Even in that case I fancy I
shall still be inclined to go home in the Autumn. If I do spend a 2^d winter abroad I think I _∧shall_[∧] renounce the idea of going to Germany. I declared to myself when I was last in Florence that in case of my being in Europe next winter, there & there only should I spend it. But next autumn is six months away & when
these have elapsed I can't but think I shall feel it best to return home & ◊◊◊ leave a residence in Italy to some future day & some new basis. You will as soon as possible let me know what money ~~you can~~ shall be able with <u>perfect comfort</u>, to let me have & I will shape my programme accordingly. One thing I beg you to
believe, that no disappointment worth taking account of is possible to me. I have now been abroad a good round year & have had a most magnificent holiday & if you should be obliged to bid me desist immediately I should feel as if I had at least bitten the fruit to the core if not wholly devoured it. If I remain
abroad the coming summer I should like to spend a month or 6 weeks of it in Switzerland. I had little idea six months ago that I should really care to go back there: but I now feel strongly that ~~I~~ if I go home in the Autumn a few weeks, walking ~~there~~ _∧in the Alps_[∧] would be a valuable preparation for getting at some sort
of work on my return. On economical grounds (even allowing for the journey) to go to Switzerland would be decidedly less expensive than to stay here. But let me without reserve & without passion reveal to you my utmost lurking thought. To go to Switzerland means in this brief synopsis more than it seems

to mean. Say I fix my return for the 20th October. If I leave
Malvern ~~I~~ towards the middle of April I shall have between then
& July 1st some ten weeks to dispose of in England. If I travel a
little I shall have small difficulty in disposing of them happily. I
should like to go ∧to∧ Switzerland via Paris & Geneva—there
being several things on the road & within a days excursion from
Paris which I had hoped recently to see but was obliged to pass
by—i.e. notably the cathedrals of Amiens, Abbeville, Rheims
Chartres & Sens. Once in Switzerland I should make no bones of
walking over to the Italian lakes. Now Milan is but an hour by
rail from the town of Como & Venice but a September
morning's journey from Milan. Oh blissful vision to spend
another week at Venice—a well man instead of the poor disease-
haunted being that I was last autumn! From Verona (an hour
this side of Venice, a railway crosses the Brenner pass into
Southern ~~Gormay~~ Germany—thro' which via Augsbürg
Nüremberg &c, one may make a very pretty journey to the
Rhineland & thence to Holland & Belgium & thence down to
Brest in time to take the French steamer for N. Y. <u>Ma foi</u>, I like
the scheme! It has a certain breadth & nobleness which please
me! On the ground that the past year has cost me 400£, the
coming 6 mos ∧including return∧ so spent would cost me £200.
<u>Allons</u>: the really economical way of spending my time would be
to remain in England as quietly as possible to July 1st. To repair
then to Switzerland for 2 mos. To spend September in Paris &
sail from Brest October 1st. Consult above all things 1st your own
necessities & conveniences. I know they must drain you most
heavily. Say but the word & I'll sail for home the next day. This is
not bravado but truth. Otherwise name the sum you can allow
me & I'll try & get the utmost out of it. The summer is the
summer wherever I spend it & that is the great thing.—But I
have written a tremendous letter. Farewell, without more words.
I shall duly report from Malvrn. Tell father that lost letter of his
persists in not turning up. Between Naples Rome & Florence

heaven know what has become of it.—I was so stupid in my last as <u>not</u> to tell you to direct to <u>Dr. Rayner</u> <u>Great Malvern</u>. I have been hoping you will have done so. Farewell. Tell father to send me all his magazinisms. ~~Lov~~ No end of things to everyone↓↑—&

5   of kisses to Alice & you.

<u>H James</u> jr.

P. S. The figure above of the sum in B.'s hands is: <u>£621</u>.

P. P. S. By talking about Money in B.'s hands I simply allude to the nominal figure of my original credit viz: £1000—purely

10   nominal as of course I know. If father has sent him $3000 in gold he holds £200 to my credit—the sum which, used properly, would enable me to carry out the programme sketched above.

— — — —

Previous publication: *HJL* 1: 193–200

∾

277.22 superscription • super= | scription

277.23 ~~above~~↓ ∧ • [∧ *overwrites* .]

277.25 managed • man= | aged

278.10 no~~w~~ • [w *blotted out*]

278.16 Lo↓! • [! *overwrites* ,]

278.17 immensely • immense= | ly

278.17 ~~o◊~~ the • [th *overwrites* o◊]

278.17–18 ~~t~~ do • [d *overwrites* t]

278.19 ~~doubling~~ doubly • [y *overwrites* in]

278.24 ~~I~~ & • [& *overwrites* I]

278.28–29 ~~economiely~~ economically • [ally *overwrites* ly]

278.33 Boulevards • Bou= | levards

279.2 edefice • [*misspelled*]

279.9–10 Notre- | Dame • Notre-Dame

279.10 edefice • [*misspelled*]

280.12 responsibility • re- | sponsibility

280.19 economist • econo= | mist

280.20 comparative • compara- | tive

280.25 I Except • [E *overwrites* I]

281.13 timp timid • [i *overwrites blotted* p]

281.20 see behold • [beh *overwrites* see]

281.20 conversation • conversa= | tion

281.32 confess • con= | fess

281.33 immediate • imme= | diate

281.34 was shall • [sh *overwrites* w; l *overwrites* s]

282.3 homeward • home- | ward

282.3 I have my • [m *overwrites* I]

282.16 ◇◇◇ leave • [lea *overwrites illegible letters*]

282.17 possible • pos= | sible

282.18 can shall • [sha *overwrites* can]

282.18 comfort • com- | fort

282.28 I if • [*proofreader's slash through* I *to indicate lowercase*]

282.32 expensive • expen= | sive

283.2 I towards • [to *overwrites* I]

283.16 Gormay Germany • [e *overwrites illegible letter;* n *overwrites* y]

283.16 Augsbürg • [*misspelled*]

283.17 Nüremberg • [*misspelled*]

284.4 Lov No • [No *overwrites* Lov]

284.4 ¦ ¦ • [. . *blotted out*]

∾

277.21 letter about a week ago • HJ to AJ 25, 27 January 1870.

277.28 régale • feast.

277.33–34 a second letter [. . .] from Willy • WJ to HJ, 19 January 1870
(*CWJ* 1: 140–41).

278.7 bonnes gens • good people.

278.7–8 Willy alludes ∧scornfully[∧] in his letter • WJ wrote: "There
was as usual the jaunty promise of a letter to me 'in a day or two,' which
will as usual be kept I suppose in 3 or 4 weeks" (*CWJ* 1: 140).

278.26 Hotel de l'Amirauté • Moderately priced hotel south of the
Boulevard de la Madeleine.

279.15 bien des choses • many good things.

279.19 Régnier · François Joseph Régnier (1807–85), French actor.

279.19 Got · François Jules Edmond Got (1822–1901), popular French actor.

279.19 Coquelin · Benoit-Constant Coquelin (1841–1909), famous Comédie Française actor who created the title role of Rostand's *Cyrano de Bergerac*. HJ and Coquelin attended the same school in Boulogne in 1857–58; HJ published an article, "Coquelin," in *Century Magazine* 33 (January 1887): 407–13, and permitted its reprinting in the 1915 U.S. edition of Coquelin's *Art and the Actor*.

283.19 Ma foi · Indeed, yes.

283.23 Allons · Come on.

WILLIAM JAMES

13, 14 February 1870

ALS Houghton

bMS Am 1094 (1942)

Great Malvern.

Sunday—February 13th '70.

Beloved Brother—I have before me two letters from you—one of Dec. 19 27th of that dead & gone old year which will have been so heavily weighted a one in my mortal career (to say nothing of yours)—the ₐother₍ₐ₎ of the ni 19th January in this lusty young '70. They were both received in Paris in those all too rich & rapid days that I tarried there on that memorable—that tragical—pilgrimage from Florence—from Naples. I may say—across the breadth of Europe, to this actual British Malvern. I A week ago I wrote to mother from London & on the following day, Monday last, came up to this place. Here I am, then, up to my neck in cold water & the old scenes & sensations of ten months ago. It's a horrible afternoon—a piercing blast, a driving snow storm & my spirits à l'avenant. I have had a cheery British fire made up in my dingy British bedroom & have thus sate me down to this ghastly mockery of a fraternal talk. My heart reverts across the awful leagues of wintry ocean to that blessed library in Quincy Street & to the image of the gathering dusk the assembled family, the possible guest, the impending—oh the impending American <u>tea</u>! In fine, if I wanted I could be as homesick as you please. All the conditions are present: <u>rien n'y manque.</u> But I'll steep myself in action but I perish with despair. I'll drive the heavy footed pen & brush away the importunate tear.—Your last letter was a real blessing & a much indispensable supplement to the ~~former~~ previous one. It contained, in your statement of your slowly dawning capacity for increased action, just the news that I had been expecting— that I had counted on as on the rising of tomorrow's sun. I have no doubt whatever that you have really entered upon the "2<u>d</u> stage." You'll find it a happier one than the first. Perhaps when I get home, six mos. hence (heaven forbid that at the present moment I should entertain any other hypothesis) I shall be able gently to usher you into the 3<u>d</u> & ultimate period of the malady. It does me good to think of you no longer ~~leadng~~ leading that dreary lonely prison-life. Before long I hope to hear ˄of˄ you trying Dr. Butler. I can assure you, it will be a great day when, having lifted, you find your'e no worse, & then, having lifted again, you find you are visibly better. This experience ~~see~~ sets the seal; in the very sanctity of truth, to your still timid & shrinking assumption that you <u>can</u> afford—that you must attempt, to indulge in action: & I almost think (as I look back hence ~~I~~ on those blessed two months that I practiced it) that the trouble is almost worth having for the joy of hugging to your heart that deep & solid conviction which you wring from those iron weights. Yet, just as I did, possibly, you may find that having brought you to a certain point the lifting will take you no further. What I gained I gained in two mos. But the gain was immense. God speed you! I see you hooked indelibly for the ringing grooves of change.—I believe that I haven't written to

287

you since my last days in Rome, & any reflections on ∧my[∧]
subsequent adventures will have reached you thro' father,
mother & Alice. Nevertheless I have had many a fancy & feeling
in the course of that extraordinary achievement—the deliberate
cold-blooded conscious turning of my back on Italy—the
gradual fatal relentless progression from Florence to Malvern—
many a ~~deep~~ ∧keen[∧] emotion & many a deep impression which I
should have been glad to submit to your genial appreciation.
Altogether, it has been a rather serious matter. I mean simply
that you feel the interest of Italy with redoubled force when you
begin to turn away from it & seek for the rare & beautiful in
other lands. Brave old bonny England of ten short months
ago—where are you ◇ now?—Where are the old thrills ∧of[∧]
fancy—the old heart-beats, the loving lingering gaze—the
charm, the fever, the desire of those innocent days? Oh but I'll
find them again. They lie nestling away with the blossoms of the
hedges—they sit waiting in the lap of the longer twilights &
they'll f burst forth once ~~in the~~ more in the green explosion of
April. This I firmly count upon. Meanwhile I sit shuddering up
to my chin in a "running sitz" & think of the olive groves at San
Remo—of the view of Florence from San Miniato—of the
Nortons at the Villa d'Elci—of Aunt Kate looking across the
Neapolitan bay to Capri. I got a◇ a letter from her yesterday. I
haven't read it properly.—I'm afraid to. I only know that it tells
of a drive to Sorrento—of a drive to Baiae—of a projected day at
Perugia on the way to Florence. When Aunt Kate gets back,
make much of her! She's not the common clay you parted with.
She has trod the perfumed meadows of Elysium—she has tasted
of the magic of the South & listened to the ~~music~~ echoes of the
past!—I was very much disappointed in not being able to write
to you at Florence, about which I fancied I had a good deal to
say. Perhaps however that this was an illusion & that of definite
statements I should not have found many rise to my pen. One
definite statement however I do feel warranted in making—[∧]

288

viz:[∧]—that I became interested in the place ⅋ attatched to it to a degree that makes me feel that it has really entered into my life ⅋ ~~was~~ [∧]is[∧] destined to a~~o~~ operate there as a motive, a prompter an inspirer of some sort.—By which I suppose I mean nothing more pregnant or sapient than that one of these days I shall be very glad to return there ⅋ spend a couple of years. I doubt that I shall ever undertake—shall ever care—to study Italian art—Italian history—for themselves or with a view to discoveries or contributions—or otherwise than as an irradiating focus of light on some other matter. <u>Ecco</u>! that I hope is sapient enough for one sitting!—I hope you managed to wring from my torpid pages some living hint of the luminous warmth ⅋ glory of my two days at Genoa ⅋ the following three days' journey to Nice. These latter were not surpassed by anything in my ∧whole[∧] Italian record; for beside their own essential divineness of beauty ⅋ purity they borrowed a fine spiritual glow from the needful heroics of the occasion. They're a precious possession of memory, at all events ⅋ even Malvern douches can't wash them out. At Nice the charm of that happy journey began to fade: at Marseilles I found it dead in my bosom—dead of cold ⅋ inanition. I tried to stop ⬦ ⅋ do a little sight-seeing in the South of France: but between being half paralysed by the <u>mistral</u> ⅋ half-sickened by the base insufficiency of the spectacle I was glad enough to push rapidly on to Paris. At ∧a[∧] first glance I found Paris strangely hollow ⅋ vulgar: but after the lapse of a few days, as soon as I ~~could~~ ∧had[∧] placed myself on a clean fresh basis I began to enjoy it—to admire it—⅋ lo! before I left, to esteem it. I should be sorry to think that for a little paltry prettiness that confounded Italy had left me with a warped ⅋ shrunken mind. Let us be just to all men! (I'm coming to England presently.) From Nice to Boulogne I was deeply struck with the magnificent order ⅋ method ⅋ decency ⅋ prosperity of France—of the felicity of <u>manner</u> in all things—the completeness of form. There was a certain <u>table d'hôte</u> breakfast

5

10

15

20

25

30

at Dijon where the whole cargo of the express train piled out ↄ
fed leisurely, comfortably, to perfection, <u>qui en disait</u> on the
subject more than I can repeat. And the excellence of the little
hotel ~~d◊~~ de l'Amirauté where I spent a week—ↄ the universal

5   merit ↄ sagacity of the cookery—ↄ above all the splendors of
arrangement—quite apart from the splendors of ~~the~~ material—
in the Louvre! The latter by the way are wondrous—a
ₐglorious₍ₐ₎ synthesis of Italy. Altogether, as I say, I enjoyed
Paris deeply. Beautiful weather came to my aid. A fortnight ago

10   this afternoon—amazing thought!—I climbed the towers of
Nôtre Dame. She is really great. Great too is the Théatre
Français where I saw Molière ↄ Emile Augier most rarely played.
En voilà, de l'art! We talk about it ↄ ◊◊◊ write about ₐit₍ₐ₎ ↄ
critique ↄ dogmatize ↄ analyse to the end of time: but those

15   brave players stand forth ₐↄ exemplify it₍ₐ₎ ↄ <u>act</u>—create—
produce! It's a most quickening ↄ health giving spectacle!—with
a strange expression of simplicity ↄ breadth ↄ dignity which I
wouldn't have gone there to find. I also went to the Palais Royal
to see a famous four act Farce of the latest fashion: but I confess

20   seeing Got as Sganarelle had spoiled me for it. Molière is every
inch as droll ↄ so much more beside ~~it~~! I saw little else. I needn't
tell you how one feels ↄ leaving Paris half-seen, ₐhalf-felt.₍ₐ₎ You
have only to remember how you left it a year ↄ ½ ago ~~to~~. I have
now been some ten days in England. In one of your last letters

25   you very wisely assure me that England like every other place
~~will~~ ₐwould₍ₐ₎ seem very flat on a second ◊ visit. For this
contingency I made the most ample ↄ providential preparation ↄ
in this way I have eluded serious disappointments. But on the
whole I don't much pretend or expect now, at best, to be

30   ravished ↄ charmed. I've been to my rope's length ↄ had my
great sensations. In spite of decidedly unpropitious
circumstances I find I like England still ↄ I expect ~~to~~ ₐher₍ₐ₎ (if I
get better) to yield me many an hour of profit and many a visible
delight. I have come upon very fierce hard weather ↄ of course I

feel it ~~much~~ ₍ₐ₎keenly₍ₐ₎ for this plunge into cold water. We have
had a week of grim winter that would do honor to Boston. I find
this house all that I remembered it—most comfortable—most
admirably & irreproachably conducted. There are some eighteen
persons here at present—from whom however (without   5
misanthropy) I ~~gain little~~ & expect little & gain less—such a
group of worthy second rate Britons as ~~lends~~ ₍ₐ₎invests with₍ₐ₎
new meaning & illuminates with a supernatural glow—the term
common-place. But as if we Americans were any better! I can't
affirm it to my knowledge! I find in Malvern itself even ◇◇ at this   10
dark season all the promise of that beauty which delighted me
last spring. The winter indeed here ~~robs~~ ₍ₐ₎strips₍ₐ₎ the landscape
far less than with us or in the South. Literally (save for the
orange trees) the country hereabouts looks less naked & out of
Season than that about Naples. The fields are all vivid with their   15
rain-deepened green—the hedges all dark & dense & damp with
immediate possibilities of verdure—the trees so multitudinously
twigged that as they rise against the watery sky a field's length
away, you can fancy them touched with early leafage. And
₍ₐ₎ah!₍ₐ₎ that watery sky—greatest of England's glories!—so high   20
& vast & various, so many lighted & many-shadowed, so full of
poetry & motion & of a strange affinity with the swarming detail
of scenery beneath. Indeed what I have most enjoyed in England
since my return—what has most struck me—is the light—or
rather, ~~or~~ if you please, the darkness: that of Du Maurier's   25
drawings. Elsewhere 'tis but a Garish world. If I can only get
started to feeling better (of wh. I have good hopes) I shall get
my fill of old England ₍ₐ₎yet.₍ₐ₎ I have had a long walk every day
of the past week. The <u>detail</u> of ₍ₐ₎the₍ₐ₎ scenery is the great point.
Beside it even Italy is vague & general. I walked this morning six   30
miles—half of them in the teeth of the snow sharpened blast—
down thro' Newlands to Maddersfield Court—a most delightful
old moated manor-house, the seat of Earl Beauchamp. In spite
of the snow it was still gentle England. English mutton was

grazing in the lee of the hedges & English smoke rolling from
the chimneys in low-latticed, steep-thatched cottages. Àpropos
of Mutton I wish I ~~gave~~ [∧]could[∧] enclose herewith one of those
unutterable joints which daily figure on our board. You don't <u>eat</u>

5   it—you devoutly ecstatically appropriate it: you put a bit into
your mouth & for the moment <u>il n'y a que ça</u>. It beats the beef.
The beef ~~various~~ varies—it has degrees, but the Mutton is
absolute, infallible, impeccable. With plenty of mutton & a great
many walks & a few books I hope to thrive & prosper. I am able

10 both to walk & read much more than when I was here before & I
am quite amused at having then objected to the place on the
ground of its giving you so much up-hill. I shall probably do no
very serious reading, but I hope at least to win back the habit. I
rec'd. your <u>Atlantic</u> with Lowell's poem, which I enjoyed largely,

15 tho' it seems to me lacking in [∧]the[∧] real poetic element thro'
excess of cleverness—the old story. I enjoyed unmitigatedly
Howells' little paper. I have enjoyed all his things more even
since being abroad than at home. They are really American. I'm
glad youv'e been liking Hawthorne. But I mean to write as good

20 a novel one of these days (perhaps) as the H. of the ~~Se 7~~ G.'s.
<u>Monday 14th</u>. With the above thrilling prophecy I last night laid
down my pen. I see nothing left but to close my letter. When I
began I had a vague intention [∧]of[∧] treating you to a grand
summing up on the subject of Italy. But it won't be summed up,

25 happily for you. I'm much obliged to you for your regret that I
didn't achieve any notes for the <u>Nation</u>. I have a vague dream, if
I get started towards a cure, of attempting a few retrospective
ones here. Oh, no words can tell of the delicious romantic look
it now suits my Italian journey to put on!—I have my heart

30 constantly burdened with messages to all my friends at home
which I never manage to discharge. Keep me in the memories of
my brothers. Give my love to T. S. P. to whom I have the best
will to write. I wrote lately to A. G. S. Tell me anything that
comes up about J. L. F. & ~~W~~ O. W. H. I am in daily hope of a

letter from Howells. A. Kate mentions that Mrs. Post has asked
Minny to go abroad with her. Is it even so? But I must be getting
up a "pre-action" for that d—d running sitz. I calculate while
here to walk from 8 to 10—or from 10 to 12 miles daily. Farewell.
Think of me as most comfortable hopeful & happy. I <u>may</u> not   5
write for a fortnight, until I have some results to announce. But
I'll not promise silence. Farewell. Love to all—

     Yours most fraternally

     <u>H James jr.</u>

P.S. An anecdote. You spoke recently of having read with   10
pleasure Lecky's <u>Hist. of Morals</u>. I found at Florence that for a
fortnight at Rome I had been sitting at breakfast opposite or
next to the elegant author. We never spoke. He is very young &
lanky & blonde & soft-looking—but most pleasant of face: with
quite the look of a better-class Cambridge Divinity student. I   15
have been sorry ever since that I never addressed him: but he
always came in to his breakfast about as I was finishing.—
Àpropos—one of these days I'll tell you my little ∧tale[∧] of
"The Little Frenchman of Padua"—just such a one as F. J. Child
likes to tell.   20

Previous publication: *HJL* 1: 200–206; *CWJ* 1: 142–47; *WHSL* 63–68

    ◍

  286.22 ~~19~~ 27 • [27 *overwrites* 19]

  286.24 ~~ni~~ 19 • [19 *overwrites* ni]

  286.28 ~~I~~ A • [A *overwrites* I]

  287.10 indispensable • indis= | pensable

  287.19 ~~leadng~~ leading • [in *overwrites* ng]

  287.23 ~~se◊~~ sets • [t *overwrites illegible letter*]

  287.26 as I look • [I *inserted*]

  287.27 ~~I~~ on • [on *overwrites blotted* I]

  288.3 Nevertheless • Neverthe= | less

  288.4 extraordinary • extraor= | dinary

  288.13 ◊ now • [n *overwrites illegible letter*]

288.18 f burst • [b *overwrites blotted* f]

288.18 ~~in the~~ more • [more *overwrites blotted* in the]

288.19 Meanwhile • Mean= | while

288.23 a◊ a • [a *overwrites* a◊]

289.1 attatched • [*misspelled*]

289.3 a◊ operate • [op *overwrites* a◊]

289.21 ◊ d • [d *overwrites illegible letter*]

290.4 d◊ de • [e *overwrites illegible letter*]

290.8 synthesis • synthe- | sis

290.11 Nôtre Dame • [*misspelled*]

290.11 Théatre • [*misspelled*]

290.13 ◊◊◊ write • [wr *overwrites blotted illegible letters;* it *overwrites illegible letter*]

290.23 ~~to.~~ • [. *overwrites blotted* t; o *blotted out*]

290.26 ◊ visit • [v *overwrites illegible letter*]

290.31 unpropitious • un= | propitious

290.32 ~~to~~ ∧her∧ (if • [(*overwrites* to]

291.4 irreproachably • irre= | proachably

291.6 misanthropy • misan- | thropy

291.10 ◊◊ at • [at *overwrites illegible letters*]

291.14 hereabouts • here- | abouts

291.17 immediate • imme= | diate

291.33 Beauchamp • Beau= | champ

292.7 ~~various~~ varies • [es *overwrites* ous]

292.19 Hawthorne • Haw= | thorne

292.20 ~~Se~~ 7 • [7 *overwrites blotted* Se]

292.27 retrospective • retro= | spective

292.34 ~~W~~ O. W. H. • [O *overwrites* W]

293.5 comfortable • comfort= | able

293.14 blonde • [e *blotted out*]

293.15 Cambridge • Cam- | bridge

293.17 breakfast • break- | fast

☙

286.21 two letters from you • 27 December 1869 (*CWJ* 1: 132–33); 19 January 1870 (*CWJ* 1: 140–41).

286.28–29 A week ago I wrote to mother from London • HJ to MWJ, 5 February [1870].

286.31 the old scenes *&* sensations • See HJ's letters from Malvern: 1 April [1869] to Sr.; 4 April [1869] to Charles Eliot Norton; 6 April [1869] to Grace Norton; 8, 9 April [1869] to WJ; 16 April [1869] to AJ; and 18 April [1869] to Grace Norton.

286.33 à l'avenant • the same in keeping.

287.6–7 rien n'y manque • nothing is missing.

287.34 ringing grooves of change • From "Locksley Hall" (1842) by Tennyson (182).

287.34–288.1 that I haven't written to you since my last days in Rome • HJ to WJ, 27, 28 December [1869]; 1 January 1870.

288.21 view of Florence from San Miniato • The church and convent of San Miniato al Monte, on a hilltop to the southeast of Florence. The Jameses also owned a Thomas Cole (1801–48) painting called *View of Florence, from San Miniato* (Habegger, *Father* 367).

289.10 Ecco! • There!

290.2 qui en disait • which said.

290.13 En voilà, de l'art! • Now that is art!

290.18 Palais Royal • Paris theater located at 38, rue Montpensier, on the northwest corner of the grounds of the Palais Royal itself.

290.20 Got as Sganarelle • Sganarelle is the name of several Molière characters: the title character of *Sganarelle, ou le cocu imaginaire* (1660), Dom Juan's servant in *Dom Juan ou le festin de pierre* (1665), and the principal character in *Le médecin malgré lui* (1666). In 1877, reflecting on his days in Paris, HJ wrote that he admired François Jules Edmond Got's portrayal of "Sganarelle of the 'Médecin Malgré Lui'" that was performed "with such an unctuous breadth of humor" ("The Théâtre Français" 445).

291.25 Du Maurier • George Du Maurier (1834–96), English illustrator and cartoonist for *Punch* magazine; HJ and Du Maurier would develop a lifelong friendship following their first meeting in May 1877. Following

Du Maurier's death, HJ published a tribute to his friend, "George du Maurier," *Harper's New Monthly* 95 (September 1897): 594–609.

291.32 Maddersfield Court • Madresfield Court, on the bank of the Severn River, east of Malvern.

291.33 Earl Beauchamp • Frederick Lygon (1830–91), Sixth Earl Beauchamp, of Madresfield Court.

292.6 il n'y a que ça • there is nothing else.

292.14 Lowell's poem • "The Cathedral."

292.17 Howells' little paper • "By Horse-Car to Boston."

292.19 youv'e been liking Hawthorne • WJ wrote in his 19 January 1870 letter: "I enjoyed last week the great pleasure of reading the 'House of 7 Gables.' I little expected so *great* a work. It's like a great symphony, with no touch alterable without injury to the harmony. It made a deep impression on me and I thank heaven that H. was an American. It also tickled my national feeling not a little to note the resemble of H's style to yours & Howell's, even as I had earlier noted the converse" (*CWJ* 1: 141).

292.32 T. S. P. • Thomas Sergeant Perry.

292.33 A. G. S. • Arthur G. Sedgwick.

292.34 J. L. F. • John La Farge.

292.34 O. W. H. • Oliver Wendell Holmes Jr.

293.1 Mrs. Post • Mary Ann King Post (1819–92), daughter of Ellen James King (1800–1823), half-sister of Sr. and James King (1788–1841); see Hastings 9–10.

293.10-11 You spoke recently of having read with pleasure Lecky's Hist. of Morals • In his 1 November 1869 letter to HJ, WJ had mentioned that he had "read lately" *History of European Morals from Augustus to Charlemagne* (1869), by William Edward Hartpole Lecky (1838–1903); WJ called it "a fascinating work, though with a strange effect of amiability" (*CWJ* 1: 120).

GRACE NORTON
18 February 1870
ALS Houghton
bMS Am 1094 (879)

Great Malvern — Feb. 18<u>th</u>. '70.
Dear Grace —

Only the other day I was in Florence thinking reluctantly of
Malvern — & now behold me in Malvern thinking regretfully of
Florence. Only the other day, too, I was in Paris reading, most   10
gratefully, your letter of Jan. 28th. It met with quite another
welcome I assure you than the missive of the "poor <u>inconnue</u>" at
Florence. What better evidence can I give you of this than the
fact that I am answering you now after only a three weeks
interval — while I ∧have_[∧] never answered the poor inconnue   15
yet — a five mos'. silence. Knowing this, esteem yourself
happy. — Circumstances, in truth, in your own case, dear Grace,
have not been propitious to a more speedy response: as you will
possibly kindly infer from the hint given ◊ you in my date of the
rate at which I have been pursuing my travels. I gave myself, out   20
of my wisdom, but ten days in Paris whereof I mostly spent the
mornings at the Louvre & the evenings at the Théâtre
Français — to say nothing of the afternoons on the Boulevard.
(Let me however here assure Jane in a parenthesis that I <u>did</u>
steal an evening from Mlle. Favart of the T. F., to bestow on   25
Miss Curtis — of whom more anon.) With all this my pen was
fairly idle. I came to this blessed old England just two weeks
ago — leaving all beauty & brilliancy & charm in Paris & finding
all the old sordid darkness & drizzle in London. At Malvern I
have now been some ten days, pretty well occupied with   30
breaking my spirit to the Malvern manner of life. Finally, this
morning I feel as if I had earned the right to fairly & squarely
think of Italy & of you. Your letter was as Florentine as I could
~~hop~~ possibly have wished — <u>c'est</u> <u>tout dire</u>. Jane's note had not

reached me at Nice. I have since made the most urgent
application for it, but it unaccountably fails to arrive. I therefore
learned first from you of the arrival of the happy little mortal
who is to boast in future years of having come into the world at
5   Florence. May she not find the world too great a falling off from
there! Do congratulate her for me in the very ~~eleve~~ cleverest &
softest Italian. And for Susan, congratulate her, pray, & give her
my love, in the very plainest & most unmistakeable English. By
this time, I hope, she is not only better but absolutely well. I
10   trust Charles too is better in such general well-being. — My last
letter I believe was from Nice, since when I have had more of a
journey than the simple run across the channel. But oh, my dear
Grace I have hardly the heart to speak of those last still southern
days — days faintly colored with a mild reflection of Italy.
15   ~~They were~~ [ʌ]Nice is[ʌ] not the rose, but she lives near it.
Avignon even has a feeble reflected perfume. But ~~it~~ [ʌ]beyond[ʌ]
Avignon the charm is utterly dead & I made the journey thence
to Paris simply with my base mechanical part. It <u>might</u> have
been pleasant enough, I confess, but for the intense cold. At
20   Marseilles I entered the belt of the <u>mistral</u> which literally blew
me before it to the very gates of Paris. I got a day at Arles & a
day at Avignon — nothing more. But even ʌin[ʌ] the kindly light
of memory they seem decidedly dreary. — Paris I largely enjoyed,
finding there plenty of sunshine & plenty of entertainment. If I
25   had not had other work on my hands I might very happily s have
spent a couple of months there & for half an hour a day, perhaps
have forgotten Florence. When I left, the recent disorders were
still in the future & no perceptible breath of revolution in the
air. I got an excellent afternoon in & about Notre Dame & I
30   basked for several successive mornings in the light of the Titians
of the Louvre. But for want of time I left many things undone
which I hope still to do within the coming six months. — For the
present I am as deeply & irreclaimably in England & part &
parcel of the stalwart English order of things as if I had never

left & were never to leave it. So fast we live! The way I have been
crowding sensations into the past ~~six~~ ₍ₐ₎three₍ₐ₎ months would
have been fatal to—what shall I say—to the intellectual
equilibrium of an <u>ordinary</u> mortal.—England is still England,
you may be sure, an England I think on the whole you're well   5
out of—so long as there is ~~still~~ an Italy to go to: full of interest,
but of an interest that somehow lies heavy on the soul & lacks
the divine lightness & brightness of one's Italian impressions.
Malvern is quite the same essentially pleasant ₍ₐ₎Malvern₍ₐ₎ as
before—as pretty a country, assuredly, as any in England—as   10
pretty as this very grim February weather will let it be. But I
needn't remind you of the sturdy misty greenness that prevails
thro' an English winter & at moments here imparts to the
landscape the air of a darksome June. On the whole I am not
sorry to be here: si je ~~n'en~~ ne m'en réjouis pas, du moins je m'en   15
console. I find in the scenery here a very audible old English
eloquence of which I am glad enough to take the burden to my
mind. Verily it's a great world, to hold at once so great an Italy &
so rich an England. He will be a wise man who ⬦⬦ shall have
learned some of the lessons of each. I find a great satisfaction   20
now that I am landed high & dry on the shores of memory &
retrospect in thinking that I have learned a few of those of Italy.
I am beginning to see those rich five months as a bright &
perfect whole. So long as I was in Italy, things stood very much
in other's way: the thrilling throbbing present crowded out the   25
past & the future. But now it's all one calm & luminous past. I
have a vague idea that your actual present is <u>not</u> very calm &
luminous: or rather I have a tolerably definite idea, gathered
from a letter just received from my Aunt, who seems to have
journeyed in a fine old New England snow-storm from Naples   30
to Florence. But we have only ten days more of February & then
indeed we have March, but I can't believe March to be as brutal
~~cloud~~ ₍ₐ₎on the₍ₐ₎ slopes of Fiesole as—on those of
Worcestershire. In fact—you must excuse me, but whatever

your sufferings may have been, I feel pretty well capable of not in the least pitying you. What! with a Florentine April, May, June shining & whispering ahead of you—& the Neapolitan Bay flinging over the ultimate future its g divine garment of azure—

5   you venture to raise a murmur! Have you been again to the Villa Landora? Have you followed up—or followed down (I might say) the acquaintance of the signorina? If the weather has really been so savage ∧you[∧] have go hardly been much, I suppose, to the Galleries & Churches. I have daily: I'm better off than you. I

10 visit the Uffizi & the Academy & Fra Angelico as an ethereal spirit, organically insensitive to the weather. On the dining room wall, opposite me as I write, straight above the heads of Irish Miss Gason & Scotch Miss Fraser hangs the great Filippo Lippi of the Academy—the one with the lilies.—But I am

15 growing transcendental: I will return to Miss Curtis. Foreseeing on my arrival in Paris that I should remain only a few days I determined to reserve the friend of my friends for a more auspicious season. But chance arranged it that the first ~~person~~ ∧individual[∧] I met at my hotel (where she had come to dine

20 with some friends) was the excellent lady in person. A mutual recognition ensued—after which I called & spent a very pleasant evening.—I have just rec'd. two Cambridge letters—one from Arthur. He mentions a piece of news which I suppose has already reached you the gift to the city of N. Y. by Mr. Lennox

25 of his magnificent collection & the wherewithal to support it. A fig for the land of the Medici! Give me the land of the Lennoxes! I don't know that I have any English news. Parliament has just opened, Mr. Gladstone has introduced his Irish Land Bill & Forster his Education scheme. Twenty years

30 hence perhaps the American visitor at Malvern as he treads the Worcestershire lanes will detect a more vivid intellectual ray in the visage of the Worcestershire rustic. The Pall Mall Gazette since its enlargement strikes me as having fallen ◇◇ off in ability. Let me take warning by its fate & not further enlarge my letter.

Farewell. We had charades last nights, but no such artists as Eliot & Sally. Give them my love & tell them to divide it with their little sister. I hope by the way Charles & Susan will name the signorina in some manner delicately suggestive of her birth-place. Why not simply <u>Florence</u>? Thinks of me as thinking   5
perpetually of you. Never mind what I'm doing: I live in my thoughts. Tell your mother that they are frequently of her. Give my most thankful love to Jane & assure her that I don't mean to rest till I have recovered her letter. <u>Bien des choses</u> to Charles & Sara. Address me (when inclined) <u>Dr. Rayner's</u>, as above.   10
Proclaim my greetings to all Italy & believe me dear Grace— unutterably yours. <u>H. James</u> jr

No previous publication

ꙮ

297.19 ◇ you • [y *overwrites illegible letter*]

297.34 h̶o̶p possibly • [p *overwrites* h; *first* s *overwrites* p]

298.6 c̶l̶e̶v̶e̶◇ cleverest • [r *overwrites illegible letter*]

298.8 unmistakeable • [*misspelled*]

298.18 mechanical • mechani= | cal

298.25 s have • [h *overwrites* s]

299.4 equilibrium • equi= | librium

299.15 n̶'̶e̶n̶ ne • [*apostrophe blotted out; second* n *blotted and struck through*]

299.19 ◇◇ shall • [sh *overwrites illegible letters*]

300.1 sufferings • suffer= | ings

300.4 g̶ divine • [d *overwrites blotted* g]

300.8 g̶o̶ hardly • [ha *overwrites* go]

300.33 ◇◇ off • [ff *overwrites illegible letters*]

301.1 nights • [s *blotted and struck through*]

301.7–12 mother that [. . .] <u>H. James</u> jr • [*written across the letter's penultimate page*]

ꙮ

297.12 <u>inconnue</u> • <u>unknown</u>.

297.34 c'est tout dire • that says it all.

298.3 the arrival of the happy little mortal • Margaret Norton, Charles Eliot and Susan Norton's third daughter, was born on 15 January 1870.

298.10–11 My last letter I believe was from Nice • HJ's 20 January 1870 letter to Grace Norton.

298.27–28 the recent disorders [. . .] breath of revolution • In January 1870 Prince Pierre Bonaparte (1815–81), an outcast of the Bonaparte family, shot and killed an employee of *La Marseillaise*, a radical anti-empire political newspaper edited by Henri Rochefort (1832–1913). During the well-publicized funeral, Rochefort incited a large mob that revolted against Emperor Napoleon III. Prince Pierre was acquitted of the murder, while Rochefort was tried, convicted, and imprisoned for the insurrection. The Second Empire of France would eventually end in a coup d'état on 4 September 1870.

299.15–16 si je n'en ne m'en réjouis pas, du moins je m'en console • if I'm not thrilled by it, at least I console myself for it.

300.5–6 Villa Landora • Villa Landor, estate of English writer Walter Savage Landor (1775–1864), located in Fiesole; he purchased the villa from Count Gherardesca on 24 August 1828.

300.7 signorina • Miss Julia Elizabeth Savage Landor (1820–84), daughter of Walter and Julia (Thuillier) Savage Landor.

300.13–14 great Filippo Lippi of the Academy • Probably the *Coronation of the Virgin*, which the *Central Italy* Murray calls "perhaps the chef d'oeuvre of the master" (184).

300.22–23 one from Arthur • Arthur G. Sedgwick to HJ, 30 January 1870 (Houghton bMS Am 1094 [398]).

300.24–25 the gift to the city [. . .] to support it • James Lenox (1800–1880), New York merchant and real-estate owner, incorporated his rare book collection into a public library in 1870. Lenox's collection included the first Gutenberg Bible brought to the United States, a Gilbert Stuart portrait of George Washington, and the original autographed manuscript of Washington's farewell address (Dain 11). The Lenox Library, along with the Astor Library and the Tilden Trust, were consolidated into the

New York Public Library in 1895. Sedgwick's 30 January 1870 letter to HJ discusses Lenox's library in some detail.

300.28 Gladstone · William E. Gladstone (1809–98) was prime minister in 1868–74, 1880–85, 1886, and 1892–94.

300.29 Irish Land Bill · Part of the Home Rule movement, Gladstone's Land Act of 1870 protected Irish tenants from arbitrary eviction and allocated funds for land improvement.

300.29 Forster his Education scheme · William Edward Forster (1818–86), privy councilor in Gladstone's 1868 government, was responsible for planning a system of national education; in 1869 he saw through the House of Commons the Endowed Schools Bill. In February 1870 he introduced an Elementary Education Bill.

301.2 Eliot & Sally · Eliot and Sally Norton.

301.9 <u>Bien des choses</u> · <u>All the best.</u>

ALICE JAMES
27, 29 [28] February 1870
ALS Houghton
bMS Am 1094 (1562)   20

Great Malvern Feb. 27th / 70.
        Sunday p.m.
Beloved Sweet—Since writing home just a fortnight ago I have
been blessed & sustained with a couple of letters—yours of   25
Jan. 31st & Willy's of Feb. 8th, inclosing an article of father's.
Many thanks for all them. The people at this house are
tremendous letter receivers. Every morning when I come down
to breakfast I see the hall table groaning beneath their weight:
but oh thrice happy I, when after yawning intervals I detect on   30
one of these shining tablets a blue American stamp! Together
with yours I received a letter from Arthur Sedgwick. Please
mention this to him & assure him that the lone exile hopes to
live to reward him. I had begun to yearn sorely, sweet sister, for

the sight of your shapely fist. Whenever I hear from Aunt Kate she speaks of having just heard from you & ~~releaves~~ ◇ me to sink into bitter wonderment why a distant Aunt should be so markedly preferred to an immediate brother. But write me a

5   good little note like that once a month & I'll rest content. Willy's letter contained ~~leo~~ later news—among other things, that you had bought the house. On the whole I applaud. The only thing that worries me is to see my poor family thus married to an eternity of Boston Winters. My sufferings from the cold

10   during the last three mos. have been such as to make ◇◇ one long to dwell forevermore in some glowing "summer-land"—which Boston can hardly be called. I feel as if I should need ten years in the tropics to take the clammy central chill out of my bones. In this accursèd world its not only the cold that's cold—but the

15   very warmth. But at any rate if I find it hard to stand American winters, by compensation I can dwell at home, rent-free, in August. None but the hottest hours of the hottest days will content me.—Willy's other news was that he was not feeling so well again—just after I had been sending up a <u>Te Deum</u> in

20   consequence of what he had told me in a preceding letter. But even now I shall not begine to lament—for I feel very sure that when he writes again he will be able to tell me that the pendulum has taken another forward swing & carried him further than ever yet. By a series of such swings he will find

25   himself finally landed in well-being again.—Your own letter was perfect in all respects save this—viz. that you didn't ~~m~~ say ◇◇ a word about the receipt of any of my recent letters—a rank Quincy St. offence. One of them I'm afraid—& one I'm sorry you should have missed—has gone astray. Did you get one dated

30   successively Rome, Assisi & Florence?—one written just before the one posted at Nice—which latter Willy acknowledges. If not you have missed the knowledge of my well-nigh richest & rarest hours in Italy—my afternoon at Assisi—my day at Perugia. It's too late now to tell the tale: I shall have to wait till I get home.—

But Italy is too far off now even to talk about talking about till
then.—I shall have been three weeks tomorrow in Malvern. As
regards my health I have as yet nothing to tell. I didn't look for
sudden & immediate results & I've not found them. While I wait
for them the time strides noiselessly along. I am very well placed
too for such waiting. Beautiful pleasant & comfortable: Malvern
is all these: what more can one ask? This house & all its
arrangements are thoroughly well-ordered & I am able to
appreciate these blessings more fully & to spend my time more
happily for, than when I was here before, owing to my being
able both to walk & to read more. I generally spin my ten miles a
day—with a theory of doing more on Sundays. But as yet I
haven't extended my walks beyond a five mile circuit—being
minded to hoard up the remoter delights for the finer weather. I
say delights because really there is no other word to apply to the
features of all this lovely English scenery. I find it in February
only a shade less lovely than I left it in all the greenness of
the verge of May. All the swarming elements of its beauty—the
crude essentials so bald & naked in other lands—now in the
absence of better things make up a landscape as warm &
complete as many an unEnglish midsummer. And it's all
intensely exquisitely English! Putting all the weeks together that
I have spent here I have got tolerably used to the look of things:
but some times as I ~~view the~~ glance at some common bit of
grouping by the wayside it will break in upon me as a revelation
& I seem to feel England for the 1st time. To <u>feel</u> <u>England</u> is a
satisfaction which I heartily wish you for some future day. It's a
good wholesome one and throws you back not too rudely on
your native ~~metal~~ mettle. To live in England, "respectably" you
have somehow to draw more heavily on your manhood—your
substance & courage than in other countries:—how much more
alas! than in that sweet relaxing Italy. But I wish my pen had
eloquence to make you feel the land as I felt it this morning—in
<u>such</u> a pleasant characteristic walk. ~~Im~~ I have been glad to take

up for company—not too often—with a poor young fellow who
is here in a wretched condition of semi-blindness—an Oxford◊
man, a good deal of a traveller (when he had his sight) & what is
more to the purpose in this pleasant England—what indeed you
5   very soon find out to be a vast deal to the purpose—a
"gentleman." It's a literal fact from my observation that a very
good Englishman who is not a gentleman is not so good as a
comparatively poor mortal who is—& to be or not to be in this
respect is to stand on one side or the other of a very visible line.
10   We walked four miles away—my gentleman & I, across a good
broad bit of this hedgy ~~w~~ Worcestershire to the banks of narrow
gliding Severn. There was nothing remarkable about the walk—
only that by chance England seemed driven home to me more
closely than ever—in the far away groups of stately blue-black
15   trees—the trees of Birket Foster (a better "artist," by the way,
than I ever fancied) taking the mist on some sheep=cropped
manorial slope—in the perpetual strip of turfy common that
borders the high-way, dotted & spotted to perfection with all the
needful figures of English story—the shaggy blind-looking
20   mouse-coloured donkey, immense of head, diminutive of body,
nosing so innocently among the very thickest brambles of the
hedge-foot—the trio of geese, cackling elongated, expanded—
the old woman—<u>the</u> very old woman in person, in her red cloak
& black bonnet, frilled all round the face & triple-ₐfrilled[ₐ]
25   ~~beneath~~ [ₐ]beside[ₐ] her decent placid cheeks—the stalwart rustic
too who calls her "Granny—as complete as herself—with his
white smock frock puckered on the chest, his standing collar &
scarlet neckerchief, his short velveteens, his vast blue-stockinged
calves & tremendous high-lows—& above all his big red rural
30   face—and then in the background, beyond the common, the
cottage of ancient England with its steep heavy thatch & its
broad low-latticed windows & its waist-high door ~~with~~ [ₐ]&[ₐ] its
curling smoke & all its innumerable patches & bits of character—
its general rich expression of having been lived & died in—&

worked & played in since a happy English day when Yankees
were babes unborn. But all this picture is nothing without the
darksome light—the mist-softened air—the damp black hedges,
the springing turf, ~~the rich horizon of crossed~~ and the great
band ~~arr~~ along the horizon—the band of watery light, playing   5
through the stems of distant copses & avenues.—By the time I
leave England I hope by dint of many walks, to have absorbed an
amount of the English <u>mise en scène</u> that will last me for a lifetime of English reading.—These walks are a sort of special
education. Willy wonders in his last letter whether England is   10
going to disappoint such hopes as I had based on the memory of
my ~~second~~ ∧first∧ visit. But I find the country doesn't suffer
from comparison with Italy at all as France or Germany would.
It's far too different in kind. Italy— ~~w~~ you cry it out at the
beginning in passion & you affirm at the end with conviction—   15
Italy to the foreigner, the stranger, is essentially <u>poetry</u>.
England, on the other hand even to ∧an∧ American is simply
excellent prose. ~~Wa~~ What you enjoy in England is the exquisite
finish of the composition of things: what moves you in Italy is
the very license & laxity of poetical passion. I have enjoyed the   20
beautiful little Abbey church beside us here more since my
return from Italy than I did before. (I enclose a couple of very
inadequate photos. of it.) It seems to me a very characteristic
building—the work of a race which had Protestantism looming
ahead of it. Of course you feel ~~in~~ everywhere after leaving Italy   25
an immense void in the air—the absence of the artistic spirit.
But English civilization ~~soo~~ woos so little the presence of any
such spirit that it seems no failure not to have won it. Nothing
you find here strikes you as a direct appeal to beauty. It comes,
hand in hand with use, but ~~soon~~ ∧<u>haud</u>∧ <u>passibus</u> <u>aequis</u>. The   30
Abbey here is certainly beautiful enough: but a part of its charm
& interest as you look at it, is in the way it prompts you to
wonder how so much of the graceful ~~of~~ ∧in∧ effect was achieved
with so little of the graceful in motive. But ~~a~~ I must make an end

of this vague babble—which reads to me very fallacious.—When
I have told you of my walks I shall have told you everything that
is matter for a tale. You'll hardly care for a record of my daily
baths. As for my fellow bathers there is very little to tell about

5   them. There is Mrs. Hooper ~~whom~~ a young widow who prattles
from morning to night—à <u>tout venant</u>, from her arm-chair by
the drawing room fire—about her Daddy & her Daddy's claret &
her Daddy's sayings—with a sort of puerile thick-waisted
English charm—but on the whole a great bore. There is

10 Mr. Bruce Campbell the swell of the house, a young barrister of
gentle lineage—very good looking, with ambrosial whiskers & a
dozen different velvet coats—beloved of silly Mrs. Hooper.
There is Captain Adams the friend of Mr. S.—a beautiful
specimen of an honest simple stammering blushing brave young

15 British officer—in the navy. There is heavy Scotch Mr. Fraser—
a "laird" tho' & a gentleman, with ∧his[∧] placid insipid lady like
spouse—and flaming-bearded Mr. Roy—another & a greater
Scotch laird, with a nice young wife who carries her arms a bit
like Minny Temple—but is to Minny as is water unto wine.

20 There, socially, with my friend Jameson are the swells—
including that tremendous old liar Major Jones who is forever
whopping about his tigers in India & his salmon in Norway & his
wild goats in Chinese Tartary—a good specimen I suppose of a
very common English figure. Besides these there are the dozen

25 ignoble vulgar—two or three of them pleasant enough. On the
whole nothing very valuable in the human line.—But if I sit
scribbling any longer I shall be ∧tomorrow morning[∧] of as
small value as the worst. A few days since came a letter from
Aunt Kate, from Florence, where she had had the great grief of

30 a great deal of rain. This I esteem a real misfortune. My present
hope is to meet her in London about April 20th. I got this
morng. a letter from Grace Norton, in wh. she spoke of Jane's
having heard from mother. They are the best of women & I am
very glad to have them as correspondents in that best of cities.

Willy wrote about my getting some photos. to replace the
vanished pictures. I wish I had got his request in Italy—or even
Paris. But I will do what I can still—& write him on the matter—
& the cognate theme of books. Tell father I read his article with
real pleasure. It's a good thing. All England just now is   5
engrossed with the Mordaunt Trial—a hideous tissue of Misery.
It strengthens the ground under father's feet. Tell him also that
a little while hence when I feel more like reading a solid book, I
mean to send to London for his Swedenborg.—
Monday 29<u>th</u>. I forebore to close my letter last night: but to day   10
gives me nothing to add—save my love to all. Mother spoke in
her last letter of Howells having told her of his having a letter
on the stocks for me. Why—oh why, doesn't it come?—
Whenever you write keep giving my love to the boys—bless
their lovely lives! Farewell. I shall probably write within the next   15
fortnight. I have said nothing of your health: I assume it to be
better & better. <u>Ton frère</u> H.
P.S. I aint the least bit homesick! Oh bless your innocent
heart no!—
I have been very sorry to hear of Minny's fresh hemmorhages—   20
& feel glad to have lately written her a long letter.—Who is the
author of the <u>Notes</u> on the Woman's Rights Question in the
Nation?

No previous publication

&

304.2   ◇ me • [m *overwrites illegible letter*]

304.4   immediate • imme= | diate

304.6   ~~le◇~~ later • [a *overwrites* e◇]

304.10 ◇◇ one • [on *overwrites illegible letters*]

304.20 preceding • pre= | ceding

304.21 begine • [*misspelled*]

304.26 ~~m~~ say • [sa *overwrites* m]

304.26 ◇◇ a • [a *overwrites illegible letters*]

305.9 appreciate • appre= | ciate

305.13 circuit • cir= | cuit

305.24 ~~view the~~ glance • [g *overwrites* the]

305.28 too • [o *inserted*]

305.29 ~~metal~~ mettle • [t *overwrites* a]

305.34 ~~Im~~ I have • [h *overwrites* m]

306.2 Oxford◊ • [*illegible letter blotted and struck through*]

306.11 ~~w~~ Worcestershire • [W *overwrites* w]

306.16 sheep=cropped • sheep= | cropped

306.22 hedge-foot • hedge- | -foot

306.22 elongated • elonga= | -ted

306.25 stalwart • stal= | -wart

307.5 ~~arr~~ along • [lo *overwrites* rr]

307.8–9 life- | time • life-time

307.14 different • differ= | ent

307.14 ~~w~~ you • [y *overwrites* w]

307.18 ~~Wa~~ What • [h *overwrites* a]

307.23 characteristic • charac= | teristic

307.34 ~~a~~ I • [I *overwrites* a]

308.1 fallacious • fal= | lacious

308.27 as • [*inserted*]

309.2 request • re= | quest

309.15 Farewell • Fare= | well

309.18 innocent • in- | nocent

309.20 hemmorhages • [*misspelled*]

∽

303.24 writing home just a fortnight ago • HJ to WJ, 13, 14 February 1870.

303.26 an article of father's • "The Woman Thou Gavest with Me."

303.32 a letter from Arthur Sedgwick • Sedgwick's letter to HJ of 30 January 1870 (Houghton bMS Am 1094 [398]).

304.7 you had bought the house • HJ apparently first became aware Sr. was negotiating the purchase of 20 Quincy Street from MWJ's lost 23 November 1869 letter to him (HJ to MWJ 21, 23 December [1869]).

304.20 he had told me in a preceding letter • WJ wrote from Cambridge, 19 January 1870, that he might be getting better (*CWJ* 1: 140–41).

304.29–30 one dated successively [. . .] Florence • HJ to WJ, 27, 28 December [1869], 1 January 1870.

304.31 one posted at Nice • HJ to Sr., 14, 17, 18, 19 January 1870.

306.15 Birket Foster • Myles Birket Foster (1825–99), celebrated Victorian landscape illustrator and watercolorist.

307.8 mise en scène • Theatrical term referring to the work of the director (i.e., staging), but here referring to the physical setting HJ witnessed.

307.30 ∧haud∧∧ passibus aequis • at an uneven pace.

308.6 à tout venant • to all comers.

309.6 the Mordaunt Trial • The sensational and lurid divorce trial of Sir Charles and Lady Mordaunt during which Lady Mordaunt was charged with adultery and insanity, the details of which were entered into testimony, and during which the Prince of Wales was called to the witness stand. The proceedings came to an end on 25 February 1870 when Lady Mordaunt was found mentally unfit for trial.

309.9 his Swedenborg • Sr.'s *The Secret of Swedenborg*.

309.10 Monday 29ᵗʰ • Monday was February 28; there was no February 29 in 1870.

309.12–13 Howells [. . .] for me • 2 January, 6 March 1870 (see Anesko 69–74).

309.17 Ton frère • Your brother.

309.21–23 the author of the Notes on the Woman's Rights Question in the Nation? • One of three articles by Lulu Gray Noble published in the *Nation*; see HJ to WJ, [7] 8, 9 March 1870.

WILLIAM JAMES
[7] 8, 9 March 1870
ALS Houghton
bMS Am 1094 (1943)

5

      Great Malvern—
          March 8<u>th</u> ’70.
Beloved Bill—
      You ask me in your last letter so “cordially” to write home
10   every week, if ◊ its only a line, that altho’ I have very little to say
on this windy ~~Su◊◊◊~~ Sunday ~~m~~ March afternoon, I can’t resist
the homeward tendency of my thoughts. I wrote to Alice some
eight days ago—raving largely about the beauty of Malvern, in
the absence of a better theme: so I haven’t even that topic to
15   make talk of. But as I say, my thoughts are facing squarely
homeward ♂ that is enough. The fact that I have been here a
month to day, I am sorry to say, doesn’t even furnish me with a
bundle of important tidings. My stay as yet is attended with very
slight results—powerful testimony to the obstinacy of my case.
20   Nevertheless I have most unmistakeably made a beginning—or
at least the beginning of one—♂ in this matter it is chiefly a
premier pas qui coûte. On the whole I’am not disappointed:
when I think from what a distance I have to return. It is
unfortunate here that the monotony ♂ gross plainness of the
25   diet (Mutton potatoes ♂ bread being its chief elements) are
rather ~~calu◊~~ calculated in this particular trouble, to combat the
effect of the baths. Ye powers immortal! how I do find myself
longing for a great succulent swash of American vegetables—for
tomatoes ♂ apples ♂ Indian meal! The narrowness of English
30   diet is something absolutely ludicrous. Breakfast cold mutton (or
chop) toast ♂ tea: dinner leg or shoulder, potatoes ♂ rice
pudding: tea cold mutton again (or chop) toast ♂ tea. I
sometimes think that I shall never get well until I get a chance
for a year at a pure vegetable diet—at unlimited tomatoes ♂

beans & pease & squash & turnips & carrots & corn—I enjoy
merely writing the words. I have a deep delicious dream of some
day uniting such a regimen with a daily ride on horseback—
walking having proved inefficient. So you see I have something
ahead of me to live for. But I have something better too than
these vain impalpable dreams—the firm resolve to recover on
my present basis—to fight it out on this line if it takes all
summer—&c! It would be too absurd not to! A ~~fornt~~ fortnight
hence I count upon being able to give you some definite good
news—to which period let us relegate the ∧further[∧] discussion
of the topic. It constantly becomes more patent to me that the
better I get of this—the more I shall be able to read ∧—up to a
certain point.[∧] During the past month I have been tasting
lightly of this pleasure—reading among other things Brownings
Ring & Book, in honor of Italy, the President de Brosses's
delightful letters, Crabbe Robinsons Memoirs & the new vol. of
Ste. Beuve. Browning decidedly gains in interest tho' he loses in
a certain mystery & (so to speak) infinitude, after a visit to Italy.
C. Robinson is disappointing I think—from the thinness of his
individuality, & the superficial character of his perceptions & his
lack of descriptive power. One of your letters contained
something to make me think ~~of~~ [∧]you[∧] have been reading him.
I have quite given up the idea of making ◊◊ a few retrospective
sketches of Italy. To begin with I shall not be well enough (I
foresee) while here; & in the scond place I had far rather let Italy
slumber in my mind untouched as a perpetual capital. whereof
for my literary needs I ~~should~~ shall draw simply the income— —
let it lie warm & nutritive at the base of my mind, manuring &
enriching its roots. I remember by the way that you recently
expressed the confident belief that I had made a series of notes
for my own use. I am sorry to say that I did nothing of the sort.
Mere bald indications (in this I was very wrong) seemed to me
useless, & for copious memoranda I was always too tired. I
expect however to find that I ∧have[∧] appropriated a good deal

from mere "soaking;" i.e. often when I <u>might</u> have been
scribbling in my room I was still sauntering & re-sauntering &
looking & "assimilating."—But now that I'm in England you'd
rather have me talk of the present ∧than of pluperfect Italy.[∧]

5   But life furnishes so few incidents here that I cudgel my brains
in vain. Plenty of gentle emotions from the scenery &c: but only
man is vile. Among my fellow-patients here I find no intellectual
companionship." Never from a single Englishman of them all
have I heard the 1ˢᵗ word of appreciation or enjoyment of the

10   things here that I find delightful. To a certain extent ~~thiu~~ this is
natural: but not to the extent to wh. they carry it. As for the
women I give 'em up, in advance. I am tired of their plainness &
stiffness & tastelessness—their dowdy heads, their dirty collars &
their linsey woolsey trains. Nay, this is peevish & brutal.

15   Personally (with all their faults) they are well enough. I revolt
from their dreary deathly want of—what shall I call it?—Clover
Hooper has it—intellectual grace—Minny Temple has it—
moral spontaneity. They live wholly in the realm of the cut &
dried. "Have you ever been to Florence?" "Oh yes." "Isn't it a

20   most peculiarly interesting city?" "Oh yes, I think its so very
nice." "Have you read <u>Romola</u>?" "Oh yes." "I suppose you
admire it." "Oh yes I think it's so very clever." "◊ The English
have such a mortal mistrust of any thing like "criticism or "keen
analysis" (wh. they seem to regard as a kind of maudlin foreign

25   flummery) that I rarely remember to have heard on English lips
any other intellectual verdict (no matter under what
provocation) than this broad synthesis—"so immensely clever."
What exasperates you is not that they can't say more, but that
they wouldn't if they could. Ah, but they are a great people, for

30   all that. Nevertheless I shd. vastly enjoy half an hour's talk with
an "intelligent American." I find myself reflecting with peculiar
complacency on American women. When I think of their
frequent beauty & grace & elegance & alertness, their cleverness
& self-assistance (if it be simply in the matter of toilet) &

314

compare E̶n̶ them with English girls, living up to their necks
among comforts & influences & advantages wh. have no place
with us, my bosom swells with affection & pride. Look at my
lovely friend Mrs. Winslow. To find in England such beauty,
such delicacy, such exquisite taste, such graceful ease & laxity & 5
t̶a̶s̶t̶e̶ freedom, you ⋄ would have to look among the duchesses—
et encore!, judging from their photos. in the shop windows. Not
that Mrs. Winslow hasn't her little vulgarities, but taking one
thing with another they are so far more innocent than those of
common English-women. But it's a graceless task abusing 10
women of any clime or country. I can't help it tho', if American
women have something which gives them a lift!—Since my
return here there is one thing that I have often wished for
strongly—i.e. that poor Jno. La Farge were with me sharing my
enjoyment of this English scenery—enjoying it that is, on his 15
own hook, with an intensity beside wh. I suppose, mine would
be feeble indeed. I never catch one of the perpetual magical
little "effects" of my walks without adverting to him. I feel sorry
at moments that a couple of months ago I didn't write to him
proposing a rendezvous at Malvern, March 1ˢᵗ, where he could 20
stay & be doctored too, & whence we might subsequently roam
deliciously forth in search of the picturesque. If I were at all sure
of my condition a couple of mos. hence & of the manner I shall
spend the spring & summer I would write to him ₍ₐ₎&₍ₐ₎ ask him if
it is at all in his power to take a three or four mos. holiday. We 25
might spend it together & return together in the Autumn. I feel
sure that as a painter he would enjoy England most intensely.
You may be a little surprised at my thus embracing for a whole
y̶e̶a̶r̶ ₍ₐ₎summer₍ₐ₎ the prospect of his undivided society. But for
one thing I feel as if I could endure his peculiarities much better 30
k̶ now than formerly; & then I feel too as if in any further
travelling I may do here—I should find it a great gain to have a
really good companion: & for observations what better
companion than he? The lack of such a companion was in Italy a

serious loss. I shall not write to him (if at all) with any such idea
until I see myself fairly on the way to be better; but meanwhile,
you, if you see him, might make some tentative inquiry ᴈ
transmit me the result. I have no doubt that he would vastly like
5   the scheme; but little hope of his finding it practicable.—Of
Wendell Holmes I get very much less news than I should like to
have. I heard recently from Arthur Sedgwick who mentioned his
being appointed at H. C. instructor in Constitutional Law. This
has a very big sound; but I never doubted of his having big
10   destinies.—Do speak of him in your next. Nor of Gray do I hear
anything. Do you often ◊◊ see him ᴈ how does he wear? I am
very nervous about a letter from Howells which Mother some
month ago mentioned his being on the point of sending. It
hasn't yet turned up ᴈ I am utterly sickened at the idea of its
15   being lost. Do ascertain from him whether it was ever sent. His
letters are really things of value ᴈ I should find it a great feast to
get one. Heaven speed it ᴈ guard it!—I rec'd. a few days since
thro' father a letter from Bob: very pleasant but with a strangely
quaint ᴈ formal tone about it. But I was very glad to hear from
20   him. It fills me with wonder ᴈ sadness that he should be off in
that Western desolation while I am revelling in England ᴈ Italy.
I should like extremely to get a line out of Wilky: but fate seems
adverse. I very much wish by the way, that some one would let
me know who ᴈ what is Wm Robeson, his partner. I simply
25   know that he is not Andrew R. Àpropos of the family property,
youv'e bought the house—an event I don't quarrel with. Since I
began my letter the afternoon has waned into dusk ᴈ by my
firelight ᴈ candles Cambridge looks like the sweetest place on
earth. And it's a good old house too ᴈ I'm not ashamed of it.
30   This reminds me of ~~your~~ [∧]what[∧] you ~~say~~ said ∧in yr. last [∧]
about ∧getting[∧] photos. ᴈ books. I some time since sent home a
statement of my complete non-purchase of the former¦ ∧ [∧] S
save 4 very handsome statues I got for Alice in Rome which
A. K. will bring her (i.e viz. the great Augustus, the boy

Augustus, the Demosthenses & the (so called "Genius of the
Vatican" (Praxiteles.)) As soon as I arrived in Italy I saw that I
must either buy more than I believed I had means for or leave
them quite alone. The mere going into the shops to buy an
occasional one would have been fatal: besides you can't carry a
few; if you get many, you provide a particular receptacle. Oh
then! the delicious things I left unbought! If I return I to the
continent I will do what I can to repair ~~my~~ discreetly my
abstinence. I very much regret now that I didn't immediately
demand of father & mother a commission of purchase. But I
seem condemned to do things in a small way. I am sure that as
notes for future reference photos. are unapproached &
indispensable. — As for books you rather amuse me by your
assumption that in Italy I went in for a certain number of <u>vellum
bindings</u>. Not for one — To get books seemed to me at that stage
of my adventures to needlessly multiply my cares: & I felt like
waiting till I had read a few of the vast accumulation on my
hands before swelling the number. I shall probably pick up a few
before going home; ~~probably~~ [ʌ]I fancy[ʌ] not many. If you want
any particular ones you 'll of course let me know. A very good
way to get books in England — modern ones — is to buy them off
Mudie's Surplus Catalogue — frequently great bargains. — But I
must put an end to my stupid letter. I have been shut up all day &
the greater part of yesterday with a bad sore-throat & feel rather
muddled & stultified. In a couple of days or so I hope again to be
hearing from home. I look very soon for a letter from you
correcting that last account of your relapse. I re-echo with all
my heart your impatience for the moment of our meeting again.
I should despair of ever making you know how your
conversation m'a manqué or how when regained, I shall enjoy it.
All I ask for is that I may spend the interval to the best
advantage — & you too. The more we shall have to say to each
other the better. Your last letter spoke of father & mother having
"shocking colds." I hope they have melted away. Among the

things I have recently read is father's <u>Marriage</u> paper in the
<u>Atlantic</u>—with great enjoyment of its manner ↄ approval of its
matter. I see he is becoming one of our prominent magazinists.
He will send me the thing from <u>Old</u> ↄ <u>New</u>. A young scotchman
here gets the <u>Nation</u>, sent him by his brother from N. Y. Whose
are the three female papers on Woman? They are "so very
clever." Àpropos—I retract all those brutalities about the
Engländerinnen. They are the mellow mothers ↄ daughters of
a mighty race.—I expect daily a letter from A. K. announcing
her ~~enjoyment~~ ∧arrival∧ in Paris. She has been having the
inappreciable sorrow of a rainy fortnight in ~~Paris,~~ ∧Florence.∧
I hope very much to hear, tho', that she has had a journey along
the Riviera divinely fair enough to make up for it. But I <u>must</u>
pull in. I have still lots of unsatisfied curiosity ↄ unexpressed
affection, but they must stand over. I never hear anything about
the Tweedies. Give them my love when you see them. T. S. P.
I suppose grows in wisdom ↄ virtue. ∧Tell him∧ I would give a
great deal for a humorous line from him. Farewell. Salute my
parents ↄ sister ↄ believe me your brother of ~~y~~ brothers

    <u>H. James</u> jr.

P.S. Tuesday, 9<u>th</u>: Don't be discouraged by what I said above of
the slowness of my progress here. I have made an impression ↄ I
mean to deepen it.—

Previous publication: Lubbock 1: 26–27; *HJL* 1: 206–12; *SL* 2: 70–76;
CWJ 1: 147–53

    ∾

    312.10 ◆ its • [i *overwrites illegible letter*]

    312.11 ~~Su◆◆◆~~ Sunday • [nda *overwrites blotted illegible letters*]

    312.11 ~~m~~ March • [M *overwrites* m]

    312.20 unmistakeably • [*misspelled*]

    312.26 ~~calu◆~~ calculated • [cu *overwrites* u◆]; calcula= | ted

    312.26 combat • com= | bat

    312.29 narrowness • narrow= | ness

313.8 ~~fornt~~ fortnight • [tn *overwrites blotted* nt]

313.18 infinitude • infini= | tude

313.19 thinness • thin= | ness

313.20 superficial • super= | ficial

313.23 ◊◊ a • [a *overwrites illegible letters*]

313.25 foresee • fore= | see

313.25 scond • [*misspelled*]

313.27 ~~should~~ shall • [all *overwrites* ould]

313.27 income— — • — | —

314.7 intellectual • intellect= | ual

314.10 ~~thiu~~ this • [s *overwrites* u]

314.17 intellectual • intellec= | tual

314.22 "◊ The • [Th *overwrites* "◊]

314.31 myself • my= | self

315.1 ~~En~~ them • [the *overwrites* En]

315.5 graceful • grace= | ful

315.6 ◊ would • [w *overwrites illegible letter*]

315.18 adverting • ad= | verting

315.19 moments • mom= | ents

315.31 ~~k~~ now • [n *overwrites* k]

316.8 instructor • instruc= | tor

316.11 ◊◊ see • [see *overwrites illegible letters*]

316.12 nervous • ner= | vous

316.24 partner • part= | ner

316.30 ~~say~~ said • [id *overwrites* y]

316.32 ╎ ∧ [∧] • [∧ *overwrites* .; *nothing inserted*]

316.32–33 S save • [s *overwrites* S]

316.34 ~~i.e~~ viz. • [viz *overwrites* i.e]

316.34 Augustus • Augus= | tus

317.1 Demosthenes • Demos= | thenes

317.2 arrived • ar= | rived

317.7 ~~I~~ to • [t *overwrites* I]

317.8 ~~my~~ discreetly • [dis *overwrites* my]

317.9 immediately • im= | mediately

317.22 frequently • fre= | quently

317.25 muddled • mud | -dled

318.3 prominent • promi= | nent

318.8 Engländerinnen • Eng= | =länderinnen

318.14 unsatisfied • un= | satisfied

318.19 ~~y~~ brothers • [b *overwrites blotted* y]

318.21 discouraged • dis= | couraged

∾

312.11 this windy ~~Su◊◊◊~~ Sunday • 8 March 1870 was actually a Monday. HJ most likely, then, misremembered the date for Sunday, which would have been 7 March, as the start date for this letter.

312.12–13 I wrote to Alice some eight days ago • HJ to AJ, 27, 29 [28] February 1870.

312.22 premier pas qui coûte • first step that is the hardest.

313.14–15 Brownings Ring ~~&~~ Book, in honor of Italy • *The Ring and the Book*, Robert Browning's long blank-verse poem, first published serially in 1868–69; the story is set in Italy.

313.15–16 President de Brosses's delightful letters • Charles de Brosses (1709–77), author of *Lettres familières écrites d'Italie en 1739–40*.

313.16 Crabbe Robinsons Memoirs • Henry Crabb Robinson (1775–1867), London solicitor remembered for his *Diary, Reminiscences, and Correspondence*.

313.16–17 the new vol. of Ste. Beuve • Sainte-Beuve's *Madame Desbordes-Valmore, sa vie et sa correspondance*.

313.21 One of your letters • See WJ to HJ, 1 November 1869 (*CWJ* 1: 118–21).

313.29–31 you recently expressed [. . .] my own use • In his 19 January 1870 letter to HJ, WJ wrote: "It's a burning shame that all the while you were in Italy you should not have been able to write any 'notes' for the Nation" (*CWJ* 1: 141).

314.16–17 Clover Hooper • Marian (Clover) Hooper (1843–83), gifted photographer, art collector, and conversationalist who married Henry Adams on 27 June 1872. Her celebrated Washington salon welcomed such notables as John and Clara Hay, Clarence King, and George Bancroft. Hooper is thought to be HJ's model for Mrs. Bonnycastle in the short story "Pandora." See also Patricia O'Toole's *The Five of Hearts* and Eugenia Kaledin's *The Education of Mrs. Henry Adams*.

314.21 <u>Romola</u> • George Eliot's *Romola* (1863).

315.4 Mrs. Winslow • Mrs. George Scott Winslow.

315.7 <u>et encore</u>! • <u>and even then</u>!

316.7 I heard recently from Arthur Sedgwick • Arthur George Sedgwick to HJ, 30 January 1870.

316.8 H. C. • Harvard College.

316.12 a letter from Howells • William Dean Howells to HJ, 2 January and 6 March 1870 (see Anesko 69–74).

316.20–21 in that Western desolation • RJ was living in Milwaukee, Wisconsin.

316.24 W<u>m</u> Robeson • William R. Robeson, to whom GWJ sold eight thousand dollars' worth of Florida land in January of 1870.

316.25 Andrew R. • Possibly Andrew Robeson Sr. or his son, Andrew Robeson.

316.31–32 I some time since sent home a statement of my complete non-purchase of the former • See HJ to MWJ, 5 February [1870].

317.1–2 "Genius of the Vatican" • The *Faun* of Praxiteles; see HJ to WJ, 8 November [1869].

317.22 Mudie's Surplus Catalogue • Mudie's Circulating Library opened on Oxford Street, London, in 1852. Subscribers were sent catalogs from which to choose current books, including a catalog of surplus copies of novels sold individually or in larger collections.

317.29–30 how your conversation m'a manqué • how I've been missing your conversation.

318.1–2 father's <u>Marriage</u> paper in the <u>Atlantic</u> • Sr.'s "Is Marriage Holy?" *Atlantic Monthly* 25 (March 1870): 360–68.

318.4 the thing from <u>Old & New</u> • A journal edited by Edward Everett Hale from 1870 to 1875. There is no record of any publication by Sr. (*CWJ* 1: 153).

318.6 three female papers on Woman • Lulu Gray Noble's "Notes on the Woman's Rights Agitation" appeared in three issues of the *Nation*.

318.8 Engländerinnen • Englishwomen.

318.21 Tuesday, 9$\underline{\text{th}}$ • 9 March 1870 was a Wednesday.

HENRY JAMES SR.

19 March 1870

ALS Houghton

bMS Am 1094 (1771)

Malvern March 19$\underline{\text{th}}$ '70. Saturday.

Dear father—I received yesterday with immense satisfaction your letter of March 3$\underline{\text{d}}$—& by its 2 weeks journey was made to feel very near to you. To get letters at this place is the only comfort—or at least the only solid delight—in life, & I think you would be what the English call extremely "diverted" to see how I handle yours—how I hoard & treasure them & flatten them out into the entertainment of ~~th~~ two or three days. Shortly before, I had got mother's of Feb. 25$\underline{\text{th}}$—& together with it a long one from A. Kate, from Paris, describing her journey from Genoa: so you see I had an ample feast of the affections—[∧]to say nothing of the intellect.[∧] I have written you so often ~~from~~ [∧]since[∧] my arrival here that I feel as if I had nothing apt to talk about & I take up my pen merely to thank you for your letter & to enjoy the sensation of looking homeward. To Willy I wrote, stupidly enough, only a week ago; & as neither of these last letters contains any particular news of him I am keenly impatient to hear from him. If good wishes could help me to a recovery I ought to be wafted on the breath of yours straight to a <u>terra firma</u> of everlasting health. Out of much tribulation I fancy it finally will come. I am pursuing my "cure" here with unfailing energy & unabated hope. I have taken a start, I think, & whatever I gain, I shall keep. I was glad to receive from mother an acknowledgement of my financial statement of six weeks ago. Your view of the future is one in which I gladly coincide. I had already quite renounced the project of travelling in England — travelling that is, in a regular way. One or two bits of the country I still cherish the hope of seeing on foot. I have now been here nearly 6 weeks, & expect to remain a month longer, when I ~~expect~~ ₍ₐ₎mean₍ₐ₎ to go up to London & meet A. Kate. A fortnight in London — a couple of days at Oxford on my way thither — & a little pedestrian turn in Devonshire & round the isle of Wight: ~~these~~ this is the amount of what I should like to accomplish. I shall then depart for the Continent — <u>i.e.</u> for Switzerland <u>via</u> Paris. Everything however will depend upon my condition at the end of my ten weeks here; so its useless at present to worry you with details. — I was of course deeply interested in your news about poor Minny. It is a wondrous thing to think of the possible extinction of that immense little spirit. But what a wretched business too that her ~~nervous~~ ₍ₐ₎nerves₍ₐ₎ should be trifled with by the false information of unwise physicians. Mother says that she asks for letters — which I'm glad to know of. Writing a dozen pages is easy terms for lightening such a miserable sorrow. But something tells me that there is somehow too much of Minny to disappear for some time yet — more life than she has yet lived out. At any rate I mean to write to her immediately. — Your letter was full of things that I don't know how to answer — beginning with your ingenious excuse for not having written before. Your letter however was worthy of your silence. You hit it perhaps more happily than you fancied when you speak of <u>dull</u> <u>Albion</u>. Dull indeed it is beside that bright immortal Italy. I feel at moments as if it were only now that I am beginning ~~to~~ to enjoy my Italian journey. My memory, at any rate, is a storehouse of treasures. I keenly envy Alice & Willy — happy mortals! — not having been to Italy. To think of having it all before one — of knowing for the 1ˢᵗ time that 1ˢᵗ month on Italian soil! I wish very much I could

exorcise this Italian ghost that haunts me. If I were feeling in
better order physically I would sit me down & never rest from
scribbling until I had written the life out of him. It may be that
in reality I never shall see Italy again: it may be that if I do see it,
half its glory will have faded: but I feel just now as if I should be
greatly disappointed if my recent visit shall have turned out to
be anything less than a beginning, a "reconnaissance" of the
ground. Your little sketch of home affairs went to my heart. I
feel a little less mean & shabby in thinking that A̶l̶ Mother &
Alice & Willy have been tasting of aesthetic joys in Fechter's
acting. I had an immense revelation of the power of good acting
at the Théatre Français. The French are certainly a great people.
So long as the Théatre Français subsists on its present basis—
there will be overwhelming testimony of this. I was deeply
moved, too, by your mention of your glorious wintry weather—
such weather as Europe knows not. But now that the spring is
coming, this grey-green old England reminds us from time to
time that she has a small t̶r̶e̶a̶s̶u̶r̶e̶ ₍ₐ₎reserve₍ₐ₎ of beautiful days.
On the whole, since coming to Malvern I have been very happy
in the absence of rain, which would have made a dismal thing of
life. The absence of rain however is rather a negative merit: but
half a dozen times the day has plucked ◊ up a spirit and burst out
in positive exquisite beauty—a beauty tempered & chastened by
the memory of former gloom & by the foresight of gloom to
come—but wonderfully delicate & perfect. The English skies
still remain my especial admiration—the more so that from
these hill sides we have a capital stand-point for watching them.
When the immense misty plain of hedge-checkered
Worcestershire lies steeped in the beautiful verdurous shades
which seem to rise as an emanation from its meadows & farm-
steads & parks, & the sky expands above it, tremendous &
Turneresque, a chaos of rolling grey—a rain of silver, a heaven
of tender distant blue—there is something to my eyes in the
sight so wonderfully characteristic & national so eloquent of the

English spirit ᶲ the English past that I half expect to hear from a thousand throats a murmur of sympathy ᶲ delight. But as a general thing all the people I see here ~~take~~ are utterly indifferent or ◇◇ densely insensible to the beauty of their Country. When I'm fairly at home again I expect to enjoy a pleasure I have never known before—to speak of—that of long walks in the Country; but I'm surely afraid that these long walks on English highways ᶲ lanes will have wrought such work on my taste that the fairest American scenery will seem wofully tame ᶲ cold. The other afternoon I trudged over to Worcester—thro' a region so thick-sown with good old English "effects"—with elm-scattered meadows ᶲ sheep-cropped commons ᶲ ₍ₐ₎the₍ₐ₎ ivy-smothered dwellings of small gentility, ᶲ high gabled heavy-timbered broken-plastered farm-houses, ᶲ ~~the beginnin~~ ₍ₐ₎stiles₍ₐ₎ leading to delicious meadow footpaths ᶲ lodge-gates leading to far off manors—with all things suggestive of the opening chapters of half-remembered novels, devoured in infancy—that I felt as iff I were pressing all England to my soul. And as I neared the good old town I saw the great Cathedral tower, high ᶲ square, rise far into the cloud-dappled blue. And as I came nearer still I stopped on the bridge ᶲ viewed the great ecclesiastical pile cast downward into the yellow Severn. And going further yet I entered the town ᶲ lounged about the close ᶲ gazed my fill at ₍ₐ₎that₍ₐ₎ most soul-soothing sight—the waning afternoon; far aloft on the broad perpendicular field of the Cathedral spire— tasted too, as deeply, of the peculiar stillness ᶲ repose of the close—saw a ruddy English lad come out ᶲ lock the door of the old foundation school which marries its hoary Gothic walls ~~of~~ to the basement of the Church ᶲ carry the vast big key into one of the still canonical houses—ᶲ stood wondering ~~wh~~ as to the effect on a man's mind of having in one's boyhood haunted the Cathedral shades as a king's scholar ᶲ yet kept ruddy with much criket in misty meadows by the Severn.—This is a sample of the meditations suggested in my daily walks. Envy me—if you can

without hating! I wish I could describe them all—Colwall Green
especially, where weather favoring I expect to drag myself this
afternoon—where ∧each₍∧₎ square yard of ground lies verdantly
brimming with the deepest British picturesque, & half begging,
half-depecrating—a sketch. You should see how a certain stile-
broken footpath here ~~wind◊◊◊◊~~ winds through the meadows to a
little grey rook-haunted church. Another region fertile in walks
◊◊ is the great line of hills. Half an hours climb will bring you to
∧the₍∧₎ top ₍∧₎of₍∧₎ the Beacon—the highest of the range—& here
in a breezy world of bounding turf with twenty counties at your
feet—& when the mist is thick something immensely English in
the situation (as if you ∧were₍∧₎ wandering on some mighty
seaward cliffs or downs, haunted by vague traditions of an early
battle₎) you may wander for hours—delighting in the great
green landscapes as it responds forever to ∧the₍∧₎ cloudy
movements of heaven—scaring the sheep—wishing horribly that
your mother & sister were—I can't say <u>mounted</u>—◊◊◊ on a
couple of little white=aproned donkeys, climbing comfortably
at your side.—But at this rate ~~of~~ I shall tire you out with my
walks as effectually as I sometimes tire myself. The feast of roast
mutton approaches. The mutton is good, but ~~nevertheless~~ where
are those rarer delights of my native larder?—the amber-tinted
surface of the scalloped oysters—the crimson ~~dye~~ die of the
tomatoes—the golden lustre of the Indian pudding—the deep
dark masses of the charlotte of apple & of peach?—You say that
you have been having all winter "plenty of society"—delightful
fact! Keep at it—the more the better. You have my complete
adherence, by the way, to the purchase of the house. It seemed
to have proved itself a residence appointed of heaven & I will do
what I can in the way of getting photos; to contribute to its
adornment. I could have done this better at Venice, Florence &
Rome than elsewhere—but I didn't feel as if I could afford to: &
I can still do well. I take great pleasure in all mention of home
people & things. How is J. T. Fields? Do you see anything of

Longfellow & Lowell? Do you go to the Club?—Have you
begun to agitate the summer question again? Write me of all
your debates & hopes & fears. I have lately received three
Nations, for wh. thanks. The notice of your Marriage paper
seemed to me rather flippant. I heard some time since that the
great Dennet had left the Nation & come to Cambridge; ~~How~~
but I ~~de~~ still detect his hand. Have you got him among you?—
But the roast mutton impends: Farewell.—I have written a very
dull letter—the less excusable as before beginning I ~~felt~~ fancied
myself full of material. If I knew just a little more about the
English I wouldn't hesitate to offer my "views" on British
character. Theyr'e a doggedly conservative lot. You come bump
up against it, in what you have innocently fancied to be friendly
sympathetic discourse, as against a Chinese Wall of cotton-
bales. But their virtues are of goodly use to the world. Kiss
mother for her letter—& for that villainous cold. I enfold you all
in an immense embrace. Your faithful son H.
P.S. Just received a letter from Howells: for which tell him I
thank him & bless him.—
P.S. You all attack me about Dr. Gully. I wish that, if you have
any special facts about him, you had communicated them. I
didn't go to him because what I had learned about his place
deterred me. He has little or nothing to do with it ∧the thing
being in the hands of another man.∧ When I was here before
he was wintering in Italy. ~~I am~~ Some time since I went to see
him, for an opinion, but he was absent for the whole spring. He
has but a few people—only men. The other day a gentleman left
his place to come here, he being the only patient. This seemed
too lonely & gloomy.—By the way, you had better address your
next letters to Barings again. I will give you any ensuing
permanent address.—

Previous publication: Lubbock 1: 28–29; *HJL* 1: 213–18

∞

322.19 ~~th~~ two • [w *overwrites* h]

322.33 unfailing • unfail= | ing

323.1 acknowledgement • acknowledge= | ment

323.3 travelling • travel= | ling

323.10 ~~these~~ this • [is *overwrites* ese]

323.30 ~~to~~ to • [o *overwrites illegible letter*]

324.9 ~~Al~~ Mother • [M *overwrites* Al]

324.12 Théatre • [*misspelled*]

324.13 Théatre • [*misspelled*]

324.22 ◊ up • [u *overwrites blotted illegible letter*]

324.25 perfect • per= | fect

324.30–31 farm- | steads • farm-steads

324.31 tremendous • tremen | dous

324.33 something • some= | thing

325.4 ◊◊ densely • [de *overwrites illegible letters*]

325.4 insensible • insensi= | ble

325.10–11 thick- | sown • thick-sown

325.17 iff • [f *blotted out*]

325.22 downward • down- | ward

325.30 ~~wh~~ as • [a *overwrites* wh]

326.2 myself • my= | self

326.5 half-depecrating • [*misspelled*]

326.6 ~~wind◊◊◊◊~~ winds through • [s th *overwrites illegible letters*]

326.7 rook-haunted • rook- | haunted

326.8 ◊◊ is • [is *overwrites blotted illegible letters*]

326.8 to • [*inserted*]

326.9 top • [p *inserted*]

326.14 ¦) • [) *overwrites period*]

326.17 ◊◊◊ on • [on *overwrites illegible letters*]

326.18 white=aproned • white= | aproned

326.19 ~~of~~ I • [I *overwrites blotted and struck through* of]

326.23 ~~dye~~ die • [i *overwrites* y]

327.7 ~~de~~ still • [st *overwrites* de]

327.9 ~~felt~~ fancied • [a *overwrites* elt]

327.18–19 P.S. Just [. . .] him.— • [*written across the letter's first page*]

327.25 ~~I am~~ Some • [Som *overwrites* I am]

∾

322.26–27 To Willy I wrote [. . .] a week ago • HJ to WJ, [7] 8, 9 March 1870.

323.1 my financial statement of six weeks ago • See 5 February [1870] letter to MWJ.

324.10–11 Fechter's acting • Charles Albert Fechter (1824–79), European actor famed for his melodramatic and romantic roles; Fechter made his U.S. debut in 1870 at Niblo's Garden playing Hugo's *Ruy Blas*.

325.19 the great Cathedral • The thirteenth-century gothic Worcester Cathedral.

326.1 Colwall • Village south of Great Malvern.

326.34 J. T. Fields • James Thomas Fields (1817–81), Boston publisher, managing partner of Ticknor and Fields, and editor of the *Atlantic Monthly* (1861–71), which Ticknor and Fields had purchased in 1859 and which published a number of HJ's earliest reviews and stories; at the end of his life, HJ wrote a commemorative article about the Fieldses, "Mr. and Mrs. James T. Fields," for the *Atlantic Monthly*. The article also appeared, with the title "Mr. & Mrs. Fields," in *Cornhill Magazine*.

327.4 your Marriage paper • "The Woman Thou Gavest with Me."

327.5–6 the great Dennet • John R. Dennett (1838–74), literary editor of the *Nation* from 1868 to 1869, had accepted a teaching post at Harvard.

327.18 Just received a letter from Howells • William Dean Howells to HJ, 2 January and 6 March 1870; see Anesko 69–74.

327.20 Dr. Gully • Dr. James Manby Gully (1808–83), British physician specializing in hydropathy. He administered his water-cure in Great Malvern at the Holyrood House for women and the Tudor House for men. Gully's writings include *An Exposition of the Symptoms, Essential Nature, and Treatment of Neuropathy, or Nervousness* (1837); *The Water Cure in Chronic Disease* (1846); and *A Guide to Domestic Hydrotherapeia* (1863).

CHARLES ELIOT NORTON
25 March 1870
ALS Houghton
bMS Am 1088 (3852)

5

Malvern, March 25<u>th</u> 1870.

My dear Charles—I received this morning with very great
satisfaction your letter of the 21<u>st</u>—& altho' I feel as if to reply
properly to certain portions of it, I ought to allow myself a little
10   longer space for reflection—yet its general effect upon my
spirits is to move me to pour forth without delay, a torrent of
thanks longings & regrets! I find it a great relief to get from
yourself rather than—optimistically—from Jane & Grace, some
report of your health, even tho' it be so poor a one. I had been
15   cheerfully nourishing the illusion that you are really better &
that your physical troubles had quite fallen into the background.
But this seems a vain hope to indulge, so long as our physics
haven't fallen into the background altogether. I most earnestly
hope that the coming spring will do for you what you speak of
20   as possible, whether with a ~~ve~~ view to sending you to ~~Sienn~~
Siena or elsewhere. But that you express an objection to going
northward I should venture to say something about the Italian
lakes—to say even that if you were to go there we possibly might
meet. But I discreetly reflect that Como is a long journey from
25   Florence—& a still longer one from London. But wherever you
spend the Summer it can hardly help being in Italy, & I suppose I
~~e~~ shan't fall short of the truth in thinking of you as backed by a
delicious <u>mise</u> <u>en scène</u>, anywhere. Not a day passes that I dont
think of your well-remembered <u>mise</u> <u>en</u> <u>scene</u> at Florence.
30   Three or four days since came to me Jane's kind letter with
Grace's well-imagined enclosure—which seemed as I opened it
to send forth a perfume of Tuscan spring. All that the spring
must be at Florence I feel as if I might almost claim that I can
vividly fancy. I had indeed, as I'm most happy to remember, a

glimpse of the divine city in early October before the Summer
was altogether dead. It was in those days that I saw the
Certosa—of which my memory tallies most lovingly with your
description. Yes, I saw it to perfection—in all its mellow
mediaevalism—uplifting those mild monastic turrets out of the
green into the blue. It gave me a very poignant pang to read
what you say of the Italy of your former visits ɟ to reflect that I
ꞟ have sate en tête à tête with a man who has really lived in the
world of the Chartreuse de Parme. À propos of the C. de P. I
have just been reading it—with real admiration. It seems to me
stronger and more truthful than the author's books of professed
observation, theory ɟc. It is certainly a great novel—great in the
facility ɟ freedom with which it handles characters ɟ passions.
On the whole I incline to agree with you that I ought to rejoice
in not being haunted by these memories of old Italy—I confess
that during my last month in the Country I was continually
led to [∧]struck[∧] with the enormous bulk of the still lingering
ineradicable past—so that at times I could think with positive
cheerfulness of that projected visit of mine, twenty years hence.
Not for twenty years, at least, shall I be willing to go ∧back[∧] to
Naples. I ꞟ rejoice most heartily over Sara's good fortune in
going to Spain. I wish I were only with you to have the benefit
of her letters. What a thankless grasping spirit a year of
travelling be◊ begets in the unregenerate mind—what a
discontentment with favors conferred—what a p◊ perpetual
demand for more! I say ◊◊ this apropos of the fierce envy I feel
of poor Sara. In reality it is only when ∧one of[∧] your Florentine
letters breaks with a momentary splash the placid surface of
my—more than resignation (if the least bit less than rapture)
that I cease to feel that in my own proper person I am a very fair
object of envy. England is certainly not Italy—but most
incontestably it is England. I feel this with less of excitement
perhaps than when I was here before but with more of
convictions. Deep aesthetic delights are constantly possible—

delights to be religiously prized by one who has a fair amount of
Cambridge, Mass. in propect ◊ retrospect. My chief amusement
here is my walks which I am able to make ◊ very long ◊ frequent,
◊ many of ◊◊ them are full to overflowing with admirably
picturesque incident ◊ matter delightful to eye ◊ fancy.
Yesterday morning if I had thought of Florence it would have
been almost in charity. I walked away across the country to the
ancient town of Ledbury, an hour of the way over the deer-
cropped slopes ◊ thro' the dappled avenues of Eastnor Park
(Earl Somers's—) a vast ◊ glorious domain ◊ as immensely idle
◊ charming ◊ uncared for as anything in Italy. And at Ledbury I
saw a noble ◊ old church (with detatched <u>Campanile</u>) ◊ a
churchyard so full of ancient sweetness—so happy in situation ◊
characteristic detail, that it seemed to me (for the time)—as so
many things do—one of the memorable sights of my European
experience. On the whole I try to make the most in the way of
culture, of all my present opportunities. I think it less of a
privilege to see England than to see Italy, but it is a privilege
nevertheless, ◊ one which I shall not in future years forgive
myself for having underestimated. It behooves me as a luckless
American diabolically tempted of the shallow ◊ the superficial,
really to catch the flavor of an old civilization (it hardly matters
which) ◊ to strive to poise myself for one brief moment at least,
in the attitude of observation. Think of me then as regretting
Italy, but making the best of England.—While I speak of regrets
let me say what I feel as to the manner in which a singularly
unsympathetic fate deals between me ◊ Grace. Jane's letter left
me no doubt as to what I had so strongly suspected—Grace's
nonreceipt of a letter I sent her almost immediately on my
arrival here—soon enough to pass muster as an answer to one
she had sent me to Paris. What has become of it I know not but
I <u>do</u> know (I think) that my standing in any quarter of Grace's
affections nearer to her heart than her charity could ill afford to
dispense with the humble testimony of that misguided missive.

Pray let her know at any rate that it ~~whe~~ [ʌ]went:[ʌ] I hope soon
to furnish her with any needful consolation (beyond this
knowledge) for its not having arrived. You ask about my plans—
concerning which I believe I recently hinted somewhat in
writing to Jane. I hope to be a couple of mos. longer in   5
England—a couple of weeks longer in this place. I am less the
better for my 8 weeks here than I hoped to be: still I am the
better. My subsequent projects are a jumble of ~~Swi◇◇~~
Switzerland—two or three German springs—Paris &c. I shall
probably return home in October. I get no home news worth   10
repeating—unless I were to enclose you bodily a very good
letter from Howells.—Susan you say is "delightfully well"—
delightfully for me, assure her with my love. Seriously, dear
Charles, for your own continued indisposition, ~~I ◇◇◇◇~~ Je
[ʌ]n'en[ʌ] reviens pas. I can only hope that you overestimate the   15
inactivity wh. results from it. At any rate I rejoice most warmly
in your uninterrupted enjoyment of the good things f about
you. With Italy in the present & your children in the future you
have de quoi vivre. You give no especial news of your Mother,
which I interpret as the best. Farewell. Love to all. Most   20
~~affectionate◇~~ affectionately yours—H. James jr.

Previous publication: Horne 32–35

ᖆ

330.8 satisfaction • satisfac= | tion

330.9 certain • cer= | tain

330.20 ~~ve~~ view • [i *overwrites* e]

330.20–21 ~~Sienn~~ Siena • [ie *overwrites* ien]

330.27 ~~e~~ shan't • [sh *overwrites* c]

330.29 scene • [*misspelled*]

331.8 ~~n~~ have • [h *overwrites* n]

331.16 continually • contin= | ually

331.19 cheerfulness • cheer- | fulness

331.21 ~~r~~ rejoice • [e *overwrites* r]

331.24 b̶e̶◊ begets • [g *overwrites illegible letter*]

331.25 p̶◊ perpetual • [er *overwrites illegible letter*]

331.26 ◊◊ this • [th *overwrites illegible letters*]

331.34 aesthetic • aes= | thetic

331.34 possible • pos= | sible

332.2 propect • [*misspelled*]

332.3 ◊ very • [v *overwrites illegible letter*]

332.4 ◊◊ them • [th *overwrites illegible letters*]

332.8–9 deer- | cropped • deer-cropped

332.10 immensely • immense= | ly

332.12 ◊ old • [o *overwrites* ◊]

332.17 opportunities • oppor= | tunities

332.18 England • En= | gland

332.29 nonreceipt • non- | receipt

333.4 somewhat • some= | what

333.8–9 S̶w̶i̶◊◊ Switzerland • [tz *overwrites illegible letters*]

333.14–15 I̶ ◊◊◊◊ Je [∧]n'en[∧] • [J *overwrites* I; n'en *inserted above struck through illegible letters*]

333.15 overestimate • overesti= | mate

333.17 f about • [a *overwrites blotted* f]

333.21 a̶f̶f̶e̶c̶t̶i̶o̶n̶a̶t̶e̶◊ affectionately • affectionate | ◊ly; [l *overwrites illegible letter*]

☙

330.8 your letter of the 21ˢᵗ • Charles Eliot Norton's 21 March 1870 letter to HJ (Houghton bMS Am 1094 [374]).

330.28 mise en scène • stage setting.

331.3 Certosa • Certosa di Val d'Ema.

331.7 what you say of the Italy of your former visits • Charles Eliot Norton, in his 21 March 1870 letter to HJ, wrote:

> Italy is a good place, however, for deadening the overactive conscience, & for killing rank ambitions. It used to be better for this than it is now. The Italians are getting tired of being the grasshoppers, & want to become thrifty ants. They sing less,—and lay up winter stores, and yet do not become happier as they become provident. [. . .] What will

our children do when all the world is depoetized, & the past dethroned by schools & railroads? To me, who remember ₐthe₍ₐ₎ Italy of the middle ages,—the Italy of Gregory XVI, and the Austrians, of the Chartreuse de Parme & the Neapolitan Bourbons,—the loss seems very great. Happy you, whose youth saves you from such a standard of comparison!

331.9 <u>Chartreuse</u> <u>de</u> <u>Parme</u> · *La Chartreuse de Parme*, the 1839 novel by Stendhal, usually entitled *The Charterhouse of Parma* in English translation.

332.8 Ledbury · A town south of Colwall and Great Malvern.

332.9 Eastnor Park · Near Ledbury, the extensive piece of parkland is home to herds of deer.

332.10 Earl Somers's · The first Earl of Somers began construction on Eastnor Castle in 1810; the third Earl of Somers, John Somers Cocks, carried out lavish embellishments during the 1860s and 1870s.

332.29–30 a letter I sent her almost immediately on my arrival here · HJ to Grace Norton, 18 February 1870.

333.14–15 Je ₍ₐ₎n'en₍ₐ₎ reviens pas · I can't get over it.

333.19 <u>de</u> <u>quoi vivre</u> · <u>something to live for.</u>

MARY WALSH JAMES
26 March [1870]
ALS Houghton
bMS Am 1094 (1772)

25

Malvern March 26ᵗʰ
Dearest mother—

I rec'd. this morning your letter with father's note, telling me of Minny's death—news more strange & painful than I can find words to express. Your last mention of her condition had   30 been very far from preparing me for this. The event suggests such a host of thought that it seems vain to attempt ₐto₍ₐ₎ utter them. You can imagine all I feel. Minny seemed such a breathing immortal reality that the mere statement of her death conveys little meaning: really to comprehend it I must wait—we must all wait—till time brings with it the poignant sense of loss & irremediable absence. I have been spending the morning letting the awakened swarm of old reccollections & associations flow into my mind—almost <u>enjoying</u> the exquisite pain they provoke. Wherever I turn in all the recent years of my life I find Minny somehow present, directly or indirectly—& with all that wonderful ethereal brightness of presence which was so peculiarly her own. And now to sit down to the idea of her <u>death</u>! As much as a human creature may, I fancy, she will survive in the unspeakably tender memory of her friends. No attitude of the heart seems tender & generous enough not to do her some unwilling hurt—now that she has meltd away into ◆◆◆ such a divine image of sweetness & weakness! Oh dearest mother! Oh poor struggling suffering <u>dying</u> creature! But who complains that she's gone or would have her back to die more painfully? She certainly never seemed to have come into this world for her own happiness—or that of others—or as anything but as a sort of divine reminder & ~~quick◆◆◆~~ quickener—a transcendent protest against our acquiescence in its grossness. To have ~~n~~ known her is certainly an immense gain: but who could have wished her to live longer on such a footing—unless he had felt within ₐhim₍ₐ₎ (what I felt little enough!) some irresistible mission to reconcile her to a world to which she ~~is~~ was essentially hostile. There is ~~bal~~ absolute balm in the thought of poor Minny & <u>rest</u>—rest & immortal absence! But viewed in a simple human light, by the eager spirit that ◆◆ insists upon its own—her death is full to overflowing of sadness. It comes home to me with irresistible power, the sense of how much I knew her & how much I loved her. As I look back upon the past, from the time I ~~be~~ was old enough to feel & perceive, her friendship seems ~~lit◆◆◆~~ literally to fill it—with proportions magnified doubtless by the mist of tears. I am very glad to have seen so little of her suffering & decline—but nevertheless every word in

which you allude to the pleasantness of that last visit has a kind
of heart-breaking force. "Dear bright little Minny!" as you most
happily say: what an impulse one feels to sum up her rich little
life in some simple compound of tenderness & awe. Time for
you at home, will have begun to melt away the hardness of the   5
thought of her being in future a simple memory of the mind—a
mere pulsation of the heart: to me as yet it seems perfectly
inadmissible. I wish I were at home to hear & talk about her: I
feel immensely curious for all the small facts & details of her last
weeks. Write me any gossip that comes into your head. By the   10
time it reaches me it will be very cheerful reading. Try &
remember anything she may have said & done. I have been
raking up all my recent ◊ memories of her & her rare personality
seems to shine out with absolutely defiant reality. Immortal
peace to her memory! I think of her gladly as unchained from   15
suffering & embalmed forever in all our souls & lives. Twenty
years hence what ~~an~~ ∧a[∧] pure eloquent vision she will be.—But
I revert in spite of myself to the hard truth that she is <u>dead</u>—
silent—absent forever—she ∧the[∧] very heroine of our common
scene. ~~of lifes~~ If you remember any talk of hers about me—any   20
kind of reference or message pray let me know of it. I wish very
much father were able to ◊◊ write me a little more in detail
concerning the funeral & anything he heard there. I feel
absolutely <u>vulgarly</u> eager for any facts whatever. Dear bright
little Minny—God bless you dear mother, for the words. What   25
~~an~~ a pregnant reference in future years—what a secret from
those who never knew her! In her last letter to me she spoke of
having had a very good photograph taken, wh. she would send.
It has never come. Can you get one—or if you have only the
home copy, can you have it repeated or copied? I should very   30
much like to have it—for the day when to think of her will be
nothing but pure blessedness. Pray, as far as possible, attend to
this. Farewell. I am melted down to such an ocean of love that
you may be sure you all ◊ come in for your share.—<u>Evening</u>.—I

have had a long walk this afternoon & feel already strangely familiar with the idea of Minny's death. But I can't help wishing that I had been in closer relations with her during her last hours⤴ —& find a solid comfort at all events in thinking of that

5 long never-to-be-answered letter I wrote to her from Florence. If ever my good genius prompted me, it was then. It is no surprise to me to find that I felt for her an affection ◊ as deep as the foundations of my being, for I always knew it: but I now become sensible how her image softened and sweetened by

10 suffering & sitting patient & yet expectant, so far away from the great world with which so many of her old dreams & impulses were ~~assose~~ associated, has ~~acted~~ [∧]operated[∧] i on my mind [*a*]s a gentle incentive to action & enterprise. There ~~were~~ have been so many things I have thought ◊ of telling her—[∧]so many stories

15 by which I had a fancy to make up her losses to her[∧]—as if she were going to linger on as a graceful invalid to listen to my stories! It was only the other day however that I dreamed of meeting her somewhere this summer with Mrs. Post. Poor Minny! how much she was not to see! It's hard to believe that

20 she is not seeing greater things now. On the dramatic fitness—as one may call it—of her early death it seems almost idle to dwell. No one who ever knew her can have failed to look at her future as a sadly insoluble problem—& we almost all had imagination enough to say, to ourselves, at least, that life—poor narrow

25 life—contained no place for her. How all her conduct & character see[*med*] to have pointed to this conclusio[*n*]—how profoundly inconsequential, in her history, continued life would have been! Every happy pleasant hour in all the long course of our friendship seems to return to me, vivid & eloquent with the

30 light of the present. I think of Newport as with its air vocal with her accents, alive with her movements. But I have written quite enough—more than I expected. I couldn't help thinking this afternoon how strange it ~~was~~ [∧]is[∧] for me to be pondering her death in the midst of this vast indifferent England which she

fancied she would have liked. Perhaps!—T[*h*]ere was no
mourning in the cold bright landscape for the loss of her liking.
Let me think that her eyes are resting on greener pastures than
even England's. But how much—how long—we have got to live
without her! It's no more than a just penalty to pay, though, for   5
the privilege of having been young with her. It will count in old
age, when we live, more than now, in reflection, to have had
such a figure in our youth. But I must say farewell. Let me beg
you once more to send me any possible talk or reminiscences—
no matter how commonplace. I only want to make up for not   10
having seen her.—I resen[*t*] thei[*r*] having buried her at
N. Roch[*elle*] She ought to lie among her ow[*n*] people. Good
night. My letter doesn't read over-wise; but I have written off
my unreason. You promise me ∧soon[∧] a letter from Alice: the
sooner the better. W[*ill*]y I trust will also be writing. Good   15
night, dearest mother—

    Your loving son
      H. James.
Write me who was at the funeral &c.—I shall write next from
here—then probably from London.   20

Previous publication: Le Clair 38–41; *SL* 1: 32–36; *HJL* 1: 218–23; Horne
35–38

    ∽

  336.4 reccollections · [*misspelled*]

  336.7 somehow · some- | how

  336.13 meltd · [*misspelled*]

  336.13–14 ◊◊◊ such · [su *overwrites illegible letters*]

  336.19 ~~quick◊◊◊~~ quickener · [ene *overwrites illegible letters*]

  336.21 n̶ known · [k *overwrites* n]

  336.24–25 i̶s̶ was · [wa *overwrites* is]

  336.25 b̶a̶l̶ absolute · [b *blotted out;* a *overwrites* al]

  336.27 ◊◊ insists · [in *overwrites illegible letters, the second of which is blotted*
out]

  336.31 b̶e̶ was · [w *overwrites* be]

336.32 ~~lit◊◊◊~~ literally • [era *overwrites blotted illegible letters*]
337.8 inadmissible • inad= | missible
337.13 ~~◊~~ memories • [m *overwrites illegible letter*]
337.17 ~~an~~ ^a[^] pure • [pu *overwrites* an]
337.20 ~~of lifes~~ If you • [If you *overwrites* of lifes]
337.22 ~~◊◊~~ write • [wr *overwrites illegible letters*]
337.26 ~~an~~ a • [a *overwrites* an]
337.27 knew • [k *inserted*]
337.34 ~~◊~~ come • [co *overwrites illegible letter*]
338.1 afternoon • after- | noon
338.4 hours~~—~~ • [— *struck through and blotted out*]
338.7 ~~◊~~ as • [a *overwrites illegible letter*]
338.8 foundations • foun= | dations
338.9 sweetened • sweet= | ened
338.12 ~~assose~~ associated • [c *overwrites* sc]
338.13 ~~were~~ have • [have *overwrites* were]
338.14 ~~◊~~ of • [o *overwrites illegible letter*]
338.33 afternoon • after- | noon
339.7 reflection • reflec= | tion
339.9 possible • pos= | sible

The original ms. is now damaged. The bracketed, italicized insertions are taken from an examination of *HJL* 1. It is possible that Edel saw the undamaged manuscripts.

335.29 Minny's death • Minny Temple died of tuberculosis on 8 March 1870 in Pelham, New York; she was twenty-four years old.

335.30 Your last mention of her condition • This does not survive, but see HJ to Sr., 19 March 1870.

337.1 that last visit • Minny Temple visited the Jameses in Cambridge in early November 1869 (see Minny Temple to HJ, 17 November 1869 [Houghton bMS Am 1094 (437)]; WJ to HJ, 1 November 1869 [*CWJ* 1: 120]; and HJ to WJ, 27, 28 December [1869]; 1 January 1870).

337.27 her last letter to me • Minny Temple's last surviving letter to HJ is dated 17 November 1869 from Pelham, New York. In it she wrote: "I

have had a very good photograph taken of myself lately, ∧one of[∧] which
I meant to send you—but they have all been taken by somebody, & I shall
have to wait till some more are struck off" (Houghton bMS Am 1094
[437]).

338.17–18 I dreamed of meeting her somewhere this summer with Mrs.
Post • See HJ to WJ, 13, 14 February 1870.

339.12 N. Roch[elle] • According to Edel, Minny Temple was removed
from New Rochelle, New York, and buried in Albany Rural Cemetery,
near her parents (*HJL* 1: 223).

WILLIAM JAMES
29, 30 March [1870]
ALS Houghton
bMS Am 1094 (1944)   15

Malvern March 2̶0̶ 29th̲
Dear Willy—
My mind is so full of poor Minny's death that altho' I
immediately wrote in answer to mother's letter, I find it easier to   20
take up my pen again than to leave it alone. A few short hours
have amply sufficed to more than reconcile me to the event & to
make it seem the most natural—the happiest, fact, almost in her
whole career. So it seems, at ~~most~~ least, on reflection: to the eye
of feeling there is something immensely moving in the sudden &   25
complete extinction of a vitality so exquisite & so apparently
infinite as Minny's. But what most occupies me, as it will have
done all of you at home, is the thought of how her whole life
seemed to tend & hasten, visibly audibly, sensibly, to this
consummation. ~~Sh~~ Her character may be almost literally said to   30
have been without practical application to life. She seems a sort
of experiment of nature—an attempt, a specimen or example—a
mere subject without an object. She was at any rate the helpless
victim & toy of her own intelligence—so that there is positive

relief in thinking of ∧her[∧] being removed from her own heroic treatment ⅋ placed in kinder hands. What a vast amount of truth appears now in all the common-places that she used to provoke—that she was restless—that she was helpless—that she

5   was unpractical. How far she may have been considered up to the time of her illness to have achieved a tolerable happiness, I don't know: hardly at all, I should say, for her happiness like her unhappiness remained wholly incomplete: but what strikes me above all is how great ⅋ rare a benefit her life has been to those

10 with whom she was associated. I ~~find~~ feel as if a very fair portion of my sense of the reach ⅋ quality ⅋ capacity of human nature rested upon my experience of her character: certainly a large portion of my admiration of it. She was a case of pure generosity—she had more even than she ever had use for—

15 inasmuch as she could hardly have suffered at the hands of others nearly as keenly as she did at her own. Upon her limitations, now, it seems idle to dwell; the list of her virtues is so much longer than her life. My own personal relations with her were always of the happiest. Every one was supposed I

20 believe to be more or less in love with her: others may answer for themselves: I never was, ⅋ yet I had the great satisfaction that I enjoyed <u>pleasing</u> her almost as much as if I had been. I cared more to please her perhaps than she ∧even[∧] cared to be pleased. Looking back upon the past half-dozen years, it seems

25 as if she <u>represented</u>, in a manner, in my life several of the elements or phases of ~~our conscious~~ life ∧at large—[∧]—her own sex, to begin with, but even more <u>Youth</u>, with which owing to my invalidism, I always felt, as in rather indirect relations. Poor Minny—what a cold thankless part it seems for her to have

30 played—an actor ⅋ setter-forth of things in which she ~~took~~ ∧had[∧] so little ∧permanent[∧] interest! Among the sad reflections that her death provokes, for me, there is none sadder than this view of the gradual change ⅋ reversal of our relations: I slowly crawling from weakness ⅋ inaction ⅋ suffering into

strength & health & hope: she sinking out of brightness & youth
into decline & death. It's almost as if she had passed away ∧—as
far as I am concerned,—[∧] from having so served her purpose
∧that of[∧]—standing well within the world, too inciting &
inviting me onward by all her ∧the[∧] bright intensity of her   5
example. She never knew how sick & disordered a creature I was
& I always felt that she knew me at my worst. I always looked
forward with a certain eagerness to the day when I should have
regained my natural level and our friendship on my part, at least
might become more active & masculine. This I have especially   10
felt during the powerful experience of the past year. In a
measure I have had worked away from the old ground of my
relations with her, without having quite taken possession of the
new: but I had it constantly in my eyes. But here I am, plucking
all the sweetest fruits of this Europe which was a dream among   15
her many dreams—while she has "gone abroa◊ abroad" in
another sense! Every thought of her is a singular mixture of
pleasure and pain. The thought of what either she or we has lost
or we, comes to one as if only to enforce the idea of her gain in
eternal freedom & rest & our's in the sense of it. Freedom & rest!   20
one must have known poor Minny to feel their value—to know
what they may contained—if one can, measure, that is, the balm
by the ache.—I have been hearing all my life of the sense of loss
wh. death leaves behind it:—now for the first time I have a
chance to learn what it amounts to. The whole past—all times &   25
places—seems full of her. Newport especially=to my mind—she
seems the very genius of the place. I could shed tears of joy far
more copious than any tears of sorrow when I think of her
feverish earthly lot exchanged for this serene promotion into the
pure fellowship of [∧]with[∧] our memories, thoughts and fancies.   30
I had imagined many a talk happy talk with her in years to
come—many a cunning device for cheering & consoling her
∧illness,[∧] ⌐ & many a feast on the ripened fruits of our
friendship: but this on the whole surpasses anything I had

conceived. You will all have felt by this time the novel delight of
thinking of Minny without ∧that₍∧₎ lurking impulse of fond
regret ⅃ uneasy conjecture so familiar to the minds of her
friends. She has gone where there is neither marrying nor giving
5   in marriage! no illusions ⅃ no disillusions—no sleepless nights ⅃
no ebbing strength. The more I think of her the more perfectly
satisfied I am to have her translated from this changing realm of
fact to ~~this~~ the steady realm of thought. There she may bloom
into a beauty more radiant than our dull eyes will ~~endure~~
10   ∧avail₍∧₎ to contemplate.—My first feeling was ◇◇ an immense
regret that I had been separated ~~by so~~ from her last days by so
great a ~~difference~~ ∧distance₍∧₎ of time ⅃ space; but this has been
of brief duration. I'm really not sorry ∧not₍∧₎ to have seen her
materially changed ⅃ thoroughly thankful to have been spared
15   the sight of her suffering. Of this you must ∧all₍∧₎ have had a
keen realization. There is nevertheless something so appealing
in the pathos of her final weakness and decline that my heart
keeps returning again ⅃ again to the scene, regardless of its pain.
When I went to bid Minny ~~g~~ farewell at Pelham before I sailed I
20   asked her about her sleep. "Sleep," she said: "Oh. I don't sleep.
I've <u>given it up</u>." And I well remember the laugh with which she
made this sad attempt at humor. And so she went on, sleeping
less ⅃ less, waking wider ⅃ wider, until she awaked absolutely! I
asked mother to tell me what she could about her ~~lo~~ last weeks ⅃
25   to repeat me any of her talk or any chance incidents, no matter
how trivial. This is a request easier to make than to ~~answer~~,
comply with ⅃ really to talk about Minny we must wait till we
meet. But I <u>should</u> like one of her last photos., if you can get
one. You will have felt for yourself I suppose how little is the
30   utmost one can <u>do</u>, in a positive sense, as regards her memory.
Her presence was so much, ∧so intent₍∧₎—so strenuous—so full
of human exaction: her absence is so modest, content with so
little. A little decent passionless grief—a little ~~rumage~~
₍∧₎rummage₍∧₎ in our little store of wisdom—a sigh of relief ~~a~~—

and we begin to live for ourselves again. If we can imagine the departed spirit ~~conscious~~ ₍ₐ₎cognizant₍ₐ₎ of our ~~actions¦ we~~ action in the matter, we may suppose it much better pleased by our perfect acceptance of the void it has left than by our quarreling with it and wishing it filled up again. What once was life is always life, in one form or another, & speaking simply of this world. I feel as if in effect and influence Minny had lost very little by her change of state. She lives as a steady unfaltering luminary in the mind rather than as a flickering wasting earth-stifled ~~spark~~ lamp. Among all my thoughts & conceptions I am sure I shall never have one of greater sereneness & purity: her ~~img~~ image will preside in my intellect, in fact, as a sort of measure and standard of ◇◇ brightness and repose. But I have scribbled enough. While I sit spinning my sentences she is <u>dead</u>: and I suppose it is partly to defend myself from ~~no~~ too direct a sense of her death that I indulge in this fruitless attempt to transmute it from a hard fact into a soft idea. Time of course will bring almost even-handedly the inevitable pain & the inexorable cure. I am willing to leave life to answer for life: but meanwhile, thinking how small at greatest, is our change as compared with her change & how vast an apathy goes to our little murmur of sympathy, I ~~taken~~ take a certain satisfaction in having simply written twelve pages. — I have been reading over the three or four letters I ₍ₐ₎have₍ₐ₎ got from her since I have been abroad: they are full of herself — or at least of a fraction of herself: they would say little to strangers. Poor living Minny! No letters would hold you. It's the <u>living</u> ones that die; the writing ones that survive. — One thought there is that moves me much — that I should be here delving into this alien England in which it was one of her fancies that she had a kind of property. It was not, I think one of the happiest. Every time that ◇ I have been out during the last three days, the aspect of things has perpetually seemed to enforce her image by simple contrast & difference. The landscape assents stolidly enough to her death: it would have ministered but scantily to her life. She was breathing protest against English grossness, English Compromises & Conventions—~~she~~ a plant of pure American growth. None the less, tho', I had a dream of telling her of England & of her

5 immensely enjoying ~~it~~ my stories. But it's only a half-change: instead of my discoursing to her I shall have her forever talking to me. Amen, Amen to all she may say! Farewell to all that she was! How much this was, & how sweet it was! How it comes back to one, the charm & essential grace of her early years. We shall

10 all have known something! How it teaches, absolutely, tenderness & wonder to the mind.—But it's all locked away, incorruptibly, within the crystal walls of the past. And there is my youth—& anything of yours you please & welcome!—turning to gold in her bright keeping. In exchange, for you, ∧dearest

15 Minny[∧] we'll all keep your future. Don't fancy that your task is done. Twenty years hence we shall be loving with your love & longing with your eagerness & suffering with your patience.

30$\underline{^{th}}$ p.m. So much I wrote last evening; but it has left me little to add, incomplete as it is. In fact it is too soon to talk of

20 Minny's death or to pretend to feel it. This I shall not do till I get home. Every now & then the ~~memory~~ ∧thought[∧] of it stops me short but it's from the life of home that I shall really miss her. With this European world of associations & art & studies, she has nothing to do: she belongs to the deep domestic moral

25 affectional realm. I can't put away the thought that ~~as~~ just as I am beginning life she has ended it. But her ∧very[∧] death is an answer to all the regrets it provokes. You remember how largely she dealt in the future—how she wondered & planned & arranged. ~~It's~~ Now it's to haunt & trouble her no longer—she

30 has her present & future in one.—To you I suppose her death must have been an unmitigated relief—you must have suffered keenly from the knowledge of her sufferi[*ng*.] Thank heaven they lasted n[*o*] longer. When I first hear[*d of*] her death I could thin[*k* . . .] of them: now I can't think of them even when I try.—

I have not heard from you for a long time: I am impatiently
expecting a letter from you. With this long effusion you will all
of have been getting of late an ample share de mes nouvelles.
From Alice too I ◇ daily expect to hear. Yesterday came to me a
very welcome ⅋ pleasantly turned note from Mr. Boott.—I hope   5
I haven't hitherto expressed myself in a way to leave room for
excessive disappointment when I sa◇ say that after now nearly
8 weeks of this place, I have made materially less progress than I
hoped. I shall be here about ten days longer. In town, I shall
immediately go [. . . s]ee a couple of as good ⅋ special   10
[physi]cians as I can hear of. Unhappily [. . .]ces of knowledge
are few. [. . .]

Previous publication: *HJL* 1: 223–29; *SL* 2: 76–81; *CWJ* 1: 153–57; *WHSL*
69–73

◯◯

341.17 2◇ 29 · [9 *overwrites illegible character*]
341.20 immediately · im= | mediately
341.24 most least · [leas *overwrites* most]
341.25 immensely · immense- | ly
341.30 Sh Her · [H *overwrites* Sh]
342.10 find feel · [eel *overwrites* ind]
343.3   s◇ served · [e *overwrites illegible letter*]
343.4   i◇◇ inciting · [nc *overwrites illegible letters*]
343.12 have had · [d *overwrites* ve]
343.16 abroa◇ abroad · [d *overwrites illegible letter*]
343.18 or we has lost · [has los *overwrites* or we]
343.22 contained— · [e *blotted out*; — *overwrites* d]
343.31 talk happy · [happy *overwrites* talk]
343.33 ⅋ ⅋ · [⅋ *overwrites* —]
344.7   satisfied · satis= | fied
344.8   this the · [e *overwrites* is]
344.10 ◇◇ an · [a *overwrites illegible letters*]
344.11 by so from · [from *overwrites* by so]
344.19 g farewell · [f *overwrites* g]

344.24 lo last • [as *overwrites blotted illegible letter*]

344.33 decent • de= | cent

344.34 a— • [— *overwrites* a]

345.2–3 actions; we action in • [on *overwrites* on *and blotted* s; *comma blotted out;* in *overwrites blotted* we]

345.6 simply • sim= | ply

345.8 unfaltering • un- | faltering

345.9–10 earth- | stifled • earth-stifled

345.10 spark lamp • [lam *overwrites blotted* spark]

345.12 img image • [a *overwrites blotted* g]

345.13 ◇◇ brightness • [br *overwrites illegible letters*]

345.15 no too • [to *overwrites* n]

345.18 even-handedly • even- | -handedly

345.21 compared • com= | pared

345.22 taken take • [e *overwrites* en]

345.23 simply • sim= | ply

345.31 ◇ I • [I *overwrites illegible letter*]

345.33 perpetually • per- | petually

346.2 protest • pro= | test

346.2 English • Eng- | lish

346.3 she a • [a *overwrites* she]

346.5 immensely • im= | mensely

346.5 it my • [m *overwrites* it]

346.24 domestic • domes= | tic

346.29 It's Now • [No *overwrites* It's]

347.1 impatiently • [im *inserted*]

347.3 of have • [h *overwrites blotted* of]

347.4 ◇ daily • [d *overwrites illegible letter*]

347.7 sa◇ say • [y *overwrites illegible letter*]

347.12 are few. [. . .] • [*remainder of ms. lost*]

∾

The original ms. is damaged. The bracketed, italicized insertions are taken from an examination of *HJL* 1. It is possible that Edel worked from an undamaged manuscript.

341.13 29, 30 March [1870] · An unidentified person wrote at the top of the letter's first manuscript page "enclosed in letter to his mother, Mar 26, [1870]."

344.19 Pelham · Suburb of New York City, where Minny Temple was living in the home of Kitty and Richard Stockton Emmet.

344.24 asked mother to tell me what she could about her ~~lo~~ last weeks · HJ to MWJ, 26 March [1870].

345.24–25 the three or four letters I ₍∧₎have₍∧₎ got from her since I have been abroad · Three letters by Minny Temple to HJ survive, all from 1869 and held at the Houghton Library: 3 June (Houghton bMS Am 1094 [435]); 15, 22 August (Houghton bMS Am 1094 [436, 438]); and 17 November (Houghton bMS Am 1094 [437]). Considering Catharine Walsh's destruction of James family papers in late 1882 or early 1883 (Habegger, *Father* 6, 155, 500) and HJ's own destruction over the years of most of the correspondence he received, it is significant that these letters survive.

347.3 de mes nouvelles · of news about me.

GRACE NORTON
1 April 1870
ALS Houghton
bMS Am 1094 (880)

25

Malvern April 1ˢᵗ 1870.
Dear Grace—If I possessed in anything like such perfection as yourself the noble art of printing, I would assure you forthwith, in the very largest & fairest capitals, that I received no longer than an hour ago, with "unfeigned delight," your good gracious   30
graphic letter of—a certain "Monday evening." A truce to all incriminations & explanations. What matters a wave more or less in the ocean?—a letter more or less in the fathomless floods of affection & sympathy which ~~dischar◊~~ discharge their equal tides

on English & Italian shores? In the letter, as in the spirit, let me
believe that we are "square." Let me nevertheless thank you for
this last note with as much <u>effusion</u> as if it were a fruit of pure
generosity (which indeed, I strongly suspect.") & no remote
response to any appealing utterance of mine. — Inexpressibly
sweet it is to hear from you & Florence — from Florence in you.
How shall I tell you what a strange look of contradictory
nearness & distance overlies all that you remind me of? so near
is it all in time — so incalculably remote in character from the
medium in which I here live & move. I could treat you to five
pages of the flattest platitudes about Italy as she dwells in my
mind <u>entre cour et jardin</u> — between memory & hope. But with
the infinite reality before you what need have you for the poor
literary counterfeit? "Oh how the March-sun feels like May!" —
exquisite truth! And what does the April sun feel like? and what
do the April hills look like? And what does the lengthening
April twilight put into one's heart — down in the city piazzas, in
front of the churches? ◇◇◇ For all your mention of your various
household facts I am duly grateful — tho hardly for the facts
themselves. I sincerely hope that by this time the colds have
melted away before the breathe of the older & kindlier spring —
the real Florentine season. Of Charles's & Susan's projected visit
to Rome I am delighted to hear. If Rome will only do a little in
the way of health-giving to Charles I will freely forgive it all its
sins & follies. For Susan — she can dispense with even the most
pious adjurations — & going to Rome t̶o̶ for the 1ˢᵗ time can easily
snap a scornful finger & thumb at poor me who have in the
vague future but the prospect of a poor second. — But in what
utterly ungracious & unlikely attitude am I thus fantastically
erecting Susan? Since I have done her a wrong, let me profit ◇◇
by it to do her the right (the fullest I know) of begging of her a
favour — that once in a while — at St. Peter's — at the Vatican in
the Coliseum, in the Campagna — out of a dozen long glances
that she takes for herself & you in Florence, she will take one

short one for me in England; & ~~out of~~ ₍ₐ₎that into₍ₐ₎ a hundred
deep thoughts which she bestows upon the ancient Romans, she
will insinuate one little heart-beat of regret that a luckless
modern American was able to see only half as much de tout cela
as he wanted.—Of immediately personal news I have none to
give you; save that in repeating to you the tidings wh. I had a
week ago from home, I shall tell you of what has been for me a
great personal sorrow. You will possibly have learned them by
your own Cambridge letters. My cousin Minny Temple died
most sudddenly some three weeks ago. I am not sure that you
ever knew her well enough to understand how great a sense of
loss this fact brings with it to those who really knew her—as I
did. I knew her well & her friendship had always been for me
one of the happiest certainties of the future. So much for
certainties! But already, after the lapse of a week, I am
strangely—most serenely—familiar with the idea of her death.
The more I think of it, the more what there is to accept—almost
with thanks—gains upon & effaces, what there is to deplore &
quarrel with. She is one about whom there would be much to
say—ₐmuch₍ₐ₎ which I know, ~~the~~ as the lapse of time tends to
clarify & simplify as it were, her memory, will seem to me so
much more & more that one of these days I shall surely say to
you a large part of it. She was a divinely restless spirit—
essentially one of the "irreconcilables;" & if she had lived to
great age, I think it would have been as the ~~toy~~ₓ ₍ₐ₎victim₍ₐ₎ &
plaything of her constant generous dreams & dissatisfactions.
During the last year moreover it had become obvious that her
life would be one of ~~ime~~ immense suffering—suffering far
harder to think of than (to me at least) even the death which has
cut short the sweetness of her youth. A fortnight before she died
she had her lungs examined by some great New-York authority,
who told her point-blank that she had less than two years to live.
From this moment she sank. Other physicians offered her far
more cheerful hopes & her family (on the testimony of

351

Dr. Metcalf) had made up their minds that she would even
recover. But she had never been afraid of the truth: & it seemed
as if she had no care to accept the respite which had been
granted her in charity. She died apparently from simple
exhaustion. Her memory will be full of interest & delight to all
her friends. I feel not only much the wiser for having known her,
but—I find—really the happier for knowing her at absolute
peace & rest. Her life was a strenuous, almost passionate
question, which <u>my</u> mind, at least, lacked the energy to offer the
elements of an answer for. It would be a really great spirit that
should contain a power to affirm & illumine & satisfy, equal to
her exquisite energy of wonder, & conjecture & unrest.—Her
peculiar personal charm & grace you will doubtless all
remember. This had never been greater, I am told, than ~~shortly~~
ʌduring the year[ʌ] before her death. She was to have come ~~af~~
abroad this next summer—but one little dream the more in a life
which was so eminently a life of the spirit—one satisfied
curiosity the less in a career so essentially incomplete on its
positive side—these seem to make her image ʌonly[ʌ] more
eloquent~~ly~~ & vivid & purely youthful & appealing. She had a
great fancy for knowing England.—Meanwhile here I sit
stupidly scanning it with these dull human eyes!—But in
speaking of her one must return~~s~~ to what one begins with—her
~~rae~~ rare simple superficial charm of physiognomy & presence.
Amen! Her absence, too, has its sweetness.—But I am scribbling
all this my dear ~~Jane~~ Grace, in a wretchedly cold room—made
~~tolerably~~ tolerable only by the thought that I am writing to a
very warm heart.—For the moment farewell. I can talk of
<u>moments</u>: I feel as if I were going to write so soon again. I am
full of wonder & sympathy & interest in all your coming days of
spring & summer. It's a great boon to my imagination to have
you there on duty for me in Italy! To Baron Mackay, if he
comes, you might venture, tentatively, to present my warm
regards. To your mother—abruptly, recklessly—my love. The

same to Susan Charles & Jane—as opportunity—of time & ◇
humour—seems to favor. To Jane I will write ∧not[∧]—"when
inclined¡ —" ~~Let her not call this end till she sees how soon it is¡~~
[∧]wh. she is not to confound with "when <u>not</u> inclined."[∧] Happy
Spain-faring Sara! Addio. Get well of everything—save a   5
lingering kindness for
    Yours most faithfully
       <u>H. James</u> jr.

Address me next please to <u>Barings</u>. I shall be in London 10 days   10
hence. "The rest is <u>Silence</u>."

Previous publication: *HJL* 1: 229–32; *SL* 2: 81–84

  ∾

349.31 Monday · Mon= | day

349.34 ~~dischar◇~~ discharge · [g *overwrites illegible letter*]

350.5 Inexpressibly · Inex= | pressibly

350.9 incalculably · in= | calculably

350.15 does · [es *inserted*]

350.18 ◇◇◇ For · [For *overwrites illegible letters*]

350.21 breath◇ · [*illegible letter blotted and struck through*]

350.24 health-giving · health= | -giving

350.26 ~~to~~ for · [for *overwrites* to]

350.30–31 ◇◇ by · [by *overwrites blotted illegible letters*]

350.33 Campagna · [*second a inserted*]

351.10 sudddenly · [*misspelled*]

351.10–11 ◇ ever · [e *overwrites illegible letter*]

351.11 understand · under= | stand

351.20 ~~the~~ as · [as *overwrites* the]

351.26 dissatisfactions · dissatis= | factions

351.28 ~~ime~~ immense · [m *overwrites* e]

352.12 ~~d~~ conjecture · [c *overwrites* d]

352.15–16 ~~af~~ abroad · [b *overwrites blotted* f]

352.20 eloquent~~ly~~ · [ly *blotted out*]

352.23 returns · [s *blotted out*]

352.24 ~~rae~~ rare · [r *overwrites* c]

352.26 ~~Jane~~ Grace · [Grace *overwrites* Jane]

352.27 ~~tolerably~~ tolerable · [e *overwrites blotted* y]

353.1–2 ⬦ humour · [h *overwrites struck through illegible letter*]

353.3 inclined┊ — · [— *overwrites* .]

∾

350.12 <u>entre</u> <u>cour</u> <u>et jardin</u> · Literally, <u>between courtyard and garden</u>, which is a theatrical expression meaning "between stage left and stage right."

351.4 <u>de tout cela</u> · of all that.

352.1 Dr. Metcalf · Minny Temple had consulted Dr. Metcalfe, a former acquaintance of her late father, who had given her hope that she could recover (Gordon 120). This is probably Dr. John T. Metcalfe, who, according to the New York City directories of this period, had an office at 86 Fifth Avenue and a house at 34 East 14th Street (the 1869 directory also lists a Dr. Orrick Metcalfe, residing at 224 East 14th Street) (Wilson, *Trow's* [1868] 710; *Trow's* [1869] 748; *Trow's* [1870] 761).

352.32 Baron Mackay · Donald Mackay, Scottish nobleman in the Dutch diplomatic service (Turner 211).

353.11 "The rest is <u>Silence</u>." · In Shakespeare's *Hamlet*, the last lines spoken by Hamlet before he dies (5.2.369).

25 GRACE NORTON
28 April [1870]
ALS Houghton
bMS Am 1094 (881)

30 London Bath Hotel
         Piccadilly—
             April 28th
Dear Grace—I have time only for a single word—a sad sad word: farewell. I received your blessed birth-day letter. Many

many thanks. I have been a week in London: I sail on Saturday
M April 30th in the <u>Scotia</u>. Many reasons combine. I am not
altogether well—that's one: & hope to mend rapidly at home—
that's another. But I have no heart to dilate on it. It's a good deal
like dying. Farewell, beloved survivors. My heart's affection to
one & all. I shall write you dear Grace, in some calmer
transatlantic hour. Meanwhile do me this kind office with Sara.
Thank her warmly for a certain note she lately sent me; assure
her it was deeply appreciated & beg her to wait for a Cambridge
answer. I trust she is ₍ₐ₎really₍ₐ₎ enjoying Spain. Have Charles &
Susan come back? But I can't ask Italian questions. I can only
think of you dear Grace mournfully, joyfully & in all friendship
& shake your hand all across Europe. Say for me the very
tenderest things to your Mother & to Jane. & to Charles & Susan
if they are there. All health & peace! Kiss the children. On the
whole I'm very well disposed toward going—!

    Your's ever—more than ever

      <u>H James</u> jr.

₍ₐ₎P.S.₍ₐ₎ I am to have on the <u>Scotia</u> the excellent company &
kindness of my Aunt.

Previous publication: *HJL* 1: 233

∾

355.2 M April • [A *overwrites* M]

355.9 appreciated • appre= | ciated

∾

355.2 the <u>Scotia</u> • Last of the Cunard paddle-wheel steamers, the <u>Scotia</u>
entered service in 1862 as a first-class ship only and set both east- and
west-bound crossing records in 1863.

HENRY WADSWORTH LONGFELLOW
[May 1870–May 1872]
ALS Houghton
bMS Am 1340.2 (2993) 2

5

My dear Mr. Longfellow—
I found the volumes of Tourgéneff of which we spoke the other
evening, were in the hands of a friend, but here they are at last—
to be kept during your uttermost convenience.—Three or four
10 of the <u>Nouvelles</u>, I think, are the best short stories ever
written—to my knowledge.
 Yours very truly
  H. James jr.
Quincy St.
15 Thursday a.m.

Previous publication: *HJL* 1: 468

  ⇛

356.2 [May 1870–May 1872] • Letter written while both men lived
in Cambridge and presumably after Longfellow first met the Jameses
(12 March 1867, according to his journal), and before Longfellow's death
on 24 March 1882. Evidence from HJ's handwriting makes any date after
the winter of 1873 unlikely. Thus the letter was probably written during
the May 1870–May 1872 period, when both HJ and Longfellow were in
Cambridge. In addition, Longfellow's journal indicates he read Turgenev
during this period: "Lisa" on 5–6 May 1871 and an unidentified "novel"
by "Tourgenief" on 15 January 1872; nowhere else in his journal does he
record reading Turgenev. HJ's "Nouvelles" is probably a reference to Turgenev's *Nouvelles moscovites*, which was published in 1869. Also during this
period, Longfellow and HJ encountered each other at a number of social
and cultural events: Howells's 27 February 1871 dinner for Bret Harte (see
Longfellow's journal for that date and HJ to Lizzie Boott, [24 February
1871]; HJ was a guest at Longfellow's 1 March 1871 dinner for Harte (see
Longfellow journal for that date and HJ to Grace Norton, 13 April [1871]);

HJ and Longfellow "spent a pleasant evening" together in the early winter of 1872 (see HJ to Charles Eliot Norton, 4, 5 February 1872); and both Longfellow and HJ attended Susan Sedgwick Norton's funeral at Shady Hill (see Longfellow journal for 23 March 1872 and HJ to Charles Eliot Norton, 6 May [1872]).

356.10 the <u>Nouvelles</u> • Probably Turgenev's *Nouvelles moscovites* (1869).

GRACE NORTON
20, 22 May 1870
ALS Houghton
bMS Am 1094 (882)

Cambridge May 20<u>th</u> 1870.
My dear Grace—
        Nothing more was needed to make me feel utterly at home—utterly <u>revenu</u> a❖ and awake from my dreams again— than to get your letter of May 2<u>d</u>. Hearty thanks for it! Here I am—here I have been for the last ten days—the last ten years. It's very hot: the window is open before me: opposite thro' the thin trees I see the scarlet walls of the presidents' <u>palazzo</u>. Beyond, the noble grey mass—the lovely outlines, of the library: ๏ above this the soaring <u>campanile of</u> the wooden church on the <u>piazza</u>. In the distance I hear the carpenters hammering at the great edefice in process of erection in the college yard—๏ in sweet accordance the tinkle of the horse-cars. Oh how the May-wind feels like August. But never mind: I am to go into town this p.m. ๏ I shall get a charming breeze in the cars crossing the bridge.—Nay, <u>do</u> excuse me: I should be sorry wilfully to make you homesick. I could find in my heart to dwell considerately only on the drawbacks of Cambridge life, but really I know of none: or at least I have only to look at that light elegant campanile—that simple devout Gothic of the library—or indeed at that dear quaint old fence of wood—of stone (which is it

most?) before the houses opposite—to melt away in ecstasy &
rapture.—My voyage I am happy to say, was as prosperous as if I
had received your good wishes at its beginning instead of its
close. We made it in nine days & a half, without storms or
serious discomforts. I will agree with you in any abuse of the
cabins & state-rooms of the Scotia: but the deck is excellent &
there I chiefly spent my time. I find all things here prosperous,
apparently, & all people decently happy. My own family may be
well reported of. My sister is in strength & activity quite an
altered person & my brother inspires me with confident hopes.
My parents are particularly well. I lately spent an evening in
Kirkland street—where of course I found many questions to
answer; & boasted hugely of all your favors. Miss Theodora is a
most delightful young lady: I say it because I don't believe you
adequately know it. Arthur I have seen several times: we enjoy
very much reminding each other of you. The Gurneys too I
have seen & ₐthe₍ₐ₎ Howells—all very well. Howells is lecturing
very pleasantly on Italian literature. I go to the lecture room in
Boylston hall; & ◊ sit with my eyes closed, listening to the sweet
Italian names & allusions & trying to fancy that the window
behind me opens out into Florence. But Florence is within & not
without. When I'm hopeful of seeing Florence again not ten
years hence—that <u>is</u> Florence!— —All that you tell me is
delightful. I can fancy what a game Florence & m̶ May are
playing between them. Poor May just here has a̶n̶ rather an
irresponsive playmate. But when May is a month older she will
amuse herself alone.—I congratulate you on Charles & Susans
having returned from Rome. When I think that a̶t̶ ₐin₍ₐ₎ this
latter season they have made that journey thro' the very vitals of
Italy. I feel almost as if it were a merry world. Indeed when I
hear that you really think of summering (not simmering) in
Venice, ₹ I pronounce it altogether a mad world—using the term
in no invidious sense. Thrice happy thought! I could say
horrible things—invent the fiercest calumnies, about Siena, to

drive you to Venice. If you write to me not from Venice — I shall — I shall almost delay to answer your letter. Siena would be all very well if you had never thought of Venice — but having done this I don't see how you can escape going there. There are things the immortal gods don't forgive. Beware then. — I wish I were able to tell you where I am going to outlast the genial season — or what, now that I have got America again, I am going to do with it. Like it enormously <u>sans doute</u>: they say there is nothing like beginning with a little aversion. On My only fear is that mine is too mild to end in a grand passion. But America is American; that is incontestable, & consistency is a jewel. I wish I could tell you how characteristic every thing strikes me as being — everything from the vast white distant sky — to the stiff sparse individual blades of grass.

22ᵈ. a.m. I went yesterday to lunch at Hi Shady Hill. Don't think me very cruel when I tell you ⬥⬥⬥ how lovely it was — in the very sweetest mood of the year — the fullness of the foliage just all but complete & the freshness of the verdure all undimmed. The grass was all golden with buttercups — the trees all silver with apple blossoms, the sky a glorious storm of light, the air of a perfect hurricane of zephyrs. We sat (Miss C. Hooper, Miss Boott &c) ⬥⬥t on a verandah a long time immensely enjoying the fun. But oh my dear Grace it was ghostly. For me the breeze was heavy with whispering spirits. Down in that glade to the right three women were wading thro' the long grass & a child picking the buttercups. One of them was you, the others Jane & Susan — the child Eliot. Mesdemoiselles Hooper & Boott talked of Boston, I thought of Florence. I wanted to go down to you in the glade & we should play it was the villa Landor. Susan would enact Miss Landor — But the genius of my beloved country — in the person of Miss Hooper — detained me. I dont know indeed whether I most wanted you to be there or to ₍ₐ₎be₍ₐ₎ be myself in Florence. Or rather I do very well know & I am quite ashamed of my fancy of robbing that delightful scene of its simple American

beauty. I wished you all there for an hour, enjoying your own. —
But my intended note is turning into a very poor letter. One of
these days I shall intend a letter. —I ought to tell you by the way,
that my having taken a turn for the worse in England, was partly
concerned in my return home. I was wise in doing as I did
apparently: for I am already vastly better. At all events, economy
had begun to make my return necessary. I don't feel very much
further from you ⊙ now than I was in England. I may safely
assume—mayn't I?—that you are to be abroad two or three
years yet. Largely within that time we shall meet again. When I
next go to Italy it will be not for months but years. These are
harmless visions, but I utter them only to you. —Wherever you
go this summer remember that I care most about hearing the
whole story. This is not modest, but I maintain it. Live, look,
enjoy, write, a little for me. Tell all your companions how fondly
I esteem them. I implore your mother to exert her maternal
authority in favor of Venice. I perceived no bad smells there: ⅆ
as for mosquitoes I imagine that a private house properly
furnished with curtains needn't in the least fear them. Howells
tells me they never suffered. Whereever you go, however, I shall
be happy in your contentment ⅆ shall believe you blessed with
peace ⅆ prosperity. Farewell. Love to one ⅆ all. Believe me dear
Grace your's most faithfully Henry James jr.

I dont ask about Sara because I have just written to her ⅆ have
hopes of an answer, if she has time before her return.

— — — —

Previous publication: *HJL* 1: 238–41; *SL* 1: 87–90

∾

357.17 a⊙ and • [n *overwrites illegible letter*]
357.25 edefice • [*misspelled*]
357.26-27 May- | wind • May-wind
358.10 confident • confi= | dent

358.11 particularly · partic= | ularly

358.19 ◊ sit · [s *overwrites illegible letter*]

358.22 hopeful · hope= | ful

358.23 — — · — | —

358.24 ~~m~~ May · [M *overwrites* m]

358.25 ~~an~~ rather · [ra *overwrites* an]

358.27 Susans · [s *blotted out*]

359.9 ~~On~~ My · [M *overwrites* On]

359.11 consistency · con= | sistency

359.15 ~~Hi~~ Shady · [Sh *overwrites* Hi]

359.16 ◊◊◊ how · [how *overwrites illegible letters*]

359.20 ~~of~~ a · [a *overwrites* of]

359.22 ◊◊t on · [on *overwrites illegible letters*]

359.26 buttercups · butter= | cups

359.32 ~~be~~ myself · [m *overwrites* be]

360.8 ◊ now · [n *overwrites illegible letter*]

360.12 harmless · harm= | less

360.20 Whereever · [*misspelled*]

360.23 faithfully · faith= | fully

᠀

357.17 <u>revenu</u> · <u>returned</u>.

357.21 presidents' <u>palazzo</u> · Harvard's fifth residence for its president, located at 17 Quincy Street, opposite the James house, had been built in 1860 by E. C. Cabot. It was demolished in 1913 after a new, adjacent residence, also numbered 17 Quincy Street, now called Loeb Hall, was completed in 1911 (see Bunting 320–21).

357.22 the library · Gore Hall, built in 1838–41 by Richard Bond and altered in 1876, 1895, and 1906, housed the Harvard Library until the building was demolished in 1913 to make way for the current Widener Library (Bunting 36).

357.23–24 the soaring <u>campanile of</u> the wooden church on the <u>piazza</u> · Probably the steeple of Cambridge's First Parish Unitarian Church, at the Harvard Square end of Church Street.

357.24–25 the great edefice in process of erection • Memorial Hall, just outside the northern entrance of Harvard Yard, was under construction from 1864 to 1878 and best fits HJ's description of a "great edefice." However, when Charles W. Eliot became president of Harvard in 1869, he embarked on an ambitious plan of building that radically transformed the geography of Harvard's campus. As a result, Thayer Hall was built in 1869, Holyoke House and Weld Hall in 1870, and Matthews Hall in 1871, and HJ could have heard the work on any of these from his parents' house (Bunting 320).

357.25 college yard • The center of Harvard University's extensive campus, bounded today by Massachusetts Avenue, Harvard Square, Broadway, and Cambridge and Quincy Streets.

357.28–29 the cars crossing the bridge • In 1870 two bridges carried trolley lines between Boston and Cambridge: the West Boston Bridge (occupying the location of the Main Street and Longfellow Bridge) and Craigie's Bridge (on or near the site of the Charles River Dam). The West Boston Bridge carried the Main Street (now part of Massachusetts Avenue) trolley while the Craigie's Bridge carried the Cambridge Street one.

358.11–12 spent an evening in Kirkland street • The Ashburner/ Sedgwick house, 71 Kirkland Street.

358.13 Miss Theodora • Theodora Sedgwick.

358.19 Boylston hall • Boylston Hall was built in 1857 by Schultze and Schoen and altered in 1871, 1876, and 1959; it housed the early chemistry laboratory (Bunting 320).

359.8 sans doute • without a doubt.

359.21 Miss C. Hooper • Clover Hooper.

359.21–22 Miss Boott • Lizzie Boott.

LYDIA (LILLA) CABOT [PERRY]
[late May 1870 or 1871]
ALS Special Collections, Colby College, Waterville, Maine

My dear Miss Cabot— 5

I had of course wildly dreamed of keeping, wearing &
cherishing your locket—but I must part from it just as I'm
getting used to it.—In sterner truth I had quite forgotten having
taken it & it was sojourning sweetly in my waistcoat pocket, just 10
over my heart, when your note was handed me. I'm sorry you
should have ₍^₎had₍^₎ the trouble of sending for it—though I can't
altogether regret an accident which has opened a
correspondence between us. Who can tell where it may end? I
dont say <u>when</u>: I hope never—never till I cease to be your most 15
faithful—
    <u>H. James</u> jr.
    I will look up Miss Poke's poem. It was very kind of her not to
have written a <u>Dunciad</u>, <u>à mon addresse</u>.

Previous publication: Horne 6–7

   ℳ

363.10 waistcoat • waist= | coat
363.19 <u>addresse</u> • [*misspelled*]

   ℳ

Lilla Cabot Perry herself wrote on the back of an envelope that is part of
the Colby collection the following:

My first letter from H. James when I was a school girl. I was staying
with Aunt Anna Lowell and was going to Harvard Square to post some
letters after supper in late May—I heard steps running after me and
H. J. asked if he might go with me. After posting the letters I said
goodnight as I had to go to my cousin's for a locket I had left there the
night before. He proposed that I sh'ld let him go with me and go for a

walk afterwards. I got my locket and dropped it when he picked it up and gave it to me. I was a shy girl and feeling embarrassed by his man of the world manner and by knowing he was "an author." I accidentally dropped it again and this time he picked it up and put it in his pocket and said it was the will of Providence he sh'ld always keep it. I had the dignity of my youth and said nothing meaning to ask for it again when he took me home from our walk but we went to the top of a hill to see a view he knew of and he talked so interestingly that we did not get home till 10.30 and I hurried into the house and forgot the locket till the next morning when I wrote him a stiff little note asking him to give my locket to the bearer and finding it very stiff and prudish I added in a P.S. "Did you see Miss Poke's poem in the Cambridge Chronicle this morning called the "Rape of a Locket". This is his reply and I kept it because I knew he was an author! My brother, who was my messenger (he was in College *&* had come to call on me) said "Well Lilla I never knew a man take so long to write a short note"! But never was a note read with such pride! H James seemed so grown up to me! Seldom has any note been kept so long but the author's celebrity has quite justified my youthful sense of its value.

363.2 [late May 1870 or 1871] • We have arrived at the probable date of this letter on the basis of the description Lilla Cabot Perry left of the circumstances in which HJ wrote this letter and through a process of elimination. The letter has to have been written prior to Cabot's marriage to Thomas Sergeant Perry on 9 April 1874. It was almost certainly written after the Jameses moved to 20 Quincy Street, Cambridge, in late 1866; Cabot's "Aunt Anna Lowell" was Anna Cabot Jackson (Mrs. Charles Russell) Lowell (1811–74), wife of James Russell Lowell's older brother, who resided at 24 Quincy Street, the property adjoining the Jameses' (*The Cambridge Directory* 195; *The Cambridge Directory for 1874* 245; Duberman 393 n.6, 396 n.9); the proximity explains how Cabot and HJ ran into each other. If the letter was indeed written in "late May," we rule out 1869, 1872, and 1873 due to HJ's travels in Europe (in 1872 HJ sailed from New York to England on 11 May). We also rule out 1867 and 1868 because none of Cabot's brothers attended Harvard in the spring of those years; her brothers Arthur Tracy Cabot (1852–1912) and James Jackson Cabot (1854–75) attended Harvard, respectively, from fall 1868 to spring 1872 and from fall 1870 to spring 1874 (Briggs 686; Harvard University Archives).

363.5 Miss Cabot · Lydia (Lilla) Cabot (1848–1933) became engaged to Thomas Sergeant Perry in the spring of 1873 (see HJ's 23 June 1873 letter to Perry, congratulating him on the engagement); the couple married in April 1874.

363.18 Miss Poke's poem · There is no poem in the *Cambridge Chronicle* by Miss Poke.

363.19 a <u>Dunciad</u> · An obvious reference to the mock-heroic satire, *The Dunciad* (1728), by Alexander Pope (1688–1744), whose "The Rape of the Lock" appeared in 1712.

363.19 <u>à mon addresse</u> · about me.

GEORGE ABBOT JAMES
6 June [1870]
ALS Houghton   15
bMS Am 1094.1 (139), letter 1

My dear George—

Many thanks for your kind note of welcome, which has gone far to complete my not unwilling sense of being really at home   20 again. I wish you were still within the compass of a journey into town—t~~o~~ though in the actual state of the thermometer the wish is a purely selfish one. Until the moment I left Europe I cherished a vague hope of hearing from you, & I expect you to make up for your silence by ◇◇ an immense communicativeness   25 when we meet. I on my own side will be able I suppose to pump up a slender stream of European gossip which ~~I supp~~ [ʌ]the[ʌ] memory of your own journey is still vivid enough, doubtless to make you not wholly indifferent to. By all means come and see me when you are again in this part of the world. I shall bear in   30 mind your invitation to Nahant & count upon some delightful hours there.—You say nothing about your health: I hope no news is good news. I envy you hugely having all the drives and piazzas and breezes to yourself—in whom I of course include

Mrs. James. Recall me to her indulgent memory. Preserve me in
your own affections, let me hear from you again & believe me
yours most faithfully

Cambridge   H. James jr.

June 6th

No previous publication

∾

365.22 t~~o~~ though • [h *overwrites illegible letter*]

365.25 ◇◇ an • [a *overwrites illegible letters*]

365.27 European • Euro= | -pean

365.29 indifferent • in= | different

∾

365.31 Nahant • An oceanside resort on a peninsula north of Boston.

GEORGE ABBOT JAMES

22 June [1870]

ALS Houghton

bMS Am 1094.1 (139), letter 3

Cambridge June 22^d.

My dear George—

I find your amiable note on my return from Newport & feel
none the less kindly to Nahant for having realled to my jaded
senses the charms of maritime ~~se~~ scenery. You are so good as to
ask me to "name the day" as regards my visit. I wish I could! It
would be not far off. But exactly how I am to dispose of my
summer I have not quite yet determined. There are half-a-dozen
conflicting possibilities which I must reduce to some sort of
harmony. I shall endeavor to make your invitation ~~I~~ a kind of
<u>nucleus</u>, with my various other engagements clustering
deferentially about it. If you will allow me therefore to ◇◇ leave
the date of my advent uncertain for the present, I will endeavor

366

to propose a day at my earliest convenience. Meanwhile I shall think of you most greedily. I am very sorry to hear of your losing your horse. I can't speak from knowledge (for I never owned a quadruped of any sort) but I fancy it a trial to part with a noble steed. No more misfortunes I hope—until I come down 5 on you. Recommend me kindly to your wife & to Mrs. Lodge, if she is at Nahant, & believe me, my dear George

    Yours most faithfully

      H. James jr.

No previous publication

∾

    366.25 realled · [*misspelled*]

    366.26 s̶e̶ scenery · [c *overwrites* e]

    366.33 ◇◇ leave · [ea *overwrites illegible letters*]

JAMES THOMAS FIELDS
15 July [1870]
TLC Houghton 20
bMS Am 1237.16, Box 1 (A–G, Fields)

Cambridge, July 15th.

My dear Mr. Fields— 25

    I leave you the manuscript of a story. I have tried to keep it within the compass of a single no., but it may have exceeded it. Probably it has. If this appears, I have marked a place for division; page 85.—Let me add that I should be grateful for a more or less immediate cheque. 30

    Yours very truly

      H. James Jr.

Previous publication: Horne 39

∾

367.26 the manuscript of a story · The *Atlantic Monthly* would publish "Travelling Companions," 26 (November–December 1870): 600–614, 684–97; and "A Passionate Pilgrim," 27 (March–April 1871): 352–71, 478–99. It is not clear which of these, if either, HJ is sending.

JAMES THOMAS FIELDS
25 July [1870]
10 TLC Houghton
bMS Am 1237.16, Box 1 (A–G, Fields)

Saratoga Springs, July 25th.

15 My dear Mr. Fields.
        I have just received from home your note with the enclosed cheque. I am sorry you had to puzzle out my story yourself—and feel that, under the circumstances, you have treated me very well. Many thanks!
20   Yours very truly
            H. James Jr.
P.S. My devotions, please, to Mrs. Fields.

Previous publication: Horne 39–40
        ∾

368.22 Mrs. Fields · Annie Adams Fields (1834–1915), author famous for her literary salon at the Fieldses' home on Charles Street, Boston; after Fields's death, she became the companion of author Sarah Orne Jewett (1849–1909).

GEORGE ABBOT JAMES
16 September [1870]
ALS Houghton
bMS Am 1094.1 (139), letter 2

5

Cambridge Sept. 16th

Dear George—

I find your letter awaiting me on my return from Newport—
not having been sent me because my return was expected &
deferred from day to day. You have had time almost to forget 10
having written it. Many thanks for it—& many hopes that you
won't think me unfriendly if I say that my much-wished visit
seems hopelessly defeated—as if some diabolical Von Moltke
were in the councils of fate & were heading me off from the
Nahant of my dreams, on every side, with hideous strategy. I 15
return from a long & various summer absence to a long & urgent
& momentous piece of Autumn work, which I should have been
up to my neck in, a fortnight since. I feel as if I should blast my
prospects forever if I were to delay for another hour in buckling
down to this momentous task. Do therefore instead of so fatally 20
multiplying your attractions—do, dear George, for once be
repulsive—send me some impudent & abusive message wh. will
cause me for the time to think of you as one whom I would fain
forget. Trust me to remember again, when the pinch of winter
comes! Then I shall come and offer forgiveness for all your 25
horrible kindness!—infest you, bore you, devour you! Seriously,
I find that work has accumulated "on me" to that degree, during
the summer, that unless you take me & keep me, clothe me &
feed me forever, at your cost, I shall have to spend the coming
weeks in fighting with impending bankruptcy. But I do hope to 30
see you long & often in Beacon St.—In all this your wife & Mrs.
Lodge are immensely sous-entendues. If they could only forbid
me the house—I might come! My devotions to them. & to
yourself dear George my friendliest friendship. Yours ever
H. James jr. 35

No previous publication

∾

369.34-35 friendship. Yours ever <u>H. James</u> jr. • [*written across the letter's last page*]

∾

369.13 some diabolical Von Moltke • Count Helmuth von Moltke (1800–1891), chief of the Prussian military general staff and architect of the German victory over France in the Franco-Prussian War of 1870–71; HJ's reference to Moltke's "heading me off [. . .] with hideous strategy" evokes the Prussian army's encircling of the French at Sedan, which led to the capitulation of Napoleon III on 2 September 1870.

369.16-17 long & urgent & momentous piece of Autumn work • Possibly HJ was beginning *Watch & Ward*, three out of five installments of which he had delivered by 15 November to James T. Fields, editor of the *Atlantic Monthly*; the novel would not begin to appear, however, until August 1871 (see HJ's 15 November [1870] letter to Fields). The only piece HJ published between 16 September 1870 and March 1871 was "Travelling Companions," which appeared in the November and December issues of the *Atlantic*. HJ had been busy during the summer of 1870, for he published two reviews in the *Atlantic*, of Disraeli's *Lothair* and of *Selections from de Musset* (however the attribution to HJ of this unsigned review may not be correct), and four travel pieces in the *Nation*: "Saratoga," "Lake George," "From Lake George to Burlington," and "Newport."

369.32 <u>sous-entendues</u> • <u>included, of course, it goes without saying.</u>

JAMES THOMAS FIELDS
24 September [1870]
TLC Houghton
bMS Am 1237.16, Box 1 (A–G, Fields)

5

Cambridge Sept. 24th.

My dear Mr. Fields:
      The Atlantic was so good, a couple of months ago, as to
accept the m.s. of a story from my pen. May I take the liberty of   10
suggesting through you, that Messers. [T]. and F. should send
me a cheque in payment at their earliest convenience, instead of
awaiting the publication of the story?—I should be much
obliged to you for your intercession.—
    Yours very truly   15
      Henry James Jr.

Previous publication: *HJL* 1: 241–42

    371.11 Messers. [T]. and F. • *[copy text reads* F. and F. *The context and*
the recipient of this letter as well as of HJ's 29 September [1870] letter to Fields
indicate that HJ is referring to Ticknor and Fields. The error was likely the
transcriber's, not HJ's.]

    371.2 24 September [1870] • Year based on Fields's retirement from
publishing and from the *Atlantic Monthly* by 1871 (see Gollin 189, Roman
89) and on "Travelling Companions" being the story HJ published in the
Atlantic Monthly in 1870–71 that best fits the time line implied in this letter.
    371.9–10 to accept the m.s. of a story • Probably "Travelling Com-
panions," which the *Atlantic Monthly* would publish in its November and
December 1870 issues.

GRACE NORTON
26 September [1870]
ALS Houghton
bMS Am 1094 (883)

5

Cambridge Sept 26<u>th</u>
My dear Grace—
    I have before me two letters: your long & most delectable
one of last June & eighteen pages of an answer written to it a few
10 weeks later at Saratoga. Nay, I have three—Jane's being ᴴ the
third, received just after I had written the pages above
mentioned. Why I never finished these pages I am quite unable
to say—nor exactly why I am ~~unable~~ ^unwilling[ᴧ] to send them
now. In truth, they are pervaded by an unutterable staleness. I
15 speak of them because I want you to know that I haven't been
quite so silent as you think. It is many many weeks since I got
your letter; but not too long ago yet for me to recall, my dear
Grace, the deep delightful pleasure it gave me. I have vaguely
felt, I think, that to such an utterance neither my nature nor my
20 circumstances could furnish an adequate or pertinent answer.
You put me in possession, thus, at the beginning of the summer,
of a picture, which thro' much of its fierce discomfort & barren
<u>ennui</u>, remained suspended in the line of my bitterly yearning
vision, to cool my fever & illuminate my mind. Now that I have
25 really & vitally <u>used</u> your letter. I can formally reply to it. I
wrote to you from Saratoga where I spent a month, taking the
waters, but somehow I felt that S̲aratoga had no vocation to
commune with Sienna, & I left my letter unfinished. While I was
in this state of mind came Jane's benignant missive—all the
30 perfumes of whose Araby couldn't make me feel near to you.
But now I am back in Cambridge—our dear detestable common
Cambridge & I have seen Sara arrive from the Villa Spanochi &
Theodora depart unto it—& have grown able a little to believe
that I may pitch my voice to ~~an~~ your Italianized ear.—Yes I have

seen Sara & I have bidden God=speed to her sister. I spent with
Sara a week ago a goodly private afternoon, discoursing of the
priceless possessions of memory. She seems to me as well &
prosperous as you would like to have her, and kindly disposed to
the mysteries of re-initiation here. May they be gentle to her—   5
even as they have been to me!—She brought with her a number
of Siennese photos., which I have literally <u>devoured</u>. My brother
says that to him, for several days, they have been as meat &
drink. Be thus assured that your pictures, verbal & other, have
been duly appreciated. By this time your summer is over, I   10
suppose, but Sienna must continue to please—the more,
doubtless that you can be more in the open air. With your five
or six months in that rare old city you will have had a rich
experience—how rich Shady Hill one of these days will tell
you.—But you had rather I talked of home at first hand than of   15
Siena at second. Of distinctly home-news there is little to tell
you; we are all living in these days on your side of the Atlantic.
The war is wonderfully present to us, thanks to the abundance &
~~immediacit~~ immediacy of our telegrams. And then, in heart &
mind, during these later days, we have been living in Italy as well 20
as France. Heaven reward the Italians, amid this hideous tumult
of carnage, for their silent & bloodless revolution. Its other
merits—whatever they are—seem just now as nothing beside the
consoling fact of its peacefulness. You have felt at Siena, I of
course, a ripple of that portentous wave. If I imagine rightly,   25
you apprehend as yet nothing more. The fortune of the French
Republic, it seems to me, has not as yet been so brilliant as to
offer a very enticing example to latent Republicanism elsewhere.
I rather doubt of its duration in France. But my very moderate
intelligence of current events is wholly merged into the single   30
strenuous desire that slaughter should cease. It seems to me not
over=fastidious ∧now[∧] to demand it. But who is to demand?
You have been feeling, I suppose, very much as we (<u>we</u>, I mean
of this immediate family)—feeling, that is, strongly with the

Germans. The war up to this time, has to my perception effected such a prodigious unmasking of French depravity & folly that it has been in a measure blessed & sanctified, in spite of its horrors, by this ittuminating & disillusioning force. All the

5 French utterances I read, seem to me, almost unexceptionally, those of barbarians & madmen. As yet it has brought out little but the virtues of Germany. If it is further prolonged, however, though I don't apprehend, that French character & intelligence will rise in the scale, that of Germany may decline. You know

10 the Italians better than I do & can p̶ better establish the proportions of their virtues and vices; but for myself, I take a private sentimental satisfaction in the simple fact that while France & Germany, those great pretentious lands, were fiercely cutting each other's throats, the lovely country of my heart was

15 Italianizing Rome with barely a gunshot. As regards the occupation I have chiefly been busy thanking my stars that f̶o̶ they ɴ̶ have ∧not[∧] denied me a glimpse of Rome Roman & Papal. One reflection slightly consoles me against this heart=thrust at the picturesque: viz: that Rome being of its

20 nature a city of relics & memories, perhaps it ∧may[∧] gain (<u>almost</u>!) as much as it will lose by this reduplication within its walls of the pure melancholy memorial reminiscential element! Another reflection I have also ventured upon: to the purpose that the departure of the capital from Florence may ~~make~~

25 ∧reconvert[∧] it in some degree ∧into[∧] the Florence of old & arrest the rank modernization wh. we used to deplore. But I stand aghast at these crude ratiocinations on a Cambridge basis: — especially as on coming to consult a couple of newspapers, I find that there <u>was</u> a goodly amount of shelling &

30 shooting on the occupation of Rome. I have followed your fortunes of late as much in detail as I have been able to; — having heard with particular sympathy of your mother's illness & of her convalescence. Do not fail to assure her of my most affectionate remembrance. I don't know that there is anything of weight to

tell you either regarding Cambridge or myself. We are still up to
our necks in obstinate, implacable fine weather—a monotony of
blue skies which has lasted for upwards of four months. During
the summer our <u>beau</u> <u>temps</u> took the shape of the most hideous
& infernal ~~fu~~ heat—heat which enlarged one's conception of the
range & reach of nature. But of this you must have heard. I spent
the summer agreeably enough _∧in spite of_[∧] having been a
month at Saratoga. Even there however, I cunningly noted many
of the idiosyncrasies of American civilization. I was a week at
Lake George—a fortnight with my family at Pomfret—the
lovely—the <u>quasi</u>-Italian!— ~~& ~~& a fortnight at Newport, where
nature was perhaps more attractive & man rather less so, than
ever. I was recently down at Beverley, where I saw, among other
folk, the serene & conjugal Gurneys. All <u>ce~ monde-là</u> seems
invested with a steady prosperous immobility. I have seen no
strangers of importance. I spent lately a couple of days with
Mr. Emerson at Concord—pleasantly, but with slender profit.
J. R. Lowell I haven't seen since my return. Howells I frequently
see & find prosperous and fairly contented. He has just come
into possession of a new domicile, opposite Richard H. Dana's
former one. He is to deliver a dozen of Lowell lectures this
winter on Italian poetry. Arthur Sedgwick I often see: ◇ our
principal theme of discussion is a plan of going abroad together
in the spring of 1873—from which you may infer that our
domestic & contemporary interests are not thrilling. <u>Que faire</u> ⊖
<u>en un gîte à moins que l'on ne songe</u>? My own household is not
prolific of news. My brother's health has small fluctuations of
better & worse, but maintains steadily a rather lowly level. My
parents and sister are fairly well. Publicly, the time is so
interesting that I think we none of us feel that life is void of
meaning or promise. (The cast of that sentence is desperately
cynical but not its spirit.) I take so much satisfaction in reading
the papers that I largely manage to forget that I am doing no
work of consequence & that the time when I shall be able to do it

seems indefinitely postponed. What I best succeed in doing is
looking flagrantly well & wantonly idle. If others could see us as
we see ourselves!—My year in Europe is fading more & more
into the incredible past. The continuity of life & routine &
5   sensation has long since so effectually re-established itself here,
that I feel my European gains sinking gradually out of sight and
sound & American experience closing <u>bunchily</u> together over
them, as flesh over a bullet—the simile is àpropos! But I have
only to probe a little to hear the golden ring of that precious
10 projectile. I am thoroughly content to have returned just when I
did—it was a wise act. When I go abroad again it will be on a
better basis. I enjoy America with a poignancy that perpetually
surprises me; & have become "reconciled" to it so many times
since the first tribulations of my return that by this time, I ought
15 to a formidable rival to the most popular fourth of July
lecturers. I will not deny however that I am constantly beset by
the vision of my return to Europe. A large part of this desire I
set down as morbid; for I am very sure that I should be very
much less subject to it, if I were engaged here in some regular &
20 absorbing work. It is the simple feeling that idleness in Europe is
so much ◇◇se more graceful & profitable than here.—The rest of
it, however, stands firm as a definite and religious intention. I
think time has fairly tested the quality of my Italian sympathies,
I feel that they have not been ~~founding~~ wanting. The wish—the
25 absolute sense of need—to see Italy & especially Florence
again—increases in force every week that I live. I dream,
therefore, of going forth before the chill of age has completely
settled upon me, & spending a long series of months in that
world of my choice. Since my next stay in Europe however, (if
30 nothing disturbs my plans) will be a long one, I shall undertake
it without precipitancy & give my purpose ample time to mature
& accumulate beneath this Western sky. Meanwhile I shall see all
I can of America & <u>rub it in</u>, with unfaltering zeal. I know that if
I ever go abroad for a long residence, I shall at best be haunted &

racked, whenever I hear an American sound, by the fantasy of thankless ignorance and neglect of my native land — & I wish in self defense to make up a little list of accomplished devotions & emotions, which may somewhat abbreviate that sentimental purgatory. — I decline to entertain the idea of your coming home in two years. If you should however, I fear my ˄own₍˄₎ departure would be still further shoved along into the future; for I should, with affectionate e̶o̶ economy, insist on drawing you dry of <u>your</u> Europe before I began the process of direct absorption. — There! dear Grace: I think I have treated you to a very pretty piece of egotism. Let me once more become objective. But I cast about in vain for objects. We are smashing & hammering with great fury in our lower domiciliary regions, with a view to removing the kitchen from beneath my bedroom, as I am beginning to be a little overdone. — Do you know Henry Adams? — son of C. F. A. He has just been appointed t̶u̶t̶o̶r̶ ₍˄₎professor₍˄₎ of History in College; & is I believe a youth of genius & enthusiasm — or at least of talent and energy. If you were interested in collegiate matters & I knew any thing about them, I fancy that I might a tale unfold which would excite you to a lofty pitch. I believe the University is just now very lively; but I am unititiated. The P̶r̶o̶f̶f̶e̶s̶s̶ Professorship of History was (I believe it's no secret) offered to G̶u̶r̶n̶e̶y̶ ˄Godkin₍˄₎, who declined. I am glad to have him stick to the <u>Nation</u>: which, by the way, has been (as you will have observed) excellent in its treatment of the war. — I should like to hear f̶r̶o̶m̶ ˄what₍˄₎ you think & what Charles thinks of the present political temper of Italy & what is to follow this last move. You must observe much. I suppose much will depend on the stability of the Republic in France. If it should fall, it will probably, be a great positive gain to monarchy elsewhere. Poor dispapalized — disaetheticized Rome! I can't get over it. But I selfishly exult in having had a glance at the old regimen. — I learn from Sara that you are probably to return to Florence for the winter & to go in the spring to Venice. A very neat arrangement!—Of your present life & mise en scène, dear Grace, your picture was as vivid as it was ~~masterle~~ masterly. ~~But~~ What an admirable spot must be that great concave ~~palazzo~~ [∧]piazza[∧], with the Palazzo Publico! The

5 tower of the latter, seems to me finer than any I saw in Italy. I noted with sympathy Jane's account of Mr. Ruskin's visit. It must be rather a spectacle to have Ruskin in juxtaposition with his subjects.—I want vastly to hear from Charles; but of course he is not to believe this till he receives a direct demand for a

10 letter. I will not do Jane the injustice to add anything herein to the mention of her received letter. Occasion shall yet wait upon her. I feel as if it were half impertinent to send my sentiments to Susan; such a richly sentient envoy is even now on the way to her. But ask her to remember me a little till her sister comes. I

15 have asked you no questions about yourself. I have only set you an example of the most effusive confidence. Show me it's not lost upon you; write me that you are well & happy. Repeat to your mother my most favoring wishes & offer them also to Charles. Greet the children all round—& Jane—all round too.

20 Answer my letter but not my silence & believe me dear Grace— yours most faithfully

H. James jr.

Previous publication: *HJL* 1: 242–48

∞

372.10 ~~f~~ the • [t *overwrites* r]

372.34 ~~an~~ your • [yo *overwrites* an]

372.34 Italianized • Italian= | =ized

373.19 ~~immediacit~~ immediacy • [c *overwrites* cit]

373.24 ~~I~~ of • [f *overwrites* I]

373.28 Republicanism • Repub= | licanism

373.34 immediate • imme= | diate

374.3 sanctified • [t *inserted*]

374.4 ittuminating • [*misspelled*]

374.10 ~~p~~ better • [b *overwrites struck through* p]

374.12 sentimental • senti= | mental

374.16–17 ~~f◊~~ they • [th *overwrites struck through* f◊]

374.17 ~~n~~ have • [h *overwrites* n]

374.26 modernization • moderniza= | tion

375.5 ~~fu~~ heat • [he *overwrites struck through* fu]

375.11 — ~~—~~& • [& *overwrites* —; — *inserted to the left of the* &]

375.14 ce~~-~~ monde-là • [*hyphen blotted out*]

375.22 ~~◊~~ our • [ou *overwrites illegible letter*]

375.25 domestic • domes= | tic

375.25–26 ~~o~~ en • [e *overwrites* o]

376.13 surprises • sur= | prises

376.21 ~~◊◊so~~ more • [mo *overwrites* ◊◊so]

376.24 found~~ing~~ • [ing *blotted and struck through*]

376.27 completely • com= | pletely

377.8 ~~e◊~~ economy • [c *overwrites illegible letter*]

377.15 overdone • over= | =done

377.16 appointed • ap= | pointed

377.22 unititiated • [*misspelled*]

377.22 ~~Proffess~~ Professorship • [e *overwrites blotted* f; ss *overwrites* ess]

377.23 ~~Gurney~~ ^Godkin[^] • [urney *struck through and* odkin *written above*]

377.27 political • po= | litical

377.31 disaetheticized • dis= | =aetheticized; [*misspelled*]

378.3 ~~masterle~~ masterly • [l *overwrites* le]

378.3 ~~But~~ What • [Wha *overwrites* But]

378.12 sentiments • senti= | ments

372.32 Sara • Sara Sedgwick.

372.32 Villa Spanochi • Villa Spannocchi, the Nortons' residence in Siena.

372.33 Theodora • Theodora Sedgwick.

373.18 The war • The Franco-Prussian War.

373.22 their silent & bloodless revolution • Italy united when French troops withdrew from Rome after the fall of Napoleon III, 20 September 1870.

374.24 the departure of the capital from Florence • Florence was the capital city of Italy from 1865 to 1870.

375.4 beau temps • beautiful weather.

375.10 Lake George • Located in New York's Adirondack Mountains.

375.13 Beverley • Beverly, Massachusetts, coastal town twenty miles north of Boston; many of HJ's acquaintances summered and vacationed there.

375.14 ce⁄ monde-là • all those people.

375.17 Mr. Emerson at Concord • Ralph Waldo Emerson, whom the Jameses knew, lived in Concord, Massachusetts.

375.18 Lowell • James Russell Lowell.

375.18–20 Howells [. . .] new domicile • Howells's new residence was no. 3 Berkeley Street, Cambridge.

375.20 Richard H. Dana • Richard Henry Dana Jr. (1815–82), American writer and lawyer, had lived at no. 2 Berkeley Street, Cambridge.

375.25–26 Que faire [. . .] songe? • What can one do in one's lodging other than dream?

377.15–16 Henry Adams • Henry Adams (1838–1918), American author, historian, and man of letters. HJ first met Adams in 1870, shortly before his appointment to Harvard College as assistant professor of history. Adams's wife, Marian "Clover" Hooper, a close friend of HJ's during his Cambridge days, fostered their early friendship. Adams frequently traveled abroad, visiting HJ regularly. His works include *The Life of Albert Gallatin* (1879), *History of the United States During the Administrations of Jefferson and Madison* (1889–91), and *The Education of Henry Adams* (1907).

377.16 C. F. A. • Charles Francis Adams (1807–86), father of Henry Adams, and son of John Quincy Adams.

378.2 mise en scène • Theatrical term referring to the play's overall staging, but here referring to the arrangement of Grace Norton's life.

378.4–5 great concave [. . .] tower of the latter • The Palazzo Publico in Siena, built between 1250 and 1315. The tower on the building is the Torre del Mangia.

JAMES THOMAS FIELDS
29 September [1870]
TLC Houghton
bMS Am 1237.16, Box 1 (A–G, Fields)

5

Cambridge. September 29th.

My dear Mr. Fields.
Many thanks for your "intervention", the result of which
was in a high degree satisfactory.   10
Faithfully yours
H. James Jr.   J. T. Fields esq.

No previous publication

∾

381.2 29 September [1870] · Year based on the assumption that this
letter follows HJ's 24 September [1870] letter to Fields.

381.9 your "intervention" · Probably Fields had seen to it that HJ was
sent the check he had requested in his letter of 24 September [1870].

JAMES THOMAS FIELDS
15 November [1870]
TLC Houghton
bMS Am 1237.16, Box 1 (A–G, Fields)

25

Cambridge. Nov. 15th.

I told Howells this morning, on his mention of your proposal
to defer for a couple of months the publication of my story, that   30
my own preference was for immediate publication—and this he
said he would communicate to you. I find, however, on reflection
that if it suits you better to delay it, I shall be well pleased to
have it lie over. My wish to have it appear in the January number

was prompted by the desire to "realize" upon it without delay. If, as it is, you can enable me to do so, I shall not regret your keeping back the work—to do so, of course I mean, on the three parts already in your hands. The two others then will have been joined with them before publication begins—which probably will turn out to be a relief to my own mind. There is only one drawback: if you wish to take cognition of the tale, you lose the comfort of doing so in the proof: the m.s. I can reccomend to no man's tolerance. Perhaps you will content yourself with my assurance that the story is one of the greatest works of "this or any age."

Yours very truly, H. James Jr.

P.S. I should like Mrs. Fields to know that I last night heard our friend [N]illson. What a pity she is not the heroine of a tale, and I didn't make her!

Previous publication: Horne 40–41; *HJL* 1: 248–49

∾

382.4 hands. The • [*TLC shows* hands, .The; *comma probably transcriber's error.*]

382.8 reccomend • [*Misspelled. It is not possible to determine whether the misspelling is HJ's or the transcriber's.*]

382.11–12 age." Yours • [*TLC gives* age." / Yours, *because use of such a slash was not HJ's habit, the handwritten slash is possibly the transcriber's correction of his own transcription or an effort to save space at the end of the page.*]

382.14 [N]illson • [*TLC reads* Millson. *HJ here probably refers to Christine Nilsson. The spelling of her name with an initial M is unlikely to be HJ's error. It is not possible to determine whether the other errors in the spelling of the singer's name are HJ's or the transcriber's.*]

∾

381.29 Howells • William Dean Howells was then the subeditor of the <u>Atlantic Monthly</u> (he would become editor in chief in July 1871).

381.30 my story • Probably either *Watch and Ward*, HJ's first novel, which the *Atlantic Monthly* published from August thru December, 1871, or "A Passionate Pilgrim," published from March thru April, 1871.

382.13–14 I last night heard our friend [N]illson • Celebrated Swedish singer Christina Nilsson (1843–1921) toured the United States in 1870–71 with a star-studded company that included Belgian virtuoso violinist Henri Vieuxtemps (1820–81). Nilsson gave a concert at Boston's Music Hall on 14 November 1870 (see "Entertainments," *Boston Post* 14 November 1870: 3).

1871

CHARLES ELIOT NORTON
16 January 1871
ALS Houghton
bMS Am 1088 (3854)

5

Cambridge Jan. 16. 71
My dear Charles—
    If I had needed any reminder ᵭ quickener of a very
old=time intention to take some morning ᵭ put into most
ineffective words my very frequent thoughts of you, I should   10
have found one very much to the purpose, in a most lovely letter
from Grace, received some ten days ago: for which pray thank
her, both as from a devoted friend ᵭ from an emulous
fellow=artist in literature. But really, I needed no deeper
consciousness of my great desire to punch a hole in the massive   15
silence which has grown up between us. There have been
moments indeed when I f have felt not ill at ease in this roomy
interval of speech, because of a firm conviction that it was, after
all, but the hollow in a larger wave꜀ of gathering utterance ᵭ re-
attested sympathies. But I have felt more than this that the long   20
run in human affairs is not so very long as that one may be
careless of tolerable occasion—such as this cold hard
long=deferred rainy morning seems to furnish—when the near
common world being forbidden to our feet, we sit and make
fireside pictures of the far=off worlds of memory and desire.—It   25
is something more than a year to day, I think, since I bade you
farewell at Florence at the outset of that reluctant northern ᵭ
western pilgrimage. Then commenced for us a great
divergence—or for me, rather; for I hold that you, in your
subsequent Italian days ᵭ scenes, have but adhered to the normal   30
medium of the man of supreme sense. The recurrence of the
precise season of my last stay ⋄ in Florence p̶ brings all the time
ᵭ place back to me with irresistible vividness. It was but a few
days ago that I sate on that little knee=high parapet of your

Bellosguardo gazing=place and saw beneath me the ample
hollow of the mountain circle filled with Florence & beauty,—
like an alms=giving hand with gold. The day before I stood on
the terrace of San Miniato & saw the landscape steaming with
5 irridescent vapors—as if on every hillside I had kindled a fire of
sacrificial thanks for Italy. But you will be amused at receiving
instructions in Florentine landscape from Cambridge! Of what
you have done & how you have done it, all this while, I have a
deeper sense than I can expound just the method of my getting.
10 I was one of you, all last summer at Siena. The cunning of Jane's
& Grace's pens ~~wer~~ was assuredly for much in my metaphysical
presence there; but let me claim credit, too, for a willing mind!
If you had listened hard, you might have heard in the noonday
stillness of your August hours the panting flutter of its hovering
15 wings.—But in that noonday stillness, I take it, you were
listening to the echos of French battle=fields. What a cloud of
battle smoke there is between us! And how I wish I were on your
side of it, to guess with you & hope with you at all the chances
and changes it conceals. Grace hinted in her letter most vividly
20 at the way you felt the overwhelming presence of the war, so that
it seemed to form a background sombre enough to absorb the
cares and trials of your mother's illness & her own. I confess I
am light=minded enough to feel how, in a way, this very
gloominess may have deepened (to the distant observer at least)
25 the romantic color of your situation—made it seem more
mediaeval & intensely Italian. To live in a Sienese palace, with
the sense of a sombre & perturbed world outside, with the
monotonous echo, in the air, of battle=sounds & death=blows &
public suffering—must have given you a glimpse of a really
30 antique state of mind. A glimpse however was probably more
than enough. To talk of the war seriously requires one to take up
a great many threads. I have a strong impression that the history
of your sympathies has been very much that of our own. Every
day, at least, confirms my impression that the upshot of the

matter will have been to leave the French completely &
deservedly beaten, with a large range of possibilities of
recuperation & self=redemption; & the Germans thoroughly &
deservedly victorious, with a considerable share of actual & a
vast amount of possible, demoralization & disorder. But the
Germans will have grown a vastly bigger people through it all &
the bigger body & bigger life must of necessity bring with it
them more chances for evil as well as for good. If you still have
any plan of spending some months in Germany you will perhaps
find it a different Germany from the one you used to talk of
with such moderate enthusiasm—a less local & provincial one &
therefore the less picturesque; but on the whole a milder dose of
◇◇ pure Teutonism.—Italian affairs, I suppose, give you plenty
to reflect & moralize upon.—there being little more morality in
them than what one supplies. As regards the occupation of
Rome, I confess, my most definite feeling has been one of
gratitude that my own particular occupation preceded it. What
Rome loses in its dreadful old aesthetic interest by the
extinction of its temporal sanctity, I think Italy gains in the same
line by the completion of her ideal unity. There is a
picturesqueness in that, too. But perhaps I don't sufficiently
allow for your having got tired of picturesqueness. Call it by
some other name then—there are names which more fairly
express it! But dont deny that it's a primordial passion of the
human, or at any rate, of the American heart. We should, each
of us, be ill occupied just now, in so horribly blaspheming;
inasmuch as the keenest of my recent pleasures has been in
looking over, with my brother W$^{\underline{m}}$. (& with the most reverent
care) several port=folios of photos. & prints, the fruits of your
previous journey to Italy, which Arthur Sedgwick has very
kindly lent us. Let your wit, who collected them, & ours who
now enjoy them, attest the dignity of Italianism in the aspect of
things—& in the sympathies of mankind! I don't know when you
last looked at the portfolios in question; but the photos. (among

the earliest taken I suppose) have the most lovely old=time
mellowness & softness. The technique is better now but the
effect harsh in proportion. We have spent over them the most
deeply agreeable hours. — Of what more I see & do & enjoy there
are no great things to tell. Cambridge & Boston society still
rejoices in that imposing fixedness of outline which is ever so
inspiring to contemplate. In Cambridge I see Arthur S. &
Howells; but little of any one else. Arthur seems not perhaps an
enthusiastic, but a well=occupied, man & talks much in a
wholesome way of meaning to go abroad. Howells edits, and
observes & produces — the latter ~~will~~ ∧in∧ his own particular
line with more & more perfection. His recent sketches in the
<u>Atlantic</u>, collected into a volume, belong I think, by the
wondrous cunning of their manner, to very good literature. He
seems to have resolved himself, however, in one who can write
solely of what his fleshly eyes have seen; & for this reason I
wishe~~d~~ he were "located" where they would rest upon richer and
fairer things than this immediate landscape. Looking about for
myself, I conclude that the face of nature & ~~cili~~ civilization in
this out country is to a certain point a very sufficient literary
field. But it will yield its secrets only to a really <u>grasping</u>
imagination. This I think Howells lacks. (Of course <u>I</u> don't!) To
write well & worthily ~~of well~~ of American things one needs even
more than elsewhere to be a <u>master</u>. But unfortunately one is

less! — You have heard, I suppose, how Henry Adams has taken
the N. A. R. & feel a grandfatherly interest in the matter. Your
grandson promises extremely well. The <u>Nation</u> throughout the
war has been excellent & has written of matters in a far
better=instructed way than any of our papers. But it has been
good to notice that having to deal with the war has been to some
of them, (the <u>Tribune</u> e.g.) a rather useful education. They have
had to pitch their tone to a certain gravity & this has reacted on
their general manner. When I say that Bayard Taylor has
published a very good (I believe) translation in verse of Faust &

that Lowell is to re=publish ~~his~~ more of his delectable essays
(with, I believe, a title no more to your taste than his last—~~I~~ title
that babbles of J. T. Fields) I shall have mentioned the only
serious literary facts of our hemisphere. I myself have been
scribbling some little tales, which in the course of time, you will
have a chance to read. To write a series of good little tales I
deem ample work for a lifetime. I dream that my lifetime shall
have done it. It's at least a relief to have arranged one's
lifetime!—All this time, my dear Charles, my soul is full of
impatient questions & protesting desires as to your own work,
your own humor, health, occupations, opinions & prospects.
What are you making out of Italy & Italy out of you? Do you
find yourself able to do any manner of work? Even with the
minimum of regular occupation you must have learned many
things, absorbed innumerable impressions & assimilated much
Italian matter. These things can be but narrowly expressed in a
letter; but I look hopefully forward to the day when, by the
library fire at Shady Hill, you may utter them in gentle streams
of discourse. The actual state of public affairs is of such
commanding interest that I can imagine it in a measure to dwarf
the attraction of remoter times & questions; but on the other
hand it is so largely fraught with the tragical & the insoluble that
one may readily turn for relief to the contemplation of issues
from which we catch no side=wind of responsibility. Do you
continue to hear from any of your English friends? There is an
immensity of stupid feeling & brutal writing prevalent here
about recent English conduct & attitude (innocuous to some
extent I think from its very stupidity) but I confess there are
now, to my mind, few things of a more appealing interest than
the various problems with which England finds herself
confronted: & this owing to the fact that, on the whole, the
country is so e deeply—so ~~heavily~~ ₍ₐ₎tragically₍ₐ₎—charged with a
consciousness of her responsibilities, dangers & duties. She
presents in this respect a wondrous contrast to ourselves. We,

retarding our healthy progress by all the gross weight of our massive contempt of the refined idea; England striving vainly to compel her lumbering carcass by the straining wings of conscience & desire. Of course I speak of the better spirits there
5   & the worse here. But the former are just now uppermost in my mind through my just having read in the <u>Fortnightly</u> for December last two articles by your two friends F Harrison & J. Morley, on Bismark & Byron respectively. They are red=radical & intemperate, each; but they have a great tone:
10   & I can't despair of ◆◆ the situation of a country in which that tone is so positively represented. Morley's article (if youv'e not read it) is really remarkable. It's a view of Byron from the <u>quasi</u>=~~political~~=political standpoint and reveals in the writer (more, decidedly, than his previous things) a broad critical
15   genius & a most admirable style. We have over here the high natural light of chance and space & prosperity; but at moments ∧dark∧ things seem to be almost more blessed by the dimmer radiance shed by impassioned thought. (This is a pretty tribute to Jno. Morley; but of course arrant nonsense.)—But I must stay
20   my gossiping hand. Methinks I could inflict upon you a world of questions & of fond assurances. Do kindly imagine my curiosity & affection. Does Florence wear well? Oh vulgar demand ⸮ ! I see you coming down ~~from~~ ∧along∧ that winding channel, between garden walls, from Bellosguardo & stopping on
25   midbridge to look once more at the Arno, & passing at the base of those mosaic mountain=walls of the Duomo. Grace gave me so vivid a sketch of your household <u>mise</u> <u>en</u> <u>scène</u> that I almost feel as if I had yesterday been dining with you. Do you still go to the galleries & churches? Do you see any Florentines?—This
30   letter of mine such as it is, is none the less addressed equally to Susan because I have not specifically invoked her gracious presence. The interests of life must be so deepening & multiplying for her in the growth of her children that it seems hardly worth while to wish her any great ~~realizaia~~ realization of

the interests of Italy in particular: but I have no doubt she finds
means to combine them ℸ conjure a great united contentment
out of ~~each↓~~ ₍∧₎both.₍∧₎ The last definite fact with regard to your
mother of which we have heard ℏ was her gradual recovery from
her summer's illness but she is altogether a very definite fact ~~and~~
₍∧₎to me,₍∧₎ ℸ I beg you, by that token, to define to her the very
affectionate nature of my sentiments. I wish her all strength ℸ
repose. — I have been wondering whether I could in any way
match the stoicism of Grace's brief allusion to her own illness by
some stern intimation of assent to her recovery. But tho' one
may be stoical on one's own behalf, one can't, successfully, on
that of the friends of one's heart: ℸ I therefore confess to a
weak=minded — ℸ in fact <u>maudlin</u>, satisfaction in ₍∧₎her₍∧₎ great
tribulation having slowly melted away — I trust forever. I wrote
some time since to Jane; as Grace⊘ mentions the receipt of my
letter↓⌀, I regard a bountiful response as one of the bright
certainties of the future. — While I am in this lonesome mood I
wonder if I may venture to lay my heart at the feet of Miss
Theodora? She will at least not trample on it. Silvia Watson is, I
believe, still in Florence. Pray recall me in spite ₍∧₎of₍∧₎ time ℸ
space to her cheerful remembrance. I have not said half I wanted
to: but there chiefly remains to say I want vastly to hear from
you. Heaven speed the day. Your's ever — <u>H. James</u> jr.

5

10

15

20

Previous publication: Lubbock 1: 30–31; *HJL* 1: 249–55

∞

387.10 ineffective • ineffec= | tive

387.15 consciousness • conscious= | ness

387.17 f have • [h *overwrites blotted* f]

387.19–20 re- | attested • re-attested

387.32 ⊘ in • [i *overwrites illegible letter*]

387.32 ᵽ brings • [b *overwrites blotted* p]

388.2 mountain • moun= | tain

388.5 irridescent • [*misspelled*]

388.5 hillside • hill= | side

388.11 ~~wer~~ was • [a *overwrites* er]

388.13 noonday • noon= | day

388.25 romantic • roman= | =tic

389.1 completely • com= | pletely

389.7–8 ~~it~~ them • [th *overwrites* it]

389.13 ◇◇ pure • [pu *overwrites illegible letters*]

389.15 occupation • occupa= | tion

390.9 enthusiastic • enthusias= | tic

390.11 particular • partic= | ular

390.13 collected • collec= | ted

390.19 ~~cili~~ civilization • [v *overwrites* li]

391.1 ~~his~~ more • [m *overwrites* his]

391.24 responsibility • respon= | sibility

391.32 ~~c~~ deeply • [d *overwrites* c]

392.10 ◇◇ the • [th *overwrites illegible letters*]

392.13 quasi=+political=political • quasi= | +political | =political

392.22 ~~?~~! • [! *overwrites* ?]

392.25 midbridge • mid= | bridge

392.34 ~~realizaia~~ realization • [e *overwrites illegible letter; second* a *over-*
writes ia]

393.4 ~~h~~ was • [w *overwrites* h]

393.5 altogether • alto= | gether

393.16 letter⸝~~ʒ~~, • [, *overwrites* ,ʒ]

393.22–23 but there chiefly [. . .] H. James jr. • [*written across the letter's*
first page]

❧

388.1 Bellosguardo • Hilltop village on the south side of Florence, to
which HJ would return frequently in later years (after Francis and Lizzie
Boott would take up permanent residence there), at Villa Castellani (now
known as Villa Mercede). He would also rent part of the Villa Brichieri-
Colombi, in December 1886 and the spring of 1887, while Constance
Fenimore Woolson inhabited neighboring apartments (Gordon 208–9, 212,
217–19). After spending the summer and fall of 1870 in Siena, the Nortons

resided at Villa d'Ombrellino at Bellosguardo until they left Florence for Venice in April 1871 (Turner 240, 243).

388.4 San Miniato · Church of San Miniato al Monte, built in phases from 1018 to 1207, located on top of the Monte alle Croci, on the south side of the Arno River. Probably the most famous view of Florence is from in front of San Miniato.

388.16 French battle=fields · The Franco-Prussian War began in August 1870.

388.26 a Sienese palace · Villa Spannocchi.

389.30 previous journey to Italy · Charles Eliot Norton, with his mother and two sisters, Grace and Jane Norton, traveled throughout Europe from October 1855 to August 1857.

390.12–13 sketches in the Atlantic, collected into a volume · William Dean Howells's *Suburban Sketches* (1871).

390.25–26 Henry Adams has taken the N. A. R. · Henry Adams assumed editorship of the *North American Review* from 1870 to 1876.

390.33 Bayard Taylor · Bayard Taylor (1825–78), Pennsylvania-born writer, diplomat, and professor of German at Cornell University.

390.34 translation in verse of Faust · Two volumes, published in Boston by Fields, Osgood (1870–71), in original meters.

391.1 Lowell is to re=publish his more of his delectable essays · James Russell Lowell's *My Study Windows* (1871).

391.2 his last · Lowell's *Among My Books* (1870).

392.7–8 F Harrison & J. Morley, on Bismark & Byron · Frederic Harrison's "Bismarckism" and John Morley's "Byron," *Fortnightly Review* 8 (1 December 1870): 631–49 and 650–73, respectively.

392.26 the Duomo · The Cathedral or Il Duomo of Florence, designed by Arnolfo di Cambio at the end of the thirteenth century.

392.27 mise en scène · setting.

393.18–19 Miss Theodora · Theodora Sedgwick.

ELIZABETH BOOTT
[24 February 1871]
ALS Houghton
bMS Am 1094 (500)

My dear Miss Lizzie—

A destiny at once cruel & kind forbids my acceptance of your amiable proposition for Monday evening. I am engaged to meet the Bret Hartes at Mrs. Howells's. An opportunity to encounter these marvellous creatures is, I suppose, not lightly to be thrown aside. On the other hands I shall pine for the marvellous creatures assembled in your <u>atelier</u> & <u>salon</u>. But such is life!— Such as it is, however, I pray it may last till we meet again.— Primed with your compliment, & your father's, about the P. P., I shall really quite hold up my head to the author of the Heathen Chinee. With cordial regards to your father & many regrets—

Your's most faithfully
<u>H. James jr.</u>
Cambridge
<u>Friday</u>

Previous publication: *HJL* 1: 255

∾

396.19 Cambridge · [*inserted*]
396.20 <u>Friday</u> · [*inserted*]

∾

396.2 [24 February 1871]; Monday; Friday · The date of this letter depends on the Hartes' arrival in Boston on Saturday, 25 February 1871. They attended a dinner party hosted by the Howellses on Monday the 27th at which HJ was also a guest (Howells, *Letters of Elinor Mead Howells* 142).

396.9 Bret Hartes · Bret Harte (1836–1902), American teacher, journalist, editor, and local-color fiction writer who gained notoriety with his western writings.

396.9 Mrs. Howells's · Elinor Gertrude Mead Howells (1837–1910).

396.12 atelier • studio.

396.14 the P. P. • HJ's story "A Passionate Pilgrim," published in the *Atlantic Monthly* 27 (March–April 1871): 352–71, 478–99; Elizabeth and Francis Boott, apparently, had just read the first installment, in the March issue, which would have come out in February.

396.15–16 the author of the Heathen Chinee • Bret Harte's popular comic ballad, "Plain Language from Truthful James," pirated in pamphlet editions as "The Heathen Chinee."

GRACE NORTON
13 April [1871]
ALS Houghton
bMS Am 1094 (885, 882)

Cambridge April 13<u>th</u>

Though I have not formally notified you, dear Grace, of the receipt of your last letter, you will have learned thro' my communication to Charles of its having been welcomed & cherished. Yesterday came to Alice from Theodora a letter telling of your having started for Venice with your mother & Jane & this tidings thrusts the pen into my hand. By this time you will have gained all needful relief & rest, I trust, in the fluid repose of gondolas—the perfection of inaction & ~~repose~~ [∧]peace.[∧] I hope with all my heart to hear that your mother has borne her journey fairly well & has been able in some degree to taste of the quality of Venetian enjoyments. She has had my frequent memory in her recent illness; pray assure her of this, with my most affectionate wishes for her amendment. You too, dear Grace, have been no stranger to my thoughts; but a very honored guest in them; so that, really (understand me aright) it is with a certain effort I remind~~ed~~ myself that you have a strictly objective & fleshly existence out of them, several thousand miles away, at a convenient distance for the receipt of letters. Of

Charles's ⅋ Susan's journey ⅋ of Theodora's share in it I heard with keen satisfaction. The ~~memory~~ ^sense~[∧]~ of its pleasures must have been, I can readily imagine, for the time, deeply merged in the anxiety ⅋ trouble which brought it to a sudden
5   close: but with brighter hours, I hope to hear, it has begun to glow with its native colors. I congratulate Susan heartily upon having had a glimpse of Naples. It was little more than a glimpse that I had; yet I value it now beyond utterance. To have been to Naples is to have been (within the limits of regular civilization)
10 to the point furthest removed from Cambridge. When you wrote me (not long after your return to Florence) your were apparently not in the best spirits ⅋ in circumstances (especially as regards weather) not conducive to great <u>allegrezza</u>. To say that I hope your spirits rose is to say more than I exactly mean:
15 for I deem that a certain depression of mind is no more than a proper tribute to the nature of things ⅋ where melancholy is <u>à propos</u>, 'tis folly to be cheerful: but I hope at least that your weather mended ⅋ that Fair Florence didn't carry coquetry to quite so grim a point as to ~~mak~~ set the price of her sunshine at a
20 whole winter's darkness. I hope too that your own strength ⅋ health have been steadily coming back to you: for you see if I am content to have you the least bit grave in spirit, I wish ^it~[∧]~ to be for none but remote ⅋ abstract causes. I got from your letter ⅋ from Jane's a very goodly sense of your Florentine interior ⅋
25 domestic <u>mise en scène</u>. The broad image of the thing I think I have: I must wait ~~too~~ for the long talks of the future for that rich filling in of detail which my fond intelligence demands.—But you have done with Florence ⅋ doubtless, just now, you don't care to be burdened with the past. The present, for you, means
30 Venice—⅋ Venice means—if any earthly sensation can mean it—the timeless ⅋ boundless infinite of beauty ⅋ charm. If only I might put myself into some sort of <u>rapport</u> with you. I have conceived the bold design (I am very glad of ~~an~~ a chance to reveal it) of procuring from Shady Hill, thro' Arthur, Charles's

copy of Ruskin's <u>Stones</u>: & in this gentle early spring of ours (no joke!) sitting by ∧my[∧] open ~~air~~ window & steeping my vision ~~with~~ ∧in[∧] ◊ that gorgeous prose, & resting it fitfully—& ah longingly & dreamingly, on the deepening green of President Eliot's front yard. (Let me assure Charles that his volumes shall be handled with all the tenderness involved in my regard for all ∧things & persons[∧] concerned. So again shall I shift along beneath palace windows on a gurgling keel & linger forever on that pavement of the Scuola of San Rocco!—But really, I'm at my old tricks again: as if you cared to look at Venice by refraction from Cambridge.—Look at Cambridge then! Honestly, just now, it is very good to look at. . Everything is more or less touched with the spring & shining with a genuine April light. The ground rejoices in a glorious carpet of good simple tough American grass and the trees are beginning to make a good thick tangle of twiggery against the blazing blue of the sky. This same blue is as usual the inimitable feature. Venice may do as well but I doubt whether Venice can do better than just this azure abyss of heaven which meets my eyes as I ~~regret~~ [∧]write:[∧] so deep & fierce & yet so cool and clear! I have been walking a great deal of late, of afternoons, countrywards; with a great pleasure in the prettiness of many of our roads & lanes hereabouts. In a hundred places there are some charming bits of the picturesque—the Yankee picturesque of course I mean— which I devour as I go; but the more I go the larger grows my appetite, & my sense aches at times for richer fare. When I go to Europe again, it will be I think, from inanition of the eyes. I have been having a quiet, low=toned sort of winter: reading somewhat, ◊ writing a little & "going out" occasionally. In the latter pursuit I have encountered no very novel or noticeable forms of humanity. My dissipations have been in Boston chiefly: Cambridge society is a little ~~aril~~ arid. I have gone wherever I have been bidden, but biddings are infrequent. Meanwhile the college is expanding & multiplying its elements: Cambridge

ought to have a <u>monde</u> of its own. I hope by the time you come
back there may be some interchange of amenities: or rather
when you come back I shan't care what otherwise happens. Of
persons known to you & yours I have encountered few. I dined
5 not long since at Mr. Longfellow's, to celebrate Mr. Bret Harte,
the imported California poet—a clever writer & pleasant man,
but with a monstrous newspaper=made reputation which
vulgarizes him in spite of himself. A little while hence when
something else has crowded him out of the newspapers he will
10 do himself justice: tho' ℏ it remains to be seen whether he is the
bard of California or of things in general. Our friend J. T.
Fields, esq. & lady have been having Friday evening receptions
for a couple of months: struggling bravely against a certain
thinness of tissue ◊ in the received & succeeding prettily enough.
15 Howells I generally see every week: his cares as husband & father
& editor weigh rather heavily on him: but his charming genius
holds its own. He has been writing a series of articles descriptive
of a western tour he made last summer—which have greater
finish & beauty than any thing he ever wrote. But there is to me
20 a somewhat pathetic discordance in his talent—the need of
applying really first class handling to subjects belonging to
<u>la petite</u> <u>littérature</u>. The more I think of it, the more I ~~tend to~~
deprecate the growing tendency—born of the very desperation
of the writer—to transfer directly and bodily, without any
25 intellectual transmutation, ◊◊◊◊ all the crude accidents of his life
as they successively befall, into the subject matter of literature.
Before we are fairly launched here, we are being swamped by the
dire vulgarity of it.—Just now all Boston is supposed to be
absorbed in the French Fair, which is raging away (rather
30 languidly, I'm afraid) at the Boston Theatre. I have been there
once—but after the sage remarks just above I'm afraid I oughtn't
even to attempt to make it the theme of a paragraph in a
letter.—There is a certain not altogether unnatural feeling
abroad, I think, that we are after all trying to ~~hep~~ help the

French against their will—that they prefer to be foolish &
miserable & that they are welcome to it. I confess that the
history of the French people for the past many weeks is
something ~~for~~ from which I as one <u>qui</u> <u>les a</u> <u>beaucoup aimés</u> am
fain to avert my face. I havent the heart to talk of them. The
Revue des 2 Mondes has begun to come to us again. I find in ◊
2 recent numbers a journal by Geo. Sand kept during the war. I
may in saying so do little more than betray my own want of
imagination & inability to change at need my point of view: but
this same journal contains passages about the Germans of a
foolishness so abject & incredible, that you blush for the poor
human mind as you read it & weep ~~at~~ to see a noble intellect so
basely self=dishonored. These & many cognate utterances on
the part of the wise heads of France offer matter, I think, for
solemn cogitation. Dont they prove, in a way, how essentially
our mind is the product of events & on how long & unbroken a
line culture has to be pursued, to prevent in certain situations
from lapsing into its native puerility? Every one hereabouts just
now is talking about Darwin's <u>Descent of Man</u>—many of ◊◊
course with great horror of his fundamental proposition: but
here is poor old France, doing its very best apparently to
convince a reluctant world that we have only to be scratched a
bit in certain places to reveal a very fair intimation of the
missing link? But its useless talking or guessing or sorrowing
about France. She's a grim object enough. She holds her fate in
her own hands & no one can help her or advise her but herself—
she who feels—poor creature!—her bosom torn and shaken with
all the raging elements of the problem. All one can say is <u>poor</u>
<u>poor</u> <u>France</u>! & yet there is a kind of resignation in ones pity: the
healthy sentiment of satisfaction that we <u>must</u> feel in seeing
folly & vanity & iniquity attended by a smothering, stifling,
trampling succession of mortifications, defeats & penances.
What Germany has done, in a broad way, has simply been to
give France over to herself: that self apparently is so weak so

vicious, so unveracious (as Carlyle would say) that she receives the great gift & charge into a yawning bloody gulf of disorder — a vainer vanity than ever! The Germans have done more than they deem — haven't they? — and builded better than they knew.

5 They have enforced certain homely truths as never in all history they can have been enforced, & the silent economy of one's ◊ moral life draws vigor from their example. Live for the shows & names and glory of things & not for ~~this~~ their bitter, nutritive essential forces and values — and you'll have the trampling

10 Germans of the universe let loose upon you. — But you must feel dear Grace as if you had at least a regiment of trampling Teutons let loose upon <u>you</u>. I have written by this time all you will care to read and more possibly than you will care to agree with. In my secret heart I do nothing but ~~but~~ weep for the

15 French; but when I come to talk aloud, even to myself, I find that propriety heals my tears. They have suffered unutterably, but they have sinned unutterably. As for the Germans, you may be very sure I don't care a straw for them! — And how are my dearly beloved Italians, all this time? — would that I could gaze

20 upon a few dozen or so! — Theodora mentions in her letter neither how long you are to be in Venice nor where you are to go afterward. If only the angel of charity may have guided your fingers ~~into~~ ∧toward∧ a little Venetian note to me! But you, Grace, are yourself the angel of charity and no lesser seraph can

25 have ventured to give you any advice: if you didn't write it's because I really don't deserve it. ~~B◊~~ But I notify you that I mean to deserve great things in future. I have never, I think, really told you as plainly as I might, that writing has from its mere <u>modus</u> <u>operandi</u> always been for me an effort and that this and

30 not baser motives have caused ◊ those prolonged flashes of silence which, on my side, have so plentifully adorned our correspondence. But now I feel as if the tax was somewhat lightened. I feel better & I shall write more. For this once, I close. Charles, I believe, received my letter of some weeks ago. If

he doesn't feel as if I had fairly earned an answer I will write
again. "I ain't proud." Give him my love ∂ my benediction on
his exit from Italy; against whom ◇ my only complaint is that she
hasn't treated more kindly a man who has done so much for her.
I hope Charles will find that much of his invalidism has been
Italy's fault ∂ not his own. <u>Bien des</u> <u>choses</u> to Susan. She will
perhaps be interested to hear that I go this evening to Kirkland
St, to a festival in honor of her kinswoman Mrs. Butler of N. Y:
with whom I shall talk all the evening about <u>her</u>. My dear
Grace—when once I fairly write to you, I wonder I ever do
anything else: unless it be, by way of a change to write to Jane.
Thank her for her letter—or rather tell her that I mean soon to
thank her solidly, myself.—But I <u>must</u> close. Farewell.
Commend me warmly to the children, if their memories haven't
outgrown me.—Do write to me, Grace, as soon ∂ as copiously
as your virtue ∂ my vices allow. I have thought of a dozen things
still unsaid; but I keep them for the answer to your letter.—
Heaven bless you all! Yours ever ∂ devotedly—<u>Henry James</u> jr.
P.S. You will be interested to h◇◇◇ hear that within the past ~~few~~
[∧]couple[∧] of months my brother W<u>m.</u> is in markedly better
health. He is, I think, ~~well~~ nearly out of the woods.—I wish I
could persuade him or enable him to go abroad for 6 mos! I
think 'twould help him.—Doubtless however he is wise to
wait—∂ perhaps fortunate in being unable ∂ unwilling to risk
anything.—My father ∂ mother are well ∂ my sister more or less
so.—I may on their behalf, as one familiar with their moral
sentiments, assure you of their fond ∂ constant remembrance.—
They are just arranging to go for the Summer to a suburb of
Portland, Me: a ravishing spot, I believe!
P.S. I am in season (at writing) to give you cordial <u>birthday</u>
wishes!

No previous publication

397.14 (885, 882) · [*final page of ms. incorrectly filed with bMS Am 1094 (882)*]

397.32 remind~~ed~~ · [ed *blotted out*]

398.19 ~~mak~~ set · [set *overwrites* mak]

398.26 t~~◇◇~~ for · [for *overwrites* t◇◇]

398.33 ~~an~~ a · [a *overwrites* an]

399.2 ~~air~~ window · [w *overwrites* air]

399.3 ◇ that · [t *overwrites illegible letter*]

399.21 countrywards · country= | wards

399.29 ◇ writing · [w *overwrites illegible letter*]

399.32 ~~aril~~ arid · [d *overwrites blotted* l]

400.2 interchange · inter= | change

400.10 ~~h~~ it · [it *overwrites* h]

400.14 ◇ in · [in *overwrites illegible letter*]

400.25 ◇◇◇◇ all · [all *overwrites illegible letters*]

400.26 successively · successive= | ly

400.34 ~~hep~~ help · [l *overwrites blotted* p]

401.4 ~~for~~ from · [ro *overwrites* or]

401.6–7 ◇ 2 · [2 *overwrites illegible letter*]

401.12 ~~at~~ to · [to *overwrites* at]

401.17 certain · cer= | tain

401.19–20 ◇◇◇ course · [ou *overwrites illegible letter*]

401.22 reluctant · reluc= | tant

401.30 sentiment · sen= | timent

402.6–7 ◇ moral · [m *overwrites illegible letter*]

402.8 ~~this~~ their · [ei *overwrites* is]

402.26 ~~B◇~~ But · [u *overwrites illegible letter*]

402.30 ◇ those · [th *overwrites illegible letter*]

403.3 ◇ my · [m *overwrites illegible letter*]

403.11 anything · any= | thing

403.19 ~~h◇◇◇~~ hear · [ea *overwrites illegible letters*]

403.21 ~~well~~ nearly · [nea *overwrites* well]

403.24 fortunate · for= | tunate

403.30–31 P.S. [. . .] wishes! · [*written across the top of the letter's first page*]

∾

397.19 communication to Charles • HJ to Charles Eliot Norton, 16 January 1871.

397.20 Theodora • Theodora Sedgwick.

398.13 allegrezza • lightness.

398.25 mise en scène • Literally, stage setting, here the Nortons' domestic setting.

399.1 Ruskin's Stones • *The Stones of Venice*.

400.1 monde • Literally, world, but in this context, high society.

400.4–5 I dined not long since at Mr. Longfellow's • According to Longfellow's journal for 1 March 1871, William Dean Howells, James Russell Lowell, and "Harry" James were among the guests at the dinner for Harte (66).

400.17–18 series of articles [. . .] western tour • William Dean Howells's *Their Wedding Journey* was serialized in the *Atlantic Monthly*, July to December 1871, before its 1872 book publication.

400.22 la petite littérature • minor literature.

400.29 the French Fair • The week-long event, held at the Boston Theatre, began 11 April 1871.

401.2–5 I confess [. . .] avert my face • HJ refers to the March–May 1871 battle between the Paris Commune and the Army of Versailles.

401.4 qui les a beaucoup aimés • who liked them very much.

401.6–7 I find in ⊕ 2 recent numbers a journal by Geo. Sand kept during the war • George Sand's "Journal d'un voyageur pendant la guerre," which appeared in three consecutive issues of the *Revue des Deux Mondes*: 1 March 1871: 5–39; 15 March 1871: 209–55; and 1 April 1871: 417–45.

403.6 Bien des choses • All the best.

403.8 Mrs. Butler of N. Y • Most likely Susan Ridley Sedgwick Butler (1828–83), wife of Charles E. Butler (1818–97) of New York.

403.28–29 suburb of Portland, Me • Sr., MWJ, and AJ spent the summer of 1871 at Scarborough Beach, Maine, five miles south of Portland. See HJ to Grace Norton, 16 July 1871.

GRACE NORTON
16 July 1871
ALS Houghton
bMS Am 1094 (886)

5

    Cambridge July 16th 71.
Dear Grace—This rsponse to your last lovely letter and missive
from Venice can hardly be called speedy: it is not so speedy by
half as I dreamed of its being, in that glowing hour when I
10 received them. But my thoughts have been winged, tho' my
hand has not ᴓ they have fluttered about you in all gratitude.
Your letter was a master=piece ᴓ divinely redolent of Venetian
things. I must believe that beside the great pleasure it brought to
me, the very writing of it must have brought much to yourself, ᴓ
15 your ~~Veni~~ Venetian satisfactions have profited largely by your
projecting them so vividly from your mind. At all events, the
letter is here—re-read, prized, preserved. The photo. was
admirably to the point—when I look i at it, I feel again that
liquid swing of the gondola ᴓ ~~feel~~ that cooling shadow of those
20 melancholy walls. But now these things are, for you, as well as
for me, memories ᴓ musings ᴓ melancholies altogether. And
what now are ₐyour₍ₐ₎ realities? I have been looking up
Innsprück in various works at the Athenaeum, so that I may at
least spend a few summer hours with you in spirit. They all
25 agree upon its great picturesqueness—I hope it's not too
picturesque for comfort. You are sure to have had an admirable
journey getting there: I hope your mother endured it fairly well,
ᴓ as far as possible enjoyed it. The Tyrol! I have great notions of
the Tyrol. From they standpoint of mid=July in Cambridge
30 they acquire peculiar vividness. Of all this, dear Grace, as well as
the thousand and one other reserved plums of discussion, we
will confabulate, in that teeming future. Have you ever a
superstitious sense of having to give some <u>quid</u> <u>pro</u> <u>quo</u> for your
particular pleasures? If so, know hereby that the penalty is

fixed—infinite narration & endless retrospection in the library at
Shady Hill, of winter nights, to a fond but inexorable listener!—
My chronic eastward hankerings & hungerings have been very
much quickened of late by the perusal of a little book by our
friend ~~Lest~~ Leslie Stephen ◊ called the <u>Playground</u> of Europe.   5
He has possibly sent it to Charles & you may have read it. It is
much charminger than I should have fancied him likely to make
it—and ~~my~~ fond memory & fonder hope lending a hand—it was
altogether charming to me. I want hugely to know how your are
lodged and "located". I don't deserve to, I know; but neither   10
Jane nor you have ever treated me according to my deserts, & I
take it you are not going to begin at this time of day. A summer
of summers to you—with long days too short to hold their
peaceful hours. From Charles, just before getting your letter, I
recd. a most interesting account of some of his Venetian   15
impressions. Pray tell him with my love, that he shall receive the
answer he deserves. His letter came to me as a real benefit and
aroused a swarm of the most substantial memories. I hope he ~~is~~
continues well enough to observe and reflect to as good purpose
as when he wrote. But thank him in especial, until I do so   20
directly, for his generous estimate of my <u>Passionate Pilgrim</u>. I
wrote it, in truth, for him & his more than for anyone, & I'm
glad to find it going so straight to its address.—And while you
are about it, dear Grace, just take yourself by the two hands and
shake yourself handsomely, with the ardor of appreciated   25
genius. My writing may be good but your reading is quite a
match for it. If you could only be ~~intimately~~ infinitely multiplied
into my public!—At all events, I shall write in future for you—
as much better and better, as I can—and the "public" may take
what suits it.—I am ~~alone in~~ ‸dwelling‸ here, in midsummer   30
solitude, with my brother Wilky; my family being established at
Scarboro' Beach, ~~m~~ Coast of Maine; whence, good folk! they
write in gentle raptures of all things. It is evidently a charming
place & they are very well off to be there. Later in the season I

shall take a look at them. They are hearty and revelling in the
sea=breezes and bathing—on which line my brother is
especially engaged in working out his salvation. With them are
Mr. Boott & his daughter who on Aug. 1ˢᵗ—detestably happy
5   creatures!— —return for an indefinite period to Italy.—This is
a warm still Sunday morning; as I sit scribbling in this empty
house the scratching of my pen seems the only sound in Nature.
Wilky, with a friend who is staying with him—has gone round
to breakfast with Arthur—ₐof with₍ₐ₎ whom, as he too is
10   forsaken of his family, we frequently commingle solitude. It's a
clear warm equal summer, as far as we've got, & Cambridge
comes in for a fair share of the good and bad. For myself, I make
a very pleasant life of it. I lounge in a darkened room all the
forenoon, reading lightish books in my shirt=sleeves; the
15   afternoons I spend abroad; the evenings, generally gossiping
with Arthur on the piazza. I have of late taken to frequenting
these Waltham and Arlington hills & I fancy I like them very
nearly as well as Jane—of on whom, as I lie deliciously stretched
on their bosky slopes, I chiefly meditate. They remind me, tell
20   her, of Italy only in so far as they remind me of her. They are
utterly uninfested, full of sylvan seclusion and sweet shady
breezy coverts which look down on the great blue plain of
Boston and its bluer cope of ocean. I lie there, often, on the
grass, with a book in my pockets, thinking hungry eastward
25   thoughts: but thinking too that we have very goods things
nearer home—witness these untrodden hills and woods—so
utterly unhaunted that I can people them with what shapes I
will—with their vast outlook into purple distances and nameless
inland horizons fretted by superb undulations—which all simply
30   mean honest Massachusetts.—This is a little private fact of my
own. The main public fact just now is not nearly as pretty—
being nothing less than the murderous Irish riot in about which,
I suppose, you'll see in the Nation all you'll care to see. For a
few hours it was really quite Parisian. The belief seems to be,

however, that the thing will have punctured a leak in the Irish
dispensation there. For the present, very little politics seem to
be talked.—You will now gradually be creeping into the
Germanic zone of feeling—I shall be curious to hear your
impressions of it. You are booked, I take it, for Germany next
winter; you will 'ere long begin to smoke with German culture
& I shall have to "consult" upon your letters as ◇ my brother W͞m
does on those of his correspondent Frau Grimm.—I am drifting
to a close, dear Grace—with the sense, as usual of leaving unsaid
what I most want to say. Much of what I have in mind belongs
perhaps to the unutterable; but I should like to get you to do it
some sort of justice.—I wish very much to ~~gett~~ get fairly into
relation with you in your new medium and atmosphere. Bear
this in mind and whenever you are afflicted with an excess of
impressions, remember whitherward to work them off.—◇ Not
hearing otherwise, I assume your mother's condition to be for
the present, comfortable. I know, of course, how at best, it must
color your days & thoughts. Pray let her know, with my most
affectionatel sympathy, how distinctly present it is to mine.—I
hope the children are well again and their poor little coughing
throats at rest. How they must be growing while I write. Don't
let them grow out ∧of[∧] all memory of me; for when they grow
older (Lily especially) I propose to claim privileges dating from
infancy. And to ensure this, commend me most devotedly to my
friend their mother. Tell Susan I would give a deal to know what
she has to say in these days; but of course she has plenty of
people to say it to, without minding me. But I love her still the
same. Tell Miss Theodora◇ that I lament my sister's absence
chiefly because of a haunting fear that she is about now getting a
letter from her which I shan't hear.—I have on my pen's end a
special message to Jane—but it's too long for this sheet & this
hour—I shall give it very soon a letter to itself. Farewell. I send
you herewith a little story—not meant for folks as fresh from
Italy as you—the fruit of a vague desire to ~~reproduced~~

5

10

15

20

25

30

409

reproduce a remembered impression & mood of mind. The lady
herself is a gross fib. At the time, I wanted something to happen;
I have improved on vulgar experience by supposing that
something <u>did</u>. It is not much you'll see, & such as it is, not

5   perhaps an improvement. Yours ever, dear G.—H. J. jr.

Previous publication: *HJL* 1: 256–59

∾

406.7   rsponse • [*misspelled*]

406.15 ~~Veni~~ Venetian • [e *overwrites* i]

406.18 ~~i~~ at • [a *overwrites* i]

406.25 picturesqueness • picturesque= | ness

406.29 the~~y~~ • [y *blotted out*]

407.5   ~~Lest~~ Leslie • [l *overwrites blotted and struck through* t]

407.5   ◇ called • [c *overwrites illegible letter*]

407.5   <u>Playground</u> • <u>Play</u>= | <u>ground</u>

407.9   you~~r~~ • [r *blotted out*]

407.18–19 ~~is~~ continues • [co *overwrites* is]

407.27 ~~intimately~~ infinitely • [finitely *overwrites* timately]

407.30 ~~alone in~~ ∧dwelling[∧] here • [h *overwrites* in]

407.32 ~~m~~ Coast • [C *overwrites* m]

408.5   — — • — | —

408.9   ~~of~~ with • [h *overwrites* of]

408.18 ~~of~~ on • [n *overwrites* f]

408.18 whom, • [m, *inserted*]

408.25 good~~s~~ • [s *blotted out*]

409.7   ◇ my • [m *overwrites illegible letter*]

409.11 unutterable • unutter= | able

409.12 ~~gett~~ get • [t *overwrites* tt]

409.15 ◇ Not • [N *overwrites illegible letter*]

409.19 affectionate~~l~~ • [l *blotted out*]

409.28 Theodora◇ • [*illegible letter blotted out*]

409.34–410.1 ~~reproduced~~ reproduce • [e *overwrites* e *and blotted* d]

∾

407.5 Leslie Stephen ⬦ called the <u>Playground</u> <u>of Europe</u> • Stephen's *The Playground of Europe* (1871), a collection of Alpine articles.

408.17 Waltham and Arlington hills • Waltham and Arlington are hilly towns immediately west of Cambridge, Massachusetts.

408.32 the murderous Irish riot • The Orange riots occurred on 12 July 1871, between pro-British, Protestant, and Irish Orangemen and Irish Catholics in the Hell's Kitchen neighborhood of New York City. A U.S. militia regiment responded to the clash by firing indiscriminately into the crowd, resulting in fifty deaths and over one hundred injuries.

409.8 Frau Grimm • Gisela von Armin Grimm (1827–89), wife of German critic and author Herman Friedrich Grimm; WJ visited the Grimms in 1867 on the strength of a letter of introduction from Ralph Waldo Emerson (see *CWJ* 4: 241, 253, 265, 609).

409.33 a little story • "At Isella" was published in the *Galaxy* 12 (August 1871): 241–55.

WILLIAM CONANT CHURCH or FRANCIS PHARCELLUS CHURCH
21 July [1871]
AL NYPL, William Conant Church Papers   20

Cambridge July 21<u>st</u>
My dear Mr. Church—
Many thanks for your cheque; it reached me this morning.
May I express the hope that you will be able to print <u>Master</u>   25
<u>Eustace</u> in the <u>large</u> <u>type</u>—undivided page—of the magazine?
As the text is very little broken up by paragraphs ⅋ talk, there
will be little waste of space in so doing⁊ .

No previous publication
∾

[*The ms. consists of one side of one half sheet. Since it is not signed, we are not able to determine whether the letter is complete.*]

411.28 ⁊ . • [*upper part of* ⁊ *struck through*]

∾

411.24 your cheque • Payment for the *Galaxy* publication of "At Isella,"
12 (August 1871): 241–55.

411.25–26 <u>Master</u> <u>Eustace</u> • Published in the *Galaxy* 12 (November
1871): 595–612.

CHARLES ELIOT NORTON
9 August 1871
10 ALS Houghton
bMS Am 1088 (3855)

    Cambridge Aug. 9th 71.
Dear Charles—Your delightful Carpaccios came to me a couple
15 of days ◇◇ since—just in time to catch the letter I was
meditating. Hearty thanks for them. They bring back all my
surprised enjoyment of the painter, two years ago. He is
certainly one of the best of the best—& I would quite prefer
(with you, I fancy) to have painted those admirable postulants
20 before the king than all the Andrea del Sartos & hoc genus omne
in Florence—well as I love it. So real and yet so graceful—so
simple and yet so deep—it does one good to look at him. It ~~was~~
ₐis₍ₐ₎ I think, from the painters of his stamp—the early fellows,
who wrought into their work their own hard aesthetic
25 experience & not that of others, transmitted & diluted—that one
learns most. These photos. give the hand to your excellent letter
of now two months since. It was no small pleasure to me, I
assure you, to catch ~~y~~ the afterglow of your impression of our
friend Tintoret. It's a portentous thought that you should have a
30 couple of his things & that Shady Hill—& I—shall yet behold
them. To all you said of him I breathed a fervent Amen. ~~The~~ My
own memory of him remains singularly distinct & vivid & I ~~find~~
feel as ₐif₍ₐ₎ the emotions wrought by his pictures had worked
themselves into the permanent substance of ~~of~~ my mind, more

412

than I can feel ~~of~~ it of any other painter—or of any works of art perhaps, save those good people at San Lorenzo.—May you know this good fact in later years! The only trouble is to express ~~the~~ at all adequately the breadth and depth of the ~~f~~ sensation he provokes. Even Ruskin, I think, has failed to do it. He appeals to such nameless feelings & faculties & seems as it were, to reveal to one one's own imagination.—Your letter had a melancholy note which afflicted me—tho' I wouldnt have a letter from Venice too cheerful. I know what you mean by it all—the change, the lapse, the decay, the hard fare measured out to the beautiful. ◇ It does indeed seem as if a certain sense that ◇◇◇ once flourished and was mighty had now passed out of the world & that, herein, what civilization ∧had[∧] ◇ grasped with one hand she ∧had[∧] let drop with the other. But oh, for some such high view of facts as would suggest that tho' eclipsed this sense, this need, were not lost; that they are masquerading awhile in strange garments, but that some day we shall see them stand forth with unforgotten faces. Narrow optimism, however, is as bad as narrow pessimism, and if the love of beauty as the renaissance possessed it, is dead, let us sing a splendid requiem. Let us build for it a mighty tomb— as grand as those in Verona. Let us take ages to carve it & adorn it & finish it & inscribe it & then let us perform a daily service around it forevermore. By that time perhaps, We shall all have become so good, that beauty as such, will ~~have become~~ ∧be altogether[∧] de trop & we shall be wrapped about in virtue as in so much Titianesque brocade. Then we shall have the satisfaction of at least having kept up the tradition. But I'm scribbling this sweet prattle as if you were still where the shadow of St. Mark's lies blue on the white piazza. You are now, I take it, ~~wors◇~~ worshipping beauty, as the Germans understand it, in goodly Innsprück, whither I have got news of your at least partial removal. With this too I hear of your mother's amended condition—in which I feel with you warmly. This must ∧be[∧] an interesting moment for you—the passage into a new society &

atmosphere. I should like vastly to know how it all strikes you. Some day perhaps you'll drop me a hint. Remember there is but one Italy ~~& the~~ don't be too hard on poor Germany. I suppose there is a Germanic charm as well as—say an American! When
5 you have found it out—you see I don't hurry you—let me ~~here~~ hear.—Your'e sure at all events to have been seeing brave things <u>en route</u>—my notion of all that journey is of a perfect revel of picturesqueness: Am I not right? But when I remember how pitiless in spirit I was to poor old France (with the shadow of
10 coming misery even then upon her) when I passed out of Italy, I can't exact much mercy for Germany.—I talk of these things (as if you hadn't settled them all among yourselves) because Cambridge at Midsummer is not prolific in themes. ◊ Did you ever try it? I am summering here alone in this empty house, and
15 in a quiet way ~~rest◊◊~~ ∧quite[∧] enjoying it. Every now & then I vaguely scheme to take up my valise & walk; but the days one by one are melting away, ~~& I~~ the crickets are filling the nights and the rare yellow leaves beginning to syllable the autumn: yet here I am still, taking it all out in reading the time=tables in the
20 <u>Advertiser</u> & ◊ wondering which were the deeper joy—Cape Cod or Mount Mansfield. I have taken a good many near=◊home rambles ∧however,[∧] & made great discoveries in prettiness roundabout Cambridge. Every one apparently is away but Arthur, F. J. Child & Miss G. Ashburner. We sit a good deal
25 evenings on the Kirkland Street piazzas and await the cool midnight with warm weather talk. Howells too is here (tho' soon to go for ~~to~~ a month to Canada with his wife & young ones) & him I generally see on Sunday afternoons. I don't know that there is anything ~~now~~ ∧"rich[∧] and strange" to tell about
30 anyone. Howells is now monarch absolute of the ~~Advertiser~~ [∧]Atlantic,[∧] to the increase of his profit and comfort. His talent grows constantly in fineness, but hardly, I think, in ◊◊◊ range of application. I remember your saying some time ago that in a couple of years when he had read Ste. Beuve &c, he

would come to his best. But the trouble is he never will read Ste.
Beuve, nor care to. He has little intellectual curiosity; so here he
stands with his admirable organ of style, like a poor man ◊◊
holding a diamond & wondering ~~when~~ ₍ₐ₎how₍ₐ₎ he can wear it.
It's s rather sad, I think, to see Americans of the younger sort so   5
unconscious and unambitious of the commission to do the <u>best</u>.
Our friend Dennett <u>e.g.</u>, who began with such excellent promise
a few years ago seems to come to little. For myself, the love of
art and letters grows steadily with my growth & I hugely wish,
my dear Charles, that you were in the neighborhood, to gossip   10
withal; as, save my brother W<u>m</u>., you are the only man I know
who loves as I love. I find myself tending more and more to
become interested in the things for which you have cared so
much—art and the history of art and multifarious Italian
matters. My passion is ludicrously <u>a priori</u>, however, & my gossip   15
would be rather poor fun for you until I had mastered a handful
of facts. But the sentiment is there & whatever becomes of it, I
trust it will at least last me out as a pretext for going again to
Italy. <u>À propos</u>; I have omitted to thank you for your very kindly
estimate of my <u>Passionate Pilgrim</u>. I know no one whom I   20
should have cared more to have like it so well. I have begun to
print in the <u>Atlantic</u> a short serial story wh. you will see. The
subject is something slight; but I have tried to make a work of
art, & if you are good enough to read it I trust you will detect
my intention. A certain form will be its chief merit.—I should   25
like much to know what you are occupied with, all these
months. One of these days I shall learn. Meanwhile all peace &
happy purpose to your hours. Will your stay in Germany
interrupt your Italian studies—or complete them? or shall
₍ₐ₎you₍ₐ₎ dabble in something new?—I believe I never close a   30
letter without saying I have left the heart of the matter untold.
So it must be this time. I seem to see a great vague surplus—
chiefly sentimental, perhaps—lying unhonored & unsung—~~tho'~~
₍ₐ₎and₍ₐ₎ quite "unwept," doubtless by you. I must compress it

roughly into a message of universal affection to all of you, from your mother down to that young daughter of Florence to whom I lack an introduction but love none the less.—

Yours ever dear Charles—

5   H. James jr.

Previous publication: *HJL* 1: 259–63

∾

412.15 ◆◆ since • [sin *overwrites illegible letters*]

412.28 y̶ the • [t *overwrites* y]

412.31 T̶h̶e̶ My • [M *overwrites* The]

412.32–33 f̶i̶n̶d̶ feel • [eel *overwrites* ind]

412.34 themselves • them= | selves

412.34 of o̶f̶ my • [my *overwrites* of; of *inserted in front of the overwriting*]

413.4 t̶h̶e̶ at • [at *overwrites* the]

413.4 f sensation • [s *overwrites* f]

413.10 ◆ It • [I *overwrites illegible letter*]

413.11 ◆◆◆ once • [onc *overwrites illegible letters*]

413.13 ◆ grasped • [g *overwrites illegible letter*]

413.18 however • how= | ever

413.20 splendid • splen= | =did

413.27 I'm • ['m *inserted*]

413.30 w̶o̶r̶s̶◆ worshipping • [h *overwrites illegible letter*]

414.3 t̶h̶e̶ don't • [do *overwrites* the]

414.5–6 h̶e̶r̶e̶ hear • [ar *overwrites* ere]

414.13 ◆ Did • [D *overwrites illegible letter*]

414.17 ◆ I̶ the • [the *overwrites* ◆ I]

414.20 ◆ wondering • [w *overwrites illegible letter*]

414.21 near=◆home • [h *overwrites illegible letter*]

414.25 Kirkland • Kirk= | land

414.32–33 ◆◆◆ range • [ra *overwrites illegible letters*]

415.3–4 ◆◆ holding • [hol *overwrites illegible letters*]

415.5 s rather • [r *overwrites* s]

415.6 unconscious • uncons= | cious

416.4–5 Yours ever [. . .] <u>H. James</u> jr. • [*written across the letter's last page*]
&

412.20 Andrea del Sartos • Andrea del Sarto (1486–1530), Italian painter.

412.20 hoc genus omne • all this sort.

413.21 those in Verona • The Tombs of the Scaligers.

413.25 <u>de trop</u> • <u>superfluous</u>.

413.29 the white piazza • Piazza San Marco, Venice.

414.8–9 how pitiless in spirit I was to poor old France • See HJ to Charles Eliot Norton, 16 January 1871.

414.21 Mount Mansfield • Mount Mansfield, highest point in Vermont at 4,393 feet.

414.30–31 Howells [. . .] <u>Atlantic</u> • William Dean Howells was editor of the *Atlantic Monthly* from 1871 to 1881.

415.7 Dennett • John R. Dennett.

415.21–22 I have begun to print in the <u>Atlantic</u> a short serial story wh. you will see • *Watch and Ward* appeared in the *Atlantic Monthly*, August–December 1871.

JAMES R. OSGOOD & CO.
4 October 1871
ALS University of Kansas
MS P159 A:1

25

Cambridge S Oct. 4<u>th</u> '71.
Messrs. J. R Osgood & Co.
Dear Sirs:—
    I beg to enclose to you the accompanying order from
Mr. Howells—   30
        Yours very truly
            H. James jr.
                (Quincy St.
                    Cambridge
                        Mass.)   35

No previous publication

∾

417.26 S Oct. · [O *overwrites* S]

GRACE NORTON
27, 30 November [1871]
ALS Houghton
bMS Am 1094 (884)

10

Cambridge Nov. 27ᵗʰ '70.
My dear Grace.

Your excellent photograph has come—accompanied by
your still more excellent note. Blessings innumerable upon your
15 head for your ingenious kindness in sending the picture. Yes, my
well-remembered <u>Frati</u> are all there ɗ my little <u>compagnon de
voyage</u>—ɗ <u>almost</u> the Prior. It's a leaf out of my own unwritten
journal.—I won't interpolate here any vain apologies for my
long delayed notice of your magnificent letter of August last
20 from Innsprück—deep in the tangled web of my existence some
palpable excuse might be discovered; but I thank you now as
freshly and heartily as if the letter had come yesterday. I have
just been reading it over. It is charmingly graphic about poor old
Innsprück ɗ charmingly amiable about poor old me, —poor
25 Roger, Nora, the Signora <u>e tutti</u> <u>quanti</u>. It is hardly worth while,
now, attempting to enlighten you upon any point of the
master=piece in which the former creations figure; by the time
you get this you will have ~~persu~~ perused it to the bitter end—ɗ
you will have been confirmed or confuted as fate ɗ occasion
30 decree. But if it has beguiled a few of your something dolorous
Germanic half=hours ɗ given you a theme for a moment's
thought or talk—"this author will not have labored in vain."
Really, I'm not writing a preface; I merely wish to thank you
before hand for any sort of final sentiment you may entertain on

the subject. Have you or Charles or any of you, by the way, been reading in the recent <u>Revues</u> <u>des 2. M.</u> V. Cherbuliez's new novel? If not, do it at your earliest convenience. It is tremendously fine—with all sorts of fineness & is quite the author's <u>magnum</u> <u>opus</u> as yet. But this en parenthèse. In looking over your letter, there is everything to re-read; but nothing definitely to answer—save indeed, those confidential remarks about Howells and his wedding=j Journeyers. But touching them, too, you will by this time have been confirmed or confuted. I suppose I'm not far wrong in guessing the former. Poor Howells is certainly difficult to defend, if one takes a stand=point the least bit exalted; make any serious demands & it's all up with him. He presents, I confess, to my mind, a somewhat melancholy spectacle—in that his charming style & refined intentions are so poorly & meagrely served by our American atmosphere. There is no more inspiration in an American journey than <u>that</u>! Thro' thick and thin I continue ~~you~~ however to enjoy him—or rather thro' thin & ~~m~~ thinner. There is a little divine spark of fancy which never quite goes out. He ~~is~~ has passed into the stage which I suppose is the eventual fate of all secondary & tertiary talents—worked off his less slender primitive capital, found a place and a routine & an income, and now is destined to fade slowly & softly away in ~~f~~ self=repetition and reconcilement to the common=place. But he will always be a <u>writer</u>—small but genuine. There are not so many after all now going in English—to say nothing of American.—These are Cambridge topics—what have I to add to them? Really nothing—save that I count off the days like a good Catholic a rosary, praying for your return.

Nov. 30<u>th</u> I was interrupted the other day & now that I begin afresh, it's a terrifically cold windy dusty Thanksgiving. I'm glad I didn't finish my letter, for scribbling thus to you is a service very appropriate to the day. Alice & Sara S. have gone down to spend it at Newport & you may believe that your health will be drunk in the two places in this hemisphere which know you best. I believe I was on the point, just above, of attempting a sketch of the <u>vie</u> intime of Cambridge at the present moment; but it's well I came to a stop; it would have been a sketch

5 without a model. Shady Hill still exists, I believe—I take it on trusts—I shan't fairly know it till you are back again. There are no new social features. Mrs. Dr. Freünd <u>née</u> Washburn, & husband have come to dwell here—the latter a graceful winning distingué ~~of Germans~~ German—a German Jew, yet apparently a

10 Christian Gentleman! Mrs. W<u>m</u> Washburn, <u>née</u> Sedgwick=Valerio, is also expected, I believe, on a visit. This will interest Susan. Also Mr. J. T. Fields lectured here on <u>Cheerfulness</u> lately (as who should say: I know I'm a humbug & a fountain of depression, but grin and bear it) & Mr. Longfellow

15 feasted him afterwards at supper. À propos of wh: Mr. Longfellow is just issuing a new poem <u>The Divine Tragedy</u>, on the Passion & Crucifixion. I don't suppose it will be quite as strong a picture as the San Cassano Tintoretto; but it will have its points. Lowell seems to write nothing. I believe he is given

20 over to the study of Low French—I use the term in a historic & not a moral sense. ~~I'm~~ I am told furthermore that he is going abroad in the Spring; but this of course you know.—You lead quiet lives; but you can match this base gossip, I imagine.—Your tremendous sally on the beauties of the German Tongue did me

25 good. I have an apprehension that I shall ~~always~~ ◇◇◇ ∧never[∧] know it decently & I am ravished to believe it's not worth my while. But don't come & tell me ~~k~~ now that you like it better for knowing it better; for I count upon you for backing me in my scorn.— —I try & figure Dresden & your walks and haunts (if

30 the word is not too flattering) as I have always tried to do, with your successive <u>emménagements</u>; & with tolerable success, perhaps this time, as I have my brother W<u>m</u> to prompt and suggest. But he, poor creature, speaks kindly of Dresden, knowing it only in Summer, & especially—miserable mortal!—

35 never having been to Italy.—You allude, with a kind of mitigated

enthusiasm, of the Gallery. Has Deutschland rubbed off on
Titian & P. Veronese?—do they—have they learned to—speak
Italian with a German accent?—I think I can say as something
more than a figure of speech that I envy you your musical
opportunities; for I find as I grow older that I listen a little less
stupidly than of yore, & as I ~~zealy~~ zealously cultivate my
opportunities, I don't despair of being able someday to
recognize an air at the five hundredth repetition. Tell Sally, with
an embrace, that I hope in a couple of years, to be wise enough
to know how well she fiddles.—I should like vastly to get a hint
of Charles's e impressions & opinions of Germany. I hope they
are not all as unfriendly as I am sorry to hear Germany
threatens to be to him. I wish he would write a couple of letters
or so to the Nation, which does n't seem to grow rich as it grows
old. But really I am very generous, wishing ₍ₐ₎him₍ₐ₎ to write to
the Nation; if he has any spare inclinations in that line, do tell
him with my love, that I wish he would direct his letter to me.
(I suppose, by the way¡—I believe I never mentioned it—that he
got safely a letter of mine of some three months since.)—I must
leave myself space to assure you of the interest I take in your
various recent mysterious hints about the "nearness" of your
return. I dont know whether I care exactly to have this
"nearness" translated into literal months—whether I don't
prefer to leave it vague & shadowy & shrouded in ◇ the hundred
potentialities born of my mingled wish to see you & my desire
that you continue to see ~~as~~ ₍ₐ₎what₍ₐ₎ you may in Europe. I wish
you at once to stay as long as you can & to come as soon as you
can. Does that mean next autumn—& does that ◇ mean next
summer in England? I think the ideal ~~think~~ thing for a long stay
in Europe is to spend the first & the last few months in England.
But these are doubtless very premature & importunate inquiries
& reflections. ~~Ther~~ I have only one distinct request—do come,
for heaven's sake, so that we ł can have a good stretch together
before I realize that fantastic dream of mine of another
visitation of England and Italy. I want to talk things thredbare

with you before I see them. But you'll think I've made a pretty good beginning now! I begin to sniff the sacred turkey, & to hear the rattling evolutions of the parlor=maid. You have I suppose a little corner of patriotic piety in your mind—sufficient to feel the pleasant pang I would fain evoke at this image of the classic Yankee feast. Farewell. Commend me most affectionately to one & all—especially to your mother—Yours always,

    dear Grace—

      H. <u>James</u> jr.

5

Previous publication: *HJL* 1: 263-67; Horne 41-45

    ∾

    418.19 magnificent • magnifi= | cent

    418.28 ~~persu~~ perused • [us *overwrites* su]

    419.8 wedding=j Journeyers • [J *overwrites* j]

    419.13 confess • con= | fess

    419.18 ~~you~~ however • [how *overwrites* you]

    419.18 ~~m~~ thinner • [th *overwrites* m]

    419.20 ~~is~~ has • [a *overwrites* i]

    419.23-24 ~~r~~ self=repetition • [s *overwrites* r]

    419.27 I • [*inserted*]

    419.31 terrifically • terrifi= | cally

    420.6 trusts— • [— *overwrites* s]

    420.9 ~~Germans~~ German • [an *overwrites* ans]

    420.21 ~~I'm~~ I am • [am *overwrites* 'm]

    420.25-26 ~~always~~ ◇◇◇ ₍ₐ₎never₍ₐ₎ know • [never *written above struck through* always; know *overwrites illegible letters*]

    420.27 ~~k~~ now • [n *overwrites* k]

    420.29 — — • — | —

    421.6 as I • [I *inserted*]

    421.6 ~~zealy~~ zealously • [*first* l *overwrites* ly]

    421.11 ~~e~~ impressions • [i *overwrites* e]

    421.12 unfriendly • un= | friendly

    421.18 ₍— • [— *overwrites* ,]

    421.24 ◇ the • [th *overwrites illegible letter*]

421.28 ◊ mean • [m *overwrites illegible letter*]

421.29 ~~think~~ thing • [g *overwrites* k]

421.31 importunate • im= | portunate

421.32 ~~Ther~~ I have • [av *overwrites* er *and* T *becomes* I]

421.33 ~~l~~ can • [c *overwrites* l]

421.35 visitation • visita= | tion

421.35 thredbare • [*misspelled*]

422.6–9 Farewell. [. . .] H. James jr. • [*written across the letter's fifth page*]

∾

418.7, 11 [1871] [. . .] Nov. 27th '70 • HJ misdated this letter, as we can tell from the reference to "Roger, Nora, the Signora" from *Watch and Ward*, published in the *Atlantic Monthly* 28 (August–December 1871): 232–46, 320–39, 415–31, 577–96, 689–710; and to "Thanksgiving," which did fall on "Nov. 30" in 1871 but on November 26 in 1870; furthermore, the Nortons were not in Germany until 1871.

418.16 Frati • Friars.

418.16–17 compagnon de voyage • traveling companion.

418.24–25 poor Roger, Nora, the Signora • Characters in *Watch and Ward*.

418.25 e tutti quanti • and all the others.

418.27–28 by the time you get this you will have ~~persu~~ perused it to the bitter end • The final installment of *Watch and Ward* appeared in the *Atlantic Monthly* December 1871 issue.

419.2–3 in the recent Revues des 2. M. V. Cherbuliez's new novel • *La Revanche de Joseph Noirel* ran in the *Revue des Deux Mondes* (94–95 [15 July, 1 August, 15 August, 1 September, 15 September, 7 October 1871]: 381–417, 465–508, 719–60, 5–45, 306–38, 487–522, respectively) in 1871 and appeared in book form in 1872.

419.5 en parenthèse • incidentally.

419.8 and his wedding=j Journeyers • Howells's *Their Wedding Journey* ran in the *Atlantic Monthly*, July–December 1871, before its book publication in 1872.

419.31 Thanksgiving • 30 November 1871 was Thanksgiving Day.

420.3 vie intime • intimate life.

420.7 Mrs. Dr. Freünd <u>née</u> Washburn, & husband • Dr. Maximilian Bernhard Freund (b. 1833), German physician, and his wife, Ellen Washburn Freund, sister of Frank Washburn, Lucy Washburn, and William T. Washburn.

420.9 <u>distingué</u> • <u>distinguished</u>.

420.10-11 Mrs. W<u>m</u> Washburn, <u>née</u> Sedgwick=Valerio • Katherine Sedgwick (1831–84), daughter of Robert Sedgwick (1787–1841) and Elizabeth Dana Ellery Sedgwick (1799-1862), married William T. Washburn, brother of Ellen Washburn Freund, on 22 November 1871; she was previously married to Joseph Valerio.

420.12-13 Mr. J. T. Fields lectured here on <u>Cheerfulness</u> • Upon his retirement from Fields, Osgood & Co. in 1870, James T. Fields lectured frequently in New York, Philadelphia, and all over New England; the lectures were based on his reminiscences of a fading literary era.

420.16 Mr. Longfellow is just issuing a new poem <u>The Divine Tragedy</u> • Osgood published Longfellow's *The Divine Tragedy* in December 1871.

420.31 <u>emménagements</u> • <u>removals</u>.

421.1 the Gallery • Probably the picture gallery at the Zwinger Palace, now part of the Dresden State Art Collections.

421.19 a letter of mine of some three months since • HJ to Charles Eliot Norton, 9 August 1871.

25 GEORGE ABBOT JAMES
28 November 1871
ALS Houghton
bMS Am 1094.1 (139), letter 4

30   Cambridge
   Nov. 28<u>th</u> 71.
    <u>a.m.</u>
Dear George—
  I tried to see you yesterday & as I shall perhaps miss you again
35 to day—I scribble this line—on <u>business</u> as you see—I shall

ₐleave₍ₐ₎ pleasure to some future early day or evening. In two words: How, when that devil of a <u>Mr. T. Cook, Tailor, London,</u> sends you a box of clothes (as I believe he has often done) does he send it, & do you get it? I appeal to you for possible assistance in my own nudity. He wrote me two weeks since that he had sent   5
me a small case, without indication of how or where or when; meanwhile it doesn't turn up & I shiver. What has been the <u>modus</u> <u>operandi</u> in your experience? Do the shipping people send you notice—or do you have to run after them (horrid thought)—& who, where and what the deuce are they? My box is   10
somewhere between this and London I suppose; but I can't come & see you some eveg. without a coat d̶o̶ to do it in—which accounts for my impatience. Could you very kindly consult m̶y̶ your memory, transmit me in three words the result & win my eternal gratitude? I make no apologies for troubling you,   15
retaining as I do a lively memory of past favors to yours most truly

     H. James jr

No previous publication

   ∾

   425.12 d̶o̶ to • [t *overwrites* do]

   425.13–14 m̶y̶ your • [your *overwrites* my]

   425.14 transmit • trans= | mit

   ∾

   425.2 <u>Mr. T. Cook, Tailor, London</u> • The *Post Office London Directory* for 1870 lists Thomas William Cook, "tailor, 8 Clifford st. Old Bond st W" (772).

1872

ELIZABETH BOOTT
24 January 1872
ALS Houghton
bMS Am 1094 (501)

Cambridge Jan. 24th 1872.

My dear Miss Lizzie—There came to us this morning from you
a letter—not, alas, addressed to me! But as I had the pleasure of
hearing the greater part of it, I cannot refuse myself the ~~licen◇◇~~
license of answering, & thanking you for, that which I
appropriated, whether lawfully or not. Your letter was so
redolent of Italy and delicious old memories that I must work off
in some fashion the ecstasy into which it has plunged me; & who
knows but that by doing it thus, I may not incur the favor of
your despatching me directly some fine day half-a-dozen pages
ₐworth₍ₐ₎ of the same divine aroma?—My brother, too, would
like to express without delay his great pleasure in hearing from
you & as his eyes still remain unserviceable, conveying you his
thanks gives me a further pretext. I relish vastly hearing that you
still enjoy Italy so much & that the good old land comes up to
time. If it is still fresh & eloquent to you after your twenty years
of it, what will it be to me, with my appetite whetted by ₐmy₍ₐ₎
five months?—We have been most sympathetically interested in
your visit to Rome, of which we had already heard; & I think I
may claim to have outdone the rest of the family, knowing, as I
do, just what a visit to Rome means. Your happy touch about the
"afternoon light" of the Campagna & Italian scenery generally
was worthy of Shelley & brought tears to my eyes. To your
raptures about Perugia I say <u>Amen</u> with all my soul. It is a place
to make a painter of the dullest Yankee ◇◇◇ clod & to give a real
painter brain=fever. I long since registered a vow to spend some
month of May there. Cant we agree to rendez=vous there for
that of next year? But aren't all the old towns on the road from
Florence to Rome—perched on their mountain sides & boxed

and belted in their black walls—the most enchanting old visions in the world?—My ideal of perfect earthly happiness is a slow Spring pilgrimage through the whole chain of them, from Arezzo to Narni.—But a truce to this desperate drivel! let me turn to sterner facts! The Winter here is working itself away without the help of the Beato Angelico, the Bargello or the Pitti, but with that of a good deal of splendid Yankee sunshine & a certain amount of Yankee sociality. I am leading a rather quiet stay at home life, but my brother goes out for two, (or nearly so) & is becoming an accomplished diner=out. He has just been describing to me ~~an~~ a dinner yesterday at Mrs. Crafts' (née Haggarty) in honor of Miss Nina Greenough's (your cousin's?) engagement to Mr. ~~A◇◇~~ Atherton Blyte, of Phila. Mr. A. B. has a name as in a novel, but Miss G. is certainly a good solid reality. Willy met ~~the~~ there Miss Nina Mason, whose name and charms this winter almost crowd those of Miss Amy Shaw off the lips of mankind. I met the latter magnificent being by the way, a month ago at a dinner at Mrs. ~~B~~ Dorr's—who is at her old tricks—and our talk was much of you. You were a Godsend under the circumstances & I assure you, were turned & re=turned & thoroughly discussed. So you see that in your absence, you still play an important part in society. Miss A. S. is hugely handsome. ~~Miss~~ Mrs. Tappan says that Boston is agog about her simply because she has a straight line from the part of her hair to the end of her nose. So she has—◇ & various other charms; chiefly the "grand air." My only other festivity save the above was to go the other night with Mrs. Bell to a concert of the "Dolby Troupe"—i.e. Santley, Cummings, Edith Wynne, &c., which was pretty well for an unmusical man. Do you read the new musical critiques in the Atlantic? They are (if you don't know it) by your friend Apthorp junior. How sound they are, I don't know, of course; but they seem to me mighty "smart"—or rather, very well written, as literature. I hardly dare in the same breath, to mention that the little art-notices, if you look at 'em,

430

are by your humble servt. The thing is hard to do, for want of
matter & occasion. If I only had Beato Angelico to start me up!
But he, poor man, has been done to death!—That is the worst of
all Italy—to me who must some day scribble my way through
it!—But I must not veer about to Italy again, until I have
finished my home gossip. There is not much left however, but to
say that Alice has gone for a week, with Mrs. Walsh, to N. Y—
chiefly, I believe, to buy a "party=dress"—though her parties
are rare. My brother Bob lately spent a week with us—& Wilky
pursues the even tenor of his Western work. It is rather odd
getting as we do these opposite blasts from East & West—I
mean from you & from my brothers. Sometimes, when,
impatient of Cambridge, I hanker fiercely after Rome, I remind
myself that I <u>might be</u> lodged in one of the innermost circles of
the Inferno—in Wisconsin.—I have seen little of any of your
own especial friends—by whom I mean the Gurney & Hooper
race. Miss C. H. is holding a German club, to which my brother
& I belong, nominally, but as yet not practically.—John Gray
came home from Europe in the autumn the same old John & I
believe hankers vaguely to return.—From ‸the rest of₍ᴧ₎ your
great circle of course you receive direct news—they form, to
me, a vague outlying swarm of "swells."—I ~~am~~ congratulate ⬧
you on Mr. Gryzanowski & his metaphysical lessons. My brother
has just helped to found a metaphysical club, in Cambridge,
(consisting of Chauncey Wright, C. Peirce &c) to which you
may expect to be appointed corresponding member.—I
congratulate ~~you~~ ‸Mr. G.₍ᴧ₎ moreover on not having come to
Cambridge. I have a subtle conviction that he would have
detested it. We are just now witnessing the forlorn & homesick
state of poor Dr. Freŭnd—husband of Miss Washburn that was,
who is striving vainly & pitifully to acclimatize & domesticate
himself.—I remember M. Hillebrand very well in the Rev. des
2. M. He writes French so well that I always fancied him a
native.—I'm afraid that I can give you no native literary news of

an at all high flavor. If you have seen the last 2 <u>Atlantics</u> you will
have probably read the beginning of the very charming and
promising papers by Dr. Holmes. So at least they seem to me.
How does your father like them? I heard read in M S. the other
evening a new story by Bret Harte (for the next Atlantic) better
than anything in his "second manner"—though not quite so
good as his first. Everyone here is reading Taine's English
Literature, provoked by the late translation, ℴ fancying it
something new under under the sun. You ℴ your father have
read ℴ relished it, I suppose, of old. What of the remaining
literary group in Florence? Is Miss Blagden productive—do you
see the Trollopes—does the shadow of Browning hover through
the city? By the time you get this, you will be sniffing great mild
perfumes of Spring. What must it be to see it deepening and
blooming over the hills from the terrace at San Miniato! Even
with the faint far=off foretaste ℴ whisper that we shall soon be
getting of it here, it seems a thing so divine, that I can imagine
the sense of it at Florence only as a kind of treacherous dream or
ecstasy.—You say nothing of your plans for the later months ℴ
the summer. Is it impertinent to wonder what they may be? I
take a kind of artistic pleasure in thinking what people in I
Europe <u>may</u> do. A month hence I suppose, my father will be
writing to poor old Scarboro to retain rooms. I went there, you
know, shortly after that parting of ours over your open trunks—
ℴ found it a charming sort of raw Paradise.—Àpropos of my
own doings, I feel like—first writing <u>Private</u> in huge letters, ℴ
then, in a "burst of confidence," as Dickens says, uttering a
certain~~ly~~ absurdly vague hope I have of getting to Europe by
hook or by crook, in the late summer or early Autumn next. If I
should, I don't see how, for the winter, I could stop short of
Rome ℴ Florence. Then we might see a thing or two together!
"Porphyro grew faint." This plan is ∧so[∧] pitifully embryonic,
that it is really cruel to expose it to the rude blasts of the World.
Take it up tenderly—lift it with care!—I am glad to hear my

432

letter reached your father safely—it was not good enough to get lost.—Give him my tender regards. He is kept in my mind by the commiseration I feel for him when, in my frequent walks over the bridge, I think he has lost this pleasure!—Farewell. Write to me with an amiable absence of delay & believe me ever my dear Miss Lizzie, yours most truly <u>H. James</u> jr.

5

Previous publication: *HJL* 1: 267–71

∾

429.9-10 licen◊◊ license • [se *overwrites illegible letters*]

429.11 lawfully • law=| fully

429.23 interested • interes=| ted

429.30 ◊◊◊ clod • [clo *overwrites illegible letters*]

430.10 accomplished • accom= | plished

430.11 an a • [a *overwrites* an]

430.13 A◊◊ Atherton • [th *overwrites illegible letters*]

430.15 the there • [e *overwrites illegible letter*]

430.18 B Dorr's • [D *overwrites* B]

430.20 circumstances • cir= | cumstances

430.23 Miss Mrs. • [rs. *overwrites* iss]

430.25 ◊ & • [& *overwrites illegible letter*]

431.8 party=dress • party= | dress

431.13 impatient • im= | patient

431.22 am congratulate • [con *overwrites* am]

431.22-23 ◊ you • [yo *overwrites illegible letter*]

431.23 Gryzanowski • Gryzan= | =owski

431.26 appointed • appoin= | ted

431.27 congratulate • con= | gratulate

431.28 conviction • con= | viction

431.30 Washburn • Wash= | =burn

431.33 fancied • fan= | cied

432.9 under under • under | under

432.12 Browning • Brow= | =ning

432.21-22 I Europe • [E *overwrites* I]

432.33 it is really • [is *inserted*]

433.4-6 Farewell. [. . .] <u>H. James</u> jr. • [*written across the letter's first page*]

∾

430.6 Bargello • Museo Nazionale del Bargello, Florence; art museum especially noteworthy for its treasures of Renaissance bronzes and marble sculptures.

430.18 Mrs. B̶ Dorr's • Probably Mary Gray Ward Dorr (1820-1901), wife of Massachusetts politician Charles H. Dorr (d. 1893), who resided at 18 Commonwealth Avenue, Boston. The Dorrs were old acquaintances of the Jameses. HJ mentioned meeting Charles Dorr in Paris (see HJ to WJ, 1, [2] December 1872) and attended a masquerade ball with their son, George Bucknam Dorr (1853-1944). WJ later corresponded with both George Bucknam and Mary Gray Ward Dorr. AJ tells of attending a "Ladies Social Club" hosted by a Mrs. Dorr of Boston while Bessy Ward was staying there (4 February 1866, AJ to Fanny Morse [Houghton bMS Am 1094 (1496)]; AJ, *Her Life in Letters* 5).

430.23 Mrs. Tappan • Caroline Sturgis Tappan (1819-88).

430.28 "Dolby Troupe"—i.e. Santley, Cummings, Edith Wynne, &c. • The Handel and Haydn Society and Mr. George Dolby's Company of Vocalists in Oratoria gave three performances at the Music Hall in Boston: Rossini's *Stabat Mater* on January 13, Mendelssohn's *Elijah* on January 14, and the Farewell Concert on January 20. The troupe included English baritone Charles Santley (1834-1922), English tenor William Hayman Cummings (1831-1915), and prominent soprano Edith Wynne (1842-97).

430.31 Apthorp junior • William Foster Apthorp (1848-1913), music critic, son of Robert and Eliza (Hunt) Apthorp; he became music editor of the *Atlantic Monthly* in 1872 (*Dictionary of American Biography*).

431.9-10 Wilky pursues the even tenor of his Western work • GWJ moved to Milwaukee in the fall of 1871 to work with the Chicago, Milwaukee, and St. Paul Railway.

431.17 Miss C. H. • Marian "Clover" Hooper.

431.23 Mr. Gryzanowski • Dr. Ernst Georg Friedrich Gryzanovski (1824-88), German educator.

431.24 a metaphysical club • Informal philosophical club including

Chauncey Wright, WJ, Charles S. Peirce, and Oliver Wendell Holmes Jr. that met regularly in the early 1870s.

431.25 Chauncey Wright • Chauncey Wright (1830–75), Northampton, Massachusetts-born philosopher and mathematician and mentor of WJ, Charles S. Peirce, and Oliver Wendell Holmes Jr.

431.25 C. Peirce • Charles Sanders Peirce (1839–1914).

431.30 poor Dr. Freŭnd • Dr. Maximilian Bernhard Freund.

431.32 M. Hillebrand • Karl Hillebrand (1829–84), German writer.

431.32–33 Rev. des 2. M. • *Revue des Deux Mondes*.

432.2–3 the very charming and promising papers by Dr. Holmes • Holmes's "The Poet at the Breakfast-Table" appeared as a serial publication in the *Atlantic Monthly* during 1872.

432.5 a new story by Bret Harte • Harte's story "How Santa Claus Came to Simpson's Bar," *Atlantic Monthly* 29 (March 1872): 349–58.

432.7–8 Taine's English Literature, provoked by the late translation • Taine's *Histoire de la littérature anglaise* (1863), translated by H. Van Laun as *History of English Literature* (1871).

432.11 Miss Blagden • Isabella J. Blagden (1816–73).

432.32 "Porphyro grew faint" • From John Keats's "The Eve of St. Agnes" (1820; l. 224).

432.34 Take it up tenderly—lift it with care • From Thomas Hood's "The Bridge of Sighs" (1844; ll. 5–6, 80–81).

CHARLES ELIOT NORTON   25
4, 5 February 1872
ALS Houghton
bMS Am 1088 (3856)

Cambridge Feb. 4ᵗʰ '72.   30
My dear Charles—

I hear of you from time to time, but I have an unsatisfied desire to hear from you—or at any rate, to talk <u>at</u> you directly, myself. Alice received a couple of days since a charming ~~news~~

note from Susan, which was an approach to immediate news of
you & has done much to put my pen into my hand. Let me use it
first to thank Susan most tenderly for her altogether amiable
mention of myself—both as man & author!—I am in constant
expectation of a letter from Jane or from Grace & I come down
to breakfast every morning & stride to my plate with a spiritual
hunger for this possible letter hugely in excess of that which
coffee & rolls can satisfy. But as yet I have to content myself
grimly with the coffee & rolls. Jane & Grace may be affected by
the knowledge that this state of things is not conducive ˄to₍˄₎
that breakfast=table cheerfulness & smilingness which I
presume figures in their programme for a Christian life.—It is
not that I have any thing very new & strange to relate. In fact,
when one sits down to sum up Cambridge life <u>plume</u> en <u>main</u>,
the strange thing seems its aridity. A big bustling drifting
snow=storm is the latest episode—& we try to believe that,
owing to the remarkably "open weather" that has preceded it, it
has a certain charm. I have been spending a quiet stay=at=home
winter, reading a good deal and writing a little. Of people or
things in which, ˄or whom,₍˄₎ you are interested especially I
have seen little. But who and what are the particular objects of
your interest? You must write and tell me—for I hardly know
what tastes ~~of~~ ˄and₍˄₎ ◊ sympathies you may be forming in these
many months of silence and absence. To the formation of what
tastes does a winter in Dresden conduce? A few <u>dis</u>tastes,
possibly, come into shape. Tell me of these too, for I want to be
assured ˄that₍˄₎ in the interest of ~~my~~ "general culture" a winter
in Germany is not <u>de</u> <u>rigueur</u>.—I have vague impressions of
your being disappointed in the gallery. But happy man, to have a
gallery even to be disappointed in!—But it will be made up to
you in New York, when you come back, by the rare collection of
old masters who are to form the germ of what it seems so odd to
have the Revue des 2. Mondes calling the <u>Musée</u> de N. Y. You
will of course adjourn thither from shipboard!—But I'll not talk

of your coming back yet awhile, but try rather to forward you
some native odds & ends.—The public mind seems to be rather
vacant just now, save as to a vague contemplation of the close of
the English Treaty. I fancy there is something irrational and
premature in the present English irritation on the subject. I
doubt whether our direct demands, in so far as the country
supports them, are not such as can be fairly satisfied. The
English seem exasperated by the very copious setting forth of
our injuries; I suppose we have stated our case strongly, to gain
moderately. At all events the matter is not, thank heaven, in the
hands, of ₐthe₍ₐ₎ two big foolish nations, but, I trust, in that of
men of the last discretion, who ~~believe~~ ₍ₐ₎feel that₍ₐ₎ the vexing
ghost <u>must</u> be laid.—Among those who ask about you when we
meet is Gurney—though we meet but rarely. I don't know
whether it's fancy, but he has to me the air of a man almost
oppressed and silenced and saddened by perfect comfort and
happiness.—Lowell, to my regret, I never see.—ₐWith₍ₐ₎
Longfellow I lately spent a pleasant evening & found him bland
and mildly anecdotical. Have you seen his new book—the
<u>Divine Tragedy</u>? I believe it's noted but a partial success. He is
not quite a Tintoretto of verse. Howells is making a very careful
and business=like editor of the <u>Atlantic</u>. As a proof of his
energy—he has induced me to write a monthly report of the
Fine Arts in Boston!! It's pitiful work and I shall of course soon
collapse for want of material.—You, like all the world here I
suppose, have been reading Forster's <u>Dickens</u>. It interested, but
disappointed me—through having too many opinions &
"remarks" & not enough facts & documents. You have always, I
think, rated Dickens higher than I; so far as the book <u>is</u>
documentary, it does not, to my sense, add to his intellectual
stature. But of this we shall discourse in coming days over the
succeeding volumes.—Have I come to the end of our common
acquaintance? You know, I suppose, the Charles Perkinses—
with whom I lately spent an evening. Mrs. P. is spicy & Mr. P.—

sugary, shall I say?—No, full of sweetness and light—especially
sweetness. He is ~~delivering~~ ∧repeating[∧] before the Lowell Inst.
a course of lectures on Ancient Art, which he gave last winter to
the University. Careful and sound, but without the divine

5 afflatus.—There is more or less good lecturing going on. John
Fiske is giving a long course in town on Positivism—quite a
large performance, in bulk & mass, at any rate; & Wendell
Holmes is about to discourse out here on Jurisprudence. The
latter, some day, I think, will <u>percer</u>, as the French say, & become

10 eminent—in a specialty, but to a high degree. He, my brother, &
various other long~~ed~~=headed youths have combined to form a
metaphysical club, where they wrangle grimly & stick to the
question. It gives me a headache merely to know of it.—I belong
to no club myself and have no great choice of company either to

15 wrangle or to agree with. If it didn't sound weak=mindedly
plaintive & fastidious, I would say I lacked society. I know no
"nice men"—that is, passing few, to converse withal. The only
one we often see is Arthur S.—who by the way, has gone to
N. Y. to comfort & assist Godkin in ~~his~~ a sudden illness.—I

20 suppose of course you always see the <u>Nation</u>. I don't know
whether it strikes you as it does us; but I fancy its tone has been
a good deal vitiated—& in a miserable, fatal sort of way.—
Godkin seems to me to ~~bee~~ ∧come[∧] less rather than more into
sympathy with our "institutions." Journalism has brutalized him

25 a good deal, & he has too little tact, pliancy and "perception."—
I confess that my best company now-a-days is that of various
vague moonshiny dreams of getting to your side of the world
with what speed I may.—I carry the desire (this confession is
mainly for Jane) to a morbid pitch, & I exaggerate the merits of

30 Europe. It's the same world there after all & Italy isn't the
absolute any more than Massachusetts. It's a complex fate, being
an American, & one of the responsibilities it entails is fighting
against a superstitious valuation of Europe.—It will be rather a
sell, getting over there and finding the problems of the universe

rather multiplied than diminished. Still, I incline to risk the discomfiture! <u>Feb. 5th a.m.</u> I was obliged to interrupt myself yesterday & must now bring my letter to a close—if not to a point! The 24 hours have brought forth nothing momentous— save a little party last night at Mrs. Dorr's (<u>arida nutrix leonum!</u> as some one called her) where I communed with a certain Miss Bessie Minturn of N. Y., whom Mrs D. tenders you as "<u>probably</u> the most learned woman now living!" Imagine the grimace with which you accept her! But if she's blue—it's a heavenly blue. She's a lovely girl.—I was going on to say above that no small part of this scandalous spiritual absenteeism of mine consists of fantastic encounters with you and yours in various choice spots of the shining Orient—so that I shall listen with infinite zeal to any hint of your future movements & tendencies.—It seems to me I have now been about as egotistical as the most friendly heart can desire. Be thus assured of the value I set on the practice! Tell me how you are & where you are,—morally & intellectually. I suppose you can bring yourself once in ◇ a while to read something not German. If so, I recommend: <u>Taine's</u> Notes sur l'Angleterre & Renan's Réforme Morale: the latter curiously fallacious in many ways, but a most interesting picture of a deeply conservative soul. And in the way of a novel, Cherbuliez's last. I don't see how <u>talent</u> can go further. I have heard of Grace, Theodora & Eliot's journey to Berlin. If I might have the story from Grace! Your mother, I trust, continues well. Give her my filial regards—& commend me fraternally to Susan, Jane & the rest. Your children, I suppose, are turning into so many burly little heroes & heroines for Otto Pletsch. Farewell, dear Charles. Respond only at your perfect convenience & believe me ever yours H. James jr.

Previous publication: *HJL* 1: 271-75; *SL* 2: 90-94; Horne 45-49

℁

435.34-436.1 ~~news~~ note • [ote *overwrites* ews]

436.17 preceded • pre= | ceded

436.23 ◇ sympathies • [s *overwrites illegible letter*]

436.34 shipboard • ship= | board

438.11 long~~ed~~=headed • [= *overwrites blotted* ed]

438.19 ~~his~~ a • [a *overwrites* his]

438.32 responsibilities • responsibili= | ties

439.2 discomfiture! Feb. 5ᵗʰ a.m. • discomfiture! | Feb. 5ᵗʰ a.m.

439.2 myself • my= | self

439.9 heavenly • heaven= | ly

439.11 scandalous • scan= | dalous

439.18 ◇ a • [a *overwrites illegible letter*]

439.25 continues • contin= | ues

439.25 well. • [*inserted*]

❧

436.14 <u>plume</u> en <u>main</u> • <u>pen in hand</u>.

436.28 <u>de</u> rigueur • <u>necessary</u>.

436.29 the gallery • Dresden Gallery, in Dresden, Germany. The Nortons lived in Dresden from September 1871 to early April 1872.

436.33 Revue des 2. Mondes calling the <u>Musée</u> de N. Y. • The Metropolitan Museum of Art was founded in 1870 and moved into its first home in early 1872 at 681 Fifth Avenue in New York City. It formally opened its doors to the public on February 20. In June of this same year, HJ reiterated in the *Atlantic Monthly* that "the collection of pictures forming the germ of what it is so agreeable to have the *Revue des Deux Mondes* talking of currently as the *Musée de New York*, has recently been lodged in a handsome and convenient gallery" ("Art: The Dutch and Flemish Pictures in New York" 757).

437.3–4 the close of the English Treaty • In the Washington Treaty of 1871, the United States and Great Britain agreed to submit several disputes for arbitration by an international commission. The disputes were monetarily settled, largely favoring the United States, the following year.

437.26 Forster's <u>Dickens</u> • John Forster's *The Life of Charles Dickens* (1872–74).

437.33–438.3 the Charles Perkinses [. . .] a course of lectures on An-

cient Art • Charles and Frances Perkins; Perkins lectured at the Lowell
Institute on Greek and Italian art and engraving several times in the 1870s.

438.5–6 John Fiske • A history and philosophy scholar, John Fiske conducted a series of popular lectures called "The Positive Philosophy" from
1869 to 1872 at Harvard College.

438.9 percer • make a name for himself.

439.5 arida nutrix leonum! • "The parched nurse of lions," from
Horace's twenty-third ode.

439.7 Bessie Minturn • Elizabeth T. Minturn contributed to the *Nation*
after 1876.

439.19–20 Taine's Notes sur l'Angleterre & Renan's Réforme Morale •
Taine's *Notes sur l'Angleterre* (1872); HJ reviewed this work in the *Nation*
14 (25 January 1872): 58–60. Ernest Renan (1823–92) published *La Réforme
intellectuelle et morale* in 1871.

439.23 Cherbuliez's last • Victor Cherbuliez's *La revanche de Joseph
Noirel.*

439.28 Otto Pletsch • Oscar Pletsch (1830–88), German illustrator of
such children's books as *Chimes and Rhymes for Youthful Times!* (1871) and
Aunt Bessie's Picture Book (1872).

CHARLES ELIOT NORTON
7 March [1872]
ALS Houghton
bMS Am 1088 (3857)   25

Cambridge March 7ᵗʰ
My dear Charles—
    We have just received the news of your overwhelming sorrow.
Friendship itself for the present must seem to you far=off and   30
unreal; but the image of all Susan's loveliness has been so vivid
with me for the past twenty four hours that I feel as if I might
speak to you almost by right of measuring your loss. A memory
of such perfect sweetness as her's seems untenderly used by

anything but silence. And yet when I find myself writing of her as a <u>memory</u> instead of as the living brightness that she was, it seems to me that I could say a great deal. But you will not thank me now for any but the simplest word of sympathy. You have had long talks, by this time, with yourself and have found in your own wise heart sturdier friends and counsellors than any the world can offer you. Yet about me here the world feels deeply with you—and for your children. They will have a fast friend in future in one who can tell them—and be reminded by them—of their mother's loveliness. We are all united in sympathy. My father tells me he means to write to you.

  Your's always

   <u>Henry James</u> jr.

No previous publication

∿

442.4 sympathy · sympa= | thy

∿

441.29 overwhelming sorrow · Susan Sedgwick Norton died 17 February 1872 from complications following the birth of her son, Richard.

JANE NORTON

8 March [1872]

ALS Houghton

bMS Am 1088.1 (61)

  Cambridge March 8$\underline{^{th}}$

My dear Jane—I know you need no assurance that I feel with you in your trouble; but I must for my own relief send you a line to say that I comprehend your loss & the infinite change that has come to you. I knew that I had the liveliest admiration and affection for Susan—but I have been feeling for the last two days how deep & tender ~~these feelings were~~ this [ʌ]appreciation[ʌ] was

& what an ineffaceable impression she had made on me. She had
an incomparable brightness and fineness, which will be a lovely
memory in many minds. I wrote yesterday to Charles a line
which ought to have been but an expression of my perfect
confidence that the time can demand nothing of him that he will
not more than yield. Indeed, my dear Jane, the pain of sympathy
with you all is strangely lightened and made to seem even a
personal weakness, by the sense that your sorrow finds you as
wise and strong and unconfounded as it is heavy & cruel. I saw
Sara yesterday & found her admirably tranquil & natural. In our
talk I had Theodora too in my thoughts. They all value greatly,
I think, Theodora's having been with Susan & envy her sad
privilege. I have been remembering many things—incidents of
our meetings abroad, to which all the foreignness of
circumstance that clusters about them seems to give, to my
imagination, a sort of providential charm. I recall in this d way
with peculiar vividness a the day I went with Susan down into
Kent from London, & ₍ₐ₎when₍ₐ₎ after lunching with those good
Darwins we took a really memorable stroll through old
Holwood park and felt the first breath of Spring there. There
was a charm on the day then—there is a deeper one now. We
You are of course so full of cares and of constant need for effort
and courage that I feel as if I had no right to prolong this idle
letter—though I must add to it the wish that I were near you &
able to lend some helping hand. When I think of all that there is
in your circumstances to multiply and deepen your cares, I
feel that ₍ₐ₎need₍ₐ₎ to remind myself afresh of your fortitude.
The blessings of heaven rest on it! I write this to you, but I think
of your mother & Grace as well. My especial remembrances to
Theodora. Your's ever <u>H. James jr</u>

No previous publication

∾

442.34 these feelings were this ₍ₐ₎appreciation₍ₐ₎ was • [is *overwrites*
ese; appreciation *written above struck through* feelings; as *overwrites* ere]

443.13 privilege • privi= | lege

443.15 them • [*inserted*]

443.16 d̶ way • [w *overwrites* d]

443.17 a̶ the • [th *overwrites* a]

443.18 London, • [*comma inserted*]

443.18 ⅋ ∧ • [∧ *overwrites* ⅋]

443.19 we • [*inserted*]

443.21–22 W̶e̶ You • [Yo *overwrites* We]

∾

442.30 your trouble • The death of Susan Sedgwick Norton.

443.3 I wrote yesterday to Charles • 7 March [1872] to Charles Eliot Norton.

443.17–18 the day I went with Susan down into Kent • HJ describes their visit to Darwin in his 26 March [1869] letter to MWJ.

GRACE NORTON

17 March 1872

ALS Houghton

bMS Am 1094 (887)

Cambridge March 17$\underline{\text{th}}$ 72.

Dear Grace—I have been meaning to write to you any time this last month, and I little thought that when I should really do so, it would be over Susan's grave. My thoughts and sympathies have been with you continually of late—like those of every one who, either more or less, had known Susan and received the vivid impression of her perfect loveliness. Your immediate confusion and trouble have by this time begun somewhat to subside, I suppose, ꝸ your sense of loss to work itself, with that inexorable logic of its own, into the substance of your lives and your future. You hold among you certainly a memory of the purest brightness, and those ∧who[∧] can never dissociate Susan's image from that of her children will feel that there is a divine

injunction upon their lives. My own memory of her will always
be a bright presence in the foreground of that year of mine in
Europe which seems to me now weighted with so many things.
There is nothing I ~~f~~ would fancy otherwise in those various days
of my seeing her—except possibly that I never told her how ~~I~~
deeply I admired her.—It's a great illusion, I imagine, dear
Grace, to suppose I must write you a funereal letter, as that you
are not still on generous terms with life. I was confident of this
from the moment I heard of your trouble—confident of it as
regards Charles and ~~as regards the other most pain~~ [∧]in spite of
all the imaginable trials[∧] of your situation.—Nothing of
consequence has befallen us here. The only change that has
come to us is that we have allowed ourselves to begin to think of
your return as something nearer at hand. I needn't say that you
will have a doubly tender welcome.—The winter in this hideous
month of ~~m~~ March is making a great fight, ઠ returning again
and again, after being for the moment melted down by a March
sun which, like your's in Florence, really felt some thing like
May.—The news of Susan's death came in the midst of a period
of cold as cruel as any I remember. But when you come, all our
bareness ઠ bleakness will be muffled in the kindliest green.—I
have seen Sara two or three times of late ઠ ∧spent[∧] an hour a
couple of evenings since, in Kirkland Street. Sara is perfect—so
are they all.—The current of your life, I fancy, is flowing
steadily again and you have resumed such quietly=aesthetic
habits as Dresden makes ~~possibly~~ possible. When the time draws
nigh for you to take your last looks at things, take a few for me
and remember our prospective talks.—When I said just now
nothing had happened I was guilty of an unwitting impertinence
to the four happy mortals who are (as one may say) about to
resolve themselves into two: W. Holmes ઠ Miss Dixwell:
Miss C. Hooper ઠ Henry Adams. You know them all more or
less, I think, ઠ will be duly interested.—You are more occupied I
suppose than I can fairly imagine; but if some day your

good=will can find time for a line, remember I am waiting
~~patiently~~ [∧]anxiously[∧] not less than patiently. Tell me then how
Charles is bearing himself, & how it is with your mother. Give
them my love—as well as to Theodora & Jane. For yourself, dear
Grace, I devoutly trust you are fairly strong. My blessings on
the Boy! Yours ever

H J. jr.

No previous publication

∾

444.33 brightness • bright= | ness

445.4 f would • [w *overwrites struck through* f]

445.16 m̶ March • [M *overwrites* m]

445.26 ~~possibly~~ possible • [e *overwrites blotted* y]

445.33 interested • inter= | ested

∾

445.31 W. Holmes & Miss Dixwell • Oliver Wendell Holmes Jr. and
Fanny Dixwell were married 17 June 1872.

445.32 Miss C. Hooper & Henry Adams • Marian (Clover) Hooper and
Henry Adams were married 27 June 1872.

446.5–6 blessings on the Boy • Richard Norton (1872–1918).

JOHN S. CLARK

21 March [1872]

ALS Pierpont Morgan Library, New York

MA 2032

My dear Mr. Clark—

I regret extremely that as I expect to go on Saturday to New
York I shall be deprived of the pleasure of spending Sunday
evening with you. I should have been happy to make Prof.
Hartt's acquaintance—having often heard him spoken of by my
brother, who knew him in Brazil.—With apologies to Mrs.
Clark

Yours very truly
Henry James jr
Cambridge
March 21st

No previous publication

∾

446.33 acquaintance · ac= | quaintance

∾

446.25 [1872] · The year of this letter is based upon Professor Hartt's activity in the Boston area as well as the watermark. According to several contemporary sources, Hartt conducted a series of popular lectures in Boston in 1872 (Hay 160; Rathbun 347). Also, the watermark (ORIGINAL | TURKEY MILL | KENT) on this letter appears on stationery used by HJ in 1872.

446.29 Mr. Clark · John S. Clark (1835–1920), partner in the publishing firms Ticknor and Fields and, later, Fields, Osgood and Co., Boston.

446.32-33 Prof. Hartt's · Charles Frederick Hartt (1840–78), Canadian-born geologist who was part of the same 1865–66 scientific expedition to Brazil as WJ that was led by Harvard zoologist and geologist Louis Agassiz (1807–73). In his [31 March 1865] letter to MWJ, WJ calls Hartt "*Hartt* of the Museum" (*CWJ* 4: 98).

CHARLES ELIOT NORTON
6 May [1872]   25
ALS Houghton
bMS Am 1088 (3858)

Cambridge May 6th
My dear Charles—   30
It was very kind in you to answer my note ở very brave in you to answer it just as you did. But as the weeks have passed away you have more ở more I suppose, sounded the depths of your loss—only of course to find ◇ deep within deep—ở if we

were sitting together would speak to me now with even more intelligent calmness. You have always appeared to me to have so profound & sincere a religious sentiment that I have found great satisfaction in thinking of what it must lately have been to you.

5　To have had this tested by a cruel sorrow and found not wanting is something that an observer (feeling at once all the force & all the vanity, of sympathy) is almost tempted to speak of as a gain.—And yet indeed when I think of how the daily lapse of life must at every step deepen to anguish your sense of the

10　difference—as Wordsworth calls it—I wonder I can do anything but lay down my pen, overwhelmed by the fatal, absolute fact. One thing however by this time you know a good deal about:— the mysteries of sorrow & what the soul finds in it for support as well as for oppression. The human soul is mighty, & it seems to

15　me we hardly know what it may ◊ achieve (as well as suffer) until it has been plunged deep into trouble. Then indeed, there seems something infinite in pain & it opens out before us, door within door, & we seem doomed to tread its whole infinitude; but there seems also something infinite in effort and something supremely

20　strong by its own right in the ~~in the~~ grim residuum of conscious manhood with which we stand faith to faith to the hard reality of things. I venture to talk to you thus, dear Charles, out of my own unshaken security, because I have in my own fashion learnt the lesson that life is effort, unremittingly repeated, and because

25　I feel ~~as~~ somehow as if real pity were for those who have been beguiled into the perilous delusion that it isn't. Their hard day when it comes, is hard indeed. The voluntary life seems to me the only intelligent one, & if there be such a thing as heaven, I take it to mean ~~the~~ a state in which <u>inoluntary</u> life is secure.—

30　A woman like Susan can have only one fault; that of making this life seem better ₍ₐ₎& safer₍ₐ₎ than it is. The effacement of a personality so pure, so charming, so instinct with nature's deepest sweetness as hers, seems the very essence & symbol of death. But against such effacement your heart of course protests

with every ~~way~~ wave of her influence ∧that[∧] it transmits to your
coming life and that of your children.—I felt many more of
these things than I can write or you would care to hear, at the
funeral at Shady Hill. You will understand what I mean when I
say that the saddest part was there, rather than at the grave.
Dr. Newell's short service was perfectly simple touching *&*
irreproachable. You would have been satisfied. The day was
extremely sombre—a momentary relapse into winter. While we
stood at the grave the snowflakes began to fall heavily. We had
been having a horribly garish winter—dry, monotonous blue sky
for months together; *&* I remember feeling, as we drove to
Mount Aburn, a supreme relief in the first rolling grey clouds I
had seen in an age—*&* a sense of the ∧superior[∧] seriousness of
cloud=scenery. I ~~rec'd~~ received yesterday Grace's inestimable
letter from Cologne—as I had of course done the note she
enclosed with yours. Thank her warmly, pray, for both. She shall
soon hear from me. It is ~~true~~ ∧proper[∧] even to talk about
seeing, I trust, as well as hearing, for my departure for England
with my aunt *&* Sister is now but five days off. (May 11ᵗʰ.) ~~W~~ I am
very anxious to hear ~~th~~ what the date of your own arrival in
England is likely to be, *&* your movements when you get there,
so that I may narrow down my confidence in our meeting to a
certainty. Our own plans are vague. Alice wishes to leave
London *&* its fatigues to the last; *&* I think we shall try *&* find
rural diversion on the North Devon Coast (Ilfracombe *&*c) for
the first three or four weeks. Then to Switzerland *&* thence, in
the late Summer, I trust, to Italy, for a month.—Very welcome
was Grace's mention of your having found, on your way from
Dresden, some incidental diversions at Halle *&* Brunswick. I can
imagine your mind turning not unkindly to ~~your~~ ∧the[∧] *&*
chance of talking Dante with ~~with~~ your German friend. I trust
Paris will have something to interest you; though Paris has
remained to me now for a long time, an obstinately sombre
fact.—Alice has just come in to announce—from Annie

Ashburner—the arrival of Theodora S., safe & well. I shall see
her early to morrow & have late news of you. You will ~~have~~ have
heard of <u>Greeley's</u> nomination at Cincinnati. He will carry but a
small fraction of the country (I suppose) as against Grant, & the
5   C. Convention is therein a failure. It is not a pure misfortune
however that it should be forced to await a stronger maturity.
With all deeply affectionate messages to every one, dear
Charles, & the hope of a speedy meeting, yours ever—
H. James jr.

Previous publication: *HJL* 1: 275–77

∾

447.34 ⬦ deep • [d *overwrites illegible letter*]

448.15 ⬦ achieve • [a *overwrites illegible letter*]

448.21 manhood • man =| =hood

448.25 ~~as~~ somehow • [so *overwrites* as]

448.26 perillous • [*misspelled*]

448.29 ~~the~~ a • [a *overwrites* the]

448.29 <u>inoluntary</u> • [*misspelled*]

449.1 ~~way~~ wave • [ve *overwrites blotted* y]

449.9 snowflakes • snow= | flakes

449.12 Aburn • [*misspelled*]

449.14 ~~rec'd~~ received • [ei *overwrites* 'd]

449.14 inestimable • inesti= | mable

449.19 ~~W~~ I • [I *overwrites* W]

449.20 ~~th~~ what • [wh *overwrites* th]

449.30–31 ⬦ chance • [c *overwrites illegible letter*]

450.2 ~~have~~ have • [e *overwrites illegible letter*]

450.7–9 With all [. . .] H. James jr. • [*written across the letter's first page*]

∾

447.31 you to answer my note • Charles Eliot Norton's 28 March 1872
letter to HJ, which answered HJ's 7 March [1872] letter to Norton.

449.3–4 the funeral at Shady Hill • 23 March 1872 (see Longfellow
journal, 23 March 1872).

449.6 Dr. Newell · Reverend William Newell, minister of Cambridge's First Parish-Unitarian Church.

449.12 Mount Aburn · Mount Auburn cemetery, Cambridge's largest cemetery.

449.31 your German friend · Karl Witte (1800–1883), an eminent Dante scholar and professor at Martin Luther University, Halle-Wittenberg, in Halle, Germany. Witte dedicated his critical edition of Dante's *Vita nuova* to Norton (Turner 247).

449.34–450.1 Annie Ashburner · Annie Ashburner (1846–1909), a close friend of AJ and a cousin of the Sedgwicks and their Ashburner aunts. She married Francis Gardiner Richards in 1879 (see A. James 28 n.41).

450.3 Greeley's nomination · Horace Greeley was the Liberal Republican Party nominee for the U.S. presidency in 1872.

GEORGE ABBOT JAMES
8 May [1872]
ALS Houghton
bMS Am 1094.1 (151), letter 2   20

Cambridge May 8th
Dear George—
   My regret at not seeing you has been in some degree alleviated by your amiable note of yesterday. I knew in a general   25 way that you were to leave ₐtown₍ₐ₎ early, but fancied I should still find you. But I can do nothing but grudge you Nahant breezes these first & most trying days of summer. May they blow you nothing but health & happiness all summer long & may I find you in the crowned, even to oppression, with both! In ~~goo~~ all   30 good wishes I of course include your wife—to whom pray give my most regretful farewell.—While I am jolting amid dust & cinders on some blessed European railway or scrambling for rooms—against a couple of hundred enterprising fellow

451

Yankees—near one of the hallowed shrines, I shall think of you
with no small envy, ⋄ lounging at your ease on your great piazza
& watching our good indigenous spectacle of the blue Atlantic
tickled into foam by quiet far=off shoals! May your new house
5   be founded on a rock—& your prospective heir (or heiress) be a
thing to delight your heart forever!—Good bye! An espcial
farewell to your sister—

      Yours ever, dear George¦,

        <u>H James</u> jr.

10   <u>G. A. James esq.</u>

No previous publication

    ∾

  451.25 yesterday • yester= | =day

  451.30 g̶o̶o̶ all • [all *overwrites* goo]

  452.2 ⋄ lounging • [l *overwrites illegible letter*]

  452.5 prospective • pros- | pective

  452.6 espcial • [*misspelled*]

  452.8 George¦, • [, *overwrites* !]

    ∾

  451.18 [1872] • Year based on the letter's reference to a pending departure for Europe; 1872 was the only year HJ lived in Cambridge,
Massachusetts, and departed for Europe during the month of May.

Biographical Register

This register is intended to help readers of *The Complete Letters of Henry James* keep track of the many people James mentions in his letters. It lists family members and friends and public, literary, and artistic figures of HJ's day whom the editors consider now to be relatively obscure. Well-known people that James mentions—for instance, Dickens, President Grant, Prime Minister Gladstone—are omitted, as are canonical authors of James's past, like Shakespeare or Molière. Such well-known contemporary authors and artists as Arnold, Ruskin, Sand, Thackeray, Burne-Jones, and Morris do appear in this register when the editors have deemed that they were significant in James's life or work.

ABOUT, EDMOND (1828–85), French journalist and novelist whom HJ admired. *Tolla* (1855), which HJ read in Boulogne in 1857, may have exerted an influence on the American's own novels. About's other works include *Germaine: Deuxième Série* (1857), *Le Roi des Montagnes* (1861), and *L'homme à l'oreille cassée* (1862). HJ and About would meet in 1879.

ACLAND, SIR HENRY WENTWORTH (b. 1815), M.D. 1848 from All Souls College, named Regius Professor of Medicine in 1857 and clinical professor of medicine, 1857–80; he treated Charles Eliot Norton at Oxford in 1857.

ADAMS, CHARLES FRANCIS (1807–86), father of Henry Adams and son of President John Quincy Adams.

ADAMS, HENRY (1838–1918), American author, historian, and man of letters; HJ first met Adams in 1870, shortly before his appointment to Harvard College as assistant professor of history. Adams's wife, Marian (Clover) Hooper, a close friend of HJ's during his Cambridge days, fostered their early friendship. Adams frequently traveled abroad, visiting HJ regularly.

ADAMS, MARIAN (CLOVER) HOOPER (MRS. HENRY) (1843–85), gifted photographer, art collector, and conversationalist who married Henry Adams on 27 June 1872. Her celebrated Washington salon welcomed such notables as John and Clara Hay, Clarence King, and George Bancroft. She is thought to be HJ's model for Mrs. Bonnycastle in the short story "Pandora." Henry Adams was devastated by her suicide.

AGASSIZ, ELIZABETH CABOT CARY (1822–1907), noted writer, educator, naturalist/scientist, founded the Harvard Annex for the collegiate education of women, who were not allowed as students at Harvard. The Annex later became Radcliffe College, and Agassiz served as the first president. Although she was related to many of Boston's distinguished families, Elizabeth Cary received no formal education. In 1850 she married Louis Agassiz and became an invaluable asset to his career. Her notes on his lectures were the raw material of much of his published work, and together they organized his expeditions and founded the Anderson School of Natural History, a marine laboratory on Penikese Island in Buzzard's Bay, Massachusetts. Elizabeth Agassiz's own published work includes *A First Lesson in Natural History* (1859), *Seaside Studies in Natural History* (1865, with her stepson Alexander Agassiz), *A Journey in Brazil* (1868, with her husband), and *Louis Agassiz: His Life and Correspondence* (1885).

AGASSIZ, LOUIS (1807–73), Swiss-born naturalist and Harvard professor of zoology and geology. He led the 1864–65 expedition to Brazil that included WJ, and his Cambridge house was on Quincy Street, near the Jameses'.

AGNEW, JOAN, not actually one of John Ruskin's "charming young nieces," as HJ called her in his 26 March [1869] letter to his mother, but the caretaker to Ruskin's mother.

APTHORP, WILLIAM FOSTER (1848–1913), music critic, son of Robert and Eliza (Hunt) Apthorp; he became music editor of the *Atlantic Monthly* in 1872.

ARMSTRONG, LILY. HJ described her as a "charming young niece" of John Ruskin's when he met her at Denmark Hill in March 1869. She was actually a friend of Rose La Touche's. Ruskin had met both girls at Winnington Hall.

ARNOLD, MATTHEW (1822–88), English poet and critic; HJ reviewed his *Essays in Criticism* for the *North American Review* (July 1865) and published a longer article on him, in January 1884, for the *English Illustrated Magazine*. HJ would meet him for the first time, in Rome, in 1873. HJ later became a close friend of Arnold's niece, Mary Augusta Arnold (Mrs. Humphry) Ward.

ASHBURNER, ANNE (1807–94), elder sister of the mother of HJ's friends Susan Sedgwick Norton, Arthur George Sedgwick, Sara Sedgwick Darwin, and Theodora Sedgwick. She lived on Kirkland Street, in Cambridge, near the Jameses' Quincy Street home, in a house that she shared with her sister Grace and her unmarried Sedgwick nieces and nephews.

ASHBURNER, ANNIE (1846–1909), a close friend of AJ and a cousin of the Sedgwicks and their Ashburner aunts. She married Francis Gardiner Richards (1879).

ASHBURNER, GRACE (1814–93), maternal aunt of HJ's friends Susan Sedgwick Norton, Arthur George Sedgwick, Sara Sedgwick Darwin, and Theodora Sedgwick. She lived on Kirkland Street, in Cambridge, near the Jameses' Quincy Street home, in a house that she shared with her sister Anne and her unmarried Sedgwick nieces and nephews.

AUGIER, ÉMILE (1820–89). Augier and Victorien Sardou (1831–1908) dominated the French stage in the late nineteenth century. HJ published a notice on Augier's *Les Fourchambault* in the *Nation* (27 June 1878), and Augier's *Le Gendre de M. Poirier* (1854) may have been part of the inspiration for HJ's *The Golden Bowl* (1904).

BANCROFT, HARRIET JAMES (MRS. JOHN CHANDLER) (d. 1906), sister of HJ's Harvard Law School friend, George A. James.

BANCROFT, JOHN CHANDLER (1835–1901), American painter and businessman.

BEESLY, EDWARD SPENCER (1831–1915), British historian and writer. He edited the *Positivist Review* and was the author of translations as well as the biographer of Comte.

BENSON, EUGENE (1839-1908), American painter who also supported himself by writing reviews for the *Galaxy*, the *Atlantic Monthly*, and *Putnam's*, among others.

BLAGDEN, ISABELLA J. (1818-73), East Indies–born poet who lived in Bellosguardo, Florence. She published under the name Ivory Beryl and was a friend of Elizabeth Barrett Browning, Bulwer Lytton, and Walter Savage Landor.

BOOTT, ELIZABETH (LIZZIE) (1846-88), and her father, Francis Boott (1813-1904), were friends of the Temples and of the Jameses. HJ was particularly close to them all their lives. Lizzie's talent as an artist was recognized early, and she pursued this passion all her life. One of her major tutors was Frank Duveneck, who was to become her husband in March 1886. HJ did much to support and promote her career as an artist and visited Lizzie and her father at Bellosguardo, their Italian home. Lizzie is said to be the model for Pansy Osmond in *The Portrait of a Lady*.

BOOTT, FRANCIS (1813-1904), an amateur composer and musician who raised his daughter, Lizzie (born in Boston), in Italy after the death of her mother and infant older brother. He was a devoted father who took delight in her education.

BOWDITCH, HENRY PICKERING (1840-1911), a medical school classmate of WJ's and a cousin to Fanny Dixwell (Holmes). After earning his medical degree in 1868, Bowditch went to Europe and became a physiologist and a well-respected researcher. In 1871 he became a teacher of physiology at Harvard. Throughout both of their careers, WJ and Bowditch remained friends.

BRIDGES, DR. JOHN HENRY (1832-1906), a positivist who wrote a number of books and contributed regularly to the *Fortnightly Review*. He was also an early follower of Auguste Comte and translated many of his works, including *Positivism* (1848).

BRODRICK, GEORGE CHARLES (1831-1903), son of William John Brodrick (1789-1870), Seventh Viscount of Middleton. HJ met him at breakfast at Albert Rutson's on 19 March 1869.

BRONSON, ARTHUR (1824–85), married Katharine de Kay in New York on 11 October 1855. After he began to have mental health problems in 1880, he lived separately from his wife.

BRONSON, KATHARINE DE KAY (1834–1901), probably first met the Jameses when she and her husband lived in Newport in the late 1850s. She would later become a close friend of Robert Browning's and of HJ's; both authors visited her at her Venice palazzino, Casa Alvisi, its guest accommodations in the neighboring Palazzo Giustiniani-Recanati, and her house, Casa La Mura, in nearby Asolo. HJ commemorated his friendship with Mrs. Bronson in his memorial article, "Casa Alvisi," which appeared in *Cornhill Magazine* and *The Critic* (both February 1902) before HJ reprinted it in *Italian Hours* (1909).

BROWNING, ROBERT (1812–89), English poet. HJ would publish three articles on Browning: a review of *The Inn Album* for the *Nation* (20 January 1876), the commemorative "Browning in Westminster Abbey" for the *Speaker* (4 January 1890), and "The Novel in *The Ring and the Book*," which HJ initially gave as a lecture to the academic committee of the Royal Society of Literature (7 May 1912) and then published in the *Quarterly Review* (July 1912) and *Notes on Novelists* (1914). HJ and Browning met occasionally when HJ lived in London and would share an intimate, mutual friend in Katharine de Kay Bronson, and HJ knew Browning's son, Pen, who lived in Asolo and Venice.

BURNE-JONES, EDWARD, FIRST BARONET (1833–98), English painter and designer and disciple of Rossetti. HJ met Burne-Jones before his return to America in April 1870 and developed a lifelong friendship with him, as well as later writing reviews of his artwork in such periodicals as the *Galaxy*, *Nation* and *Atlantic Monthly*.

BUSHNELL, HORACE (1802–76), theologian and Congregational pastor in Hartford; Bushnell's criticism of transcendentalism in general—and of Sr.—in his *Nature and the Supernatural* (1858) provoked Sr. to write five angry letters to the *New York Tribune* during the winter of 1859.

BUTLER, DR. DAVID P., Boston physician and physical therapist (his practice at 53 Temple Place included a gymnasium) who treated WJ, HJ, and AJ.

BUTLER, SUSAN RIDLEY SEDGWICK (1828–83), wife of Charles E. Butler (1818–97) of New York.

CABOT, ARTHUR TRACY (1852–1912), brother of James and Lydia (Lilla) Cabot.

CABOT, JAMES JACKSON (1854–75), brother of Arthur and Lydia (Lilla) Cabot.

CABOT (PERRY), LYDIA (LILLA) (1848–1933), became engaged to Thomas Sergeant Perry in the spring of 1873; the couple married in April 1874. She was a talented painter.

CARLYLE, THOMAS (1795–1881), Victorian essayist, historian, and acquaintance of Sr. Recommended by Emerson, Sr. met Carlyle in England during his transatlantic trip of 1838. HJ reviewed *The Correspondence of Thomas Carlyle and Ralph Waldo Emerson* for the *Century Magazine* (June 1883).

CHERBULIEZ, VICTOR (1829–99), Swiss-born French novelist whom the young HJ admired and who is perhaps best remembered today, at least to English-language readers, for the reference to his 1866 novel, *Paule Méré*, at the opening of part 3 of "Daisy Miller." Thomas Sergeant Perry reviewed Cherbuliez's *Prosper Randoce* in the *Atlantic Monthly* (April 1874).

CHILD, ELIZABETH ELLERY SEDGWICK (MRS. FRANCIS JAMES) (1824–98), married Francis James Child in 1860. They lived on Kirkland Street, in Cambridge, near the Jameses' home at 20 Quincy Street, next to the Nortons' Shady Hill estate and adjoining the house inhabited by her unmarried Sedgwick cousins (their father, Theodore Sedgwick III, was her first cousin), Sara, Arthur George, and Theodora, and their maternal aunts, Anne and Grace Ashburner. Katharine Sedgwick Valerio Washburn was her younger sister, and Robert Sedgwick Watson was her first cousin.

CHILD, FRANCIS JAMES (1825–96), Harvard professor of English and editor of *English and Scottish Popular Ballads*; his wife, Elizabeth Ellery Sedgwick Child, and their children lived in Cambridge and were family friends of the Jameses.

CHURCH, FRANCIS PHARCELLUS (1839–1906), co-founder, with his brother, William Conant Church, of the *Galaxy*, to which HJ contributed early in his career.

CHURCH, WILLIAM CONANT (1836–1917), founding editor, with his brother Francis Pharcellus Church, of the *Galaxy*, and biographer of Ulysses S. Grant and of John Ericsson.

CLARK, JOHN SPENCER, editor at Ticknor and Fields and its later permutations: Fields, Osgood and Osgood and Co.; he lived in Cambridge but then moved to Boston.

CLARKE, DUMONT, assistant librarian of the Redwood Library, Newport, until late 1859.

CLARKE, SARAH FREEMAN, an artist who befriended the Jameses and the Emersons.

COCHRAN, THOMAS, JR., married HJ's first cousin Emilie Walsh (daughter of MWJ's older brother) in 1867.

COCKS, JOHN SOMERS, third Earl of Somers, proprietor of Eastnor Park near Ledbury, which HJ visited in March 1870. Somers carried out lavish entertainments there during the 1860s and 1870s.

COQUELIN, BENOIT-CONSTANT (1841–1909), famous Comédie Française actor who created the title role of Rostand's *Cyrano de Bergerac*. HJ and Coquelin attended the same school in Boulogne in 1857–58; HJ published an article, "Coquelin," in the *Century Magazine* (January 1887) and permitted its reprinting in the 1915 U.S. edition of Coquelin's *Art and the Actor*.

COUGNARD, JEAN-MARC (1821–96), pastor in Geneva (1851–65) and professor of Christian morality and practical theology, 1865–96. In 1870 Cougnard lived in Geneva at the rue des Philosophes, 12.

CUMMINGS, WILLIAM HAYMAN (1831–1915), English tenor who toured the United States in 1871–72 with the Dolby Troupe.

CURTIS, JOHN G., classmate and brief roommate at Harvard of HJ's close friend, Thomas Sergeant Perry.

DANA, RICHARD HENRY, JR. (1815–82), American writer, author of *Two Years Before the Mast* (1840), lawyer, and son of the founder of the *North American Review*, lived at 2 Berkeley Street, Cambridge.

DARWIN, CHARLES (1809–92), his home in Downe, Kent, was near one rented in 1868 by the Nortons in nearby Keston, and Susan Sedgwick Norton brought HJ there for lunch in March 1869. Darwin's son, William Erasmus Darwin (1839–1914), married Sara Sedgwick.

DARWIN, EMMA (1808–96), wife of Charles Darwin.

DARWIN, SARA SEDGWICK (Mrs. William Erasmus). *See* Sedgwick, Sara Price Ashburner.

DEACON, EDWARD (NED) PARKER, attended the Berkeley Institute with HJ and Thomas Sergeant Perry in 1859.

DE KAY, HELENA, American artist and sister of Katharine de Kay Bronson; Helena de Kay married poet and *Scribner's Monthly* and *Century* editor Richard Watson Gilder (1844–1909) in 1874. She was a close school friend of Minny Temple's.

DENNETT, JOHN R. (1838–74), literary editor of the *Nation* from 1868 to 1869 and then a teacher at Harvard.

DENNISTON, DR. EDWARD E., ran the Springdale spa in Northampton, where HJ resided in 1864.

DE VERE, AUBREY (1814–1902), Irish poet, lecturer, and essayist.

DICKENS, KATE MACCREADY (1839–1929), daughter of Charles Dickens; she married twice: first to Collins Charles Allston (1828–73) and then to Carlo Perugini (1839–1918).

DIXWELL, EPES SARGENT, graduated from Harvard College in 1827; read law in the office of Oliver Wendell Holmes Jr.'s grandfather, Judge Jackson; spent three years in practice; and was named headmaster of the Boston Latin School in 1836. He married the daughter of Nathaniel Bowditch, the renowned author of the *Practical Navigator*, and of their six children, the eldest, Fanny Bowditch Dixwell, would marry Oliver Wendell Holmes Jr. in 1872.

DIXWELL (HOLMES), FANNY BOWDITCH, daughter of Epes Sargent Dixwell, married Oliver Wendell Holmes Jr. on 17 March 1872.

DODGE, MARY ABBY. *See* Hamilton, Gail.

DRESEL, MRS. OTTO, wife of Otto Dresel (ca. 1826–90), German concert pianist and composer who, after 1852, resided primarily in Boston with her.

DUFFY, DR., Irish doctor in Florence, a fellow of the College of Surgeons in Ireland, who treated HJ's constipation.

DUMAS, ALEXANDRE, FILS (1824–95), son of novelist Alexandre Dumas (the author of *Les Trois Mousquetaires*); best known today for his novel *La Dame aux camélias*, Dumas fils was one of the two or three most successful French playwrights during the second half of the nineteenth century. HJ published a review of Dumas's novel *Affaire Clémenceau* in the *Nation* of 11 October 1866.

DU MAURIER, GEORGE (1834–96), Paris-born English artist and writer who later became a friend of HJ's. He did illustrations for a number of important late-Victorian novelists, including HJ, and is best remembered for his novel *Trilby* (1894).

ELIOT, CHARLES WILLIAM (1834–1926), president of Harvard, 1869–1909.

ELIOT, GEORGE (1819–80), pseudonym of Mary Ann Evans. HJ first met the great mid-nineteenth century novelist and her consort, George Henry Lewes, in 1869. Seven months before her death she married the forty-year-old John Walter Cross.

EMERSON, EDWARD WALDO (1844–1930), son of Ralph Waldo Emerson and a friend of the James family.

EMERSON, RALPH WALDO (1803–82). Sr. was a great admirer of the great transcendentalist author and showed Emerson HJ's 1869–70 letters from Europe.

EMERSON, SYLVIA HATHAWAY WATSON (MRS. WILLIAM RALPH). *See* Watson, Sylvia Hathaway.

EMMET, CHRISTOPHER TEMPLE (1822–84), married HJ's cousin Ellen Temple in 1869.

EMMET, RICHARD STOCKTON (1821–1902), married HJ's cousin Katharine (Kitty) Temple in 1868.

FELTON, CORNELIUS CONWAY (1807–62), president of Harvard at the time of his death.

FELTON, MARY LOUISA CARY (MRS. CORNELIUS CONWAY), wife of Harvard's president and sister of Elizabeth Cary Agassiz.

FERGUSSON, SIR WILLIAM (1808–77), Scottish surgeon, professor of surgery at King's College, London (1840–70), afterward clinical professor of surgery and senior surgery at the same college; named sergeant-surgeon to the queen in 1867, elected to the council of the College of Surgeons in 1861 and president in 1870.

FEUILLET, OCTAVE (1821–90), popular French novelist and playwright and frequent contributor to the prestigious *Revue des Deux Mondes*; HJ reviewed his *Monsieur de Camors* in 1868 and his *Les Amours de Philippe* in 1877, both for the *Nation*.

FIELDS, ANNIE ADAMS (1834–1915), author famous for her literary salon at the Fieldses' home on Charles Street, Boston; after James T. Fields's death, she became the companion of author Sarah Orne Jewett (1849–1909).

FIELDS, JAMES THOMAS (1817–81), Boston publisher, managing partner of Ticknor and Fields, and editor of the *Atlantic Monthly* (1861–71), which Ticknor and Fields had purchased in 1859 and which published a number of HJ's earliest reviews and stories; at the end of his life, HJ wrote a commemorative article about the Fieldses, "Mr. and Mrs. James T. Fields," for the *Atlantic Monthly* (July 1915; the article also appeared the same month, with the title "Mr. & Mrs. Fields," in the *Cornhill Magazine*).

FISKE, JOHN (1842–1901), history and philosophy scholar and author, a lecturer at Harvard and later professor at Washington University (in Saint Louis); a follower of Spencer and Comte, he conducted a series of popular lectures at Harvard, called "The Positive Philosophy," from 1869 to 1872.

FORSTER, JOHN (1812–76), English critic and biographer remembered for his biography of Dickens (1872–74); he also wrote biographies of Oliver Goldsmith (1848), Walter Savage Landor (1869), and Jonathan Swift (unfinished, 1875).

FORSTER, WILLIAM EDWARD (1818–86), privy councilor in Gladstone's 1868 government; he was responsible for planning a system of national education. In 1869 he saw through the House of Commons the Endowed Schools Bill, and in February 1870 he introduced the Elementary Education Bill.

FOSTER, MYLES BIRKET (1825–99), celebrated Victorian landscape illustrator and watercolorist.

FREUND, DR. MAXIMILIAN BERNHARD (b. 1835), German physician known to WJ; his wife, Ellen Washburn, was the sister of Frank Washburn.

GARRATT, DR. ALFRED CHARLES (ca. 1813–91), American physician; WJ corresponded with him about medical uses of electricity.

GILDER, RICHARD WATSON (1844–1909), poet, assistant editor of *Scribner's Monthly* (1870–81), and editor of the *Century* (1881–1909); he married Helena de Kay in 1874.

GODKIN, EDWIN LAWRENCE (1831–1902), founded the liberal weekly *Nation* in 1865 and published many of HJ's earliest, mostly unsigned, reviews and articles. In 1881 the *Nation* merged with the *New York Evening Post*, which Godkin edited from 1883 to 1900.

GOT, FRANÇOIS JULES EDMOND (1822–1901), Comédie Française actor whom HJ admired.

GOULD, DR. JAMES BREWSTER, American doctor in Rome whom HJ saw in 1869 for his constipation.

GRAHAM, JAMES LORIMER, JR., a New Yorker and American consul to Florence, whom HJ met in October 1869.

GRAY, JOHN CHIPMAN (1839–1915), a friend of Minny Temple's, was a distinguished lawyer and Harvard law professor. He and his law partner, John Ropes, established the *American Law Review* in 1866, which they edited until 1870. HJ met Gray in August 1865 when Oliver Wendell Holmes Jr. brought him on a trip to the White Mountains. Gray preserved all his life the letters he had received from Minny Temple, and near the end of his life, he turned them over to WJ's widow, Alice H. James, who in turn sent them to HJ, who made use of them in *Notes of a Son and Brother.*

GREENOUGH, CHARLOTTE (b. 1850), daughter of Horatio and Louisa Gore Greenough.

GREENOUGH, LOUISA GORE (MRS. HORATIO) (1812–92), wife of sculptor Horatio Greenough. She was born in Boston and died in Florence.

GRINNELL, CHARLES E., identified by Harlow as one of the fourteen members who formed "The Club," a dinner and conversation club. The founding members included HJ and WJ, William Dean Howells, Arthur Sedgwick, Henry Adams, Oliver Wendell Holmes Jr., and Thomas Sergeant Perry (46).

GROGAN, ALEXANDER EDWARD, a passenger with WJ on the *Great Eastern*, when they traveled to Europe in the spring of 1867.

GRYMES, MARY (NELLY) HELEN JAMES (MRS. CHARLES ALFRED) (1840–81), was the daughter of John Barber James, HJ's uncle, and the wife of Dr. Charles Alfred Grymes of New York.

GRYZANOVSKI, DR. ERNST GEORG FRIEDRICH (1824–88), German educator and author.

GULLY, DR. JAMES MANBY (1808–83), British physician specializing in hydropathy. He administered his water-cure in Great Malvern at the Holyrood House for women and the Tudor House for men. His writings include *An Exposition of the Symptoms, Essential Nature, and Treatment of Neuropathy, or Nervousness* (1837), *The Water Cure in Chronic Disease* (1847), and *A Guide to Domestic Hydrotherapeia* (1863).

GURNEY, EPHRAIM (1829–86), assistant professor of Latin, assistant professor of modern languages, and later dean of the faculty at Harvard. He was also the editor of the *North American Review* before Henry Adams. Gurney married Adams's sister-in-law, Ellen Sturgis Hooper (1838–87). While the Nortons were abroad (1868–72), the Gurneys resided at Shady Hill, Charles Eliot Norton's Cambridge home.

HAMILTON, GAIL (1833–96), pseudonym for Mary Abigail Dodge, a popular, inspirational author and women's reformer.

HARCOURT, A. VERNON, a young Oxford chemist, met the Nortons in 1868 when they lived briefly in Oxford and served as host to HJ when he visited Oxford in 1869.

HARRISON, FREDERIC, Comtist author and public servant and acquaintance of Charles Eliot Norton's in London.

HARTE, BRET (1836–1902), American teacher, journalist, editor, and local-color fiction writer who gained notoriety with his western writings; he was appointed secretary of the United States Branch Mint at San Francisco and later United States consul at Crefeld, Germany. HJ mentions being present at an 1871 dinner given by Longfellow in Harte's honor.

HATCH, CORA L. V., lecturer on such religious topics as "Patriotism and Religion," "The Summer Land," and "The Harmonial Man: A Plea for Humanity," whom HJ heard speak in New York in November 1863.

HELPS, SIR ARTHUR (1813–75), clerk of the privy council (1860–75) and a successful writer. He was an admirer of the writings of Sr., but HJ nevertheless passed up an opportunity to meet him at the Nortons' in May 1869.

HOLMES, AMELIA JACKSON (1843–89), sister of Oliver Wendell Holmes Jr.; she married John Turner Welles Sargent.

HOLMES, AMELIA LEE JACKSON (1818–88), wife of Dr. Oliver Wendell Holmes and mother of Oliver Wendell Holmes Jr.

HOLMES, EDWARD JACKSON (1846–84), brother of Oliver Wendell Holmes Jr.

HOLMES, OLIVER WENDELL (1809–94), well-known author and one of the original contributors to the *Atlantic Monthly* and father of HJ's friend, Oliver Wendell Holmes Jr.

HOLMES, OLIVER WENDELL, JR. (1841–1935), lawyer, essayist, judge, and Supreme Court justice; close friend of HJ when both were young men.

HOOPER, MARIAN (CLOVER). *See* Adams, Marian (Clover) Hooper.

HORTON, SAMUEL DANA (1844–95), enjoyed a relatively short career as a diplomat working with the American minister in Florence before the unification of Italy.

HOSMER, BURR GRISWOLD, author of the 1868 *Poems.*

HOUGHTON, RICHARD MONCKTON MILNES, LORD (1809–85), was a passionate supporter of young writers and an intimate to many established writers of the day. He secured the laureateship for Tennyson, promoted Emerson among the British, and recognized Swinburne's brilliance. Houghton also wrote *Life of Keats* (1848). He and HJ later became friends.

HOWELLS, ELINOR GERTRUDE MEAD (1837–1910), married William Dean Howells in 1862.

HOWELLS, JOHN MEAD (1868–1959), William Dean Howells's only son.

HOWELLS, WILLIAM DEAN (1837–1920), American author, editor, and literary critic who, together with HJ, is largely credited for ushering in literary realism in the United States. His and HJ's first meeting probably occurred in the summer of 1866 (Anesko 11–13). Despite their different upbringings, the two became lifelong friends. As assistant editor, and then editor, of the *Atlantic Monthly*, Howells accepted HJ's work for publication, and throughout their careers they exchanged literary advice.

HUMPERT, DOCTOR, and family. HJ and GWJ resided with this family, which apparently regularly took in students, during the summer of 1860, in order to practice German. The Jameses' letters from this period are inconsistent in their spelling of the doctor's name.

HUNT, WILLIAM HOLMAN (1827–1910), Pre-Raphaelite painter whose illustrations for "The Ballad of Oriana," in the 1857 edition of Tennyson's *Poems*, HJ remembered when writing home from London in March 1869.

HUNT, WILLIAM MORRIS (1824–79), was born in Brattleboro, Vermont, spent his childhood in New Haven, Connecticut, and studied sculpture at Harvard. He went on to Europe, studying at Düsseldorf

Academy in Germany and then in France; first under Thomas Couture (1815–79), and then as a disciple of the Barbizon school of landscape painting, at which point he was particularly influenced by Jean-François Millet. He returned to the United States in 1855 and set up residence in Newport, Rhode Island, where he taught John La Farge, WJ, and HJ, among others. He finally settled in Boston, where he became famous both for introducing the Barbizon method of landscape painting to American audiences and as a portrait painter.

HUNTER, GEORGE GRENVILLE (b. 1892), the only child of Ellen James Temple Emmet Hunter and her second husband, George Hunter (1847–1914).

HUNTINGTON, ELLEN GREENOUGH (1814–93), was the second wife of Charles Phelps Huntington and sister-in-law to Francis Boott; she resided in Florence.

INMAN, DR. THOMAS (1820–76), HJ called this Liverpool doctor "our friend" in his 27 February [1869] letter to his family; Inman was a distinguished physician and an author of many publications on hygiene, archaeology, and mythology.

JAMES, ALICE (1848–92) (AJ), was the fifth and youngest child and only daughter of Sr. and MWJ. She is remembered for her eloquent and candid journal, written during the last three years of her life and preserved and posthumously printed by her close friend Katharine Peabody Loring.

JAMES, ELIZABETH CABOT LODGE (b. 1843), sister of Henry Cabot Lodge and wife of HJ's Harvard Law School friend, George Abbot James (married in 1864).

JAMES, GARTH WILKINSON (1845–83) (GWJ), the third child of Sr. and MWJ, referred to by the family as Wilky. Unlike his older brothers, he served in the Civil War, in which he was badly wounded. After the war, he and RJ tried to run a plantation in Florida. In 1873 he married Caroline Cary (Carrie James), and they had two children: Joseph Cary and Alice.

JAMES, GEORGE ABBOT (b. 1838), met HJ during HJ's brief stint at Harvard Law School in 1862. Their lifelong friendship (they were not related) was maintained through decades of letters and a visit HJ made to Nahant in the early summer of 1911. He recalled their early friendship in *Notes of a Son and Brother* (368).

JAMES, HENRY, SR. (1811–82) (Sr.), was born in Albany, New York, graduated from Union College in Schenectady, New York, worked in business and law, and then studied at Princeton Theological Seminary (1835–37). Although raised in a strict Presbyterian family, he was repelled by orthodox Protestantism and gave up adherence to institutional religion. He is remembered as an author and theological philosopher and was heavily influenced by Swedenborg. His books include *Christianity the Logic of Creation* (1857), *The Secret of Swedenborg* (1869), and *Society the Redeemed Form of Man* (1879). He and MWJ married in 1840 and had five children.

JAMES, HOWARD (1828–87), youngest brother of Sr.

JAMES, JEANNETTE (1814–42), Sr.'s younger sister; in 1832 she married William H. Barker, brother of Anna Barker Ward.

JAMES, JOHN BARBER (1816–56), younger brother of Sr.; he became a drunkard and committed suicide.

JAMES, MARY ROBERTSON WALSH (1810–82) (MWJ), married Sr. in 1840. She is most often described as having been a stable and comforting mother and wife. HJ continued his devotion to her until her death.

JAMES, ROBERTSON (1846–1910) (RJ), the fourth and youngest son of Sr. and MWJ, usually called Bob by the family. He served in the Civil War and worked with GWJ on his plantation in Florida. In 1872 he married Mary Holton, and they had two children, Edward (Ned) Holton and Mary Walsh (later Mary James Vaux).

JAMES, WILLIAM (OF ALBANY) (1771–1832), HJ's paternal grandfather; an immigrant from Ireland in the eighteenth century, he made a fortune in real estate in Albany and upstate New York.

JAMES, REVEREND WILLIAM (1797–1868), older half-brother of Sr. and father of Katharine (Mrs. William Henry) Prince (1834–90).

JAMES, WILLIAM (1842–1910) (WJ), HJ's older brother and pioneering psychologist and pragmatist philosopher best remembered for *The Principles of Psychology* (1890), *The Will to Believe* (1897), *The Varieties of Religious Experience* (1902), and *Pragmatism* (1907). He began teaching at Harvard in 1872, three years after he had received his M.D. there, and retired in 1907. In 1878 he married Alice Howe Gibbens (1849–1922), and they had five children: Henry (Harry) (1879–1947), William (Bill) (1882–1961), Herman (1884–85), Margaret (Peggy) Mary (Mrs. Bruce Porter) (1887–1950), and Alexander (Aleck) Robertson (1890–1946).

JEWETT, SARAH ORNE (1849–1909), author and companion of Annie Adams Fields (1834–1915).

KING, ANNIE, daughter of MWJ's first cousin, Charlotte Elizabeth Sleight Matthews, and Clarence W. King.

KING, ARTHUR, son of MWJ's first cousin, Charlotte Elizabeth Sleight Matthews, and Clarence W. King.

KING, CHARLOTTE (COUSIN CHARLOTTE) ELIZABETH SLEIGHT MATTHEWS, daughter of MWJ's aunt, Charlotte Walsh, and her husband, Reverend James Matthews. She married Clarence W. King.

KING, CLARENCE W., husband of Charlotte Elizabeth Sleight Matthews, MWJ's first cousin.

KING, ELLEN JAMES (1800–23), half-sister of Henry James Sr. and mother of Mary Ann King Post.

KING, JAMES (1788–1841), husband of Sr.'s half-sister, Ellen King.

KING, WILLIAM VERNON (d. 1864), son of Charlotte Elizabeth Sleight Matthews and Clarence W. King; he was killed in the battle at Petersburg.

LADD, ANNA RUSSELL WATSON (MRS. WILLIAM JONES). *See* Watson, Anna Russell.

LA FARGE, JOHN (1835–1910), was an American painter, stained-glass designer, and writer. He studied art under William Morris Hunt (who would later teach WJ, and to some extent HJ) during his time in Newport, where he met the Jameses in 1858. La Farge had a major influence on both WJ and HJ, as he encouraged HJ to pursue writing and the study of literature, and mentored WJ in the Hunt studio. In *Notes of a Son and Brother*, HJ says "John La Farge became at once [. . .] quite the most interesting person we knew" (84–85). In 1860 La Farge married Thomas Sergeant Perry's older sister Margaret. He also provided the original illustrations for "The Turn of the Screw" when it appeared in *Collier's Weekly*. HJ later recalled La Farge to Mary Cadwalader Jones as one of his oldest friends.

LA FARGE, MARGARET MASON PERRY (MRS. JOHN). *See* Perry, Margaret Mason.

LANDOR, JULIA (THUILLIER), married Walter Savage Landor in 1811 and separated from him in 1835.

LANDOR, JULIA ELIZABETH SAVAGE (1820–84), daughter of Walter and Julia (Thuillier) Savage Landor.

LANDOR, WALTER SAVAGE (1775–1864), English poet admired by Robert Browning. He resided in Italy from 1811 to 1835, when he separated from his wife.

LECKY, WILLIAM EDWARD HARTPOLE (1838–1903), author of *History of European Morals from Augustus to Charlemagne* (1869).

LENOX, JAMES (1800–1880), New York merchant and real-estate owner who incorporated his rare book collection into a public library in 1870. Lenox's collection included the first Gutenberg Bible brought to the United States, a Gilbert Stuart portrait of George Washington, and the original autographed manuscript of Washington's farewell address. The Lenox Library, along with the Astor Library and the Tilden Trust, were consolidated into the New York Public Library in 1895.

LEVERETT, REVEREND WILLIAM C., ran the Berkeley Institute, the James boys' Newport school, which in 1858 was located at 10 Washington Square. According to HJ, he was an uninspiring teacher. See also *Notes of a Son and Brother* (81–82).

LEWES, GEORGE HENRY (1817–78), English philosopher, dramatist, actor, literary critic, editor, and scientist, who engaged in a twenty-four-year liaison with Mary Ann Evans (George Eliot). He married Agnes Jervis in 1841 and the couple lived communally with their friend Thornton Leigh Hunt, Hunt's wife, and two other couples. The arrangement failed after Mrs. Lewes gave birth to two of Hunt's children. His publications include *Life of Goethe* (1855), *Seaside Studies* (1858), *The Physiology of Common Life* (1859–60), *Studies in Animal Life* (1862), and the ambitious *Problems of Life and Mind* (1873–79).

LEWES, MRS. *See* Eliot, George.

LEWES, THORNTON ARNOTT (1844–69), second son of George Henry Lewes, whom HJ observed, when he first met George Eliot on 9 May 1869, suffering from back pains caused by spinal tuberculosis. Lewes died five months later.

LODGE, ANNA SOPHIA CABOT (1821–1900), mother of Elizabeth Cabot Lodge James.

LOMBARD, MRS. According to AJ's biographer, the Lombards were family friends (Strouse 142).

LONGFELLOW, HENRY WADSWORTH (1807–82), celebrated poet, who had lived in Cambridge since 1836 (he taught French and Spanish at Harvard 1836–54); HJ mentions attending an 1871 dinner Longfellow hosted in honor of Bret Harte.

LOWELL, ANNA CABOT JACKSON (1811–74), aunt of Lilla Cabot Perry and wife of Charles Russell Lowell, the elder brother of James Russell Lowell. She lived at 24 Quincy Street, Cambridge, the property adjoining the Jameses'.

LOWELL, CHARLES RUSSELL, JR. (1835–64), the son of James Russell Lowell's brother, Charles Russell Lowell, and Anna Cabot Jackson Lowell and the husband to social reformer and charity activist Josephine Shaw Lowell; he died in the Civil War.

LOWELL, JAMES RUSSELL (1819–91), well-known poet, American diplomat (ambassador to Spain, 1877–80, and to England, 1880–85), and Harvard professor of French and Spanish, 1855–76. He was the first editor of the *Atlantic Monthly* (1857–61) and in 1864 helped Charles Eliot Norton edit the *North American Review*. He and HJ later became close friends, especially when Lowell was posted in England.

LOWELL, MABEL (1847–98), James Russell Lowell's only surviving daughter.

LYGON, FREDERICK (1830–91), sixth Earl Beauchamp, of Madresfield Court, on the bank of the Severn River, east of Malvern. HJ described visiting this estate in February 1870.

MACKAY (OR MACKAYE), BARON DONALD, Scottish nobleman in the Dutch diplomatic service who visited the Nortons in Cambridge.

MARSH, GEORGE PERKINS (1801–82), American attorney and politician; he was appointed by Lincoln in 1861 to be the first U.S. minister to Italy.

MATHEWS, FLORENCE WILKINSON, the daughter of Emma and Dr. James John Garth Wilkinson and sister of Mary Wilkinson. Florence married St. John Mathews.

MATHEWS, FRANK, cousin of Florence Wilkinson Mathews's husband, St. John Mathews, and a London solicitor.

MCKAYE, COLONEL JAMES, father of Steele McKaye and an old friend of Sr., whose summer house at 13 Kay Street, Newport, the Jameses rented from the fall of 1860 to the spring or summer of 1862.

MCKAYE (OR MACKAYE), STEELE (1842–94), the son of Colonel James McKaye; he studied art under Thomas Couture in Paris, later became an actor, dramatist, and producer. He created and patented more than one hundred inventions for the theater, which include overhead lighting, moving double stages, and folding theater seats.

METCALFE, DR. JOHN T., New York City physician who examined Minny Temple; his office was at 86 Fifth Avenue.

MILNES, RICHARD MONCKTON. *See* Houghton, Lord.

MINTURN, ELIZABETH (BESSIE) T., contributed to the *Nation* after 1876.

MORLEY, JOHN (1838–1923), editor of the *Fortnightly Review* and *Pall Mall Gazette* and also a statesman, historian, and writer. He served as chief secretary for Ireland (1886, 1892–95) and secretary for India (1905–10). Morley's works include *Diderot and the Encyclopoedists* (1878), *Ralph Waldo Emerson* (1884), and *Life of Gladstone* (1903).

MORRIS, JANE BURDEN (1840–1914), the wife of William Morris (they married in 1859) and a frequent model for Pre-Raphaelite painters; HJ met her in 1869.

MORRIS, WILLIAM (1834–96), English poet and designer whom HJ met in 1869. Among his most remembered works are *The Defence of Guenevere and Other Poems* (1858); *The Life and Death of Jason* (1867), which HJ reviewed for the October 1867 *North American Review*; *The Earthly Paradise* (1868–70), the first part of which HJ reviewed for the *North American Review* (July 1868) and the *Nation* (9 July 1868); *Sigurd the Volsung* (1876); *A Dream of John Bull* (1888); and *News from Nowhere* (1891).

MORSE, FRANCES (FANNY) ROLLINS (1850–1928), AJ's first intimate and lifelong friend and WJ's lifelong correspondent.

MOTLEY, JOHN LOTHROP (1814–77), appointed American minister to Great Britain in March 1869, he played a role in attempting to negotiate the *Alabama* Claims.

NEWELL, REVEREND WILLIAM, minister of Cambridge's First Parish–Unitarian Church.

NILSSON, CHRISTINA (1843–1921), celebrated Swedish singer; HJ heard her at Boston's Music Hall on 14 November 1870 while she was touring the United States in 1870–71 with a star-studded company that included Belgian virtuoso violinist Henri Vieuxtemps (1820–81).

NOBLE, LULU GRAY, author of "Notes on the Woman's Rights Agitation" (*Nation*, 20 January 1870, 10 February 1870, and 17 February 1870), about which HJ questioned WJ on [7], 8, 9 March 1870.

NORTON, ANDREWS (1786–1853), biblical scholar, Harvard teacher, and Boston merchant, the father of Grace, Jane, and Charles Eliot Norton.

NORTON, CATHARINE ELIOT (1793–1879), married Andrews Norton in 1821; after her husband's death, she lived with her unmarried daughters, Jane and Grace, and her son, Charles.

NORTON, CHARLES ELIOT (1827–1908), influential author, editor, and scholar, professor of the history of fine art at Harvard (1873–98), translator of Dante, editor of the *North American Review* (1864–68), one of the founders of the *Nation*; he lived in Cambridge, at Shady Hill, near the Jameses and was an early mentor of HJ's career, publishing some of his first review articles and introducing him in 1869 to prominent cultural figures in London. He married Susan Ridley Sedgwick in 1862; they had six children.

NORTON, ELIOT (1863–1932), oldest child of Charles Eliot and Susan Sedgwick Norton.

NORTON, ELIZABETH (LILY) (b. 1866), the second daughter of Charles Eliot Norton and Susan Sedgwick Norton.

NORTON, GRACE (1834–1926), Charles Eliot Norton's youngest sister; she lived most of her life with her brother, helping to raise his children, but in the early twentieth century she published several studies of Montaigne, including *Studies in Montaigne* (1904), *The Spirit of Montaigne* (1908), and *The Influence of Montaigne* (1908). She and HJ maintained a lengthy and intimate correspondence from 1868 to the end of his life.

NORTON, JANE (1824–77), Charles Eliot Norton's elder sister; she lived with her brother during her adult years and helped to raise his children.

NORTON, MARGARET (1870–1947), the third daughter of Charles Eliot and Susan Sedgwick Norton.

NORTON, RICHARD (1872–1918), the sixth and last child of Charles Eliot and Susan Sedgwick Norton.

NORTON, RUPERT (1867–1914), the second son of Charles Eliot and Susan Sedgwick Norton.

NORTON, SARA (SALLY) (1864–1922), the eldest daughter of Charles Eliot and Susan Sedgwick Norton.

NORTON, SUSAN RIDLEY SEDGWICK (1838–72), married Charles Eliot Norton in 1862. Her death following the delivery of her sixth child in ten years of marriage was a terrible blow to her husband. She was the sister of HJ's friend Arthur G. Sedgwick and of AJ's friend Sara Sedgwick Darwin.

PAGET, GEORGE EDWARD (K.C. B. in 1885), physician to Addenbrooke's Hospital, bursar of Caius College, Cambridge, elected to the Royal College of Physicians, London (1839), president of the General Council of Medical Education and Registration (elected 1869).

PATTISON, EMILIA (b. 1840), wife of Mark Pattison, classical scholar; Mrs. Pattison became friendly with the Nortons when they stayed in Oxford in 1868.

PEABODY, LUCIA MARIA (1828-1919), a resident of Roxbury, Massachusetts, and secretary and an active member of the New England Women's Club (founded in 1868), of which Sr. and MWJ were members in 1869.

PEARSON, CHARLES HENRY (1830-94), English (and later Australian) historian and educator; author of *The Early and Middle Ages of England* (1861) and *History of England during the Early and Middle Ages* (1867).

PEIRCE, BENJAMIN (1844-70), a mining engineer, was in Paris with his brother, James Mills Peirce, at the same time as Thomas Sergeant Perry. Both Peirce brothers were professors of mathematics at Harvard College and became intimate friends of Perry's.

PEIRCE, CHARLES SANDERS (1839-1914), pragmatic philosopher and semiotician who was a close friend of WJ.

PELL, DUNCAN ARCHIBALD (ARCHIE) (1840-74), one year older than WJ and three years older than HJ, was their friend and schoolmate in Newport. He was the son of Duncan Campbell Pell, lieutenant governor of Rhode Island and a friend of Sr.'s. The Pells lived at 14 Mary Street in Newport.

PEPPER, FRANCES (FANNY) PERRY. *See* Perry, Frances (Fanny).

PERKINS, CHARLES CALLAHAN (1823-86), Boston art critic, he lectured at the Lowell Institute on Greek and Italian art and engraving several times in the 1870s. In 1855 he married Frances D. Bruen.

PERKINS, FRANCES D. BRUEN, wife of Charles Callahan Perkins.

PERKINS, HELEN (COUSIN HELEN) RODGERS WYCKOFF (1807–87), maternal first cousin of MWJ, she had grown up almost as a third sister to MWJ and Catharine Walsh. Cousin Helen and her husband, Leonard, shared a house across Sixth Avenue in New York from the Jameses.

PERKINS, JANE SEDGWICK WATSON (MRS. EDWARD CRANCH). *See* Watson, Jane Sedgwick.

PERKINS, LEONARD (d. 1869), husband of MWJ's first cousin Helen Rodgers Wyckoff Perkins. He was once a custom house officer, and he died while touring Europe with Catharine (Aunt Kate) Walsh, Helen Ripley, his wife, and her brother, Henry.

PERRY, FRANCES (FANNY), younger sister of Thomas Sergeant Perry; she later married Dr. William Pepper, who became provost of the University of Pennsylvania.

PERRY, FRANCES SERGEANT, mother of Thomas Sergeant Perry.

PERRY, LILLA CABOT (MRS. THOMAS SERGEANT). *See* Cabot, Lilla.

PERRY (LA FARGE), MARGARET MASON (1840–1925), sister of HJ's close friend Thomas Sergeant Perry. She married painter John La Farge in 1860.

PERRY, OLIVER HAZARD (1842–1913), older brother of Thomas Sergeant Perry.

PERRY, THOMAS SERGEANT (1845–1928), writer, scholar, educator, translator, and a close friend of HJ's for over fifty years, until HJ's death. They first met in Newport in 1858.

PLETSCH, OSCAR (1830–88), German illustrator of such children's books as *Chimes and Rhymes for Youthful Times!* (1871) and *Aunt Bessie's Picture Book* (1872).

PORTER, ANNIE, daughter of a family, apparently in Louisiana, that Thomas Sergeant Perry and his mother and sister visited during the winter of 1860.

PORTER, MARY, daughter of a family, apparently in Louisiana, that Thomas Sergeant Perry and his mother and sister visited during the winter of 1860.

POST, MARY ANN KING (1819-92), daughter of Ellen James King, half-sister of Sr., and James King; she proposed taking Minny Temple with her to Europe during the summer of 1870.

PRATT, HERBERT JAMES (b. 1841), a graduate of Harvard Medical School (1868) and an army surgeon during the Civil War. He traveled to Europe in 1867 on the same ship as WJ.

PRESCOTT (SPOFFORD), HARRIET ELIZABETH (1835-1921), prolific American author; HJ's second publication for the *North American Review* was an unsigned review of her novel *Azarian: An Episode.*

PRINCE, KATHARINE (KITTY) JAMES (1834-90), the youngest daughter of Reverend William James (1797-1868), the half brother of Sr. She married Dr. William Henry Prince in 1861.

RAYNER, DR., director of the water-cure in Malvern, England, where HJ sought treatment, in April 1869 and March 1870, for constipation and back pain.

REILLY, MISS A., apparently an Irish maid in the La Farges' Newport home.

RHOADES, BENJAMIN H. (d. 1880), librarian of the Redwood Library in 1859, when the Jameses moved to Newport, and until his death.

RIPLEY, GEORGE (1802-80), American literary reviewer and critic, was also a founder of the Brook Farm commune.

RIPLEY, HELEN, HJ's second cousin; her mother, Catherine Walsh Andrews (Mrs. Joseph) Ripley (1806-65), was the daughter of Catharine Walsh (Mrs. David) Andrews (1785-1829), who was the younger sister of MWJ's and Aunt Kate's father, James Walsh (c. 1780-1820).

RIPLEY, SOPHIA WILLARD DANA (MRS. GEORGE), wife of George Ripley and a fellow founder of the Brook Farm commune; HJ met her in Rome in December 1869.

RISTORI, ADELAIDE (1822-1906), Italian tragedienne who gained international fame. HJ first witnessed her performance in the title role of *Maria Stuart* when the family was staying in Bonn, Germany, during 1860. Ristori toured the United States in 1866 with *Medea*, and her success encouraged her return in 1867, 1875, and 1884.

RITCHIE, ANNE ISABELLA THACKERAY (1837–1919), later Lady Ritchie, wrote impressionistic essays and novels and also published reminiscences of the literary figures she knew in her youth, including Tennyson, Ruskin, and Elizabeth and Robert Browning. HJ met her in 1877, and they remained friends for decades.

ROBESON, ANDREW, JR. (b. 1843), a schoolmate of HJ's at the Berkeley Institute in Newport and the son of Andrew Robeson Sr.

ROBESON, ANDREW, SR. (1817–74), the father of HJ's Berkeley Institute schoolmate Andrew Robeson Jr., who owned a house in Newport at the corner of Bellevue Avenue and Perry Street; he was instrumental in developing steamship (and later railway) travel between Boston and New York.

ROBESON, WILLIAM (1843–1922), GWJ's partner in their Florida plantation during the late 1860s; he studied at Harvard (1860–64) and later became a railroad executive.

ROBIN, CHARLES-PHILIPPE (1821–85), French doctor and physiologist.

ROBINSON, HENRY CRABB (1775–1867), London solicitor remembered for his *Diary, Reminiscences, and Correspondence* (1869), which was first published in London by Macmillan.

ROCHETTE, GUSTAVE, was the director of the polytechnic school in Geneva that HJ attended from about mid-October 1859 until approximately April 1860. He resided at rue St. Léger, 61, in 1860. The Institut Rochette was located at the rue de l'Evêché, 7, directly behind the Cathédrale de Saint Pierre. HJ describes the school in *Notes of a Son and Brother* (2–13).

RODGERS, ALEXANDER ROBERTSON (b. 1807), father of Katherine (Katie) and Henrietta (Nettie) Rodgers; he was MWJ's and Aunt Kate's first cousin.

RODGERS, HENRIETTA (NETTIE) (1843–1906), sister of Katherine (Katie) Rodgers.

RODGERS, KATHERINE (KATIE) OUTRAM (b. 1841), granddaughter of MWJ's maternal aunt, Hellen Robertson (d. 1818), and of her husband, John Richardson Bayard Rodgers (d. 1833); her parents were Alexander Robertson Rodgers (b. 1807) and his wife, Mary Ridgely Darden (d. 1888).

RODGERS, MARY RIDGELY DARDEN (MRS. ALEXANDER ROBERTSON) (d. 1888), mother of Katherine (Katie) and Henrietta (Nettie) Rodgers and wife of MWJ's first cousin Alexander Robertson Rodgers.

ROMANOV, OLGA NIKOLAEVNA (1822–92), queen of Würtemberg, grand duchess of Russia, was married to Karl I, king of Würtemberg, who reigned from 1864 to 1891. HJ mentioned Sophia Ripley's audience with her in Rome in late December 1869.

ROSSETTI, DANTE GABRIEL (1828–82), English painter and poet who helped found the Pre-Raphaelite Brotherhood with William Holman Hunt and John Millais. Charles Eliot Norton introduced HJ to him in 1869.

RUSKIN, JOHN (1819–1900), English critic, scholar, and artist, whose work HJ knew rather well. In 1869 HJ visited him near Dulwich at Denmark Hill, Ruskin's family home in London.

RUTSON, O. ALBERT, private secretary at the Home Office, Whitehall, under Secretary of State Henry Austin Bruce. He lived at 7 Half-Moon Street, Piccadilly, and helped HJ secure a lodging in the same building during March 1869. HJ met him through Charles Eliot Norton.

SAINT-BEUVE, CHARLES-AUGUSTIN (1804–69), leading French literary critic, best known for his *Causeries du lundi* (15 vols., 1851–62) and *Nouveaux lundis* (13 vols., 1861–69), which collected his regular Monday column for *Le Constitutionnel*, *Le Moniteur*, and *Le Temps*. HJ reviewed several of his books and was considerably influenced by Sainte-Beuve. When HJ noted Sainte-Beuve's death in the postscript to his 13, 16, [17] October [1869] letter to his mother, he wrote: "I have lost my best friend."

SAND, GEORGE (1804–76), pseudonym of the prolific French novelist Aurore Dupin, Baronne Dudevant, whose own vivacious life rivaled that in her fictional works. HJ reviewed the 1868 American translation of her novel *Mademoiselle Merquem* for the *Nation* (16 July 1868) and went on to publish seven other articles on her during his life.

SANTLEY, CHARLES (1834–1922), English baritone who toured the United States in 1871–72 with the Dolby Troupe.

SARDOU, VICTORIEN (1831–1908), playwright who dominated the French stage in the late nineteenth century. He was elected to the Académie Française in 1877 and is best remembered today as the author of *Tosca*, the source for Puccini's opera.

SCHÉRER, EDMOND (1815–89), French critic of Swiss ancestry; HJ published an unsigned review of Schérer's *Nouvelles Études sur la littérature contemporaine* in the *Nation* (12 October 1865).

SEDGWICK, ARTHUR GEORGE (1844–1915), lawyer, writer, and editor. The novelist Catharine Maria Sedgwick was his great-aunt. HJ knew him when both were young men in Cambridge. Their friendship would intersect at the professional level when Sedgwick worked as an editorial assistant on the *Nation* (1872–84) and then later at the *New York Evening Post* (1881–85). Sedgwick's sister, Susan, married Charles Eliot Norton in 1862. Before he moved to New York in 1872, he lived with his sisters Sara and Theodora and their maternal aunts, Anne and Grace Ashburner, on Kirkland Street, between the Nortons' Shady Hill estate and the Jameses' house at 20 Quincy Street, Cambridge.

SEDGWICK, SARA MORGAN ASHBURNER (MRS. THEODORE) (1812–56), mother of Susan Ridley Sedgwick Norton, Sara Price Ashburner Sedgwick Darwin, Arthur George Sedgwick, and Theodora Sedgwick.

SEDGWICK, SARA PRICE ASHBURNER (1839–1902), sister of Charles Eliot Norton's wife, Susan Sedgwick Norton, and of HJ's friend Arthur G. Sedgwick; she married Charles Darwin's son, William Erasmus Darwin, in 1879.

SEDGWICK, THEODORA (1851–1916), youngest sister of Susan Sedgwick Norton and Arthur George Sedgwick.

SEDGWICK, THEODORE, III (1811–59), father of Susan Sedgwick Norton, Sara Sedgwick Darwin, Arthur George Sedgwick, and

Theodora Sedgwick; the novelist Catharine Maria Sedgwick was his aunt, and Elizabeth Ellery Sedgwick Child, Katharine Sedgwick Valerio Washburn, and Robert Sedgwick Watson were his first cousins.

SEEMÜLLER, ANNE MONCURE (1838–72), author of *Emily Chester: A Novel* (1864), which HJ reviewed for the January 1865 *North American Review*.

SENIOR, NASSAU WILLIAM (1790–1864), British economist and author of political articles and biographical and critical essays and lectures, including a famous series of reviews of Scott's Waverley novels. HJ's first published review for the *North American Review* was on Senior's 1864 *Essays on Fiction*.

SIMON, SIR JOHN (1816–1904, knighted in 1887), a friend of Charles Eliot Norton and a physician and member of the Royal College of Surgeons.

SMITH, ALFRED, a Newport realtor to whom Sr. wrote in the summer of 1860 about finding a residence in Newport and who arranged for the Jameses to buy a house at the corner of Spring and Lee Streets in Newport.

SPOFFORD, HARRIET ELIZABETH PRESCOTT. *See* Prescott (Spofford), Harriet Elizabeth.

STEPHEN, LESLIE (1832–1904), British intellectual, essayist, philosopher, editor, biographer, and literary critic, best remembered today as the father of Virginia Woolf. He gained access into the literary community through his brother, James Fitzjames Stephen, who was a contributor to the *Saturday Review*. Stephen edited the *Cornhill Magazine* from 1871 to 1882 and established himself as one of the first serious critics of the novel. During his editorship, Stephen encouraged young authors (socially as well as professionally), including HJ. Stephen's most enduring professional success came with the *Dictionary of National Biography*, which he edited from 1882 to 1891. In 1902 Stephen was created Knight Commander of Bath in recognition of his service to letters.

STOREY, MOORFIELD (1845–1929), was a Harvard classmate and friend of Thomas Sergeant Perry's. He became a prominent Boston attorney and politician, an overseer of Harvard College and a member of "The Club"—the dinner and conversation group that included HJ, WJ, Perry, William Dean Howells, and Oliver Wendell Holmes Jr. In 1910 Storey was elected president of the newly formed NAACP.

STORY, EDITH (1857–1919), daughter of sculptor William Wetmore Story. She later married the Florentine marquis Simone Peruzzi, a descendant of the Medicis.

STORY, EMELYN ELDREDGE (1821–94), wife of William Wetmore Story.

STORY, WILLIAM WETMORE (1819–95), sculptor, his most famed piece, *Cleopatra*, was immortalized in Hawthorne's *The Marble Faun*. In 1903 HJ wrote Story's biography about his art and life in Rome, *William Wetmore Story and His Friends*.

STRATTON, CHARLES, a lifelong friend and a classmate at Harvard of Thomas Sergeant Perry's, he became an attorney.

STRONG, ELEANOR FEARING (MRS. CHARLES EDWARD), was estranged from her husband and resided abroad with their daughter.

SUMNER, CHARLES (1811–74), U.S. senator from Massachusetts (1851–74). He was an outspoken abolitionist and in 1856 was savagely beaten on the floor of the U.S. Senate by Congressman Preston S. Brooks. He was also one of the founders of the Republican Party. In 1869 he was serving as chairman of the Senate Foreign Relations Committee and gave a speech in April against a compromise in the dispute between the United States and England over American Civil War damage claims against the British.

SWINBURNE, ALGERNON CHARLES (1837–1909), English poet, playwright, and literary critic. HJ reviewed Swinburne's *Chastelard: A Tragedy* for the *Nation*, 18 January 1866.

TAINE, HIPPOLYTE (1828–93), influential critic, philosopher, and historian, perhaps best remembered for his *Histoire de la littérature anglaise* (1863), a U.S. edition of which HJ reviewed for the *Atlantic Monthly* (April 1872).

TAPPAN, CAROLINE STURGIS (1819–88), transcendentalist poet and friend of Emerson, Margaret Fuller, and Sr.

TAYLOR, BAYARD (1825–78), Pennsylvania-born writer, diplomat, and professor of German at Cornell.

TAYLOR, DR. CHARLES FAYETTE (1827–99), New York orthopedic surgeon who treated AJ in 1867 and from whom HJ planned to obtain a corset for his back trouble. Dr. Taylor was a practical psychotherapist, treating numerous neurasthenic women through a series of exercises he documented in *The Theory and Practice of the Movement Cure* (1861).

TAYLOR, TOM (1817–80), was a successful dramatist and editor of *Punch.* He married Laura Barker in 1855 (she died in 1905); she was a composer and contributed the overture and entr'acte to Taylor's *Joan of Arc* (1870).

TEMPLE (EMMET HUNTER), ELLEN JAMES (1850–1920), Minny Temple's younger sister, she married her cousin, Christopher Temple Emmet, in 1869, and they had six children: Mary (b. 1872), Rosina Hubley (b. 1873), Ellen (Bay) Gertrude (Mrs. William Blanchard Rand) (1876–1941), Edith (b. 1877), Christopher, and Katharine. She later married George Hunter (1847–1914), with whom she had one child, George Grenville (b. 1892).

TEMPLE (EMMET), KATHARINE (KITTY) (1843–95), Minny Temple's elder sister, she married her cousin, Richard Stockton Emmet, in 1868. They had six children: William (1869–1918), Richard Jr. (1871–97), Katharine (b. 1873), Elizabeth (b. 1874), Grenville (1877–1937), and Eleanor (b. 1880).

TEMPLE, MARY (MINNY) (1845–70), HJ's vivacious first cousin; her mother was Sr.'s sister, Catharine (1820–54). Orphaned by her parents' deaths in 1854, she and her siblings lived during the early 1860s in Newport with their paternal aunt, Mary Temple, and her husband, Sr.'s friend, Edmund Tweedy. After the latter began to have money problems, Minny and her younger sisters moved to Pelham, New York, to live with her sister, Kitty, and her husband, Richard Stockton Emmet. Minny's death from tuberculosis was a great shock to HJ, and many scholars believe her memory was one of his most lasting inspirations, inspiring, among others, his characters Daisy Miller, Isabel Archer, and Milly Theale.

TEMPLE, ROBERT (BOB) EMMET, JR. (b. 1840), HJ's cousin and Minny Temple's oldest brother. He developed a drinking problem and became "a charming rogue, leaning to the wrong side of the law" (Gordon 43). HJ devotes a section to Bob Temple in *Notes of a Son and Brother* (142–50).

THACKERAY, ANNE. *See* Ritchie, Anne Isabella Thackeray.

THACKERAY, WILLIAM MAKEPEACE (1811–63), the author of *Vanity Fair* (1847), *Pendennis* (1848–50), and *The Newcomes* (1853–55), visited the Jameses at their home in New York in 1852, during his 1851–53 American lecture tour. HJ recalled this meeting and an 1857 encounter in Paris in *A Small Boy and Others* (87–91), and he reviewed *Thackerayana*, a posthumous collection of notes, anecdotes, and sketches, for the *Nation* (9 December 1875) and became a friend of the novelist's daughter, Anne Thackeray Ritchie.

THIES, LOUIS, curator of the Gray Collection of Engravings at Harvard; he was the Jameses' landlord at 20 Quincy Street, Cambridge, until Sr. bought the house from him in 1870.

TROLLOPE, T. ADOLPHUS (1810–92), English novelist; the *North American Review* published HJ's unsigned review of Trollope's *Lindisfarn Chase: A Novel* (1864) in January 1865.

TWEEDY, EDMUND (ca. 1812–1901), a friend of Sr., a follower of Fourier, and a contributor to the *Harbinger*; his wife, Mary Temple Tweedy, was the paternal aunt and guardian of HJ's Temple cousins.

TWEEDY, MARY TEMPLE (d. 1891), the paternal aunt of HJ's cousins, the Temples; she was the sister of Robert Emmet Temple (1808–54), who married Sr.'s sister, Catharine James (1820–54), in 1839; after the deaths in 1854 of Robert and Catharine Temple, Mary Tweedy and her husband, Edmund, took in the orphaned Temple children, Robert (Bob), William, Katharine (Kitty), Mary (Minny), Ellen (Elly), and Henrietta.

VAN BUREN, CATHARINE (KITTY) BARBER (b. 1849), HJ's first cousin, daughter of Ellen King James and Smith Thompson Van Buren. RJ become secretly engaged to her in 1869, but apparently the family convinced them to break it off. She later married Peyton Farrell Miller, divorced him in 1888, and married a man named Wilson.

VAN BUREN, ELLEN (ELLY) (b. 1844), HJ's first cousin, daughter of Sr.'s sister, Ellen King James Van Buren. She lived in Albany and occasionally visited the Jameses with the Temple sisters. She married Stuyvesant Fish Morris in 1868.

VAN BUREN, ELLEN KING JAMES (1823–49), Sr.'s sister; she married Smith Van Buren, son of former U.S. president Martin Van Buren.

VAN WINKLE, EDGAR (EDDY) (1842–1920), lived at 62 W. 14th St., New York City, while the James family lived at 58 W. 14th St. (1847–55); he went on to attend Union College and to become a civil engineer and chief engineer of New York's Department of Parks. Boyhood letters (1856–59) and a 1903 letter by WJ to Van Winkle have survived.

VAUGHAN, ROBERT, author of *Revolutions in English History* (1859), the purpose of which was to reveal the various causes of British national character and institutions. HJ was reading this book in October 1864.

WALSH, CATHARINE (AUNT KATE) (1812–89) (AK), sister of HJ's mother, she remained a constant and usually present member of the James family until her death. She lived and traveled with her sister's family and became something of a second mother to the children. Catharine is usually described as having been much more outgoing and opinionated than her quieter sister. In 1853 she married Captain Charles H. Marshall, but the union lasted for only twenty-eight months. She died after a fall in her home in March of 1889.

WALSH, EMILIE BELDEN (b. 1844), was the daughter of Alexander Robertson Walsh, MWJ's brother. She married Thomas Cochran Jr. on 28 November 1867.

WARD, ANNA HAZARD BARKER (ca. 1813–1900), an intimate friend of Sr. during the 1840s and 1850s and wife of Samuel G. Ward, New York and Boston banker and U.S. partner of the Barings Bank. Her brother, William H. Barker, married Sr.'s sister, Jeannette James.

WARD, ARTEMUS (1834–67), pseudonym of Charles Farrar Browne, one of the most popular nineteenth-century American humorists;

he commented on a variety of subjects in his letters to *Plain Dealer*, *Punch*, and *Vanity Fair*.

WARD, ELIZABETH (BESSY), a daughter of Anna Barker Ward.

WARD, ELLEN M., resided at the Hotel Pelham, in Boston, in 1867; in 1869 HJ met her and her sister, Judy E. Ward, in Glion, Switzerland, and called on them in Lucerne.

WARD, JUDY E., resided at the Hotel Pelham, in Boston, in 1867; in 1869 HJ met her and her sister, Ellen M. Ward, in Glion, Switzerland, and called on them in Lucerne.

WARD, LYDIA (LILY), a daughter of Anna Barker Ward.

WARD, MRS. SAM. *See* Ward, Anna Barker.

WARE, WILLIAM ROBERT (1832–1915), American architect and educator. A fashionable exponent of gothic style, Ware built St. John's Chapel at the Episcopal Theological Seminary on Brattle Street in Cambridge, Massachusetts. Six years later, he and his partner, Henry Van Brunt, started the First Church in Boston, and in 1870 they began Memorial Hall at Harvard, a prominent paradigm of the style. Ware was also appointed to establish and head the school of architecture at the Massachusetts Institute of Technology (1865).

WASHBURN, FRANCIS (FRANK) TUCKER (1843–73), a friend of WJ's who graduated from Harvard (1864), attended Harvard Divinity School, and became a Unitarian minister.

WASHBURN, KATHARINE SEDGWICK VALERIO (MRS. WILLIAM T.) (1831–84), younger sister of Elizabeth Ellery Sedgwick Child; she was married twice: to Joseph Valerio and to William T. Washburn.

WASSON, DAVID ATWOOD (1823–87), transcendentalist minister and author; he contributed to the *Radical* and the *Atlantic Monthly*. Thomas Sergeant Perry published an article on him in *Harvard Magazine*'s April 1864 issue.

WATSON, ADELAIDE (ADDY) HOWARD (1841–69), was a sister of Anna, Jane, and Sylvia Watson and one of nine children of Robert Sedgwick Watson of Milton, Massachusetts; she was a second cousin of Susan Sedgwick Norton, Sara Sedgwick Darwin, Arthur George Sedgwick, and Theodora Sedgwick.

WATSON, ANNA RUSSELL (1843-1909), a sister of Adelaide (Addy), Jane, and Sylvia Watson, of Milton, Massachusetts; she married William Jones Ladd in 1869.

WATSON, JANE SEDGWICK (1838-1914), a sister of Adelaide (Addy), Anna, and Sylvia Watson; she married Edward Cranch Perkins in 1869.

WATSON, ROBERT SEDGWICK (1809-88), father of Adelaide (Addy), Anna, Jane, and Sylvia Watson and first cousin of Elizabeth Ellery Sedgwick Child, Katharine Sedgwick Valerio Washburn, and Theodore Sedgwick III. He lived in Milton, Massachusetts.

WATSON, SYLVIA HATHAWAY (b. 1834), eldest child of Robert Sedgwick Watson of Milton, Massachusetts, and sister of Adelaide (Addy), Anna, and Jane Watson. She married William Ralph Emerson in 1873.

WETMORE, GEORGE PEABODY (1846-1921), may have been a boyhood friend of the Jameses during their Newport days. His father, William Wetmore, was quite wealthy due to his business in the China trade and in banking and had the famous Château-sur-Mer, the family's residence, built in Newport in 1852. George Wetmore graduated from Yale and Columbia Law School and later became governor of Rhode Island and a U.S. senator.

WHITE, WILLIAM, London journalist who published Swedenborgian and spiritual books and journals.

WILKINSON, EMMA, the wife of Dr. James John Garth Wilkinson.

WILKINSON, JAMES (b. 1844), son of Emma and Dr. James John Garth Wilkinson.

WILKINSON, DR. JAMES JOHN GARTH (1812-99), an eminent Swedenborgian; he and his wife, Emma, befriended the Jameses during their European sojourn of 1843-44.

WILKINSON, MARY WALSH (b. 1846), daughter of Emma and Dr. James John Garth Wilkinson, named after her godmother, MWJ;

she was a playmate of HJ's when the Jameses lived in St. John's Wood, London, in 1856–57. Mary Wilkinson married Frank Mathews, cousin of her brother-in-law, St. John Mathews.

WILLSON, FORCEYTHE (1837–67), a Civil War poet-annalist and friend of the Holmeses. Interested in war politics, he wrote Union editorials for the *Louisville Journal*. His poem "Old Sergeant," a transcript of Civil War history, propelled Willson to nationwide recognition. Dr. Oliver Wendell Holmes strongly favored the work and read it during his lectures on "The Poetry of the War." In 1864 Willson bought an old mansion in Cambridge, situated upon the Charles River close to the Holmeses.

WINSLOW, SARAH TRAIN (MRS. GEORGE SCOTT) (ca. 1839–1925), American socialite whom HJ first met in Boston.

WITTE, KARL (1800–83), an eminent Dante scholar and professor at Martin Luther University, Halle-Wittenberg, in Halle, Germany. Witte dedicated his critical edition of Dante's *Vita Nuova* to Charles Sanders Eliot Norton.

WRIGHT, CHAUNCEY (1830–75), Northampton, Massachusetts-born philosopher and mathematician and mentor of WJ, Charles Sanders Peirce, and Oliver Wendell Holmes Jr.

WYCKOFF, HENRY (1815–90), first cousin of MWJ (his mother, Mary Robertson Wyckoff, was the sister of MWJ's mother, Elizabeth Robertson Walsh). HJ considered him insane.

WYNNE, EDITH (1842–97), prominent soprano who performed in 1871–72 with the Dolby Troupe.

YOUMANS, EDWARD LIVINGSTON (1821–87), co-founder, with his brother, of the *Popular Science Monthly* (later *Scientific Monthly*).

YOUMANS, WILLIAM JAY (1838–1901), co-founder, with his brother, of the *Popular Science Monthly* (later *Scientific Monthly*).

Genealogies

The James Family

(1) William James (1771–1832) m. (1796) Elizabeth Tillman (1774–97)

    Robert James (1797–1821)
        Lydia Lush James (1820–97) m. Henry Mason (1819–91)

    Rev. William James (1797–1868)
        Katharine (Kitty) James (1834–90) m. (1861) William Henry Prince (1817–83)

(2) William James m. (1798) Mary Ann Connolly (1778–1800)

    Ellen James (1800–1823) m. (1818) James King (1788–1841)
        Mary Ann King (1819–92) m. Mr. Post

(3) William James m. (1803) Catharine Barber (1782–1859)

    Augustus (Gus) James (1807–66)

    Henry James Sr. (1811–82) [Sr.] m. (1840) Mary Robertson Walsh (1810–82) [MWJ]
        William James (1842–1910) [WJ]
        Henry James (1843–1916) [HJ]
        Garth Wilkinson (Wilkie) James (1845–83) [GWJ]
        Robertson (Bob) James (1846–1910) [RJ]
        Alice James (1848–92) [AJ]

    Jeannette James (1814–42) m. (1832) William H. Barker
        Augustus (Gus) Barker (1842–63)

    John Barber James (1816–56) m. (1834) Mary Helen Vanderburgh (1816–46)
        John (Johnny) Vanderburgh James (1835–58)
        Mary (Nellie) Helen James (1840–81)
            m. (1868) Charles Alfred Grymes (1829–1905)

    Catharine Margaret James (1820–54) m. (1839) Robert Emmet Temple (1808–54)
        Robert (Bob) Temple (1840–?)
        William James Temple (1842–63)
        Katharine (Kitty) Temple (1843–95)
            m. (1868) Richard Stockton Emmet (1821–1902)
                William Temple Emmet (1869–1918)
                Richard Stockton Emmet (1871–97)
        Mary (Minny) Temple (1845–70)
        Ellen Temple (1850–1920) m. (1) (1869) Christopher Temple Emmet
            (1822–84); (2) George Hunter (1847–1914)
        Henrietta (1853–1934) m. (1876) Leslie Pell-Clarke (1853–1904)

    Ellen King James (1823–49) m. (1842) Smith Thompson Van Buren (1817–76)
        Ellen Van Buren (1844–1929) m. (1868) Stuyvesant Fish Morris (1843–1925)
            Elizabeth Marshall Morris (1869–?)
        Catharine (Kitty) Van Buren (1849–?)

    Howard James (1828–87)

The Temple Family

Robert Temple and Clarina Hawkins

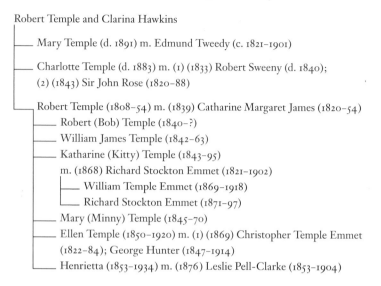

Mary Temple (d. 1891) m. Edmund Tweedy (c. 1821–1901)

Charlotte Temple (d. 1883) m. (1) (1833) Robert Sweeny (d. 1840); (2) (1843) Sir John Rose (1820–88)

Robert Temple (1808–54) m. (1839) Catharine Margaret James (1820–54)

Robert (Bob) Temple (1840–?)

William James Temple (1842–63)

Katharine (Kitty) Temple (1843–95)
m. (1868) Richard Stockton Emmet (1821–1902)

William Temple Emmet (1869–1918)

Richard Stockton Emmet (1871–97)

Mary (Minny) Temple (1845–70)

Ellen Temple (1850–1920) m. (1) (1869) Christopher Temple Emmet (1822–84); George Hunter (1847–1914)

Henrietta (1853–1934) m. (1876) Leslie Pell-Clarke (1853–1904)

The Robertson and Walsh Families

Alexander Robertson (1733–1816) m. Mary Smith

    Hellen Robertson (d. 1818) m. John Richardson Bayard Rodgers (d. 1833)

        Alexander Robertson Rodgers (b. 1807) m. Mary Ridgely Darden (d. 1888)

            Katherine (Katie) Rodgers (b. 1841)

            Henrietta (Nettie) Dorrington Rodgers (1843–1906)

    Mary (great-aunt Wyckoff) Robertson (1778–1855) m. Albert Wyckoff (1771–1840)

        Helen Rodgers Wyckoff (1807–87) m. Leonard Perkins (d. 1869)

        Henry A. Wyckoff (1815–90)

            Hugh Walsh (1745–1817) m. (1775) Catharine Armstrong (1755–1801)

    Elizabeth Robertson (1781–1847)

    m. (1806) James Walsh (c. 1780–1820)

        Alexander Robertson Walsh (1807–84)

        m. (1838) Emily Brown (1816–81)

            Emily Belden Walsh (b. 1844)

            m. (1867) Thomas Cochran Jr.

        Mary Robertson Walsh (1810–82) [MWJ]

        m. (1840) Henry James Sr. (1811–82) [Sr.]

            William James (1842–1910) [WJ]

            Henry James (1843–1916) [HJ]

            Garth Wilkinson (Wilkie) James (1845–83) [GWJ]

            Robertson (Bob) James (1846–1910) [RJ]

            Alice James (1848–92) [AJ]

        Catharine (Aunt Kate) Walsh (1812–89) AK

        m. Charles H. Marshall

    Catharine Walsh (1785–1829)

    m. (1805) David Andrews

        Catherine Walsh Andrews (1806–65)

        m. Joseph Ripley

            Helen Ripley

    Charlotte Walsh (1789–1816)

    m. Rev. James Matthews

        Charlotte Elizabeth Sleight Matthews m. C. W. King

            William Vernon King

            Annie King

            Arthur King

The Sedgwick Family

Theodore Sedgwick (1746–1813) m. (1774) Pamela Dwight (1753–1807)

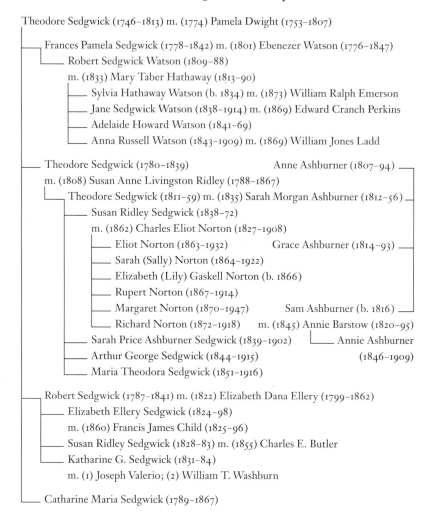

Frances Pamela Sedgwick (1778–1842) m. (1801) Ebenezer Watson (1776–1847)

Robert Sedgwick Watson (1809–88)

m. (1833) Mary Taber Hathaway (1813–90)

Sylvia Hathaway Watson (b. 1834) m. (1873) William Ralph Emerson

Jane Sedgwick Watson (1838–1914) m. (1869) Edward Cranch Perkins

Adelaide Howard Watson (1841–69)

Anna Russell Watson (1843–1909) m. (1869) William Jones Ladd

Theodore Sedgwick (1780–1839)   Anne Ashburner (1807–94)

m. (1808) Susan Anne Livingston Ridley (1788–1867)

Theodore Sedgwick (1811–59) m. (1835) Sarah Morgan Ashburner (1812–56)

Susan Ridley Sedgwick (1838–72)

m. (1862) Charles Eliot Norton (1827–1908)

Eliot Norton (1863–1932)   Grace Ashburner (1814–93)

Sarah (Sally) Norton (1864–1922)

Elizabeth (Lily) Gaskell Norton (b. 1866)

Rupert Norton (1867–1914)

Margaret Norton (1870–1947)   Sam Ashburner (b. 1816)

Richard Norton (1872–1918)   m. (1845) Annie Barstow (1820–95)

Sarah Price Ashburner Sedgwick (1839–1902)   Annie Ashburner

Arthur George Sedgwick (1844–1915)   (1846–1909)

Maria Theodora Sedgwick (1851–1916)

Robert Sedgwick (1787–1841) m. (1822) Elizabeth Dana Ellery (1799–1862)

Elizabeth Ellery Sedgwick (1824–98)

m. (1860) Francis James Child (1825–96)

Susan Ridley Sedgwick (1828–83) m. (1855) Charles E. Butler

Katharine G. Sedgwick (1831–84)

m. (1) Joseph Valerio; (2) William T. Washburn

Catharine Maria Sedgwick (1789–1867)

The Norton Family

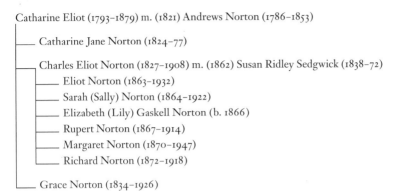

Catharine Eliot (1793–1879) m. (1821) Andrews Norton (1786–1853)

Catharine Jane Norton (1824–77)

Charles Eliot Norton (1827–1908) m. (1862) Susan Ridley Sedgwick (1838–72)

Eliot Norton (1863–1932)

Sarah (Sally) Norton (1864–1922)

Elizabeth (Lily) Gaskell Norton (b. 1866)

Rupert Norton (1867–1914)

Margaret Norton (1870–1947)

Richard Norton (1872–1918)

Grace Norton (1834–1926)

493

Works Cited

List of Works Cited by Abbreviation

Anesko	Anesko, Michael. *Letters, Fictions, Lives: Henry James and William Dean Howells*. New York: Oxford University Press, 1997.
CWJ	James, William. *The Correspondence of William James*. Ed. Ignas Skrupskelis and Elizabeth Berkeley. 12 vols. Charlottesville: University of Virginia Press, 1992–2004.
HJL 1–4	James, Henry. *Henry James Letters*. Ed. Leon Edel. 4 vols. Cambridge: Belknap/Harvard University Press, 1974–84.
Horne	James, Henry. *Henry James: A Life in Letters*. Ed. Philip Horne. New York: Viking, 1999.
La Farge	La Farge, John, S.J. "Henry James's Letters to the La Farges." *New England Quarterly* 22 (1949): 173–92.
Le Clair	Le Clair, Robert C. "Henry James and Minnie Temple." *American Literature* 21 (Mar. 1949): 35–48.
Lubbock 1–2	James, Henry. *The Letters of Henry James*. Ed. Percy Lubbock. 2 vols. New York: Scribner's, 1920.
SL 1	*The Selected Letters of Henry James*. Ed. Leon Edel. New York: Farrar, 1955.
SL 2	*Henry James: Selected Letters*. Ed. Leon Edel. Cambridge: Belknap/Harvard University Press, 1987.
WHSL	James, William, and Henry James. *William and Henry James: Selected Letters*. Ed. Ignas Skrupskelis and Elizabeth Berkeley. Charlottesville: University of Virginia Press, 1997.
Zorzi, *Palazzo Barbaro*	James, Henry. *Henry James: Letters from the Palazzo Barbaro*. Ed. Rosella Mamoli Zorzi. London: Pushkin, 1998.

Additional Works Cited

Adams, Henry. *The Education of Henry Adams*. Washington: [Adams], 1907.

———. *History of the United States during the Administrations of Jefferson and Madison*. New York: Scribner's, 1889–91.

———. *The Life of Albert Gallatin.* Philadelphia: Lippincott, 1879.

Annuaire-Almanach du Commerce, de l'Industrie, de la Magistrature et de l'Administration. Paris: Didot, 1869.

Arnold, Matthew. *Poems.* London: Longman, 1853.

Baedeker, Karl. *Central Italy and Rome.* Coblenz: Bædeker, 1867.

———. *London and Its Environs; Including Excursions to Brighton, the Isle of Wight, etc.* London: Dulau, 1867.

———. *Northern Italy, as Far as Leghorn, Florence, and Ancona, and the Island of Corsica.* Coblenz: Bædeker, 1868.

———. *La Suisse et les parties limitrophes de l'Italie, de la Savoie et du Tyrol: Manuel du Voyageur.* 8th ed. Coblenz: Baedeker, 1869.

———. *Switzerland and the Adjacent Portions of Italy, Savoy with the Tyrol: Handbook for Travelers.* Coblenz: Bædeker, 1869.

Balzac, Honoré de. *Le Lys dans la vallée.* Paris: Werdet, 1836.

Bolton, Charles Knowles. *The Athenaeum Centenary.* Boston: Boston Athenæum, 1907.

Briggs, L. Vernon. *History and Genealogy of the Cabot Family: 1475–1927.* 2 vols. Boston: Goodspeed, 1927.

Brosses, Charles de. *Lettres familières écrites d'Italie en 1739–1740.* Paris: Perrin, 1885.

Browning, Robert. *Men and Women.* London: Chapman, 1855.

———. *The Ring and the Book.* Boston: Fields, 1869.

Bunting, Bainbridge, assisted by Margaret Henderson Floyd. *Harvard: An Architectural History.* Cambridge: Harvard University Press, 1985.

Byron, George Gordon, Lord. *The Prisoner of Chillon, and Other Poems.* London: Murray, 1816.

The Cambridge Directory. Boston: Dudley, 1869.

The Cambridge Directory for 1874. Boston: Greenough, 1874.

Catalan, Ad., and Ch[arles] Page. *Indicateur des 25,000 Adresses genevoises, dit Bottin genevois.* Geneva: Carey, 1870.

Cherbuliez, Victor. "La revanche de Joseph Noirel," *Revue des Deux Mondes* 94 (1871): 381–418, 465–509, 719–61; 95 (1871): 5–46, 306–39, 481–523.

———. *Le revanche de Joseph Noirel.* Paris: Hachette, 1872.

Constant, Benjamin. *Adolphe.* Paris: Treuttel, 1816.

Dain, Phylis. *The New York Public Library: A History of Its Founding and Early Years.* New York: New York Public Library, 1972.

Darwin, Charles. *Descent of Man, and Selection in Relation to Sex.* New York: Appleton, 1871.

"Deaths." *New York Times* 4 June 1869: 5.

Dictionary of American Biography. Ed. John Allen, Dumas Malone, and Harris E. Starr. 20 vols. New York: Scribner, 1928–37.

Dictionary of National Biography. Ed. Sir Leslie Stephen and Sidney Lee. 66 vols. London: Smith, 1885–1901.

Duberman, Martin. *James Russell Lowell*. Boston: Houghton, 1966.

Edel, Leon. *Henry James*. 5 vols. Philadelphia: Lippincott, 1953–72.

Eliot, George. *Romola*. London: Smith, 1863.

"Entertainments." *Boston Post* 14 Nov. 1870: 3.

Explication des ouvrages de peinture, sculpture, architecture, gravure et lithographie des artistes vivants exposés au Palais des Champs-Elysées le 1er mai 1869. Paris: Mourgues, 1869.

Fitzgerald, Penelope. *Edward Burne-Jones: A Biography*. London: Joseph, 1975.

Forster, John. *The Life of Charles Dickens*. 3 vols. London: Chapman, 1872–74.

Gardner, Helen, Horst de la Croix, and Richard G. Tansey. *Gardner's Art Through the Ages*. 6th ed. New York: Harcourt, 1975.

Gautier, Théophile. *Italia*. Paris: d'Aujourd'hui, 1976.

Gollin, Rita K. *Annie Adams Fields: Woman of Letters*. Amherst: University of Massachusetts Press, 2002.

Gordon, Lyndall. *A Private Life of Henry James*. New York: Norton, 1998.

Gully, James Manby. *An Exposition of the Symptoms, Essential Nature, and Treatment of Neuropathy, or Nervousness*. London: Churchill, 1837.

———. *A Guide to Domestic Hydrotherapeia: A Water Cure in Acute Disease*. London: Simpkin, 1863.

———. *The Water Cure in Chronic Disease*. London: Churchill, 1846.

Habegger, Alfred. *The Father: A Life of Henry James, Sr*. New York: Farrar, 1994.

Harrison, Frederic. "Bismarckism." *Fortnightly Review* 8 (1 December 1870): 631–49.

Harte, Bret. "How Santa Claus Came to Simpson's Bar." *Atlantic Monthly* 29 (Mar. 1872): 349–58.

———. "Plain Language from Truthful James." *Overland Monthly & Out West Magazine* 5 (Sept. 1870): 287–88.

Hastings, Katharine. *William James of Albany, N. Y. (1771–1832) and His Descendants*. New York: n.p., 1924.

Hawthorne, Nathaniel. *The House of the Seven Gables*. Boston: Ticknor, 1851.

Hay, G. U. *The Scientific Work of Professor Chas. Fred. Hartt*. Ottawa: Hope, 1899.

Heyer, Henri. *L'église de Genève: 1555–1909*. Geneva: Jullien, 1909.

Hirst, Robert H. "Editing Mark Twain, Hand to Hand, 'Like All D—d

Fool Printers.'" *Papers of the Bibliographical Society of America* 88.2 (1994): 157–88.

Holmes, Oliver Wendell. "The Poet at the Breakfast-Table" *Atlantic Monthly* 29 (Jan.–June 1872): 90–105, 224–236, 338–349, 485–496, 606–619, 731–743; 30 (July–Dec. 1872): 98–110, 225–40, 352–64, 426–38, 513–26, 720–34, 744.

Holy Bible, People's Parallel Edition. Wheaton: Tyndale, 1997.

Hood, Thomas. "The Bridge of Sighs." *The Complete Poetical Works of Thomas Hood*. London: Oxford University Press, 1935. 649–50.

Horace. *Epistriac, Ars poetica*. Edinburgh: Blackwood, 1880.

Howells, Elinor Mead. *If Not Literature: Letters of Elinor Mead Howells*. Columbus: Ohio State University Press, 1988.

Howells, William Dean. "By Horse-Car to Boston." *Atlantic Monthly* 25 (Jan. 1870): 114–22.

———. "Jubilee Days." *Atlantic Monthly* 24 (Aug. 1869): 245–54.

———. "A Pedestrian Tour." *Atlantic Monthly* 24 (Nov. 1869): 591–603.

———. *Suburban Sketches*. New York: Hurd, 1871.

———. "Their Wedding Journey." *Atlantic Monthly* 28 (July–Dec. 1871): 29–40, 162–76, 345–57, 442–59, 605–23, 721–40.

———. *Their Wedding Journey*. Boston: Osgood, 1872.

Hugo, Victor. *Ruy Blas*. Paris: Delloye, 1838.

James, Alice. *Her Life in Letters*. Ed. Linda Anderson. Bristol: Thoemmes, 1996.

James, Henry, Jr. "Art: The Dutch and Flemish Pictures in New York." *Atlantic Monthly* 29 (June 1872): 757–63.

———. "At Isella." *Galaxy* 12 (Aug. 1871): 241–55.

———. "Coquelin." *Century Magazine* 33 (Jan. 1887): 407–13.

———. Rev. of *The Correspondence of Carlyle and Emerson*. *Century Magazine* 26 (June 1883): 265–72.

———. *Daisy Miller*. New York: Harper, 1879.

———. "Florentine Notes." *Independent* (21 May 1874): 1–2.

———. "From Lake George to Burlington." *Nation* 11 (1 Sept. 1870): 135–36.

———. "Gabrielle de Bergerac." *Atlantic Monthly* 24 (July–Sept. 1869): 55–71, 231–41, 352–61.

———. "George du Maurier." *Harper's New Monthly* 95 (Sept. 1896): 594–609.

———. [unsigned] "Henry Beyle." Rev. of Andrew A. Paton's *Henry Beyle (otherwise De Stendahl): A Critical and Biographical Study*. *Nation* 19 (17 Sept. 1874): 187–89.

———. "An Italian Convent." *Independent* (2 July 1874): 3–4.

———. *Italian Hours*. In *Collected Travel Writings: The Continent*. New York: Library of America, 1993.

———. "Lake George." *Nation* 11 (25 Aug. 1870): 119–20.

———. "The Late Mrs. Arthur Bronson." *Critic* 40 (Feb. 1902): 162–64.

———. "A Light Man." *Galaxy* 8 (July 1869): 49–68.

———. "Lothair." *Atlantic Monthly* 26 (Aug. 1870): 249–51.

———. "Master Eustace." *Galaxy* 12 (Nov. 1871): 595–612.

———. "Mr. & Mrs. Fields." *Cornhill Magazine* 39 (July 1915): 29–43.

———. "Mr. and Mrs. James T. Fields." *Atlantic Monthly* 116 (July 1915): 21–31.

———. "Newport." *Nation* 11 (15 Sep. 1870): 170–72.

———. *Notes of a Son and Brother*. New York: Scribner's, 1914.

———. [Unsigned] Rev. of *Notes sur l'Angleterre*, by Hippolyte Taine. *Nation* 14 (25 Jan. 1872): 58–60.

———. *The Painter's Eye: Notes and Essays on the Pictorial Arts*. Ed. John L. Sweeney. London: Hart-Davis, 1956.

———. "A Passionate Pilgrim." *Atlantic Monthly* 27 (Mar.–Apr. 1871): 352–71, 478–99.

———. "Saratoga" [unsigned]. *Nation* 11 (11 Aug. 1870): 87–89.

———. "Selections from de Musset" [unsigned]. *Atlantic Monthly* 26 (Sept. 1870): 379–81.

———. *Stories Revived*. London: Macmillan, 1885.

———. "The Théâtre Français." *Galaxy* 23 (Apr. 1877): 437–49; rpt. in *The Scenic Art: Notes on Acting and the Drama, 1872–1901*. Ed. Allan Wade. New Brunswick NJ: Rutgers University Press, 1948. 68–92.

———. "Travelling Companions." *Atlantic Monthly* 26 (Nov.–Dec. 1870): 600–614, 684–97.

———. "Watch and Ward." *Atlantic Monthly* 28 (Aug.–Dec. 1871): 232–46, 320–39, 415–31, 577–96, 689–710.

———. *William Wetmore Story and His Friends*. Edinburgh: Blackwood, 1903.

James, Henry, Sr. "Is Marriage Holy?" *Atlantic Monthly* 25 (Mar. 1870): 360–68.

———. *The Secret of Swedenborg: Being an Elucidation of His Doctrine of the Divine Natural Humanity*. Boston: Fields, 1869.

———. [Unsigned letter]. *Nation* 9 (16 Dec. 1869): 534.

———. "The Woman Thou Gavest with Me." *Atlantic Monthly* 25 (Jan. 1870): 66–72.

James, William. Rev. of *The Subjection of Women*, by John Stuart Mill, and *Women's Suffrage: The Reform against Nature*, by Horace Bushnell. *North American Review* 109 (Oct. 1869): 556–65.

Kaledin, Eugenia. *The Education of Mrs. Henry Adams*. Philadelphia: Temple University Press, 1981.

Keats, John. *Lamia, Isabella, the Eve of St. Agnes, and Other Poems*. London: Taylor, 1820.

Lecky, William Edward Hartpole. *History of European Morals from Augustus to Charlemagne*. New York: Appleton, 1869.

Lewis, R.W.B. *The Jameses: A Family Narrative*. New York: Farrar, 1991.

Longfellow, Henry Wadsworth. *The Divine Tragedy*. Boston: Osgood, 1871.

———. Longfellow journal, Longfellow Papers, 1 January 1863–17 December 1869, Houghton MS 1340 (210).

———. Longfellow journal, Longfellow Papers, 1 January 1870–16 November 1873, Houghton MS 1340 (213).

Lowell, James Russell. "The Cathedral." *Atlantic Monthly* 25 (Jan. 1870): 1–15.

———. *My Study Windows*. Boston: Osgood, 1871.

Maher, Jane. *Biography of Broken Fortunes: Wilkie and Bob, Brothers of William, Henry and Alice James*. Hamden CT: Archon, 1986.

Meilhac, Henri, and Ludovic Halévy. *Froufrou: Comédie en cinq actes*. Paris: Lévy, 1870.

Michelet, Jules. *L'Amour*. Paris: Hachette, 1858.

———. *Histoire de France*. 17 vols. Paris: Hachette, 1833–67.

———. *L'Oiseau*. Paris: Hachette, 1856.

Mill, John Stuart. *The Subjection of Women*. London: Longmans, 1869.

Morley, John. "Byron." *Fortnightly Review* 7 (Dec. 1870): 650–73.

Murray, John. *A Handbook for Travellers in Central Italy*. London: Murray, 1867.

———. *Handbook for Travellers in Northern Italy*. London: Murray, 1866.

———. *A Handbook for Travellers in the Alps of Savoy and Piedmont*. London: Murray, 1867.

———. *A Handbook of Rome and Its Environs*. 9th ed. London: Murray, 1869.

"New Publications: The July Magazines." *New York Daily Tribune* 18 June 1869: 6.

Noble, Lulu Gray. "Notes on the Woman's Rights Agitation." *Nation* 10 (20 Jan. 1870): 38–39; (10 Feb. 1870): 88–89; (17 Feb. 1870): 101–4.

O'Conner, Richard. *Bret Harte: A Biography*. Boston: Little, 1966.

O'Toole, Patricia. *The Five of Hearts: An Intimate Portrait of Henry Adams and His Friends, 1880–1918*. New York: Potter, 1990.

Paton, Andrew A. *Henry Beyle (otherwise De Stendahl): A Critical and Biographical Study*. London: Trübner, 1874.

Pletsch, Oscar. *Aunt Bessie's Picture Book*. London: Routledge, 1872.

———. *Chimes and Rhymes for Youthful Times!* London: Routledge, 1871.

Post Office London Directory, 1870. London: Kelly, 1870.

Rathbun, Richard. *Sketch of the Life and Scientific Work of Prof. Charles Fred. Hartt.* Boston: Kingman, 1878.

Renan, Ernest. *La Réforme intellectuelle et morale.* Paris: Lévy, 1871.

Robinson, Henry Crabb. *Diary, Reminiscences, and Correspondence.* London: Macmillan, 1869.

Ruskin, John. *The Stones of Venice.* London: Smith, 1851–53.

Sainte-Beuve, Charles-Augustin. *Madame Desbordes-Valmore, sa vie et sa correspondance.* Paris: Lévy, 1870.

———. *Volupté.* Paris: Charpentier, 1834.

Sand, George. "Journal d'un voyageur pendant la guerre." *Revue des Deux Mondes* 1 Mar. 1871: 5–39; 15 Mar. 1871: 209–55; 1 Apr. 1871: 417–45.

———. *Lélia.* Brussels: Meline, 1833.

Scudder, Horace. *James Russell Lowell: A Biography.* Cambridge: Riverside-Houghton, 1901.

Senancour, Étienne Pivert de. *Oberman.* Paris: Cerioux, 1804.

Shakespeare, William. *The Riverside Shakespeare.* Ed. G. Blakemore Evans. 2nd ed. Boston: Houghton, 1997.

Staël, Madame de (Anne-Louise-Germaine). *Corinne, ou L'Italie.* Paris: Nicolle, 1807.

———. *Delphine.* Geneva: Paschoud, 1802.

Stendhal (Henri Beyle). *La Chartreuse de Parme.* Paris: Dupont, 1839.

———. *Chroniques italiennes.* Paris: Lévy, 1855.

———. *Histoire de la peinture en Italie.* Paris: Didot, 1817.

———. *Promenades dans Rome.* Paris: Delaunay, 1829.

———. *Rome, Naples et Florence en 1817.* Paris: Delaunay, 1817.

———. *Le Rouge et le noir: Chronique de 1830.* Paris: Levasseur, 1831.

Stephen, Leslie. *The Playground of Europe.* London: Longmans, 1871.

Stowe, Harriet Beecher. *Old Town Folks.* Boston: Fields, 1869.

Strouse, Jean. *Alice James: A Biography.* Boston: Houghton, 1980.

Taine, Hippolyte. *Histoire de la littérature anglaise.* 4 vols. 1863–64; *History of English Literature.* Trans. H. Van Laun. 2 vols. New York: Holt, 1871.

———. *Notes sur l'Angleterre.* Paris: Hachette, 1872.

Tanselle, G. Thomas. "The Editing of Historical Documents." *Studies in Bibliography* 31 (1978): 1–56.

———. "The Editorial Problem of Final Intention." *Studies in Bibliography* 29 (1975): 167–211.

———. "Recent Editorial Discussion and the Central Questions of Editing." *Studies in Bibliography* 34 (1981): 23–65.

Tennyson, Alfred. *Poems.* London: Moxon, 1857.

Turgenev, Ivan. *Nouvelles moscovites*. Paris: Hetzel, 1869.

Turner, James. *The Liberal Education of Charles Eliot Norton*. Baltimore: Johns Hopkins University Press, 1999.

"The United States: From an American Correspondent." *Times* [London] 9 Sept. 1869: 5.

[Unsigned letter]. "A Swedenborgian." *Nation* 9 (25 Nov. 1869): 458.

Wilson, H. *Trow's New York City Directory*. New York: Trow, 1868.

———. *Trow's New York City Directory*. New York: Trow, 1869.

———. *Trow's New York City Directory*. New York: Trow, 1870.

Index

This index includes every person, place, published work, work of art, and institution mentioned in James's letters. Letters addressed to a person are listed under "Letters to:" at the end of the entry. Letters written by Henry James from a particular place are listed under "Letters from:" at the end of the entry.

Works by James are indexed under his name. Works by other people are indexed under both the author/artist and the title of the work.

Page numbers in boldface indicate an entry in the biographical register. Numbers in italics indicate the photographs in the separate section following page 252.

The Complete Letters of Henry James

The Complete Letters of Henry James, 1855–1872
    Volume 1 (1855–1869)
    Volume 2 (1869–1872)